Frommer's

Austria

POSTCARDS FROM

W9-CPE-029

Hiking vacations are favorite summer pastimes in the Tyrol. See chapter 10. © Peter Cade/
Getty Images.

Café Tomaselli is a great place to sit and talk and feast on homemade pastries in Salzburg's Altstadt. See chapter 7.
© Bob Krist Photography.

You can sample Vienna's famous Sacher torte, a glazed chocolate cake filled with apricot jam, in the city's many coffeehouses. See chapter 3. © Dave Bartruff Photography.

Stroll among the fountains and statues of the Imperial Gardens, then explore the State Apartments at Vienna's Schönbrunn Palace. See chapter 4. © David R. Frazier/Folio, Inc.

See the world-famous Lipizzaner stallions perform in the chandeliered ballroom at the Spanish Riding School in Vienna. See chapter 4. © Jerry Cooke/Corbis.

Discover Hansel and Gretel villages in the Tyrol. See chapter 10. © Kevin Galvin Photography.

The spectacular Virgental in East Tyrol is a winter wonderland. See chapter 10. © Walter Geiersperger/
The Stock Market.

At Graz's famous Opera House, you can see everything from opera to touring Broadway musicals. See chapter 13. © Bob Krist Photography.

Marvel at the rich baroque interior of Salzburg Cathedral. See chapter 7.
© Walter Geiersperger/ The Stock Market.

Hand-painted town signs abound in the Lech valley of the Tyrol. See chapter 10. © *Shaun Egan/ Getty Images.*

Beautiful Innsbruck is your gateway to the Tyrol's famous ski slopes. See chapter 10. © *Dave Bartruff Photography.*

The Traunsee, one of Upper Austria's largest lakes, is ringed by famous summer resorts. See chapter 9. © Geopress/Getty Images.

One look at baroque Melk Abbey and you'll know why Empress Maria Theresa said, "If I had never come here, I would have regretted it." See chapter 5. © Walter Bibikow/Folio, Inc.

Hailed as one of northern Europe's "most perfect" Renaissance buildings, Salzburg Cathedral sparkles in the snows of winter. See chapter 7. © Connie Coleman/Getty Images.

A New Star-Rating System & Other Exciting News from Frommer's!

In our continuing effort to publish the savviest, most up-to-date, and most appealing travel guides available, we've added some great new features.

Frommer's guides now include a new **star-rating system.** Every hotel, restaurant, and attraction is rated from 0 to 3 stars to help you set priorities and organize your time.

We've also added **seven brand-new features** that point you to the great deals, in-the-know advice, and unique experiences that separate travelers from tourists. Throughout the guide, look for:

Finds   Special finds—those places only insiders know about

Fun Fact   Fun facts—details that make travelers more informed and their trips more fun

Kids   Best bets for kids—advice for the whole family

Moments   Special moments—those experiences that memories are made of

Overrated   Places or experiences not worth your time or money

Tips   Insider tips—some great ways to save time and money

Value   Great values—where to get the best deals

We've also added a **"What's New"** section in every guide—a timely crash course in what's hot and what's not in every destination we cover.

Here's what the critics say about Frommer's:

Other Great Guides for Your Trip:

Frommer's®

Austria
10th Edition

by Darwin Porter &
Danforth Prince

WILEY

Wiley Publishing, Inc.

About the Authors

Veteran travel writers **Darwin Porter** and **Danforth Prince** have written numerous best-selling Frommer's guides, notably to Germany, France, Italy, England, and Spain. Porter was bureau chief for the *Miami Herald* when he was 21. Prince, who began writing with Porter in 1982, worked for the Paris bureau of the *New York Times*. Together, they wrote and researched the first-ever Frommer's guide to Austria. As frequent travelers to this alpine country, they know their destination well.

Published by:

Wiley Publishing, Inc.

111 River Street, 5ᵗʰ Floor
Hoboken, NJ 07030

ISBN 0-7645-2438-0
ISSN 0899-3297

Editor: Paul Prince
Production Editor: Tammy Ahrens
Cartographer: Elizabeth Puhl
Photo Editor: Richard Fox
Production by Wiley Indianapolis Composition Services

Front cover photo: Salzkammergut Area: Two ladies outside a typical house with summer flowers
Back cover photo: View of Hallstadt

For information on our other products and services or to obtain technical support, please contact our Customer Care Department within the U.S. at 800-762-2974, outside the U.S. at 317-572-3993 or fax 317-572-4002.

Wiley also publishes its books in a variety of electronic formats. Some content that appears in print may not be available in electronic formats.

Manufactured in the United States of America

5   4   3   2

Contents

List of Maps

An Invitation to the Reader

In researching this book, we discovered many wonderful places—hotels, restaurants, shops, and more. We're sure you'll find others. Please tell us about them, so we can share the information with your fellow travelers in upcoming editions. If you were disappointed with a recommendation, we'd love to know that, too. Please write to:

Frommer's Austria, 10th Edition
Wiley Publishing, Inc. • 111 River Street, 5th Floor • Hoboken, NJ 07030

An Additional Note

Please be advised that travel information is subject to change at any time—and this is especially true of prices. We therefore suggest that you write or call ahead for confirmation when making your travel plans. The authors, editors, and publisher cannot be held responsible for the experiences of readers while traveling. Your safety is important to us, however, so we encourage you to stay alert and be aware of your surroundings. Keep a close eye on cameras, purses, and wallets, all favorite targets of thieves and pickpockets.

New! Frommer's Star Ratings & Icons

Every hotel, restaurant, and attraction listing in this guide has been ranked for quality, value, service, amenities, and special features using a star-rating scale. In country, state, and regional guides, we also rate towns and regions to help you narrow down your choices and budget your time accordingly. Hotels and restaurants in the Very Expensive and Expensive categories are rated on a scale of one (highly recommended) to three stars (exceptional). Those in the Moderate and Inexpensive categories rate from zero (recommended) to two stars (very highly recommended). Attractions, towns, and regions are rated according to the following scale: zero stars (recommended), one star (highly recommended), two stars (very highly recommended), and three stars (must-see).

In addition to the rating system, we also use seven icons to highlight insider information, useful tips, special bargains, hidden gems, memorable experiences, kid-friendly venues, places to avoid, and other useful information:

(*Finds*   (*Fun Fact*   (*Kids*   (*Moments*   (*Overrated*   (*Tips*   (*Value*

The following abbreviations are used for credit cards:

AE American Express	DISC Discover	V Visa
DC Diners Club	MC MasterCard	

FROMMERS.COM

Now that you have the guidebook to a great trip, visit our website at **www.frommers.com** for travel information on nearly 2,500 destinations. With features updated regularly, we give you instant access to the most current trip-planning information available. At Frommers.com, you'll also find the best prices on airfares, accommodations, and car rentals—and you can even book travel online through our travel booking partners. At Frommers.com, you'll also find the following:

- Online updates to our most popular guidebooks
- Vacation sweepstakes and contest giveaways
- Newsletter highlighting the hottest travel trends
- Online travel message boards with featured travel discussions

What's New in Austria

In the vanguard of world tourism, Austria is always changing, but its imperial monuments, alpine majesty, and scenic wonders remain eternal. Nonetheless, here are some of the latest developments.

VIENNA In the Hotel Ambassador, **Mörwald,** Kärntner Strasse 22 (© 01/961-61-0), has become the most stylish restaurant in Vienna. From bankers to hipsters, *haute* Vienna is flocking to these precincts for a refined and classic Viennese cuisine as created by master chef Christian Domschitz. He takes time-tested recipes and gives them innovative modern twists.

Vienna's newest grand museum is also the site of a trend-setting rendezvous point, the chic **Café Leopold,** in the Leopold Museum, Museumsplatz 1 (© 01/523-67-32). The cafe, which serves top-notch international dishes, operates long after the museum has closed for the day. Most dishes come from the kitchens of middle Europe or Southeast Asia, including Vietnam.

A direct competitor of Café Leopold is **Café Restaurant Halle,** in the Kunsthalle Wien, Museumsplatz 1 (© 01/523-7001). More spacious than the Café Leopold, it boats a somewhat more sophisticated menu, which is frequently changed and adjusted according to the seasons.

The biggest cultural news coming out of middle Europe is the opening of the **MuseumsQuartier Complex,** Vienna's major statement for the new millennium. The complex has been compared to combining the Guggenheim Museum with New York's Museum of Modern Art and tossing in a few more institutions as well. Contemporary art and classic modern art are showcased at **Kunsthalle Wien** (© 01/521-89-0). The **Leopold Museum** (© 01/525-70), contains the world's largest treasure trove of the works of Egon Schiele (1890–1918), among other artists. One of the most outstanding collections of contemporary art is presented at **MUMOK (Museum of Modern Art Ludwig Foundation)** (© 01/525-00). American Pop Art is mingled with major continental movements such as Hyperrealism. See chapters 3 and 4 for information about all of these establishments.

SALZBURG In the City of Mozart, more visitors are discovering that some of Salzburg's best accommodation deals lie only a 20-minute or so ride from the historic center, in the city's leafy suburbs. More locals are opening up charming little inns to catch the overflow from the city's downtown core. Chief among these is **Hotel Am Nussdorferhof,** Moosstrasse 36 (© 0662/824838), a renovated 70-year-old building that charges affordable rates and houses guests in considerable comfort.

In the same vein, **Rosenvilla,** Höfelgasse 4 (© 0662/621765), has opened in a residential suburb across from the Salzach River and the Altstadt, or Old Town. A graceful turn-of-the-20th-century villa has been renovated, offering beautifully furnished, cozy bedrooms. With its wrought-iron supports and a small garden, Rosenvilla is a cliché of Austrian charm.

On the restaurant front, another establishment, the restaurant **Pfefferschiff,** Sollheim 3, in the suburb of Hallwang (© **0662/661242**), is luring Salzburgers out to its country precincts for a superb continental cuisine. In a converted country-baroque rectory some 3 centuries old, the owner/chef Klaus Fleischhaker will dazzle and delight you with his frequently changing menu that always emphasizes what's fresh and good in any season. Every dish is given an original touch, even the desserts, which include a succulent version of rhubarb tart with buttermilk ice cream.

Back in Salzburg itself, the **Restaurant Bristol** in the Hotel Bristol, Makartplatz 4 (© **0662/8735577**), is giving other top dining choices, such as the Goldener Hirsch, serious competition. Even if you are not a guest of the deluxe hotel, you might want to visit to sample a continental cuisine that truly lives up to its potential. The adjacent club-style bar is also a stylish and comfortable place for a drink.

Those in the know about Salzburg sightseeing will find that two brothers have opened **Ristorante/Pizzeria Il Sole,** Gstättengasse 15 (© **0662/843284**), near the Monchsberg elevator. They not only serve the best pizzas—more than a dozen different flavors—in the Old Town, but they offer a most respectable and affordable Italian cuisine as well. For more details about all of these establishments, refer to chapter 7.

UPPER AUSTRIA In Linz, the capital of Upper Austria, the dining secret is out. Linzers have jealously guarded the address of the **Restaurant Verdi,** at Pachmayrstrasse 137 in the village of Lichtenberg, 3km (2 miles) from the center. Now with foreign press coverage in 2002, visitors to Linz are also heading here for its excellent modern continental and Austrian cooking. The building itself is a century old, but the cuisine is contemporary: Time-tested recipes are lightened but made equally as tasty for the modern palate. See chapter 9.

INNSBRUCK Those seeking a decent, affordable hotel in the capital of the Tyrol might gravitate to **Best Western Hotel Mondschein,** Mariahilfstrasse 6 ((© **0512/22784**), which has now joined the Best Western chain and has been much improved. During its restoration, the antique interior was carefully preserved—the building originally dates from 1473—but all the modern comforts have been added.

Innsbruck has seen an explosion of new and good restaurants. Chief among these is **Jörgele,** Herzog-Friedrich-Strasse 13 (© **0512/582217**), serving a top-notch Austrian and Tyrolean cuisine that's known locally for its good value and most affordable meals. The building that houses this restaurant was a wine tavern dating from the 16th century. Another good choice making local culinary news is **Sweet Basil,** Herzog-Friedrich-Strasse 31 (© **0512/584996**), with its sophisticated international cuisine. The chefs here roam the world for culinary inspiration.

Austria, a land of meat-eaters, is not known for its vegetarian restaurants, but **Philippine,** Templstrasse 2 (© **0512/589157**), serves some of Innsbruck's finest vegetarian dishes, along with an assortment of fish specialties. For information about all of these establishments, refer to chapter 10.

VORALBERG The world's largest museum devoted to the Rolls-Royce automobile, appropriately called **The Rolls-Royce Museum,** 11A Gütle (© **05572/52652**), has opened in Dornbirn, "The City of Textiles," in the heart of Voralberg. A world-class collector of these deluxe vehicles has assembled the collection of swanky cars, owned by everybody from John Lennon to Queen Elizabeth II. Vehicles are spread across three floors. See chapter 11 for more details.

CARINTHIA In the capital of Klagenfurt, the center of the Austrian lake district, **Maria Loretto,** Lorettoweg 54 (© **0463/24465**), has suddenly been discovered by the regional gourmet guides. It specializes in seafood and does so exceedingly well, using imported ingredients from the Atlantic Ocean along with the North and Mediterranean seas. For excellent food and romantic and cozy dining in this region of Austria, it doesn't get much better than Maria Loretto.

A challenger in Klagenfurt is **Restaurant Oscar,** Sankt Veiter Ring 43 (© **0463/5001-77**), which ranks along with Maria Loretto as the finest dining choice in the city. With its refined Austrian and Italian cuisine, it is waking up

the taste buds of this once-sleepy dining town. Its sea bass and sea trout are reason enough to visit.

Good news is also emerging from the former capital of Carinthia, St. Veit an der Glan, where the **Rogner Dorint Hotel,** Friesacherstrasse 1 (© **04212/46600**), has opened as the town's first art-filled hotel. Designed by Ernst Fuchs, doyen of the country's "Fantastic Realists," the hotel sits behind a Tiffany-style glass exterior and is filled with luxury and comfort. For information about all of these establishments, refer to chapter 12.

STYRIA In the capital of this region, the city of Graz, **Johan,** Landhausgasse 1 (© **0316/821312-0**), has emerged as the premier and most stylish restaurant in the city. Its setting in a medieval building might be old, but the chef prepares a "new Austrian" cuisine for palates demanding lighter fare. His continental dishes are refined and sophisticated. Johan is also the site of the best bar in Graz. See chapter 13.

1

The Best of Austria

There's so much to do in Austria, from exploring historic castles and palaces to skiing some of the world's finest alpine slopes. All the choices you'll have to make when planning your trip can be a bit bewildering. We've tried to make your task easier by compiling a list of our favorite experiences and discoveries. In the following pages you'll find the kind of candid advice we'd give our close friends.

1 The Best Travel Experiences

- **Skiing in the Alps:** This is the reason thousands of visitors come to Austria in the first place; skiing is the Austrian national sport. The country abounds in ski slopes, and you'll find the best ones in Tyrol, Land Salzburg, and Vorarlberg, although most parts of Carinthia, Western Styria, and Lower Austria also have slopes. The season lasts from late November to April, depending on snow conditions. At 1,739m (5,700 ft.), the Obertauern region extends its ski season until May. The daredevils among you can ski glaciers at 3,355m (11,000 ft.), even in summer. See section 8, "The Best Ski Areas," in this chapter.
- **Feasting on the "Emperor's Dish,"** *Tafelspitz:* No Austrian dish is more typical than the fabled *Tafelspitz* (boiled beef dinner) favored by Emperor Franz Joseph. Boiled beef might sound dull, but *Tafelspitz* is far from bland. Boiled to a tender delicacy, the "table end" cut is flavored with a variety of spices, including juniper berries, celery root, and onions. An apple-and-horseradish sauce further enlivens the dish, which is usually served with fried, grated potatoes. The best *Tafelspitz* is served in

Vienna, where the chefs have been making the dish for decades. We recommend several restaurants where you can sample this dish. See chapter 3.
- **Listening to Mozart:** It is said that at any time of the day or night in Austria, someone, somewhere is playing the music of Wolfgang Amadeus Mozart. You might hear it at an opera house, a church, a festival, an open-air concert, or more romantically in a Belle Epoque cafe performed by a Hungarian orchestra. Regardless, "the sound of music" drifting through Vienna is likely the creation of this child prodigy. Try to hear Mozart on his home turf, especially in Vienna and Salzburg. See chapters 4 and 7.
- **Watching the Lipizzaner Stallions (Vienna):** Nothing evokes the heyday of imperial Vienna more than the Spanish Riding School. Here, the sleek white stallions and their expert riders demonstrate the classic art of dressage in choreographed leaps and bounds. The stallions, a crossbreed of Spanish thoroughbreds and Karst horses, are the finest equestrian performers on earth. Riders wear brass buttons, doeskin

breeches and black bicorne hats. You can watch the performances, but you'll need to make reservations 6 to 8 weeks in advance. See p. 129.

- **Cruising the Danube (Donau):** Johann Strauss took a bit of poetic license in calling the Donau "The Blue Danube," as it's actually a muddy-green color. But a Danube cruise is a highlight of any Austrian vacation. The legendary DDSG, Blue Danube Shipping Company, Handelskai 265, offers mostly 1-day trips. On board, you'll pass some of the most famous sights in eastern Austria, including Krems and Melk. See "Boating on the 'Blue' Danube" (p. 149).

- *Heurigen* **Hopping in the Vienna Woods:** *Heurigen* are rustic wine taverns that celebrate the arrival of each year's new wine (*Heuriger*) by placing a pine branch over the door. Austrians rush to these taverns to drink the new local wines and feast on a country buffet. Some *Heurigen* have garden tables with panoramic views of the Danube Valley, whereas others provide shaded, centuries-old courtyards where revelers can enjoy live folk music. Try the red wines from Vöslau, the Sylvaner of Grinzing, or the Riesling of Nussberg, while listening to a *Schrammelmusik* quartet with all the revelers singing "*Wien bleibt Wien.*" See "The Wienerwald (Vienna Woods)" in chapter 5.

- **Reliving** *The Sound of Music:* In 1964, Julie Andrews, Christopher Plummer, and a gaggle of kids imitating the von Trapp family filmed one of the world's great musicals. The memory of that Oscar-winning movie lingers on, as a steady stream of visitors heads to Salzburg just to take *The Sound of Music* tour. You visit the Nonnberg Abbey where the nuns sang "How Do You Solve a Problem like Maria?" as well as that little gazebo where Rolf and Liesl danced in the rain. There's also a stop at the Felsenreitschule (Rock Riding School), where the von Trapps gave their final performance. See p. 241.

- **Driving on Top of the World on the Grossglockner Road (Land Salzburg):** For the drive of a lifetime, you can take Europe's longest and most panoramic alpine highway, with hairpin turns and bends around every corner—the stuff Grand Prix is made of. It begins at Bruck an der Grossglocknerstrasse at 757m (2,483 ft.); continues through the Hochtortunnel, where the highest point is 2,507m (8,220 ft.); and ends in the province of Carinthia. The mountain part of the road, stretching some 22km (13½ miles), often at 1,983m (6,500 ft.), has a maximum gradient of 12%. You can drive this stunning engineering feat from mid-May to mid-November, although the road is safest from mid-June to mid-September. The views are among the greatest in the world, but keep your eye on that curvy road! See p. 282.

- **Exploring the Alps:** There are few places in the world that are as splendid as the limestone chain of mountains shared between Austria and Bavaria. Moving toward the east, the Alps slope away to the Great Hungarian Plain. The Austrian Alps break into three chains, including the High or Central Alps, the Northern Limestone Alps, and the Southern Limestone Alps. In the west, you discover fairy-tale Tyrolean villages, the Holy Roman Empire attractions of Innsbruck, and some of the world's greatest ski resorts, including St. Anton, Zürs, Lech, and Kitzbühel. Filled with quaint little towns, the Eastern

Alps sprawl across the Tyrolean country, West Styria, and Land Salzburg. Centuries-old castles and stunning views await you at every turn. See chapters 8, 10, 11, and 13.

2 The Most Romantic Getaways

• **Hof bei Salzburg (Land Salzburg):** Lying on Lake Fuschl (Fuschlsee), this chic resort is only a 15-minute ride from the congestion of Salzburg; it boasts a breathtaking alpine backdrop of blue clear but chilly waters, mountains, and evergreen forests. Based here, you can also easily get to Fuschlsee as well as Wolfgangsee and Mondsee. The town offers some romantic places to stay, notably the Hotel Schloss Fuschl (© 06229/22530), whose main section dates from 1450. See p. 287.

• **St. Wolfgang (Upper Austria):** On the Wolfgangsee, one of Austria's loveliest lakes, St. Wolfgang lies in the mountains of the Salzkammergut. It's the home of the White Horse Inn (© 06138/2306-0), which served as the setting for Ralph Benatzky's operetta *The White Horse Inn.* Lying 50km (31 miles) east of Salzburg, the resort is a summer paradise, with lakefront beaches and cafes and hiking opportunities in all directions, plus skiing in winter. See section 3, "St. Wolfgang & Bad Ischl," in chapter 9.

• **Mutters (Tyrol):** On a sunny plateau above Innsbruck, this little resort has been called the most beautiful village in Tyrol (quite a compliment). Mutters, a central base of the 1964 and 1976 Olympics, attracts visitors year-round. The most romantic place to stay is the Hotel Altenburg (© 0512/54-85-34), a restaurant back in 1622 and later a farmhouse before its conversion into an elegant hotel. See p. 357.

• **Stuben (Vorarlberg):** The rich and famous might flock to Vorarlberg's stellar ski resorts, Zürs or Lech, but we think you should sneak away to the little village of Stuben, 10km (6 miles) north of Lech on the west side of the Arlberg Pass. A way station for alpine travelers for centuries, Stuben was the birthplace of the great ski instructor Hannes Schneider. In winter, you can take a horse-drawn sleigh from Lech to Stuben. Once here, stay at Hotel Mondschein (© 05582/511), a 1739 house converted to a hotel. See p. 413.

• **Pörtschach (Carinthia):** Many wealthy Viennese have lavish summer homes in this resort town on the northern perimeter of Lake Wörther. Known for its lakeside promenade, it attracts a sports-oriented crowd that wants to hike, play golf, ride, sail, and water-ski, or just enjoy scenic drives through the countryside. Lake Wörther itself is Carinthia's largest alpine lake, yet its waters are warm, often going above 80°F (27°C) in summer. We recommend staying and dining at the romantic Hotel Schloss Leonstain (© 04272/281-60), where Johannes Brahms composed his Violin Concerto and Second Symphony. See p. 432.

• **Bad Aussee (Styria):** An old market town and spa in the "green heart" of the Salzkammergut, Bad Aussee is 80km (50 miles) southeast of Salzburg. In the Valley of Traun, it's set against the backdrop of Totes Gebirge and the Dachstein massif. June is a lovely time to visit, when fields of narcissus burst into bloom. Bad Aussee lies only 5km

(3 miles) north of the lake, Altausee, and is situated in one of the most beautiful parts of Austria. Long known as a summer spa resort, it's also developing into a winter ski center. The best place to stay is the Eurotel Erzherzog Johann (© **03622/52507**), with its rustic interior and spa facilities that include an indoor swimming pool. See section 4, "Bad Aussee," in chapter 13.

3 The Best Castles & Palaces

- **Schönbrunn Palace (Vienna):** This Hapsburg palace of 1,441 rooms was the summer residence of this powerful family that ruled much of Europe. The great baroque architect J. B. Fischer von Erlach modeled his plans on Versailles, though he ultimately surpassed the French palace in size. Even so, Maria Theresa spoke of the palace as "cozy," where she could retreat with her many children and paint watercolors or work on her embroidery. The Hapsburg dynasty came to an end here when Karl I signed his Act of Abdication on November 11, 1918. See p. 136.

- **Hofburg (Vienna):** The winter palace of the Hapsburgs, Hofburg was the seat of an imperial throne that once governed the mighty Austro-Hungarian Empire. The sprawling palace reads like an architectural timeline of the Hapsburg family, dating from 1279 with subsequent additions continuing until 1918. Truly a city within a city, the Hofburg houses everything today from the offices of the president of Austria to the Spanish Riding School with its Lipizzaner stallions—even the Vienna Boys' Choir. See section 1, "The Hofburg Palace Complex," in chapter 4.

- **Österreichische Galarie Belvedere (Belvedere Palace) (Vienna):** On a slope above Vienna, this palace was designed by Johann Lukas von Hildebrandt, the last major architect of the baroque in Austria.

Belvedere served as a summer home for Prince Eugene of Savoy, the country's greatest military hero, who routed the Ottomans in the late 17th century. The palace was a gift from the imperial throne in recognition of the prince's military achievements, although he was (at the time) richer than the Hapsburgs. Not exactly pleased with his "gift," the hero made stunning new baroque additions and improvements. As a collector and patron of the arts, he filled the palace with objets d'art. See p. 134.

- **Schloss Esterházy (Eisenstadt):** This castle in Eisenstadt, capital of Burgenland, was the seat of the Esterházy princes, a great and powerful Hungarian family that helped the Hapsburgs gain control of Hungary. The seat of their power was built around an inner courtyard and designed by Carlone, the Italian architect. Work started on the castle in 1663, but the design was subsequently altered over the years and later received the baroque treatment. The family invited Haydn here to work on his music, and in the Haydnsaal, the great composer conducted an orchestra for the family's entertainment. See p. 193.

- **Residenz (Salzburg):** The seat of the Salzburg prince-bishops, this opulent palace dates from 1120. Over the years, newer palaces were added to form an ecclesiastical complex. On the palace's second floor is a 15-room art gallery filled with the works of 16th- to

18th-century European masters. You can also walk through more than a dozen richly decorated staterooms. The Residenz fountain, which dates from the 1660s, is one of the largest and most impressive baroque fountains north of the Alps. See p. 234.

- **Hofburg (Innsbruck):** This imperial palace, built in the 14th to 16th centuries, was the seat of Emperor Maximilian I. In the 18th century, Empress Maria Theresa made major structural changes, giving it a rococo appearance; the Giant's Hall is an architectural marvel of 18th-century Austrian architecture. In the palace's main hall hangs a portrait of Maria's famous youngest daughter, Marie Antoinette—with her head. See p. 334.

4 The Best Cathedrals & Abbeys

- **Domkirche St. Stephan (Vienna):** Crowned by a 137m (450-ft.) steeple, St. Stephan's, the Cathedral of Vienna, is one of Europe's great Gothic structures. The great Austrian writer Adalbert Stifter claimed that its "sheer beauty lifts the spirit." The Viennese regard this monument with great affection, calling it *Der Steffl.* The cathedral's vast tiled roof is exactly twice the height of its walls. Intricate altarpieces, stone canopies, and masterful Gothic sculptures are just some of the treasures that lie within. Climb the spiral steps to the South Tower for a panoramic view of the city. See p. 131.

- **Melk Abbey (Melk):** This abbey church, situated on a promontory above the Danube, is one of the world's finest baroque buildings. Melk figures in the *Nibelungenlied,* the great German epic poem, as well as Umberto Eco's best-selling *The Name of the Rose.* The view from here is one of the most panoramic in a country known for its views. This baroque masterpiece has burned many times, the first time in 1297 and then in 1683 and 1735, but each time has risen from the ashes. After a 1947 fire, the golden abbey church was restored yet again, even to the regilding of statues and altars with gold bullion. See p. 188.

- **Salzburg Cathedral (Salzburg):** World renowned for its 4,000-pipe organ, this cathedral is the "most perfect" Renaissance structure in the Germanic countries, with a rich baroque interior and elaborate frescoes. It towers 76m (250 ft.) into the air and holds 10,000 worshippers. The present cathedral was consecrated with great ceremony in 1628, although records show a cathedral on this spot since the 8th century. In 1756, Mozart was baptized in the Romanesque font. See p. 234.

- **Abbey of St. Florian (St. Florian, Near Linz):** Austria's largest abbey is a towering example of the baroque style. On a site occupied by the Augustinians since the 11th century, the present structure was constructed mainly from 1686 to 1751. Honoring a 4th-century Christian martyr and saint, the abbey has as its chief treasure the Altdorfer Gallery, whose most valuable pictures are those by Albrecht Altdorfer, master of the Danubian school. Anton Bruckner, Austria's greatest composer of church music in the 1800s, became the organist at St. Florian as a young man and composed many of his masterpieces here. See p. 298.

THE BEST HISTORIC TOWNS   9

5 The Best Museums

- **Kunsthistorisches Museum (Vienna):** This art gallery, across from Hofburg Palace, houses the stellar art collection of the Hapsburg dynasty. It's especially strong in the Flemish, Dutch, and German schools, with works ranging from Rubens to Dürer, Pieter Bruegel the Elder to Van Dyck. Also strong are the Italian, Spanish, and French collections, with works by Veronese, Caravaggio, and Tintoretto. See p. 133.

- **MuseumsQuartier (Vienna):** Vienna launched its new millennium with one of the major cultural centers to open in Middle Europe in some 2 decades. Architecturally stunning, this complex contains a treasure trove of art, being especially strong in modern works. The three major museums to visit here are Kunsthalle Wien, Leopold Museum, and MUMOK (Museum of Modern Art Ludwig Foundation). See p. 129.

- **Mozart Geburtshaus (Salzburg):** Music pilgrims flock to see the typical old burgher's house where Mozart was born. You can still see many of his childhood belongings, including a lock of hair from his egg-shape noggin, his first viola, and a pair of keyboard instruments. Mozart's first violin is also displayed. Even at the age of 4, he was a musical genius. See p. 236.

- **Mauthausen (Upper Austria):** The most unusual and horrifying museum in Austria lies 29km (18 miles) down the Danube from Linz. Mauthausen was a notorious concentration camp, used in World War II for the slaughter of Austria's Jews. It's estimated that some 200,000 victims were killed here. Visitors today can bear witness to this scene of holocaust. See p. 297.

- **Tiroler Volkskunst-Museum (Innsbruck):** In an abbey with 16th-century origins, this museum of popular art contains Austria's most impressive collection of Tyrolean artifacts. You'll see everything from mangers to monumental stoves from peasant's homes. The collections sweep from the Gothic decorative style through the Renaissance to the rich and opulent baroque era. The first floor contains models of Tyrolean houses. See p. 335.

- **Landeszeughaus (Armory) (Graz):** This armory, built between 1642 and 1645, displays 3 centuries of weaponry, one of Europe's great collections. Here you'll see some 30,000 harnesses, coats of mail, helmets, swords, pikes, and muskets of various kinds, along with pistols and harquebuses. There are richly engraved and embossed jousting suits and a parade of armor. See p. 464.

- **Österreichisches Freilichtmuseum (Outside Graz):** Sixteen kilometers (10 miles) from Graz in a wooded valley is one of Austria's great open-air museums. This museum of vernacular architecture, spread across 50 hectares (120 acres), features some 80 rural homes with ancillary buildings that have been reassembled. The site presents an excellent overview of the country's rural heritage, from a Carinthian farmstead to alpine houses from the Tyrol. See p. 466.

6 The Best Historic Towns

- **Krems (Lower Austria, Outside Vienna):** In the eastern part of the Wachau, on the river's left bank, this 1,000-year-old town incorporates the little village of Stein, with narrow streets terraced above the river. Many houses date from the 16th century. See p. 149.

- **Wels (Upper Austria):** Even in Roman times, Wels, on the left bank of the Traun River, was a flourishing town. Emperor Maximilian I died here in 1519. Its town parish church has a 14th-century chancel with a tower from 1732. Across from the church is the house of Salome Alt, the notorious mistress of Prince-Archbishop Wolf Dietrich of Salzburg who bore him 15 children. See section 6, "Wels," in chapter 9.

- **St. Christoph (Tyrol):** St. Christoph, the mountain way station of St. Anton in Tyrol, sits at an elevation of 1,784m (5,850 ft.). It was a famous settlement on the road to the Arlberg Pass and was the site of a fabled hospice established in 1386. Members of the hospice patrolled the pass looking for frozen bodies and assisting wayfarers in trouble. See p. 376.

- **Lienz (East Tyrol):** Not to be confused with Linz in Upper Austria, Lienz with an *e* is the capital of remote East Tyrol. Set at the junction of three valleys, this colorful town stretches along the banks of the Isel River. In summer, mountain climbers use it as a base to scale the Dolomites. The town is presided over by Schloss Bruck, the fortress of the counts of Gorz. See p. 400.

- **Mariazell (Styria):** Pilgrims come here to see the Mariazell Basilica, dating from the early 1200s, with a trio of prominent towers. Both Fischer von Erlachs, senior and junior, the famed baroque architects, helped transform the church. The Chapel of Grace inside is the national shrine of Austria, Hungary, and Bohemia. If you're exploring Styria, this old town, both a winter playground and a summer resort, is worth a stop. See section 3, "Mariazell," in chapter 13.

7 The Best Outdoor Adventures

Skiing is the name of the game in Austria, of course; see section 8, below, for a list of the best ski areas.

- **Biking Along the Danube:** The Lower Danube Cycle Track is a biker's paradise. The most exciting villages and stopovers along the Danube, including Melk and Dürnstein, are linked by a riverside bike trail between Vienna and Naarn. As you pedal along, you'll pass castles, medieval towns, and latticed vineyards. You can rent bikes from the train or ferry stations, and all tourist offices provide route maps. See section 6, "The Active Vacation Planner," in chapter 2.

- **Ballooning Over Styria:** Styria has some of the best alpine ballooning in Europe, as experienced by participants who have sailed over the alpine ranges of the Salzkammergut and a *steppe*-like landscape that evokes the Great Hungarian Plain. A typical ballooning excursion will cross river valleys, mountain peaks, glaciers, and vineyards. For outfitters, see p. 458.

- **Canoeing & Rafting in the Salzburg Alps (Land Salzburg):** Known for their beautiful alpine lakes and roaring white-water streams, the lakes in and around Salzburg are some of the most ideal in Europe for canoeing, rafting, and kayaking. Waters aren't polluted and powerboats are restricted, making these safe and idyllic adventures. See p. 254.

• **Hiking in the Zillertal Alps (Tyrol):** This mountain paradise is the best place to hike in Western Austria. Instead of roads, you'll find footpaths winding through the scenic Zillertal Valley, east of Innsbruck. Alpine guides lead you to some of the most panoramic scenery you've ever seen. At Zell am Ziller's tourist office, you can purchase a Z-Hiking Ticket valid on all lift stations in the Zillertal. After that, this alpine world is yours as you hike across mountain trails or ascend on lifts to higher elevations. You can even find year-round skiing at Tuxer Gletscher, a glacier. See section 7, "The Ziller Valley," in chapter 10.

• **Traversing Ice Age Valleys:** No scenic thrill in all of Europe quite matches that available in the Hohe Tauern National Park, Europe's largest national park. Part of the Austrian Central Alps, the Hohe Tauern range cuts across Land Salzburg, Tyrol, and Carinthia. Molded during the Ice Age, these valleys are filled with pastureland, alpine heaths, vast expanses of snow and ice, forested bulwarks, fields of rock, and gargantuan alluvial and mudflow cones. The park is also home to numerous nearly extinct species. Much of this vast and remote area has never been explored, but parts are accessible by car or government-owned Bundesbus (the route goes from Böckstein to Badgastein and from Zell am Ziller to Krimml). You can get car or bus information from the local tourist offices. See chapter 8.

8 The Best Ski Areas

• **Innsbruck:** Tyrol's capital, the medieval city of Innsbruck, is set against a scenic backdrop of high mountain peaks, with good skiing in virtually all directions. Two Olympic Winter Games have been staged in the Innsbruck area. It's somewhat inconvenient to get to the slopes, but it's worth the effort. There are five ski resorts around Innsbruck. Hungerburg is the local favorite because a funicular from the city heads directly to the base station at Hoch Innsbruck at 300m (984 ft.). Nearby Igls also enjoys great favor with its extensive slopes under the Patscherkofel peak. For the most extensive all-around skiing, head for Axamer Lizum, although it's the farthest from Innsbruck. Good snow conditions are generally the rule. See section 1, "Innsbruck: The Capital of Tyrol," in chapter 10.

• **St. Anton am Arlberg:** This picture-postcard Tyrolean village sits at 1,304m (4,277 ft.), although its upper slopes climb to more than 2,801m (9,185 ft.). Massive snow falls attract intermediate and expert skiers from all over. St. Anton lies at the eastern base of the Arlberg Pass. St. Christoph, 10km (3 miles) west, lies almost on the Arlberg Pass and is another chic winter enclave. Four major ski areas at St. Anton—Galzig, Valluga, St. Christoph, and Gampen-Kapall—are interlinked to form one big ski circuit. See p. 369.

• **Seefeld (Tyrol):** One of the major international ski resorts of Europe, Seefeld hosted the Nordic events for the 1964 and 1976 Olympic Winter Games and the 1985 Nordic Ski World Championships. On a sunny plateau at 1,052m (3,450 ft.), it has prime skiing conditions and a network of surface lifts, chairlifts, and cable cars that appeal to skiers of all levels. In addition, there are 200km

(124 miles) of prepared cross-country tracks. Seefeld is also known for its other winter sports, including curling and outdoor skating. See section 6, "Seefeld," in chapter 10.

- **Kitzbühel:** This home of the world's original lift circuit is a medieval walled city and regal resort that in the 1960s blossomed into a premier international spot. Visitors flock here in winter to ski forested trails and broad alpine ridges. The Hahnenkamm ski circus has more than 50 lifts at elevations of 800m to 2,000m (2,624 ft.–6,560 ft.). The main season runs from Christmas to mid-March. See p. 387.

- **Lech & Zürs:** In Vorarlberg, these neighboring resorts feature the best skiing in Austria. They are also among Europe's most exclusive ski resorts, drawing a chic crowd. Both resorts cater to novice and intermediate skiers with broad boulevards winding between peaks and runs that fall straight back to the resorts. The resorts also offer high altitudes and good snow conditions, plus a high-tech lift system. Huge chunks of skiable terrain above both resorts provide a 20km (12½-mile) long circuit with generally superior ski conditions. See p. 406 for Lech and p. 414 for Zürs.

9 The Best Lake Resorts & Spas

- **Baden bei Wien (Lower Austria):** Developed by the ancient Romans and then studded with ocher-colored Biedermeier buildings during the early 19th century, this was once known as the "dowager empress" of Austrian spas. Today frequent chamber concerts and elaborate flower beds keep the aura of old-fashioned grandeur alive. See section 2, "The Spa Town of Baden bei Wien," in chapter 5.

- **Bad Hofgastein (Land Salzburg):** A select annex of the larger, better-known resort of Badgastein, it appeals to anyone in search of peace, healing, and quiet. Civic architecture and hotels are appropriately grand and solemn. See section 3, "Bad Hofgastein," in chapter 8.

- **Badgastein (Land Salzburg):** This is Austria's premier spa, with a resort industry dating from the 1400s. Hotels are almost universally excellent, offering the densest concentration of fine lodgings in Land Salzburg. See section 4, "Badgastein: Austria's Premier Spa," in chapter 8.

- **St. Wolfgang (Upper Austria):** The landscapes around this lake are so lovely that they served as the setting for the popular musical work *The White Horse Inn,* by Ralph Benatzky. Adjacent to the grander and somewhat more formal resort of Bad Ischl, St. Wolfgang offers ample options for outdoor diversions. See section 3, "St. Wolfgang & Bad Ischl," in chapter 9.

- **Bad Ischl (Upper Austria):** For more than 60 years, Franz Joseph selected Bad Ischl as the summer holiday seat of the Hapsburg Empire. No other Austrian resort captures the glamour of the long-departed empire quite like this one. See section 3, "St. Wolfgang & Bad Ischl," in chapter 9.

- **Pörtschach (Carinthia):** It's the premier resort in Carinthia, the southeasterly Austrian province bordering the edge of Slovenia. Site of dozens of fine villas, it's unmistakably linked to the good life. See p. 445.

- **Velden (Carinthia):** The region's most sophisticated resort, Velden is the heart of the so-called Austrian Riviera. Despite the traffic, it offers a convenient combination of bucolic charm and Viennese style. See p. 447.
- **Villach (Carinthia):** The second-largest town in the province, it's the gateway to Austria's lake district, northeastern Italy, and Slovenia. The nearby village of Warmbad-Villach offers warm springs that were favored by the ancient Romans. See section 4, "Villach," in chapter 12.
- **Bad Gleichenberg (Styria):** Set within one of the most undiscovered regions of Austria, near the Slovenian border, this is the most important summer spa in Styria. It stands among rolling hills and vineyards. This is an area rich in history, natural beauty, and imperial nostalgia. See section 2, "Bad Gleichenberg," in chapter 13.
- **Bad Aussee (Styria):** Lying at the junction of two tributaries of the region's most important river, Bad Aussee is known for its verdant beauty, healthful waters, and bracing climate. It's also the center of a network of hiking and cross-country ski trails. See section 4, "Bad Aussee," in chapter 13.

10 The Best Luxury Hotels

- **Hotel Bristol** (Vienna; ✆ 888/625-5144 in the U.S., or 01/515-160): Facing the Staatsoper, this classic six-story building is a Viennese symbol of luxury and class. It ranks with the Imperial as the city's most glamorous hotel. The luxuriously appointed and often exquisite rooms boast a cornucopia of amenities. Velvet and silk, chandeliers, and double doors adorn the place and the ever-attentive, gracious staff adds to the allure. See p. 77.
- **Hotel Imperial** (Vienna; ✆ 800/325-3589 in the U.S., or 01/501100): Once a ducal palace—now Vienna's most glamorous hotel—the Imperial is a landmark 2 blocks east of the Staatsoper. Built in 1869, it's Austria's official "guesthouse," often hosting visiting musicians (Wagner stayed here long ago). A wealth of antiques adorn the gracious public areas, and everything is gilt-edged, from the polished marble to the glittering chandeliers. Opulently appointed rooms vary in size but are generally regal. See p. 80.
- **Hotel Schloss Dürnstein** (Dürnstein, along the Danube; ✆ 02711/212): A 10-minute walk from the medieval village in Wachau, this fairy-tale castle is perched above a bend in the river. Above the hotel are the ruins of a castle where Richard the Lion-Hearted was imprisoned. This exquisite gem of a hotel brims with history, glamour, art, and fantasy. See p. 187.
- **Goldener Hirsch** (Salzburg; ✆ 800/325-3535 in the U.S., or 0662/8084): For some 6 centuries, this mellow old hostelry has been welcoming guests to its patrician precincts. With the city's best and most professional staff, the Goldener Hirsch is the finest hotel in Salzburg. In the Old Town, near Mozart's birthplace, the building is a historical monument, rich in legend and lore. Although rooms vary, all are furnished with antiques in traditional taste but have modern plumbing and appointments. See p. 208.
- **Hotel Grüner-Baum** (Badgastein; ✆ 06434/2516-0): A veritable village has grown up around this

converted hunting lodge. The family-run hotel has sheltered everybody from Toscanini to the Shah of Iran. Scattered chalets house some of the finest rooms at this fashionable spa—each in the typical alpine style. The hospitality is unequaled in the area. See p. 269.

- **Hotel Schloss Fuschl** (Hof bei Salzburg; ℂ **06229/22530**): East of Salzburg, this medieval castle and its outbuildings have origins dating from 1450. Everybody from Eleanor Roosevelt to Khrushchev has stayed in this rich, lush setting of oriental rugs, antiques, fine art, and vaulted ceilings. Diners sit on a terrace taking in panoramic lake and alpine views. The spacious rooms are beautifully furnished and well maintained. Sports lovers feel at home here with a nine-hole golf course, indoor pool, and Turkish bath and sauna. See p. 288.

- **Grand Hotel** (Zell am See; ℂ **06542/788**): Three "grand hotels" have stood on this site over the years, and the latest incarnation is the grandest of them all. Windows open onto incredible views of the lake and the Alps. Flanked by pillars, the glassed-in pool also offers lake views, and the hotel has an array of facilities ranging from a gym to a sauna. The contemporary rooms, which vary in size and design, are the best in town. Split-level suites are also great. See p. 285.

- **Romantik Hotel Post** (Villach; ℂ **04242/26-10-10**): With architectural origins from 1500, this is the most fabled hotel in Carinthia. A hotel since the 1730s, it is a cozy and charming retreat on the town's main square. A pianist plays on the terrace in summer. Rooms are richly furnished, often with oriental rugs on parquet floors, including the suite where Emperor Charles V once slept in the 1500s. A solarium, gym, and sauna keep the hotel up-to-date. See p. 451.

11 The Best Affordable Hotels

- **Hotel Kaiserin Elisabeth** (Vienna; ℂ **01/515260**): Lots of famous folks, from Wagner to Franz Liszt, have stayed in this building, which dates from the 14th century. It manages to be stately and homey at the same time. Public areas are richly furnished with oriental rugs, a dome skylight, and marble floors. The most desirable rooms are furnished in a neobaroque style with parquet floors. See p. 86.

- **Gasthof-Pension Sänger Blondel** (Dürnstein; ℂ **02711/253**): Along the Danube sits this charmingly old-fashioned place, painted a bright lemon and accented with green shutters. It's named for the faithful minstrel who searched the countryside for the imprisoned Richard the Lion-Hearted. Today guests are housed in traditionally styled and cozy rooms; if your windows are open, you can sometimes hear zither music drifting in from the courtyard.

- **Hotel Auersperg** (Salzburg; ℂ **0662/889-44-0**): A traditional family-run hotel, with rooms of generous size, this charmer has an old-fashioned atmosphere but is still beautifully maintained, from its antiques-filled drawing room to its convivial library bar. It is a warm, inviting, and cozy place to base yourself in the city of Mozart. See p. 213.

- **Hotel Seehof** (Goldegg; ℂ **06415/8137**): This hotel, on a small alpine lake south of Salzburg, dates from 1449. Rustic artifacts and local painted furnishings add to its old-fashioned charm. In summer, guests can enjoy the outdoor terrace, but in winter, they come here for skiing. The hotel rents ski equipment and directs guests to the nearby slopes. See p. 259.

- **Schlosshotel Freisitz Roith** (Gmunden; ℂ 07612/64905): Built as a summer house by the Hapsburg Emperor Rudolf II in 1597, this castle hotel, in one of the most popular summer resorts in the Salzkammergut, is now open to all. Converted into a hotel in 1965, it's a winning combination of a baroque private residence and a Victorian hotel. See p. 320.
- **Hotel Goldener Adler** (Innsbruck; ℂ 0512/57-11-11): This hotel, which has hosted everyone from Goethe to Paganini, has a history spanning 6 centuries. Genuine art decorates the public areas, and the four dining rooms (including a Tyrolean cellar) are local favorites for eating and drinking. Rooms vary in size but are nicely appointed, with Tyrolean touches. The place isn't

luxurious, but is it ever historic and comfortable. See p. 340.
- **Romantik Hotel Traube** (Lienz; ℂ 04852/644-44): Deep in the heart of East Tyrol, this classic hotel rebuilt after World War II damage is the most desirable in this remote and offbeat part of Austria. Yet its prices are reasonable, and it also offers the best restaurant in East Tyrol. Open your window, see the mountains, and imagine you're Julie Andrews. See p. 403.
- **Hotel Alte Post-Wrann** (Velden; ℂ 04274/2141): In the sophisticated summer resort of Carinthia, at the western end of the Wörther See, this is an ideal choice for an "Austrian Riviera" vacation. Once the headquarters of a postal route station, it was long ago renovated, enlarged, and turned into this welcoming hotel. Rooms are sunny and traditionally furnished. The restaurant, with its massive ceiling beams, is very good. There's also a Viennese-style *Heurige* (rustic wine tavern) serving the finest local wines. See p. 449.

12 The Best Restaurants

- **Sacher Hotel Restaurant** (Vienna; ℂ 01/514560): A celebrity favorite since the days of the Empire, this is the home of one of the world's most famous pastries, the Sacher torte. Against a flaming scarlet background, you can enjoy dishes that pleased emperors— notably Vienna's famous dish *Tafelspitz*, the most savory and herb-flavored boiled beef you'll ever taste. Come dressed to the nines and prepare to enjoy a banquet fit for a king. See p. 101.
- **Drei Husaren** (Vienna; ℂ 01/512-1092): Drei Husaren has been a Viennese landmark for decades. It's a lavish, sophisticated setting in which to enjoy both

classic and creative Viennese specialties. If money's no object, you might sample some of the 35 tempting items offered on a roving hors d'oeuvre cart. A meal here is nothing short of exquisite. See p. 100.
- **Goldener Hirsch** (Salzburg; ℂ 0662/80-84-0): Hospitality has been served up within its thick walls since 1407, but today the victuals are vastly improved and the clientele is a little more refined. Few other places are as elegant, and during the Salzburg Music Festivals, this is definitely the place to be. The chef prefers the *grand bourgeois* tradition and prepares meals with both a

jeweler's precision and a poet's imagination. See p. 208.

- **Restaurant Ferwall** (St. Anton; © 05446/32-49): Set in the high Alps near the Arlberg Pass, this place attracts some of the most discerning palates in Europe. Since 1972, this restaurant has been serving some of the finest fare in Tyrol, a traditional Austrian and international menu with innovative modern twists. The restaurant celebrates Tyrolean country life. See p. 374.

- **Europastüberl** (Innsbruck; © 0512/5931): Head here for

spectacular food served among meticulously re-created traditional Tyrolean decor. As business travelers and corporate bigwigs know, its setting manages to be simultaneously rustic and sumptuous. See p. 344.

- **Maria Loretto** (Klagenfurt; © 0463/24465): This is the premier restaurant in the capital of Carinthia, site of Austria's summer lake district. A specialist in seafood, the restaurant hauls in raw ingredients from the Mediterranean and Atlantic, and its chefs fashion them into delectable platters. See p. 439.

13 The Best Dining Bargains

- **Plachutta** (Vienna; © 01/512-1577): The Viennese are fanatical about their *Tafelspitz* the way Italian chefs are firm in their standards for tomato sauce, or American Southerners insist that theirs is the only true fried chicken. No place in all of Austria serves better *Tafelspitz* than Plachutta, which produces 10 different variations! See p. 104.

- **Gulaschmuseum** (Vienna; © 01/512-1017): Imagine a "museum" devoted to goulash. Here you can find 15 varieties of this savory kettle of goodies inspired by neighboring Hungary, once part of the Austro-Hungarian Empire. Each dish is redolent with the taste of paprika, Hungary's national spice. There's even an all-vegetarian version. See p. 110.

- **Herzl Tavern** (Salzburg; © 0662/808-4889): Owned by the city's most glamorous hotel, the super-expensive Goldener Hirsch, the Herzl—in the center of town—is frequented by some of Europe's most celebrated musicians, who for some reason always demand the finest in cuisine. Here they get hearty food prepared in a

traditional style but with only the finest ingredients. See p. 222.

- **Weinhaus Attwenger** (Bad Ischl; © 06132/23327): Some parts of it, built in 1540, were already well established when 19th-century composers Bruckner and Lehar adopted it as one of their preferred wine houses. See p. 314.

- **Restaurant Wirt am Berg** (Wels; © 07242/45059): With a pedigree dating from 1630, Wirt am Berg boasts a vast wine cellar and flavorful food. Its modest prices draw diners from as far away as Munich. See p. 323.

- **Auerhann** (Zug; © 05583/27-54-14): Warm and woodsy, and permeated with the aroma of good food and a convivial hubbub from the other tables, this inexpensive restaurant is in a building erected during the 1600s. Its three types of fondue and its fresh trout from nearby streams are among the best in the province. See p. 412.

- **Landhaus-Keller** (Graz; © 0316/830276): In a historic building with outdoor tables in summer, this cellar serves some of the best local specialties, many based on old recipes handed down from generation to generation. It's hearty drinking and dining here. See p. 470.

- **Hirschen-Stuben** (Innsbruck; C **0512/58-29-79**): This charming restaurant in a restored 17th-century house is known for its good Austrian and Italian cuisine served at affordable prices. From stewed deer to the best of alpine lake fish, this one is a winner. See p. 345.

14 The Best Classic Cafes

- **Café Demel** (Vienna; C **01/533-5516**): This most famous cafe in Vienna has a long-standing feud with the Sacher Hotel as to who has the right to sell the legendary and original Sacher torte. Demel claims that the chef who invented the torte left the Sacher to work for Demel, bringing his recipe with him. Why not be good to yourself and sample the torte? See p. 114.
- **Café Imperial** (Vienna; C **01/5011-0389**): Owned and operated by a grand hotel, this cafe was a favorite of composer Gustav Mahler. Favored as a lunchtime stop by a chic local crowd, it offers "the most regal" cup of coffee, pastry, or glass of wine in town. See p. 115.
- **Café Landtmann** (Vienna; C **01/532-0621**): The newspapers it provides for its patrons are tattered by the end of every day, and a haze of smoke evokes the backroom machinations of a meeting of political cronies from another era. Sigmund Freud claimed it as his favorite cafe, and after your first 15 minutes inside, you might, too. See p. 115.
- **Café-Restaurant Glockenspiel** (Salzburg; C **0662/84-14-03-0**): Some readers of this guidebook have written that their time at one of this cafe's outdoor tables represented everything they ever liked about Europe. Inside it's a little heavy on the "Mozart drank coffee here" theme, but despite that, everybody likes the Glockenspiel. See p. 224.
- **Café Tomaselli** (Salzburg; C **0662/84-44-88**): Established in 1705, it competes neck and neck with the above-mentioned Glockenspiel. As such, it provides a rich atmosphere as well as delectably fattening pastries and endless cups of coffee. See p. 224.
- **Café Frauenschuh** (Mondsee; C **06232/2312**): Deliciously loaded with every imaginable kind of high-calorie pastry, this time-honored place is a cliché of old-fashioned Austrian charm. See p. 309.
- **Konditorei-Kafé Zauner Gesellschaft** (Bad Ischl; C **06132/233100**): It's the oldest pastry shop in Austria and the emporium that satisfied the long-ago sugar cravings of such Hapsburg monarchs as Franz Joseph. Today it trades heavily on the aristocratic associations of yesteryear, attracting droves of tourists to its baroque-inspired setting in the resort's center. See p. 314.
- **Café Munding** (Innsbruck; C **0512/58-41-18**): Plushly decorated and upholstered, this cafe offers a setting from 1720, torrents of Tyrolean color, unusual murals, and platters of food followed by a scrumptiously fattening array of creamy pastries. See p. 351.

2

Planning Your Trip to Austria

This chapter is devoted to the where, when, and how of your trip—the advance-planning issues required to get it together and take it on the road.

1 The Regions in Brief

The forests, mountains, and lowlands of the Austrian landscape were divided early in their history into nine distinctly different regions (see the map on the inside back cover of this guide). In addition to their topographical diversities, each region has its own history, cultural identity, and—in some cases—oddities of language and dialect.

VIENNA

Austria's capital, the former hub of a great empire, and a province in its own right, Vienna is one of Europe's most beautiful cities. Images spring to mind of imperial palaces, the angelic voices of choir boys, the Spanish Riding School, and rich cakes served in cafes. In this former seat of the once-powerful Hapsburg dynasty, you follow in the footsteps of Schubert, Strauss, Brahms, Mahler, Mozart, and Beethoven, among others. Of course, the Blue Danube (even if it's not blue) cuts through the city that controlled a great deal of Europe for more than 6 centuries until it suffered humiliating defeats in both world wars of the 20th century. After a long, dreary slumber during the postwar years, Vienna has regained its old *joie de vivre* and is today one of Europe's most vital capitals. This economic power stands today at the crossroads of eastern and western Europe.

LOWER AUSTRIA

Set at Austria's northeastern corner, bordering the Czech Republic and Slovakia, this is Austria's largest province. Known for its fertile plains, renowned vineyards, and prosperous bourgeoisie, it's very different from the alpine regions of western Austria. Although the region's administrative capital is the culturally ambitious city of **Sankt Pölten,** most of the region directs its focus toward Vienna, which it completely surrounds. Visitors to Lower Austria typically come on a day trip from Vienna to explore the **Weinerwald (Vienna Woods)** romanticized in operetta, literature, and the famous Strauss waltz. One of the best places to explore the Vienna Woods is **Klosterneuburg,** a major wine-producing center. Other places to explore include **Mayerling,** in the heart of the woods, and **Heiligenkreuz,** one of Austria's oldest Cistercian abbeys. The district's leading spa is **Baden bei Wien,** a lively casino town in the eastern sector of the Vienna Woods.

The other major attraction of Lower Austria is the **Wachau-Danube Valley,** rich in scenic splendor and castles. In the valley, you can visit the ancient town of **Tulln,** the early-12th-century **Herzogenburg Monastery,** the 1,000-year-old city of **Krems,** and the lovely town of **Dürnstein. Melk Abbey** is one of the world's finest baroque buildings.

BURGENLAND

The newest of the Austrian provinces was formed in 1921 from the German-speaking region of what had once been part of the Hungarian half of Austria-Hungary. Located at Austria's southeastern tip, its plains, reef-fringed lakes, and abundant bird life resemble the landscapes of Hungary. Its capital is **Eisenstadt,** the native city of composer (Franz) Joseph Haydn. Largely agricultural, with an unusual demographic mixture of Hungarians, Croats, and German-speaking Austrians, Burgenland lacks the visual drama and grand alpine scenery of other parts of Austria. Lakes remain its primary attraction, and they are best visited in summer.

SALZBURG

A city rich with the splendors of the baroque age and the melodies of Mozart, Salzburg is one of Europe's premier architectural gems. It's also the setting for Austria's most prestigious music festival. Its natural setting is panoramic—hugging both banks of the Salzach River and "pinched" between two mountains, Mönchsberg and Kapuzinerberg.

Many travelers come here to follow in the footsteps of Julie Andrews in the fabled 1965 musical *The Sound of Music.* The von Trapps and Mozart have put Salzburg on international tourist maps.

LAND SALZBURG

The only area of Austria that can compare with Tyrol in both outdoor activities and scenic grandeur is Land Salzburg, which lies at the doorstep of Salzburg. It's easy to spend weeks in this mountainous area. In summer, the greatest attraction is the **Grossglockner Road,** Europe's longest and most splendid highway. In winter, **Zell am See** is the most popular resort in the region, located on a lake against a mountain backdrop, but there are many other options to consider. **Golling,** in the Salzach Valley south of Salzburg, is one of the most inviting. Visitors frequently visit the winter and summer spa resorts of **Badgastein** and **Bad Hofgastein** in the Gastein Valley. Two major ski resorts are **Saalbach** and **Hinterglemm.**

UPPER AUSTRIA

Tied to of the Danube's fertile plains, which straddle that famous river, this region produces much of Austria's agricultural bounty. Its capital is the historic but heavily industrialized city of **Linz,** famous for a raspberry-chocolate concoction known as the Linzer torte. Upper Austria doesn't offer the resorts and attractions of Tyrol, Land Salzburg, or Vorarlberg. But there's charming scenery here, especially in summer at **Attersee,** the largest lake in the Austrian Alps. Another major summer resort is **Mondsee (Moon Lake),** the warmest lake in the Salzkammergut. Also in the Salzkammergut, **St. Wolfgang,** one of Austria's most romantic lakes, draws visitors to its White Horse Inn, the setting for the fabled operetta of the same name. **Bad Ischl,** once the summer retreat of Emperor Franz Joseph, is one of the country's most fashionable spas. Hallstatt is the best center for exploring the province's major attractions: the salt mines of **Salt Mountain** and the spectacular **Dachstein Caves.**

TYROL

One of Austria's most historic and colorful provinces, this breathtaking mountainous district was once the medieval crossroads between the Teutonic world and Italy. Its capital is the beautiful city of **Innsbruck,** both a summer resort and a winter ski center. Filled with attractions, it's the third-most important city to visit in Austria (after Vienna and Salzburg). But the glories of the Tyrolean country hardly end in Innsbruck. The province is riddled with valleys, each filled with resorts drawing both summer and winter visitors. These valleys include the beautiful Stubai and Wipp, where the major resorts of **Fulpmes** and **Neustift** offer vistas of glacier tops and alpine peaks.

The **Upper Inn district** is also worth a visit. The old market town of **Imst** makes a good stop along the Upper Inn. On the eastern side of the Arlberg are the resorts of **St. Anton am Arlberg,** an old village on the Arlberg Pass, and **St. Christoph,** the mountain way station of St. Anton. **Seefeld** is also a great ski resort, offering both summer and winter outdoor activities. In the Ziller Valley is another sophisticated resort, **Zell am Ziller.** The **Kitzbühel Alps** offer some of Austria's best skiing. If you have enough time, journey to **East Tyrol** to **Lienz,** a rich, folkloric town on the Isel River with many romantic old inns and guest houses.

VORARLBERG

Located at the country's westernmost tip, sharing most of its borders with the wild and mountainous eastern border of Switzerland, Vorarlberg contains some of Austria's most sophisticated ski resorts, highest alpine peaks, and most beautiful scenery. Its capital is **Bregenz,** a pleasant town at any time of the year, although it hardly competes with the scenic grandeur of the province's resorts, such as **Lech** and **Zürs.** In winter, Lech and the even more chic and elegant Zürs, on the western side of the Arlberg, are among Europe's leading ski resorts.

The **Montafon Valley,** known for its powdery snow and sun, has been called a winter "ski stadium." The best places for skiing here are the hamlets of **Schruns** and **Tschagguns.** If you're

---

 Destination: Austria—Red Alert Checklist

- Citizens of EC countries can cross into Vienna or Austria for as long as they wish. Citizens of other countries must have a passport.
- If you purchased traveler's checks, have you recorded the check numbers and stored the documentation separately from the checks?
- Did you pack your camera and an extra set of camera batteries, and purchase enough film? If you packed film in your checked baggage, did you invest in protective pouches to shield film from airport X-rays?
- Do you have a safe, accessible place to store money?
- Did you bring your ID cards that could entitle you to discounts, such as AAA and AARP cards, student IDs, etc.?
- Did you bring emergency drug prescriptions and extra glasses and/or contact lenses?
- Do you have your credit card PINs?
- If you have an E-ticket, do you have documentation?
- Did you leave a copy of your itinerary with someone at home?
- Did you check to see if any travel advisories have been issued by the **U.S. State Department** (http://travel.state.gov/travel_warnings.html) regarding your destination?
- Do you have the address and phone number of your country's embassy with you?

here in summer, you might want to explore the **Bregenz Forest (Bregenz-erwald)**, although it's hardly the Black Forest in Germany. The northern part of the Vorarlberg alpine range is a prime place for outdoor activities. You'll want to dine and stay at **Bezau.** If you have time, the towns of **Dornbirn, Feldkirch,** and **Bludenz** are interesting to explore.

CARINTHIA
Noted for its forests, rolling hills, and hundreds of freshwater lakes, Carinthia shares most of its border with Slovenia. Although landlocked, the province has just a hint of Mediterranean flavor, which permeates its gardens, lakeside resorts, and the verdant capital city, **Klagenfurt.** Outside the capital is the striking hilltop **Hochosterwitz Castle.** The province's biggest alpine lake is **Wörther See,** where you can stay at the idyllic summer resorts of **Krumpendorf** or **Pörtschach.** The sophisticated resort of **Velden,** at the western end of Wörther See, is called the heart of the Austrian "Riviera." In the center of the lake district, **Villach,** with its nearby warm springs, is another major destination.

STYRIA
One of the most heavily forested of the Austrian provinces, Styria has landscapes that rise from lush valleys to towering alpine peaks. With a strong medieval tradition, this area originated the loden-colored jackets and felt hats with feathers that many newcomers assume are the Austrian national costume. The district's capital is **Graz,** boasting one of the best-preserved medieval cores of any Austrian city. You'll also want to visit **Bad Gleichenberg,** the province's most important summer spa, and **Mariazell,** a major pilgrimage site because of its Mariazell Basilica. Another spa, **Bad Aussee,** is in the "green heart" of the Salzkammergut, in an extremely beautiful part of Austria. You'll find the area's best skiing in the **Dachstein-Tauern,** where you can stay at the twin resorts of **Schladming** and **Rohrmoos.**

2 Visitor Information

VISITOR INFORMATION
TOURIST OFFICES Contact the **Austrian National Tourist Office,** P.O. Box 1142, New York, NY 10108-1142 (✆ **212/944-6880;** www.Austria.info.com).

In Canada, you'll find offices at 2 Bloor St. E., Suite 3330, Toronto, ON M4W 1A8 (✆ **416/967-3381**). In London, contact the Austrian National Tourist Office at 14 Cork St., W1X 1PF (✆ **020/7629-0461**).

Dispensing information for the entire country, the **Austrian National Tourist Office** is at Margaretenstrasse 1, A-1040 Vienna (✆ **01/588-660**). It cannot, however, make reservations for you. As you travel throughout the towns and villages of Austria, you'll see a sign emblazoned with a fat I (for information) in front of the local tourist office where you likely can obtain maps and might even get assistance in finding a hotel if you arrive without a reservation.

You might want to ask for the free English-language booklet *Art and Architecture in Austria,* which lists examples and photos of Austria's most renowned architectural sites.

WEBSITES To begin your exploration of Austria, check out the sites for the **Austrian National Tourist Office** (www.Austria.info.com), **Tourist-Net: Austria** (www.tourist-net.co.at), **Vienna Tourist Board** (www.info.wien.at), **Mozart Concerts** (www.mozart.co.at), and **LiveCam Vienna** (http://rhw cam.markant.at).

3 Entry Requirements & Customs

ENTRY REQUIREMENTS

Citizens of the United States, Canada, the United Kingdom, Australia, Ireland, and New Zealand need only a valid passport to enter Austria. No visa is required. Safeguard your passport in an inconspicuous, inaccessible place like a money belt. If you lose it, visit the nearest consulate of your native country as soon as possible for a replacement. It's always a good idea to have a photocopy of your passport to expedite replacement.

CUSTOMS

Visitors who live outside Austria in general are not liable to pay duty on personal articles brought into the country temporarily for their own use, depending on the purpose and circumstances of each trip. Customs officials have great leeway here. Likewise, travelers 17 years of age and older may carry up to 200 cigarettes or 50 cigars or 250 grams of tobacco, 1 liter of distilled liquor, and 2.25 liters of wine or 3 liters of beer duty-free. Gifts not exceeding a value of 230€ are also exempt from duty.

Returning U.S. citizens who have been away for 48 hours or more are allowed to bring back, once every 30 days, $800 worth of merchandise duty-free. You'll be charged a flat rate of 10% duty on the next $1,000 worth of purchases. Be sure to have your receipts handy. On gifts, the duty-free limit is $100. For more specific guidance, contact the **U.S. Customs Service,** 1300 Pennsylvania Ave., Washington, DC 20229 (② **202/354-1000;** www.customs. ustreas.gov), and request the free pamphlet "Know Before You Go." For a clear summary of Canadian rules, request the book *I Declare* from **Revenue Canada,** 1165 St. Laurent Blvd., Ottawa, KIG 4KE (② **800/461-9999** in Canada, 204/983-3500; www.ccra-adrc.gc.ca). If you're a citizen of the United Kingdom, contact **Her Majesty's Customs and Excise Office,** National Advise Service, Dorset House, Stamford Street, London SE1 9PY (② **020/7202-4510;** fax 020/7202-4131; www. hmce.gov.uk). Australian citizens should contact the **Australian Customs Service,** GPO Box 8, Sydney NSW 2001 (② **1300/1363-263** in Austria, 02/6275-6666; www.customs. gov.au). New Zealanders should contact **New Zealand Customs,** 17–21 Whitmore St., P.O. Box 2218, Wellington, NZ (② **09/359-66-55;** www.customs.govt.nz). And citizens of Ireland should contact **The Revenue Commissioner,** Dublin Castle (② **01/679-27-77;** fax 01/679-3261; www.revenue.ie), or write The Collector of Customs and Excise, The Custom House, Dublin 1.

4 Money

Foreign money and euros can be brought into Vienna without any restrictions. There is no restriction on taking foreign money out of the country, either.

CURRENCY

The **euro,** the new single European currency, became the official currency of Austria and 11 other participating countries on January 1, 1999. Greece joined the group in 2001. However, the euro didn't go into general circulation until early in 2002. The old currency, the Austrian schilling, disappeared into history on March 1, 2002, replaced by the euro, whose official abbreviation is "EUR." The symbol of the euro is a stylized E: €. Exchange rates of the participating countries are locked into a common currency fluctuating against the dollar.

The Euro, the U.S. Dollar & the British Pound

Regarding the Euro   At the time of this writing, the U.S. dollar and the euro traded almost on par (i.e., $1 = approximately 1€). But that relationship can and probably will change during the lifetime of this edition. For more exact ratios between these and other currencies, check an up-to-date source at the time of your arrival in Europe.

For British Readers   At this writing, £1 = approximately $1.56, at approximately the same rate against the euro. These were the rates of exchange used to calculate the values in the table below.

€	US$	UK£	€	US$	UK£
1	1	0.64	75	75	48.23
2	2	1.29	100	100	64.30
3	3	1.93	125	125	80.38
4	4	2.57	150	150	96.45
5	5	3.22	175	175	112.53
6	6	3.86	200	200	128.60
7	7	4.50	225	225	144.68
8	8	5.14	250	250	160.75
9	9	5.79	275	275	176.83
10	10	6.43	300	300	192.90
15	15	9.65	350	350	225.05
20	20	12.86	400	400	257.20
25	25	16.08	500	500	321.50
50	50	32.15	1000	1000	643.00

For more details on the euro, check out **www.europa.eu.int/euro**.

The relative value of the euro fluctuates against the U.S. dollar, the pound sterling, and most of the world's other currencies, and its value might not be the same by the time you actually travel to Vienna. A last-minute check is also advised before beginning your trip.

Exchange rates are more favorable at the point of arrival. Nevertheless, it's often helpful to exchange at least some money before going abroad (standing in line at the exchange bureau in the Vienna airport isn't fun after a long overseas flight). Check with any of your local American Express or Thomas Cook offices or major banks. Or, order in advance from the following:

American Express (✆ **800/721-9768**, cardholders only), **Thomas Cook** (✆ **800/223-7373**; www.thomascook. com), or **Capital for Foreign Exchange** (✆ **888/842-0880**; www. afex.com).

It's best to exchange currency or traveler's checks at a bank, not at a cambio, hotel, or shop. Currency and traveler's checks (for which you'll receive a better rate than cash) can be changed at all principal airports and at some travel agencies, such as American Express and Thomas Cook. Note the rates and ask about fees; it can sometimes pay to shop around and ask the right questions.

If you need to prepay a deposit on hotel reservations by check, it's cheaper and easier to pay with a check drawn on an Austrian bank. This can be arranged by a large commercial bank or **Ruesch International,** 700 11th St. NW, Washington, DC 20001 (☎ **800/424-2923** or 202/408-1200; www.ruesch.com), which performs many conversion-related tasks, usually for only $15 per transaction.

CREDIT CARDS

To get the best rate of exchange, use your credit cards whenever possible. They virtually always offer the best exchange rate, and there's no accompanying service charge. Credit cards are widely accepted in Austria; American Express, Visa, and Diners Club are the most commonly recognized. A EUROCARD or ACCESS sign displayed at an establishment means that it accepts MasterCard.

ATMS

ATMs are prevalent in all Austrian cities and even the smaller towns. ATMs are linked to a national network that most likely includes your bank at home. Both the **Cirrus** (☎ **800/424-7787**; www.mastercard.com) and the **PLUS** (☎ **800/843-7587**; www.visa.com) networks have automated ATM locators listing the banks in Austria that'll accept your card. Or, just search out any machine with your network's symbol emblazoned on it.

Important note: Make sure that the PINs on your bank cards and credit cards will work in Austria. You'll need a **four-digit code** (six digits won't work); if you have a six-digit code, you'll have to go into your bank and get a new PIN for your trip. If you're unsure about this, contact Cirrus or PLUS (above). Be sure to check the daily withdrawal limit at the same time.

TRAVELER'S CHECKS

These days, traveler's checks seem less necessary because most Austrian cities and towns have 24-hour ATMs, allowing you to withdraw small amounts of cash as needed. But if you prefer the security of the tried and true, you might want to stick with traveler's checks—provided that you don't mind showing an ID every time you want to cash a check.

You can get traveler's checks at almost any bank. **American Express** offers denominations of $20, $50, $100, $500, and (for cardholders only) $1,000. You'll pay a service charge ranging from 1% to 4%. You can also get American Express traveler's checks over the phone by calling ☎ **800/721-9768;** Amex gold and platinum cardholders who use this number are exempt from the 1% fee. AAA members can obtain checks without a fee at most AAA offices.

 Emergency Cash—The Fastest Way

If you need emergency cash over the weekend when all banks and American Express offices are closed, you can have money wired to you from **Western Union** (☎ 800/325-6000; www.westernunion.com). You must present valid ID to pick up the cash at the Western Union office. However, in most countries, you can pick up a money transfer even if you don't have valid identification, as long as you can answer a test question provided by the sender. Be sure to let the sender know in advance that you don't have ID. If you need to use a test question instead of ID, the sender must take cash to his or her local Western Union office rather than transfer the money over the phone or online.

What Things Cost in Vienna	Euros
Taxi from the airport to the city center	32€
U-Bahn (subway) from St. Stephan's to Schönbrunn Palace	1.50€
Local phone call	.18€
Double room at Hotel Astoria (expensive)	190€
Double room at the Am Parkring (moderate)	129€
Double room at the Pension Nossek (inexpensive)	105€
Lunch for one, without wine, at Drei Husaren (expensive)	32€
Lunch for one, without wine, at Griechenbeisl (moderate)	23€
Dinner for one, without wine, at Vincent (expensive)	39€
Dinner for one, without wine, at Plachutta (moderate)	32€
Dinner for one, without wine, at Apostelkeller (inexpensive)	16€
Glass of wine	2€–3€
Half-liter of beer in a *Beisl*	3€
Coca-Cola in cafe	3€
Cup of coffee ("*ein kleine Braun*")	3€
Roll of color film, 36 exp.	6.50€–8€
Movie ticket	9.50€
Admission to Schönbrunn Palace	9.80€

Visa offers traveler's checks at Citibank locations nationwide, as well as at several other banks. The service charge ranges between 1.5% and 2%; checks come in denominations of $20, $50, $100, $500, and $1,000. Call ✆ 800/732-1322 for information. **MasterCard** also offers traveler's checks. Call ✆ 800/223-9920 for a location near you.

5 When to Go

Vienna experiences its high season from April to October, with July and August and the main festivals being the most crowded times. Bookings around Christmastime are also heavy, as many Austrians themselves visit the capital during this festive time. Always arrive with reservations during these peak seasons. During the off-seasons, hotel rooms are generally plentiful and less expensive, and there is less demand for tables in the more popular restaurants.

CLIMATE

In Austria, the temperature varies greatly depending on your location.

The national average ranges from a low of 9°F (–13°C) in January to a high of 68°F (20°C) in July. However, in Vienna the January average is 32°F (0°C); for July, it's 66°F (19°C). Snow falls in the mountainous sectors by mid-November. Road conditions in winter can be very dangerous in many parts of the country. The winter air is usually crisp and clear, with many sunny days. The winter snow cover lasts late December through March in the valleys, November through May at about 1,830m (6,000 ft.), and all year at 2,592m (8,500 ft.) or higher. The

Vienna's Average Temperature & Rainfall

	Jan	Feb	Mar	Apr	May	June	July	Aug	Sept	Oct	Nov	Dec
Temp. (°F)	30	32	38	50	58	64	68	70	60	50	41	33
Temp. (°C)	–1	0	4	10	14	18	20	21	16	10	5	0
Rainfall (in.)	1.2	1.9	3.9	1.3	2.9	1.9	.8	1.8	2.8	2.8	2.5	1.6

Salzburg's Average Temperature & Rainfall

	Jan	Feb	Mar	Apr	May	June	July	Aug	Sept	Oct	Nov	Dec
Temp. (°F)	28	35	37	45	55	64	68	67	60	50	39	33
Temp. (°C)	−2	2	3	7	13	18	20	19	16	10	4	0
Rainfall (in.)	2.5	2.6	2.8	3.5	5.3	6.8	7.5	6.4	3.6	2.9	2.7	2.7

Innsbruck's Average Temperature & Rainfall

	Jan	Feb	Mar	Apr	May	June	July	Aug	Sept	Oct	Nov	Dec
Temp. (°F)	30	39	52	59	68	73	77	75	70	59	45	36
Temp. (°C)	−1	4	11	15	20	23	25	24	21	15	7	2
Rainfall (in.)	3.4	2.5	3.2	4.1	4.5	5.4	5.8	5.3	4.2	3.5	3.3	3.7

ideal times for visiting Vienna are spring and fall, which have mild, sunny days. "Summer" generally means from Easter until about mid-October. By the end of July, alpine wildflowers are in full bloom.

HOLIDAYS

Bank holidays in Austria are as follows: January 1, January 6 (Epiphany), Easter Monday (April 21 in 2003, April 12 in 2004), May 1, Ascension Day (May 29 in 2003, May 20 in 2004), Whitmonday (June 9 in 2003, May 31 in 2004), Corpus Christi Day (June 19 in 2003, June 10 in 2004), August 15, October 26 (Nationalfeiertag), November 1, December 8, and December 25 and 26.

AUSTRIA CALENDAR OF EVENTS

For more information about these and other events, contact the various tourist offices throughout Austria. Dates given below are for 2003 unless otherwise indicated.

January

New Year's Eve/New Year's Day. Vienna's biggest night is launched by the famed concert of the Vienna Philharmonic Orchestra. The New Year also marks the beginning of **Fasching,** the famous Vienna Carnival season, which lasts through Shrove Tuesday (Mardi Gras). For

tickets and information, contact the Wiener Philharmoniker, Bösendorferstrasse 12, A-1010 Vienna (© 01/505-6525; www.wienerphilharmoniker.at). The concert is followed by the **Imperial Ball** in the Hofburg. For information and tickets, contact the WKV, Hofburg, Heldenplatz, A-1014 Vienna (© 01/587-3666).

Eistraum (Dream on Ice). During the coldest months of Austrian winter, the monumental plaza between the Town Hall and the Burgtheater is flooded and frozen; lights, loudspeakers, and a stage are hauled in, and the entire civic core is transformed into a gigantic ice-skating rink. Sedate waltz tunes accompany the skaters during the day, and DJs spin rock, funk, and reggae after the sun goes down. Around the rink, dozens of kiosks sell everything from hot chocolate and snacks to wine and beer. For information, call © 01/532-05-45 or visit www.wienereistraum.com. Last week of January to mid-March.

Berg Isel Ski Jumping Competition, Innsbruck. One of the country's most daredevil ski-jump competitions kicks off the new year at a platform built for the 1964 Olympics. First week in January.

Hahnenkamm World Cup Ski Race, Kitzbühel. Since 1931, this major sporting event has drawn world-class skiers from around the globe to compete for the prestigious World Cup. It is televised across Europe and America. Skiers compete over 2 days, but the whole town parties for a week. Entry tickets are available at the gate. Mid-January.

Mozart Week, Salzburg. This festival features opera, orchestral works, and chamber music. Get tickets at the Mozarteum, Schwarzstrasse 26, A-5024 Salzburg (© **0662/88-940-22**). January 24 to February 2, 2003.

February

International Seniors' Giant Slalom, Saalfelden. Competitors whip around poles stuck into the snow, trying to weave speed, agility, and precision into a winning combination. This event is scheduled for February 23, 2003.

Opera Ball. On the last Thursday of the Fasching, Vienna's high society gathers at the Wein Staatsoper for the grandest ball of the Carnival season. The evening opens with a performance by the Opera House Ballet. You don't need an invitation, but you do need to buy a ticket, which, as you might guess, isn't cheap. For information contact the Vienna Opera House (© **01/514-44-2606;** www.wiener-staatsoper.at) directly.

Ski Festival. Gaschurn, in the heart of Vorarlberg (9.6km/6 miles from Schruns), is the resort that lies closest to the downhill runs of the Silvretta-Nova subdivision of the Montafon Valley. It's the site of a 1-week ski festival sponsored by the Belgian-Austrian chocolate manufacturer Suchard. The men's and women's events are the Montafon Valley's most important ski competition. Late February to early March.

March

Bregenz Spring Festival. The Vienna Symphony Orchestra usually appears at these concerts, which usher in the greening of the surrounding Alps. For information, contact the Bregenz Tourist Office, Anton-Schneider-Strasse 4-A, A-6900 Bregenz (© **05574/49-590**). First 3 weeks of March.

April

Vienna Mozart Week. Celebrating the festival's eighth year in 2003, Vienna's musicians devote an entire week to the works of Wolfgang Amadeus Mozart. The Neues Wiener Barockensemble sets the tone with orchestral works by the musical genius, followed by performances by the Vienna Philharmonic. Mozart Week culminates in a performance of the Coronation Mass and church sonatas during Sunday Mass at the Church of the Augustinian Friars. Organizers of the festival also conduct guided walks following in "Mozart's Footsteps in Vienna." For bookings, contact Wiener Mozartwoche, Postfach 55, A-1181 Vienna (© **01/408-7586**). Festival dates change every year but usually begin the end of the first week in April, lasting for 1 week.

Vienna Spring Festival. The festival has a different central theme every year, but always count on music by the world's greatest composers, including Mozart and Brahms, at the Konzerthaus. The booking address is Karlsplatz 6, Lothringerstrasse 20, A-1010 Vienna (© **01/505-8190**). Mid-April through the first week of May.

May

International Music Festival. This traditional highlight of Vienna's concert calendar features top-class international orchestras, distinguished conductors, and classical greats. You can hear Beethoven's *Eroica* as it was meant to be played, Mozart's *Jupiter* Symphony, and perhaps Bruckner's *Romantic*. The list of conductors and orchestras reads like a Who's Who of the international world of music. The venue and also the booking address is Wiener Musikverein, Lothringer-Strasse 20, A-1030 Vienna (© 01/ 242-002). Early May through the first 3 weeks of June.

Vienna Festival. An exciting array of operas, operettas, musicals, theater, and dances are performed. New productions of treasured classics are presented alongside avant-garde premieres, all staged by international leading directors. In addition, celebrated productions from renowned European theaters offer guest performances. Anticipate such productions as Mozart's *Così fan tutte*, Monteverdi's *Orfeo*, and Offenbach's *La Vie Parisienne*. For bookings, contact Wiener Festwochen, Lehárgasse 11, A-1060 Vienna (© 01/589-220). The second week of May until mid-June.

June

Danube Lower Austria Festival, along the Danube River, in various locations and at St. Pölten, the state capital. Dance and theater, music and art, poetry, and ecology are presented at a number of venues, including a riverboat. Mid-June to mid-July.

Midsummer Night Celebration. This celebration is held all over Austria, with bonfires and folkloric events. The liveliest observances are in the Tyrolean valley towns and in the Wachau region along the Danube in Austria. June 20.

Styriarte Graz. This grand annual cultural celebration features a different theme every year. For tickets and information, contact Styriarte Graz, Palais Attems, Sackstrasse 17,

A-8010 Graz (© 0316/81-29-410). Last 2 weeks of June and first 3 weeks of July.

Vienna Jazz Festival. This is one of the world's top jazz events, using the Vienna State Opera as its central event venue. The program calls for appearances by more than 50 international and local stars. For information and bookings, contact the Vienna Jazz Festival, Frankenberggasse 13 (© 01/503-561). June 23 to July 6, 2003.

July

Vienna Summer of Music. This premier event fills the cultural calendar with concerts at City Hall, at Schönbrunn Palace, and at many landmark homes of great 19th-century Viennese musicians. Densely packed with musical options, the festival often features a series of different musical events on any given night. For tickets, schedules, and information, contact the Wiener Musiksommer, Laudongasse 4, A-1010 Vienna (© 01/ 4000-84-722). July 1 to August 31.

Salzburg Festival. Since the 1920s, this has been one of the premier cultural events of Europe, sparkling with opera, chamber music, plays, concerts, appearances by world-class artists, and many other cultural presentations. Always count on stagings of Mozart operas. Performances are staged at various venues throughout the city. For tickets, write several months in advance to the Salzburg Festival, Postfach 140, A-5010 Salzburg (© 0662/8045). July 26 to August 31, 2003.

Festival of Early Music, Innsbruck. Everything from plain song to baroque operas to recitals featuring historical instruments characterizes this annual event. Concerts are presented at the Hofburg, the Tyroler Landestheater, and the Castle

Ambras. For tickets and information, contact the Innsbruck Tourist Office, Burggraben 3, A-6020 Innsbruck (℡ **0512/598500**). Mid July into August.

Summer Stage, Vienna. Along the quays of the Donau Inlet, adjacent to the Friedensbrücke, midsummer is celebrated by hundreds of the young, the upwardly mobile, and the trendy who converge on the periphery of the city to enjoy the night air and one another's company. Temporary stages present everything from skits to performance art to live music. Adding to the revelry are the 20 or so seasonal bars that open their doors to the milling summer crowd every night from 5pm to 2am. July and August.

Klangbogen. A wealth of musical events, ranging from opera, operetta, and chamber music to orchestral concerts. World-renowned orchestras perform in the Golden Hall of the Vienna Musikverein. For bookings and information, contact Klangbogen, Stadiongassse 9, A-1010 Vienna (℡ **01/427-17**). The second week of July through the last week of August.

Music Film Festival. Opera, operetta, and masterful concert performances captured on celluloid are enjoyed free under a starry sky in front of the neo-Gothic City Hall on the Ringstrasse. Programs focus on works by Franz Schubert, Johannes Brahms, or other composers. You might view Rudolf Nureyev in *Swan Lake* or see Leonard Bernstein wielding the baton for Brahms. For more information, contact Ideenagentur Austria, Opernring 1R, A-1010 Vienna (℡ **01/587-0150**). July and August.

September

Haydn Days, Eisenstadt, in Burgenland. Held in Eisenstadt, where Haydn lived for 40 years, this festival presents the composer's trios, quartets, symphonies, operas, and choral works. Venues include the Esterházy castle, local churches, and even the city's public parks. For tickets and information, contact the Burgenlandische Haydn Festspiele, Schloss Esterházy, A-7000 Eisenstadt (℡ **02682/61-866**). September 11–21, 2003.

International Bruckner Festival, Linz. This month-long festival features concerts, theatrical presentations, art exhibits, and fireworks. For tickets and information, contact Festspiele, Untere Donaulände 7, A-4010 Linz (℡ **0732/775230**). September.

October

Viennale. This film festival shows everything from the most daringly avant-garde to golden oldies of the (mostly European) silver screen. Check the program to see which films will be in English or have English subtitles. For tickets and information, contact the Wiener Festwochen Viennale, Stiftgasse 6, A-1070 Vienna (℡ **01/526-59-47**). Throughout October.

Wien Modern, in its 16th year in 2003, was founded by Claudio Abbado and is devoted to the performance of contemporary works in music. The emphasis is not just on Austrian composers, but it has included works from Scandinavian and Baltic countries, Iceland, Romania, Portugal, and other nations. Some of the composers make live appearances and discuss their compositions. Concerts usually last 1½ to 2 hours. Performances are at Verein Wien Modern, Lothingerstrasse 20 (℡ **01/712-468**), but the booking address is Wiener Konzerthaus, Lothringerstrasse 20 (℡ **01/712-1211**). End of October to November.

November

Vienna Schubert Festivale. A relative newcomer to the Viennese music scene, this all-Schubert celebration marks its 21st annual observance in 2003. For information, contact Wiener Musikverein, Karlsplatz 6, A-1010 Vienna (*©* **01/505-81-90**). Third week of November.

December

Christkindlmarkt. Look for pockets of folkloric charm (and, in some cases, kitsch) associated with the Christmas holidays. Small outdoor booths known as Christkindlmarkt—usually adorned with evergreen boughs, red ribbons, and, in some cases, religious symbols—sprout up in clusters around Vienna. They're selling old-fashioned toys, *Tannenbaum* (Christmas tree) decorations, and gift items. Food vendors will also be nearby offering sausages, cookies and pastries, roasted chestnuts, and *Kartoffel* (charcoal-roasted potato slices). The greatest concentrations of these open-air markets can be found in front of the Rathaus, in the Spittelberg Quarter (7th District), at Freyung, the historic square in the northwest corner of the Inner City. Late November to New Year's.

6 The Active Vacation Planner

Austrians love sports and the outdoors. Although skiing is a national obsession, there are great opportunities to participate in a variety of activities. Here are the best places to go. You'll find more specific information in each regional chapter.

BALLOONING

Hot-air ballooning over the dramatic landscapes of Austria, including alpine terrain, can be a real thrill ride. One of the best centers for this is Voralberg in western Austria. The balloon specialist here is **Günter Schabus,** Bruderhof 12A, A6833 (*©* **05523/51121**), which features ballooning 7 days a week year-round—weather permitting, of course—near the German and Swiss borders. The cost of ballooning is 290€ per person, with reductions if 2 to 5 persons join you.

BIKING

Holland Bicycling Tours, P.O. Box 6086, Huntington Beach, CA 92615 (*©* **800/852-3258;** fax 714/593-1710; www.hollandbicyclingtours.com), is the North American representative for a Dutch-based company that leads 10-day bicycle tours in Austria. You'll bike along well-laid-out paths and quiet country roads, which are thankfully flat and mostly downhill. One of the most interesting jaunts begins in Vienna and goes along Hungary's Lake Balaton, ending in Budapest. Highlights include Sopron, a lovingly restored walled town, and Keszthely, a cultural center and one of Balaton's most inviting towns. The tour price is $1,900 per person based on double occupancy. In Austria itself, another tour goes through the Valley of Achental to Salzburg. This is a landscape of waterfalls and serene countryside with unspoiled villages. At Hallein in Land Salzburg, you can ride a cable car for a memorable visit to the salt mines. The cost of this tour is also $1,900 per person based on double occupancy.

From the beginning of April to the beginning of November, you can rent a bicycle at larger Austrian railroad stations. A photo ID must be presented at the time of rental. The charge is 10€ per day, which is reduced to 6€ if you hold a railroad ticket to the point of rental. You can reserve a bicycle in advance. The vehicle can be returned to where it was rented or to any other Austrian railroad station during business hours.

Backroads, 801 Cedar St., Berkeley, CA 94710 (℗ **800/GO-ACTIVE** in the U.S., or 510/527-1555; www.backroads.com), offers 6-day, 5-night trips that take you from Prague to Vienna going along the Danube. Lodging is in either castles or first-class country inns. The trip also includes most meals.

David Zwilling, David Zwilling, GmbH, Waldhof 64, A-5441 Abtenau (℗ **06243/3069-0;** fax 06243/306917), organizes Austria's best mountain-biking trips, as well as other adventure activities such as rafting, rock climbing, and paragliding.

FISHING

Austria is an angler's paradise, with many clear, unpolluted streams and deep rivers and lakes. You can try for trout, char, pike, sheatfish (monster catfish), and pike perch in well-stocked mountain streams. In the right tributaries of the Danube, you might catch a huch, a land-locked salmon that's an excellent fighter and a culinary delight, usually fished for in late fall. The Wörther See in Carinthia sometimes yields the North American big-mouth black bass, with which an owner of Velden Castle once stocked the lake by accident. Intended for a pond on his estate, one barrel fell into the lake and burst, introducing the immigrants from America to a new happy home. All local tourist offices in every province offer information about local fishing conditions and can advise you of the best local outfitters. Fishermen generally need two permits—a general license issued by the state for 67€ and, according to the province, a private permit from the local owner of the land. You can also write for information from **Asterreichischen Arbeiter-Fischerei-Vereine,** Lenaugasse 14, A-1080 Vienna (℗ **01/403-2176**).

GOLF

One of the country's most outstanding 18-hole courses is at the Murhof in Styria, near Frohnleiten. Others are the Igls/Rinn near Innsbruck, Seefeld-Wildmoos in Seefeld, Dallach on the shores of the Wörther See in Carinthia, Enzefeld and Wiener Neustadt-Foehrenwald in Lower Austria, and the oldest of them all, Vienna-Freudenau, founded in 1901. There are numerous nine-hole courses throughout the country. The season generally extends from April to October or November. For more information, contact **Österreichischer Golfverband,** Prinz Eugen-Strasse 12, A-1040 Vienna (℗ **01/505-3245**).

HIKING & MOUNTAINEERING

More than 70% of Austria's total area is covered by mountains of all shapes and sizes, and the rugged beauty of the Alps demands exploration. Walking, hiking, or mountain climbing across these hills and glaciers is an unforgettable experience. Paths and trails are marked and secured, guides and maps are readily available, and there's an outstanding system of huts to shelter you. Austria has more than 450 chairlifts or cable cars to open up the mountains for visitors.

Certain precautions are essential, foremost being to inform your innkeeper or host of your route. Also, suitable hiking or climbing shoes and protective clothing are imperative. Camping out overnight is strongly discouraged because of the rapidly changing mountain weather and the established system of keeping track of hikers and climbers in the mountains. More than 700 alpine huts—many of which are really full-service lodges with restaurants, rooms, and dormitories—are spaced about 4 to 5 hours apart so that you can make rest and lunch stops. Hikers are required to sign into and out of the huts and to give their destination before setting off. If you don't show up as planned, search parties go into action.

If you're advised that your chosen route has difficulties, hire a mountain guide or get expert advice from some qualified local person before braving the unknown. Certified hiking and climbing guides are based in all Austrian mountain villages and can be found by looking for their signs or by asking at the local tourist office. Above all, *obey signs.* Even in summer, if there's still snow on the ground, you could be in an area threatened by avalanches. There are other important rules to follow for your own safety if you're going walking, hiking, or mountaineering. You can obtain these from the Austrian National Tourist Offices, from bookstores, at the branches of various alpine clubs, or at local tourist offices in villages throughout the Alps.

For information about alpine trekking, contact **Österreichischer Alpenverein (Austrian Alpine Club),** A-6020 Wilhelm-Greil-Strasse 15, Innsbruck (© **0512/595470**). Membership in this alpine club costs 50€. Members receive a 50% reduction for overnight stays in mountain refuges. One of the best trekking adventure companies in Austria is **Waymark Holidays,** 44 Windsor Rd., Slough, Berkshire SL1 2EJ England (© **01753/516-477;** www.waymark holidays.com). Run by avid naturalists and mountaineers, it offers hiking tours through Austria for moderately experienced hikers in good physical condition. Tours usually last about 2 weeks.

The most cutting-edge sporting outfit in Austria, the kind of place that merges California cool with alpine adventure, is **David Zwilling,** Waldhof 64, A-5441 Abtenau (© **06243/ 3069-0;** fax 06243/306917). It organizes the best mountain-biking trips in Austria and is also the front-runner in mountain- and rock-climbing tours. This outfitter also arranges paragliding adventures over nerve-jangling cliffs and some incredible white-water rafting trips.

There are summer and winter mountaineering schools in at least 3 dozen resorts in all Austrian provinces except Burgenland, with regular courses, mountain tours, and camps for all ages.

SKIING

Austria today is world renowned for its downhill skiing facilities. Across the country, some 3,500 lifts transport skiers and sightseers to the summits of approximately 20,113km (12,500 miles) of marked runs. Don't forget to look around on the way up; the view above is as amazing as the runs below. Intricate networks cover whole mountainsides so you don't have to take a step uphill on your own. Ski "circuses" allow skiers to move from mountain to mountain, and ski "swings" opening up opposite sides of the same mountain tie villages in different valleys into one big ski region.

Shuttle buses, usually free for those with a valid lift ticket, take you to valley points where you board funiculars, gondolas, aerial trains, or chairlifts. Higher up, you can leave the larger conveyance and continue by another chairlift or T-bar.

Because competition among ski resorts is so fierce, you'll probably find roughly equivalent prices at many resorts for 1-, 2-, and 3-day passes. For example, at the Arlberg in Tyrol, one of the most famous ski areas of Europe, a 1-day pass costs 30€ to 35€. Discounts are granted for longer stays. A 6-day pass ranges from 150€ to 175€ per person. Prices for skiing in other regions of Austria, such as the area around Lech and Zürs in the Vorarlberg, and the Ötzal region of the Tyrol, tend to be similar. And skiers who buy passes valid for more than 2 days are rewarded with a much wider diversity of skiing options.

The Austrian Ski School is noted for its fine instruction and practice techniques, available in many places: Arlberg; the posh villages of Zürs and Lech/Arlberg, where the rich and famous gather; the Silvretta mountains; and Hochgurgl, Obergurgl, Hochsölden, and Sölden in the Tyrolean Ötzal, to name a few. Year-round skiing is possible in the little villages of the Stubaital through use of a cableway on the Stubai glacier, more than 3,050m (10,000 ft.) above sea level. Kitzbühl is known to all top skiers in the world, while Seefeld lures the trendy.

Skiing is a family sport in Europe, and ski centers usually have bunny slopes and instruction for youngsters, plus babysitting services for very small children. Many of these areas offer more than just fine powder. The Valley of Gastein was known for its medicinal thermal springs long before it became a ski center. The people of Schladming, in the Dachstein mountains, wore their local costumes and lodens well before the first cross-country skier discovered the high plateau surrounding the small, unspoiled village of Ramsau.

Among the most attractive large-scale skiing areas are the Radstädter Tauern region and Saalbach/Hinterglemm in Salzburg province. Here, as in most of the winter-sports areas, you can rest your tired legs by the crackling fire of a ski hut while enjoying hot spiced wine or a *Jägertee,* hot tea heavily laced with rum.

Snowboarding, whose popularity is spreading each year, is making inroads in Austria. The best outfitter is **Ski Europe** (𝒞 **800/333-5533** or 713/960-0900; www.ski-europe.com). They can arrange all sorts of vacations focused on skiing and snowboarding, also including winter hiking.

Cross-country skiing is popular among those who want to enjoy the winter beauty in quiet and get a great workout. Many miles of tracks are marked for this sport, and special instructors are available.

In the summer, you can give grass skiing a try. Ask at the Austrian National Tourist Office for a list of resorts providing this sport, as well as for details about centers offering summer snow skiing.

For complete information about the best skiing in Austria, contact **Österreichischer Skiverband (Austrian Ski Federation),** Olympiastrasse 10, A-6020 Innsbruck (𝒞 **0512/33501**).

SPAS & HEALTH RESORTS

Austrians have long been aware of the therapeutic faculties of mineral water, thermal springs, and curative mud in their own country. More than 100 spas and health resorts are found here, including the Oberlaa Spa Center on the southern hills of Vienna. These institutions not only use the hidden resources of nature to prevent physical ailments, but they offer therapy and rehabilitation as well.

You can "take the waters" at baths (*Baden*), with springs ranging from thermal brine to thermal sulfur water, some rich in iodine or iron and some rich with radon. (Many hot-water springs in Europe contain trace amounts of radon, which is not harmful in the doses that doctors prescribe.) Users of these facilities have found them effective treatment for digestive troubles, rheumatism, cardiac and circulatory diseases, and gynecological and neurological ills, to name just a few that are eased at various health centers.

Information about these spas and treatments is available from **Österreichischer Hellbäder-und Kurotelverband,** Josefsplatz 6, A-1010 Vienna (𝒞 **01/512-19-04**). Ask for a copy of the brochure "Nature the Healer: Spas and Health Resorts in Austria." You can also learn about "Kneipp Cures," a method developed in the 19th century as a restorative treatment and still hailed as "a magic formula in the world of natural medicine." This cure, popular among seniors with limited circulation, involves simple stretching exercises and moderate amounts of low-impact aerobics. The exercise session is then followed by immersing the feet in icy, nonsulfurous water.

WATERSPORTS

Austria has no seacoast, but from Lake Constance (Bodensee) in the west to Lake Neusiedl (Neusiedl See) in the east, the country is rich in lakes and boasts some 150 rivers and streams.

Swimming is, of course, possible year-round if you want to use an indoor pool or to swim at one of the many health clubs in winter. Swimming facilities have been developed at summer resorts, especially those on the warm waters of Carinthia, where you can swim from May to October, and in the Salzkammergut lake district between Upper Austria and Land Salzburg.

The beauty of Austria underwater is attested to by those who have tried diving in the lakes. Most outstanding are the diving and underwater exploration possibilities in the Salzkammergut lake district and in the Weissen See in Carinthia. You can receive instruction and obtain necessary equipment at both places.

If you prefer to remain on the surface, you can go sailing, windsurfing, or canoeing on the lakes and rivers.

The sailing (yachting) season lasts from May to October, with activity centered on the Attersee in the Salzkammergut lake district, on Lake Constance out of Bregenz, and on Lake Neusied, a large shallow lake in the east. Winds on the Austrian lakes can be treacherous, but a warning system and rescue services are alert. For information on sailing, contact **Österreichischer Segel-Verband,** Zetschegasse 21 (© **01/662-44-62-0**).

Most resorts on lakes or rivers where windsurfing can be safely enjoyed have equipment and instruction available. This sport is increasing in popularity and has been added to the curriculum of several sailing schools, especially in the area of the Wörther See in Carinthia, the warmest of the alpine lakes.

If you're interested in riding the rapids of a swift mountain stream or just paddling around on a placid lake, don't miss the chance to go canoeing in Austria. You can canoe down slow-flowing lowland rivers such as the Inn or Mur, or tackle the wild waters of glacier-fed mountain streams suitable only for experts. Special schools for fast-water paddling operate May through September in the village of Klaus on the Steyr River in Upper Austria, in Opponitz in Lower Austria on the Ybbs River, and in Abtenau in Salzburg province.

7 Insurance, Health & Safety

TRAVEL INSURANCE AT A GLANCE

Since Austria is far from home for most of us, and since a number of things could go wrong—lost luggage, trip cancellation, a medical emergency—consider the following types of insurance.

Check your existing insurance policies before you buy travel insurance to cover trip cancellation, lost luggage, medical expenses, or car rental insurance. You're likely to have partial or complete coverage. But if you need some, ask your travel agent about a comprehensive package. The cost of travel insurance varies widely, depending on the cost and length of your trip, your age and overall health, and the type of trip you're taking. Insurance for extreme sports or adventure travel, for example, costs more than coverage for a European cruise. Some insurers provide packages for specialty vacations, such as skiing or backpacking. More dangerous activities might be excluded from basic policies.

For information, contact one of the following popular insurers:

- **Access America** (℃ **800/284-8300;** www.accessamerica.com)
- **Travel Assistance International** (℃ **800/821-2828;** www.travelassistance.com)
- **Travel Guard International** (℃ **800/826-1300;** www.travelguard.com)
- **Travel Insured International** (℃ **800/243-3174;** www.travelinsured.com)
- **Travelex Insurance Services** (℃ **800/228-9792;** www.travelex-insurance.com)

TRIP-CANCELLATION INSURANCE (TCI)

There are three major types of trip-cancellation insurance. One type covers you in the event that you prepay a cruise or tour that gets canceled, and you can't get your money back. The second reimburses you when you or someone in your family gets sick or dies, and you can't travel (but beware that you might not be covered for a pre-existing condition). The third covers you when bad weather makes travel impossible. Some insurers provide coverage for events like jury duty; natural disasters close to home, like floods or fire; or even the loss of a job. A few have added provisions for cancellations because of terror activities. Always check the fine print before signing on, and don't buy trip-cancellation insurance from the tour operator that might be responsible for the cancellation; buy it only from a reputable travel insurance agency. Don't overbuy. You won't be reimbursed for more than the cost of your trip.

MEDICAL INSURANCE

Most health insurance policies cover you if you get sick away from home, but check before you go, particularly if you're insured by an HMO. With the exception of certain HMOs and Medicare/Medicaid, your medical insurance should cover medical treatment—even hospital care—overseas. However, most out-of-country hospitals make you pay your bills up front and send you a refund after you've returned home and filed the necessary paperwork. Members of **Blue Cross/Blue Shield** can now use their cards at select hospitals in most major cities worldwide. Call ℃ **800/810-BLUE** or visit www.bluecares.com for a list of hospitals.

Some credit cards (American Express and certain gold and platinum Visas and MasterCards, for example) offer automatic flight insurance against death or dismemberment in case of an airplane crash if you charged the cost of your ticket.

If you require additional insurance, try one of the following companies:

- **MEDEX International,** 8501 LaSalle Rd., Suite 200, Towson, MD 21286 (℃ **888/MEDEX-00** or 410/453-6300; fax 410/453-6301; www.medexassist.com)
- **Travel Assistance International** (℃ **800/821-2828;** www.travelassistance.com), 9200 Keystone Crossing, Suite 300, Indianapolis, IN 46240 (for general information on services, call the company's Worldwide Assistance Services, Inc., at ℃ **800/777-8710**).

The cost of travel medical insurance varies widely. Check your existing policies before you buy additional coverage. Also check to see if your medical insurance covers you for emergency medical evacuation. If you have to buy a one-way same-day ticket home and forfeit your nonrefundable round-trip ticket, you could be out big money.

LOST-LUGGAGE INSURANCE

On international flights (including the U.S. portions of international trips), baggage is limited to approximately

> ## Tips   Quick ID
>
> Tie a colorful ribbon or piece of yarn around your luggage handle, or slap a distinctive sticker on the side of your bag. This makes it less likely that someone will mistakenly appropriate it. And if your luggage gets lost, it will be easier to find.

$9.07 per pound, up to approximately $635 per checked bag. If you plan to check items more valuable than the standard liability, you can purchase "excess valuation" coverage from the airline, up to $5,000. Be sure to take any valuables or irreplaceable items with you in your carry-on luggage. If you file a lost luggage claim, be prepared to answer detailed questions about the contents of your baggage, and be sure to file a claim immediately; most airlines enforce a 21-day deadline. Before you leave home, compile an inventory of all packed items and a rough estimate of the total value, to ensure you're properly compensated if your luggage is lost. You will be reimbursed only for what you've lost, no more. Once you've filed a complaint, persist in securing your reimbursement; there are no laws governing the length of time it takes for a carrier to reimburse you. If you arrive at a destination without your bags, ask the airline to forward them to your hotel or to your next destination; they will usually comply. If your bag is delayed or lost, the airline might reimburse you for reasonable expenses, such as a toothbrush or a set of clothes, but the airline is under no legal obligation to do so.

Lost luggage might also be covered by your homeowner's or renter's policy. Many platinum and gold credit cards cover you as well. If you choose to purchase additional lost-luggage insurance, be sure not to buy more than you need. Buy in advance from the insurer or a trusted agent (prices will be much higher at the airport).

CAR RENTAL INSURANCE (LOSS/DAMAGE WAIVER OR COLLISION DAMAGE WAIVER)

If you hold a U.S. private auto insurance policy, you probably are covered in the United States but not abroad for loss or damage to the car and liability in case a passenger is injured. The credit card you used to rent the card also might provide some coverage.

Car rental insurance probably does not cover liability if you caused the accident. Check your own auto insurance policy, the rental company policy, and your credit card coverage for the extent of coverage. Is your destination covered? Are other drivers covered? How much liability is covered if a passenger is injured? (If you rely on your credit card for coverage, you might want to bring a second credit card with you: Damages might be charged to your card, and you could find yourself stranded with no money.)

Car rental insurance costs about $20 a day.

STAYING HEALTHY

You'll encounter few health problems while traveling in Austria. The tap water is generally safe to drink, the milk is pasteurized, and health services are good. Occasionally, the change in diet and water could cause some minor disturbances, so you might want to talk to your doctor.

WHAT TO DO IF YOU GET SICK AWAY FROM HOME

If you worry about getting sick away from home, consider purchasing **medical travel insurance** and carry your

ID card in your purse or wallet. In most cases, your existing health plan will provide the coverage you need. See the section on insurance earlier in this chapter for more information.

If you suffer from a chronic illness, consult your doctor before your departure. For conditions like epilepsy, diabetes, or heart problems, wear a **Medic Alert Identification Tag** (℡ 800/825-3785; www.medicalert.org), which will immediately alert doctors to your condition and give them access to your records through Medic Alert's 24-hour hotline.

Pack **prescription medications** in your carry-on luggage, and carry prescription medications in their original containers. Also bring along copies of your prescriptions, in case you lose your pills or run out. Carry the generic name of prescription medicines, in case a local pharmacist is unfamiliar with the brand name.

And don't forget sunglasses and an extra pair of contact lenses or prescription glasses.

Contact the **International Association for Medical Assistance to Travelers (IAMAT)** (℡ 716/754-4883 or 519/836-3412; fax 519/836-0102; www.iamat.org) for tips on travel and health concerns and for lists of local English-speaking doctors. In Canada,

call 519/836-0102. The United States **Centers for Disease Control and Prevention** (℡ 800/311-3435; www.cdc.gov) provides up-to-date information on necessary vaccines and health hazards by region or country. (The CDC's booklet *Health Information for International Travel* is $25 by mail; on the Internet, it's free.) Any foreign consulate can provide a list of area doctors who speak English. If you get sick, consider asking your hotel concierge to recommend a local doctor—even his or her own. You can also try the emergency room at a local hospital; many have walk-in clinics for emergency cases that are not life-threatening. You might not get immediate attention, but you won't pay the high price of an emergency room visit (usually a minimum of $300 just for signing your name).

THE SAFE TRAVELER
Never leave valuables in a car, and never travel with your car unlocked. A U.S. State Department travel advisory warns that every car (whether parked, stopped at a traffic light, or even moving) can be a potential target for armed robbery. In these uncertain times, it is always prudent to check the U.S. State Department's travel advisories at http://travel.state.gov.

8 Tips for Travelers with Special Needs

FOR TRAVELERS WITH DISABILITIES
Laws in Austria have compelled rail stations, airports, hotels, and most restaurants to follow a stricter set of regulations about **wheelchair accessibility** to restrooms, ticket counters, and the like. Even museums and other attractions have conformed to the regulations, which mimic many of those presently in effect in the United States. Always call ahead to check on the accessibility in hotels, in restaurants, and at sights you want to visit.

AGENCIES/OPERATORS
- **Flying Wheels Travel** (℡ 507/451-5005; www.flyingwheelstravel.com) offers escorted tours and cruises that emphasize sports and private tours in minivans with lifts.
- **Access Adventures** (℡ 716/889-9096), a Rochester, New York–based agency, offers customized itineraries for a variety of travelers with disabilities.
- **Accessible Journeys** (℡ 800/TINGLES or 610/521-0339;

www.disabilitytravel.com) caters specifically to slow walkers and wheelchair travelers and their families and friends.

ORGANIZATIONS

• **The Moss Rehab Hospital** (℗ 215/456-5882; www.moss resourcenet.org) provides helpful phone assistance through its **Travel Information Service.**

• **The Society for Accessible Travel and Hospitality** (℗ 212/447-7284; fax 212/725-8253; www. sath.org) offers a wealth of travel resources for all types of disabilities and informed recommendations on destinations, access guides, travel agents, tour operators, vehicle rentals, and companion services. Annual membership costs $45 for adults and $30 for seniors and students.

• **The American Foundation for the Blind** (℗ 800/232-5463; www.afb.org) provides information on traveling with Seeing Eye dogs.

PUBLICATIONS

• **Mobility International USA** (℗ 541/343-1284; www.miusa. org) publishes *A World of Options,* a 658-page book of resources, covering everything from biking trips to scuba outfitters, and a biannual newsletter, "Over the Rainbow." Annual membership is $35.

• **Twin Peaks Press** (℗ 360/694-2462) publishes travel-related books for travelers with special needs.

• *Open World for Disability and Mature Travel* magazine, published by the Society for Accessible Travel and Hospitality (see above), is full of good resources and information. A year's subscription is $14 ($21 outside the U.S.).

FOR BRITISH TRAVELERS

The **Royal Association for Disability and Rehabilitation (RADAR)**, Unit 12, City Forum, 250 City Rd., London EC1V 8AF (℗ 020/7250-3222; www. radar.org.uk), publishes three holiday "fact packs" for £2 each or £5 for all three. The first provides general information, including tips for planning and booking a holiday, obtaining insurance, and handling finances; the second outlines transportation available when going abroad and equipment for rent; and the third deals with specialized accommodations. Another good resource is **Holiday Care,** Imperial Building, 2nd Floor, Victoria Rd., Horley, Surrey RH6 7PZ (℗ 01293/774-535; www.holidaycare.org.uk), a national charity advising on accessible accommodations for the elderly and persons with disabilities. Annual membership is £35.

FOR GAYS & LESBIANS

Unlike Germany, Austria still has a prevailing antihomosexual attitude, in spite of the large number of gay people who live there. There is still much discrimination; gay liberation has a long way to go. Vienna, however, has a large gay community with many bars and restaurants. For information about gay-related activities in Vienna, call the **Gay/Lesbian Visitor Center** at Novargasse 40 (℗ 01/216-6604; www.gay.or.at).

In Austria, the minimum age for consensual homosexual activity is 18.

The **International Gay & Lesbian Travel Association (IGLTA)** (℗ 800/448-8550 or 954/776-2626; fax 954/776-3303; www.iglta.org) links travelers with gay-friendly hoteliers, tour operators, and airline and cruise-line representatives. It offers monthly newsletters, marketing mailings, and a membership directory that's updated once a year. Membership is $200 yearly, plus a $100 administration fee for new members.

AGENCIES/OPERATORS

• **Above and Beyond Tours** (℗ 800/397-2681; www.above beyondtours.com) offers gay and lesbian tours worldwide and is the exclusive gay and lesbian tour operator for United Airlines.

- **Now, Voyager** (© **800/255-6951;** www.nowvoyager.com) is a San Francisco–based gay-owned and operated travel service.
- **Olivia Cruises & Resorts** (© **800/631-6277** or 510/655-0364; http://oliviatravel.com) charters entire resorts and ships for exclusive lesbian vacations all over the world.

PUBLICATIONS

- *Out and About* (© **800/929-2268** or 415/644-8044; www.out andabout.com) offers guidebooks and a newsletter 10 times a year (for $49) packed with solid information on the global gay and lesbian scene.
- *Spartacus International Gay Guide* and *Odysseus* are good annual English-language guidebooks focused on gay men, with some information for lesbians. You can get them from most gay and lesbian bookstores, or order them from **Giovanni's Room** bookstore, 1145 Pine St., Philadelphia, PA 19107 (© **215/923-2960;** www.giovannisroom.com).
- *Gay Travel A to Z: The World of Gay & Lesbian Travel Options at Your Fingertips,* by Marianne Ferrari (Ferrari Publications), is a very good gay and lesbian guidebook series.

SENIOR TRAVEL

Mention the fact that you're a senior when you first make your travel reservations. All major airlines and many Austrian hotels offer discounts for seniors.

Members of **AARP** (formerly known as the American Association of Retired Persons), 601 E St. NW, Washington, DC 20049 (© **800/424-3410** or 202/434-2277; www.aarp.org), get discounts on hotels, airfares, and car rentals. AARP offers members a wide range of benefits, including a magazine and a monthly newsletter. Anyone 50 or older can join.

Alliance for Retired Americans, 888 16 St. NW, Washington, DC 20006 (© **888-373-6497** or 202/974-8256; www.retiredamericans.org), offers a newsletter six times a year and discounts on hotel and auto rentals; annual dues are $10 per person or couple. *Note:* Members of the former National Council of Senior Citizens receive automatic membership in the Alliance.

AGENCIES/OPERATORS

- **Grand Circle Travel** (© **800/221-2610** or 617/350-7500; www.gct.com) offers package deals for the 50-plus market, mostly of the tour-bus variety, with free trips thrown in for those who organize groups of 10 or more.
- **Elder Travelers,** 1615 Smelter Ave., Black Eagle, MT 59414 (www.eldertravelers.com), aids those who are more than 50 years old and like to travel and meet people. The group's stated purpose is to provide members with "zero cost lodging" anywhere in the world, including Austria, as seniors are hooked up with their counterpart hosts in the lands in which they travel. For $40 annually, subscriptions are given to its informative newsletter, which provides links to the best travel data sites worldwide. For more information on this unique group, visit its website.

PUBLICATIONS

- *The Book of Deals* is a collection of more than 1,000 senior discounts on airlines, lodging, tours, and attractions around the country; it's available for $9.95 by calling © **800/460-6676.**
- *101 Tips for the Mature Traveler* is available from Grand Circle Travel (© **800/221-2610**

or 617/350-7500; fax 617/346-6700).

- *The 50+ Traveler's Guidebook* (St. Martin's Press).
- *Unbelievably Good Deals and Great Adventures That You Absolutely Can't Get Unless You're Over 50* (Contemporary Publishing Co.).

FAMILY TRAVEL

Austria is a great place to take your kids. The pleasures available for children (which most adults enjoy just as much) range from watching the magnificent Lipizzaner stallions at the Spanish Riding School in Vienna to exploring the country's many castles and dungeons.

Another outstanding and kid-friendly Viennese attraction is the Prater amusement park, with its giant Ferris wheel, roller coasters, merry-go-rounds, arcades, and tiny railroad that loops around the park. Even if your kids aren't very interested in touring palace state rooms, take them to Schönbrunn, where the zoo and coach collection will tantalize. In summer, beaches along the Alte Donau (an arm of the Danube) are suitable for swimming. And don't forget the lure of the *Konditorei,* those little shops where scrumptious Viennese cakes and pastries are sold.

Babysitting services are available through most hotel desks or by applying at the Tourist Information Office in the town where you're staying. Many hotels have children's game rooms and playgrounds.

Throughout the guide, look for our child-friendly "Kids" icons.

AGENCIES/OPERATORS

- **Familyhostel** (© 800/733-9753; www.learn.unh.edu) takes the whole family on moderately priced domestic and international learning vacations. All trip details are handled by the program staff, and lectures, field trips, and sightseeing are guided by a team of academics. These packages are geared toward kids ages 8 to 15 accompanied by their parents and/or grandparents.

PUBLICATIONS

- *How to Take Great Trips with Your Kids* (The Harvard Common Press) is full of good general advice that can apply to travel anywhere, including Austria.

WEBSITES

- **Family Travel Network** (www.familytravelnetwork.com) offers travel tips and reviews of family-friendly destinations, vacation deals, and thoughtful features such as "What to Do When Your Kids Are Afraid to Travel" and "Kid-Style Camping."
- **Travel with Your Children** (www.travelwithyourkids.com) is a comprehensive site offering sound advice for traveling with children.

STUDENT TRAVEL

If you're planning to travel outside the United States, you'd be wise to arm yourself with an **international student ID card,** which offers substantial savings on rail passes, plane tickets, and entrance fees. It also provides you with basic health and life insurance and a 24-hour help line. The card is available for $22 from the **Council on International Educational Exchange,** or CIEE (www.ciee.org). The CIEE's travel branch, **Council Travel Service** (© **800/226-8624;** www.counciltravel.com), is the biggest student travel agency in the world. If you're no longer a student but are still under 26, you can get a **GO 25 card** from the same organization, which entitles you to insurance and some discounts (but not on museum admissions). **STA Travel** (© **800/781-4040;** www.statravel.com) is another travel agency catering especially to young travelers, although their bargain-basement prices are available to people of all ages.

In Canada, **Travel Cuts** (℗ **800/ 667-2887** or 905/361-2022; www. travelcuts.com) offers similar services. In London, **Usit Campus** (℗ **0870/**

240-1010; www.usitworld.com), opposite Victoria Station, is Britain's leading specialist in student and youth travel.

9 Getting There

BY PLANE

Since the collapse of the Iron Curtain, Vienna has played an increasingly important role as a gateway between western and eastern Europe. Consequently, air traffic into the city has markedly increased. Although Vienna is serviced by a number of well-respected European airlines, most flights coming from the western hemisphere require a transfer in other European cities such as London or Frankfurt.

If you're planning to travel to western Austria—Innsbruck, Salzburg, Tyrol, Vorarlberg, and parts of Land Salzburg—keep in mind that these destinations are closer to Munich than to Vienna. It might be easier to fly to Munich and then rent a car or take a train to your final destination.

Also, if your destination lies somewhat off the beaten track, note that more connections are possible into the secondary airports of Austria from Frankfurt than from any other non-Austrian city. These connections are usually made by Lufthansa, Austrian Airlines, or Tyrolean Air, or on flights maintained cooperatively by some combination of those three.

Most flights from London to Vienna depart from London's Heathrow Airport. The flight takes 2 hours and 20 minutes.

THE MAJOR AIRLINES

From the United States, you can fly directly to Vienna on **Austrian Airlines** (℗ **800/843-0002** in the U.S. and Canada; www.austrianair.com), the national carrier of Austria. There's nonstop service from New York to Vienna (approximately 9 hr.) and

more recently from Chicago and Washington to Vienna.

British Airways (℗ **800/AIRWAYS** in the U.S. and Canada; www.ba.com) provides excellent service to Vienna. Passengers fly first to London—usually nonstop—from 18 gateways in the United States, 3 in Canada, 2 in Brazil, and 1 in Bermuda, Mexico City, and Buenos Aires. From London, British Airways has two to five daily nonstop flights to Vienna from either Gatwick or Heathrow airports.

Flights on **Lufthansa** (℗ **800/ 645-3880** in the U.S. and Canada; www.lufthansa-usa.com), the German national carrier, depart from North America frequently for Frankfurt and Düsseldorf, with connections to Vienna.

American Airlines (℗ **800/433-7300** in the U.S. and Canada; www. aa.com) funnels Vienna-bound passengers through gateways in Zurich or London.

If you're traveling from Canada, you can usually connect from your hometown to **British Airways** (℗ **800/ AIRWAYS** in Canada; www.ba.com) gateways in Toronto, Montréal, and Vancouver. Separate nonstop flights from both Toronto's Pearson Airport and Montréal's Mirabelle Airport depart every day for London, and flights from Vancouver depart for London three times a week. In London, you can stay for a few days (arranging discounted hotel accommodations through the British Airways tour desk) or head directly to Vienna on any of the two to five daily nonstop flights from either Heathrow or Gatwick.

There are frequent flights between London and Vienna, the majority of which depart from London's Heathrow Airport. Flight time is 2 hours and 20 minutes.

Austrian Airlines (© 0845/601-0948 in London; www.aua.com) has four daily nonstop flights into Vienna from Heathrow.

British Airways (© 08457/733-377 in London; www.ba.com) surpasses that, offering three daily nonstops from Heathrow and two from Gatwick, with easy connections through London from virtually every other part of Britain.

The lowest fares are offered to travelers who stay a Saturday night abroad and return to London on a predetermined date within 1 month of their initial departure. To qualify for this type of ticket on either of the above-mentioned airlines, no advance purchase is necessary.

NEW AIR TRAVEL SECURITY MEASURES

In the wake of the terrorist attacks of September 11, 2001, the airline industry began implementing sweeping security measures in airports. Expect a lengthy check-in process and extensive delays. Although regulations vary from airline to airline, you can expedite the process by taking the following steps:

- **Arrive early.** Arrive at the airport at least 2 hours before your scheduled flight.
- **Try not to drive your car to the airport.** Parking and curbside access to the terminal might be limited. Call ahead and check.
- **Don't count on curbside check-in.** Some airlines and airports have stopped curbside check-in altogether, whereas others offer it on a limited basis. For up-to-date information on specific regulations and implementations, check with the individual airline.
- **Be sure to carry plenty of documentation.** A government-issued photo ID (federal, state, or local) is now required. You might need to show this at various checkpoints. With an E-ticket, you might be required to have with

---

Tips What You Can Carry On—and What You Can't

The Federal Aviation Administration (FAA) has devised new restrictions on carry-on baggage, not only to expedite the screening process, but to prevent potential weapons from passing through airport security. Passengers are now limited to bringing just one carry-on bag and one personal item onto the aircraft (previous regulations allowed two carry-on bags and one personal item, like a briefcase or a purse). For more information, go to the FAA's website www.faa.gov. The agency has released a new list of items passengers are not allowed to carry onto an aircraft.

Not permitted: knives and box cutters, corkscrews, straight razors, metal scissors, metal nail files, golf clubs, baseball bats, pool cues, hockey sticks, ski poles, ice picks.

Permitted: nail clippers, tweezers, eyelash curlers, safety razors (including disposable razors), syringes (with documented proof of medical need), walking canes, umbrellas (must be inspected first).

The airline you fly might have additional restrictions on items you can and cannot carry on board. Call ahead to avoid problems.

you a printed confirmation of your purchase and perhaps even the credit card with which you bought your ticket (see "All About E-Ticketing," below). This varies from airline to airline, so call ahead to make sure you have the proper documentation. And be sure that your ID is **up-to-date;** an expired driver's license, for example, might keep you from boarding the plane altogether.

- **Know what you can carry on— and what you can't.** Travelers in the United States are now limited to one carry-on bag, plus one personal bag (such as a purse or a briefcase). The FAA has also issued a list of newly restricted carry-on items; see the box "What You Can Carry On—and What You Can't."

- **Prepare to be searched.** Expect spot-checks. Electronic items, such as a laptop computer or cellphone, should be readied for additional screening. Limit the metal items you wear on your person.

- **It's no joke.** When a check-in agent asks if someone other than you packed your bag, don't decide that this is the time to be funny. The agents will not hesitate to call an alarm.

- **No ticket, no gate access.** Only ticketed passengers are allowed beyond the screener checkpoints, except for those people with specific medical or parental needs.

FLYING FOR LESS: TIPS FOR GETTING THE BEST AIRFARE

Passengers within the same airplane cabin are rarely paying the same fare. Business travelers who need to purchase tickets at the last minute, change their itinerary at a moment's notice, or get home for the weekend pay the premium rate. Passengers who can book their ticket long in advance, who can

stay over Saturday night, or who are willing to travel on a Tuesday, Wednesday, or Thursday after 7pm pay a fraction of the full fare. Here are a few other easy ways to save.

- **Take advantage of APEX fares.** Advance-purchase booking, or APEX, fares are often the key to getting the lowest fare. You generally must be willing to make your plans and buy your tickets as far ahead as possible: The **21-day APEX** is seconded only by the **14-day APEX,** with a stay in Austria of 7 to 30 days. Because the number of seats allocated to APEX fares is sometimes less than 25% of plane's capacity, the early bird gets the low-cost seat. There's often a surcharge for flying on a weekend, and cancellation and refund policies can be strict.

- **Watch for sales.** You'll almost never see sales during July and August or the Thanksgiving or Christmas seasons, but at other times you can get great deals. In the last couple of years, there have been amazing prices on winter flights to Austria. If you already hold a ticket when a sale breaks, it might pay to exchange it, even if you incur a $50 to $75 penalty charge. Note, however, that the lowest-priced fares are often nonrefundable, require advance purchase of 1 to 3 weeks and a certain length of stay, and carry penalties for changing dates of travel. Make sure you know exactly what the restrictions are before you commit.

- If your schedule is flexible, ask if you can secure a cheaper fare by **staying an extra day** or by **flying midweek.** (Many airlines won't volunteer this information.)

- **Consolidators,** also known as bucket shops, are a good place to find low fares, often below even the airlines' discounted rates. Basically,

Tips   All About E-Ticketing

Only yesterday, **electronic tickets (E-tickets)** were the fast and easy ticket-free alternative to paper tickets. E-tickets allowed passengers to avoid long lines at airport check-in, all while saving the airlines money on postage and labor. With the increased security measures in airports, however, an E-ticket no longer guarantees an accelerated check-in. You often can't go straight to the boarding gate, even if you have no bags to check. You'll probably need to show your printed E-ticket receipt or confirmation of purchase, as well as a photo ID and some-times even the credit card with which you purchased your E-ticket. That said, buying an E-ticket is still a fast, convenient way to book a flight; instead of having to wait for a paper ticket to come through the mail, you can book your fare by phone or on the computer, and the airline will immediately confirm by fax or e-mail. In addition, airlines often offer frequent-flier miles as incentive for electronic bookings.

they're just big travel agents who get discounts for buying in bulk and pass some of the savings on to you. Before you pay, however, be aware that consolidator tickets are usually nonrefundable or come with stiff cancellation penalties. We've gotten great deals on many occasions from **Cheap Tickets** (② 800/377-1000; www.cheap tickets.com). **Council Travel** (② 800/2COUNCIL; www.coun ciltravel.com) and **STA Travel** (② 800/781-4040; www.statravel. com) cater especially to young trav-elers, but their bargain-basement prices are available to people of all ages. Other reliable consolidators include **Cheap Seats** (② 800/ 451-7200; www.cheapseatstravel. com) and **1-800/FLY-CHEAP** (www.flycheap.com).

• Join a travel club such as **Moment's Notice** (② 718/234-6295; www. moments-notice.com) or **Sears Discount Travel Club** (② 800/ 433-9383, or 800/255-1487 to join; www.travelersadvantage.com), which supply unsold tickets at dis-counted prices. You pay an annual membership fee to get the club's hot line number. Of course, you're limited to what's available, so you have to be flexible.

• Join **frequent-flier clubs.** It's best to accrue miles on one program so you can rack up free flights and achieve elite status faster. But it makes sense to open as many accounts as possible, no matter how seldom you fly a particular airline. It's free, and you'll get the best choice of seats, faster response to phone inquiries, and prompter service if your luggage is stolen, if your flight is canceled or delayed, or if you want to change your seat

• Search the **Internet** for cheap fares—though it's still best to compare your findings with the research of a dedicated travel agent, if you're lucky enough to have one, especially when you're booking more than just a flight. Among the better-respected vir-tual travel agents are **Travelocity** (www.travelocity.com), **Expedia** (www.expedia.com), and **Yahoo! Travel** (http://travel.yahoo.com).

> **Tips   Canceled Plans**
>
> If your flight is canceled, don't book a new fare at the ticket counter. Find the nearest phone and call the airline directly to reschedule. You'll be relaxing while other passengers are still standing in line.

A NOTE FOR BRITISH TRAVEL-ERS   A regular fare from the United Kingdom to Vienna is extremely expensive, so call a travel agent about a charter flight or special air-travel promotions. If this is not possible, then an APEX ticket (see above) might be the way to trim costs. You might also ask the airlines about a "Eurobudget ticket," which carries restrictions or length-of-stay requirements.

British newspapers are always full of classified ads touting "slashed" fares from London to other destinations. One good source is *Time Out,* a magazine filled with cultural information about London. The *Evening Standard* maintains a daily travel section, and the Sunday editions of virtually any newspaper in the British Isles will run ads.

Although competition among airline consolidators is fierce, one well-recommended company is **Trailfind-ers** (© 020/7937-5400 in London; www.trailfinder.com). Buying blocks of tickets from such carriers as British Airways, Austrian Airlines, and KLM, it offers cost-conscious fares from London's Heathrow or Gatwick airports to Vienna.

In London, many bucket shops around Victoria and Earl's Court offer low fares. Make sure that the company you deal with is a member of the IATA, ABTA, or ATOL. These umbrella organizations will help you if anything goes wrong.

CEEFAX, a British television information service, airs on many home and hotel TVs and runs details of package holidays and flights to Vienna and beyond. Just switch to your CEEFAX channel, and you'll find a menu of listings that includes travel information.

Make sure that you understand the bottom line on any special deal. Ask if all surcharges, including airport taxes and other hidden costs, are included before committing. Upon investigation, some of these "deals" are not as attractive as advertised. Also, find out about any penalties incurred if you're forced to cancel at the last minute.

BY TRAIN

If you plan to travel a lot on the European or British railroads on your way to or from Vienna, you'd do well to secure the latest copy of the "Thomas Cook European Timetable of Railroads." It's available exclusively in North America from **Forsyth Travel Library,** 44 S. Broadway, White Plains, NY 10601 (© **800/FORSYTH;** www.forsyth. com), at a cost of $27.95 plus $4.95 postage (priority airmail) in the United States, and $2 (U.S.) for shipment to Canada.

Vienna has rail links to all the major cities of Europe. From Paris, a train leaves the Gare de l'Est at 7:49am, arriving in Vienna at 9:18pm. From Munich, a train leaves daily at 9:24am (arriving in Vienna at 2:18pm) and then again at 11:19pm (arriving in Vienna at 6:47am). From Zurich, you can take a 9:33pm train that arrives in Vienna at 6:45pm.

Rail travel within Austria itself is superb, with fast, clean trains taking you just about anywhere in the country and going through some incredibly scenic regions.

Train passengers using the **Chunnel** under the English Channel can go from London to Paris in just 3 hours and then on to Vienna (see above). Le Shuttle transports passengers along the 31-mile journey in just 35 minutes. The train also accommodates passenger cars, charter buses, taxis, and motorcycles through a tunnel from Folkestone, England, to Calais, France. Service is year-round, 24 hours a day.

RAIL PASSES FOR NORTH AMERICAN TRAVELERS

EURAILPASS   If you plan to travel extensively in Europe, the **Eurailpass** might be a good bet. It's valid for first-class rail travel in 17 European countries. With one ticket, you travel whenever and wherever you please; more than 100,000 rail miles are at your disposal. Here's how it works: The pass is sold only in North America. A Eurailpass good for 15 days costs $588, a pass for 21 days is $762, a 1-month pass costs $946, a 2-month pass is $1,338, and a 3-month pass goes for $1,654. Children under 4 travel free if they don't occupy a seat; all children under 12 who take up a seat are charged half-price. If you're under 26, you can buy a **Eurail Youthpass,** which entitles you to unlimited second-class travel for 15 days ($414), 21 days ($534), 1 month ($664), 2 months ($938), or 3 months ($1,160). Travelers considering buying a 15-day or 1-month pass should estimate rail distance before deciding whether a pass is worthwhile. To take full advantage of the tickets for 15 days or a month, you'd have to spend a great deal of time on the train. Eurailpass holders are entitled to substantial discounts on certain buses and ferries as well. Travel agents in all towns and railway agents in such major cities as New York, Montréal, and Los Angeles sell all of these tickets. For information on Eurailpasses and other European train data, call **RailEurope** at © **800/438-7245,** or visit it on the Web at **www.rail europe.com**.

Eurail Saverpass offers a 15% discount to each person in a group of three or more people traveling together between April and September, or two people traveling together between October and March. The price of a Saverpass, valid all over Europe for first class only, is $498 for 15 days, $648 for 21 days, $804 for 1 month, $1,138 for 2 months, and $1,408 for 3 months. Even more freedom is offered by the **Saver Flexipass,** which is similar to the Eurail Saverpass, except that you are not confined to consecutive-day travel. For travel over any 10 days within 2 months, the fare is $592; for any 15 days over 2 months, the fare is $778.

Eurail Flexipass allows even greater flexibility. It's valid in first class and offers the same privileges as the Eurailpass. However, it provides a number of individual travel days over a much longer period of consecutive days. Using this pass makes it possible to stay longer in one city and not lose a single day of travel. There are two Flexipasses: 10 days of travel within 2 months for $694, and 15 days of travel within 2 months for $914.

With many of the same qualifications and restrictions as the Eurail Flexipass, the **Eurail Youth Flexipass** is sold only to travelers under age 25. It allows 10 days of travel within 2 months for $488 and 15 days of travel within 2 months for $642.

RAIL PASSES FOR BRITISH TRAVELERS

If you plan to do a lot of exploring, you might prefer one of the three rail passes designed for unlimited train travel within a designated region during a predetermined number of days. These passes are sold in Britain and several other European countries.

An **InterRail Pass** is available to passengers of any nationality, with some restrictions—passengers must be under age 26 and able to prove residency in a European or North African country (Morocco, Algeria, and Tunisia) for at least 6 months before buying the pass. It allows unlimited travel through Europe, except Albania and the republics of the former Soviet Union. Prices are complicated and vary depending on the countries you want to include. For pricing purposes, Europe is divided into eight zones; the cost depends on the number of zones you include. The most expensive option (£249) allows 1 month of unlimited travel in all eight zones and is known to BritRail staff as a "global." The least expensive option (£119) allows 12 days of travel within only one zone.

Passengers age 25 and older can buy an **InterRail 26-Plus Pass,** which, unfortunately, is severely limited geographically. Many countries—including France, Belgium, Switzerland, Spain, Portugal, and Italy—do not honor this pass. It is, however, accepted for travel throughout Denmark, Finland, Norway, and Sweden. Second-class travel with the pass costs £169 for 12 days or £209 for 22 days. Passengers must meet the same residency requirements that apply to the InterRail Pass (described above).

For information on buying individual rail tickets or any of the just-mentioned passes, contact **National Rail Inquiries,** Victoria Station, London (© **08705/848-848** or 0845/748-4950). Tickets and passes also are available at any of the larger railway stations as well as selected travel agencies throughout Britain and the rest of Europe.

BY CAR

If you're traveling from continental Europe and don't want to fly, there are several other options for getting to Austria. If you're coming over from Britain and have arrived at a Channel port in France, by either ferry or the Chunnel, Vienna is about 1,287km (800 miles) and Salzburg is about 1,030km (640 miles). It's faster to travel on the motorways going through Frankfurt, Cologne, Passau (Germany), and Linz (Austria). One of the main roads into Austria is the autobahn from Munich via Salzburg to Vienna. From Switzerland, the main arteries are via Feldkirch to Innsbruck (capital of Tyrol), or from Basel via Karlsruhe to Munich and then on that busy autobahn to either Salzburg or Vienna.

BY BUS

Because of the excellence of rail service from all parts of the Continent into both Salzburg and Vienna, bus transit into Austria is not especially popular. But there is some limited service. **Eurolines,** 52 Grosvenor Gardens, Victoria, London SW1 England (© **020/7730-8235;** www.eurolines.co.uk), operates two express buses per week between London's Victoria Coach Station and Vienna. The trip takes about 29 hours and makes 45-minute rest stops en route about every 4 hours during the transit through France, Belgium, and Germany. Buses depart from London at 8:30am every Friday and Sunday, and are equipped with reclining seats, toilets, and reading lights. The one-way London–Vienna fare is £67. If you opt for a round-trip fare, priced at £111, you won't need to declare your intended date of return until you actually use your ticket (although advance reservations are advisable), and the return half of your ticket will be valid for 6 months. The return to London departs from Vienna every Sunday and Friday at 7:45pm, arriving at Victoria Coach Station about 29 hours later. You can reserve tickets in advance through the Eurolines office listed above, through most British travel agencies, or through Eurolines' largest sales agent, National Express (© **020/7529-2000;** www.nationalexpressgroup.com).

Eurolines also maintains affiliates in every major city of western Europe, including Munich (Deutsch Touring Office, ℂ **069/790-3250**) and Vienna (ℂ **01/712-04-53**). In Paris, contact Eurolines at Gare Routière International de Paris-Gallieni, at the bus station in the Paris suburb of Bagnolet (ℂ **08/36-69-52-52**).

10 Getting Around

BY TRAIN

Rail travel is superb in Austria, with fast, clean trains taking you through scenic regions. If you don't have a car, this is the preferred way to travel, as trains will take you nearly every place in Austria except for remote hamlets tucked away in almost-inaccessible mountain districts. Many other services tie in with railroad travel, among them car or bicycle rental at many stations, bus transportation links, and package tours, including boat trips and cable-car rides.

Inter-City Express trains connect Vienna with all major cities in the country, including Salzburg, Klagenfurt, Graz, and Linz. A train trip from Salzburg to Vienna takes about 3 hours.

RAIL PASSES See "Getting There," earlier in this chapter, for information on the **Eurailpass,** which is valid in Austria.

If you plan rail travel just within Austria, consider the **Austrian Railpass,** available at most travel agents. You get 3 days of unlimited train travel in a 15-day period, with a choice of first class for $158 or second class for $107. Children 6 to 12 pay half the adult fare (free for 5 and under). Bonuses include 50% discount on most Danube steamers, 40% discount on bike rentals at rail stations, 10% to 15% on some rack railways, and 20% discount on steamers operating on Wolfgangsee.

SENIORS DISCOUNT In Austria, women 60 years of age and over and men age 65 and over, regardless of nationality, can travel on half-fare passes valid on the Austrian Federal Railways and on the bus systems of the Federal Railways and the Postal Service. The reduction is not applicable on municipal transit lines such as subways, streetcars, or buses, even in towns where the Postal Service operates the local bus service.

To purchase a half-fare ticket, a Railway Senior Citizen's Identification must be obtained in advance. This is issued at all railroad stations, at certain major post offices, and at the central railroad station (Hauptbahnhof) in Frankfurt and Munich, Germany. In Zurich, Switzerland, both the Senior Citizen and the Austrian Network passes are available at the rail station at the Zurich airport. At the main rail station, the Zurich Hauptbahnhof, you can purchase only the Senior Citizen pass. This makes it possible to take a train into Austria without having to break your trip at the border.

The price of the identification is 25€, and it's valid from January 1 to December 31. A passport photo is required, and you must present your passport to prove your age. With this Senior Citizen's Identification—not available in the United States—you can buy tickets for your half-fare travel in Austria. The reduction is also granted for express trains, first-class tickets, and checked luggage. If a TEE (Trans European Express) train is used, any supplement must be paid in full.

This ID for seniors, called a *Seniorenauswels,* is sold at railroad stations as well as major post offices.

OTHER RAILWAY DATA For information on short-distance round-trip tickets, cross-country passes, and passes for all lines in the individual provinces, as well as piggyback transportation for your car through the Tauern Tunnel, check with the **Austrian Federal Railways,** c/o the Austrian National Tourist Office, P.O. Box 1142, New York, NY 10108-1142 (© **212/944-6880).**

BY PLANE

Austrian Airlines (© **800/843-0002** in the U.S. and Canada; www.austrian air.com) offers flights that link Vienna to the country's leading cities. Outgoing flights from Vienna are carefully timed to coincide with the arrivals of most of the company's transatlantic flights.

Cities in Austria not serviced by Austrian Airlines are usually the domain of the company's wholly owned subsidiary, Austrian Air Services (A.A.S.; same telephone number and website as above). A.A.S. offers frequently scheduled domestic flights connecting Vienna to most of the country's provincial capitals: Graz, Klagenfurt, Linz, and Salzburg, among others. The timetable for these flights is often adjusted to coincide with the arrival in Vienna of international flights. Austrian Airlines is the general representative and sales agent for A.A.S.

Tyrolean Airways (same telephone number and website as Austrian Airlines), an airline partially owned by Austrian Airlines, offers a very useful airborne network whose home base is the Tyrolean capital of Innsbruck. Its regular flight network consists of up to four flights per day between Vienna and Innsbruck, and four flights each between Innsbruck and both Frankfurt and Zurich. The airline also offers about five flights a week between Innsbruck and the Styrian capital of Graz. Reservations on Tyrolean Airways can be made through Austrian Airlines. Its fleet consists almost entirely of turbo-prop planes containing no more than 49 seats. The airline specializes in domestic flights and commuter runs to destinations close to the border, including Munich and Budapest.

BY BUS

It's easiest to get around Austria on the country's excellent rail network, but many Austrian villages are not near rail lines. Reaching some of these areas can be best accomplished by car or bus. To facilitate travel, the Austrian government maintains two different bus networks: those maintained by the **Austrian Postal Service** (whose vehicles, in most cases, are painted a reddish-orange) and those maintained by the **Austrian Federal Railways** (which, in some, but not all, cases are painted blue and white). In recent years, efforts have been made to merge both of these systems into one overall administration identified as the **Bundesbus System,** but many Austrians continue to make a distinction between the two networks. There are also a limited number of privately owned bus companies that specialize in long-haul transits to major cities outside Austria.

Buses (some of which also carry mail) cover a network of almost 30,500km (19,000 miles) of often very remote secondary roads. One of their primary functions involves retrieving passengers at railway stations for the continuation of journeys. Bus departures are usually timed to coincide with the arrival of trains from other parts of Austria. Buses are particularly helpful at the bottom of alpine valleys, where transit is needed to carry passengers from the local railway station up toward ski resorts and hamlets at higher altitudes. Children under 6 travel free on many of these buses, and children under 15 usually receive a 50% discount.

Information about bus schedules and routings is available at most post offices, at the reception desks of most hotels whose business relies on clients arriving by bus, and at travel agencies.

Specifics about routes and schedules are in the *Kursbuch* (Austrian Motor Coach Schedule), a timetable that is usually updated annually and that forms part of the basic library maintained by virtually every tourist office in Austria. Bus information is usually also merged into the thousands of railway timetables that are posted at train stations throughout the country. An especially convenient way to find out about bus schedules, if you're heading for a hotel in a remote area, is to call the hotel and ask. Austrian hoteliers usually keep up-to-date schedules on hand.

BY CAR

All main roads in Austria are hard-surfaced. Between Salzburg and Vienna there's a four-lane autobahn, and between Vienna and Edlitz the autobahn has six lanes. Part of the highway system includes mountain roads, and in the alpine region drivers face gradients of 6% to 16%, or even steeper in some places. When driving in Austria, always plot your course carefully. If you have had no experience in mountain driving—much less alpine mountain driving—you might want to take a train or a bus to get to some of the loftier mountain alpine retreats.

In summer, driving conditions are good, but in winter, December though March, motorists must reckon with snow on the roads and passes at higher altitudes. Roads at altitudes of up to 1,700m (5,580 ft.) are kept open in winter, although they can be temporarily closed because of heavy snowfall or avalanche danger. If you're planning to drive in Austria in winter, you'll need snow tires or chains.

Don't take chances. Ask about road conditions before you start on a trip. This information is available in English 7 days a week from 6am to 8pm from the **Österreich- ischer Automobil-, Motorrad- und Touringclub (ÖAMTC),** Schubertring 1–3, A-1010 Vienna (② **01/711-997**).

CAR RENTALS All drivers in Austria must have been in possession of a valid driver's license for at least 1 year before renting a vehicle. They must also present a valid passport when they sign the rental agreement. Drivers not in possession of a major credit card must pay in advance a minimum deposit, plus the estimated rental cost and the estimated tax. Cars rented from most rental companies can be dropped off in major cities of Germany for no additional charge. Drop-offs in Switzerland or Italy, however, require an extra charge, which can be quite high.

Tax on Car Rentals Be aware that car rentals in Austria are taxed at a whopping rate of 21.2%. This is in addition to a 6% municipal airport tax added to the cost of any car rented at an airport. Clarify in advance whether the rates you're quoted include the taxes. You might consider taking a taxi to your hotel upon arrival and then renting your vehicle from an inner-city location, to avoid the 6% airport surcharge.

When you reserve a car, be sure to ask if the price includes insurance. The rental outfits offer an optional insurance policy known as a loss-damage waiver (LDW). If you accept it, you'll be charged around 25€ per day. It allows you to waive all financial responsibility for any damage to your car, even if it's eventually determined that you were the driver at fault. In some instances, certain credit-card companies offer free insurance if you use the card to pay for the rental. Check directly with your credit-card issuer to see if you are covered.

Budget-Rent-a-Car (② **800/472-3325;** www.budget.com) is among the least expensive options in Austria. It maintains more than a dozen locations throughout the country, including branches at all the major airports and at downtown locations in most of the provincial capitals.

Hertz (✆ **800/654-3001;** www. hertz.com) maintains offices in about 18 cities throughout Austria. During limited periods, it sometimes publicizes price promotions worth inquiring about, depending on the season, as well as discounts to employees of some large North American corporations.

Avis (✆ **800/331-1084;** www.avis. com) operates offices in 19 Austrian cities, at airports and downtown, as well as at some of the country's larger ski resorts. Avis usually offers 10% discounts for members of such organizations as the AAA and AARP. Like Budget and Hertz, it offers seasonal price promotions.

ROAD MAPS Some of the most useful maps for touring the countryside include Michelin's *Austria* (no. 426) and Freytag & Berndt's *Autokarte Austria.* Even more detailed are Freytag & Berndt's *Grosse Strassen Karten,* which covers Austria in three separate breakdowns, with the enlargement of certain regions of Land Salzburg available on a fourth. Some visitors find it more convenient to buy these same four maps in the form of the 12-page atlas, *Grosser Auto Atlas Österreich.* It includes helpful blowups of the centers of many of the country's large and medium-size cities.

Freytag & Berndt also publish detailed maps (in either atlas or foldaway form) of Greater Vienna. Maps of Vienna's public transport system are available from the city's tourist offices.

Hill-climbers and trekkers appreciate Freytag & Berndt's detailed topographical maps known as the *Wanderkarten* (*W.K.*). The company also publishes canoeing maps of specific regions, including the Carinthian lakes.

Most of the maps mentioned above are available in bookstores throughout Austria and in larger bookstores in the rest of Europe and North America. Freytag & Berndt's shops are at Kohlmarkt 9 in Vienna, and at Wilhelm-Greil-Strasse 15 in Innsbruck.

If you'd like a map before your trip to plan your itinerary, you can obtain one from Rand McNally, Michelin, or AAA. These are sold at bookstores all over America. Rand McNally has retail stores at 150 E. 52nd St., New York, NY 10022 (✆ **212/758-7488;** www. randmcnally.com); at 595 Market St., San Francisco, CA 94105 (✆ **415/ 777-3131**); and at many other outlets. The U.S. headquarters of Michelin is at P.O. Box 19008, Greenville, SC 29602 (✆ **800/423-0485**).

The **AAA** (American Automobile Association) (✆ **800/222-4357** or 407/444-4300; www.aaa.com) publishes a regional map of Austria that's available free to members at most AAA offices throughout the United States. Also available free to members is a guide of approximately 60 pages, *Motoring in Europe,* which gives helpful data about road signs, insurance regulations, speed limits, and other concerns in Europe.

GASOLINE Regular-grade unleaded (*Blei-frei*) motor fuel is generally available in Austria. Gasoline prices vary from place to place but are generally lower at discounted gasoline stations or self-service operations. Austrian service stations don't accept U.S. oil company or general-purpose credit or charge cards.

DRIVING RULES Traffic regulations are similar to those in other European countries where you *drive on the right.* The speed limit is 50kmph (31 mph) in built-up areas within the city limits unless otherwise specified. Out of town, the limit is 130kmph (80 mph) on motorways and 100kmph (62 mph) on all other roads.

Driving under the influence of alcohol is severely punished. The permissible alcohol content of the blood is very low—two beers or 8 ounces of wine can put you over the mark. The *minimum* fine is 335€ and possible loss of a driver's license.

The minimum driving age in Austria is 18. If you're over 18 and have a valid U.S., Canadian, or British license, you're not required to have an International Driver's License. However, you should inquire at your travel agency, an Austrian consulate, or an Austrian National Tourist Office about official validation of your home driver's license for use in Austria.

Use of seat belts is compulsory, and children under 12 may not sit in the front passenger seat unless a child's seat belt or a special seat has been installed.

If you're involved in or witness an accident resulting in bodily injury, you must report it immediately. If only property damage is involved, you may exchange identification with the other person. If you can't find the owner of a vehicle you might have damaged, you must report the incident to the police. Otherwise, you might be considered a hit-and-run driver.

PARKING   A number of Austrian cities and towns have restricted parking zones, where you can park for 90 minutes in specially marked "blue zones," so-called because of blue lines on the road.

In Vienna, Graz, Linz, Klagenfurt, Innsbruck, and other major towns, you must use a parking voucher to stop in limited-parking zones. You must purchase a voucher and then, when you park, write in the time you arrived and display it on the dashboard inside the windshield. You can buy vouchers at banks, gas stations, or tobacconists.

Parked vehicles that are obstructing traffic are quickly towed away at the owner's or driver's expense.

Out at country resorts, parking is not a problem—except in winter, when you might have to pay extra for indoor or covered parking. However, in Austria's congested cities, such as Vienna, parking is a real problem. If your hotel doesn't have a private garage, the police will usually let you park in front of a hotel long enough to unload your luggage; then someone from the hotel staff will direct you to the nearest garage, often in the same neighborhood.

AUTOMOBILE CLUBS   The leading auto club of Austria is the ÖAMTC (Österreichischer Automobil-, Motorred- und Touringclub), Schubertring 1–3, A-1010 Vienna (✆ **01/711-997**). ARBÖ (✆ **01/891-21-7**) is another.

BREAKDOWNS/ASSISTANCE In case of car breakdown, foreign motorists can call the two auto clubs mentioned above. Call **ARBÖ** (✆ **123**) or **ÖAMTC** (✆ **120**) anywhere in Austria. You don't need to use an area code for either number. However, if you're not a member of either of these clubs, you'll pay for emergency road service.

MOTORCYCLES   The same requirements for operating cars in Austria hold for operating motorcycles. Both drivers and passengers of motorcycles must wear crash helmets. Lights must be kept on when the vehicle is being driven.

BY TAXI

In large Austrian cities, taxis are equipped with officially sealed taximeters that show the cost of your trip in euros. If a rate change has recently been instituted, a surcharge might be added to the amount shown on the meter, pending adjustment of the taximeter. Surcharges are posted in the cab. A supplement is charged for luggage carried in the vehicle's trunk. Zone charges or set charges for standard trips are the rule in most resort areas. Tip the driver 10% of the fare.

BY BOAT

Why not take a boat trip on the Danube or on one of Austria's beautiful lakes? Passenger boats on the Danube are operated by the **DDSG-Blue**

Danube Shipping Co. (See "Boating on the 'Blue' Danube," in chapter 4.) **Lake Constance boats** visit the most popular tourist destinations daily May through October. A special ticket, the Bodenseepass, is valid for 15 days, during which time you can go on excursions on any scheduled boat. Also, during the time the pass is valid, you can purchase tickets at reduced fares for any railroad, bus, and cable-car trips in the Lake Constance area. Information on Lake Constance offerings is available at Schiffshafen, A-6900 Bregenz (© **05574/42868**).

BY BICYCLE

From April to the beginning of November, you can rent a bicycle at leading Austrian railroad stations. Photo ID must be presented at the time of rental. The charge is 10€ per day, which is reduced to 6€ if a railroad ticket to the point of rental is held. You can reserve a bicycle in advance, but you can almost always get a bike without making reservations. The vehicle can be returned to where it was rented or to any other Austrian railroad station during business hours.

11 Organized Tours

For many destinations, you can book airfare, hotel, ground transportation, and even some sightseeing just by making one call to a travel agent or packager for a lot less than if you tried to put the trip together yourself. But be aware that packages vary in quality and cost. Some packages offer a better class of hotels than others. Some offer the same hotels for lower prices. Some offer flights on scheduled airlines, while others book charters. In many packages, your choices of accommodations and travel days is limited. In other words, do a little research and decide which package most meets your needs.

British Airways' Holidays (© **877/428-2228;** www.ba.com) offerings tend to incorporate the scenery and architecture of Austria with similar attractions across the border in Germany and Switzerland. BA can arrange a stopover in London en route for an additional fee and allows extra time in either Vienna or Zurich before or after any tour, for no additional charge.

Other attractive options are provided by **Delta Vacations** (© **800/872-7786;** www.deltavacations.com), **American Express Travel** (© **800/446-6234;** www.travelimpressions.com), and an unusual, upscale (and

very expensive) tour operator, **Abercrombie and Kent** (© **800/323-7308;** www.abercrombiekent.com), known for its carriage-trade rail excursions through eastern Europe and the Swiss and Austrian Alps.

The oldest travel agency in Britain, **Cox & Kings,** Gordon House, 10 Greencoat Place, London SW1P 1PH (© **020/7873-5000;** www.coxandkings.co.uk), specializes in unusual, if pricey, holidays. Offerings in Austria include organized tours through the country's many regions of natural beauty and tours of historic or aesthetic interest. Also available are opera tours to Salzburg and Vienna.

Other companies featuring offbeat adventure travel include **HF Holidays,** Imperial House, Edgware Road, Colindale, London NW9 5AL (call © **020/8905-9388** or visit www.hfholidays.co.uk for a brochure). It offers a range of 1- to 2-week packages to Austria. **Sherpa Expeditions,** 131 A Heston Rd., Hounslow, Middlesex TW5 0RF (© **020/8577-2717;** www.sherpaexpeditions.com), offers treks through off-the-beaten-track regions of Europe, especially the Alps.

The best deals for families are often package tours put together by some of the giants of the British travel industry.

Well positioned among them is **Thomson's Holiday Tours.** Through its cost-conscious subsidiary, **Skytours,** Hampstead Rd., Greater London House, London NW1 7SD (© **020/7387-9321,** www.thomson-holidays.com), it offers land, rail, self-driving, and air packages to continental Europe. To qualify, clients must book airfare and hotel accommodations lasting 2 weeks or more. Book as far in advance as possible.

12 Planning Your Trip Online

Researching and booking your trip online can save time and money. Then again, it might not. It is simply not true that you always get the best deal online. Most booking engines do not include schedules and prices for budget airlines, and from time to time you'll get a better last-minute price by calling the airline directly. It's best to call the airline to see if you can do better before booking online.

On the plus side, Internet users today can tap into the same travel-planning databases that were once accessible only to travel agents—and do it at the same speed. Sites such as **Frommers.com, Travelocity.com, Expedia.com,** and **Orbitz.com** allow consumers to comparison-shop for airfares, access special bargains, book flights, and reserve hotel rooms and rental cars.

But don't fire your travel agent just yet. Though online booking sites offer tips and hard data to help you bargain-shop, they cannot endow you with the hard-earned experience that makes a seasoned, reliable travel agent an invaluable resource, even in the Internet age. And for consumers with a complex itinerary, a trusty travel agent is still the best way to arrange the most direct flights to and from the best airports.

Some sites, such as Expedia.com, send you **e-mail notification** when a cheap fare becomes available to your favorite destination. Some also tell you when fares to a particular destination are lowest.

TRAVEL-PLANNING & BOOKING SITES
Keep in mind that because several airlines are no longer willing to pay commissions on tickets sold by online travel agencies, these agencies might either add a $10 surcharge to your bill if you book on that carrier or neglect to offer those carriers' schedules.

The list of sites below is selective, not comprehensive. Some sites will have evolved or disappeared by the time you read this.

Travelocity (www.travelocity.com or http://frommers.travelocity.com) and **Expedia** (www.expedia.com) are among the most popular, offering an excellent range of options. Travelers can search by destination, dates, and cost.

Qixo (www.qixo.com) is another search engine that allows you to search for flights and accommodations from some 20 airline and travel-planning sites (such as Travelocity) at once. Qixo sorts results by price.

SMART E-SHOPPING
The savvy traveler is one armed with good information. Here are a few tips to help you navigate the Internet successfully and safely.

- **Know when sales start.** Last-minute deals can vanish in minutes. If you have a favorite booking site or airline, find out when last-minute deals are released to the public. (For example, Southwest's specials are posted every Tuesday at 12:01am Central Standard Time).

- **Shop around.** Compare results from different sites and airlines—and against a travel agent's best fare. If possible, try ranges of times and alternate airports before making a purchase.
- **Follow the rules of the trade.** Book in advance, and choose an off-peak time and date, if possible. Some sites tell you when fares to a particular destination tend to be cheapest.
- **Stay secure.** Book only through secure sites (some airline sites are not secure). Look for a key icon (Netscape) or a padlock (Internet Explorer) at the bottom of your Web browser before you enter credit-card information or other personal data.
- **Avoid online auctions.** Sites that auction airline tickets and frequent-flier miles are the number-one perpetrators of Internet fraud, according to the National Consumers League.
- **Maintain a paper trail.** If you book an E ticket, print a confirmation or write down your confirmation number, and keep it safe and accessible—or your trip could be a virtual one!

ONLINE TRAVELER'S TOOLBOX

Veteran travelers usually carry some essential items to make their trips easier. Following is a selection of online tools to bookmark and use.

- **Visa ATM Locator** (www.visa.com) or **MasterCard ATM Locator** (www.mastercard.com). Find ATMs in hundreds of cities in the United States and around the world.
- **Foreign Languages for Travelers** (www.travlang.com/languages). Learn basic terms in more than 70 languages, and click on any underlined phrase to hear what it sounds like.
- **Intellicast** (www.intellicast.com). Get weather forecasts for all 50 states and cities around the world. *Note:* Temperatures are in Celsius for many international destinations.
- **Mapquest** (www.mapquest.com). The best of the mapping sites, Mapquest lets you choose a specific address or destination, and in seconds, returns a map and detailed directions.
- **Cybercafes.com** (www.cybercafes.com) or **Net Café Guide** (www.netcafeguide.com). Locate Internet cafes around the globe. Catch up on your e-mail and log onto the Web for a few dollars per hour.
- **Universal Currency Converter** (www.xe.com). See what your dollar or pound is worth in more than 100 other countries.
- **U.S. State Department Travel Warnings** (www.travel.state.gov). Get reports on places where health concerns or unrest might threaten U.S. travelers. This site also lists the locations of U.S. embassies around the world.

13 Tips on Accommodations

Hotels, inns, and pensions (boardinghouses) are classified by the government into five different categories in Austria and are rated with stars. A five-star rating is deluxe, and four stars is first class. Two and three stars classify middle-bracket establishments, and one star designates a simple inn or hotel; there's a chance that not all rooms have private bathrooms. However, one-star hotels are most often clean and decent establishments where you get more value for your euro than anywhere else in the country.

Reservations are advised, especially if you're visiting in high season. High season means different things in different parts of the country. For example, summer is high season in Salzburg and Vienna. Innsbruck actually has two high seasons: It enjoys a great deal of summer tourist business but is also the center of the bustling Tyrolean ski industry in winter. High season at ski resorts is usually from Christmas to mid-April; most resorts actually lower their prices in summer. Sometimes hotels offer a "shoulder" rate in spring and fall when business lessens; sometimes these hotels close if business is slow.

The local tourist office in any Austrian city or resort can assist you in making the necessary reservations. If a certain hotel is booked and cannot accept your reservation, the tourist office will be able to make an alternative reservation in a hotel of comparable price and character. Send your request via airmail and enclose an International Reply Coupon, obtainable at your local post office, for an airmail reply. Be sure to give the following information: hotel category (deluxe, first class, standard, or budget), desired location (center, edge of town, near a lake or ski lifts). Address your request to *Verkehrsverein* in small towns or *Tourismusverband* in large resorts and cities, adding the postal code, the town name, and *Austria*.

Regional service organizations are your best bet if you want to visit several towns or resorts in one Austrian province or one of Austria's major cities. These addresses are available from the Austrian National Tourist Office abroad.

BED & BREAKFASTS

Look for the signs that say ZIMMER FREI attached to the front of a house or to a short post at the front-yard gate or driveway. This means that the proprietors rent rooms on a bed-and-breakfast basis to travelers. You'll encounter these signs along Austria's highways and along some of the most scenic byways.

Such accommodations have hot and cold running water in the bedrooms, although private bathroom and toilet facilities are rare. (There's usually a toilet on every floor and one bathroom in the house.) A continental breakfast is served.

Few homes accept advance reservations, so just stop in and inquire. When the rooms are filled, the sign is taken down or covered. The local tourist office can also help you find B&B accommodations.

You might need a few words of basic German to converse with the owner, as only a few proprietors speak a little English. If you're staying for only 1 night, you might be asked to pay your bill in advance, and it must be paid in euros.

FARMHOUSE ACCOMMODATIONS

Groups or whole families can stay on a farm, renting several rooms or even a wing of the house. However, a stay of at least a week is generally required, and advance reservations through a local tourist office or regional tourist board are necessary. The correct form of address for the local offices is *Verkehrsverein,* then the postal code and the name of the town near which you want to stay, and *Austria.* Regional boards should be addressed by writing to *Landesfremdenverkehrsamt,* followed by the postal code and the name of the capital of the respective Austrian province, and *Austria.* Your reservation will be confirmed upon receipt of a deposit.

CASTLE HOTELS (SCHLOSSHOTELS)

Graced with a rich and ornate imperial tradition, Austria poured funds and resources throughout its history into constructing palaces and castles. Many of these ancestral buildings, partly from lack of funds, have been transformed into hotels. Information on these hotels can be obtained through **Euro-Connection,** 7500 212th St. SW, Suite 103, Edmonds, WA 98026 (© **800/645-3876;** www. euro-connection.com), which represents castle hotels throughout Europe.

CHALETS, VILLAS & APARTMENTS

Many cottages, chalets, and condominiums, built as second homes by Austrian entrepreneurs, are available for short-term rentals to qualified visitors when they're not otherwise occupied. These rental properties are usually at or near sites of natural or historic beauty or in ski or lakeside resorts.

Pego Leasing Centre, Sageweg 1, A-6700 Bludenz (© **05552/65666;** www.pego.at), inventories more than 1,000 rental properties (chalets, villas, cottages, farmhouses, and apartments) in Austria. The company arranges rentals of 1 week to a year or more for 1 to 30 occupants at a time; rentals traditionally begin and end on a Saturday. Pego usually collects most of its fee directly from the owners of the rental property, but the tenant usually pays an agency fee to Pego of around 10% for each booking.

PENSIONS

A pension is generally more intimate and personal than a hotel. Of course, the nature and quality of the welcome depends largely on the host or hostess, who might also be the cook and chief maid. As a general rule, a first-class

pension in Austria is equal to a second-class hotel; a second-class pension is equal to a third-class hotel. Usually a continental breakfast is served; some pensions also offer dinner. Expect to be on your own for lunch.

HOME EXCHANGES

You can arrange a home exchange—swapping your home with that of an Austrian family, often with a car included—through several U.S.-based organizations. **Intervac U.S. & International,** 30 Corte San Fernando, Tiburon, CA 94159 (© **800/756-HOME** or 415/435-3497; www.inter vacus.com), publishes three catalogs a year containing listings of more than 9,000 homes in more than 36 countries. Members contact each other directly. Depending on your type of membership, fees begin at 65€.

YOUTH HOSTELS

Austria has 108 youth hostels distributed throughout the provinces. Rates for a bed and breakfast run from $13 to $19 per person daily. Some hostels lock their doors between 10pm and 6am to discourage late arrivals. Dormitories must be empty between 10am and 5pm. You must have an International Youth Hostel Federation membership card to use Austria's youth hostels, and advance reservations are recommended. In Austria, you can get information regarding hostels from Österreichischer Jugendherbergsverband, Schottenring 28, A-1010 Vienna (© **01/533-53-53**). A detailed brochure is available at any branch of the Austrian National Tourist Office.

For information on finding a hostel worldwide, visit www.findhostels.com.

14 Recommended Books

BIOGRAPHY

Gay, Peter. *Freud: A Life for Our Times.* Norton. Gay's biography is a good introduction to the life of one of the seminal figures of the 20th century. Freud, of course, was a Viennese until he fled from the Nazis in 1938, settling with his sofa in London.

Geiringer, Karl and Irene. *Haydn: A Creative Life in Music.* University of California. This is the best biography of composer (Franz) Joseph Haydn, friend of Mozart, teacher of Beethoven, and court composer of the Esterházys.

Gutman, Robert W. *Mozart: A Cultural Biography.* Harvest. Music historian Gutman places Mozart squarely in the cultural world of 18th-century Europe.

Pic, Robert. *Empress Maria Theresa.* Harper & Row. The life and times of the greatest, most colorful Hapsburg monarch is richly treated in this engrossing biography.

HISTORY

Brook-Shepherd, Gordon. *The Austrians: A Thousand-Year Odyssey.* Carroll & Graf. Historian Brook-Shepherd looks at Austria's long history to explain its people: who they are, how they got there, and where they're going.

Schorske, Carol E. *Fin-de-Siecle Vienna: Politics and Culture.* Vintage. This landmark book takes you into the political and social world of Vienna during the late 19th and early 20th centuries.

Morton, Frederic. *A Nervous Splendor: Vienna 1888–1889.* Viking Penguin. Morton uses the mysterious deaths of Archduke Rudolf and Baroness Marie Vetsera at Mayerling as a point of departure to capture in detail the life of Imperial Vienna at its glorious height.

Wheatcroft, Andrew. *The Hapsburgs: Embodying Empire.* Viking Penguin. Here is the full sweep of the Hapsburg dynasty, from the Middle Ages to the end of World War I, focusing on such remarkable personalities as Rudolph I, Charles V, Maria Theresa, and Franz Joseph I.

ART, ARCHITECTURE & MUSIC

Aurenhammer, Hans. *J. B. Fischer von Erlach.* Harvard University Press. This entertaining volume illuminates the life, times, and aesthetic vision of the court-appointed architect who transformed the face of 18th-century Vienna and Salzburg.

Varnedoe, Kirk. *Vienna 1900: Art, Architecture, and Design.* New York Museum of Modern Art. During the late 19th century, Vienna's artistic genius reached dazzling heights of modernity. These movements are explored in this appealing primer.

Burgess, Anthony. *On Mozart.* Ticknor & Fields. Set in heaven, amid a reunion of the greatest composers of all time, this controversial book creates debates about music that never occurred but should have. Condemned by some critics as gibberish, and praised by others as brilliant and poetic, Burgess's work is highly recommended for musical sophisticates with a sense of humor.

Rickett, Richard. *Music and Musicians in Vienna.* Hienemann. Few countries in Europe pride themselves as thoroughly as Austria does for its music. This brief, wisely created volume offers a broad overview of the country's musical heritage. It makes a good introduction to the subject.

 FAST FACTS: Austria

American Express This company has agents in Vienna, Salzburg, and Innsbruck. See "Fast Facts" under the individual cities, or check its website (www.amex.com) for office locations and hours.

Business Hours In the federal provinces, banking hours vary according to the region. The exchange counters at airports and railroad stations are generally open from the first to the last plane or train, usually from 8am to 8pm daily. Many stores are open from 8am to 6pm Monday through Friday, and from 8am to noon on Saturday; they close for 2 hours during the middle of each day.

Drug Laws Penalties for violations are severe and could lead to either imprisonment or deportation. Selling drugs to minors is dealt with particularly harshly.

Drugstores In Austrian cities, at least one pharmacy stays open 24 hours. If a particular pharmacy is closed, a sign on the door will list the address and phone number of the nearest one that is open.

Electricity Austria operates on 220 volts AC (50 cycles). That means that U.S.-made appliances that don't come with a 110/220 switch will need a transformer (sometimes called a converter). Many Austrian hotels stock adapter plugs but not power transformers.

Embassies & Consulates The main U.S., Canadian, British, Australian, and New Zealand offices are all located in Vienna. See "Fast Facts: Vienna" in chapter 3 for addresses and hours.

Emergencies Emergency phone numbers throughout the country (no area code needed) are as follows: ℂ **133** for the police, **144** for accident service, **122** to report a fire, and **120** to report a car breakdown on the highway.

Language German is the official language of Austria, but since English is taught in the high schools, it's commonly spoken throughout the country, especially in tourist regions. Certain Austrian minorities speak Slavic languages, and Hungarian is commonly spoken in Burgenland. See the appendix for a glossary of common and useful German words and phrases.

Liquor Laws Eighteen is the legal drinking age for buying or ordering alcohol. Alcohol is sold day and night year-round, and there are few restrictions on its sale.

Mail Post offices (*Das Postamt*) in Austria are usually located in the heart of the town, village, or urban district they service. If you're unsure of your address in any particular town, correspondence can be addressed care of the local post office by labeling it either POST RESTANTE or POSTLAGERND. If you do this, it's important to clearly designate the addressee, the name of the town, and its postal code. To claim any correspondence, the addressee must present his or her passport.

As an alternative to having your mail sent *post restante* to post offices, you might opt for the mail services offered in Salzburg, Innsbruck, and Vienna by American Express (see above). There's no charge for this service to anyone holding an American Express card or American Express traveler's checks.

The postal system in Austria is, for the most part, efficient and speedy. You can buy stamps at a post office or from the hundreds of news and tobacco kiosks, designated locally as *Tabac/Trafik*. Mailboxes are painted yellow, and older ones are emblazoned with the double-headed eagle of the Austrian Republic. Newer ones usually have the golden trumpet of the Austrian Postal Service. A blue stripe on a mailbox indicates that mail will be picked up there on a Saturday.

Both postcards and airmail letters weighing under 20 grams cost 1.09€ for delivery to North America.

Newspapers & Magazines In major cities, you'll find the *International Herald Tribune* or *USA Today,* as well as other English-language newspapers and magazines, including the European editions of *Time* and *Newsweek,* at hotels and news kiosks.

Police Dial ✆ **133** anywhere in Austria to summon the police.

Radio & Television The Austrian Radio Network (ÖRF) broadcasts English-language news daily at 8:05am. "Blue Danube Radio" broadcasts in English daily from 7 to 9am, noon to 2pm, and 6 to 7:30pm in the Vienna area. The Voice of America broadcasts news, music, and feature programs at 1197 AM (middle wave, here) from 7am to 1pm, as well as midafternoon and early evening. Many deluxe and first-class hotels subscribe to CNN, BBC, and some British channels. Many second-class hotels also provide TVs in the room, but you're likely to hear only German-language telecasts. However, many English and American films and programs are shown in their original language with German subtitles.

Restrooms All airport and railway stations have restrooms, rarely with attendants. Bars, nightclubs, restaurants, cafes, and hotels have facilities as well. You'll also find public toilets near many major sights.

Safety No particular caution is needed other than what a discreet person would maintain anywhere. Compared with the rest of the world, Austria is a very safe country in which to travel.

Smoking Many Austrians are heavy smokers, and unlike in the United States, smoking is not prohibited in many restaurants. If you're sensitive to smoke, ask the headwaiter to sit you in a nonsmoking section, if possible. If not, ask to be seated away from the smoke or outside on a terrace.

Taxes Depending on the object or service, a Value-Added Tax (*Mehrwertsteuer Rückvergütung,* or VAT) of between 7% and 34% is included in the price of items sold. Items such as food in grocery stores is taxed at 7%; luxury items such as jewelry are taxed at 34%, and many items, such as clothing and souvenirs, are taxed at 20%. Austrian residents have no recourse but to pay this tax; short-term visitors from other countries, however, can arrange for a refund of the VAT if they can prove that they carried it out of Austria unused and in nearly new condition, and that the purchase was part of a sale totaling more than 75.01€ per store. To get the refund, you must fill out Form U-34, which is available at most stores (a sign will read TAX-FREE SHOPPING). Get one for ÖAMTC quick refund if you plan to get your money at the border. Check whether the store gives refunds itself or uses a service. Sales personnel will help you fill out the form and will affix the store-identification stamp. You show the VAT (*MWSt*) as a separate item or state that the tax is part of the total price. Keep your U-34 forms handy when you leave the country, and have them validated by the Viennese Customs officer at your point of departure.

Know in advance that you'll have to show the articles for which you're claiming a VAT refund. Because of this, it's wise to keep your purchases in a suitcase or carry-on bag that's separate from the rest of your luggage, with all the original tags and tickets, and the original receipts nearby.

Don't check the item within your luggage before you process the paper-work with the Customs agent. In some instances, if your paperwork is in order, you'll receive a tax refund on the spot. If your point of departure is not equipped to issue cash on the spot, you'll have to mail the validated U-34 form or forms back to the store where you bought the merchandise after you return home. It's wise to keep a copy of each form. Within a few weeks, the store will send you a check, bank draft, or international money order covering the amount of your VAT refund. Help is available from the Austrian Automobile and Touring Club (ÖAMTC), which has instituted methods of speeding up the refund process. Before you go, call the Austrian National Tourist Office for the ÖAMTC brochure "Tax-Free Shopping in Austria."

Telephone Remember, never dial abroad from your hotel room unless it's an emergency. Place phone calls at the post office or some other location. Viennese hotels routinely add 40% surcharges, and some add as much as 200% to your call! For help dialing, contact your hotel's operator; or dial 𝄽 **09** for placement of long-distance calls within Austria or for information about using a telephone company credit card; dial 𝄽 **1611** for **local** direc-tory assistance, 𝄽 **1613** for European directory assistance, and 𝄽 **1614** for overseas directory assistance; and dial 𝄽 **08** for help in dialing international long distance. Coin-operated phones are all over Vienna. Despite the increasing automation of many aspects of Viennese life, most of the public phones in Vienna are still operated by coins instead of by credit card. Using one of them requires picking up the receiver, inserting a minimum of .10€, waiting for the dial tone, and dialing the number. Know in advance that .10€ will allow no more than about 2 minutes of talk time even to a num-ber you're calling within Vienna. When your talk time is finished, a recorded telephone announcement instructs you in German to put in more coins. To avoid this unwelcome interruption to their calls, most Viennese insert up to .40€ at the beginning of their call. In theory, at least, the phone will return whatever unused coins remain at the end of your call, although many Viennese admit that getting money back for the unused portion of your call is "iffy." On some older phones, you'll need to push a clearly designated button before the coins drop into the phone and the call is connected.

Avoid carrying lots of coins by buying a **Wertkarte** at tobacco/news kiosks or at post offices. Each card is electronically coded to provide 3€, 7€, 14€, or 35€ worth of phone calls. Buyers receive a slight discount because cards are priced slightly lower than their face value.

AT&T's USA Direct plan enables you to charge calls to your credit card or to call collect. The access number, 𝄽 **0800/200-288,** is a local call all over Austria. For **Sprint,** dial 𝄽 **0800/200-236;** for **Worldcom,** dial 𝄽 **0800/200-235;** for **British Telecom,** dial 𝄽 **0800/200-209;** and for **Canada Direct,** dial 𝄽 **0800/200-217.**

The international access code for both the United States and Canada is **001,** followed by the area code and the seven-digit local number.

Time Austria operates on central European time, which makes it 6 hours later than U.S. Eastern Standard Time. It advances its clocks 1 hour in sum-mer, however.

Tipping A service charge of 10% to 15% is included on hotel and restaurant bills, but it's a good policy to leave something extra for waiters and 2€ per day for your hotel maid.

Railroad station, airport, and hotel porters get 1.50€ per piece of luggage, plus a .75€ tip. Your hairdresser should be tipped 10% of the bill, and the shampoo person will be thankful for a 1.50€ gratuity. Toilet attendants are usually given .50€, and hat-check attendants expect .50 to 1.50€, depending on the place.

Water Tap water is generally safe to drink in Austria. However, don't drink from fresh alpine springs. Regardless of how clean they look, they could be contaminated.

3

Settling into Vienna

City of music, cafes, waltzes, parks, and pastries—that's Vienna. The capital of Austria has been a showplace city since the tumultuous reign of the Hapsburg dynasty, and unlike many other European capitals, it has managed to survive two world wars with most of its beautiful landmarks unscathed.

Vienna is a truly cosmopolitan city. For centuries, different tribes, races, and nationalities have fused their cultural identities into the intriguing and often cynical Viennese of today. From the time the Romans chose a Celtic settlement on the Danube for one of their most important central European forts, Vienna has played a vital role in European history. Austria grew up around this city and, in doing so, developed into one of Europe's mightiest empires. The face of the city has been altered time and again by war, siege, victory, defeat, death of an empire, birth of a republic, bombing, occupation, and the passage of time. But fortunately, the Viennese character, which includes a strict devotion to the good life, has remained intact.

1 Orientation

ARRIVING

BY PLANE **Vienna International Airport (VIE)** (© **01/70070;** english. viennaairport.com) is about 19km (12 miles) southeast of the city center. Austrian Airlines and United Airlines offer nonstop service from New York (JFK), Chicago, and Washington, D.C., Austrian Airlines and British Airways fly nonstop from London (Heathrow). Other transatlantic airlines connect to Vienna via major European hubs.

The official **Vienna Tourist Information Office** in the arrival hall of the airport is open daily October through May from 9am to 10pm and June through September from 8:30am to 9pm.

There's regular bus service between the airport and the **City Air Terminal,** adjacent to the Vienna Hilton and directly across from the **Wien Mitte/Landstrasse** rail station, where you can easily connect with subway and tram lines. Buses run every 20 minutes from 6:30am to 11:30pm, and hourly from midnight to 5am. The trip takes about 25 minutes and costs 5€ per person. Tickets are sold on the bus and must be purchased with Austrian money. There's also bus service between the airport and two railroad stations, the Westbahnhof and the Südbahnhof, leaving every 30 minutes to an hour. Fares are also 5€.

There's also local train service, Schnellbahn (S-Bahn), between the airport and the Wien Nord and Wien Mitte rail stations. Trains run hourly from 4:30am to 9:30pm and leave from the basement of the airport. Trip time is 40 to 45 minutes, and the fare is 3€.

BY TRAIN   Vienna has four principal rail stations, with frequent connections from all Austrian cities and towns and from all major European cities. For train information for all stations, call ✆ **05/1717.**

Westbahnhof (West Railway Station), on Europaplatz, is for trains arriving from western Austria, France, Germany, Switzerland, and some eastern European countries. It has frequent links to major Austrian cities such as Salzburg, which is a 3-hour train ride from Vienna. The Westbahnhof connects with local trains, the U3 and U6 underground lines, and several tram and bus routes.

Südbahnhof (South Railway Station), on Südtirolerplatz, has train service to southern and eastern Austria, Italy, Hungary, Slovenia, and Croatia. It is linked with local rail service and tram and bus routes.

Both of these stations house useful travel agencies (**Österreichisches Verkehrsbüro**) that provide tourist information and help with hotel reservations. In the Westbahnhof, it's in the upper hall; at the Südbahnhof, it's in the lower hall.

Other stations in Vienna include **Franz-Josef Bahnhof,** on Franz-Josef-Platz, used mainly by local trains, although connections are made here to Prague and Berlin. You can take the D-tram line to the city's Ringstrasse from here. **Wien Mitte,** at Landstrasser Hauptstrasse 1, is also a terminus for local trains, plus a depot for trains to the Czech Republic and to Vienna International Airport.

BY BUS   The **City Bus Terminal** is at the Wien Mitte rail station, Landstrasser Hauptstrasse 1. This is the arrival depot for Post and Bundesbuses from points all over the country, as well as the arrival point for private buses from various European cities. The terminal has lockers, currency-exchange kiosks, and a ticket counter open daily from 6:15am to 6pm. For bus information, call ✆ **05/1717** daily from 6:15am to 6pm.

BY CAR   Vienna can be reached from all directions via major highways (*Autobahnen*) or by secondary highways. The main artery from the west is Autobahn A1, coming in from Munich (468km/291 miles), Salzburg (336km/209 miles), and Linz (186km/116 miles). Autobahn A2 arrives from the south, from Graz (200km/124 miles) and Klagenfurt (308km/192 miles). Autobahn A4 comes in from the east, connecting with Route E58, which runs to Bratislava and Prague. Autobahn A22 takes traffic from the northwest, and Route E10 connects to the cities and towns of southeastern Austria and of Hungary.

VISITOR INFORMATION

Once you've arrived safely in Vienna, head for either of two information points that make it their business to have up-to-the-minute data about what to see and do in Vienna. The more centrally located of the two is the **Wien Tourist-Information** office at Albertinaplatz (✆ **01/211-140;** tram: 1 or 2). Located directly behind the Vienna State Opera, on the corner of Philharmoniker Strasse, in the heart of the Innere Stadt (Inner City), it's open daily from 9am to 7pm. The staff will make free hotel reservations for anyone in need of lodgings. Larger and more administrative, but also willing to handle questions from the public, is the headquarters of the **Vienna Tourist Board,** at Obere Augartenstrasse (✆ **01/2111-4412;** tram: 31). Both branches stock free copies of a tourist magazine, *Wien Monatsprogramm,* which lists what's going on in Vienna's concert halls, theaters, and opera houses. Also worthwhile here is *Vienna A to Z,* a general, pocket-size guide with descriptions and locations for a slew of attractions. This booklet is also free, but don't rely on its cluttered map.

For information on Vienna and Austria, including day trips from the city, visit the **Austrian National Tourist Office** (© **01/58866**) at Margaretenstrasse 1, A-1040. Lower Austria (Niederösterreich), the region surrounding the city, contains dozens of attractions worth a visit (see chapter 5). For a rundown on the Wachau (Danube Valley) and the Weinerwald (Vienna Woods), you might want to contact **Niederösterreich Information,** Fishhoffe 3 (© **01/53-610-0**).

CITY LAYOUT

From its origins as a Roman village on the Danubian plain, Vienna has evolved over the years into one of the largest metropolises of central Europe, with a surface area covering 414 sq. km (160 sq. miles). That area has been divided into 23 districts (*Bezirke*), which are rather cumbersomely identified with a Roman numeral. Each district carries its own character or reputation; for example, the 9th District is known as Vienna's academic quarter, whereas the 10th, 11th, and 12th districts are home to blue-collar workers and are the most densely populated.

The 1st District, known as the **Innere Stadt (Inner City),** is where most foreign visitors first flock. This compact area is Vienna at its most historic and boasts the city's astounding array of monuments, churches, palaces, and museums, in addition to its finest hotels and restaurants. Its size and shape roughly correspond to the original borders (then walls) of the medieval city; however, other than **St. Stephan's Cathedral,** very few buildings from that era remain.

The Inner City is surrounded by **Ringstrasse,** a circular boulevard about 4km (2½ miles) long. Constructed between 1859 and 1888, it's one of the most ambitious examples of urban planning and restoration in central European history. Built over the foundations of Vienna's medieval fortifications, the Ring opened new urban vistas for the dozens of monumental 19th-century buildings that line its edges today. The name of this boulevard changes as it moves around the Inner City, which can get confusing. Names that correspond with the boulevard end in *Ring*: Schottenring, Dr.-Karl-Lueger-Ring, Burgring, Opernring, Kärntner Ring, Stubenring, Parkring, and Schubertring.

Ironically, the river for which Vienna is so famous, the **Danube,** doesn't really pass through the center of the city at all. Between 1868 and 1877, the river was channeled into its present muddy banks east of town and was replaced with a small-scale substitute, the **Donaukanal (Danube Canal),** which was dug for shipping food and other supplies to the Viennese. The canal is set against Ringstrasse's eastern edge and is traversed by five bridges in the 1st District alone.

Surrounding Ringstrasse and the Inner City, in a more or less clockwise direction, are the inner suburban districts (2–9), which contain many hotels and restaurants popular for their proximity to the city center. The villas and palaces of Vienna's 18th-century aristocrats can be found here, as well as modern apartment complexes and the homes of 19th-century middle-class entrepreneurs. These districts are profiled later in this chapter under "Neighborhoods in Brief."

The outer districts (10–23) form another concentric ring of suburbs, comprising a variety of neighborhoods from industrial parks to rural villages. **Schönbrunn,** the Hapsburg's vast summer palace, is located in these outlying areas in the 13th District, **Hietzing.** Also noteworthy is the 19th District, **Döbling,** with its famous *Heurigen* villages, like Grinzing and Sievering (see "The Heurigen," p. 165), and the 22nd District, **Donau-stadt,** home to the verdant Donau Park and the adjoining UNO-City, an impressive modern complex of United Nations agencies.

FINDING AN ADDRESS   Street addresses are followed by a four-digit postal code, or sometimes a Roman numeral, that identifies the district in which the address is located. Often the code is preceded by the letter *A.* The district number is coded in the two middle digits, so if an address is in the 1st District ("01"), the postal code would read A-1010; in the 7th District, A-1070; and in the 13th District, A-1130.

A rule of thumb used by hotel concierges and taxi drivers involves the following broad-based guidelines: Odd street numbers are on one side of the street, and even numbers are on the other. The lowest numbers are usually closest to the city's geographic and spiritual center, St. Stephansplatz, and get higher as the street extends outward. Naturally, this system won't work on streets running parallel to the cathedral, so you'll have to simply test your luck.

What about the broad expanses of Vienna's Ring? Traffic always moves clockwise on the Ring, and any backtracking against the direction of the traffic must be done via side streets that radiate from the general traffic flow. Numeration on the Ring always goes from high numbers to lower numbers, as determined by the direction of the prevailing traffic: Odd street numbers appear on a driver's left, and even numbers appear on the right.

STREET MAPS   You'll need a very good and detailed map to explore Vienna, as it has some 2,400km (1,500 miles) of streets (many of them narrow). Since so many places, including restaurants and hotels, lie in these alleyways, routine overview maps that are given away at hotels or the tourist office won't do. You'll need the best city map in Vienna, which is published by **Falk** and sold at all major newsstands, at bookstores, and in many upscale hotels.

NEIGHBORHOODS IN BRIEF

Many of Vienna's hotels and restaurants are conveniently located within or just outside the 1st District. In this section, we profile the Inner City, or Innere Stadt, and the adjacent districts.

INNERE STADT (1ST DIS-TRICT) This compact area, bounded on all sides by the legendary Ring, is at the center of Viennese life. The Inner City has dozens of streets devoted exclusively to pedestrian traffic, including **Kärntnerstrasse,** which bypasses the Wiener Staatsoper (Vienna State Opera), and the nearby **Graben,** which backs up to Stephansplatz, home to the famous cathedral. Competing with both the cathedral and the Staatsoper as the district's most famous building is the **Hofburg,** the famous Hapsburg palace that includes the National Library, the Spanish Riding School, and six museums. Other significant landmarks include the Rathaus (City Hall), Parlament (Parliament), the Universität (University of Vienna), the Naturhistorisches (Natural History) and Kunsthistorisches (Art History) museums, and Stadtpark.

LEOPOLDSTADT (2ND DIS-TRICT) Once inhabited by Balkan traders, this area doesn't physically border the Ringstasse, but it lies on the eastern side of the Danube Canal, just a short subway ride (U1) from the Inner City. Here you'll find the massive **Prater** park, which boasts an amusement park, miles of tree-lined walking paths and numerous sports facilities, including a large stadium. Vienna's renowned trade-fair exhibition site is also in this district.

LANDSTRASSE (3RD DIS-TRICT) The bucolic **Stadtpark** spreads into this district, where you'll also discover more of Vienna's imperial charm. Streets are dotted

Impressions

The streets of Vienna are surfaced with culture as the streets of other cities are with asphalt.

—Karl Kraus (1874–1936)

with churches, monuments, and palaces, such as the grand **Schwarzenburg Palace** and the looming **Konzerthaus (concert house).** However, the top attraction remains Prince Eugene Savoy's exquisite baroque **Belvedere Palace.** Several embassies make their home in a small section of Landstrasse known as Vienna's diplomatic quarter. The **Wien Mitte rail station** and the **City Air Terminal** are also located here.

WIEDEN (4TH DISTRICT)

This small neighborhood extends south from Opernring and Kärtnerring, and it's just as fashionable as the 1st District. Most activity centers on **Karlsplatz,** a historical city square that features its domed namesake, Karlskirche. Also seated around this hub are Vienna's Technical University and the **Historical Museum of the City of Vienna.** Kärntnerstrasse, the main boulevard of the city center, turns into **Wiedner-Hauptstrasse** as it enters this district, and the **Südbahnof,** one of the two main train stations, lies at its southern tip.

MARGARETEN (5TH DISTRICT)

Southwest of the 4th District (Wieden), this area does not border the Ring and thus lies a bit farther from the Inner City. The historic homes of composers Franz Schubert and Christoph Gluck still stand here among modern apartment complexes and industrial centers.

MARIAHILF (6TH DISTRICT)

One of Vienna's busiest shopping streets, **Mariahilferstrasse,** runs

through this bustling neighborhood. The sprawling and lively **Naschmarkt (Produce Market),** selling fresh fruits, vegetables, breads, cheeses, and more, is an ideal scene for people-watching. On Saturday, the adjacent **Flea Market** adds to the lively but sometimes seedy atmosphere as vendors sell antiques and other junk. The surrounding streets are packed with *Beisls* (small eateries), theaters, cafes, and pubs. As you wander farther from the city center, however, you'll find that the landscape becomes more residential.

NEUBAU (7TH DISTRICT)

Bordering the expansive Museum Quarter of the Inner City, this is an ideal place to stay, as its easily accessible by public transportation. The picturesque and once neglected **Spittleburg quarter** lies atop a hill just beyond Vienna's most famous museums. It's a vibrant, cultural community that's popular with both young and old visitors. The old Spittleburg houses have been renovated into boutiques, restaurants, theaters, and art galleries—a perfect backdrop for an afternoon stroll.

JOSEFSTADT (8TH DISTRICT)

This, the smallest of Vienna's 23 districts, is named after Hapsburg Emperor Joseph II and was once home to Vienna's civil servants. Like Neubau, this quiet, friendly neighborhood sits behind the city hall and the adjacent grand museums of the Ringstrasse. You'll find everything from shady and secluded parks to charming cafes, to elaborate

Vienna Neighborhoods

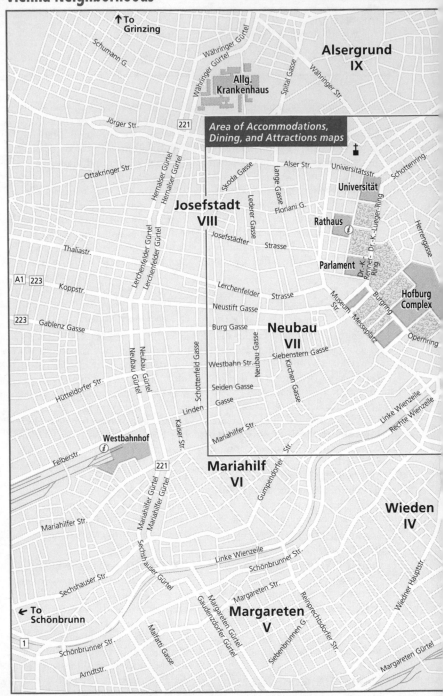

↑ To Grinzing

Schumann G.

Währinger Gürtel

Währinger Str.

Spital Gasse

**Alsergrund
IX**

**Allg.
Krankenhaus**

Jörger Str.

221

Ottakringer Str.

Hernalser Gürtel

**Area of Accommodations,
Dining, and Attractions maps**

Skoda Gasse

Lange Gasse

Alser Str.

Universitätsstr.

Schottenring

Universität

Lederer Gasse

Floriani G.

**Josefstadt
VIII**

Josefstädter Strasse

Rathaus ⓘ

Dr.-K.-Lueger-Ring

Herrengasse

Thaliastr.

Lerchenfelder Gürtel

Parlament

Dr.-K.-Renner-Ring

**Hofburg
Complex**

A1 223

Koppstr.

Lerchenfelder Strasse

Museum Str.

Burgring

223

Gablenz Gasse

Neustift Gasse

Burg Gasse

**Neubau
VII**

Messeplatz

Opernring

Neubau Gürtel

Schottenfeld Gasse

Westbahn Str.

Neubau Gasse

Siebenstern Gasse

Kirchen Gasse

Hütteldorfer Str.

Seiden Gasse

Linden Gasse

Linke Wienzeile

Rechte Wienzeile

Kaiser Str.

Westbahnhof ⓘ

Mariahilfer Str.

Felberstr.

221

**Mariahilf
VI**

Gumpendorfer Str.

**Wieden
IV**

Mariahilfer Gürtel

Mariahilfer Str.

Sechshauser Gürtel

Linke Wienzeile

Schönbrunner Str.

Wiedner Hauptstr.

Sechshauser Str.

Schönbrunner Str.

Margareten Str.

Margareten Gürtel

Gaudenzdorfer Gürtel

Reinprechtsdorfer Str.

**Margareten
V**

Siebenbrunnen Str.

← To
Schönbrunn

1

Malfatti Gasse

Arndtstr.

Margareten Gürtel

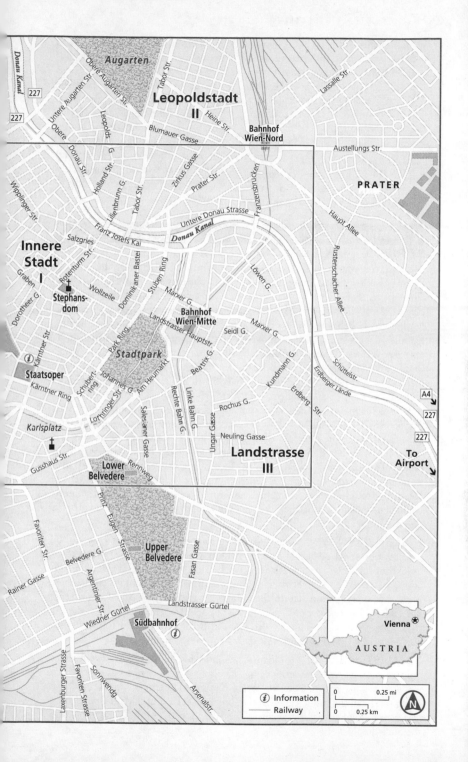

Donau Kanal

227
227

Augarten

Obere Augarten Str.

Untere Augarten Str.

Obere

Tabor Str.

Leopoldstadt
II

Heine Str.

Leopolds G.

Blumauer Gasse

Bahnhof
Wien-Nord

Wipplinger Str.

Obere Donau Str.

Holland Str.

Lilienbrunn G.

Tabor Str.

Zirkus Gasse

Prater Str.

Franzensbrucken

Austellungs Str.

PRATER

Lassalle Str.

Franz Josefs Kai

Untere Donau Strasse

Donau Kanal

Salzgries

Rotenturm Str.

Dominikaner Bastei

Stuben Ring

Löwen G.

Haupt Allee

Rustenschacher Allee

Innere
Stadt
I

Graben

Dorotheer G.

Stephans-
dom

Wollzeile

Marxer G.

Bahnhof
Wien-Mitte

Landstrasser Hauptstr.

Seidl G.

Marxer G.

Park Ring

Stadtpark

Kärntner Str.

Staatsoper

Kärntner Ring

Schubert-
ring

Lothringer Str.

Johannes G.

Am Heumarkt

Beatrix G.

Rechte Bahn G.

Linke Bahn G.

Kundmann G.

Erdberg Str.

Schüttelstr.

Erdberger Lände

A4
227

227

To
Airport

Karlsplatz

Gusshaus Str.

Salesianer Gasse

Rochus G.

Ungar Gasse

Neuling Gasse

Landstrasse
III

Lower
Belvedere

Rennweg

Prinz Eugen Strasse

Favoriten Str.

Belvedere G.

Argentinier Str.

Rainer Gasse

Upper
Belvedere

Fasan Gasse

Landstrasser Gürtel

Wiedner Gürtel

Südbahnhof

Laxenburger Strasse

Favoriten Strasse

Sonnwendg.

Arsenalstr.

Vienna

AUSTRIA

ⓘ Information
— Railway

0   0.25 mi
0   0.25 km

N

monuments and churches. Vienna's oldest and most intimate theater, **Josefstadt Theater** (Josefstadtterstrasse 26), was built in 1788. The clientele among Josefstadt's shops and restaurants is varied, featuring lawmakers from City Hall as well as students from the university.

ALSERGRUND (9TH DISTRICT) This area is often referred to as the academic quarter, not just because of its position near the University of Vienna, but also because of its many hospitals and clinics. This is Freud territory, and you can visit his home, now the Freud Museum, on Berggasse. Here you'll also stumble upon the Liechtenstein Palace, which today houses the federal Museum of Modern Art. At the northern end of Alsergrund is the **Franz-Josef Bahnhof,** an excellent depot for excursions to Lower Austria.

2 Getting Around

BY PUBLIC TRANSPORTATION

Whether you want to visit the Inner City's historic buildings or the outlying Vienna Woods, Vienna Transport (Wiener Verkehrsbetriebe) can take you there. This vast transit network—U-Bahn (subway), streetcar, or bus—is safe, clean, and easy to use. If you plan on taking full advantage of it, pay the 1€ for a map that outlines the U-Bahn, buses, streetcars, and local trains (Schnellbahn, or S-Bahn). It's sold at the **Vienna Public Transport Information Center (Informationdienst der Wiener Verkehrsbetriebe),** which has five locations: Opernpassage (an underground passageway adjacent to the Wiener Staatsoper), Karlsplatz, Stephansplatz (near Vienna's cathedral), Westbahnhof, and Praterstern. For information about any of these outlets, call ℂ **01/790-9105.**

Vienna maintains a uniform fare that applies to all forms of public transport. A ticket for the bus, subway, or tram costs 1.50€ if you buy it in advance at a Tabac-Trafiks (a store or kiosk selling tobacco products and newspapers) or 2€ if you buy it on board. Smart Viennese buy their tickets in advance, usually in blocks of at least five at a time, from any of the city's thousands of Tabac-Trafiks or at any of the public transport centers noted above. No matter what vehicle you decide to ride within Vienna, remember that once a ticket has been stamped (validated) by either a machine or a railway attendant, it's valid for one trip in one direction, anywhere in the city, including transfers.

U-BAHN (SUBWAY)   Most of the top attractions in the Inner City can be seen by foot, tram, or bus, but the U-Bahn is your best bet to get across town quickly or reach the suburbs. It consists of five lines labeled as U1, U2, U3, U4, and U6 (there is no U5). Karlsplatz, in the heart of the Inner City, is the most important underground station for visitors, as the U1, U2, and U4 converge here. The U2 traces part of the Ring, the U4 goes to Schönbrunn, and the U1 stops in Stephansplatz. The U3 also stops in Stephansplatz and connects with the Westbanhof. The U-Bahn runs daily 6am to midnight.

TRAM (STREET CAR)   Riding the red-and-white trams (*Strassenbahn*) is not only a practical way to get around, but it's also a great way to see the city. Tram stops are well marked and lines are labeled as numbers or letters. Lines 1 and 2 will bring you to all the major sights on the Ringstrasse. Line D skirts the outer Ring and goes to the Südbahnhof, whereas line 18 goes between the Westbahnhof and the Südbahnhof.

Vienna U-Bahn

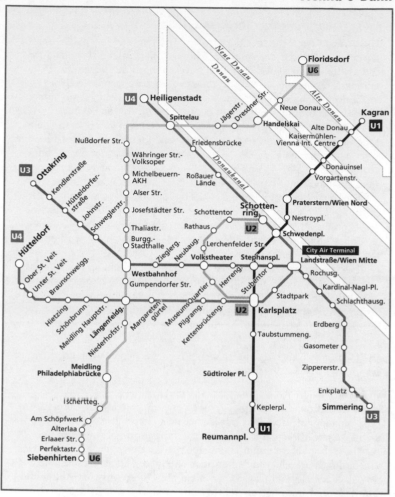

BUS Buses traverse Vienna in all directions and operate Monday through Saturday from 6am to 10pm and Sunday from 6am to 8pm. Buses 1A, 2A, and 3A will get you around the Inner City. Convenient night buses are available on weekends and holidays starting at 12:15am. They go from Schwedensplatz to the outer suburbs (including Grinzing). Normal tickets are not valid on these late "N" buses. Instead, you pay a special fare of 1.50€ on board.

BY TAXI

Taxis are easy to find within the city center, but be warned that fares can quickly add up. Taxi stands are marked by signs, or you can call ☎ **01/31300,** 60160, 81400, 91011, or 40100. The basic fare is 4€, plus 1.09€ per kilometer. There are extra charges of 1€ for luggage in the trunk. For night rides after 11pm, and for trips on Sunday and holidays, there is a surcharge of 1€. There is an additional charge of 2€ if ordered by phone. The fare for trips outside the Vienna

Tips Transportation for Less

The **Vienna Card** is the best ticket to use when traveling by public transportation within the city limits. It's extremely flexible and functional for tourists because it allows unlimited travel, plus various discounts at city museums, restaurants, and shops. You can purchase a Vienna Card for 17€ at tourist information offices, public transport centers, and some hotels, or order one over the phone with a credit card (© **01/7984-40028**).

You can also buy tickets that will save you money if you plan to ride a lot on the city's transport system. A ticket valid for unlimited rides during any 24-hour period costs 5€; an equivalent ticket valid for any 72-hour period goes for 12€. There's also a green ticket, priced at 24€, that contains eight individual partitions. Each of these, when stamped, is good for 1 day of unlimited travel. An individual can opt to reserve all eight of the partitions for his or her own use, thereby gaining 8 days of cost-effective travel on the city's transport system. Or, the partitions can be subdivided among a group of several riders, allowing—for example—two persons 4 days each of unlimited rides.

These tickets are also available at Tabak-Trafiks, vending machines in underground stations, the airport's arrival hall (next to baggage claim), the DDSG landing pier (Reichsbrücke), and the travel agencies (Österreichisches Verkehrsbüro) of the two main train stations.

---

area (for instance, to the airport) should be agreed upon with the driver in advance, and a 10% tip is the norm.

BY CAR

See "Getting Around," in chapter 2, for general tips on renting a car in Austria. Use a car only for excursions outside Vienna's city limits; don't try to drive around the city. Parking is a problem; the city is a maze of congested one-way streets, and the public transportation is too good to endure the hassle of driving.

If you do venture out by car, information on road conditions is available in English 7 days a week from 6am to 8pm from the **Österreichischer Automobil-, Motorrad- und Touringclub (ÖAMTC),** Schubertring 1–3, A-1010 Vienna (© **01/711-997**). This auto club also maintains a 24-hour emergency road service number (© **120,** 123, or 0660/7500).

RENTALS   It's always best to reserve rental cars in advance (see chapter 2), but you can rent a car once you've arrived in Vienna. You'll need a passport and a driver's license that's at least 1 year old. Avoid renting a car at the airport, where there is an extra 6% tax, in addition to the 21% value-added tax on all rentals.

Major car-rental companies include **Avis,** Opernring 1 (© **01/700-732-700**); **Budget Rent-a-Car,** Hilton Air Terminal (© **01/714-6565**); and **Hertz,** in the Marriott Hotel, Parkring 12A (© **01/512-8677**).

PARKING   Curbside parking in Vienna's 1st District, site of most of the city's major monuments, is extremely limited—almost to the point of being nonexistent. Coin-operated parking meters as they exist within North America are not common. When curbside parking is available at all, it's within one of the city's "blue zones" and is usually restricted to 90 minutes or less from 8am to 6pm. If you find an available spot within a blue zone, you'll need to display a *Kurzpark*

Scheine (short-term parking voucher) on the dashboard of your car. Valid for time blocks of only 30, 60, or 90 minutes, they're sold at branch offices of Vienna Public Transport Information Center (see above) and, more conveniently, within tobacco/news shops. You'll have to write in the date and the time of your arrival, before displaying the voucher on the right side of your car's dashboard. Be warned that towing of illegally parked cars is not an uncommon sight here. Frankly, it's much easier to simply pay the price that's charged by any of the city's dozens of underground parking garages and avoid the stress of looking for one of the virtually impossible-to-find curbside parking spots.

Parking garages are scattered throughout the city, and most of them charge between 3.50€ and 6€ per hour. Every hotel in Vienna is acutely aware of the location of the nearest parking garage—if you're confused, ask. Some convenient 24-hour garages within the first district include **Parkgarage Am Hof** (© 01/ 533-5571); **Parkgarage Freyung,** Freyung (© 01/535-0450); and **Tiefgarage Kärntnerstrasse,** Mahlerstrasse 8 (© 01/512-5206).

DRIVING & TRAFFIC REGULATIONS   In general, Austria's traffic regulations do not differ much from those of other countries where you *drive on the right.* In Vienna, the speed limit is 50kmph (about 30 mph). Out of town, in areas like the Wienerwald, the limit is 130kmph (80 mph) on motorways and 100kmph (62 mph) on all other roads. Honking car horns is forbidden everywhere in the city.

BY HORSE-DRAWN CARRIAGE

A horse-drawn carriage (called a *Fiaker* in German) has been used as a form of transportation in the Inner City for some 3 centuries. You can clip-clop along in one for about 30 minutes at a cost of about 45€. Prices and the length of the ride must be negotiated in advance. In the 1st District, you'll find a *Fiaker* for hire at the following sites: on the north side of St. Stephan's, on Heldenplatz near the Hofburg, and in front of the Albertina on Augustinerstrasse.

BY BIKE

Vienna has more than 250km (155 miles) of marked bicycle paths within the city limits. In the summer, many Viennese leave their cars in the garage and ride bikes. You can take bicycles on specially marked U-Bahn cars for free, but only Monday through Friday from 9am to 3pm and 6:30pm to midnight. On weekends in July and August, bicycles are carried free from 9am to midnight.

Rental stores abound at the Prater (see chapter 4) and along the banks of the Danube Canal, which is the favorite bike route for most Viennese. One of the best of the many sites specializing in bike rentals is **Pedalpower,** Ausstellungsstrasse 3 (© 01/729-7234), which is open May through October from 9am to 8pm. The Vienna Tourist Board can also supply a list of rental shops and more information about bike paths. Bike rentals begin at about 27€ per day.

 FAST FACTS: Vienna

American Express The office at Kärntnerstrasse 21–23 (© 01/51540-770), near Stock-im-Eisenplatz, is open Monday through Friday from 9am to 5:30pm and Saturday from 9am to noon.

Babysitters Most hotels will provide you with names of babysitters if they do not provide their own service. Sitters charge roughly 8€ to 11€ per hour, and you'll need to provide transportation home, via a cab, if they sit beyond 11pm.

Business Hours Most shops are open Monday through Friday from 9am to 6pm and Saturday from 9am to noon, 12:30pm, or 1pm, depending on the store. On the first Saturday of every month, shops customarily remain open until 4:30 or 5pm. The tradition is called *langer Samstag.*

City Code The telephone city code for Vienna is **01**. It is used only when you're calling from outside Vienna.

Dentists For dental problems, call ℭ **01/512-2078.**

Doctors A list of physicians can be found in the telephone directory under "Arzte." If you have a medical emergency at night, call ℭ **141** daily from 7pm to 7am.

Drug Laws Penalties are severe and could lead to either imprisonment or deportation. Selling drugs to minors is dealt with particularly harshly.

Drugstores Drugstores (chemist's shops) are open Monday through Friday from 8am to noon and 2 to 6pm, and Saturday from 8am to noon. At night and on Sunday, you'll find the names of the nearest open shops on a sign outside every drugstore.

Electricity Vienna operates on 220 volts AC (50 cycles). That means that U.S.-made appliances without a 200/110 switch will need a transformer (sometimes called a converter). Many Viennese hotels stock adapter plugs but not power transformers. Electric clocks, record players, and tape recorders, however, will not work well even with transformers.

Embassies & Consulates The main building of the **Embassy of the United States** is at Boltzmanngasse 16, A-1090 Vienna (ℭ **01/31339**). However, the consular section is at Gartenbaupromenade 2–4, A-1010 Vienna (ℭ **01/31339**). Lost passports, tourist emergencies, and other matters are handled by the consular section. Both the embassy and the consulate are open Monday through Friday from 8:30am to noon and 1 to 4pm.

   Canada's Embassy, Laurenzerberg 2 (ℭ **01/531-380**), is open Monday through Friday from 8:30am to 12:30pm and 1:30 to 3:30pm; the **United Kingdom**'s, Jauresgasse 12 (ℭ **01/71613-0**), is open Monday through Friday from 9am to 1pm and 2 to 4pm; **Australia**'s, Mattiellistrasse 2–4 (ℭ **01/50674**), is open Monday through Thursday from 8:30am to 1pm and 2 to 5:30pm, and Friday 8:30am to 1:15pm; and **New Zealand**'s, Springsiedelgasse 28 (ℭ **01/318-8505**), is open Monday through Friday from 8:30am to 5pm, but it's best to call to see if it's actually open. **Ireland's Embassy,** at Hilton Center, Landstrasser Hauptstrasse 2 (ℭ **01/715-4246**), is open Monday though Friday from 9 to 11:30am and 1:30 to 4pm.

Emergencies Call ℭ **122** to report a fire, **133** for the police, or **144** for an ambulance.

Hospitals The major hospital is **Allgemeines Krankenhaus,** Währinger Gürtel 18–20 (ℭ **01/40400**).

Internet Access **Café Stein,** Währingerstrasse 6 (ℭ **01/319-72-41**), offers Internet access at the rate of 3€ every half-hour and is open daily from 5 to 11pm.

Luggage Storage & Lockers All four main train stations in Vienna have lockers available on a 24-hour basis, costing 3€ for 24 hours. It's also possible to store luggage at these terminals daily from 4am to midnight (1:15am at the Westbahnhof) at a cost of 2.50€.

Money During off-hours, you can exchange money at *bureaux de change* (exchange bureaus) throughout the Inner City (there's one at the intersection of Kohlmarkt and the Graben), as well as at travel agencies, train stations, and at the airport. There's also a 24-hour exchange service at the post office (Hauptpostamt) at Fleischmarkt 19.

Newspapers & Magazines Most newsstands at major hotels or news kiosks along the streets sell copies of the *International Herald Tribune* and *USA Today,* and also carry copies of the European editions of *Time* and *Newsweek.*

Police The emergency number is ℭ **133.**

Post Offices Post offices in Vienna can be found in the heart of every district. Addresses for these can be found in the telephone directory under "Post." Post offices are generally open for mail services Monday through Friday from 8am to noon and 2 to 6pm. The central post office (Hauptpostamt), Barbaragasse 2 (ℭ **01/515090**), and most general post offices are open 24 hours a day, 7 days a week. Postage stamps are available at all post offices and at tobacco shops, and there are stamp-vending machines outside most post offices.

Safety In recent years, Vienna has been plagued by purse-snatchers. In the area around St. Stephan's Cathedral, signs (in German only) warn about pickpockets and purse-snatchers. Small foreign children often approach sympathetic adults and ask for money. As the adult goes for his wallet or her purse, full-grown thieves rush in and grab the money, fleeing with it. Unaccompanied women should hold on to their purses tightly and never open them in public.

Taxes Vienna imposes no special city taxes, other than the national value-added tax that's tacked on to all goods and services. The tax depends on the item but can range up to 32% on luxury goods and 20% on car rentals.

Telegrams, Telexes & Faxes The central telegraph office is at Börseplatz 1.

Transit Information Information, all types of tickets, and maps of the transportation system are available at Vienna Transport's main offices on Karlsplatz or at the Stephansplatz underground station Monday through Friday from 8am to 6pm and Saturday, Sunday, and holidays from 8:30am to 4pm. Alternatively, you can call ℭ **01/7909** 24 hours a day for information in German and English about public transport anywhere within Greater Vienna.

Useful Telephone Numbers Dial ℭ **05/1717** for rail information, ℭ **01/711-01** for bus schedules, and ℭ **01/211140** for tourist information Monday through Friday from 8am to 4pm. For hotel reservations, call the Vienna Tourist Board's room reservations system at ℭ **01/2111-4444** Monday through Saturday from 8am to 6pm.

3 Where to Stay

Vienna has some of the greatest hotels in Europe and more than 300 recommendable ones. But finding a room can be a problem, especially in August and September, if you arrive without a reservation. During these peak visiting months, you might have to stay on the outskirts, in the Grinzing or the Schön-brunn district, for example, and commute to the Inner City by streetcar, bus, or U-Bahn. If you're looking to cut costs, staying outside the Inner City is not a bad option, as you can pay a fifth to a quarter less for a hotel in the areas out-side the Ringstrasse.

High season in Vienna encompasses most of the year: from May to October or early November, and during some weeks in midwinter, when the city hosts major trade fairs, conventions, and other cultural events. If you're planning a trip around Christmas and New Year's Day, room reservations should be made *at least* 1 month in advance. Some rate reductions (usually 15%–20%) are avail-able during slower midwinter weeks—it always pays to ask.

Any branch of the **Austrian National Tourist Office** (② **01/58-86-60**), including the Vienna Tourist Board, will help you book a room. They have branch offices in the arrival halls of the airport, train stations, and major highways that access Vienna. They will not, however, reserve a room in advance for you.

If you prefer to deal directly with an Austrian travel agency, three of the city's largest are **Austropa,** Friedrichsgasse 7, A-1010 (② **01/588-000**); **Austrobus,** Dr. Karl Lueger-Ring 8, A-1010 (② **01/534-110**); and **Blaguss Reisen,** Wied-ner Hauptstrasse 15 A-1040 (② **01/50180**). Any of them can reserve hotel space, sell airline tickets, and procure hard-to-get tickets for music festivals. Many of their employees speak English fluently.

INNERE STADT (INNER CITY)
VERY EXPENSIVE

Grand Hotel Wien 🌟🌟🌟　Some of the most discerning hotel guests in Europe, often music lovers, prefer this seven-story deluxe hotel to the more traditional and famous Imperial or Bristol. Only a block from the Wiener Staatsoper, it's a honey. The luxurious service begins with a doorman ushering you past the columns at the entrance into the stunning lobby and reception area. You enter a world of beveled mirrors, crystal chandeliers, a "Grand Hotel" staircase, marble in various hues, and brass-adorned elevators. Off the lobby is a complex of elegant shops selling expen-sive perfumes and pricey clothing. The spacious accommodations are posh, with all the modern luxuries, such as heated floors, beverage makers, and phones in marble bathrooms (which contain shower-tub combinations and even antifogging mirrors). The more expensive units have more elaborate furnishings and decora-tion, including delicate stuccowork. The main dining room specializes in Austrian and international dishes, and there is also a Japanese restaurant that serves the town's best sushi brunch on Sunday.

Kärnter Ring 9, A-1010 Vienna. ② **01/515-800.** Fax 01/515-13-13. www.grandhotelwien.com. 205 units. 370€–450€ double; from 660€ suite. AE, DC, MC, V. U-Bahn: Karlsplatz. **Amenities:** 3 restaurants; 2 bars; fitness center; salon; boutiques; room service; massage; babysitting; laundry; dry cleaning. *In room:* A/C, TV, coffeemaker, minibar, hair dryer, safe.

Hilton International Vienna Plaza 🌟🌟　This is Vienna's "other Hilton," and it is a much newer version, having opened in 1989. It rises imposingly for 10 sto-ries, opening onto Ringstrasse just opposite the stock exchange. Its financial-district location draws many business clients from around the world, but it's also near many attractions, such as the Burgtheater, City Hall, and the Kunsthis-torisches and Naturhistorisches museums. Designed with flair for the modern traveler, the luxury hotel offers spacious guestrooms and suites. Room rates increase with altitude and view; two floors are smoke-free. Furnishings tend to be traditional, and many extras are included, such as electronic locks, three phones, and fluffy robes. Each unit has floor-to-ceiling windows and a large marble bathroom fitted with a shower-tub combination. The hotel also offers a penthouse floor with balconies. You shouldn't have trouble finding a place to eat or drink at this hotel, as it has three restaurants, a piano bar, a cocktail lounge, and a sidewalk terrace.

Am Schottenring 11, A-1010 Vienna. (© 800/445-8667 in the U.S., or 01/31390. Fax 01/31390-22009. www.hilton.com. 255 units. 336€–376€ double; from 420€ suite. AE, DC, MC, V. Parking 27€. U-Bahn: U2 to Schottentor. Tram: 1 or D. Bus: 40A. **Amenities:** 3 restaurants; 2 bars; health club; Jacuzzi; sauna; room service; massage; laundry; dry cleaning. *In room:* A/C, TV, minibar, hair dryer, safe.

Hotel Ambassador 🏵🏵   Until it became a hotel in 1866, the six-story Ambassador was a warehouse for wheat and flour, a far cry from its status today as one of the four or five most glamorous hotels in Vienna. It's no Bristol or Imperial, but it's quite posh nonetheless. The Ambassador couldn't be better located: It's between the Vienna State Opera and St. Stephan's Cathedral, on the square facing the Donner Fountain. Shop-lined Kärntnerstrasse is on the other side. Mark Twain stayed here, as have a host of diplomats and celebrities, including Theodore Roosevelt.

The hotel's trademark color, red, crops up all over: in the silk wall coverings, the bedspreads, the upholstery, and the long carpet that's often unrolled to the limousine of some famous personage. These sumptuous accommodations are an ideal choice for devotees of rococo fin-de-siècle or early-20th-century decor. Bedrooms are furnished with Biedermeier and Art Nouveau period pieces. The quieter rooms open onto Neuer Markt, although you'll miss the view of lively Kärntnerstrasse. Comfortable beds, marble bathrooms with shower-tub combinations and toiletries, and ample closet space add to the hotel's allure. Five rooms are nonsmoking. The restaurant, Léhar, serves high-quality Austrian and international cuisine.

Kärntnerstrasse 22, A-1010 Vienna. (© 01/961610. Fax 01/513-29-99. www.ambassador.at. 86 units. 235€–425€ double. AE, DC, MC, V. Parking 28€. U-Bahn: Stephansplatz. **Amenities:** Restaurant; bar; room service; laundry; dry cleaning. *In room:* A/C, TV, minibar, hair dryer, safe.

Hotel Bristol 🏵🏵🏵   From the outside, this six-story landmark looks no different from Vienna's other grand buildings. But connoisseurs of Austrian hotels maintain that this is a superb choice. Its decor evokes the height of the Hapsburg Empire—only the Hotel Imperial is grander. The hotel was constructed in 1894 next to the Vienna State Opera but has been updated to provide guests with black-tile bathrooms and other modern conveniences.

Many of the architectural embellishments rank as objets d'art in their own right, including the black carved marble fireplaces and the oil paintings in the salons. All rooms have thermostats, bedside controls, and ample storage, plus generous marble bathrooms with scales, robes, and shower-tub combinations. The Bristol Club Rooms in the tower offer comfortable chairs, an open fireplace, a self-service bar, library, stereo, deck, and sauna. Each bedroom includes a living-room area, and many have a small balcony providing a rooftop view of the Vienna State Opera and Ringstrasse. Corkscrew columns of rare marble grace the Korso, Bristol's restaurant, which is one of the best in Vienna.

Kärntner Ring 1, A-1015 Vienna. (© 888/625-5144 in the U.S., or 01/515-160. Fax 01/515-16-550. www. westin.com/bristol. 146 units. 208€–345€ double; from 590€ suite. AE, DC, MC, V. Parking 28€. U-Bahn: Karlsplatz. Tram: 1 or 2. **Amenities:** 2 restaurants; bar; fitness center; sauna; room service; babysitting; laundry; dry cleaning. *In room:* A/C, TV, minibar, hair dryer, safe.

Hotel de France 🏵   Hotel de France is right on the Ring and has long been a favorite. It is neighbor to the university and the Votivkirche, which makes it a

Vienna Accommodations

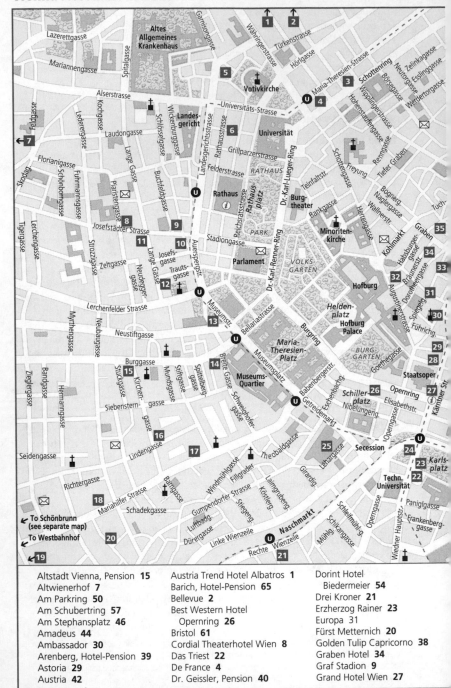

Altstadt Vienna, Pension **15**	Austria Trend Hotel Albatros **1**	Dorint Hotel
Altwienerhof **7**	Barich, Hotel-Pension **65**	Biedermeier **54**
Am Parkring **50**	Bellevue **2**	Drei Kroner **21**
Am Schubertring **57**	Best Western Hotel	Erzherzog Rainer **23**
Am Stephansplatz **46**	Opernring **26**	Europa **31**
Amadeus **44**	Bristol **61**	Fürst Metternich **20**
Ambassador **30**	Cordial Theaterhotel Wien **8**	Golden Tulip Capricorno **38**
Arenberg, Hotel-Pension **39**	Das Triest **22**	Graben Hotel **34**
Astoria **29**	De France **4**	Graf Stadion **9**
Austria **42**	Dr. Geissler, Pension **40**	Grand Hotel Wien **27**

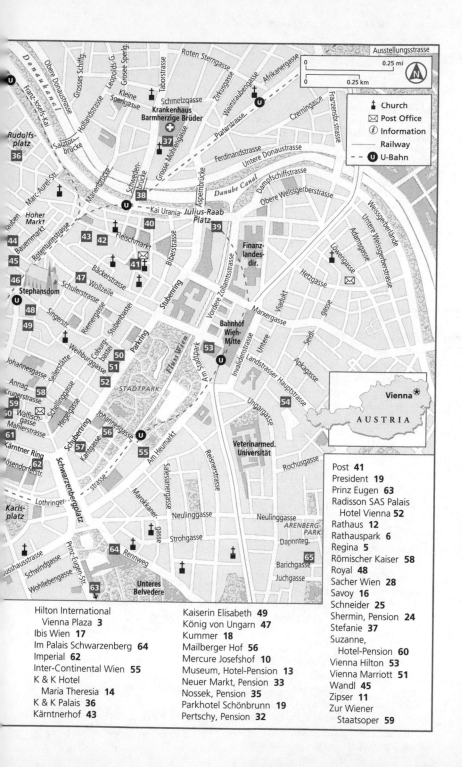

Map legend:

- ✠ Church
- ✉ Post Office
- ⓘ Information
- .... Railway
- Ⓤ U-Bahn

0 — 0.25 mi
0 — 0.25 km

Vienna ✦
AUSTRIA

centrally located choice. Its chiseled gray facade looks basically as it did when it was first erected in 1872. After World War II, the building was transformed into a hotel. Its modern elements and unobtrusively conservative decor are the result of extensive renovation. In such a subdued and appealing ambience, you often encounter businesspeople from all over the world. They appreciate the high-ceilinged public rooms and oriental carpets, the generously padded armchairs, and the full-dress portrait of Franz Joseph. The bedrooms are among the finest for their price range in Vienna. Housekeeping is of a high standard; furnishings are traditional, with firm beds and double-glazed windows that really keep noise pollution down. Roomy bathrooms have shower-tub combinations and toiletries. The best units are on the fifth floor, although windows there are too high for you to absorb the view unless you're very tall.

Schottenring 3, A-1010 Vienna. ⓒ 01/31368. Fax 01/3195969. www.austria-hotels.co.at/defrance. 212 units. 245€ double; 380€ suite. AE, DC, MC, V. Parking 17€. U-Bahn: U2, Schottentor. Tram: 1, 2, 37, or D. Bus: 1A. **Amenities:** 2 restaurants; 3 bars; sauna; room service; laundry; dry cleaning. *In room:* A/C, TV, minibar, hair dryer, safe.

Hotel Imperial 𝓪𝓪𝓪   This hotel is definitely the grandest in Vienna. Luminaries from around the world use it as their headquarters, especially musical stars who prefer the location—2 blocks from the Vienna State Opera and 1 block from the Musikverein. Richard Wagner stayed here with his family for a few months in 1875 (some scholars claim that he worked out key sections of both *Tannhäuser* and *Lohengrin* during that period). Other artists who have soothed opening-night jitters here over the years include Plácido Domingo, Monserrat Caballé, José Carreras, Eugene Ormandy, and Herbert von Karajan, along with thousands of music lovers who have come to see and hear them.

The hotel was built in 1869 as the private residence of the Duke of Württemberg. The Italian architect Zanotti designed the facade, which resembles a massive governmental building with a heroic frieze carved into the pediment below the roofline. It was converted into a private hotel in 1873. The Nazis commandeered it for their headquarters during World War II, and the Russians requisitioned it in 1945, turning it into a ghost of its former self. Massive expenditures have returned it to its former glory. The Austrian government puts up official state visitors at the Imperial, which was recently renovated, with special care paid to its fourth and fifth floors, now among the most desirable rooms.

On the staircase leading up from the glittering salons are archways supported by statues of gods and goddesses, along with two Winterhalter portraits of Emperor Franz Joseph and his wife, Elisabeth. Everything is set against a background of polished red, yellow, and black marble; crystal chandeliers; Gobelin tapestries; and fine rugs. The salons have arched ceilings, intricately painted with garlands of fruit, ornate urns, griffins, and the smiling faces of sphinxes. Some of the royal suites are downright palatial, but even the regular rooms today are soundproof and generally spacious. Accommodations vary greatly in size, as befits a hotel of this era. Those on the mezzanine and first floors are lavishly baroque; as you go higher, appointments diminish, as do bathroom sizes. Except for some top-floor rooms, bathrooms are generous in size, with heated marble floors, robes, and shower-tub combinations. Courtyard rooms are more tranquil but lack the view of the city.

The elegant restaurant Hotel Imperial Restaurant has a turn-of-the-20th-century atmosphere, accented by antique silver, portraits of Franz Joseph, and superb service.

Kärntner Ring 16, A-1015 Vienna. © **800/325-3589** in the U.S., or 01/501100. Fax 01/5011-0410. www. luxurycollection.com/imperial. 138 units. 510€–625€ double; from 880€ suite. AE, DC, MC, V. Parking 30€. U-Bahn: Karlsplatz. **Amenities:** 2 restaurants; bar; health club; sauna; room service; massage; babysitting; laundry; dry cleaning. *In room:* A/C, TV, hair dryer, safe.

Hotel Inter-Continental Wien ★★

Opposite the Stadtpark and a few minutes from the Ringstrasse, this government-rated five-star deluxe property has forged ahead of the Marriott and the Hilton even though it cloaks its charms in a dull "white tower." Once inside, however, the hotel is inviting and elegant, with a tasteful lobby lit by some of the best hotel chandeliers in Vienna. Many musical stars make this their hotel of choice. The higher the room, the better the view, of course. Rooms are spacious and richly furnished but are not necessarily evocative of Vienna. All the luxuries are here: dataports with voice mail, soundproofing, comfortable beds, and robes and toiletries in bathrooms with marble sinks and shower-tub combinations. Three floors are reserved for nonsmokers.

The Four Seasons Restaurant is one of the best for hotel dining in town, serving an international menu with regional specialties featured daily.

Johannesgasse 28, A-1037 Vienna. © **01/711-22-0.** Fax 01/713-44-89. www.vienna.interconti.com. 453 units. 225€–330€ double; from 350€ suite. AE, DC, MC, V. Parking: 16.10€. U-Bahn: Johannesgasse. **Amenities:** 3 restaurants; 2 bars; health club; sauna; room service; massage; babysitting; laundry; dry cleaning. *In room:* A/C, TV, minibar, hair dryer, safe.

Hotel Sacher Wien ★★★

The Sacher was built in 1876 and still has an air of Hapsburg-era glory. Red velvet, crystal chandeliers, and brocaded curtains in the public rooms evoke Old Vienna. If you want truly grand, we think the Imperial and Bristol are superior, but the Sacher has its diehard admirers. The facade is appropriately elaborate, with neoclassical detailing, a striped awning over the sidewalk cafe, and flags from seven nations displayed near the caryatids on the second floor. Despite its popularity as a setting for spy novels, both the crowned heads of Europe and the deposed heads (especially those of eastern European countries) have safely dined and lived here.

In addition to intrigue, the Sacher has produced culinary creations that still bear its name. Franz Sacher, the celebrated chef, left the world a fabulously caloric chocolate cake called the Sacher torte.

Most rooms contain antiques or superior reproductions; those facing the Vienna State Opera have the best views. Rooms near the top are small with cramped bathrooms, but most accommodations are generous in size and often have sitting areas and midsize marble bathrooms with shower-tub combinations. Interior rooms tend to be dark, however. Thick towels are endlessly supplied by the eagle-eyed housekeeping staff.

Demi-suites and chambers with drawing rooms are more expensive. The reception desk is fairly flexible about making arrangements for salons or apartments, or joining two rooms together, if possible.

Philharmonikerstrasse 4, A-1010 Vienna. © **01/514560.** Fax 01/512-56-810. www.sacher.com. 112 units. 294€–633€ double; from 989€ suite. AE, DC, MC, V. Parking 29€. U-Bahn: Karlsplatz. Tram: 1, 2, 62, 65, D, or J. Bus: 4A. **Amenities:** 2 restaurants; bar; fitness center; room service; massage; babysitting; laundry/dry cleaning. *In room:* A/C, TV, minibar, hair dryer, safe.

Radisson/SAS Palais Hotel Vienna ★

This hotel is one of Vienna's grandest renovations. An unused neoclassical palace was converted into a hotel in 1985 by SAS, the Scandinavian airline; in 1994, another palace next door was added, allowing the hotel to double in size. Near Vienna's most elaborate park (the Stadtpark), the hotel boasts facades accented with cast-iron railings, reclining nymphs, and elaborate cornices. The interior is plushly outfitted with 19th-century architectural motifs, all impeccably restored and dramatically illuminated. The lobby contains arching palms, a soaring ceiling, and a bar with evening piano music. The result is an uncluttered, conservative, and well-maintained hotel that is managed in a breezy, highly efficient manner. Bedrooms are outfitted in either pink or blue and, in the new wing, in summery shades of green and white. Ample closet space is an attractive feature, as are the good beds and generous-size marble bathrooms with heated floors, makeup mirrors, and shower-tub combinations. Smoke-free units can be arranged. The hotel also offers several duplex suites, or *maisonettes*, conventional suites, and rooms in the Royal Club, which has upgraded luxuries and services.

Parkring 16, A-1010 Vienna. ℂ 800/333-3333 in the U.S., or 01/515170. Fax 01/512-2216. www.radisson. com. 247 units. 212€–276€ double; from 337€ suite. AE, DC, MC, V. Parking 30€. U-Bahn: Stadtpark. Tram: 2. **Amenities:** Restaurant; 2 bars; fitness center; Jacuzzi; sauna; room service; babysitting; laundry; dry cleaning. *In room:* A/C, TV, minibar, hair dryer, safe.

EXPENSIVE

Hotel Amadeus ⚐   Cozy and convenient, this boxlike hotel is only 2 minutes away from the cathedral and within walking distance of practically everything else of musical or historical note in Vienna. It was built on the site of a once-legendary tavern (Zum roten Igel) that attracted the likes of Johannes Brahms, Franz Schubert, and Moritz von Schwind. Behind a dull 1960s facade, the hotel maintains its bedrooms and carpeted public rooms in reasonable shape. Bedrooms are furnished in a comfortable, modern style, and many open onto views of the cathedral, but ceilings are uncomfortably low. Double-glazing on the windows quiets but does not obliterate street noise. Some of the carpeting and fabrics look a little worse for wear. Tiled bathrooms are midsize, but there's not enough room to lay out your toiletries. Eight rooms have showers but no tubs. Expect a somewhat dour welcome: No one on the staff will win any Mr. and Mrs. Sunshine contests.

Wildpretmarkt 5, A-1010 Vienna. ℂ 01/533-87-38. Fax 01/533-87-38-38. www.tiscover.com/amadeus. 30 units. 142€–160€ double. Rates include breakfast. AE, DC, MC, V. Parking 22€. U-Bahn: Stephansplatz. **Amenities:** Breakfast room; lounge; babysitting; laundry; dry cleaning. *In room:* A/C, TV, minibar, hair dryer, safe.

Hotel Astoria ⚐   Hotel Astoria is for nostalgists who want to experience life as it was in the closing days of the Austro-Hungarian Empire. A first-class hotel, the Astoria has an eminently desirable location, lying on the shopping mall near St. Stephan's Cathedral and the Vienna State Opera. Decorated in a slightly frayed turn-of-the-20th-century style, the hotel offers well-appointed and traditionally decorated bedrooms. The interior rooms tend to be too dark, and singles are just too cramped. The place is, in fact, a bit on the melancholy side. Rooms contain built-in armoires and well-chosen linens and duvets on good beds and bathrooms that, for the most part, are spacious (although the fixtures are old) and have such extras as dual basins, heated racks, shower-tub combinations, and bidets. Of course, it has been renovated over the years, but the old style has been preserved, and management seems genuinely concerned about offering high-quality service and accommodation for what is considered a reasonable price in Vienna. The Astoria has long been a favorite with visiting performers like the late Leonard Bernstein.

Kärntnerstrasse 32-34, A-1015 Vienna. ℂ 01/515770. Fax 01/515-7782. www.austria-trend.at. 118 units. 190€–212€ double; 292€ suite. Rates include breakfast. AE, DC, MC, V. Parking 22€. U-Bahn: Stephansplatz. **Amenities:** Restaurant; bar; room service; babysitting; laundry; dry cleaning. *In room:* TV, minibar, hair dryer, safe.

Hotel Das Triest ★★ *(Finds)*   Sir Terence Conran, the famous English architect and designer, has created the interior decoration for this contemporary hotel in the center of Vienna, a 5-minute walk from St. Stephan's Cathedral. Conran has done for Das Triest what Philippe Starck did for New York's Paramount Hotel: created a stylish address in the heart of one of the world's most important cities. An emerging favorite with artists and musicians, this hip hotel has such grace notes as a courtyard garden. The building was originally used as a stable for horses pulling stagecoaches between Vienna and Trieste—hence its name, "City of Trieste." Its old cross-vaulted rooms, which give the structure a distinctive flair, have been transformed into lounges and suites. Bedrooms are midsize to spacious, tastefully furnished, and comfortable. The white-tiled bathrooms have heated racks, shower-tub combinations, deluxe toiletries, and vanity mirrors. You're carried to your bedroom by one of two black-glassed elevators. In the afternoon, some guests gather for tea in front of the cozy fireplace.

Wiedner Hauptstrasse 12, A-1040 Vienna. ℂ 01/589-18. Fax 01/589-18-18. www.nethotels.com/das_triest. 73 units. 245€ double; from 299€ suite. Rates include buffet breakfast. AE, DC, MC, V. Parking: 21€. U-Bahn: Stephansplatz. **Amenities:** Restaurant; bar; fitness center; sauna; salon; room service; massage; babysitting; laundry; dry cleaning. *In room:* A/C, TV, minibar, hair dryer, safe.

Hotel Europa ★   The welcoming parapet of this glass-and-steel hotel extends over the sidewalk almost to the edge of the street. You'll find the 10-story hotel midway between the Vienna State Opera and St. Stephan's Cathedral. It offers comfortable bedrooms furnished in Scandinavian modern. Some bedrooms are spacious, with lots of light coming in from the large windows, but nearly all the shower-only bathrooms are microscopic. The Europa has a Viennese cafe and a first-class restaurant, Zum Donnerbrunnen, which features zither music at night.

Kärntnerstrasse, A-1010 Vienna. ℂ 01/515940. Fax 01/513-8138. www.austria-trend.at. 116 units. 152€–190€ double. Rates include buffet breakfast. AE, DC, MC, V. Parking 23€. U-Bahn: Stephansplatz. **Amenities:** Restaurant; bar; room service; laundry; dry cleaning. *In room:* A/C, TV, minibar, hair dryer, safe.

Hotel König Von Ungarn ★   On a narrow street near St. Stephan's, this hotel occupies a dormered building that dates back to the early 17th century. It has been receiving paying guests for more than 4 centuries and is Vienna's oldest continuously operated hotel—in all, an evocative, intimate, and cozy retreat. It was once a pied-à-terre for Hungarian noble families during their stays in the Austrian capital. In 1791, Mozart reportedly resided and wrote some of his immortal music in an apartment upstairs, where you'll find a Mozart museum.

The interior abounds with interesting architectural details, such as marble columns supporting the arched ceiling of the King of Hungary restaurant, which is one of Vienna's finest and most famous. There's also a mirrored solarium/bar area with a glass roof over the atrium, and a live tree growing out of the pavement. Tall hinged windows overlook the Old Town, and Venetian mirrors adorn some walls. Everywhere you look, you'll find low-key luxury, tradition, and modern convenience. Try for the two rooms with balconies. Guestrooms have been newly remodeled with Biedermeier accents and traditional furnishings. Most bathrooms are generous in size and have dual basins, shower-tub combinations, and tiled walls. The professional staff is highly efficient, keeping the hotel spotless.

Schulerstrasse 10, A-1010 Vienna. ℂ 01/515840. Fax 01/515848. www.kvu.at. 33 units. 182€ double; 210€–290€ apartment. Rates include breakfast. AE, DC, MC, V. U-Bahn: Stephansplatz. **Amenities:** Restaurant; bar; room service; babysitting; laundry; dry cleaning. *In room:* A/C, TV, minibar, hair dryer, safe.

Hotel Römischer Kaiser ★ *(Kids)*   A Best Western affiliate, this hotel is housed in a national trust building that has seen its share of transformations. It's located in a traffic-free zone between St. Stephan's Cathedral and the Vienna State Opera, on a side street off Kärntnerstrasse. It was constructed in 1684 as the private palace of the imperial chamberlain and later housed the Imperial School of Engineering before becoming a hostelry at the turn of the 20th century. The hotel rents romantically decorated rooms (our favorite has red satin upholstery over a chaise lounge). Thick duvets and custom linens make the rooms homelike and inviting, and bathrooms are generous in size, often luxurious, with showers and half tubs, vanity mirrors, and enough shelf space to spread out your toiletries. Double-glazed windows keep down the noise, and baroque paneling is a nice touch. Some rooms—notably nos. 12, 22, 30, and 38—can accommodate three or four beds, making this a family-friendly place. The red-carpeted sidewalk cafe has bar service and tables shaded with flowers and umbrellas. It evokes memories of Vienna in its imperial heyday.

Annagasse 16, A-1010 Vienna. ℭ **800/528-1234** in the U.S., or 01/512-7751. Fax 01/5127-75113. info@ rkhotel.bestwestern.at. 23 units. 145€–238€ double. Rates include breakfast. AE, DC, MC, V. Parking 17€. U-Bahn: Stephansplatz. **Amenities:** Restaurant; bar; room service; laundry; dry cleaning. *In room:* A/C, TV, minibar, hair dryer, safe.

K & K Palais Hotel ✦   This hotel, with its severely dignified facade, sheltered the affair of Emperor Francis Joseph and his celebrated mistress, Katherina Schratt, in 1890. Occupying a desirable position near the river and a 5-minute walk from the Ring, it remained unused for 2 decades until the Best Western chain renovated it in 1981.

Vestiges of its imperial past remain, in spite of the contemporary but airy lobby and the lattice-covered bar. The public rooms are painted a shade of imperial Austrian yellow, and one of Ms. Schratt's antique secretaries occupies a niche near a white-sided tile stove. The bedrooms are comfortably outfitted and stylish. Rooms have a certain Far East motif, with light wood, wicker, and rattan. The tiled bathrooms are equipped with shower-tub combinations, decent shelf space, and state-of-the-art plumbing. Two floors are nonsmoking.

Rudolfsplatz 11, A-1010 Vienna. ℭ **800/537-8483** in the U.S., or 01/533-1353. Fax 01/5331-35370. www.kkhotels.com. 66 units. 205€ double. Rates include breakfast. AE, DC, MC, V. Parking 16€. U-Bahn: Schottenring. **Amenities:** Restaurant; bar; room service; babysitting; laundry; dry cleaning. *In room:* A/C, TV, minibar, hair dryer, safe.

Vienna Marriott ✦   The Marriott has a striking exterior and holds its own against SAS, the K&K Palais Hotel, and the Hilton, although the latter two hotels manage to evoke a more Viennese atmosphere. Opposite Stadtpark, the hotel is ideally located for visitors, as it's within walking distance of such landmarks as St. Stephan's Cathedral, the Vienna State Opera, and the Hofburg. Its Mississippi-riverboat facade displays expanses of tinted glass set in finely wrought enameled steel. About a third of the building is occupied by the American Consulate offices and a few private apartments.

The hotel's lobby culminates in a stairway whose curved sides frame a splashing waterfall that's surrounded with plants. Many of the comfortably modern bedrooms are larger than those in the city's other contemporary hotels. Spacious mirrored closets are a feature, as are great bathrooms with large sinks and shower-tub combinations. Furnishings are a bit commercial. There are four smoke-free floors and adequate soundproofing.

Parkring 12A, A-1010 Vienna. ℭ **800/228-9290** in the U.S., or 01/515180. Fax 01/51518-6736. 313 units. 270€ double; 360€–490€ suite. AE, DC, MC, V. Parking 27€. Tram: 1 or 2. **Amenities:** 2 restaurants; 2 bars; pool; fitness center; Jacuzzi; sauna; salon; room service; massage; babysitting; laundry; dry cleaning. *In room:* A/C, TV, minibar, hair dryer, safe.

MODERATE

Best Western Hotel Opernring *(Kids*   Across from the Vienna State Opera, and lying along the Ring, this government-rated four-star hotel has been much improved under new owners, who have carried out a major rejuvenation of a formerly tired property. Accommodations are fairly large and tastefully furnished, with such extras as dataports, duvet-covered beds, and spacious tiled bathrooms equipped with shower-tub combinations. Double-glazed windows cut down on the noise in the front bedrooms. Some units are reserved for nonsmokers, and some of the accommodations can sleep three to four family members comfortably. Don't judge the hotel by its rather cramped reception area or its entrance. The third-floor lounge is large and inviting; its bay window opens onto the activity of central Vienna.

Opernring 11, A-1010 Vienna. © **800/528-1234** in the U.S., or 01/587-55-18. Fax 01/587-55-18-29. www. bestwestern.com. 35 units. 119€–155€ double; 280€ suite. Rates include breakfast. AE, DC, MC, V. Parking 22€. U-Bahn: Karlsplatz. **Amenities:** Breakfast room; lounge; room service; babysitting; laundry; dry cleaning. *In room:* TV, minibar, hair dryer, safe.

Golden Tulip Capricorno   In the heart of Vienna, this government-rated four-star hotel, a short stroll from St. Stephan's, has more than a convenient location going for it. Next to the Danube Canal, it is solidly commercial and undramatic architecturally on the outside (a dull, cube-shape building), but rather warm and inviting inside. The reception area is decorated in a modern Art Nouveau style with tiles and brass trim. Rooms are compact—even cramped, in many cases— but they are well furnished and maintained. Singles are particularly small, mainly because the beds are more spacious than most. All units have neatly kept bathrooms mostly equipped with shower-tub combinations. Some units, especially those on the lower levels, suffer from noise pollution. The hotel sends its guests to its sibling, the Hotel Stefanie, across the street, for dining in a first-class restaurant, Kronprinz Rudolph, offering both Viennese and international cuisine.

Schwedenplatz 3-4, A-1010 Vienna. © **01/5333-1040.** Fax 01/5337-6714. www.hotels-austria.com/Vienna-center/capricorno.htm. 46 units. 147€–172€ double. AE, DC, MC, V. Rates include buffet breakfast. U-Bahn: Stephansplatz. **Amenities:** Breakfast room; lounge; room service; laundry; dry cleaning. *In room:* A/C, TV, minibar, hair dryer.

Graben Hotel   Back in the 18th century, this was called Zum Goldener Jägerhorn; over the years, it has attracted an array of bohemian writers and artists. The poet Franz Grillparzer was a regular guest, and during the dark days of World War II, it was a gathering place for such writers as Franz Kafka, Max Brod, and Peter Altenberg. There aren't too many bohemians around anymore, but what's left of them can be seen gathered at the fabled Café Hawelka across the street. The hotel stands on a narrow street off the Kärntnerstrasse, in the very center of the city. One journalist in Vienna wrote that "its staff was lent by Fawlty Towers," but we're sure he meant that lovingly, as they're helpful and bright. Guests gather around the stone fireplace in winter and look at the original postcards left by Altenberg. Rooms are high ceilinged but rather cramped, with shower-tub combinations in the bathrooms. Although there are some Art Nouveau touches, much of the furniture is a bit drab and spartan for our tastes. If there's any sunlight streaming in, it'll come from the front rooms, not the darker havens in the rear. On-site is the excellent trattoria San Stefano, serving some of the best Italian dishes in the area. The Restaurant Altenberg specializes in Austrian dishes. The chef is known for his creamy cake named in honor of Kaiser Franz Josef.

Dorotheergasse 3, A-1010 Vienna. © **01/512-15-31-0.** Fax 01/512-15-31-20. www.kremslehner.hotels. or.at/graben. 41 units. 127€–167€ double. Rates include buffet breakfast. AE, DC, MC, V. U-Bahn: Karlsplatz. **Amenities:** Restaurant; lounge; room service; babysitting. *In room:* TV, minibar, hair dryer.

Hotel Am Parkring This well-maintained hotel occupies the top three floors of a 13-story office building near the edge of Vienna's Stadtpark. A semiprivate elevator services only the street-level entrance and the hotel's floors. There are sweeping views of the city from all of its bedrooms, some of which overlook nearby St. Stephan's Cathedral. Bedrooms are furnished in a conservative but comfortable style and are favored by business travelers and visitors alike, although the atmosphere is a bit sterile if you're seeking nostalgic Vienna. Bedrooms have well-kept bathrooms that are small but functional (some with showers instead of tubs). Eighteen units were recently equipped with sparkling new bathrooms. This hotel is not the kindest to the lone tourist, as single accommodations tend to be too small, and often sofa beds are used. Rooms here are a standard, reliable choice, but don't expect fireworks.

Parkring 12, A-1015 Vienna. © **01/514800.** Fax 01/514-8040. www.bestwestern.com. 64 units. 129€–215€ double; 210€–315€ suite. Rates include breakfast. AE, DC, MC, V. Parking 18€. U-Bahn: Stadtpark or Stuben-tor. Tram: 1 or 2. **Amenities:** Restaurant; bar; room service; babysitting; laundry; dry cleaning. *In room:* A/C, TV, minibar, hair dryer.

Hotel Am Schubertring ★ *Kids* In a historic building in the very center of town, this small hotel has a certain charm and style. On the famous Ringstrasse, next to the opera, it has Viennese flair, especially in the use of Art Nouveau and Biedermeier-style furnishings in its moderate size and comfortable bedrooms with small bathrooms containing shower-tub combinations. Rooms are generally quiet, and eight units are suitable for three guests or more. The top-floor rooms look out over the rooftops of Vienna. At this family-friendly place, children under age 6 are housed free if sharing accommodations with their parents.

Schubertring 11, A-1010 Vienna. © **01/717-020.** Fax 01/713-99-66. www.schubertring.at. 39 units. 128€–182€ double. AE, DC, MC, V. U-Bahn: Karlsplatz. **Amenities:** Restaurant; bar; room service; baby-sitting; laundry; dry cleaning. *In room:* TV, minibar, hair dryer, safe.

Hotel Am Stephansplatz Walk out the door, and you'll be facing the front entrance to Vienna's cathedral if you stay here. The location, admittedly, is virtually unbeatable, although a lot of other hotels have more charm and more helpful staffs. Nevertheless, the place has many winning qualities; for example, it receives individual bookings and is not overrun with group package tours. Marble, granite, crystal, and burled woods set the tone for the renovated lobby. Some of the bedrooms contain painted reproduction rococo furniture and red-flocked wallpaper. All have firm beds. Most rooms, however, are rather sterile and functional, and 10 come with showers only instead of tub baths. Bathrooms tend to be small. Lack of air-conditioning could be a problem in the evening, especially if guests must open their windows onto noisy Stephansplatz. The singles are so plain and cramped that they're hardly recommendable.

Stephansplatz 9, A-1010 Vienna. © **01/534-05-0.** Fax 01/534-05-711. hotel@stephansplatz.co.at. 57 units. 145€–230€ double. Rates include breakfast. AE, DC, MC, V. Parking 25€. U-Bahn: Stephansplatz. **Amenities:** Restaurant; lounge; room service; laundry; dry cleaning. *In room:* TV, minibar, hair dryer.

Hotel Kaiserin Elisabeth This yellow-stoned hotel is conveniently located near the cathedral. The interior is decorated with oriental rugs on well-maintained marble and wood floors. The main salon has a pale-blue skylight suspended above it, with mirrors and half-columns in natural wood. The small, quiet rooms have been considerably updated since Wolfgang Mozart, Richard Wagner, Franz Liszt, and Edvard Grieg stayed here, and their musical descendents continue to patronize the place. Polished wood, clean linen, and perhaps another oriental rug grace the rooms. Bathrooms are a bit cramped, with not enough room for your toilet articles, but they are tiled and equipped with shower-tub combinations, vanity mirrors, and, in some cases, bidets.

Weihburggasse 3, A-1010 Vienna. ℂ 01/515260. Fax 01/515267. kaiserin@ins.at. 63 units. 193€ double; 215€ suite. Rates include buffet breakfast. AE, DC, MC, V. Parking 25.44€. U-Bahn: Stephansplatz. **Amenities:** Restaurant; bar; room service; laundry; dry cleaning. *In room:* A/C, TV, minibar, hair dryer, safe.

Hotel-Pension Arenberg *⋌*   This genteel but unpretentious hotel-pension occupies the second and third floors of a six-story apartment house that was built around the turn of the 20th century. Set in a prestigious neighborhood on Ringstrasse, it offers soundproof bedrooms outfitted in old-world style with oriental carpets, conservative furniture, and intriguing artwork. The place is rather old-fashioned but has a certain Viennese charm. One enthusiastic reader described it as a small luxury hotel where the English-speaking staff couldn't be more delightful or helpful. "On your second visit, they treat you like family," the reader wrote. The bedrooms are furnished the way your Viennese grandmother might have found inspiring, although they are a bit small. The shower-only bathrooms are a bit cramped. But in spite of it all, this hotel remains exceptionally appealing to those with a sense of history.

Stubenring 2, A-1010 Vienna. ℂ **800/528-1234** in the U.S., or 01/512-5291. Fax 01/513-9356. www.best western.com. 23 units. 118€–148€ double; 142€–172€ triple suite. Rates include breakfast. AE, DC, MC, V. Parking 21€. U-Bahn: Schwedenplatz. **Amenities:** Restaurant; lounge; room service; babysitting; laundry; dry cleaning. *In room:* A/C, TV, minibar, hair dryer, safe.

Hotel Royal *⋌⋌*   This dignified, nine-story hotel is on one of the more prestigious streets of the old city, less than a block from St. Stephan's Cathedral. The lobby contains the piano where Wagner composed *Die Meistersinger von Nürnberg*. Each of the good-size rooms is furnished differently, with some good reproductions of antiques and even an occasional original. Built in 1960, the hotel was rebuilt in 1982. Try for a room with a balcony and a view of the cathedral. Corner rooms with spacious foyers are also desirable, although those facing the street tend to be noisy. The midsize bathrooms have mosaic tiles, dual basins, heated towel racks, and, in most cases, a tub bath along with a shower unit. Firenze Enoteca (p. 105), under separate management, serves savory Italian food and has the largest selection of Italian wines in Austria.

Singerstrasse 3, A-1010 Vienna. ℂ 01/515680. Fax 01/513-9696. 81 units. 127€–167€ double; 211€ suite. Rates include breakfast. AE, DC, MC, V. U-Bahn: Stephansplatz. **Amenities:** Restaurant; bar; room service; laundry; dry cleaning. *In room:* TV, minibar, hair dryer.

Mailberger Hof   This old palace was built in the 13th century as a mansion for the knights of Malta and was converted into a hotel in the 1970s. Off the main drag, Kärntnerstrasse, it lies on a typical Viennese cobblestone street. The two large wooden doors at the entrance still boast a Maltese cross. The vaulted ceiling, the leather armchairs, and maybe the marbleized walls are about all that would remind the knights of their former home. Everywhere the place has been renewed, although a cobblestone courtyard, set with tables in fair weather, remains. A family-run place with a cozy atmosphere, the hotel features moderate-size bedrooms that are often brightened with pastels, each with comfortable beds, plus shower-tub combinations in the small bathrooms. In general, though, the public rooms are more inviting than the private ones.

Annagasse 7, A-1010 Vienna. © **01/512-0641.** Fax 01/512-0641-10. 40 units. 160€–185€ double; from 196€ suite. AE, DC, MC, V. Parking 19€. U-Bahn: Karlsplatz. **Amenities:** Restaurant; bar; room service; babysitting; laundry; dry cleaning. *In room:* A/C, TV, minibar, hair dryer, safe.

INEXPENSIVE

Drei Kronen 🅐   The celebrated architect Ignaz Drapala designed this splendid Art Nouveau building in a charming section of Vienna close to the famous Naschmarkt. The "three crowns" in the German name Drei Kronen refer to Austria, Hungary, and Bohemia from the old Austro-Hungarian empire. A symbol of the crowns is displayed on top of the building. The hotel enjoys one of Vienna's best locations, close to such monuments as the Vienna State Opera and St. Stephan's Cathedral. Built in 1894, the five-story hotel was completely renovated in 1999. The midsize to spacious bedrooms are fresh and bright, with comfortable furnishings along with immaculate bathrooms with showers. Some of the rooms are large enough to contain three beds.

Schleifmuehlgasse 25, A-1040 Vienna. © **01/587-3289.** Fax 01/710-1920. http://vienna.nethotels.com/ nethotels/deutsch/hotels/drei_kronen/default.htm. 41 units. 72€–101€ double; 91€ triple. AE, DC, MC, V. Parking 13€. U-Bahn: Karlsplatz. **Amenities:** Breakfast room; lounge; babysitting. *In room:* TV, safe in some.

Hotel Austria   The staff here always seems willing to tell you where to go in the neighborhood for a good meal or a glass of wine, and often distributes typed sheets explaining the medieval origins of this section of the city center. This unpretentious, family-owned hotel sits on a small, quiet street whose name will probably be unfamiliar to many taxi drivers—a corner building on the adjoining street, Fleischmarkt 20, is the point where you'll turn onto the narrow lane. The comfortable furnishings in the lobby and in the chandeliered breakfast room are maintained in tip-top shape. Every year one of the four floors of the hotel is completely renovated with wallpapering, a change of furniture, and a replacement of bedding. The tiled shower-only bathrooms are small but adequate unless you have a lot of toilet articles to spread out. The decor is rather functional, although the hotel is immaculately maintained and inviting.

Wolfengasse 3A, A-1011 Vienna. © **01/51523.** Fax 01/5152-3506. www.hotelaustria-wien.at. 46 units, 42 with bathroom. 70€–90€ double without bathroom; 98€–136€ double with bathroom; 110€–174€ triple with bathroom. Rates include breakfast. AE, DC, MC, V. Parking 19€. U-Bahn: Schwedenplatz. Tram: 1 or 2. **Amenities:** Breakfast room; lounge; massage; babysitting; laundry; dry cleaning. *In room:* TV, minibar, hair dryer.

Hotel Kärntnerhof 🅐 *(Kids)*   Only a 4-minute walk from the cathedral, the Kärntnerhof advertises itself as a *gutbürgerlich* (bourgeois) family-oriented hotel. The decor of the public rooms is tastefully arranged around oriental rugs, well-upholstered chairs and couches with cabriole legs, and an occasional 19th-century portrait. The midsize to spacious units are more up-to-date, usually with the original parquet floors and striped or patterned wallpaper set off by curtains. Many of the guestrooms are large enough to handle an extra bed or so, making this a family favorite. The small private bathrooms glisten with tile walls and floors; about half of them contain shower-tub combinations. The owner is quite helpful, directing guests to the post office and nearby Vienna landmarks.

Grashofgasse 4, A-1011 Vienna. © **01/512-1923.** Fax 01/5132-22833. www.karntnerhof.com. 44 units. 105€–143€ double; 180€–225€ suite. Rates include buffet breakfast. AE, DC, MC, V. Parking 16€. U-Bahn: Stephansplatz. **Amenities:** Breakfast room; lounge; room service; laundry; dry cleaning. *In room:* TV.

Hotel Pension Shermin   The Voshmgir family welcomes you into its small, inviting, homelike boardinghouse in the city center. Bedrooms are big and comfortable, and the hotel-pension draws many repeat guests. The location is convenient for such sights as the opera house, the Imperial Palace, and the

Spanish Riding School, all a 5-minute walk away. Bathrooms are small but have good showers and well-maintained plumbing. Furnishings are modern and without much flair, but are exceedingly comfortable.

Rilkeplatz 7, A-1040 Vienna. ⓒ **01/58-66-18-30.** Fax 01/58-66-18-310. www.hotel-pension-shermin.com. 11 units. 72€–108€ double. Rates include breakfast. AE, DC, MC, V. Parking 7€. U-Bahn: Karlsplatz. **Amenities:** Breakfast room; lounge; room service. *In room:* TV, hair dryer.

Hotel Pension Suzanne (★) (*Kids*)   Only a 45-second walk from the opera house, this is a real discovery. Once you get past its post-war facade, the interior warms considerably, brightly decorated in a comfortable, traditional style with antique beds, plush chairs, and the original molded ceilings. Now into its second generation of managers, the hotel-pension is run by the welcoming Strafinger family, who like its classic Viennese turn-of-the-20th-century styling. Rooms are midsize and exceedingly well maintained, facing either the busy street or a court-yard. Families often stay here because some of the accommodations contain three beds. Some bedrooms are like small apartments, with kitchenettes. Each unit comes with a private bathroom with a shower-tub combination.

Walfischgasse 4. ⓒ **01/513-25-07.** Fax 01/513-25-00. 26 units. 83€–108€ double; 105€ double with kitchenette; 99€–139€ triple. AE, DC, MC, V. U-Bahn: Karlsplatz. **Amenities:** Breakfast room; lounge; babysitting. *In room:* TV, hair dryer.

Hotel Post   Hotel Post lies in the medieval slaughterhouse district, today an interesting section full of hotels and restaurants. The dignified front of this hotel is constructed of gray stone, with a facade of black marble covering the street level. The manager is quick to tell you that both Mozart and Haydn frequently stayed in a former inn at this address. Those composers would probably be amused to hear recordings of their music played in the coffeehouse/restaurant, Le Café/Alte Weinstube, attached to the hotel. Bedrooms, most of which are midsize, are streamlined and functionally furnished, each well maintained and most with small shower-only bathrooms.

Fleischmarkt 24, A-1010 Vienna. ⓒ **01/51-58-30.** Fax 01/515-83-808. 107 units, 77 with bathroom. 93€ double without bathroom; 111€ double with bathroom; 110€ triple without bathroom; 136€ triple with bathroom. Rates include buffet breakfast. AE, DC, MC, V. Parking 16€. Tram: 1 or 2. **Amenities:** Restaurant; lounge; salon; room service; laundry; dry cleaning. *In room:* TV, hair dryer.

Hotel Wandl   Stepping into this hotel is like stepping into a piece of a family's history—it has been under the same ownership for generations. The Wandl lies in the Inner City and offers views of the steeple of St. Stephan's Cathedral from many of its windows, which often open onto small balconies. The breakfast room is a high-ceilinged, two-toned room with hanging chandeliers and lots of ornamented plaster. The bedrooms usually offer the kind of spacious dimensions that went out of style 60 years ago; bathrooms, most of which contain shower only, are small but adequate, tiled, and well maintained. Beds are frequently renewed—all in all, this is a comfortable choice if you're not too demanding. The hotel faces St. Peter's Church.

Petersplatz 9, A-1010 Vienna. ⓒ **01/53-45-50.** Fax 01/53-455-77. reservation@hotelwandl.com. 138 units, 134 with bathroom. 100€ double without bathroom; 135€–170€ double with bathroom. Rates include breakfast. AE, DC, MC, V. Parking 20€. U-Bahn: Stephansplatz. **Amenities:** Breakfast room; lounge; room service; laundry; dry cleaning. *In room:* TV, safe.

Pension Dr. Geissler (*Value*)   Unpretentious lodgings at reasonable prices are offered here, near the well-known Schwedenplatz at the edge of the Danube Canal. The bedrooms in this attractive, informal guesthouse are furnished with simple blond headboards and a few utilitarian pieces. Hallway bathrooms are generous. Most units, however, have their own private bathrooms, which are tiled and well maintained but a bit cramped. Most bathrooms here have shower-tub combinations.

Postgasse 14, A-1010 Vienna. © **01/533-2803.** Fax 01/533-2635. 35 units, 21 with bathroom. 52€ double without bathroom; 89€ double with bathroom. Rates include buffet breakfast. AE, DC, MC, V. U-Bahn: Schwedenplatz. **Amenities:** Breakfast room; bar; room service; babysitting; laundry; dry cleaning. *In room:* TV.

Pension Neuer Markt Near the cathedral, in the heart of Vienna, this pension is housed in a white baroque building that faces a square with an ornate fountain. The carpeted but small rooms are clean and well maintained in an updated motif of white walls and strong colors, with large windows in some. Some of the comfortable, duvet-covered beds are set into niches. Each of the units has central heating. Bathrooms with shower-tub combinations are small, seemingly added as an afterthought, but for Vienna the price is delicious. We recommend reserving 30 days in advance.

Seilergasse 9, A-1010 Vienna. © **01/512-2316.** Fax 01/513-9105. 36 units. 88€–120€ double. Rates include breakfast. AE, DC, MC, V. Parking 10€. U-Bahn: Stephansplatz. **Amenities:** Breakfast room; bar; room service; babysitting; laundry; dry cleaning. *In room:* TV, safe.

Pension Nossek Mozart lived in this building in 1781 and 1782, when he wrote the *Haffner* symphony and *The Abduction from the Seraglio.* The pension lies on one of Vienna's best shopping streets, just blocks away from the major sights. In 1909, the building was converted into a guesthouse and has always been a good bet for clean, comfortable accommodations with decent beds—most comfortable. Most of the bedrooms have been renovated, and all but a few singles contain small private bathrooms with shower-tub combinations.

Graben 17, A-1010 Vienna. © **01/5337-0410.** Fax 01/535-3646. pension.nossek@faxvia.net. 26 units (4 with shower only, 22 with tub). 105€ double with tub or shower; 130€ suite with tub or shower. Rates include breakfast. No credit cards. Free parking. U-Bahn: Stephansplatz. **Amenities:** Breakfast room; lounge; laundry; dry cleaning. *In room:* TV, minibar, hair dryer (in some).

Great Summer Savings: Staying in Dorms

In Vienna, from July to September, a number of student dormitories are transformed into fully operational hotels. Three of the most viable and popular of these are the **Academia Hotel,** Pfeilgasse 3A; the **Avis Hotel,** Pfeilgasse 4; and the **Atlas Hotel,** at Lerchenfelderstrasse 1. Each is a rather unimaginative-looking, angular, 1960s-style building, and the lodgings will definitely take you back to your college dorm days, though each room does have a phone and a private bathroom. But it's a comfortable and reasonably priced alternative, only a 20-minute walk west of St. Stephan's. Many of them are booked well in advance by groups, but individual travelers are welcome if space is available. Depending on the hotel, doubles cost from 40€ to 80€ a night, and triples run from 62€ to 99€ each. Breakfast is included in the rates. Bookings at all three hotels are arranged through the receptionists at the Academia Hotel, which functions as the headquarters for the entire Academia chain. For reservations and information, call © **01/401-76-55** or fax 01/401-76-20. To get to the Academia and Avis hotels, take the U-Bahn to Thaliastrasse, and then transfer to tram no. 46 and get off at Strozzistrasse. For access to the Atlas Hotel, take the U-Bahn to Lerchenfelderstrasse. These hotels accept American Express, Diners Club, MasterCard, and Visa for payment.

Pension Pertschy   Well-scrubbed and reputable, this simple but historic pension was originally built in the 1700s as the Palais Carviani with a restrained baroque style. Several rooms overlook a central courtyard and are scattered among six or seven private apartments, whose residents are used to foreign visitors roaming through the building. Midsize bedrooms are high-ceilinged and outfitted in old-fashioned, almost dowdy tones of cream and pink, with good beds and rather cramped shower-only bathrooms. Most appealing is its prime location in the heart of Old Vienna (between Habsburgasse and Bräunergasse, just off the Graben).

Habsburgergasse 5, A-1010 Vienna. © **01/534490.** Fax 01/534-4949. 50 units (2 with kitchen). 95€–110€ double without kitchen; 110€–135€ suite. AE, DC, MC, V. Parking 3.60€–15€. U-Bahn: Stephansplatz. **Amenities:** Breakfast room; lounge. *In room:* TV, minibar, hair dryer.

Zur Wiener Staatsoper   You'll probably stop to admire the elaborately baroque facade of this family-run hotel even if you don't plan to stay here. Rooms are clean and comfortable, although the furnishings are rather simple. Private bathrooms with shower units are bigger than those found on a cruise ship, but not by much. The hotel's location, near most Inner City monuments, is convenient.

Krugerstrasse 11, A-1010 Vienna. © **01/513-1274.** Fax 01/5131-27415. www.zurwienerstaatsoper.at. 22 units. 109€–135€ double. Rates include breakfast. AE, DC, MC, V. Parking 17€. U-Bahn: Karlsplatz. Tram: 1, 2, D, or J; Opernring. **Amenities:** Breakfast room; lounge. *In room:* TV, hair dryer, safe.

LEOPOLDSTADT (2ND DISTRICT)
MODERATE

Hotel Stefanie   This updated government-rated four-star hotel is across the Danube Canal from St. Stephan's Cathedral, but it's still easily accessible to the rest of the city. It has had a long and distinguished history, dating back to 1630. A century later, a famous inn, Weisse Rose, stood on this site. Ever since 1870, the hotel has been run by the Schick family. The interior is partially decorated in beautifully finished wall paneling and gilded wall sconces. Upon closer examination, much of the decor is reproductions, yet the hotel emits a hint of 19th-century rococo splendor. The bar area is filled with black leather armchairs on chrome swivel bases, and the concealed lighting throws an azure glow over the artfully displayed bottles. Over the past 20 years, all the bedrooms have had major renovations and today are well furnished in sleek Viennese styling. Some are a bit small, but they are beautifully maintained, with excellent beds and small tiled bathrooms that, for the most part, contain shower-tub combinations but not enough shelf space.

Taborstrasse 12, A-1020 Vienna. © **800/528-1234** in the U.S., or 01/211500. Fax 01/21150-160. stefanie@schick-hotels.com. 131 units. 124€–199€ double. Rates include buffet breakfast. AE, DC, MC, V. Parking 17€. U-Bahn: Schwedenplatz. Tram: 21. **Amenities:** Restaurant; bar; room service; laundry; dry cleaning. *In room:* A/C, TV, minibar, hair dryer, safe.

LANDSTRASSE (3RD DISTRICT)
VERY EXPENSIVE

Hotel im Palais Schwarzenberg ✦✦✦   Just outside the Ring, this hotel—more a museum, really—is hidden amid 15 acres of manicured gardens. It's an excellent choice if you want a noble and elegant ambience. Unlike the Bristol and the Imperial, this hotel has the aura of a country estate in a formally landscaped and statue-dotted park. The palace was built 300 years ago by Hildebrandt and Fischer von Erlach, masters of baroque architecture, and has held on to its splendid original touches. It was gutted during the Nazi era but was completely reconstructed after the Soviet occupation of Vienna. Today the same striated marble, crystal chandeliers, mythical beasts, oval mirrors, and gilt—lots of it—fill the public rooms between painted murals of festive deities. The posh bedrooms and suites contain exquisite objets d'art and antique pieces, although they vary greatly in size. The large marble or tile bathrooms have bidets, robes, and shower-tub combinations.

Guests enjoy the terrace restaurant, Wintergarten, which serves classical French and Viennese cuisine and overlooks the park. The Palais Bar is one of the most elegant in Vienna.

Schwarzenbergplatz 9, A-1030 Vienna. ☎ 01/798-4515. Fax 01/798-4714. www.palais-schwarzenberg.com. 44 units. 265€–400€ double; from 450€ suite. AE, DC, MC, V. Free parking. Tram: D. U-Bahn: Karlsplatz. **Amenities:** Restaurant; bar; pool; fitness center; room service; babysitting; laundry; dry cleaning. *In room:* A/C, TV, minibar, hair dryer, safe.

Vienna Hilton 🎯🎯 This 18-story box overlooks the Danube Canal and offers plush accommodations and elegant public areas. Despite the hotel's modernity, it manages to provide plenty of Viennese flavor. Its soaring atrium and bustling nightlife make it a vibrant home for business travelers. The hotel offers well-appointed bedrooms in a range of styles, including Biedermeier, contemporary, baroque, and Art Nouveau. Regardless of the style, the hotel offers the highest level of comfort. Because the Hilton towers over the city skyline, it also affords great views from the top floors. Its suites and executive floors provide extra comfort for frequent travelers, but standard extras in all bedrooms include shower-tub combinations and a basket of toiletries in the good-size bathrooms. The adjacent Stadtpark is connected to the hotel and the City Air Terminal by a bridge, which strollers and joggers use during excursions into the landscaped and bird-filled park.

Am Stadtpark, A-1030 Vienna. ☎ 800/445-8667 in the U.S., or 01/717000. Fax 01/7170-0339. www.hilton. com. 629 units. 155€–311€ double; from 390€ suite. AE, DC, MC, V. Parking is free. The Hilton is attached to the City Air Terminal, the drop-off point for buses coming in at frequent intervals from the airport. U-Bahn: Landstrasse. **Amenities:** 4 restaurants; 2 bars; fitness center; sauna; room service; babysitting; laundry; dry cleaning. *In room:* A/C, TV, minibar, hair dryer, safe.

EXPENSIVE

Dorint Hotel Biedermeier This hotel was established in 1983 in a reno-vated late-19th-century apartment house. It boasts a pronounced Biedermeier style in both the public areas and the bedrooms. Although the hotel is adjacent to the Wien Mitte bus station and has roaring traffic on all sides, most bedrooms overlook a pedestrian-only walkway lined with shops and cafes. Duvets cover the firm beds, and double glazing keeps the noise level down. Bathrooms are small and tiled, with fake-marble counters and mostly shower-tub combinations. On the premises are the formal restaurant Zu den Deutschmeistern and the simpler Weissgerberstube.

Landstrasser Hauptstrasse 28, A-1030 Vienna. ☎ 800/780-5734 in the U.S., or 01/716710. Fax 01/7167-1503. www.dorint.de/wien. 203 units. 179€–191€ double; 203€–299€ suite. Rates include breakfast. AE, DC, MC, V. Parking 14€. U-Bahn: Rochusgasse. **Amenities:** 3 restaurants; 2 bars; room service; babysitting; laundry; dry cleaning. *In room:* A/C, TV, minibar, hair dryer, safe.

MODERATE

Hotel-Pension Barich This spot might be the choice for guests who prefer serene residential surroundings. Northeast of the Südbahnhof, behind an unpre-tentious facade, this small hotel is quiet and well furnished. The proprietors, Ulrich and Hermine Platz, speak fluent English. Small soundproofed bedrooms have well-kept tiled bathrooms equipped with shower-tub combinations.

Barichgasse 3, A-1030 Vienna. ☎ 01/712-2275. Fax 01/7122-27588. www.nethotels.com/barich. 17 units. 99€–129€ double. Rates include buffet breakfast. AE, DC, MC, V. Parking 17€. U-Bahn: Rochusgasse. Bus: 74A. **Amenities:** Breakfast room; lounge; laundry; dry cleaning. *In room:* TV, minibar, hair dryer, safe.

(Kids) Family-Friendly Hotels

Best Western Hotel Opernring (p. 85)   For the family who'd like to lodge in a government-rated four-star hotel, this much improved property offers a number of bedrooms spacious enough to sleep three or four in comfort.

Hotel Am Shubertring (p. 86)   At this family-friendly place, parents with their kids enjoy a Ringstrasse location next to the opera in the center of Vienna. Its especially large accommodations are eagerly booked by families who also enjoy the affordable prices, with kids under 6 staying free.

Hotel Graf Stadion (p. 97)   Many rooms at this hotel—a longtime favorite of families on a tight budget—contain two double beds, suitable for parties of three or four.

Hotel Kärntnerhof (p. ###)   At this family-oriented *gutbürgerlich* hotel, right in the center of Vienna, the helpful management welcomes kids.

Hotel Mercure Josefshof (p. 98)   This Biedermeier mansion lies close to the Parliament and the English Theater in a central location. Families get a big welcome here and are housed in one of the spacious accommodations equipped with kitchenettes.

Hotel Pension Suzanne (p. 89)   At this hotel adjacent to the opera in the historic core, families are welcomed by the family owners, the Strafingers, and housed in comfort. Clients keep expenses down in Vienna by booking one of the small apartments with kitchenettes.

Hotel Römischer Kaiser (p. 83)   The former palace of the imperial chamberlain, this edifice, a Best Western affiliate, offers a glimpse of Imperial Vienna from around 1684, when it was constructed. Kids will feel like young royalty. Its staff is extremely hospitable and gracious to visiting families.

Hotel Schneider (p. 95)   Between the Wiener Staatsoper and the flower market, this is one of Vienna's best small hotels. Families rent rooms with kitchenettes to cut down on the high cost of dining in Vienna.

WIEDEN & MARGARETEN (4TH & 5TH DISTRICTS)

MODERATE

Hotel Erzherzog Rainer   Popular with groups and business travelers, this government-rated four-star, family-run hotel was built just before World War I and was gradually renovated room by room between 1992 and 1994. It's only 5 minutes by foot to the Vienna State Opera and Kärntnerstrasse, with a U-Bahn stop just steps away. The bedrooms are well decorated but come in a variety of sizes; you'll find radios and good beds, but not soundproofing, in all. Bathrooms are tiled and small, with about half equipped with both showers and tubs. The singles are impossibly small; on certain days, air-conditioning is sorely missed.

An informal brasserie serves Austrian specialties, and the cozy bar is modishly decorated with black and brass.

Wiedner Hauptstrasse 27-29, A-1040 Vienna. ℂ **01/501110.** Fax 01/5011-1350. www.schick-hotels.com. 84 units. 123€–179€ double. Rates include breakfast. AE, MC, V. Parking 17€. U-Bahn: Taubstummengasse. **Amenities:** Restaurant; bar; room service; babysitting; laundry; dry cleaning. *In room:* TV, minibar, hair dryer.

Hotel Prinz Eugen 𝒜   In a section of Vienna favored by diplomats, this hotel is immediately opposite the Belvedere Palace and the Südbahnhof rail station. Subways will carry you quickly to the center of Vienna, and there are good highway connections as well. Renovated between 1992 and 1996, the hotel has soundproof windows opening onto private balconies. The decor is a mixture of antiques, oriental rugs, and some glitzy touches like glass walls with brass trim. Suites are nothing more than slightly larger double rooms with an additional bathroom. Bedrooms come in a wide range of sizes, although all are comfortable and have firm, duvet-covered beds. Bathrooms, only fair in size, are well maintained, although 50 rooms have showers only (no tubs). The single accommodations, however, are decidedly small, suitable for one traveling light.

Wiedner Gürtel 14, A-1040 Vienna. ℂ **01/505-1741.** Fax 01/5051-74119. www.hotelprinzeugen.at. 114 units. 110€–160€ double; 121€–218€ suite. Rates include breakfast. AE, DC, DISC, MC, V. Parking 16€. U-Bahn: Südtiroler Platz or Südbahnhof. **Amenities:** Restaurant; bar; room service; babysitting; laundry; dry cleaning. *In room:* TV, minibar, hair dryer, safe.

MARIAHILF (6TH DISTRICT)
EXPENSIVE
Hotel Kummer   Established by the Kummer family in the 19th century, this hotel was built in response to the growing power of the railways as they forged new paths of commerce and tourism through central Europe. A short walk from Vienna's Westbahnhof, the hotel sits in a busy, noisy location, but looks as ornamental as any public monument constructed during those imperial days. The facade is richly embellished with Corinthian capitals on acanthus-leaf bases, urn-shape balustrades, and representations of four heroic demigods staring down from under the building's eaves. The hotel was restored and renovated in 1994.

The modern public rooms inside are not as delightful as the building's exterior, but they are satisfactory. The bedrooms have soundproof windows and often come with stone balconies. Not all rooms are alike—some feature superior appointments and deluxe furnishings. If possible, opt for a corner room—they are better lit and more spacious. Tiled bathrooms contain tubs in about half the accommodations (otherwise showers), along with vanity mirrors. Some of the singles are so small and dimly lit that they aren't recommendable.

Mariahilferstrasse 71A, A-1060 Vienna. ℂ **01/58895.** Fax 01/587-8133. www.hotelkummer.at. 100 units. 225€ double. Rates include buffet breakfast. AE, DC, MC, V. Parking 18€. U-Bahn: Neubaugasse. Bus: 13A or 14A. **Amenities:** Restaurant; bar; salon; room service; laundry; dry cleaning. *In room:* TV, minibar, hair dryer, safe.

MODERATE
Fürst Metternich Hotel 𝒜 *Finds*   Pink-and-gray paint and ornate stone window trim identify this solidly built 19th-century hotel, formally an opulent private home. It's located between the Ring and the Westbahnhof near Mariahilferstrasse, about a 20-minute walk from the cathedral. Many of the grander architectural elements were retained, including a pair of red stone columns in the entranceway and an old-fashioned staircase guarded with griffins. The high-ceilinged bedrooms have a neutral decor, with laminated furnishings and feather pillows. The partly marbled bathrooms have modern fixtures and tubs. They aren't generally roomy, however. Windows in the front units are soundproof in theory, but not in practice. If you want a more tranquil night's sleep, opt for a room in the rear. The Barfly's Club, a popular hangout open daily, offers 120 different exotic drinks.

Esterházygasse 33, A-1060 Vienna. © **01/588-70.** Fax 01/58-75-268. metternich@austrotel.at. 55 units. 131€ double; 182€–210€ suite. Rates include breakfast. AE, DC, MC, V. Parking 14€. U-Bahn: Zieglergasse. **Amenities:** Breakfast room; bar; babysitting; laundry; dry cleaning. *In room:* TV, minibar.

Hotel President   This seven-story concrete-and-glass hotel was designed in 1975 with enough angles in its facade to give each bedroom an irregular shape. Usually the units have two windows that face different skylines. Aside from the views, each of the decent-size bedrooms has comfortable furnishings and good beds. Bathrooms, though small, are well maintained, brightly lit, and equipped with shower-tub combinations. Opt for a room—really a studio with a terrace—on the seventh floor, if one is available. The hotel also has a public rooftop terrace where guests sip drinks in summer.

Wallgasse 23, A-1060 Vienna. © **800/387-8842** in the U.S., or 01/59990. Fax 01/596-7646. 77 units. 122€–204€ double; 240€ suite. Rates include buffet breakfast. AE, DC, MC, V. Parking 15€. U-Bahn: Gumpendorfer. Bus: 57A. **Amenities:** Breakfast room; bar; room service; babysitting; laundry; dry cleaning. *In room:* A/C, TV, minibar, hair dryer, safe.

Hotel Schneider 🌟 *Kids*   Sitting at the corner of a well-known street, Lehargasse, this hotel is in the center of Vienna between the Vienna State Opera and the famous Nasch Market. It's a modern five-story building with panoramic windows on the ground floor and a red-tile roof. The interior is warmly decorated with some 19th-century antiques and comfortably upholstered chairs. Musicians, singers, actors, and other artists form part of a loyal clientele. This is one of Vienna's best small hotels; families are especially fond of the place as 35 of the accommodations contain kitchenettes. All the small units have neatly kept bathrooms with shower-tub combinations. Most of the units are at the lower end of the price scale, which barely keeps this hotel in the inexpensive category—that's inexpensive in terms of Vienna.

Getreidemarkt 5, A-1060 Vienna. © **01/588380.** Fax 01/5883-8212. www.best-of-austria.com/hotel/schneider. 70 units. 130€–171€ double. Rates include buffet breakfast. AE, DC, MC, V. Parking 18€. U-Bahn: Karlsplatz. **Amenities.** Breakfast room; bar; room service; babysitting; laundry; dry cleaning. *In room:* A/C, TV, minibar, hair dryer, safe.

NEUBAU (7TH DISTRICT)
EXPENSIVE

K + K Hotel Maria Theresia 🌟   The hotel's initials are a reminder of the empire's dual monarchy (*Kaiserlich und Königlich*—"by appointment to the Emperor of Austria and King of Hungary"). Even the surrounding neighborhood, home to some major museums that lie just outside the Ring, is reminiscent of the days of Empress Maria Theresa. The hotel is in the artists' colony of Spittelberg, within walking distance of the Winter Palace gardens, the Volkstheater, and the famous shopping street Mariahilferstrasse. The hotel, built in the late 1980s, offers amply sized contemporary rooms. The beds (usually twins) are comfortable, and the medium-size bathrooms with shower-tub combinations are attractively tiled.

Kirchberggasse 6-8, A-1070 Vienna. © **800/537-8483** in the U.S., or 01/52123. Fax 01/521-2370. www.kkhotels.com. 123 units. 205€ double; from 240€ suite. Rates include breakfast. AE, DC, MC, V. Parking 14€. U-Bahn: Volkstheater. Bus: 48. **Amenities:** Restaurant; bar; room service; babysitting; laundry; dry cleaning. *In room:* A/C, TV, minibar, hair dryer, safe.

MODERATE

Pension Altstadt Vienna 🌟   A noted connoisseur of modern art, Otto Wiesenthal, converted a century-old private home into this charming and stylish hotel in the mid-1990s. Otto comes from a long line of artists. Grandmother Greta was an avant-garde opera dancer in the 1930s and 1940s and the duenna of a salon frequented by artists and writers. Works by Mr. Wiesenthal's great-great-grandfather Friedrich hang in the Vienna Historic Museum as well as the hotel. Although part of the structure remains a private home, the remainder of the building contains a series of comfortable and cozy bedrooms. Each is outfitted with a different color scheme and contains at least one work of contemporary art, usually by an Austrian painter. Many of the good-size units are a bit quirky in decor, as exemplified by a club chair in leopard prints set against a sponge-painted wall. Nearly all have high ceilings, antiques, parquet floors, double-glazed windows, and good beds. The white-tiled bathrooms are midsize, with a second phone and decent shelf space. About half of the accommodations contain a shower instead of a tub.

Kirchengasse 41, A-1070 Vienna. ✆ **01/1526-3399.** Fax 01/523-4901. hotel@altstadt.at. 36 units. 129€–149€ double; 149€–249€ suite. AE, DC, MC, V. No parking. U-Bahn: Volkstheater. **Amenities:** Breakfast room; bar; salon; room service; babysitting; laundry; dry cleaning. *In room:* TV, minibar, hair dryer, safe.

INEXPENSIVE

Hotel Ibis Wien   If you'd like a reasonably priced choice near the Westbahnhof, the main rail station, this is one of your best bets. The station itself is about an 8-minute walk away. Although this is a chain and its units are no better than a good motel in the United States, for Vienna the price is right. Behind a graceless facade that looks like a small-town department store, the Ibis Wien offers modern comforts. The furnishings, though well maintained, might not always be tasteful. One guest called the upholstery "psychedelic." The bedrooms are bland but snug and inviting, with streamlined furnishings and small, neatly kept private bathrooms with shower units. The roof terrace provides a panoramic view of Vienna. Groups are booked in here, and you'll meet all of them in the impersonal restaurant, where reasonably priced meals and wine are served. Some accommodations are suitable for persons with disabilities, and others are reserved for nonsmokers.

Mariahilfer Gurtel 22, 1060 Vienna. ✆ **01/599-98.** Fax 01/597-9090. www.accorhotels.com. 341 units. 84€ double. Parking 9.90€. U-Bahn: Gumpendorfer. **Amenities:** Restaurant; bar; room service; laundry; dry cleaning. *In room:* A/C, TV.

Hotel-Pension Museum   This hotel was originally built in the 17th century as the home of an aristocratic family. But its exterior was transformed around 1890 into the elegant Art Nouveau facade it has today. It's across from the Imperial Museums, and there are plenty of palaces, museums, and monuments nearby to keep you busy for days. Bedrooms come in a wide variety of sizes; some are spacious, while others are a bit cramped. Bathrooms are small but tiled, with shower-tub combinations and not much counter space. However, for Vienna the price is right, and this place has its devotees.

Museumstrasse 3, A-1070 Vienna. ✆ **01/5234-4260.** Fax 01/5234-42630. www.tiscover.com/hotel.museum. 15 units. 105€–120€ double. Rates include breakfast. AE, DC, MC, V. Parking 12€. U-Bahn: Volkstheater. **Amenities:** Breakfast room; lounge; room service. *In room:* TV, hair dryer.

Hotel Savoy   Built in the 1960s, this well-managed hotel rises six stories above one of Vienna's busiest wholesale and retail shopping districts. Within walking distance of Ringstrasse, opposite a recently built station for the city's newest U-Bahn line (the U3), the hotel prides itself on tastefully decorated units with good beds to make you feel at home and get a comfortable night's sleep. The small but tiled bathrooms contain only tubs. Most units offer picture-window views of the neighborhood. Although the only meal served in the hotel is breakfast, there are dozens of places to eat in the neighborhood.

Lindengasse 12, A-1070 Vienna. ℭ **01/523-4640.** Fax 01/934640. 43 units. 93€–105€ double; 120€ suite. Rates include breakfast. AE, DC, MC, V. Free parking. U-Bahn: Neubaugasse. **Amenities:** Breakfast room; lounge; room service; babysitting; laundry; dry cleaning. *In room:* TV, minibar, hair dryer, safe.

JOSEFSTADT (8TH DISTRICT)
EXPENSIVE

Cordial Theaterhotel Wien   This hotel was created from a 19th-century core that was radically modernized in the late 1980s. Today it's a favorite of Austrian business travelers, who profit from the hotel's proximity to the city's wholesale buying outlets. Each simply furnished room contains its own small but efficient kitchenette, which allows guests to save on restaurant bills. The well-maintained bedrooms, available in a variety of sizes, have good beds and adequate tiled bathrooms with shower-tub combinations. The on-site Theater-Restaurant is especially busy before and after performances next door.

Josefstadter Strasse 22, A-1080 Vienna. ℭ **01/405-3648.** Fax 01/405-1406. chwien@cordial.at. 54 units. 183€–200€ double; 248€ suite. Rates include breakfast. AE, DC, MC, V. Parking 14€. U-Bahn: Rathaus. **Amenities:** Restaurant; bar; fitness center; sauna; room service; babysitting; laundry; dry cleaning. *In room:* TV, minibar, hair dryer.

Rathauspark Hotel   A 5-minute walk from the city center, this government-rated four-star hotel stands behind an elaborate wedding cake facade, installed in an old palace dating back to 1880. The interior doesn't quite live up to the promise of the exterior, but the hotel does tastefully combine the old with the new. Guestrooms vary in size from average to spacious, and all have been updated with contemporary furnishings. Each room has a well-kept bathroom with a shower-tub combination.

Rathausstrasse 17, A-1010 Vienna. ℭ **01/404-120.** Fax 01/404-12-761. www.austria-trend.at. 117 units. 178€ double; 220€ triple; 290€ suite. AE, DC, MC, V. Rates include buffet breakfast. No parking. U-Bahn: Rathaus. **Amenities:** Breakfast room; bar; babysitting; laundry; dry cleaning. *In room:* TV, minibar, hair dryer, safe.

INEXPENSIVE

Hotel Graf Stadion ℛ *(Kids)*   This is one of the few genuine Biedermeier-style hotels left in Vienna. It's right behind the Rathaus, a 10-minute walk from most of the central monuments. The facade evokes the building's early 19th-century elegance, with triangular or half-rounded ornamentation above many of the windows. The bedrooms have been refurbished and are comfortably old-fashioned, and many are spacious enough to accommodate an extra bed for couples traveling with small children. Bathrooms are equipped with shower units and kept sparklingly clean.

Buchfeldgasse 5, A-1080 Vienna. ℭ **01/405-5284.** Fax 01/4050-111. www.graf-stadion.com. 40 units. 89€–137€ double; 111€ triple. Rates include buffet breakfast. AE, DC, MC, V. Parking 11€. U-Bahn: Rathaus. **Amenities:** Breakfast room; bar; room service; babysitting; laundry; dry cleaning. *In room:* TV, hair dryer.

Hotel Rathaus   Located behind a wrought-iron gate, Hotel Rathaus offers small bedrooms that are simple and functional. The shower-only bathrooms are just adequate, definitely designed for one person at a time; some of the singles lack bathrooms. This is a no-frills place, but because it's so well situated near the university and Parliament, and because its prices are so reasonable, we consider it a worthy choice.

Lange Gasse 13, A-1080 Vienna. ℭ **01/406-4302.** Fax 01/408-4272. 40 units, 36 with bathroom. 75€ double with bathroom. Rates include breakfast. AE, DC, MC, V. Parking 14€. U-Bahn: Lerchenfelderstrasse. Bus: 13. **Amenities:** Breakfast room; lounge. *In room:* TV, hair dryer, safe.

Hotel Zipser   A 5-minute walk from the Rathaus, this pension offers rooms with wall-to-wall carpeting and central heating, many overlooking a private garden. Much of the renovated interior is tastefully adorned with wood detailing. Generous-size bedrooms are furnished in a functional, modern style, with some opening onto balconies above the garden. Bathrooms with shower units are small, but housekeeping rates high marks.

Lange Gasse 49, A-1080 Vienna. € **01/404540.** Fax 01/404-5413. www.zipser.at. 47 units. 94€–116€ double. Rates include breakfast. AE, DC, MC, V. Parking 15€. U-Bahn: Rathaus. Bus: 13A. **Amenities:** Breakfast room; bar, lounge. *In room:* TV, hair dryer.

ALSERGRUND (9TH DISTRICT)
MODERATE
Austria Trend Hotel Albatros   A 10-minute ride from the center, this government-rated four-star choice is dull on the outside but lively inside. The well-furnished bedrooms were completely renovated in 1998. Bedrooms are midsize, with comfortable upholstery and small but efficient bathrooms with shower units.

Liechtensteinstrasse 89, A-1090 Vienna. € **01/317-35-08.** Fax 01/317-35-08-85. www.hotels-austria.com/ Vienna-josefstadt/albatros.htm. 70 units. 115€–145€ double. Rates include breakfast. AE, DC, MC, V. Parking: 13€. U-Bahn: Friedensbrücke. **Amenities:** Breakfast room; bar; sauna; laundry; dry cleaning. *In room:* A/C, TV, minibar, hair dryer, safe.

Hotel Bellevue   This hotel, with its ornate sandstone facade and Italianate embellishments, was built in 1873, at about the same time as the Franz-Josefs Bahnhof, which lies a short walk away and whose passengers it was designed to house. Its wedge-shape position on the acute angle of a busy street corner is similar to the Flatiron Building in Manhattan.

Most of the antique details have been stripped from the public rooms, leaving a clean series of lines. At least 100 of the hotel's bedrooms are in a new wing added in 1982. All bedrooms are clean, functional, and well maintained. Rooms are decorated in monochromatic color schemes of brown or blue and contain comfortable low beds and utilitarian desks and chairs. Bathrooms, most with shower-tub combinations, are midsize.

Althanstrasse 5, A-1091 Vienna. € **01/31348.** Fax 01/3134-8801. www.hotelbellevue.at. 173 units. 122€– 180€ double; from 204€ suite. Rates include breakfast. AE, DC, MC, V. Parking 7.27€. U-Bahn: Friedensbrücke. Tram: 5 or D. **Amenities:** Restaurant; bar; sauna; room service; babysitting; laundry; dry cleaning. *In room:* TV, minibar, hair dryer, safe (in most).

Hotel Mercure Josefshof ✿ *Kids*   Close to the Parliament and next to the English Theater, this Biedermeier mansion is located down a narrow cobblestone street. The hotel's gilded touches include a baroque lobby with marble checkerboard floors and a lounge brimming with antiques. Standard-size bedrooms have double-glazed windows, and a few accommodations come with kitchenettes, great for families. The corner rooms are the most spacious; bathrooms are small, however, and a dozen come with showers (no tubs). Several rooms are suitable for persons with disabilities. A lavish breakfast buffet is served in the morning and can be enjoyed in summer in an inner courtyard with plants and flowers.

Josefsgasse 4, A-1090 Vienna. € **01/404-190.** Fax 01/404-191-50. www.mercure.com. 68 units. 165€–173€ double; from 179€ suite. AE, DC, MC, V. U-Bahn: Rathaus. **Amenities:** Bar; fitness center; sauna; room service; babysitting; laundry; dry cleaning. *In room:* A/C, TV, minibar, hair dryer.

Hotel Regina   Established in 1896 near the Votive Church, this hotel has a structure that every Viennese would instantly recognize: the "Ringstrasse" style. The facade is appropriately grand, reminiscent of a French Renaissance palace.

The tree-lined street is usually calm, especially at night. The Regina is an old-world hotel with red salons and interminable corridors. Bedrooms are well maintained and traditionally furnished, some with half-canopied beds and elaborate furnishings. Despite variation in style and size, all have comfortable beds and small, well-maintained shower-only bathrooms.

Rooseveltplatz 15, A-1090 Vienna. ℂ **01/404-460.** Fax 01/408-8392. 128 units. 138€–167€ double. Rates include breakfast. AE, DC, MC, V. Parking 17€. U-Bahn: Schottenring. Tram: 1, 2, 38, 40, or 41. **Amenities:** Restaurant; bar; cafe; room service; laundry; dry cleaning. *In room:* TV, minibar, hair dryer.

NEAR SCHÖNBRUNN
EXPENSIVE

Parkhotel Schönbrunn 🅰   Called the "guesthouse of the kaisers," this government-rated four-star hotel—1½ miles from the Westbahnhof, 3 miles from the City Air Terminal—is today part of the Steigenberger reservations system. It has had a long history since Franz Joseph I ordered its construction in 1907. The first performances of *Loreleyklänge* by Johann Strauss, and of *Die Schönbrunner,* the famous Josef Lanner waltz, took place here. During the hotel's heyday, guests ranged from Thomas Edison to Walt Disney.

Today the hotel complex is modern and updated. The original part of the building is used for public rooms, which have lost some of their elegance. Contemporary wings and annexes include the Stöckl, Residenz, and Maximilian (which has the most boring and cramped rooms), together with a villa formerly inhabited by Van Swieten, the personal doctor of Empress Maria Theresa. Rooms are generally spacious and well appointed, and all accommodations have good beds. The well-furnished guest rooms are done in a variety of styles ranging from classical to modern. All are equipped with a small private bathroom with a shower-tub combination. Opposite the magical Schönbrunn Castle and its park, the hotel is only a 10-minute tram ride from the Inner City.

Hietzinger Hauptstrasse 10-20, A-1131 Vienna, ℂ 01/87804. Fax 01/0700-4322U. www.austria-trend.at. 402 units. 170€ 203€ double; 255€–330€ suite. Rates include breakfast. AE, DC, MC, V. Parking 19€. U-Bahn: Hietzing. Tram: 58 or 60. **Amenities:** 2 restaurants; 3 bars; cafe; pool; fitness center; sauna; room service; babysitting; laundry; dry cleaning. *In room:* TV, minibar, hair dryer.

INEXPENSIVE

Altwienerhof 🅰 *Finds*   This is mainly a highly acclaimed restaurant, one of the finest and most expensive in the city. But it's also a reasonably priced hotel, with traditionally furnished bedrooms, many of which were renovated in 1993. The owners, Rudolf and Ursula Kellner, and their helpful and welcoming staff carefully nurture its old-world charm. Bedrooms are quite large, with luxurious bathrooms with separate toilets. Bathrooms are equipped with mirrors, towel warmers, double tubs, and showers with an aquamassage. (See p. 99, in "Where to Dine," for a complete description of the restaurant.)

Herklotzgasse 6, A-1150 Vienna. ℂ **01/892-6000.** Fax 01/892-60-00-8. www.altwienerhof.at. 27 units. 90€ double; 131€ suite. Rates include breakfast. AE, DC, MC, V. Parking 11€. U-Bahn: Gumpendorferstrasse. Tram: 6, 8, or 18. **Amenities:** Restaurant; lounge; room service; laundry; dry cleaning. *In room:* TV.

4 Where to Dine

In Vienna, eating out is a local pastime. Befitting a historically cosmopolitan capital, Viennese restaurants serve not only Austrian and French cuisine, but also Serbian, Slovenian, Slovakian, Hungarian, and Czech, as well as Chinese, Italian, and Russian. Although meals are traditionally big and hearty, innovative chefs throughout the city are now turning out lighter versions of the old classics.

Unlike those in many western European capitals, Vienna's restaurants still heed Sunday closings (marked by SONNTAG RUHETAG signs). Also, beware of those summer holiday closings, when chefs would rather rush to nearby lake resorts than cook for Vienna's visiting hordes. However, post-theater dining is fashionable in this city, and many restaurants and cafes stay open late.

INNERE STADT (INNER CITY)
VERY EXPENSIVE

Drei Husaren ★★★ VIENNESE/INTERNATIONAL   This is a longtime favorite for inventive and classic Viennese cuisine. Some consider it as much an institution as nearby St. Stephan's Cathedral. Few social or business moguls would consider a trip to Vienna without dining here. Over the years it has entertained the famous (the Duke and Duchess of Windsor) and the not-so-famous. Just off Kärntnerstrasse, it has a large plate-glass window with plaster mannequins of the Hungarian officers who established the restaurant after World War I. A look inside reveals Gobelin tapestries, antiques, fine rugs, and lots of flowers. The owner, Uwe Kohl, is the most gracious restaurant host in Vienna.

Drei Husaran is expensive and select, with delectable cuisine rated by most as Vienna's best traditional food. Enjoy Gypsy melodies as you savor lobster cream soup with tarragon, freshwater salmon with pike soufflé, or breast of guinea fowl. The chef specializes in veal, including his deliciously flavored *Kalbsbrücken Metternich*. A renowned repertoire of more than 35 hors d'oeuvres is served from a roving cart, but if you choose to indulge, your bill is likely to double, as the hors d'oeuvres aren't priced. Finish with the *Husaren Pfannkuchen* (Hussar's pancake) or the cheese-filled crepe topped with chocolate sauce, a secret recipe that's been a favorite since the 1960s.

Weihburggasse 4. ℂ 01/512-1092. Reservations required. Main courses 16€–32€; menu dégustation (6 courses) 62€; 4-course fixed-price business lunch 32€. AE, DC, MC, V. Daily noon–3pm and 6pm–1am. U-Bahn: Stephansplatz.

Kervansaray und Hummer Bar ★★ SEAFOOD   Here you'll sense the historic link between the Hapsburgs and their 19th-century neighbor, the Ottoman Empire. On the ground floor, in the Kervansaray, polite waiters announce a changing array of daily specials and serve tempting salads from an hors d'oeuvre table. Upstairs, guests enjoy the bounties of the sea at the Lobster Bar. There's also a deli.

A meal often begins with a champagne cocktail, followed by one of many appetizers, including a lobster and salmon caviar cocktail. The menu has a short list of meat dishes like filet mignon with Roquefort sauce, but it specializes in seafood, including grilled filet of sole with fresh asparagus, Norwegian salmon with a horseradish and champagne sauce, and, of course, lobster. If shellfish is your weakness, be prepared to pay for your indulgence.

Mahlerstrasse 9. ℂ 01/512-8843. Reservations recommended. Main courses 19€–44€. AE, DC, MC, V. Restaurant Mon–Sat noon–midnight. Bar Mon–Sat 6pm–midnight. U-Bahn: Karlsplatz. Tram: 1 or 2. Bus: 3A.

König von Ungarn (King of Hungary) ★ VIENNESE/INTERNATIONAL Housed in the famous hotel of the same name, this restaurant evokes a rich atmosphere with crystal chandeliers, antiques, marble columns, and vaulted ceilings. The service is superb and the menu appealing. If you're unsure of what to order, try the *Tafelspitz* (boiled beef), elegantly dispensed from a cart. Other seasonal choices include a ragout of seafood with fresh mushrooms, tournedos of beef with a mustard-and-horseradish sauce, and appetizers like scampi in caviar sauce. Chefs balance flavors, textures, and colors to create a cuisine that's long been favored by locals, who often bring out-of-town guests here.

Schulerstrasse 10. © **01/512-5319.** Reservations required. Main courses 14€–18€; fixed-price menu 34€ at lunch, 39€ at dinner. AE, DC, MC, V. Mon–Fri noon–2:30pm and 6–10:30pm. U-Bahn: Stephansplatz. Bus: 1A.

Korso bei der Oper ★★★ VIENNESE/INTERNATIONAL This chic and glittering choice is decorated with tasteful paneling, sparkling chandeliers, and, flanking either side of a baronial fireplace, two of the most breathtaking baroque columns in Vienna. Set in the elegant Hotel Bristol, the restaurant has its own entrance directly across from the Staatsoper, a position that has always attracted a legendary clientele of opera stars.

The kitchen concocts an alluring mixture of traditional and modern cuisine for discriminating palates. Your meal might feature filet of char with a sorrel sauce, saddle of veal with cepe mushrooms and homemade noodles, or the inevitable *Tafelspitz* (boiled beef). The rack of lamb is excellent, as are the medallions of beef with a shallot-infused butter sauce and Roquefort-flavored noodles. The wine list is extensive, and the service, as you'd expect, is impeccable.

In the Hotel Bristol, Kärntneering 1. © **01/5151-6546.** Reservations required. Main courses 23€–36€; fixed-price menu 38€ at lunch, 72€ at dinner. AE, DC, MC, V. Sun–Fri noon–2pm; daily 7–11pm. U-Bahn: Karlsplatz. Tram: 1 or 2.

Mörwald ★★★ VIENNESE In the Hotel Ambassador, this is the most stylish and one of the best restaurants in Vienna. Bankers, diplomats, and what one local food critic called "Helmut Lang–clad hipsters" show up here not only to see and be seen, but also to enjoy the delectable modern Viennese cuisine of Christian Domschitz. He's shown a genius for giving classic Viennese dishes a modern twist. Prepared with élan and precision, some of his best dishes include saddle of suckling pig with white cabbage dumplings, veal meat loaf with pureed spring onions, and a spicy brook char, one of the best fish offerings. You might start with his velvety smooth foie gras in Kirschwasser. For dessert, we recommend the diced semolina pancakes, which sound ordinary but aren't, as they are served with a spicy apple compote and feather dumplings with a *fromage blanc* (white cheese).

In the Hotel Ambassador, Kärntnerstrasse Strasse 22. © **01/961-61-0.** Reservations required. Main courses 21€–27€. AE, DC, MC, V. Mon–Sat noon–3pm and 6:30–11pm. U-Bahn: Stephansplatz.

Sacher Hotel Restaurant ★ AUSTRIAN/VIENNESE/INTERNATIONAL Most celebrities who visit Vienna are eventually spotted in this scarlet dining room, most likely enjoying the restaurant's most famous dish, *Tafelspitz*. The chef at Sacher prepares the boiled beef ensemble with a savory, herb-flavored sauce that is truly fit for the emperor's table. Other delectable dishes include fish terrine and veal steak with morels. For dessert, the Sacher torte enjoys world renown. It's primarily a chocolate sponge cake that's sliced in half and filled with apricot jam. This most famous of pastries in Vienna was supposedly created in 1832 by Franz Sacher when he served as Prince Metternich's apprentice.

Come dressed to the nines, and make sure to show up before 11pm, even though the restaurant officially closes at 1am. Despite the adherence to form and protocol here, latecomers will never go hungry, as the hotel maintains tables in the adjoining and less formal Red Bar, where the menu is available every day from noon to 11:30pm (last order). The Sacher has always been a favorite for dinner either before or after the opera.

Philharmonikerstrasse 4. © **01/514560.** Reservations required. Main courses 18€–29€. AE, DC, MC, V. Daily noon–3pm and 6–11:30pm. U-Bahn: Karlsplatz.

Vienna Dining

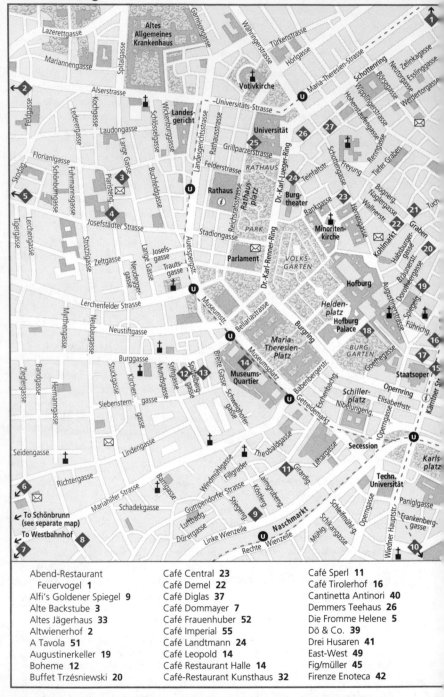

Abend-Restaurant Feuervogel **1**	Café Central **23**	Café Sperl **11**
Alfi's Goldener Spiegel **9**	Café Demel **22**	Café Tirolerhof **16**
Alte Backstube **3**	Café Diglas **37**	Cantinetta Antinori **40**
Altes Jägerhaus **33**	Café Dommayer **7**	Demmers Teehaus **26**
Altwienerhof **2**	Café Frauenhuber **52**	Die Fromme Helene **5**
A Tavola **51**	Café Imperial **55**	Dö & Co. **39**
Augustinerkeller **19**	Café Landtmann **24**	Drei Husaren **41**
Boheme **12**	Café Leopold **14**	East-West **49**
Buffet Trzésniewski **20**	Café Restaurant Halle **14**	Fig/müller **45**
	Café-Restaurant Kunsthaus **32**	Firenze Enoteca **42**

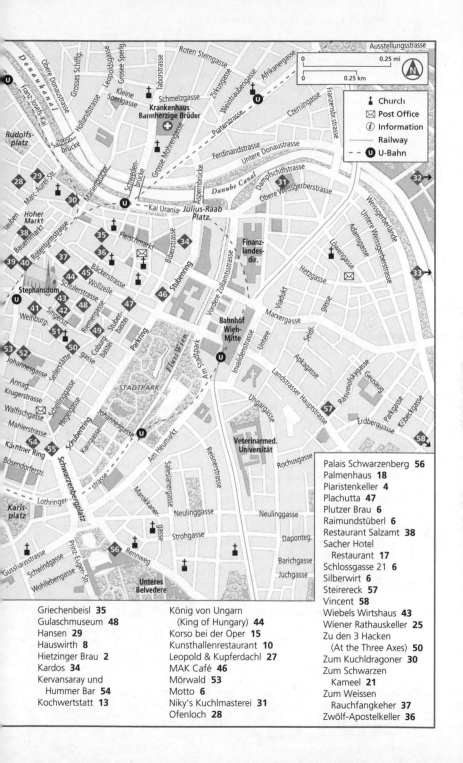

Map labels:

Ausstellungstrasse
Roten Sterngasse
Obere Donaustrasse
Grosses Schiff
Leopoldsgasse
Grosse Sperlg.
Taborstrasse
Zirkusgasse
Weintraubengasse
Afrikanergasse
Donaukanal
Franz-Josefs-Kai
Hollandstrasse
Kleine Sperlgasse
Schmelzgasse
Krankenhaus Barmherzige Brüder
Weintraubengasse
Praterstrasse
Czerningasse
Franzensbr.strasse
Rudolfs-platz
Salztor-brücke
Grosse Mohrengasse
Ferdinandstrasse
Untere Donaustrasse
Dampfschiffstrasse

Legend:
- 0.25 mi / 0.25 km
- ♱ Church
- ✉ Post Office
- ① Information
- ───── Railway
- – – ⓤ U-Bahn

Marc-Aurel-Str.
Hoher Markt
Bauernmarkt
Rotenturmstrasse
Fleischmarkt
Biberstrasse
Stubenring
Vordere Zollamtsstrasse
Danube Canal
Aspernbrücke
Schweden-brücke
Maria Hilferstr.
Kai Urania
Julius-Raab Platz
Obere Weissgerberstrasse
Weissgerberlände
Untere Weissgerberstrasse
Adamsgasse
Löwengasse
Finanzlandes-dir.
Hetzgasse

Stephansdom
Bäckerstrasse
Wollzeile
Schulerstrasse
Singerstr.
Riemergasse
Weihburg-
Coburg-bastei
Stuben-bastei
Parkring
Marxergasse
Viadukt
gasse
Seidl-
Bahnhöf Wien-Mitte
Untere
Invalidenstrasse
Apkagasse
Landstrasser Hauptstrasse
Resumofskygasse
Geusaug.
Parkgasse
Klibeckgasse
Erdberggasse
Johannesgasse
Sellerstätte gasse
Annag.
Krugerstrasse
Walfischgasse
Mahlerstrasse
Schellinggasse
Hegelgasse
Johannesgasse
STADTPARK
Am Heumarkt
Am Stadtpark
Fluss Wien
Ungargasse
Rochusgasse
Veterinärmed. Universität
Reisnerstrasse

Kärntner Ring
Bösendorferstr.
Schwarzenbergplatz
Kärntgasse
Lothringer-strasse
Salesianergasse
Marokkaner-gasse
Neulinggasse
Neulinggasse
Strohgasse
Daponteg.
Barichgasse
Juchgasse
Karls-platz
Gusshausstrasse
Schwindgasse
Wohllebengasse
Prinz-Eugen-Str.
Rennweg
Unteres Belvedere

EXPENSIVE

Dö & Co. ✸ CONTINENTAL/INTERNATIONAL   Stylish, upscale, and rather expensive, this restaurant attracts a purely Viennese clientele and very few visitors. This derives partly from its ownership by one of Austria's most esoteric food stores and partly from its inconvenient location on the seventh floor of the aggressively ultra-modern Haas Haus, which stands in jarring proximity to Vienna's cathedral. You'll navigate your way through somewhat claustrophobic passageways past a vigilant maître d'hôtel, who will lead you to tables with views of an immaculate showcase kitchen on one side and the city's historic core on the other. Menu items change with the season, but considering the rarefied nature of the organization that's presenting it, each is appropriately esoteric, rare, and unusual. Examples include Uruguayan beef, Austrian venison, grilled Norwegian baby turbot, deep-fried monkfish, and carpaccio parmigiana, as well as such traditional Austrian specialties as *Tafelspitz* and Wiener schnitzel. There's also a repertoire of Thai dishes, including crispy pork salad, red curried chicken, and sweet-and-sour red snapper. And there's a "wok buffet," wherein you assemble the ingredients for your meal on a plate and then deliver it to a uniformed chef who will quick-sear it for you with whatever sauces you want.

In the Haas Haus, Stephansplatz 4. ⓒ **01/512-26-66.** Reservations recommended. Main courses 8€–14€. V. Daily noon–3pm and 6pm–midnight. U-Bahn: Stephansplatz.

Leopold & Kupferdachl ✸ VIENNESE/AUSTRIAN   Run by the Leopold family since the 1950s, this choice is known for "new Austrian" cuisine, although the chef does prepare traditional dishes. Recommended menu items include beef tenderloin (Old Viennese style) with dumplings boiled in a napkin, lamb loin breaded and served with potatoes, and chicken breast Kiev. The interior is both rustic and elegant, decorated with oriental rugs and cozy banquettes with intricate straight-back chairs. The restaurant operates a beer pub, with good music and better prices: A large beer begins at 3€, and main courses are 4€ to 12€. The pub is open daily from 10am to midnight.

Schottengasse 7. ⓒ **01/533-9381.** Reservations recommended. Main courses 7.80€–18€. AE, DC, MC, V. Mon–Fri 10am–3pm; Mon–Sat 6pm–midnight. U-Bahn: Schottentor 7. Tram: 2, 43, or 44.

Plachutta ✸ VIENNESE   Few restaurants have built such a fetish around one dish as Plachutta has done with *Tafelspitz,* offering 10 different variations of the boiled beef dish that was the favorite of Emperor Franz Josef throughout his prolonged reign. The differences between the versions are a function of the cut of beef you request. We recommend *Schulterscherzel* (shoulder of beef) and *Beinfleisch* (shank of beef), but if you're in doubt, the waitstaff is endlessly knowledgeable about one of the most oft-debated subjects in Viennese cuisine. Hash brown potatoes, chives, and an appealing mixture of horseradish and chopped apples accompanies each *Tafelspitz* dish. There's more on the menu here than boiled beef. Other Viennese staples include goulash soup, grilled or sautéed fish, calves' liver, fried Viennese chicken, and braised pork with cabbage.

Wollzeile 10. ⓒ **01/512-1577.** Reservations recommended. Main courses 13€–25€. DC, MC, V. Daily 11:30am–11:15pm. U-Bahn: Stubentor.

Wiebels Wirtshaus ✸ *Finds* AUSTRIAN   There are only two rooms (and about 40 seats) within this wood-paneled restaurant, each on a separate floor of a building whose age is estimated at around 400 years old. During clement weather, another 30 seats become available within a garden in back. But don't be fooled by the unpretentious and cozy feel to this place, which at first glance might look like a simple tavern. Food is considerably better than the *Wirtshaus* (tavern) appellation implies, and the clientele is a lot more upscale than the usual wurst-with-potatoes-and-beer crowd. Former clients have included the mayor of Vienna, and the wine list, with more than 250 varieties of Austrian wine, looks like a patriotic, pro-Austrian statement in its own right. Menu items change seasonally, but during our visit it included pumpkinseed soup; a cold and peppery version of *Tafelspitz* (the boiled beef with potatoes and horseradish), served as an appetizer; sliced breast of duck with lentils; well-prepared schnitzels of veal and chicken; braised roulades of beef; and a superb saddle of lamb with polenta and spinach.

Kumpfgasse 2. ℂ 01/512-3986. Reservations recommended. Main courses 13€–21€; set-price menus 29€–36€. AE, MC, V. Mon–Sat 11:30am–midnight. U-Bahn: Stephansplatz.

Wiener Rathauskeller ⋆⋆ VIENNESE/INTERNATIONAL City halls throughout the Teutonic world have traditionally maintained restaurants in their basements, and Vienna is no exception. Although Vienna's famous Rathaus was built between 1871 and 1883, its cellar-level restaurant wasn't added until 1899. Today, in half a dozen richly atmospheric dining rooms, with high vaulted ceilings and stained-glass windows, you can enjoy good and reasonably priced food. The chef's specialty is a *Rathauskellerplatte* for two, consisting of various cuts of meat, including a veal schnitzel, lamb cutlets, and pork medallions. One section of the cellar is devoted every evening to a Viennese musical soirée beginning at 8pm. Live musicians ramble through the world of operetta, waltz, and *Schrammel* (traditional Viennese music) as you dine.

Rathausplatz 1. ℂ 01/4051-2190. Reservations required. Main courses 13€–19€; Vienna music evening with dinner (Tues–Sat at 8pm) 36€. AE, DC, MC, V. Mon–Sat 11:30am–3pm and 6–11pm. U-Bahn: Rathaus.

MODERATE

Cantinetta Antinori ⋆ TUSCAN This is one of three European restaurants run by the Antinori family, who own Tuscan vineyards and whose name is nearly synonymous with Chianti. The traditions and aesthetics of the original restaurant, in Florence, have been reproduced here to showcase Antinori wines and the culinary zest of Tuscany. Within a 140-year-old building overlooking the Stephansplatz and the cathedral, you'll find a high-ceilinged dining room, as well as a greenhouse-style "Winter garden" that transports you straight to Tuscany. Start off with an order of *antipasti tipico,* a medley of marinated vegetables and seafood arranged by the staff. This might be followed with a sumptuous ravioli stuffed with porcini mushrooms and summer truffles or perfectly grilled lamb steaks with sun-dried tomatoes and Mediterranean herbs. *Panna cotta,* a creamy flan, is a simple but flavorful way to finish a meal. A huge selection of wines is served by the glass.

3–5 Jasomirgottstrasse. ℂ 01/533-7722. Reservations required. Main courses 14€–24€. AE, DC, MC, V. Daily 11:30am–11pm. U-Bahn: Stephansplatz.

Firenze Enoteca ⋆⋆ TUSCAN/ITALIAN This is one of Vienna's premier Italian restaurants. Located near St. Stephan's next to the Royal Hotel, it's furnished in Tuscan Renaissance style, with frescoes by Benozzo Gozzoli. The kitchen specializes in homemade pasta served with zesty sauces. According to the chef, the cuisine is "80% Tuscan, 20% from the rest of Italy." Start with selections from the antipasti table, and then choose among spaghetti with "fruits of the sea"; penne with salmon; veal cutlet with ham, cheese, and sardines; or perhaps filet mignon in a tomato-garlic sauce. Be sure to complement any meal here with a classic bottle of Chianti.

Singerstrasse 3. ⓒ **01/513-4374.** Reservations recommended. Main courses 8€–26€. AE, DC, MC, V. Daily noon–2pm and 6–11pm. U-Bahn: Stephansplatz.

Griechenbeisl AUSTRIAN   Astonishingly, Griechenbeisl was established in 1450 and is still one of the city's leading restaurants. There's a maze of dining areas on three different floors, all with low vaulted ceilings, smoky paneling, and wrought-iron chandeliers. Watch out for the Styrian-vested waiters who scurry around with large trays of food. As you enter, look down at the grate under your feet for an illuminated view of a pirate counting his money. Inside, check out the so-called inner sanctum, with signatures of former patrons like Mozart, Beethoven, and Mark Twain. The Pilsen beer is well chilled, and the food is hearty and ample. Menu items include deer stew, Hungarian and Viennese goulash, sauerkraut garni, and venison steak. As an added treat, the restaurant features nighttime accordion and zither music.

Fleischmarkt 11. ⓒ **01/533-1941.** Reservations required. Main courses 14€–22€; fixed-price menu 23€–40€. AE, DC, MC, V. Daily 11am–1am (last orders at 11:30pm). Tram: N , 1, 2, or 21.

Ofenloch VIENNESE   Viennese have frequented this spot since the 1600s, when it functioned as a simple tavern. The present management dates from the mid-1970s and maintains a well-deserved reputation for its nostalgic, old-fashioned eating house. Waitresses wear classic Austrian regalia and will give you a menu that looks more like a magazine, with some amusing mock-medieval illustrations inside. The hearty soup dishes are popular, as is the schnitzel. For smaller appetites, the menu offers salads and cheese platters, plus an entire page devoted to one-dish meals. For dessert, choose from old-style Viennese specialties.

Kurrentgasse 8. ⓒ **01/533-8844.** Reservations required. Main courses 11€–17€. AE, DC, MC, V. Tues–Sat 11:30am–11pm. U-Bahn: Stephansplatz. Bus: 1A.

Zum Schwarzen Kameel (Stiebitz) INTERNATIONAL   This restaurant has remained in the same family since 1618. A delicatessen against one of the walls sells wine, liquor, and specialty meat items, although most of the action takes place among the chic clientele in the cafe. On Saturday mornings, the cafe is packed with weekend Viennese trying to recover from a late night. Uniformed waiters will bring you a beverage here, and you can select open-face sandwiches from the trays on the black countertops.

Beyond the cafe is a perfectly preserved Art Deco dining room where jeweled copper chandeliers hang from beaded strings. The walls are a combination of polished paneling, yellowed ceramic tiles, and a dusky plaster ceiling frieze of grape leaves. The restaurant has just 11 tables, but it's a perfect place for a nostalgic

---

Tips Picnic Paradise

The best and least expensive place to stock up for a picnic is the **Naschmarkt,** an open-air market that's only a 5-minute stroll from Karl-splatz (the nearest U-Bahn stop). Hundreds of stalls sell fresh produce, breads, meats, cheeses, flowers, tea, and more. Fast-food counters and other stands peddle ready-made foods like grilled chicken, Austrian and German sausages, sandwiches, and beer. The market is open Monday through Friday from 6am to 6:30pm and Saturday from 6am to 1pm.

Great places to picnic are the Stadtpark or the Volksgarten, each lying on the famous Ring. Even better, if the weather is right, plan an excursion to the Vienna Woods.

Dining on the Danube

In summer the Viennese flock to the Danube to dine in one of 20 or 30 restaurants on the river. Our pick of the lot is **Taverna La Carabela/La Carabelita,** Donauinsein (no phone).

This is one of the most appealing of the 20 or so restaurants that lure the Viennese out to "Danube Island" on summer evenings. Designed like an octagonal, rough-hewn *bohio* you might have expected beside a beach in Mexico, it floats on pontoons in the Danube, connected to the "mainland" with a rustic-looking gangplank. No one will mind if you just hang out with a "Danube Waltz" made from gin, blue curaçao, and seltzer. But if you want to remain for a plate of Peruvian or South American food, there's a menu that lists calamari, chicken wings with Mexican-style red sauce, chili con carne, tacos, and burgers. Staff here is an engaging blend of Austrian and Hispanic (usually from Venezuela and Colombia), and recorded versions of salsa and merengue help you forget, at least for the moment, that you're actually deep in the heart of central Europe. Most cocktails cost from 5€ to 8€. Reservations are not accepted, and main courses go from 6€ to 10€. It's open from May to September only, Monday through Friday from 6pm to 4am, and Saturday and Sunday from 4pm to 5am.

lunch in Vienna. The hearty and well-flavored cuisine features herring filet Oslo, potato soup, tournedos, Roman *saltimbocca* (veal with ham), and an array of daily fish specials.

Bognergasse 5. (℃) **01/533-8125.** Main courses 13€–25€. AE, DC, MC, V. Mon–Sat 8:30am–3pm and 6–10:30pm. U-Bahn: Schottentor. Bus: 2A or 3A.

Zum Weissen Rauchfangkehrer VIENNESE   Established in the 1860s, this dinner-only place is the former guildhall for Vienna's chimney sweeps. In fact, the restaurant's name (translated as the "white chimney sweep") comes from the story of a drunken and blackened chimney sweep who fell into a kneading trough and woke up the next day covered in flour. The dining room is rustic, with deer antlers, fanciful chandeliers, and pine banquettes that vaguely resemble church pews. A piano in one of the inner rooms provides nighttime music and adds to the comfortable ambience. Big street-level windows let in lots of light. The hearty, flavorful menu offers Viennese fried chicken, both Tyrolean and Wiener schnitzel, wild game, veal goulash, bratwurst, and several kinds of strudel. You'll certainly want to finish with the house specialty, a fabulously rich chocolate cream puff.

Weihburggasse 4. (℃) **01/512-3471.** Reservations required. Main courses 15€–26€. DC, MC, V. Tues–Sat 5pm–1am. Closed: July 15–Aug 13. U-Bahn: Stephansplatz.

INEXPENSIVE

A Tavola (℞ (Kids) ITALIAN/TUSCAN   This well-managed and likable restaurant occupies the 14th-century site of a much-venerated restaurant (Stadtkrug), which had for generations been favored by visiting artists such as Leonard Bernstein. Today mostly Tuscan cuisine is served in an informal but smoothly run venue that's fast becoming a local favorite. Start your meal with a well-rounded medley of vegetable and seafood antipasti, one of the most appealing selections in the neighborhood. Favorite pastas are penne with eggplant and tomatoes, risotto with mushrooms, and gnocchi with three or four kinds of cheeses, depending on the mood of the chef. Other dishes include entrecôte of beef and a well-prepared sea bass.

Weihburggasse 3–5. ℭ **01/512-7955.** Reservations required. Main courses 8€–16€. AE, DC, MC, V. Mon–Sat 12–3pm and 6–11pm. U-Bahn: Stephansplatz.

Augustinerkeller AUSTRIAN   Since 1857, the Augustinerkeller has served wine, beer, and food from the basement of one of the grand Hofburg palaces. It attracts a lively and diverse crowd that gets more boisterous as the *Schrammel* music is played late into the night. The vaulted brick room, with worn pine-board floors and wooden banquettes, is an inviting place to grab a drink and a simple meal. Be aware that this long and narrow dining room is usually as packed with people as it is with character. Roaming accordion players add to the festive atmosphere. An upstairs room is quieter and less crowded. This place offers one of the best values for wine tasting in Vienna. The ground-floor lobby lists prices of vintage local wines by the glass. Tasters can sample from hundreds of bottles near the stand-up stainless-steel counter. Aside from the wine and beer, the kitchen serves simple food, including roast chicken, schnitzel, and *Tafelspitz*.

Augustinerstrasse 1. ℭ **01/533-1026.** Main courses 8€–15€. AE, DC, MC, V. Daily 11am–midnight. U-Bahn: Stephansplatz.

Buffet Trzésniewski ℛ SANDWICHES   Everyone in Vienna, from the most hurried office worker to the most elite hostess, knows about this spot. Franz Kafka lived next door and used to come here for sandwiches and beer. It's unlike any buffet you've seen, with six or seven cramped tables and a rapidly moving line of people, all jostling for space next to the glass counters. Indicate to the waitress the kind of sandwich you want (if you can't read German, just point). Most people hurriedly devour the delicious finger sandwiches, which come in 18 different combinations of cream cheese, egg, onion, salami, mushroom, herring, green and red peppers, tomatoes, lobster, and many other tasty ingredients. You can also order small glasses of fruit juice, beer, or wine with your snack. If you do order a drink, the cashier will give you a rubber token, which you'll present to the person at the far end of the counter.

Dorotheergasse 1. ℭ **01/512-3291.** Reservations not accepted. Sandwiches .80€. No credit cards. Mon–Fri 9:30am–7:30pm; Sat 9am–5pm. U-Bahn: Stephansplatz.

Café Leopold ℛ INTERNATIONAL   Even before it was built, everyone expected that the cafe and restaurant within one of Vienna's newest museums would be trend-setting. And indeed, critics have defined the place as a post-modern version, in architectural form, of the Viennese Expressionist paintings (including many by Egon Schiele) that are exhibited within the museum that contain it. Set one floor above street level in the Leopold Museum, and with a schedule that operates long after the museum is closed for the night, it's sheathed in the same pale pink sandstone as the museum's exterior, but enhanced with three tones (jet black, "Sahara cream," and russet) of marble. There's a mini-malist-looking oak-trimmed bar, huge windows, vague and much-simplified references to 18th-century baroque architecture, and a chandelier that cynics say looks like a lost UFO suspended from the ceiling. During the day, the place functions as a conventional cafe and restaurant, serving a postmodern blend of *mitteleuropäische* (central European) and Asian food. (Examples include roasted shoulder of veal with Mediterranean vegetables, roulades of beef, roasted chicken, Thai curries, Vietnamese spring rolls, and arugula-studded risottos.) Three nights a week, however, from around 10pm till at least 2am, any hints of kitsch and coziness are banished as soon as a DJ begins cranking out dance tunes for a hard-drinking denizens-of-the-night crowd. For more on this cafe's role as a nightclub, see "Vienna After Dark" (in chapter 4).

In the Leopold Museum, Museumsplatz 1. 𝄞 01/523-67-32. Reservations not necessary. Main courses 4.50€–11€; 2-course set-price menu 8.50€. AE, DC, MC, V. Daily 9am-2am. U-Bahn: Volkstheater or Babenbergstrasse/MuseumsQuartier.

Café Restaurant Halle INTERNATIONAL   Set within the Kunsthalle, this is the direct competitor of the also-recommended Café Leopold, which lies in the Leopold Museum, a very short distance away. Larger and with a more sophisticated menu than the Café Leopold, but without any of its late-night emphasis on disco, it's a postmodern, airy, big-windowed quartet of wood-trimmed, cream-color rooms. The menu changes every 2 weeks, and service is efficient, conscientious, and in the old-world style. The first thing you'll see when you enter is a spartan-looking cafe area, with a trio of more formal dining rooms at the top of a short flight of stairs. Despite the commitment of its staff to changing the *carte* very frequently, the menu will always contain a half-dozen meal-size salads, many garnished with strips of steak, chicken, or shrimp; two daily homemade soups; and a rotating series of platters that, on the day of our last visit, included tasty braised filets of shark and roasted lamb, prepared delectably in the Greek style, with yogurt-and-herb dressing.

In the Kunsthalle Wien, Museumsplatz 1, in the MuseumsQuartier. 𝄞 01/523-7001. Reservations not necessary. Main courses 6€–15€. MC, V. U-Bahn: MuseumsQuartier.

East-West ASIAN   Established in 1999, this is the first pan-Asian restaurant to open within the Ring. As such, it's favored by business travelers interested in impressing their Asian clients. It's outfitted in a streamlined, monochromatic, and wood-trimmed design that you might imagine as a blend of contemporary Japanese, Chinese, and Thai architecture. The menu divides its food into dishes deriving from the north, south, west, and east of Asia, with other sections devoted to the mountains of central Asia and traditional Chinese dishes already known to most Western diners. Examples of unusual, relatively modern dishes include ginger-pepper chicken nuggets in rice wine sauce; the "Malaysian triangle" (three different preparations of pork in a satay sauce); glass-noodle salad with cucumbers, chicken, and sesame; the "Golden age of Siam" (chicken with red and green peppers and red coconut curry); and Marco Polo beef (spicy beef with scallions served on a hot stone).

Seilerstätte 14. 𝄞 01/512-9149. Reservations recommended. Main courses 9.50€–13€; fixed-price menu from 5€. AE, DC, MC, V. Daily 11:30am-2:30pm and 5:30-11pm. U-Bahn: Stephansplatz.

Figlmüller AUSTRIAN   This is the newest (2001) branch of a wine tavern whose original home lies only a few blocks away, at Wollzeille 5 (𝄞 01/512-6177) and which was established in 1905. This new branch, thanks to a location on three floors of a thick-walled 200-year-old building, and thanks to lots of old-world memorabilia attached to the walls, evokes Old Vienna with style and panache. Austrian Airlines referred to its black-and-white uniformed waiters as "unflappable," and we believe that its schnitzels are the kind of plate-filling, golden-brown delicacies that people always associate with schmaltzy Vienna. Menu items include goulash soup, the above-mentioned Weiner schnitzel, onion-flavored roast beef, Vienna-style fried chicken, and strudels. During mushroom season (autumn and early winter), expect varied dishes featuring mushrooms, perhaps most deliciously served in an herbed cream sauce over noodles. This restaurant's nearby twin, at Wollzeile 5 ((C) **01/512-6177**), offers basically the same menu at the same prices and the same richly nostalgic wine-tavern ambience.

Bäckerstrasse 6. (C) 01/512-1760. Reservations recommended. Main courses 7€–15€. AE, DC, MC, V. Daily 11am–11:30pm. Closed Aug. U-Bahn: Stephansplatz.

Gulaschmuseum 🔆 *Kids* AUSTRIAN/HUNGARIAN   If you thought that goulash was available in only one form, think again. This restaurant celebrates at least 15 varieties of it, each an authentic survivor of the culinary traditions of Hungary, and each redolent with the taste of the national spice, paprika. The Viennese adopted goulash from their former vassal centuries ago and have long since added it to their culinary repertoire. You can order versions of goulash made with roast beef, veal, pork, or even fried chicken livers. Vegetarians rejoice: Versions made with potatoes, beans, or mushrooms are also available. Boiled potatoes and rough-textured brown or black bread will usually accompany your choice. An excellent starter is the Magyar national crepe, *Hortobágy Palatschinken*, stuffed with minced beef and paprika-flavored cream sauce. If you prefer an Austrian dish, there's *Tafelspitz*, Wiener schnitzel, fresh fish from Austria's lakes, and such dessert specialties as homemade *Apfelstrudel* (apple strudel) and Sacher torte.

Schulerstrasse 20. (C) **01/512-1017**. Reservations recommended. Main courses 6€–12€. MC, V. Mon–Fri 9am–midnight; Sat–Sun 10am–midnight. U-Bahn: Wollzeile or Stephansplatz.

Hansen 🔆 MEDITERRANEAN/INTERNATIONAL/ASIAN   One of the most intriguing and stylish restaurants in Vienna opened as a partnership between a time-tested culinary team and the downtown showrooms of one of Austria's most famous horticulturists and gardening stores (Lederleitner, GmbH). You'll find them cheek-by-jowl in the vaulted cellars of Vienna's stock exchange, a beaux-arts pile designed in the 1890s by the restaurant's namesake, Theophile Hansen. Part of the charm of this place involves trekking through masses of plants and elaborate garden ornaments on your way to your dining table. Expect to be joined by the movers and shakers of corporate Vienna at lunch and at relatively early dinners, when the place is likely to be very busy. Choose from a small but savory menu that changes every week. Examples include a spicy bean salad with strips of chicken breast served in a summer broth, lukewarm vegetable salad with curry and wild greens, clear salmon soup with tofu, risotto with cheese and sour cherries, pork filet with butter beans and wild-berry relish, and poached *Saibling* (something akin to trout from the coldwater streams of the Austrian Alps) with a potato and celery puree and watercress.

In the cellar of the Börsegebäude (Vienna Stock Exchange), Wipplingerstrasse 34 at the Schottenring. (C) 01/532-05-42. Reservations recommended. Main courses 8€–17€. AE, DC, MC, V. Mon–Fri 9am–8pm (last order); Sat 9am–3pm (last order). U-Bahn: Schottenring.

Kardos HUNGARIAN/SLOVENIAN/AUSTRIAN   This folkloric restaurant specializes in the strong flavors and potent traditions that developed in different parts of what used to be the Austro-Hungarian empire. Similarly, the setting celebrates the idiosyncratic folklore of various regions of the Balkans and the Great Hungarian Plain. Newcomers are welcomed with piquant little rolls known as *Grammel*, seasoned with minced pork and spices, and a choice of grilled meats. Other specialties include Hungarian *Fogosch* (a form of pike perch) that's baked with vegetables and parsley potatoes; Hungarian goulash; and braised cabbage.

The cellar atmosphere is Gypsy schmaltz—pine-wood accents and brightly colored Hungarian accessories. During the winter, you're likely to find a strolling violinist. To begin, try a glass of *Barack,* an apéritif made from fermented apricots.

Dominikaner Bastei 8. Ⓒ **01/512-6949.** Reservations recommended. Main courses 5.50€–14€. AE, DC, MC, V. Mon–Sat 11am–2:30pm and 6pm–midnight. Closed Aug. U-Bahn: Schwedenplatz.

Kunsthallenrestaurant CONTINENTAL There's nothing particularly beautiful about this restaurant, but it's associated with one of Vienna's most respected repositories of modern art. For at least a decade, this restaurant was housed in a prefabricated metal annex to the museum, reminiscent of an oversize metallic shoebox and painted a vivid shade of orange. All of that changed around 2000, when a more tasteful glass-sided addition was built, adding a new sense of solidity and permanency. The staff here is congenial, the food is well prepared, and the other clients are highly likely to have a deeper-than-the-norm appreciation for modern art. Menu items include simple versions of homemade soups, vegetarian dishes, roulades of beef, succulent veal or roast chicken, a very satisfying roast pork, and, on most days, an intriguing roster of fresh vegetables.

Treitlstrasse 2. Ⓒ **01/586-9864.** Reservations not necessary. Main courses 4€–15€. No credit cards. Daily 10am–2am. U-Bahn: Karlsplatz.

MAK Café CONTINENTAL Of the many restaurants within Vienna's museums, this is the most unusual and the most sought after. It occupies an enormous and echoing room on the MAK museum's street level, beneath an elaborately coffered and painted late-19th-century ceiling. In deliberate contrast, the restaurant's tables, chairs, and accessories are artfully minimalist. You can opt for Czech, Swedish, Hungarian, or Austrian dishes. Examples include a savory *bollito misto* (a medley of boiled meats), stuffed breast of chicken with spinach, carpaccio with Parmesan cheese, roast duck with orange sauce, and an unusual selection of pirogies, the stuffed potato dumplings native to Poland and Russia.

In the Österreichisches Museum für Angewandte Kunst (MAK), Stubenring 5. Ⓒ **01/714-0121.** Reservations not necessary. Main courses 6.50€–16€. No credit cards. Tues–Sun 10am–midnight. U-Bahn: Stubentor.

Palmenhaus AUSTRIAN Many architectural critics consider the Jugendstil glass canopy of this greenhouse the most beautiful in Austria. Overlooking the formal terraces of the Burggarten, it was built between 1901 and 1904 by the Hapsburgs' court architect Friedrich Ohmann as a graceful architectural transition between the Albertina and the National Library. Damaged during wartime bombings, it was restored in 1998. Today, its central section functions as a chic cafe and, despite the lavishly historic setting, an appealingly informal venue. No one will mind if you drop in just for a drink and one of the voluptuous pastries displayed near the entrance. But if you want a meal, there's a sophisticated menu that changes monthly and that might include fresh Austrian goat cheese with stewed peppers and zucchini salad; young herring with sour cream, horseradish, and deep-fried beignets stuffed with apples and cabbage; squash blossoms stuffed with salmon mousse; breast of chicken layered with goose liver and served with a port-flavored mango glaze; and "various sorts of marine fish from the grill."

In the Burggarten. Ⓒ **01/533-1033.** Reservations recommended for dinner. Main courses 4€–15€; pastries 3€–3.80€. AE, DC, MC. V. Daily 10am–2am. U-Bahn: Opera.

Restaurant Salzamt ⓐ AUSTRIAN This is the best restaurant in a neighborhood—the "Bermuda Triangle"—that's loaded with less desirable competitors. It evokes a turn-of-the-20th-century Viennese bistro, replete with Weiner Werkstatte–inspired chairs and lighting fixtures, cream-color walls, and dark tables and banquettes where you're likely to see an arts-involved, sometimes surprisingly prominent clientele of loyal repeat diners. Sit within its vaulted interior or—if weather permits—move out to any of the tables on the square, overlooking Vienna's oldest church, St. Ruprecht. Well-prepared items include a terrine of broccoli and artichoke hearts, light-textured pastas, filets of pork with a Gorgonzola-enriched cream sauce, roast beef with wild lettuce salad, several kinds of goulash, and fresh fish. One of the most noteworthy of these is fried filets of *Saibling*, a fish native to the coldwater streams of western Austria, served with lemon or tartar sauce.

Ruprechtsplatz 1. ℂ 01/533-5332. Reservations recommended. Main courses 8.50€–17€. V. Mon–Fri 11am–2am; Sat–Sun 3pm–2am. U-Bahn: Schwedenplatz.

Zu den 3 Hacken (At the Three Axes) ⊛ AUSTRIAN   Cozy, small-scale, and charming, this restaurant was established 350 years ago and today bears the reputation as the oldest tavern (*Gastehaus*) in Vienna. In 1827, Franz Schubert had an ongoing claim to one of the establishment's tables as a site for entertaining his cronies. Today the establishment maintains midsummer barriers of green-painted lattices and potted ivy for tables that jut onto the sidewalk. During inclement weather, head for one of three dining rooms, each paneled and each evocative of an inn high in the Austrian Alps. Expect an old-fashioned menu replete with the kind of dishes that fueled the Austro-Hungarian Empire. Examples include *Tafelspitz*, beef goulash, mixed grills piled high with chops and sausages, and desserts that include Hungarian-inspired *Palatschinken* (crepes) with chocolate-hazelnut sauce. The Czech and Austrian beer here seems to taste especially good when it's dispensed from a keg.

Singerstrasse 28. ℂ 01/512-5895. Reservations recommended. Main courses 6.90€–15€. AE, DC, MC, V. Mon–Sat 11am–midnight. U-Bahn: Stephansplatz.

Zum Kuchldragoner AUSTRIAN   Some aspects of this place will remind you of an old-fashioned Austrian tavern, perhaps one that's perched high in the mountains, far from any congested city neighborhood. The feeling is enhanced by the pine trim and the battered gemütlichkeit of what you'll soon discover is a bustling, irreverent, and sometimes jaded approach to feeding old-fashioned, flavorful, but far-from-cutting-edge cuisine to large numbers of urban clients, usually late into the night after everyone has had more than a drink or two. You can settle for a table inside, but our preferred venue is an outdoor table, immediately adjacent to the Romanesque foundation of Vienna's oldest church, St. Ruprechts. Come here for foaming steins of beer and such Viennese staples as Wiener schnitzel, schnitzel cordon bleu, baked eggplant layered with ham and cheese, and grilled lamb cutlets.

Seitenstettengasse 3 or Ruprechtsplatz 4–5. ℂ 01-533-83-71. Reservations recommended. Main courses 6€–10€. MC, V. Mon–Thurs 11am–12:30am; Fri–Sun 11am–4am. U-Bahn: Schwedenplatz.

Zwölf-Apostelkeller VIENNESE   For those seeking a taste of old Vienna, this is the place. Sections of this old wine tavern's walls predate 1561. Rows of wooden tables stand under vaulted ceilings, with lighting partially provided by streetlights set into the masonry floor. It's so deep that you feel you're entering a dungeon. Students love this place for its low prices and proximity to St. Stephan's. In addition to beer and wine, you can get hearty Austrian fare. Specialties include Hungarian goulash soup, meat dumplings, and a *Schlachtplatte* (a selection of hot black pudding, liverwurst, pork, and pork sausage with a hot bacon and cabbage salad). The cooking is hardly refined, but it's very well prepared.

Sonnenfelsgasse 3. ℂ 01/512-6777. Main courses 5.30€–10€. AE, DC, MC, V. Daily 4pm–midnight. Closed July. Tram: 1, 2, 21, D, or N. Bus: 1A. U-Bahn: Stephansplatz.

LEOPOLDSTADT (2ND DISTRICT)
EXPENSIVE
Vincent ℛ CONTINENTAL The decor of this restaurant is smooth and cozy, and guests can opt for a seat in any of three different dining rooms, any of which might remind you of a richly upholstered, carefully decorated private home that's accented with flickering candles, flowers, and crystal. The menu here changes with the season and the whim of the chef. There's an a la carte menu, but most diners opt for one of the set-price menus, one of which is described as a "light evening supper" (4 courses, 40€), or a "tasting menu" (8–9 courses, depending on the venue that day, priced at 68€). Other options include a set-price menu featuring mussels, caviar, and truffles (3 courses for 55€). Food here is elegant, upscale, and served in convivial surroundings. The finest examples include a well-prepared rack of lamb flavored with bacon, whitefish or pike perch in white-wine sauce, turbot with saffron sauce, filet of butterfish with tiger prawns served with a consommé of shrimp, and, in season, many different game dishes, including quail and venison.

Grosse-Pfarrgasse 7. ℂ 01/214-1516. Reservations required. Main courses 18€–28€. Set menus 40€–68€. Mon–Sat 6–11pm. U-Bahn: Schwedenplatz.

INEXPENSIVE
Altes Jägerhaus AUSTRIAN/GAME Little about the decor here has changed since this place opened in 1899. Located 1 mile from the entrance to the Prater in a verdant park, it's a welcome escape from the more crowded restaurants of the Inner City. Grab a seat in any of the four old-fashioned dining rooms, where the beverage of choice is equally divided between beer and wine. Seasonal game like pheasant and venison are the house specialty, but you'll also find an array of seafood dishes that might include freshwater and saltwater trout, zander, or salmon. The menu also features a delicious repertoire of Austrian staples like *Tafelspitz* and schnitzel.

Freudenau 255. ℂ 01/7289-5770. Reservations recommended. Main courses 6.50€–16€. AE, DC, MC, V. Daily 9am–11:30pm. U-Bahn: Schlachthausgasse; then Bus 77A.

LANDSTRASSE (3RD DISTRICT)
VERY EXPENSIVE
Restaurant at Palais Schwarzenberg ℛℛ CLASSICAL VIENNESE Located in one of Vienna's premier hotels, Palais Schwarzenberg is owned by Prince Karl Johannes von Schwarzenberg, scion of one of Austria's most aristocratic families. Take your time over a cocktail in the plush lounge, where the waiter will most likely recite the daily specials. In summer you can dine Hapsburg-style on a magnificent terrace. The cuisine is refined, with many French entrees, and the chef adjusts his menu seasonally. His many specialties include filet of catfish on a ragout of potatoes and morels with leek, medallions of venison roasted with fresh morels, and, for dessert, a chocolate-mint soufflé with passion fruit. Service is first class and the wine cellar is superb.

Schwarzenbergplatz 9. ℂ 01/798-4515. Reservations required. Main courses 19€–28€; fixed-price business lunch 30€; 5-course fixed-price dinner 58€. AE, DC, MC, V. Daily 6–10:30am, noon–2:30pm and 6:30–10pm. U-Bahn: Karlsplatz. Tram: D.

Steirereck ℛℛℛ VIENNESE/AUSTRIAN *Steirereck* means "corner of Styria," which is exactly what Heinz and Margarethe Reitbauer have created in this

Coffeehouses & Cafes

Café Central ⊕, Herrengasse 14 (© **01/533-3763**; U-Bahn: Herrengasse), stands in the center of Vienna across from the Hofburg and the Spanish Riding School. This grand cafe offers a glimpse into 19th-century Viennese life–it was once the center of Austria's literati. Even Lenin is said to have met his colleagues here. The Central offers a variety of Viennese coffees and a vast selection of pastries and desserts, plus Viennese and provincial dishes, and is a delightful spot for lunch. The cafe is open Monday through Saturday from 7am to 8pm.

The windows of the venerated **Café Demel** ⊕⊕, Kohlmarkt 14 (© **01/ 533-5516**; U-Bahn: Herrengasse; Bus: 1A or 2A), are filled with fanciful spun-sugar creations of characters from folk legends. Inside you'll find a splendidly baroque landmark where dozens of pastries are available daily, including the *Pralinen,* Senegal, truffle, *Sand,* and *Maximilian* tortes, as well as cream-filled horns (*Gugelhupfs*). Demel also serves a mammoth variety of tea sandwiches made with smoked salmon, egg salad, caviar, or shrimp. If you want to be traditional, ask for a Demel-Coffee, which is filtered coffee served with milk, cream, or whipped cream. It's open daily from 10am to 7pm.

Café Diglas, Wollzeile 10 (© **01/512-5765**; U-Bahn: Stubentor), evokes prewar Vienna better than many of its competitors, thanks to a decor that retains some of the accessories from 1934, when it first opened. The cafe prides itself on its long association with Franz Lehár. It offers everything in the way of run-of-the-mill caffeine fixes, as well as more elaborate, liqueur-enriched concoctions such as a Biedermeier (with apricot schnapps and cream). If you're hungry, ask for a menu (foremost among the platters is an excellent Wiener schnitzel). The cafe is open daily from 7am to midnight.

Café Dommayer, Dommayergasse 1 (© **01/877-220811**; U-Bahn: Schönbrunn), boasts a reputation for courtliness that goes back to 1787. In 1844, Johann Strauss Jr. made his musical debut here, and beginning in 1924, the site became known as *the* place in Vienna for tea dancing. During clement weather, a garden with seats for 300 opens in back. The rest of the year, the venue is restricted to a high-ceilinged black-and-white old-world room. Every Saturday from 2 to 4pm, a pianist and violinist perform; and every third Saturday, an all-woman orchestra plays mostly Strauss. Most patrons come for coffee, tea, and pastries, but if you have a more substantial appetite, try the platters of food, including Wiener schnitzel, *Rostbraten,* and fish. It's open daily from 7am to midnight.

Even the Viennese debate the age of **Café Frauenhuber,** Himmelpfortgasse 6 (© **01/512-8383**; U-Bahn: Stephansplatz). But regardless of whether 1788 or 1824 is correct, it has a justifiable claim to being the oldest continuously operating coffeehouse in the city. The old-timey decor is just a bit battered and more than a bit smoke-stained. Wiener schnitzel, served with potato salad and greens, is a good bet, as are any of the ice-cream dishes and pastries. It's open daily from 8am to 11pm.

Housed in the deluxe Hotel Imperial, **Café Imperial** 🦮, Karntner Ring 16 (© **01/5011-0389;** U-Bahn: Karlsplatz), was a favorite of Gustav Mahler and a host of other celebrities. The "Imperial Toast" is a mini-meal in itself: white bread with veal, chicken, and leaf spinach topped with a gratin, baked in an oven, and served with hollandaise sauce. A daily breakfast/brunch buffet for 31€ is served Hapsburg style on Sunday from 7am to 11pm. It's said to be the only hotel buffet breakfast in Vienna that comes with champagne. The cafe is open daily from 7am to 11pm.

One of the Ring's great coffeehouses, **Café Landtmann,** Dr.-Karl-Lueger-Ring 4 (© **01/532-0621;** tram: 1, 2, or D), has a history dating to the 1880s and has traditionally drawn a mix of politicians, journalists, and actors. It was also Freud's favorite. The original chandeliers and the prewar chairs have been refurbished. We highly suggest spending an hour or so here, perusing the newspapers, sipping on coffee, or planning the day's itinerary. The cafe is open daily from 7:30am to midnight (lunch is served 11:30am–to 3pm and dinner is served 5–11pm).

Part of the success of **Café Sperl,** Gumpendorferstrasse 11 (© **01/586-4158;** U-Bahn: Karlsplatz), derives from the fact that the gilded-age panels and accessories that were installed in 1880 are still in place. That contributed to Sperl's designation in 1998 as "Austria's best coffeehouse of the year." If you opt for a black coffee, you'll be in good company. Platters include salads; toast; baked noodles with ham, mushrooms, and cream sauce; omelets; steaks; and Wiener schnitzels. The staff displays a bemused kind of courtliness, but in a concession to modern tastes, there's a billiard table and some dartboards on the premises. It's open Monday through Saturday from 7am to 11pm and Sunday from 11am to 8pm (closed Sun July–Aug).

Café Tirolerhof, Fürichgasse 8 (© **01/512-7833;** U-Bahn: Stephansplatz or Karlsplatz), which has been under the same management for decades, makes for a convenient sightseeing break, particularly from a tour of the nearby Hofburg complex. One coffee specialty is the Maria Theresia, a large cup of mocha flavored with apricot liqueur and topped with whipped cream. If coffee sounds too hot, try the tasty milk shakes. You can also order a Viennese breakfast of coffee, tea, hot chocolate, two Viennese rolls, butter, jam, and honey. It's open daily from 7am to midnight.

Thirty kinds of tea are served at **Demmer's Teehaus,** Mölkerbastei 5 (© **01/533-5995;** U-Bahn: Schottentor), along with dozens of pastries, cakes, toasts, and English sandwiches. Demmer's is managed by the previously recommended restaurant, Buffet Trzésniewski; however, the teahouse offers you a chance to sit down, relax, and enjoy your drink or snack. It's open Monday through Friday from 10am to 6:30pm.

intimate and rustic restaurant on the Danube Canal between the Central Station and the Prater. The Reitbauers transplanted original beams and archways from an old castle in Styria to enhance the ambience. Murals adorning the walls contribute to the cozy feel. You'll find both traditional Viennese dishes and "new Austrian" selections on the menu. Begin with a caviar-semolina dumpling or roasted turbot with fennel (served as an appetizer), or opt for the most elegant and expensive item of all, goose-liver Steirereck. Some enticing main courses include asparagus with pigeon, saddle of lamb for two, prime Styrian roast beef, or red-pepper risotto with rabbit. The menu is wisely limited and well prepared, changing daily depending on what's fresh at the market. The restaurant is popular with after-theater diners, and the large wine cellar holds some 35,000 bottles.

Rasumofskygasse 2. ℭ 01/713-3168. Reservations required. Main courses 22€–28€; 3-course fixed-price lunch 31€; 5-course fixed-price dinner 69€. AE, DC, MC, V. Mon–Fri 10:30am–2pm and 7pm–midnight. Closed holidays. Tram: N. Bus: 4.

EXPENSIVE

Niky's Kuchlmasterei VIENNESE/INTERNATIONAL   The decor features old stonework with some modern architectural innovations, and the extensive menu boasts well-prepared food. The lively crowd of loyal habitués adds to the welcoming ambience, making Niky's a good choice for an evening meal, especially in summer when you can dine on its unforgettable terrace. After a long and pleasant meal, your bill will arrive in an elaborate box suitable for jewels, along with an amusing message in German that offers a tongue-in-cheek apology for cashing your check.

Obere Weissgerberstrasse 6. ℭ 01/712-9000. Reservations recommended. Main courses 16.35€–26€; fixed-price menu 29€ for 3-course lunch, 51€ for 7-course dinner. AE, DC, MC, V. Mon–Sat noon–midnight. U-Bahn: Schwedenplatz.

INEXPENSIVE

Café-Restaurant Kunsthaus AUSTRIAN/INTERNATIONAL   One of the most distinctive architects in Austrian history was the late Friedensreich Hundertwasser, whose design philosophy called for an assimilation of nature with human building techniques, the banishment of straight lines and 90° angles, and a ferocious refusal to use symmetry as it's understood by architectural classicists. This restaurant was designed by Hundertwasser as a whimsical, tongue-in-cheek answer to the awesomely portentous collections of the Kunsthaus, the museum that contains it. The cafe occupies the street level of the museum, in a location overlooking a lavish garden through large sliding windows that remain completely open whenever the weather is clement. Hundreds of verdant potted plants, the complete absence of any 90° angles, and a defiant lack of symmetry have made the place a hot conversational topic in Vienna. Adding to the sense of creative hysteria is the artful mismatching of chairs, very few of which are exactly alike. Come here for the visuals and the artsy, chit-chatting crowd, which spills over into the garden, again on mismatched chairs, in summer, but don't expect anything terribly innovative in the cuisine. It's competent and well-prepared, but much more traditional than the bizarre decor might imply. Standard menu items include Viennese beef broth, roast beef with onions, schnitzels of veal or pork, goulash or potato soup, fried chicken, wursts, and strudels.

In the Kunsthaus, 14 Weissgerberlande. ℭ 01/712-0497. Reservations not necessary. Main courses 6.40€–13€. No credit cards. Daily 10am–11pm. U-Bahn: Schwedenplatz or Tram N to Radetskyplatz.

WIEDEN & MARGARETEN (4TH & 5TH DISTRICTS)
MODERATE

Motto THAI/ITALIAN/AUSTRIAN   This is the premier gay restaurant of Austria, with a cavernous red-and-black interior, a busy bar, and a clientele that has included many of the glam figures (Thierry Mugler, John Galliano, and lots of theater people) of the international circuit. (Even Helmut Lang worked here briefly as a waiter.) It's set behind green doors and a sign that's so small and discreet as to be nearly invisible. In summer, it's enhanced with tables set up in a garden. No one will mind if you pop in just for a dialogue, as it's a busy nightlife entity in its own right. But if you're hungry, cuisine is about as eclectic as it gets, ranging from sushi and Thai-inspired curries to *gutbürgerlich* food that reminds some clients of dishes once prepared by their grandmothers.

Schönbrunnerstrasse 30 (entrance on Rudigergasse). ℂ 01/587-0672. Reservations recommended. Main courses 7.20€–17€. MC, V. Daily 6pm–4am. U-Bahn: Pilgrimgasse.

INEXPENSIVE

Schlossgasse 21 AUSTRIAN/INTERNATIONAL   This cozy restaurant was the private turn-of-the-19th-century home of its owner until its transformation in the early 1990s. Decorated in a pleasant mishmash of old and new furnishings, the restaurant offers an eclectic menu of classic Austrian dishes, plus some interesting and palate-pleasing Asian alternatives, such as Indonesian satay and Chinese stir-fries. An enduring favorite is the expertly prepared steak.

Schlossgasse 21. ℂ 01/544-0767. Reservations recommended. Main courses 7€–15€. V. Daily 6pm–2am. U-Bahn: Pilgrimgasse.

Silberwirt VIENNESE   Despite the fact that it opened a quarter of a century ago, this restaurant oozes with Old Viennese style and resembles the traditional *Beisl* (bistro) with its copious portions of conservative, time-honored Viennese food. You can dine within a pair of dining rooms or move into the beer garden. Menu items include stuffed mushrooms, *Tafelspitz*, schnitzels, and filets of zander, salmon, and trout. Be aware that this establishment shares the same building and address as the restaurant Schlossgasse 21 listed above.

Schlossgasse 21. ℂ 01/544-4907. Reservations recommended. Main courses 7.20€–19€. V. Daily noon–midnight. U-Bahn: Pilgrimgasse.

MARIAHILF (6TH DISTRICT)
MODERATE

Raimundstüberl *(Value* VIENNESE   Appealing because of its emphasis on old-world decor and time-tested cuisine, this restaurant is also a good value, in a neighborhood loaded with simpler, and usually less worthy, choices. Established around the turn of the 19th century, it features a pair of wood-sheathed dining rooms, a garden, and copious portions of schnitzels, goulashes, and beefsteaks smothered in mushrooms. The staff is polite; the ambience is pure Viennese.

Liniengasse 29. ℂ 01/596-7784. Reservations recommended. Main courses 5.70€–19€. DC, MC, V. Mon-Fri 11am–2pm; daily 5:30pm–midnight. U-Bahn: Gumpen-dorferstrasse or Westbahnhof.

INEXPENSIVE

Alfi's Goldener Spiegel VIENNESE   By everyone's account, this is the most prominent gay restaurant in Vienna, where a mostly gay clientele enjoys food and ambience that might remind you of a simple Viennese *Beisl* in a working-class district. A congenial bar area draws a local crowd. If you do decide to sit down for a meal, expect large portions of traditional Viennese specialties such as Wiener schnitzel, roulade of beef, filet steaks with pepper sauce, and *Tafelspitz*. Its position near Vienna's Naschmarkt, the city's biggest food market, ensures that the food served is impeccably fresh.

Linke Wienzeile 46 (entrance on Stiegengasse). ℭ 01/586-6608. Reservations not necessary. Main courses 5.70€–14€. No credit cards. Wed–Mon 7pm–2am. U-Bahn: U-4 to Kettenbruckengasse.

NEUBAU (7TH DISTRICT)

EXPENSIVE

Hauswirth 🎯🎯 VIENNESE   The imposing entrance to this trendy restaurant is hidden down a rectangular corridor. Push open the leaded-glass door to discover an Art Nouveau enclave that has become a regular stomping ground for Vienna's hippest. In summer, the gardens are lovely; in winter, the dark wood paneling and crystal chandeliers inside set the tone. The chef adjusts his menu seasonally, obtaining whatever is fresh at local markets. On any night there may be quail, venison, goose liver, sweetbreads, well-prepared steaks, and seafood specialties, followed by fresh berries and tempting homemade pastries. The preparations are as excellent as the fine ingredients. The kitchen has great finesse, and everything that arrives on your table is guaranteed to be fresh and appetizing. The cellar holds not only a large variety of the finest Austrian wines, but also a well-chosen selection from some of Europe's best vineyards.

Otto-Bauer-Gasse 20. ℭ 01/587-1261. Reservations recommended. Main courses 14€–17€; 3-course fixed-price menu 35€; 4-course fixed-priced menu 60€. AE, DC, MC, V. Daily 11:30am–3pm; Mon–Sat 6pm–midnight. Closed Dec 23–Jan 8. U-Bahn: Zieglerstrasse. Tram: 52 or 58.

MODERATE

Bohème 🎯 VIENNESE/INTERNATIONAL   This one-time bakery was originally built in 1750 in the baroque style. Today its historic street is an all-pedestrian walkway loaded with shops. Since opening in 1989, Bohème has attracted a crowd that's knowledgeable about the nuances of wine, food, and the opera music that reverberates throughout the two dining rooms. Even the decor is theatrical; it looks like a cross between a severely dignified stage set and an artsy, turn-of-the-19th-century cafe. Menu items are listed as movements in an opera, with overtures (apéritifs), prologues (appetizers), and first and second acts (soups and main courses). As you'd guess, desserts provide the finales. Some tempting items include melon with thinly sliced cured ham, Andalusian gazpacho, platters of mixed fish filets with tomato risotto, *Tafelspitz* with horseradish, gourmet versions of bratwurst and sausages on a bed of ratatouille, and vegetarian dishes like soya schnitzels in sesame sauce.

Spittelberggasse 19. ℭ 01/523-3173. Reservations recommended. Main courses 7€–20€. AE, DC, MC, V. Mon–Sat 6–11:30pm. Closed Jan 7–23. U-Bahn: Volkstheater.

INEXPENSIVE

Plutzer Bräu 🎯 *Finds* AUSTRIAN   This is one of the best examples in Vienna of the explosion of hip and trendy restaurants within the city's 7th district, just to the southeast of the city's inner core. Maintained by the Plutzer Brewery, it occupies the cavernous cellar of an imposing 19th-century building. Any antique references are quickly lost once you're inside, thanks to an industrial-looking decor with exposed heating ducts, burnished stainless steel, and accessories that might remind you of the cafeteria in a central European factory. You can stay at the long, accommodating bar and drink fresh-brewed Plutzer beer. But if you're hungry (and this very good beer will probably encourage an appetite), head for

the well-scrubbed dining room, where the menu reflects Old Viennese traditions. Food is excellent and includes veal stew in beer sauce with dumplings, "brewmaster's style" pork steak, and pasta with herbs and feta cheese. Dessert might include curd dumplings with poppy seeds and sweet bread crumbs.

Schrankgasse 4. (✆ **01/526-12-15**. Reservations not necessary. Main courses 6.40€–12€. 2-course set-price lunch served daily 11:30am–3pm, 5.96€. MC, V. Daily 11am–11:45pm. U-Bahn: Volkstheater.

JOSEFSTADT (8TH DISTRICT)
EXPENSIVE

Kochwertstatt ⭐ FRENCH   The setting is hip, artfully minimalist, somewhat more spartan than you might care for, and in distinct opposition to the carefully restored antique buildings of the Spittelberg neighborhood that contains it. It's the stage upon which chef Oliver Hoffinger plays out his culinary visions and whims, many of which are based on French models with an occasional nouvelle inspiration. Amid a color scheme of soft pink, black, and white, and against a backdrop of rough-textured medieval stone columns supporting the ceiling of the dining room, you'll enjoy menu items that change frequently and that are usually accompanied by French, Italian, or Spanish wines. The finest examples include foie gras with honey-marinated apples, a chili pepper and tomato mousse served with avocado slices, roasted quail with pickled walnuts, a savory roasted rabbit with a cassis sauce, and an intensely upscale version of *Tafelspitz* (boiled beef) garnished with truffles. There are only 24 seats in this restaurant—small enough for a genuinely intimate kind of dining experience.

Spittelberggasse 8. (✆ **01/523-3291**. Reservations recommended. Main courses 20€–22€; set-price menus 35€–42€. No credit cards. Daily 6–11pm (last order). U-Bahn: Volkstheater.

MODERATE

Alte Backstube VIENNESE/HUNGARIAN   This spot is worth visiting just to admire the baroque sculptures that crown the top of the doorway. The building was originally designed as a private home in 1697, and 4 years later it was transformed into a bakery, complete with wood-burning stoves. For more than 2½ centuries, the establishment served the baking needs of the neighborhood. In 1963, the Schwarzmann family added a dining room, a dainty front room for drinking beer and tea, and a collection of baking-related artifacts. Once seated, you can order such wholesome, robust specialties as braised pork with cabbage, Viennese-style goulash, and roast venison with cranberry sauce and bread dumplings. There's an English-language menu if you need it. Try the house special dessert, cream-cheese strudel with hot vanilla sauce.

Lange Gasse 34. (✆ **01/406-11-01**. Reservations required. Main courses 9.20€–15€. AE, MC, V. Daily 11am–midnight. Closed mid-July to Aug 30. U-Bahn: Rathaus. Go east along Schmidgasse to Lange Gasse.

Die Fromme Helene ⭐ AUSTRIAN   This is the kind of upscale tavern where the food is traditional and excellent, where the crowd is animated and creative, and where the staff is hip enough to recognize and recall the names of the many actors, writers, and politicians who come here regularly. Part of its theatrical allure derives from a location that's close to several of the city's theaters (including the English Theater), and to prove it, there are signed and framed photographs of many of the quasi-celebrity clients who have eaten and made merry here. A recent celebrity of note is Annie Girardot, a French star who appeared in the films of Buñuel and Truffaut, who dined here often during 2002, usually after one of her performances at the nearby English Theater. Expect a wide range of traditional and well-prepared Austrian dishes, including schnitzels of both veal and pork, pastas, and a chocolate pudding (whose name translates as "Moor in a Shirt") served with hot chocolate sauce and whipped cream. The establishment's enduring specialty is *Alt Wiener Backfleisch,* a long-marinated and spicy version of steak that's breaded, fried, and served with potato salad. There's a range of pasta and vegetarian dishes as well. The restaurant's name, incidentally, derives from the comic-book creation of a 19th-century illustrator, Wilhelm Busch, whose harddrinking but well-meaning heroine, "pious Helen," captivated the imagination of the German-speaking world.

15 Josefstaedter Strasse. © **01/406-9144.** Reservations recommended. Main courses 7€–18€. AE, DC, MC, V. Mon–Sat 11:30am–1am. Tram J to Theater in der Josefstadt.

Piaristenkeller AUSTRIAN   Erich Emberger has successfully renovated and reassembled this wine tavern with centuries-old vaulted ceilings in a vast cellar room. The place was founded in 1697 by Piarist monks as a tavern and wine cellar. The kitchen, which once served the cloisters, still dishes out traditional Austrian specialties based on original recipes. Zither music is played beginning at 7:30pm, and in summer the garden at the church square is open from 11am to midnight. Wine and beer are available whenever the cellar is open. Advance booking is required for a guided tour of the cloister's old wine vaults. Groups of six or more pay 11€ per person for the tour.

Piaristengasse 45. © **01/405-9152.** Reservations recommended. Main courses 14€–22€. AE, DC, MC, V. Daily 6pm–midnight. U-Bahn: Rathaus.

ALSERGRUND (9TH DISTRICT)
MODERATE
Abend-Restaurant Fuervogel RUSSIAN   Since World War I, this restaurant has been a Viennese landmark, bringing Russian cuisine to a location across from the palace of the Prince of Liechtenstein. You'll eat in romantically Slavic surroundings with Gypsy violins playing Russian and Viennese music. Specialties include chicken Kiev, beef Stroganoff, veal Dolgoruki, borscht, and many other dishes that taste as if they came right off the steppes. For an hors d'oeuvre try *sakkuska,* a variety platter that's popular in Russia. You can also order a gourmet fixed-price dinner with five courses. Be sure to sample the Russian ice cream known as *plombier.*

Alserbachstrasse 21. © **01/317-5391.** Reservations recommended. Main courses 8€–14€; 5-course fixed-price menu 45€. AE, DC, MC, V. Mon–Sat 5:30pm–midnight. Closed July 15–Aug 1. U-Bahn: Friedensbrücke. Bus: 32.

NEAR SCHÖNBRUNN
VERY EXPENSIVE
Altwienerhof 🏵🏵🏵 AUSTRIAN/FRENCH   A short walk from Schönbrunn Palace lies one of the premier dining spots in Vienna. The building is completely modernized, but it was originally designed as a private home in the 1870s. Rudolf and Ursula Kellner bring sophistication and charm to the dining rooms, which retain many Biedermeier embellishments from the original construction. The chef prepares nouvelle cuisine using only the freshest and highest-quality ingredients. The menu changes frequently, and the maître d' is always willing to assist with recommendations. Each night the chef prepares a tasting menu, which is a sampling of the kitchen's best nightly dishes. The wine list consists of well over 700 wines, each of which is selected by Mr. Kellner himself. The cellar below houses about 18,000 bottles.

Herklotzgasse 6. (*) **01/892-6000.** Reservations recommended. Main courses 21€–26€; fixed-price lunch 21€–28€; menu dégustation (dinner only) 59€ for 6 courses, 85€ for 8 courses. AE, DC, MC, V. Mon–Sat noon–2pm and 6:30–10:30pm. Closed first 3 weeks in Jan. U-Bahn: Gumpendorferstrasse.

MODERATE

Hietzinger Brau AUSTRIAN   Established in 1743, this is the most famous and best-recommended restaurant in the vicinity of Schönbrunn Palace. Everything about it evokes a sense of bourgeois stability—wood paneling, a staff wearing folkloric costume, and platters heaped high with *gutbürgerlich* cuisine. The menu lists more than a dozen preparations of beef, including the time-tested boiled-beef favorite, *Tafelspitz,* as well as mixed grills, all kinds of steaks, and fish that include lobster, salmon, crab, and zander. Homage to the cuisine of Franz-Joseph appears in the form of very large Wiener schnitzels, a creamy goulash, and even a very old-fashioned form of braised calves' head. Wine is available, but by far the most popular beverage here is foaming steins of the local brew, Hietzinger.

Auhofstrasse 1. (*) **01/877-7087-0.** Reservations not necessary. Main courses 13€–23€. DC, MC, V. Daily 11:30am–3pm and 6–11:30pm. U-Bahn: Hietzing.

4

Exploring Vienna

In this chapter, we'll explore the many sights of this vibrant and storied city, including its palaces, museums, churches, parks, attractions for kids, and attractions for those with special sightseeing interests. Be warned that it's possible to spend a week here and only touch the surface of this multifaceted city. We'll take you through the highlights, but try to set aside some time for wandering and taking in the street life. We'll also take you shopping and then show you the glittering world of Vienna after dark, including a look at its rich cultural life and world-class performing-arts scene.

SIGHTSEEING SUGGESTIONS

Some visitors will have only a day or two, and with those people in mind, we've compiled a list of the major attractions a first-time traveler to Vienna will want to explore, as well as additional sights for those with more time. Regardless of time, the must-sees on everyone's list should include the Inner City, Ringstrasse, Schönbrunn Palace, Hofburg Palace, Belvedere Palace, the Kunsthistorisches Museum, and St. Stephan's Cathedral.

If You Have 1 Day

Begin at St. Stephan's Cathedral in the heart of the Inner City, or Old Town. Climb its south tower for a panoramic view of the city (you can also take an elevator to the top). Next, stroll down Kärntnerstrasse, the main shopping artery. Take time to join in the 11am ritual of coffee in a grand cafe, such as the Café Imperial. In the afternoon, visit Schönbrunn Palace, the magnificent summer seat of the Hapsburg dynasty. Have dinner in a Viennese wine tavern.

If You Have 2 Days

For Day 1, stick to the agenda above. On Day 2, explore other major attractions, including the Hofburg, the Imperial Crypt, and the Kunsthistorisches Museum. In the evening, take in an opera performance or some other musical event, perhaps at the famous Konzerthaus.

If You Have 3 Days

Spend Days 1 and 2 as above. On Day 3, try to work two important performances into your schedule: the Spanish Riding School (Tues–Sat) and the Vienna Boys' Choir (singing at Masses on Sun). Also be sure to visit the Belvedere Palace and its fine art galleries. Take a stroll through the Naschmarkt, the city's major open-air market.

If You Have 4 Days

Spend Days 1 to 3 as above. On Day 4, take a tour of the Vienna Woods and then visit Klosterneuburg Abbey, Austria's most impressive abbey (see chapter 5). Return to Vienna for some fun at the Prater amusement park.

1 The Hofburg Palace Complex (★★★

Once the winter palace of the Hapsburgs, the Hofburg sits in the heart of Vienna and is known for its vast, impressive courtyards. To reach it (you can hardly miss it), head up Kohlmarkt to Michaelerplatz 1, Burgring (© 01/ 587-5554), where you'll stumble upon two enormous fountains ornamented with statues. You can also take the U-Bahn to Stephansplatz, Herrengasse, or Mariahilferstrasse, or else tram no. 1, 2, D, or J to Burgring.

This complex of imperial edifices, the first of which was constructed in 1279, grew with the empire, so today the palace is virtually a city within a city. The earliest parts were built around a courtyard, the **Swiss Court,** named for the Swiss mercenaries who performed guard duty here. This most ancient section of the palace is at least 700 years old.

The Hofburg's complexity of styles, which are not always harmonious, is the result of each emperor or empress opting to add to or take away some of the work done by his or her predecessors. The palace, which has withstood three major sieges and a great fire, is called simply *die Burg,* or "the palace," by Viennese. Of its more than 2,600 rooms, fewer than 2 dozen are open to the public.

Albertina (★   One of the greatest graphics collections in the world—scheduled to reopen in 2003—is housed within the Hofburg. The museum, named for a son-in-law of Maria Theresa, traces the development of graphic arts since the 14th century. The most outstanding treasure is the Dürer collection. Unfortunately, what you'll usually see are copies—the originals are shown only on special occasions. Be sure to view Dürer's *Praying Hands,* which has been reproduced throughout the world. The 20,000-some drawings and more than 250,000 original etchings and prints include work by such artists as Poussin, Fragonard, Rubens, Rembrandt, Michelangelo, and Leonardo da Vinci. Exhibitions of both ancient and modern drawings and prints are always changing.

Albertinaplatz. © 01/53483. www.albertina.at. Admission 9€ adults, 7€ students, free for children under 6. Tues–Sun 10am–5pm.

Augustinerkirche (Church of the Augustinians) (★   This 14th-century church was built within the Hofburg complex to serve as the parish church for the imperial court. In the latter part of the 18th century, it was stripped of its baroque embellishments and returned to the original Gothic features. The Chapel of St. George, dating from 1337, is entered from the right aisle. The **Tomb of Maria Christina** (★, the favorite daughter of Maria Theresa, is housed in the main nave near the rear entrance, but there's no body in it. (The princess was actually buried in the Imperial Crypt, described later in this section.) This richly ornamented empty tomb is one of Canova's masterpieces. A small room in the Loreto Chapel is filled with urns containing the hearts of the imperial Hapsburg family. They can be viewed through a window in an iron door. The Chapel of St. George and the Loreto Chapel are open to the public only by prearranged guided tour.

Not everything in the church belongs to the macabre. Maria Theresa married François of Lorraine here in 1736, and the Augustinerkirche was also the site of other royal weddings: Marie Antoinette to Louis XVI of France in 1770, Marie-Louise of Austria to Napoléon in 1810 (by proxy—he didn't show up), and Franz Joseph to Elisabeth of Bavaria in 1854.

The most convenient—and most dramatic—time to visit the church is on Sunday at 11am, when a high Mass is accompanied by a choir, soloists, and an

The Hofburg

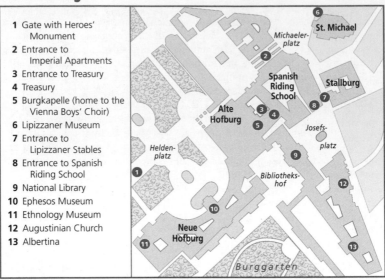

1 Gate with Heroes' Monument
2 Entrance to Imperial Apartments
3 Entrance to Treasury
4 Treasury
5 Burgkapelle (home to the Vienna Boys' Choir)
6 Lipizzaner Museum
7 Entrance to Lipizzaner Stables
8 Entrance to Spanish Riding School
9 National Library
10 Ephesos Museum
11 Ethnology Museum
12 Augustinian Church
13 Albertina

St. Michael
Michaeler-platz
Spanish Riding School
Stallburg
Alte Hofburg
Josefs-platz
Helden-platz
Bibliotheks-hof
Neue Hofburg
Burggarten

orchestra. On selected Sundays of the church year and between June and September, beautiful organ Masses are presented. Admission to the Masses is free, but donations are welcome. On Friday at 7:30pm from the end of May to September—and on selected Fridays throughout the year—organ recitals and concerts are also given. Tickets are 10€ to 25€, depending on the event.

Augustinerstrasse 3. ℰ 01/533-70-99. Free admission. Daily 6:30am–6pm. U-Bahn: Stephansplatz.

Die Burgkapelle (Home of the Vienna Boys' Choir) Construction of this Gothic chapel began in 1447 during the reign of Emperor Frederick III, but it was later massively renovated. From 1449 it was the private chapel of the royal family. Today the Burgkapelle hosts the **Hofmusikkapelle** 𝕲𝕲, an ensemble of the Vienna Boys' Choir and members of the Vienna State Opera chorus and orchestra, which performs works by classical and modern composers. Written applications for reserved seats should be sent at least 8 weeks in advance. Use a credit card; do not send cash or checks. For reservations, write to Verwaltung der Hofmusikkapelle, Hofburg, A-1010 Vienna. If you failed to reserve in advance, you might be lucky enough to secure tickets from a block sold at the Burgkapelle box office every Friday from 11am to 1pm or 3 to 5pm, plus Sunday from 8:15 to 8:45am. The line starts forming at least half an hour before that. If you're willing to settle for standing room, it's free.

The Vienna Boys' Choir boarding school is at Palais Augarten, Obere Augartenstrasse.

Hofburg (entrance on Schweizerhof). ℰ 01/533-9927. Mass: Seats and concerts 5€–29€; standing room free. Masses (performances) held only Jan–June and mid-Sept to Dec, Sun and holidays 9:15am. Concerts May–June and Sept–Oct Fri 4pm.

Kaiserappartements (Imperial Apartments) 𝕲𝕲 The Kaiserapparte-ments, on the first floor, is where the emperors and their wives and children lived. To reach these apartments, enter through the rotunda of Michaelerplatz. The rooms are richly decorated with tapestries, many from Aubusson in France. Unfortunately, you can't visit the quarters once occupied by Empress Maria

Theresa—they are now used by the president of Austria. The court tableware and silver are outrageously ornate, reflecting the splendor of a bygone era. The **Imperial Silver and Porcelain Collection,** from the Hapsburg household of the 18th and 19th centuries, provides a window into their court etiquette.

The Imperial Apartments seem to be most closely associated with the long reign of Franz Joseph. A famous full-length portrait of his beautiful wife, Elisabeth (Sissi) of Bavaria, hangs in the apartments. You'll see the "iron bed" of Franz Joseph, who claimed he slept like his own soldiers. Maybe that explains why his wife spent so much time traveling!

Michaeler Platz 1 (inside the Ring, about a 7-min. walk from Stephansplatz; entrance via the Kasertor in the Inneren Burghof). (C) 01/533-7570. Admission 7.50€ adults, 5.90€ students under 25, 3.90€ children 6–15, free for children 5 and under. Daily 9am–4:30pm. U-Bahn: U-1 or U-3 to Stephansplatz. Tram: 1, 2, 3, or J to Burgring.

Lipizzaner Museum   The latest attraction at Hofburg Palace is this newly opened museum near the stables of the famous white stallions. The permanent exhibition begins with the historic inception of the Spanish Riding School in the 16th century and extends to the stallions' near destruction in the closing weeks of World War II. Exhibits of paintings, historic engravings, drawings, photographs, uniforms and bridles, plus video and film presentations bring to life the history of the Spanish Riding School and offer an insight into the breeding and training of these champion horses. A window into the stables allows museum visitors to watch the stallions being fed and saddled.

Reitschulgasse 2, Stallburg. (C) 01/533-7811. Admission 9€ adults, 6.50€ children. Daily 9am–6pm. U-Bahn: Stephansplatz.

Neue Hofburg   The most recent addition to the Hofburg complex is the Neue Hofburg, or New Château. Construction was started in 1881 and continued through 1913. The palace was the residence of Archduke Franz Ferdinand, the nephew and heir apparent of Franz Joseph, whose assassination at Sarajevo by Serbian nationalists set off the chain of events that led to World War I.

The arms and armor collection, second only to that of the Metropolitan Museum of Art in New York, is in the **Hofjagd and Rüstkammer** ★★, on the second floor of the Neue Hofburg. On display are crossbows, swords, helmets, pistols, and other armor, mostly the property of Hapsburg emperors and princes. Some of the exhibits, such as scimitars, were captured from the Turks as they fled their unsuccessful siege of Vienna. Of bizarre interest is the armor worn by the young (and small) Hapsburg princes.

⟨Moments⟩ The Vienna Boys' Choir

In 1498, Emperor Maximilian I decreed that 12 boys should be included among the official court musicians. Over the next 500 years, this group evolved into the world-renowned Vienna Boys' Choir (*Wiener Sängerknaben*). They perform in Vienna at various venues, including the Staatsoper, the Volksoper, and Schönbrunn Palace. The choir also performs at Sunday and Christmas Masses with the *Hofmusikkapelle* (Court Musicians) at the Hofburgkapelle (see listing for details). The choir's boarding school is at Augartenpalais, Obere Augartenstrasse. For more information on where they are performing and how to get tickets, go to the choir's website (www.wsk.at).

Vienna Attractions

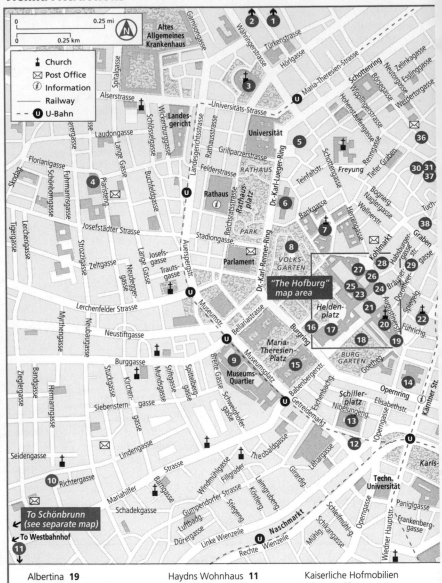

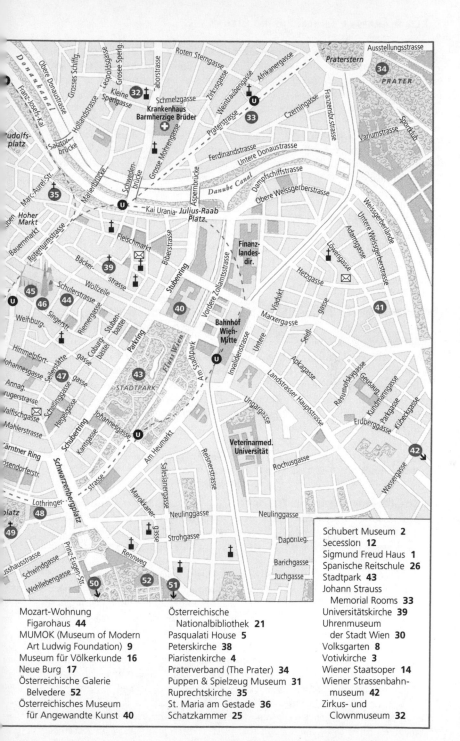

Another section, the **Musikinstrumentensammlung** ✲ (✆ **01/52524,** ext. 471), is devoted to old musical instruments, mainly from the 17th and 18th centuries, but some from the 16th century. Some of these instruments, especially among the pianos and harpsichords, were played by Brahms, Schubert, Mahler, Beethoven, and Austrian emperors who fancied themselves as having an ear for music.

In the **Ephesos-Museum (Museum of Ephesian Sculpture),** with an entrance behind the Prince Eugene monument, you'll see high-quality finds from Ephesus in Turkey and the Greek island of Samothrace. Here the prize exhibit is the Parthian monument, the most important relief frieze from Roman times ever found in Asia Minor. It was erected to celebrate Rome's victory in the Parthian wars (A.D. 161–65).

Visit the **Museum für Völkerkunde (Museum of Ethnology)** for no other reason than to see the only original Aztec feather headdress in the world. Also on display are Benin bronzes, Cook's collections of Polynesian art, and Indonesian, African, Eskimo, and pre-Columbian exhibits.

Heldenplatz. ✆ **01/525-24-484.** Admission for each museum 8€ adults, 6.50€ for children. Wed–Mon 10am–6pm.

Österreichische Nationalbibliothek (Austrian National Library)   The royal library of the Hapsburgs dates from the 14th century, and the library building, developed on the premises of the court from 1723 on, is still expanding to the Neue Hofburg. The **Great Hall** ✲✲ of the present-day library was ordered by Karl VI and designed by those masters of the baroque, the von Erlachs. Its splendor is captured in the frescoes of Daniel Gran and the equestrian statue of Joseph II. The complete collection of Prince Eugene of Savoy is the core of the precious holdings. With its manuscripts, rare autographs, globes, maps, and other historic memorabilia, this is among the finest libraries in the world.

Josefplatz 1. ✆ **01/5341-0202.** www.onb.ac.at. Summer admission 4€ adults; 2€ children, students, and seniors. Winter admission 2€ adults; 1€ children, students, and seniors. Nov–Apr Mon–Sat 10am–2pm; May–Oct Mon–Wed and Fri–Sat 10am–4pm, Thurs 10am–7pm, Sun and public holidays 10am–1pm.

Schatzkammer (Imperial Treasury) ✲✲✲   Reached by a staircase from the Swiss Court, the Schatzkammer is the greatest treasury in the world. It's divided into two sections: the Imperial Profane and the Sacerdotal Treasuries. The first displays the crown jewels and an assortment of imperial riches, while the other contains ecclesiastical treasures.

The most outstanding exhibit in the Schatzkammer is the imperial crown, which dates from 962. It's so big that, even though padded, it probably slipped down over the ears of many a Hapsburg at his coronation. Studded with emeralds, sapphires, diamonds, and rubies, this 1,000-year-old symbol of sovereignty is a priceless treasure, a fact recognized by Adolf Hitler, who had it taken to Nürnberg in 1938 (the American army returned it to Vienna after World War II). Also on display is the imperial crown worn by the Hapsburg rulers from 1804 to the end of the empire. Be sure to have a look at the coronation robes of the imperial family, some of which date from the 12th century.

You can also view the 9th-century saber of Charlemagne and the 8th-century holy lance. The latter, a sacred emblem of imperial authority, was thought in medieval times to be the weapon that pierced the side of Christ on the cross. Among the great Schatzkammer prizes is the Burgundian Treasure. Seized in the 15th century, it is rich in vestments, oil paintings, and gems. Highlighting this collection of loot are artifacts connected with the Order of the Golden Fleece, the romantic medieval order of chivalry.

Hofburg, Schweizerhof. ℭ **01/533-7931**. Admission 7€ adults; 5€ children, seniors, and students; free for children under 6. Wed–Mon 10am–6pm.

Spanische Reitschule (Spanish Riding School) ☆

This riding school is a reminder that horses were an important part of everyday Vienna life for many centuries, particularly during the imperial heyday. The school is housed in a white, crystal-chandeliered ballroom in an 18th-century building. You'll marvel at the skill and beauty of the sleek Lipizzaner stallions as their adept trainers put them through their paces in a show that hasn't changed for 4 centuries. These are the world's most famous classically styled equine performers. Many North Americans have seen them in the States, but to watch the Lipizzaners prance to the music of Johann Strauss or a Chopin polonaise in their home setting is a pleasure you shouldn't miss.

Reservations for performances must be made in advance, as early as possible. Order your tickets for the Sunday and Wednesday shows by writing to Spanische Reitschule, Hofburg, A-1010 Vienna (fax 01/533-903-240), or through a travel agency in Vienna. (Tickets for Saturday shows can be ordered only through a travel agency.) Tickets for training sessions with no advance reservations can be purchased at the entrance.

Michaelerplatz 1, Hofburg. ℭ **01/533-9032**. www.lipizzaner.at. Regular performances 33€–145€ seats, 25€ standing room. Classical art of riding with music 22€ adults, free for children 3–6 with an adult; children under age 3 not admitted. Training session 12€ adults, 5€ children. Regular shows Mar–June and Sept to mid-Dec, most Sun at 11am and some Fri at 6pm. Classical dressage with music performances Apr–June and Sept, most Sat at 10am. Training sessions Mar–June, first 2 weeks in Sept, and mid-Oct to mid-Dec Tues–Sat 10am–noon.

EXPLORING THE MUSEUMSQUARTIER COMPLEX ☆☆☆

The big cultural news of Vienna, perhaps of Europe, is the long-awaited premiere of this giant modern art complex. Art critics claimed that the assemblage of art installed in former Hapsburg stables has tipped the city's cultural center of gravity from Hapsburgian pomp into the new millennium. This massive complex, one of the largest cultural complexes in the world, is like combining the Guggenheim Museum with New York's Museum of Modern Art and tossing in the Brooklyn Academy of Music, a children's museum, an architecture-and-design center, lots of theaters, art galleries, and video workshops, and much more. There's even an ecology center, architecture museum, and, yes, a tobacco museum. U-Bahn: MuseumsQuartier.

Kunsthalle Wien ☆

Cutting-edge contemporary and classic modern art is showcased here. Exhibits focus on specific subjects and seek to establish a link between modern art and current trends. You'll find works by everyone: from Picasso and Juan Miró to Jackson Pollock and Paul Klee, from Wassily Kandinsky to Andy Warhol and, surprise, Yoko Ono. From expressionism to cubism to abstraction, exhibits reveal the major movements in contemporary art since the mid–20th century. There are five floors that can be explored in 1 to 2 hours, depending on what interests you.

Museumsplatz 1. ℭ **01/521-89-0**. Admission 8€ adults; 5€ seniors, students, and children. Daily 10am–7pm (Thurs to 10pm).

Leopold Museum ☆☆

This extensive collection of Austrian art includes the world's largest treasure trove of the works of Egon Schiele (1890–1918), who was once forgotten in art history but now takes his place alongside van Gogh and

Der Dritte Mann

The 1949 film *The Third Man,* starring Joseph Cotten, Orson Welles, and Alida Valli, remains the best record of a ruined postwar Vienna, occupied by the victorious powers of World War II: the United States, Britain, France, and the Soviet Union. Graham Greene wrote the screenplay (his screen treatment has been published by Penguin Books). Arriving in Vienna, Greene found a "city of undignified ruins which turned February into great glaciers of snow and ice." He pictured the Danube as a "gray flat muddy river, and the Russian zone, where the Prater lay, as "smashed and desolate and full of weeds."

In the closing weeks of World War II, the Soviet army attacked Nazi troops that had retreated west. Hitler was in his Berlin bunker when he learned that Vienna, the city of his youth, had fallen to the Allied advance. The Allies had been bombing Vienna since 1943, and the city that had once spawned an empire was on the verge of starvation.

The Third Man immortalized "four men in a Jeep"—that is, four military policemen from the quartet of occupying powers, as they drove around the beleaguered city.

They found a city laid to waste. By 1945, Vienna had recorded the highest death rate in Europe. Bombings had killed 12,000 people and destroyed 20% of its buildings. Some 270,000 Viennese were left homeless. The city began to rebuild immediately, but it wasn't until 1955 that Austria regained its sovereignty.

Even today, the Viennese have bitter memories of the occupation, especially by the Soviets. A major reminder of those dreaded years can be found at Schwarzenbergplatz, reached from Karlsplatz by walking along Friedrichstrasse which becomes Lothringerstrasse. When the Nazis were in power, this square was called Hitlerplatz. A patch of landscaped greenery surrounds a fountain and a Soviet statue, a gift "from Russia with love."

The city has been none too happy with this "gift" from its former conquerors. Three times officials have tried to demolish the memorial, but so far Soviet engineering has proven too strong. Here the Viennese have nicknamed the grave of an anonymous Soviet soldier "The Tomb of the Unknown Plunderer." Behind the fountain, a swastika used to fly over Hildebrandt's Schwarzenberg Palace before giving way to the Soviet Red Star and, eventually, the banner of the Austrian Republic.

As dust settles over the past, it now appears that the long Soviet occupation was an attempt to extract heavy reparations from Austria. Until their demands were met, they intended to postpone the peace treaty and their withdrawal. Austria eventually guaranteed the Soviet Union $150,000,000 in reparations.

By the time the Allies withdrew their forces, Vienna had already become a center of Cold War espionage and spying—a setting as intriguing as any James Bond movie or John Le Carré novel.

Modigliani in the ranks of great doomed artists. Although he died before he was 28, his collection of art at the Leopold includes more than 2,500 drawings and watercolors and 330 oil canvases. Other works by Austrian modernist masterpieces include paintings by Oskar Kokoschka, the great Gustav Klimt, Anton Romaki, and Richard Gerstl. Major statements in Arts and Crafts from the late 19th and 20th centuries include works by Josef Hoffmann, Kolo Moser, Adolf Loos, and Franz Hagenauer.

Museumsplatz 1. (C) **01/525-70.** Admission 9€ adults, 6€ students and children over 7. Mon and Wed–Thurs 11am–7pm; Fri 11am–9pm; Sat–Sun 10am–7pm. Closed Tues.

MUMOK (Museum of Modern Art Ludwig Foundation) ✿ This gallery presents one of the most outstanding collections of contemporary art in central Europe. It comprises mainly of works from American Pop Art mixed with concurrent continental movements such as Hyperrealism of the 1960s and 1970s. The museum features five exhibition levels (three of them above ground and two underground). To make it easier to compare works in a single art movement, such as cubism or surrealism, paintings "in the same family" are grouped together. Expect to encounter pieces by all the fabled names, such as Robert Indiana, Jasper Johns, Roy Lichtenstein, Robert Rauschenberg, George Segal, and, of course, Andy Warhol.

Museumsplatz 1. (C) **01/525-00.** Admission 8€ adults, 2€ children. Daily 9am–6pm.

2 Other Top Attractions
THE INNER CITY

Domkirche St. Stephan (St. Stephan's Cathedral) ✿✿✿ A basilica built on the site of a Romanesque sanctuary, the cathedral was founded in the 12th century in what was, even in the Middle Ages, the town's center.

Stephansdom was virtually destroyed in a 1258 fire that swept through Vienna, and toward the dawn of the 14th century the ruins of the basilica were replaced by a Gothic building. The cathedral suffered terribly in the Turkish siege of 1683 but then experienced peace until the Soviet bombardments of 1945. Destruction continued as the Germans bombarded the city to cover their retreat. Restored and reopened in 1948, the cathedral is today one of the greatest Gothic structures in Europe, rich in wood carvings, altars, sculptures, and paintings. The steeple, rising some 137m (450 ft.), has come to symbolize the very spirit of Vienna.

The 107m (352-ft.) cathedral is inextricably entwined in Viennese and Austrian history. It was here that mourners attended Mozart's "pauper's funeral" in 1791, and it was on the cathedral door that Napoléon posted his farewell edict in 1805.

The **pulpit** of St. Stephan's was carved from stone by Anton Pilgrim, his enduring masterpiece. But the chief treasure of the cathedral is the carved wooden **Wiener Neustadt altarpiece** ✿✿ that dates from 1447. Richly painted and gilded, the altar was discovered in the Virgin's Choir. In the Apostles' Choir, look for the curious **Tomb of Emperor Frederick III** ✿✿. Made of a pinkish Salzburg marble, the carved 17th-century tomb depicts hideous little hobgoblins trying to enter and wake the emperor from his eternal sleep. The entrance to the catacombs or crypt is on the north side next to the Capistran pulpit. Here you'll see the funeral urns that contain the entrails of 56 members of the Hapsburg family. (As we noted earlier, the hearts are inurned in St. George's Chapel of the Augustinerkirche, and the bodies are entombed in the Imperial Crypt of the Kapuziner Church.)

You can climb the 343-step south tower, which dominates the skyline with its needlelike spire, for a view of the Vienna Woods. Called Alter Steffl (Old Steve), the tower was built between 1350 and 1433. The North Tower (Nordturm), reached by elevator, was never finished to match the South Tower, but was crowned in the Renaissance style in 1579. From here you get a panoramic sweep of the city and the Danube.

Stephansplatz 1. ✆ **01/515-52563.** Cathedral free admission; tour of catacombs 3€ adults, 1€ children under 15. Guided tour of cathedral 3€ adults, 1€ children under 15. North Tower 3.50€ adults, 1€ children under 15; South Tower 3.50€ adults, 1€ students, 1€ children under 15. Evening tours, including tour of the roof, 10€ adults, 3.50€ children under 15. Cathedral daily 6am–10pm except times of service. Tour of catacombs Mon–Sat 10, 11, and 11:30am, 12:30, 1:30, 2, 2:30, 3:30, 4, and 4:30pm; Sun 2, 2:30, 3, 3:30, 4, and 4:30pm. Guided tour of cathedral Mon–Sat 10:30am and 3pm; Sun at 3pm. Special evening tour Sat 7pm (June–Sept). North Tower Oct–Mar daily 8:30am–5pm; Apr–Sept daily 9am–6pm. South Tower daily 9am–5:30pm. Bus: 1A, 2A, or 3A. U-Bahn: Stephansplatz.

Gemäldegalerie der Akademie der Bildenden Kunste (Gallery of Painting and Fine Arts) 𝄐 When in Vienna, always make at least one visit to this painting gallery to see the *Last Judgment* 𝄐𝄐 triptych by the incomparable Hieronymus Bosch. In this masterpiece, the artist conjured up all the demons of hell for a terrifying view of the suffering and sins that humankind must endure. You'll also be able to view many Dutch and Flemish paintings, some from as far back as the 15th century, although the academy is noted for its 17th-century art. The gallery boasts works by Van Dyck, Rembrandt, and a host of other artists. There are several works by Lucas Cranach the Elder, the most outstanding being his *Lucretia*, completed in 1532. Some say it's as enigmatic as *Mona Lisa*. Rubens is represented here by more than a dozen oil sketches. You can see Rembrandt's *Portrait of a Woman* and scrutinize Guardi's scenes from 18th-century Venice.

Schillerplatz 3. ✆ **01/58816.** Admission 3.50€ adults, 1.45€ students and children. Tues–Sun 10am–4pm. U-Bahn: Karlsplatz.

Haus der Musik 𝄐 Mozart is long gone, but Vienna finally got around to opening a full-scale museum devoted to music. This hands-on museum is high-tech. You can take to the podium and conduct the Vienna Philharmonic. Wandering the halls and niches of this museum, you can encounter nostalgic reminders of the great composers who have lived in Vienna—not only Mozart, but Beethoven, Schubert, Brahms, and others. In the rooms, you can listen to your favorite renditions of their works or explore memorabilia of the composers. As a sad note, a memorial, Exodus, pays tribute to the Viennese musicians driven into exile or murdered by the Nazis. At the Musicantino Restaurant on the top floor, you can enjoy a panoramic view of the city and some good food. On the ground floor is a coffeehouse.

Seilerstätte 30. ✆ **01/516-48-51.** Admission 8.05€ adults, 5.85€ students and seniors, 4€ children. Open daily 10am–10pm.

Hundertwasserhaus In a city filled with baroque palaces and numerous architectural adornments, this sprawling public-housing project in the rather bleak 3rd District is visited—or at least seen from the window of a tour bus—by about a million visitors annually. Completed in 1985, it was the work of self-styled "eco-architect" Friedensreich Hundertwasser. The complex, which has a facade like a gigantic black-and-white game board, is relieved with scattered splotches of red, yellow, and blue. Trees stick out at 45-degree angles from apartments designed to accommodate human tenants among the foliage.

There are 50 apartments here, and signs warn not to go inside. However, there's a tiny gift shop at the entrance where you can buy Hundertwasser posters and postcards, plus a coffee shop on the first floor. With its irregular shape, its turrets, and its "rolling meadows" of grass and trees, the Hundertwasserhaus is certainly the most controversial building in Vienna.

Löwengasse and Kegelgasse 3. No phone. U-Bahn: Landstrasse. Tram: N.

Kaiserlich Hofmobilien Depot (Imperial Furniture Collection) ⭐ A collection spanning 3 centuries of royal collecting, this museum is a treasure house of the Hapsburg attics. Exhibits range from the throne of the Emperor Francis Joseph to Prince Rudolf's cradle to a forest of coat racks. This horde of property was inherited by the new republic at the end of World War I and the collapse of the Austro-Hungarian Empire. The empress Maria Theresa had established the collection in 1747, and it eventually totaled some 55,000 objects, an antiques-collector's dream. This Hapsburg hoard has been called "one of the world's most curious collections of household artifacts."

The furnishings and trappings are on show in a century-old warehouse complex halfway between the Hofburg Palace and the Schönbrunn Palace. Allow about 2½ hours to view this collection, which sprawls across three floors. Expect cheek-by-jowl bric-a-brac and a total of some 15,000 chairs alone used by the court.

Although there's much here that is of only passing interest, such as fire screens and picture frames, there are prized examples of decorative and applied arts. You're brought into intimate contact with the humanity of the Hapsburgs by such items as chamber pots, spittoons, and porcelain toothbrush holders. Particularly stunning is Maria Theresa's imposing desk of palisander marquetry with a delicate bone inlay. You can even see the coffin that carried Emperor Maximilian's corpse, which was returned to Vienna from Mexico following his execution in 1867 by Benito Juárez's forces.

The collection is particularly rich in Biedermeier furnishings, which characterized the era from 1815 to 1848. The modern world also intrudes, with pieces designed by such 20th-century Viennese architects as Adolf Loos and Otto Wagner. On display is the apartment of the famous ceramist Lucie Rie, the contents of which she took with her to London in 1938 when she fled the Nazis. The furnishings were returned to Vienna following her death in 1995.

7 Andreasgasse. ℂ **01/524-33570.** Admission 6.90€ adults, 4.30€ students, 3.60€ children under 18. Tues–Sun 9am–5pm. U-Bahn: Zieglergasse.

Kunsthistorisches Museum (Museum of Fine Arts) ⭐⭐⭐ Across from the Hofburg Palace, this huge building houses many of the fabulous art collections gathered by the Hapsburgs as they added new territories to their empire. One highlight is the fine collection of ancient Egyptian and Greek art. The museum also has works by many of the great European masters, such as Velásquez and Titian.

On display here are Roger van der Weyden's *Crucifixion* triptych, a Memling altarpiece, and Jan van Eyck's portrait of Cardinal Albergati. But it's the work of Pieter Brueghel the Elder for which the museum is renowned. This 16th-century Flemish master is known for his sensitive yet vigorous landscapes. He did many lively studies of peasant life, and his pictures today seem almost an ethnographic study of his time. Don't leave without a glimpse of Brueghel's *Children's Games* and his *Hunters in the Snow,* one of his most celebrated pieces.

Don't miss the work of van Dyck, especially his *Venus in the Forge of Vulcan,* or Peter Paul Rubens's *Self-Portrait* and *Woman with a Cape,* for which he is said to have used the face of his second wife, Helen Fourment. The Rembrandt collection includes two remarkable self-portraits as well as a moving portrait of his mother and one of his sons, Titus.

A highlight of any trip to Vienna is the museum's Albrecht Dürer collection. The Renaissance German painter and engraver (1471–1528) is known for his innovative art and painstakingly detailed workmanship. *Blue Madonna* is here, as are some of his realistic landscapes, such as the *Martyrdom of 10,000 Christians.*

The glory of the French, Spanish, and Italian schools is also visible, having often come into Hapsburg hands as "gifts." Titian is represented by *A Girl with a Cloak*, Veronese by an *Adoration of the Magi*, Caravaggio by his *Virgin of the Rosary*, Raphael by *The Madonna in the Meadow*, and Tintoretto by his painting of Susanna caught off guard in her bath. One of our all-time favorite painters is Giorgione, and here visitors can gaze at his *Trio of Philosophers*.

Maria-Theresien-Platz, Burgring 5. ℂ 01/525-24-405. Admission 9€ adults, 6.50€ students and seniors, free for children under 6. Daily 10am–6pm, Thurs until 9pm. U-Bahn: Mariahilferstrasse. Tram: 52, 58, D, or J.

Secession Building ⭐   Come here if for no other reason than to see Gustav Klimt's *Beethoven Frieze*, a 30m (100-ft.) visual interpretation of Beethoven's *Ninth Symphony*. Built in 1898, this dome-crowned building—itself a virtual-art manifesto—stands south of the Opernring, beside the Academy of Fine Arts. Once called "outrageous in its useless luxury," the empty dome, covered in triumphal laurel leaves, echoes that of the Karlskirche on the other side of Vienna.

The Secession building was the home of the Viennese avant-garde, which extolled the glories of Jugendstil or Art Nouveau. A young group of painters and architects launched the Secessionist movement in 1897 in rebellion against the strict confines of the Academy of Fine Arts. Klimt was a leader of the movement and defied the historicism favored by the Emperor Franz Joseph. The works of Kokoschka and of the "barbarian" Gauguin were featured here. Instead of being a memorial to the great Secessionist artists of yesterday, the pavilion today displays substantial contemporary exhibits. The Belvedere Palace is still the best repository for Secessionist art.

Friedrichstrasse 12 (on the western side of Karlsplatz). ℂ 01/587-53070. www.secession.at. Admission 5.50€ adults, 3€ children 6–18. Tues–Sun 10am–6pm, Thurs 10am–8pm. U-Bahn: Karlsplatz.

Wiener Staatsoper (Vienna State Opera) ⭐   This is one of the most important opera houses in the world. When it was originally built in the 1860s, critics apparently so upset one of the architects, Eduard van der Null, that he killed himself. In 1945, at the end of World War II, despite other pressing needs, such as public housing, Vienna started restoration work on the theater, finishing it in time to celebrate the country's independence from occupation forces in 1955. It's so important to the Austrians that they don't seem to begrudge the thousands of euros a day its operation costs taxpayers. (For information on performances held at the Staatsoper, see section 11, "Vienna After Dark.")

Opernring 2. ℂ 01/5144-42960. Tours daily year-round, 2–5 times a day, depending on demand. Tour times are posted on a board outside the entrance. Tours 4.50€ per person. U-Bahn: Karlsplatz.

OUTSIDE THE INNER CITY

Österreichische Galarie Belvedere (Belvedere Palace) ⭐⭐   Southeast of Karlsplatz, the Belvedere sits on a slope above Vienna. You approach the palace through a long garden with a huge circular pond that reflects the sky and the looming palace buildings. Designed by Johann Lukas von Hildebrandt, who was the last major Austrian baroque architect, the Belvedere was built as a summer home for Prince Eugene of Savoy. It consists of two palatial buildings, made up of a series of interlocking cubes. The interior is dominated by two great flowing staircases.

Unteres Belvedere (Lower Belvedere), with its entrance at Rennweg 6A, was completed in 1716. **Oberes Belvedere (Upper Belvedere)** was completed in 1723.

The Gold Salon in Lower Belvedere is one of the most beautiful rooms in the palace. Anton Bruckner, the composer, lived in one of the buildings until his death in 1896, and the palace was also the residence of Archduke Franz Ferdinand, the slain heir and World War I spark. In May 1955, the peace treaty recognizing Austria as a sovereign state was signed in Upper Belvedere by foreign ministers of the four powers that occupied Austria at the close of World War II—France, Great Britain, the United States, and the Soviet Union.

Today visitors come to the splendid baroque palace to enjoy the panoramic view of the Wienerwald (Vienna Woods) from the terrace. A regal French-style garden lies between Upper and Lower Belvedere, both of which feature impressive art collections that are open to the public.

Lower (Unteres) Belvedere has a wealth of sculptural decorations and houses the **Barockmuseum (Museum of Baroque Art).** The original sculptures from the Neuermarkt fountain, the work of Georg Raphael Donner, are displayed here. During his life, Donner dominated the development of 18th-century Austrian sculpture, heavily influenced by Italian art. The four figures on the fountain represent the four major tributaries of the Danube. Works by Franz Anton Maulbertsch, an 18th-century painter, are also exhibited. Maulbertsch, strongly influenced by Tiepolo, was the most original and accomplished Austrian painter of his day. He was best known for his iridescent colors and flowing brushwork.

Museum Mittelalterlicher Kunst (Museum of Medieval Austrian Art) is located in the Orangery at Lower Belvedere. Here you'll see works from the Gothic period, as well as a Tyrolean Romanesque crucifix that dates from the 12th century. Outstanding works include seven panels by Rueland Frueauf portraying scenes from the life of the Madonna and the Passion of Christ.

Upper Belvedere houses the **Galerie des 19. and 20. Jahrhunderts (Gallery of 19th- and 20th-Century Art)** ⭐. In a large salon decorated in red marble, you can view the 1955 peace treaty mentioned above. A selection of Austrian and international paintings of the 19th and 20th centuries is on display, including works by Oskar Kokoschka, Vincent van Gogh, James Ensor, and C. D. Freidrich.

Most outstanding are the works of Gustav Klimt (1862–1918), one of the founders of the 1897 Secession movement. Klimt used a geometrical approach to painting, blending figures with their backgrounds in the same overall tones. Witness the extraordinary *Judith*. Other notable Klimt works on display are *The Kiss, Adam and Eve*, and five panoramic lakeside landscapes from Attersee. Sharing almost equal billing with Klimt is Egon Shiele (1890–1918), whose masterpieces include *The Wife of an Artist*. Schiele could be both morbid, as exemplified by *Death and Girl*, or cruelly observant, as in *The Artist's Family*.

Prinz-Eugen-Strasse 27. (℃ **01/79557**. www.belvedere.at. Admission 7.50€ adults, free for children 11 and under. Tues–Sun 10am–6pm. Tram: D to Schloss Belvedere.

Art-School Reject

One Austrian painter whose canvases will never grace any museum wall is Adolph Hitler. Aspiring to be an artist, Hitler had his traditional paintings, including one of the Auersberg Palace, rejected by the Academy of Fine Arts in Vienna. The building was accurate, but the figures were way out of proportion. Hitler did not take this failure well, denouncing the board as a "lot of old-fashioned fossilized civil servants, bureaucrats, devoid lumps of officials. The whole academy ought to be blown up!"

Schönbrunn Palace ☆☆☆   A Hapsburg palace of 1,441 rooms, Schönbrunn was designed by those masters of the baroque, the von Erlachs. It was built between 1696 and 1712 at the request of Emperor Leopold I for his son, Joseph I. Leopold envisioned a palace whose grandeur would surpass that of Versailles. However, Austria's treasury, drained by the cost of wars, could not support such an ambitious undertaking, and the original plans were never completed.

When Maria Theresa became empress, she had the plans altered, and Schönbrunn looks today much as she conceived it, with delicate rococo touches designed for her by Austrian Nikolaus Pacassi. Schönbrunn was the imperial summer palace during Maria Theresa's 40-year reign (1740–80), and it was the scene of great ceremonial balls, lavish banquets, and fabulous receptions held during the Congress of Vienna (1814–15). At the age of 6, Mozart performed in the Hall of Mirrors before Maria Theresa and her court, and the empress held secret meetings with her chancellor, Prince Kaunitz, in the round Chinese Room.

Franz Joseph was born within the palace walls, which became the setting for the lavish court life associated with his reign. He also spent the final years of his life here. The last of the Hapsburg rulers, Charles I, abdicated here on November 11, 1918.

Schönbrunn Palace was damaged in World War II by Allied bombs, but restoration has removed the scars. In complete contrast to the grim, forbidding Hofburg, Schönbrunn Palace, done in "Maria Theresa ochre," has the **Imperial Gardens** ☆, embellished by the **Gloriette** ☆☆, a marble summerhouse topped by a stone canopy that showcases the imperial eagle. The so-called Roman Ruins are a collection of marble statues and fountains from the late 18th century, when it was fashionable to simulate the grandeur of Rome. The park, which can be visited until sunset daily, contains many fountains and heroic statues, often depicting Greek mythological characters.

The **State Apartments** ☆☆☆ are the most stunning display in the palace. Much of the interior is decorated in the rococo style, done in red, white, and, more often than not, 23½-karat gold. Of the 40 rooms you can visit, the "Room of Millions," the grandest rococo salon in the world, decorated with Indian and Persian miniatures, is one of the more fascinating. Guided tours of the palace rooms last 50 minutes and are narrated in English every half-hour beginning at 9:30am. You should tip the guide.

Also on the grounds at Schönbrunn is the **Schlosstheater** (© 01/876-4272), which still has summer performances. Marie Antoinette appeared on its stage in pastorals during her happy youth, and Max Reinhardt, the theatrical impresario, launched an acting school here. The **Wagenburg (Carriage Museum)** ☆ (© 01/877-3244) is also worth a visit. It contains a fine display of imperial coaches from the 17th to 20th centuries. The coronation coach of Charles VI (1711–40), which was pulled by eight white stallions, is here. It was also used for several subsequent Hapsburg coronations. This intriguing museum is open from April to October daily from 9am to 6pm, and from November to March Tuesday through Sunday from 10am to 5:30pm. Admission is 4.15€ for adults and 3€ for seniors and children 10 and under.

Schönbrunner Schlossstrasse. © 01/8113. www.schoenbrunn.at. Admission 9.80€ adults, 5€ children 6–15, free for children under 6. Apartments Apr–Oct daily 8:30am–5pm; Nov–Mar daily 9am–4:30pm. U-Bahn: Schönbrunn.

Schönbrunn

THE PARK

1 Main Gate
2 Courtyard, Carriage Museum
3 Theater
4 Mews
5 Chapel
6 Restaurant
7 Hietzing Church
8 Naiad's Fountains
9 Joseph II Monument
10 Palm House
11 Neptune's Fountain
12 Schöner Brunnen
13 Gloriette
14 Small Gloriette
15 Spring
16 Octagonal Pavilion

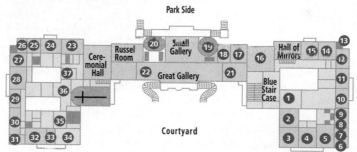

THE PALACE

1 Guard Room
2 Billiard Room
3 Walnut Room
4 Franz Joseph's Study
5 Franz Joseph's Bedroom
6 Cabinet
7 Stairs Cabinet
8 Dressing Room
9 Bedroom of Franz Joseph I & Elisabeth
10 Empress Elisabeth's Salon
11 Marie Antoinette's Room
12 Nursery
13 Breakfast Room
14 Yellow Salon
15 Balcony Room
16 17 18 Rosa Rooms
19 20 Round and Oval Chinese Cabinets
21 Lantern Room
22 Carousel Room
23 Blue Chinese Salon
24 Vieux-Laque Room
25 Napoleon Room
26 Porcelain Room
27 Millions Room
28 Gobelin Tapestry Room
29 Archduchess Sophie's Study
30 Red Drawing Room
31 East Terrace Cabinet
32 Bed-of-State Room
33 Writing Room
34 Drawing Room
35 Wild Boar Room
36 Passage Chamber
37 Bergl-Zimmer

Moments **An Evening with Mozart**

The palace's grandest summer attraction is the **Mozart Festival** in July and August. This open-air festival, initiated at Schönbrunn in 1992, is set in the Imperial Gardens. It attracts top-notch international artists and is bound to include a performance of the opera *Don Giovanni*. The most recent festivities included an all-new staging of *Die Zauberflöte,* perhaps Mozart's most enigmatic, albeit highly popular, opera. Under the starry summer sky, a night of enchantment awaits visitors in a city renowned for its charmed musical progeny. Concerts are from 7 to 10pm. Tickets are 27€ to 48€. For more information on the **Festival Mozart in Schönbrunn,** 24 Fleischmarkt, A-1010 Vienna, call ℂ **01/512-0100.**

3 Churches

For the Hofburg Palace Chapel, where the Vienna Boys' Choir performs, and the Augustinerkirche, see section 1 earlier in this chapter; for St. Stephan's Cathedral, see section 2.

THE INNER CITY

Die Deutschordenkirche (Church of the Teutonic Order) Die Deutschordenkirche and its treasury, Schatzkammer des Deutschen Ordens, will stir thoughts of the Crusades in the minds of history buffs, but the relics of vanished glory will make some visitors wish they had been among the medieval nobility. The Order of the Teutonic Knights was founded in 1190 in the Holy Land. The order came to Vienna in 1205, but the church they built dates from 1395. The building never fell prey to the baroque madness that swept the city after the Counter-Reformation. Subsequently, you see it pretty much in its original form, a Gothic church dedicated to St. Elizabeth. A choice feature is the 16th-century Flemish altarpiece on the main altar, which is richly decorated with wood carving, gilt, and painted panel inserts. Many knights of the Teutonic Order are buried here, their heraldic shields still mounted on some of the upper walls.

In the knights' treasury, on the second floor of the church, you'll see mementos such as seals and coins illustrating the history of the order, as well as a collection of arms, vases, gold, crystal, and precious stones. Also on display are the charter given to the Teutonic Order by Henry IV of England and a collection of medieval paintings. A curious exhibit is a Viper Tongue Credenza, said to have the power to detect poison in food and render it harmless.

Singerstrasse 7. ℂ **01/512-1065.** Free admission to church; treasury 3.60€ adults, 2.20€ children under 11. Church daily 9am–6pm; treasury Mon–Tues and Thurs 10am–noon, Wed and Fri–Sat 3–5pm. U-Bahn: Stephansplatz.

Kapuzinerkirche, with the Kaisergruft (Imperial Crypt) The Kapuziner Church (just inside the Ring and behind the Staatsoper) houses the Imperial Crypt, the burial vault of the Hapsburgs for some 3 centuries. Capuchin friars guard the family's final resting place, where 12 emperors, 17 empresses, and dozens of archdukes are entombed. (But only their bodies are here. Their hearts are in urns in the Loreto Chapel of the Augustinerkirche in the Hofburg complex, while their entrails are similarly enshrined in a crypt below St. Stephan's Cathedral.)

The most outstanding imperial tomb is the double sarcophagus of Maria Theresa and her consort, Emperor Francis I (François of Lorraine), the parents of Marie Antoinette. Before her own death, the empress used to descend into the tomb often to visit the gravesite of her beloved Francis. The "King of Rome," the ill-fated son of Napoléon and Marie-Louise of Austria, was also buried here in a bronze coffin after his death at 21. (Hitler managed to anger both the Austrians and the French by having the remains of Napoléon's son transferred to Paris in 1940.) Although she was not a Hapsburg, Countess Fuchs, the governess who practically reared Maria Theresa, lies in the crypt.

Emperor Franz Joseph was interred here in 1916, a frail old man who outlived his time and died just before the final collapse of his beloved empire. His wife, Empress Elisabeth, was buried in the crypt following her assassination in Geneva in 1898, as was their son, Archduke Rudolf, who allegedly committed suicide at Mayerling.

Neuer Markt. © **01/512-6853**. Admission 3.60€ adults, 2.90€ children. Daily 9:30am–4pm. U-Bahn: Stephansplatz.

Michaelerkirche (Church of St. Michael)   This church can trace some of its Romanesque portions to the early 1200s. The exact date of the chancel is not known, but it's probably from the mid–14th century. Over its long history, the church has felt the hand of many architects and designers, resulting in a medley of styles, not all harmonious. Perhaps only the catacombs could still be recognized as medieval.

Most of St. Michael's as it appears today dates from 1792, when the facade was redone in the neoclassical style; however, the spire is 16th century. The main altar is richly decorated in baroque style; the altarpiece, entitled *The Collapse of the Angels* (1781), is the last major baroque work completed in Vienna.

Michaelerplatz. © **01/533-8000**. Free admission. Mon–Sat 6:45am–8pm; Sun 8am–6:30pm. U-Bahn: Herrengasse. Bus: 1A, 2A, or 3A.

Minoritenkirche (Church of the Minorites)   If you're tired of baroque ornamentation, visit this church of the Friar Minor Conventual, a Franciscan order also called the Minorite friars (inferior brothers). Construction began in 1250 but was not completed until the early 14th century. Its tower was damaged by the Turks in their two sieges of Vienna, and it later fell prey to baroque architects and designers in the 18th century. But in 1784, Ferdinand von Hohenberg ordered that the baroque additions be removed and the simple lines of the original Gothic church be restored, complete with Gothic cloisters. Inside you'll see a mosaic copy of Leonardo's *Last Supper*. Masses are held on Sunday at 8:30 and 11am.

Minoritenplatz 2A. © **01/533-4162**. Free admission. Apr–Oct Mon–Sat 9am–6pm; Nov–Mar Mon–Sat 9am–5pm. U-Bahn: Herrengasse.

St. Maria Am Gestade   This church, the Church of Our Lady of the Riverbank, was once just that. With an arm of the Danube flowing by, it was a favorite place of worship for fishermen. The river was redirected, but the church still draws people with its own beauty. The original Romanesque church was rebuilt in the Gothic style between 1394 and 1427. The western facade is flamboyant, with a remarkable seven-sided Gothic tower; it's surmounted by a dome that culminates in a lacy crown.

At Passauer Platz. © **01/5339-5940**. Free admission. Daily 7am–7pm. U-Bahn: Stephansplatz.

Universitatskirche (Church of the Jesuits)   Built during the Counter-Reformation, this church is rich in baroque embellishments. This was the university church, dedicated to the Jesuit saints Ignatius of Loyola and Francis Xavier. The high-baroque decorations—galleries, columns, and the trompe-l'oeil painting on

the ceiling, which gives the illusion of a dome—were added in 1703 to 1705. The embellishments were the work of a Jesuit lay brother, Andrea Pozzo, at the orders of Emperor Leopold I. Look for Pozzo's painting of Mary behind the main altar. Choral and orchestral services (mostly classical) are celebrated on Sunday and Holy Days at 10am.

Dr.-Ignaz-Seipel-Platz 1. (© 01/512-13350. Free admission to church. Daily 8am–7pm. U-Bahn: Stephansplatz or Stubentor. Tram: 1 or 2. Bus: 1A.

OUTSIDE THE INNER CITY

Karlskirche (Church of St. Charles)   Construction on Karlskirche, dedicated to St. Charles Borromeo, was begun in 1716 by order of Emperor Charles VI. The Black Plague had swept Vienna in 1713, and the emperor made a vow to build the church if the disease would abate. The baroque master Johann Bernard Fischer von Erlach did the original work on the church from 1716 to 1722, and his son, Joseph Emanuel, completed it between 1723 and 1737. The lavishly decorated interior stands as a testament to the father-and-son duo who led the baroque movement.

The well-known ecclesiastical artist J. M. Rottmayr painted many of the frescoes inside the church from 1725 to 1730. The green copper dome of Karlskirche is 72m (236 ft.) high, a dramatic landmark on the Viennese skyline. Two columns, spin-offs from Trajan's Column in Rome, flank the front of the church, which opens onto Karlsplatz. There's also a sculpture by Henry Moore in a little pool.

Karlsplatz. (© 01/504-6187. Admission 4€ adults, 2.50€ children 6–18, free for children under 6. Self-guided tours .65€ adults, .35€ children. Mon–Fri 7:30am–7pm; Sat 8am–7pm; Sun 9am–7pm. U-Bahn: Karlsplatz.

Peterskirche (St. Peter's Church)   Peterskirche is the second-oldest church in Vienna, but the spot on which it stands might well be the oldest Christian church site in the city. Many places of worship have stood here; the first is believed to date from the second half of the 4th century. Charlemagne is credited with commissioning a church on the site during the late 8th or early 9th century.

The present St. Peter's, the most lavishly decorated baroque church in Vienna, was designed in 1702 by Gabriel Montani. Von Hildebrandt, the noted architect who designed the Belvedere Palace, is believed to have finished the building in 1732. The fresco in the dome, depicting the Coronation of the Virgin, is a masterpiece by J. M. Rottmayr. The church contains many other frescoes and much gilded carved wood, plus altarpieces by many well-known artists of the period.

Peterplatz. (© 01/533-6433. Free admission. Daily 9am–6:30pm. U-Bahn: Stephansplatz.

Piaristenkirche (Church of the Piarist Order)   Work on the Piaristenkirche, more popularly known as Piaristenplatz, was launched in 1716 by a Roman Catholic teaching congregation known as the Piarists (fathers of religious schools). The church, however, was not consecrated until 1771. Some of the designs submitted during that long period are believed to have been drawn by von Hildebrandt, the noted architect who designed the Belvedere Palace, but many builders had a hand in its construction. This church is noteworthy for its fine classic facade as well as the frescoes by F. A. Maulbertsch, which adorn the insides of the circular cupolas.

Piaristeng 54. (© 01/406-14530. Free admission. Mon–Fri 3–6pm; Sat 10am–noon. U-Bahn: Rathaus.

Ruprechtskirche (St. Rupert's Church)   The oldest church in Vienna, Ruprechtskirche has stood here since A.D. 740, although much that you see now, such as the aisle, is from the 11th century. Beautiful new stained-glass windows— the work of Lydia Roppolt—were installed in 1993. It's believed that much of the masonry from a Roman shrine on this spot was used in the present church. The tower and nave are Romanesque; the rest of the church is Gothic. St. Rupert is the patron saint of the Danube's salt merchants.

Ruprechtsplatz, Seittenstettengasse 4–5. © 01/553-6003. Free admission. Easter to Oct only, Mon–Fri 10am–noon. U-Bahn: Schwedenplatz.

Votivkirche   After a failed assassination attempt on Emperor Franz Joseph, a collection was taken for the construction of the Votive Church, which sits across from the site where the attempt was made. Heinrich von Ferstel began work on the neo-Gothic church in 1856, but it was not consecrated until 1879. The magnificent facade features awesome lacy spires and intricate sculpture. Most noteworthy is the Renaissance sarcophagus of Niklas Salm, commander of the Austrian forces during the Turkish siege in 1529.

Rooseveltplatz 8. © 01/406-1192. Free admission. Tues–Sun 9am–1pm and 4–6:30pm. U-Bahn: Schottenor.

4 More Museums & Galleries

See sections 1 and 2 above for additional museums and galleries.

THE INNER CITY

Judisches Museum Wien   This is the main museum tracing the history of Viennese Jewry. It's not to be confused with its annex at Judenplatz (see below). This museum opened in 1993 in the former Eskeles Palace, once one of the most patrician of town houses in Vienna and a private residence. Both temporary and permanent exhibitions are on view here, the permanent exhibitions tracing the major role that Viennese Jews played in the history of Vienna until their expulsion or deaths in the Holocaust beginning in 1938. Their valuable contributions are noted in such fields as philosophy, music, and medicine. And, of course, we must mention Sigmund Freud, who escaped the Holocaust by fleeing to London. The museum defines itself as an "archive of memory" or a "place for remembering." Many objects on view were rescued from Vienna's private synagogues and prayer-houses, concealed in 1938 from the Nazis. Many other exhibits are from the old Jewish Museum that existed in Vienna until it was closed in 1938.

Dorotheergasse 11. © 01/535-0431. Admission 5€ adults, 2.90€ students and children. Sun–Fri 10am–6pm (until 8pm Thurs). U-Bahn: Stephansplatz.

Österreichisches Museum für Angewandte Kunst (Museum of Applied Art)   Of special interest here is a rich collection of tapestries, some from the 16th century, and the most outstanding assemblage of Viennese porcelain in the world. Look for a Persian carpet depicting *The Hunt* as well as the group of 13th-century Limoges enamels. Exhibits typically display Biedermeier furniture and other antiques, glassware, and crystal; outstanding objects of the early-20th-century crafts workshop the Wiener Werkstätte; and large collections of lace and textiles. An entire hall is devoted to Art Nouveau.

Stubenring 5. © 01/711360. www.mak.at. Admission 6.60€ adults, 3.30€ children 6–18, free for children under 6. Wed–Sun 10am–6pm; Tues 10am–midnight. U-Bahn: Stubentor. Tram: 1 or 2.

Uhrenmuseum der Stadt Wien (Municipal Clock Museum)   A wide-ranging collection of timepieces—from ancient to modern—are on view here. Housed in what was once the Obizzi town house, the museum dates from 1917 and displays clocks of all shapes and sizes. From all over Europe and North

In Memory of Vienna's Jewish Ghetto

Judenplatz (U-Bahn: Stephansplatz), lying off Wiplingerstrase, was the heart of the Jewish Ghetto from the 13th to the 15th centuries. That memory of long ago has been brought back by the opening of a Holocaust memorial on this square.

This memorial, combined with a new museum devoted to medieval Jewish life, along with excavations, have re-created a center of Jewish culture on the Judenplatz. It is a place of remembrance unique in Europe.

The architect of the Holocaust memorial, Rachel Whitehead, designed it like a stylized stack of books signifying Jewish strivings toward education. The outer sides of this reinforced concrete cube are in the form of library shelves. Around the base of the monument are engraved the names of the places in which Austrian Jews were put to death during the Nazi era. Nearby is a statue of Gotthold Ephraim Lessing (1729–81), the Jewish playwright.

Museum Judenplatz, Judenplatz 8 (𝄐 01/535-0431), is a new annex of Vienna's Jewish Museum (Judisches Museum Wien). Exhibits tell the major role that Viennese Jews played in all aspects of city life, from music to medicine, until a reign of terror began against them in 1938. The main section of the museum is devoted to the exhibition on medieval Jewry in Vienna. The exhibition features a multimedia presentation of the religious, cultural, and social life of the Viennese Jews in the Middle Ages until their expulsion and death in 1420–21 during the First Viennese Gesera, as it is called. The three exhibition rooms are in the basement of the Misrachi house. An underground passage connects them to the exhibitions of the medieval synagogue. The museum is open Sunday through Thursday from 10am to 6pm and Friday from 10am to 2pm; admission is 3€ for adults and 1.50€ for students and children under 16.

An exhibition room has been installed in the **Mittelalterliche Synagogue (Medieval Synagogue)** nearby. It is visited on the same ticket as the Jewish Museum. The late medieval synagogue was built around the middle of the 13th century. It was one of the largest synagogues of its time. After the pogrom in 1420–21, the synagogue was systematically destroyed so that only the foundations and the floor remained. These were excavated by the City of Vienna Department of Urban Archaeology from 1995 to 1998. The exhibition room shows the remnants of the central room, or "men's shul" (the room where men studied and prayed), and a smaller room annexed to it, which might have been used by women. In the middle of the central room is the foundation of the hexagonal bimah (raised podium from which the Torah was read).

America, clock collectors and fans of the offbeat come here to gaze and perhaps to covet. Check out Rutschmann's astronomical clock made in the 18th century. There are several interesting cuckoo clocks and a gigantic timepiece that was once mounted in the tower of St. Stephan's.

Schulhof 2. 𝄐 01/533-2265. Admission 3.60€ adults, 1.40€ children. Tues–Sun 9am–4:30pm. U-Bahn: Stephansplatz.

OUTSIDE THE INNER CITY

Heeresgeschichtliches Museum (Museum of Military History)   The oldest state museum in Vienna, this building was constructed from 1850 to 1856, a precursor to the Ringstrasse style. The Moorish-Byzantine and neo-Gothic designs draw attention to the museum, where the military history of the Hapsburgs, including both triumphs and defeats, is delineated.

A special display case in front of the Franz-Josef Hall contains the six orders of the House of Hapsburg that Franz Joseph sported on all public occasions. The Sarajevo room is fascinating—it contains mementos of the assassination of Archduke Franz Ferdinand and his wife on June 28, 1914, the event that set off World War I. The archduke's bloodstained uniform is displayed, along with the bullet-scarred car in which the royal couple rode. Many exhibits concentrate on the navy of the Austro-Hungarian Empire, and frescoes depict important battles, including those fought against the Turks in and around Vienna.

Arsenal 3. (01/79561. Admission 5€ adults, 3€ children under 14. Sat–Thurs 9am–5pm. Closed Jan 1, Easter, May 1, Nov 1, Dec 24–25 and 31. Tram: 18 or D.

Historisches Museum der Stadt Wien (Historical Museum of Vienna)
History buffs should seek out this fascinating but little-visited collection. Here the full panorama of Old Vienna's history unfolds, beginning with the settlement of prehistoric tribes in the Danube basin. On display are Roman relics, artifacts from the reign of the dukes of Babenberg, and a wealth of leftovers from the Hapsburg sovereignty, as well as arms and armor from various eras. A scale model shows Vienna as it looked in the Hapsburg heyday. You'll see pottery and ceramics dating from the Roman era, 14th-century stained-glass windows, mementos of the Turkish sieges of the city in 1529 and 1683, and Biedermeier furniture. There's also a section on Vienna's Art Nouveau.

Karlsplatz 4. (01/505-8747. www.museum.vienna.at. Admission 3.60€ adults, 1.40€ children. Tues–Sun 9am–6pm. U-Bahn: Karlsplatz.

Sigmund Freud Haus   The museum's dark furniture (only part of it original), lace curtains, and collection of antiquities create an atmosphere into which you can imagine the doctor will walk at any moment and tell you to make yourself comfortable on the couch. His velour hat, dark walking stick with ivory handle, and other mementos are on view in the study and waiting room he used during his residence here from 1891 to 1938. The museum also has a bookshop where souvenirs are available, including a variety of postcards of the apartment, books by Freud, posters, prints, and pens.

Berggasse 19. (01/319-1596. Admission 5€ adults, 3€ seniors and students, 2€ children 10–15, free for children 9 and under. Daily 9am–6pm. Tram: D to Schlickgasse.

5 Parks & Gardens

When the weather is fine, the Viennese shun city parks in favor of the **Wienerwald (Vienna Woods),** a wide arc of forested countryside that surrounds the northwestern and southwestern sides of Vienna (for more details, see chapter 5). But if you're an aficionado of parks, you'll find some magnificent ones in Vienna, where there are more than 4,000 acres of gardens and parks and no fewer than 770 sports fields and playgrounds. You can, of course, visit **Schönbrunn Park** and **Belvedere Park** when you tour those once-royal palaces. Below, we highlight only the most popular parks of Vienna.

THE INNER CITY

The former gardens of the Hapsburg emperors, **Burggarten,** Opernring-Burgring, next to the Neue Hofburg (tram: 1, 2, 52, 58, or D), was built soon after the Volkgarten (see below). Look for the monument to Mozart, as well as an equestrian statue of Franz I, beloved husband of Maria Theresa. The only open-air statue of Franz Joseph in all Vienna is also here, and there's a statue of Goethe at the park entrance.

The lovely **Stadtpark (City Park)** ⚘, at Parkring (tram: 1, 2, J, or T), is reached from the Ring or from Lothringer Strasse. It lies on the slope where the Danube used to overflow into the Inner City before the construction of the Danube Canal. You'll find statues of Franz Schubert and Hans Makart, a well-known artist whose work you'll see in churches and museums. But the best known is of Johann Strauss Jr., composer of operettas and waltzes. These monuments are surrounded by verdant squares of grass, well-manicured flower gardens, and plenty of benches.

From Easter to October, **Café Maierei am Stadtpark** (✆ **01/714-61-590;** tram 1, 2, J, or T), built in 1867, is an old-world schmaltzy cafe with occasional bouts of waltz music. You can sit at a garden table and often enjoy live Viennese music as you sip the local wine.

Known as the people's park, **Volksgarten** stands next to the Burgtheater (tram: 1, 2, or D). This oasis was laid out on the site of the old city wall fortifications and can be entered from Dr.-Karl-Lueger-Ring. The oldest public garden in Vienna, dating from 1820, it's dotted with monuments, including a 1907 memorial to the assassinated Empress Elisabeth. Construction of the so-called Temple of Theseus, a copy of the Theseion in Athens, was begun in 1820.

OUTSIDE THE INNER CITY

The **Praterverband (The Prater)** ⚘, an extensive tract of woods and meadowland in the 2nd district, has been Vienna's favorite recreation area since 1766, when Emperor Joseph II opened it to the public. Previously, it had been a hunting preserve and riding ground for the aristocracy.

The Prater is the birthplace of the waltz, first introduced here in 1820 by Johann Strauss Sr. and Josef Lanner. However, it was under Johann Strauss Jr., who became known as "the Waltz King," that this music form reached its greatest popularity.

The best-known part of the huge park is at the end nearest the entrance from the Ring. Here you'll find the **Riesenrad** (✆ **01/729-5430;** www.wienerriesen rad.com), the giant Ferris wheel, which was constructed in 1897 and reaches 67m (220 ft.) at its highest point. In 1997, the Ferris wheel celebrated its 100th anniversary, and it remains, after St. Stephan's Cathedral, the most famous landmark in Vienna. Erected at a time when European engineers were showing off their "high technology," the wheel was designed by Walter Basset, the British engineer, trying to outdo Eiffel, who had constructed his tower in Paris a decade earlier. The wheel was designed for the Universal Exhibition (1896–97), marking the golden anniversary of Franz Joseph's coronation in 1848. Like the Eiffel Tower, it was supposed to be a temporary exhibition. Except for World War II damage, the Ferris wheel has been going around without interruption since 1897. It was immortalized in a famous scene from the 1949 film *The Third Man,* with Joseph Cotten and Orson Welles.

Just beside the Riesenrad is the terminus of the Lilliputian railroad, the 4km (2.6-mile) narrow-gauge line that operates in summer using vintage steam locomotives. The amusement park, right behind the Ferris wheel, has all the typical

Tales of the Vienna Woods

Yes, dear reader, there really are Vienna Woods (*Wienerwald* in German). They weren't simply dreamed up by Johann Strauss Jr. as the subject of musical tales in waltz time. The Wienerwald is several thousand acres of gentle paths and trees in a delightful hilly landscape that borders Vienna on its southwestern and northwestern sides. If you stroll through this area, a weekend playground for the Viennese, you'll be following in the footsteps of Strauss and Schubert. Beethoven, when his hearing was failing, claimed that the chirping birds, trees, and leafy vineyards of the Wienerwald made it easier for him to compose. Many attractions of the Wienerwald are described in chapter 5.

A round-trip through the woods takes about 3½ hours by car, a distance of some 80km (50 miles). Even if you don't have a car, the woods can be visited relatively easily. Board tram 1 near the Staatsoper, going to Schottentor; here, switch to tram 38 (the same ticket is valid) going out to **Grinzing,** home of the famous *Heurigen* (wine taverns). Here you can board bus 38A to go through the Wienerwald to **Kahlenberg.** The whole trip takes about 1 hour each way. You might rent a bicycle nearby to make your own exploration of the woods.

Kahlenberg is located on a hill that is part of the northeasternmost spur of the Alps (483m/1,585 ft.). If the weather is clear, you can see all the way to Hungary and Slovakia. At the top of the hill is the small Church of St. Joseph, where King John Sobieski of Poland stopped to pray before leading his troops to the defense of Vienna against the Turks. For one of the best views overlooking Vienna, go to the right of the Kahlenberg restaurant. From the terrace here, you'll have a panoramic sweep, including the spires of St. Stephan's. You can also go directly to Kahlenberg from the city center in about 20 minutes by U-Bahn to Heiligenstadt; then take bus 38A.

A favorite pastime, especially in summer, involves fleeing the congested city and taking tram D to either Heiligenstadt (a 30-min. ride from Stephansplatz) or Nussdorf (a 45-min. ride from Stephansplatz). At either of these points you'll see a string of *Heurigen* and a series of footpaths perfect for a relaxing stroll.

attractions—roller coasters, merry-go-rounds, tunnels of love, and game arcades. Swimming pools, riding schools, and racecourses are interspersed between woodland and meadows. International soccer matches are held in the Prater stadium.

The Prater is not a fenced-in park, but not all amusements are open throughout the year. The season lasts from March or April to October, but the Ferris wheel operates from March to November 1. Some of the more than 150 booths and restaurants stay open in winter, including the pony merry-go-round and the gambling venues. If you drive here, don't forget to observe the no-entry and no-parking signs, which apply after 3pm daily. The place is usually jammed on Sunday afternoons in summer.

Admission to the park (*©* **01/728-0516;** U-Bahn: Praterstern) is free, but you'll pay for games and rides. The Ferris wheel costs 7.50€ for adults and 3€ for children ages 4 to 14; it's free for children 1 to 3. The park is open May through September daily from 10am to midnight, October through November daily from 10am to 10pm, and from November 4 to December 1 daily from 10am to 8pm.

The lush **Botanischer Garten (Botanical Garden),** Rennweg 14 (𝄞 01/ 4277-54100; tram: 71 to Unteres Belvedere), contains exotic plants from all over the world, many of which are extremely rare. Located in Landstrasse (3rd District, right next to the Belvedere Park), the Botanical Garden originated as a place where medicinal herbs were planted on orders from Maria Theresa. The gardens may be visited from late March to late October daily from 9am to dusk, but call ahead if the weather is inclement. Admission is free.

Located in the 22nd District between the Danube Canal and the Old Danube, **Donaupark,** Wagramer Strasse (U-Bahn: Reichsbrücke), was converted in 1964 from a garbage dump to a park with flowers, shrubs, and walks, as well as a bird sanctuary. You'll find a bee house, an aviary with native and exotic birds, a small-animal paddock, a horse-riding course, playgrounds, and games. An outstanding feature of the park is the **Donauturm (Danube Tower),** Donauturmstrasse 4 (𝄞 01/2633-5720), a 253m (828-ft.) tower with two rotating cafe-restaurants from which you have a panoramic view of Vienna. One restaurant is at the 161m (528-ft.) level; the other is at 171m (561 ft.). International specialties and Viennese cuisine are served in both. There's also a sightseeing terrace at 151m (495 ft.). Two express elevators take people up in the tower. It's open daily in summer from 10am to midnight and in winter from 10am to 10pm. The charge for the elevator is 5.20€ for adults and 3.80€ for children.

6 Especially for Kids

The greatest attraction for kids is the **Prater Amusement Park,** but there's much more in Vienna that children find amusing, especially the performances of the horses at the **Spanish Riding School.** They also love the adventure of climbing the tower of **St. Stephan's Cathedral.** Nothing quite tops a day like a picnic in the **Vienna Woods.** Below, we list other fun-filled attractions that you and your children will enjoy. (See also "Outdoor Pursuits," later in this chapter.)

Schönbrunner Tiergarten, Schönbrunn Gardens (𝄞 01/8779-2940; U-Bahn: Hietzing), is the world's oldest zoo, founded by Franz Stephan von Lothringen, husband of Empress Maria Theresa. Maria Theresa liked to have breakfast here with her brood, favoring animal antics with her eggs. The baroque buildings in a historical park landscape provide a unique setting for modern animal keeping; the tranquillity makes for a relaxing yet interesting outing. Admission is 10€ for adults and 4€ for children. It's open March through September daily from 9am to 6:30pm, October through February daily from 9am to 5pm.

Puppen & Spielzeug Museum (Doll and Toy Museum), Schulhof 4 (𝄞 01/ 535-6860; U-Bahn: Stephansplatz or Herrengasse), located near the Municipal Clock Museum (see section 4, "More Museums & Galleries," above), is a museum for all ages. Its collection of dolls and dollhouses is one of the most remarkable in the world, ranging from the 1740s to the 1930s. Some of the most outstanding dolls featured in the exhibits are from Germany, which has a rich doll-making heritage. Admission is 4.70€ for adults and 2.35€ for children. The museum is open Tuesday through Sunday from 10am to 6pm.

Other worthwhile museums for children include the **Zirkus und Clown-museum (Circus and Clown Museum),** Karmelitergasse 9 (𝄞 01/369-1111; tram: 21 or N), a repository of the persona that clowns and circus performers have adopted throughout the centuries; and the **Wiener Straasenbahnmuseum (Streetcar Museum),** Erdbergstrasse 109 (℡ **01/7909-44900;** U-Bahn: Praterstern), a site commemorating the public conveyances that helped usher Vienna and the Hapsburg Empire into the Industrial Age.

7 For Music Lovers

If you're a fan of Mozart, Schubert, Beethoven, Strauss, or Haydn, you've landed in the right city. While in town, you not only can hear their music in the concert halls and palaces where the artists performed, but you can also visit the houses and apartments in which they lived and worked, and the cemeteries where they were buried.

Haydns Wohnhaus (Haydn's House)   This is where (Franz) Joseph Haydn (1732–1809) conceived and wrote his magnificent later oratorios *The Seasons* and *The Creation.* He lived in this house from 1797 until his death. Haydn also gave lessons to Beethoven here. There's a room in the house, which is a branch of the Historical Museum of Vienna, honoring Johannes Brahms.

Haydngasse 19. ℡ **01/596-1307.** Admission 1.80€ adults, .70€ students and children. Tues–Sun 9am–12:15pm and 1–4:30pm. U-Bahn: Nestroyplatz.

Johann-Strauss-Memorial Rooms   "The King of the Waltz," Johann Strauss Jr. (1825–99), lived at this address for a number of years, composing "The Blue Danube Waltz" here in 1867. The house is now part of the Historical Museum of Vienna.

Praterstrasse 54. ℡ **01/214-0121.** Admission 1.80€ adults, .70€ children. Tues–Sun 9am–12:15pm and 1–4:30pm. U-Bahn: Nestroyplatz.

Mozart-Wohnung/Figarohaus (Mozart Memorial)   This 17th-century house is called the House of Figaro because Mozart (1756–91) composed his opera *The Marriage of Figaro* here. The composer resided here from 1784 to 1787, a relatively happy period in what was otherwise a rather tragic life. It was here that he often played chamber-music concerts with Haydn. Over the years he lived in a dozen houses in all, which became more squalid as he aged. He died in poverty and was given a "pauper's" blessing at St. Stephan's Cathedral and then buried in St. Marx Cemetery. The Domgasse apartment has been turned into a museum.

Domgasse 5. ℡ **01/513-6294.** Admission 1.80€ adults, .70€ students and children. Tues–Sun 9am–6pm. U-Bahn: Stephansplatz.

Pasqualati House   Beethoven (1770–1827) lived in this building on and off from 1804 to 1814. It's likely that either the landlord was tolerant or the neighbors were deaf. Beethoven is known to have composed his *Fourth, Fifth,* and *Seventh* symphonies here, as well as *Fidelio* and other works. There isn't much to see except some family portraits and the composer's scores, but you might feel it's worth the climb to the fourth floor (there's no elevator).

Mölker Bastei 8. ℡ **01/535-8905.** Admission 1.80€ adults, .70€children. Tues–Sun 9:15am–12:15pm and 1–4:30pm. U-Bahn: Schottentor.

Schubert Museum   The son of a poor schoolmaster, Franz Schubert (1797–1828) was born here in a house built earlier in that century. Many Schubert mementos are on view. You can also visit the house at Kettenbrückengasse 6, where he died at age 31.

Nussdorferstrasse 54. ℡ **01/317-3601.** Admission 1.80€ adults, .70€ students and children. Tues–Sun 9am–12:15pm and 1–4:30pm. S-Bahn: Canisiusgasse.

8 Organized Tours

Wiener Rundfahrten (Vienna Sightseeing Tours), Stelzhamergasse 25 (② 01/
7124-6830; www.viennasightseeingtours.com), offers many tours, ranging from
a 75-minute **"Vienna—Getting Acquainted"** trip to a 1-day motor-coach
excursion to Budapest costing 100€ per person. The historical city tour costs
32€ for adults and is free for children 12 and under. It's ideal for visitors who
are pressed for time and yet want to be shown the major (and most frequently
photographed) monuments of Vienna. Tours leave the Staatsoper daily at 9:45
and 10:30am and 2:45pm. The tour lasts 3½ hours. (U-Bahn: Karlsplatz).

"Vienna Woods—Mayerling," another popular excursion, lasting about 4
hours, leaves from the Staatsoper and takes you to the towns of Perchtoldsdorf
and Modling, and also to the Abbey of Heiligenkreuz, a center of Christian culture since medieval times. The tour also takes you for a short walk through
Baden, the spa that was once a favorite summer resort of the aristocracy. Tours
cost 39€ for adults and 15€ for children.

A **"Historical City Tour,"** which includes visits to Schönbrunn and Belvedere
palaces, leaves the Staatsoper daily at 9:45am and 10:30am. It lasts about 3 hours
and costs 32€ for adults and 15€ for children.

A variation on the city tour includes an optional visit to the Spanish Riding
School. This tour is offered Tuesday through Saturday, leaving from the Staatsoper building at 9:30am. Tickets are 41€ for adults, 16€ for children 3 to 14,
and free for children under 12.

Information and booking for these tours can be obtained either through Vienna
Sightseeing Tours (see above) or through its affiliate, **Elite Tours,** Operngasse 4
(② 01/513-2225).

9 Outdoor Pursuits

BIKING

Vienna maintains almost 322km (200 miles) of cycling lanes and paths, many
of which meander through some of the most elegant parks in Europe. Depending on their location, they're identified by a yellow image of a cyclist either
stenciled directly onto the pavement or crafted from rows of red bricks set amid
the cobblestones or concrete of the busy boulevards of the city center. Some of
the most popular bike paths run parallel to both the Danube and the Danube
Canal.

You can carry your bike onto specially marked cars of the Vienna subway
system, but only during non-rush hours. Subway cars marked with a blue shield
are the ones you should use for this purpose. Bicycles are *not* permitted on the
system's escalators—take the stairs.

You can rent a bike for 3€ to 5€ per hour. You'll usually be asked to leave
either your passport or a form of ID as a deposit. One rental possibility is **Pedal
Power,** Ausstellungsstrasse 3 (② 01/729-7234). There are rental shops at the
Prater and along the banks of the Danube Canal. You can also rent from a kiosk
in the **Westbahnhof** (② 01/5800-32985).

One terrific bike itinerary, and quite popular since it has almost no interrup-
tions, encompasses the long, skinny island that separates the Danube from the
Neue Donau Canal. Low-lying and occasionally marshy, but with paved paths
along most of its length, it provides clear views of central Europe's industrial
landscape and the endless river traffic that flows by on either side.

Boating on the "Blue" Danube

Its waters aren't as idyllic as the Strauss waltz would lead you to believe, and its color is usually muddy brown rather than blue. But despite these drawbacks, many visitors to Austria view a day cruise along the Danube as a highlight of their trip. Until the advent of railroads and highways, the Danube played a vital role in Austria's history, helping to build the complex mercantile society that eventually became the Hapsburg empire.

The most professional of the cruises are operated by the **DDSG Blue Danube Shipping Co.**, whose main offices are at Fredrickstrasse 7, A-1010 Vienna ((C) **01/588800**; www.ddsg-blue-danube.at). The most appealing cruise focuses on the Wachau region east of Vienna, between Vienna and Dürnstein. The cruise departs April through October every Sunday at 8:30am from the company's piers at Handelskai 265, 1020 Vienna (U-Bahn: Vorgartenstrasse), arriving in Dürnstein 6 hours later. The cost each way is 17€ for adults; it's half-price for children 10 to 15.

An alternative route takes passengers to Melk Abbey April through October every Sunday, leaving from the company's piers at 8:30am and arriving in Melk at 1:40pm. The cost each way is 16€ for adults; it's half-price for children 15 and under. If you want to go by boat to Melk during the week, you'll have to take the train to the railway station in Krems, where you can board a boat at Schiffstation Krems, about a 15-minute walk from the station. Three river cruises depart daily at 10:15am, 1pm, and 3:45pm for the 3-hour trip between Krems and Melk. One-way fare is 10.4b€. Frankly, most travelers find the one way passage to either Dürnstein or Melk an adequate exposure to the glories of riverboat travel, so we advise taking one of the many trains back to Vienna after your visit.

A final note: April through October, DDSG operates a daily hydrofoil that departs from the Vienna piers at 9am and arrives in Budapest at 2:30pm. One-way transit is 75€ for adults; it's half-price for children 15 and under.

BOATING

Wear a straw boating hat and hum a few bars of a Strauss waltz as you paddle your way around the quiet eddies of the Alte Donau. This gently curving stream bisects residential neighborhoods to the north of the Danube and is preferable to the muddy and swift-moving currents of the river itself.

At An der Obere along the Danube, you'll find some kiosks in summer where you can negotiate for the rental of a boat, perhaps a canoe or a kayak. There are, of course, organized tours of the Danube, but it's more fun to do it yourself.

HIKING

You're likely to expend plenty of shoe leather simply navigating Vienna's museums and palaces, but if you yearn for fresh air, the city tourist offices will provide information about its eight **Stadt-Wander-Wege.** These are carefully marked hiking paths that originate at points within the city's far-flung network of trams.

A less structured option involves heading east of town into the vast precincts of the **Lainzer Tiergarten,** where hiking trails entwine themselves amid forested hills, colonies of deer, and abundant bird life. To reach it from Vienna's center, first take the U-Bahn to the Kennedy Brücke/Heitzing station, which lies a few steps from the entrance to Schönbrunn Palace. A trek among the formal gardens of Schönbrunn might provide exercise enough, but if you're hungry for more, take tram no. 60 and then bus no. 60B into the distant but verdant confines of the Lainzer Tiergarten.

ICE-SKATING

There's a public rink, the **Wiener Eislaufverein,** Lothringer Strasse 22 (© **01/ 713-6353**), within a 20-minute walk southeast of the cathedral. Located just outside the famous Am Stadtpark, near the Inter-Continental Hotel, and especially crowded on weekends, the rink rents skates and is open from late October to early March daily from 8am to 8pm. Monday through Saturday, the charge is 6€ for adults and 5€ for children 7 to 18. On Sunday, the price goes up to 7€ for adults and 5.50€ for children. Skates rent for 5.50€. The rest of the year (Apr–Sept), the site is transformed into seven public tennis courts available to anyone who wants to play. The price for rental of a court is 7.50€ for daily sessions from 8am to noon, 10€ for sessions from noon to 5pm, and 15€ for sessions from 5 to 8pm.

10 Shopping

Visitors can spend many happy hours shopping or just browsing in Vienna's shops, where handicrafts are produced in a long-established tradition of skilled workmanship. Popular for their beauty and quality are petit-point items, hand-painted Wiener Augarten porcelain, work by goldsmiths and silversmiths, handmade dolls, ceramics, enamel jewelry, wrought-iron articles, leather goods, and many other items of value and interest.

The main shopping streets are in the city center (1st District). Popular destinations can be found on **Kärntnerstrasse,** between the Staatsoper and Stock-im-Eisen-Platz; the **Graben,** between Stock-im-Eisen-Platz and Kohlmarkt; **Kohlmarkt,** between the Graben and Michaelplatz; and **Rotensturmstrasse,** between Stephansplatz and Kai. There is also **Mariahilferstrasse,** between Babenbergerstrasse and Schönbrunn, one of the longest streets in Vienna; **Favoritenstrasse,** between Südtiroler Platz and Reumannplatz; and **Land-strasser Hauptstrasse.**

The **Naschmarkt** is a vegetable-and-fruit market, which has a lively scene every day. It's at Linke and Rechte Wienzeile, south of the opera district.

ANTIQUES

D&S Antiquitäten   This store, established in 1979, specializes in the acquisition, sale, and repair of antique Viennese clocks, stocking an awesome collection that would be coveted by many world-class museums. Some of the greatest breakthroughs in clock-making technology occurred in Vienna between 1800 and 1840, and the resulting highly accurate timepieces were hand-manufactured in wood, both carved and, in some cases, gilded—in rare cases (and only for extremely wealthy patrons), in fire-gilded bronze. The shop even stocks a "masterpiece" (each craftsman made only one such piece in his lifetime, and it accompanied his bid for entrance into the clockmaker's guild); in this case, it was made by a well-known craftsman of the early 1800s, Benedict Scheisel.

Shopping Hours

Shops are normally open Monday through Friday from 9am to 6pm and Saturday from 9am to 1pm. Small shops close from noon to 2pm for lunch. Westbahnhof and Südbahnhof shops are open daily from 7am to 11pm, offering groceries, smokers' supplies, stationery, books, and flowers.

Don't come here expecting a bargain: Prices are, as expected, astronomical. But devotees of timepieces from around the world flock to this emporium, treating it like a virtual museum of clocks. Dorotheergasse 13. ℂ **01/512-1011.** U-Bahn: Stephansplatz.

Dorotheum The state-owned Dorotheum is Europe's oldest auction house, founded by Emperor Joseph I in 1707 as an auction house where impoverished aristocrats could fairly (and anonymously) get good value for their heirlooms. Today the Dorotheum also holds many art auctions. If you're interested in what's being auctioned off, pay a small fee to a *Sensal,* one of the licensed bidders, and he or she will bid in your name. The objects for sale cover a wide spectrum, including exquisite furniture and carpets, delicate objets d'art, valuable paintings, and decorative jewelry. If you're unable to attend an auction, you can browse the sales rooms at your own pace, selecting items you want to purchase directly. These auctions are responsible for some 250,000 pieces of art and antiques exchanging hands annually. Dorotheergasse 17. ℂ **01/5156-0449.** U-Bahn: Stephansplatz.

Es Brennt Just a short walk east from the MuseumsQuartier, this is a much funkier antiques store than the grander (and stuffier) shops nearby. Its specialties include Art Deco French and English antiques, as well as Austrian, Bauhaus inspired pieces and old furniture from the 1920s to the 1960s. Sift among the interesting Soviet-era kitsch from Hungary and the former Czechoslovakia. There's a lot of retro stuff here from the age of Sputnik. Haven't you always wanted a Czech chrome toaster? Gunpindorsirstrasse 15–17. ℂ **01/532-0900.** U-Bahn: Stephansplatz.

Flohmarkt You can find a little of everything at this flea market, held every Saturday from 8am to 6pm except on public holidays. The Viennese have perfected the skill of haggling, and the Flohmarkt is one of their favorite arenas for this ritual battle of wills and wallets. It takes a trained eye to spot the treasures that are scattered among the junk. Everything you've ever wanted is here, especially if you're seeking those chunky Swiss watches from the '70s, glassware from the Czech Republic (sold as "Venetian glassware"), and even Russian icons. Believe it or not, some of this stuff is original; other merchandise is merely the knockoff version. Linke Wienzeille, near the Naschmarkt. No phone. U-Bahn: Kettenbrückengasse.

Galerie dei der Albertina Come here for ceramics and furniture made during the early 20th century by the Weiner Werkstette, the famous iconoclastic group of craftspeople. They made good use, better than anyone else before them, of the machinery of the emerging industrial age in the fabrication of domestic furnishings and decor. The shop's inventories include decorative objects, sculpture, and paintings from the Art Nouveau (Jugendstil) age, paintings and etchings (including an occasional drawing by Egon Schiele and Gustav Klimt), and esoterica that might be deeply appreciated by art critics in Vienna but not completely understood or appreciated except by the hyper-cognoscenti anywhere else. Lobkowitzplatz 1. ℂ **01/513-1416.**

ANTIQUE GLASS

Glasgalerie Kovacek   Its ground floor is devoted to antique glass collected from estate sales and private collections throughout Austria. Most of these items date from the 19th and early 20th centuries, although some 17th-century pieces are displayed as well. The most appealing pieces boast heraldic devices. There's also a collection of stunning glass paperweights imported from Bohemia, France, Italy, and other parts of Austria.

The upper floor is devoted to classical paintings that the Secessionists revolted against. Look for canvases by Franz Makart, foremost of the 19th-century historic academics. Two works by Kokoscha, a noted Secessionist, are also on display. Spiegelgasse 12. ✆ 01/512-9954. U-Bahn: Stephansplatz.

ART

Ö. W. (Österreichische Werkstatten)   This three-floor, well-run store sells hundreds of handmade art objects from Austria. Leading artists and craftspeople throughout the country organized this cooperative to showcase their wares. It's easy to find, only half a minute's walk from St. Stephan's. There's an especially good selection of pewter, along with modern jewelry, glassware, brass, baskets, ceramics, and serving spoons fashioned from deer horn and bone. Be sure to keep wandering; you never know what treasure awaits you in a nook of this cavernous outlet. Even if you skip the other stores of Vienna, check out this one. Kärntnerstrasse 6. ✆ 01/512-2418. U-Bahn: Stephansplatz.

CANDY & DESSERTS

Altmann & Kühne   If asked, many Viennese will regale you with childhood memories of the chocolates and marzipan, hazelnut, or nougat desserts their parents bought for them during strolls along the Graben. Established in 1928, Altmann & Kühne is the kind of cozy and nostalgic shop where virtually nothing inside is particularly good for your waistline or your teeth, but everything is positively and undeniably scrumptious. The decadent displays themselves are a visual feast. Don't expect to devour your purchases on-site, as everything is takeout. The pastries and tarts filled with fresh seasonal raspberries are, quite simply, delectable. Graben 30. ✆ 01/533-0927. U-Bahn: Stephansplatz.

Gerstner   This competes with Café Demel (see chapter 3) as one of the great pastrymakers and *chocolatiers* of Vienna, with a long-standing history of providing ingredients for kaffeeklatches throughout Vienna and some of the most delectable-looking cakes, petits fours, and chocolate anywhere. Kärntnerstrasse 11–15. ✆ 01/512-49-63-77. U-Bahn: Stephansplatz.

CHANDELIERS & PORCELAIN

Albin Denk   Established in 1702, Albin Denk is the oldest continuously operating porcelain store in Vienna. The shop looks much the same as it did when Empress Elisabeth was a client. The decor of the three low-ceilinged rooms is beautiful, as are the thousands of objects from Meissen, Dresden, and other regions. With such a wealth of riches, it can be hard to make a selection, but the staff will help you. Graben 13. ✆ 01/512-4439. U-Bahn: Stephansplatz.

Augarten Porzellan   Established in 1718, Augarten is, after Meissen, the oldest manufacturer of porcelain in Europe. This multitiered shop is the most visible and best-stocked outlet for the prized merchandise in the world. Virtually anything can be shipped anywhere. Tableware, consisting of fragile dinner plates with 18th-century patterns as well as contemporary designs, is much sought-after. Also noteworthy are porcelain statues of Lipizzaner horses. Stock-im-Eisenplatz 3–4. ⓒ 01/512-1494. U-Bahn: Stephansplatz.

J. & L. Lobmeyr   If during your exploration of Vienna you should happen to admire a crystal chandelier, there's a good chance that it was made by this company. In the early 19th century, Lobmeyr was named as a purveyor to the imperial court of Austria, and it has maintained an elevated position ever since. The company is credited with designing and producing the first electric chandelier, in 1883. It has also designed chandeliers for the Staatsoper; the Metropolitan Opera House in New York; the Assembly Hall in the Kremlin; the new concert hall in Fukuoka, Japan; and many palaces and mosques in the Middle and Far East.

Behind its Art Nouveau facade on this main shopping street, more than 50 chandeliers of all shapes and sizes are on display. The store also sells hand-painted Hungarian porcelain, along with complete breakfast and dinner services. They'll also do engravings or sell you one of the unique pieces of modern sculptured glass from the third-floor showroom. The second floor is a museum with some outstanding pieces. Kärntnerstrasse 26. ⓒ 01/512-0508. U-Bahn: Stephansplatz.

CLOTHING (TRADITIONAL AUSTRIAN)

Lanz   A well-known Austrian store, Lanz specializes in Austrian dirndls and other folkloric clothing. It has a rustically elegant format of wood paneling and brass chandeliers. Most of their stock is for women, although they do offer a limited selection of men's jackets, neckties, and hats. Clothes for toddlers begin at sizes appropriate for a 1-year-old child; women's apparel begins at size 36 (American size 7). Kärntnerstrasse 10. ⓒ 01/512-2456. U-Bahn: Stephansplatz.

Loden Plankl   Established in 1830 by the Plankl family, this store is the oldest and most reputable outlet in Vienna for traditional Austrian clothing. You'll find loden coats, shoes, trousers, dirndls, jackets, lederhosen, and suits for men, women, and children. The building, located opposite the Hofburg, dates from the 17th century. Children's clothing usually begins with items for 2-year-olds, and women's sizes range from 36 to 50 (American 7–20). Large or tall men won't be ignored either, as sizes go up to 60 (an American size 50). Michaelerplatz 6. ⓒ 01/533-8032. U-Bahn: Stephansplatz.

Niederösterreichisches Heimatwerk   This is one of the best-stocked clothing stores in Vienna for traditional Austrian garments. Inventory covers three full floors and includes garments inspired by the folkloric traditions of Styria, the Tyrol, Carinthia, and every other Austrian province in between. If you're looking for a loden coat, a dirndl, an alpine hat (with or without a pheasant feather), or an incredibly durable pair of lederhosen for those climbs in the foothills of the Alps, this is the place. You'll also find a charming collection of handcrafted gift items, including pewter, breadboards and breadbaskets, crystal, and tableware. Wippaingerstrasse 23. ⓒ 01/533-18990. U-Bahn: Schottentor.

Sportalm Trachtenmoden   If you're a woman looking for a coy and flattering dirndl to carry home with you, this stylish women's store stocks a staggering collection. Many are crafted as faithful replicas of designs that haven't been altered for generations; others take greater liberties and opt for brighter colors and updates that are specifically geared for modern tastes. Even if you're male and wouldn't otherwise dream of stepping into this shop, consider the possibility of procuring a lace-trimmed christening dress for a favorite niece, or a dirndl or traditional Austrian jacket that would make virtually any female child look adorable. Children's sizes fit girls ages 1 to 14. You'll find the store within the jarringly modern Haas Haus, across the plaza from St. Stephan's. Braunstette 7–9. ℂ 01/535-5289. U-Bahn: Stephansplatz.

DEPARTMENT STORES

Steffl Kaufhaus   Rising five floors above the pedestrian traffic of inner Vienna's most appealing shopping street, this is the city's most prominent and well-advertised department store. Within its well-stocked premises, you'll find rambling racks of cosmetics, perfumes, a noteworthy section devoted to books and periodicals, housewares, and a huge selection of men's, women's, and children's clothing. If there's something you forgot to pack, chances are very good that Steffl Kaufhaus has it. Kärntnerstrasse 19. ℂ 01/514-310. U-Bahn: Stephansplatz.

EMBROIDERY

Petit Point Kovacec   The delicate, small-scale art of petit point, in which floral patterns are hand-embroidered using the smallest possible stitches, has always been a craft for which Austria is famous. This shop carries only work that has been completed by workers using traditional techniques and patterns, and who work in their own homes. Items for sale include purses, bookmarks, key holders, brooches and rings set into sterling silver frames, and more ambitious works, such as framed pictures of floral themes and landscapes. Kärntnerstrasse 16. ℂ **01/512-4886.** U-Bahn: Stephansplatz.

FASHIONS

Casselli   This store caters to hip younger women in search of affordable fashions. Many of the garments are Italian made or inspired; the remainder are Austrian. Many of the younger downtown Viennese swear by the place for both casual street clothes and funky evening wear. In the Ringstrassen Galleries, Kärntner Ring 5–7. ℂ 01/512-5350. U-Bahn: Karlsplatz.

Helmut Lang   Although Helmut Lang's fashion success came after many years in New York and Paris, his earliest creative years were spent in his hometown of Vienna. In 1996, this "designer of the moment" returned, with fanfare, to open a boutique within Vienna's medieval core; and he has done a booming business ever since. Here, both men and women can find something to wear to an upscale cocktail party, a business meeting, or an off-the-record weekend with their inamorata of the moment. They also sell blue jeans with the Helmut Lang logo. Seilergasse 6. ℂ 01/513-2588. U-Bahn: Stephansplatz.

Popp & Kretschmer   The staff here is usually as well dressed as the clientele, and if you appear to be a bona fide customer, the sales clerks will offer coffee, tea, or champagne as you scrutinize the carefully selected merchandise. The store, opposite the Staatsoper, contains three carpeted levels of dresses for women, along with shoes, handbags, belts, and a small selection of men's briefcases and travel bags. Kärntnerstrasse 51. ℂ **01/512-7801.** U-Bahn: Stephansplatz.

JEWELRY

A. E. Köchert   Here, the sixth generation of the family that served as court jewelers to the House of Hapsburg continues its tradition of fine workmanship.

Finds Vintage Threads

If you're looking for second-hand or vintage clothing, join Vienna's youth rifling through the racks at the year-round **Naschmarkt** (U-Bahn: Karlsplatz).

The store, founded in 1814, is in a 16th-century building with landmark status. Although the firm has designed many of the crown jewels of Europe, the staff still pays attention to customers looking for such minor items as charms for a bracelet. Neuer Markt 15. ✆ 01/512-5828. U-Bahn: Stephansplatz.

Agatha Paris   The concept here is small-scale and intensely decorative, with jewelry that manages to be both exotic and tasteful at the same time. Many are inset with semiprecious (affordable) gemstones, others combine gold and silver into attractive ornaments that are sometimes (but not always) based on antique models. In the Ringstrassen Galleries, Kärntner Ring 5–7. ✆ 01/512-4621. U-Bahn: Karlsplatz.

Rozet & Fischmeister   Few jewelry stores in Austria attain the prestige of this 200-year-old emporium of good taste and conspicuous consumption. Owned by the same family since it was established in 1770, this store specializes in gold jewelry and gemstones set into artful settings. If you're looking for flawless copies of Biedermeier silverware or pieces inspired by 18th- and 19th-century aesthetics, this is the place to go. If you opt to buy an engagement ring or a trifle for a friend, you won't be the first. The staff will quietly admit that Franz Joseph I made several discreet purchases here for his legendary mistress, actress Katharina Schratt. Kohlmarkt 11. ✆ 01/533-8061. U-Bahn: Stephansplatz.

LACE & NEEDLEWORK

Zur Schwabischen Jungfrau   This is one of the most illustrious shops in Austria, with a reputation that goes back almost 300 years. Maria Theresa bought her first handkerchiefs here, thousands of debutantes have shopped for dresses here, and brides have accumulated even the most esoteric items for their trousseaux here. Oil billionaires from the Middle East have bought out the shop's supply of hand-embroidered silk sheets, and costume designers have rummaged through the racks of material before whipping up period costumes. Come here for towels, bed linens, lace tablecloths, and some of the most elaborate needlepoint and embroidery anywhere. Know in advance that the ground-floor showrooms seem relatively small, but an elevator will take you up to two additional floors of merchandise. Service is courtly, cordial, old worldish, and impeccable. Graben 26. ✆ 01/535-5356. U-Bahn: Stephansplatz.

MUSIC

Arcadia Opera Shop   Well respected as one of Austria's best music stores, this shop offers a broad range of classical music. Its staff is well educated in the lore, legend, and availability of classical recordings and is usually eager to share its knowledge with customers. Located on the street level of the Staatsoper, with a separate entrance opening onto Kärntnerstrasse, the store also carries books on art, music, architecture, and opera, as well as an assortment of musical memorabilia. Guided tours of the splendid opera house conveniently end here. Wiener Staatsoper, Kärntnerstrasse 40. ✆ 01/513-9568. U-Bahn: Karlsplatz.

Da Caruso   Set almost adjacent to the Staatsoper, Da Caruso draws music fans and academicians from around the world for its inventory of rare and unusual recordings of historic performances by the Vienna Opera and the Vienna Philharmonic. Here's where you'll find a recording of a magical or particularly emotional performance by Maria Callas, Herbert von Karajan, Bruno Walter, or whomever your favorite might be. The staff is hip, alert, educated, and obviously in love with music. There's also a collection of taped films. Operngasse 4. ✆ 01/513-1326. U-Bahn: Karlsplatz.

Moments   Noshing Your Way Through Vienna's Open-Air Markets

Viennese merchants have thrived since the Middle Ages by hauling produce, dairy products, and meats in bulk from the fertile farms of Lower Austria and Burgenland into the city center. The tradition of buying the day's provisions directly from street stalls is so strong that, even today, it's tough for modern supermarkets to survive within the city center.

Odd (and inconvenient) as this might seem, you'll quickly grasp the fun of Vienna's open-air food stalls after a brief wander through one of these outdoor markets. Most of the hundreds of merchants operating within them maintain approximately the same hours: Monday through Friday from 8am to 6pm and Saturday from 8am to noon.

The largest is the **Naschmarkt,** Wienzeile, in the 6th District (U-Bahn: Karlsplatz), just south of the Ring. Because of its size, it's the most evocatively seedy and colorful of the bunch, as well as being the most firmly rooted in the life of the city.

Less comprehensive are the **Rochusmarkt,** at Landstrasser Hauptstrasse at the corner of the Erdbergstrasse, 3rd District (U-Bahn: Rochusgasse), a short distance east of the Ring, and the **Brunnenmarkt,** on the Brunnengasse, 16th District (U-Bahn: Josefstädterstrasse), a short walk north of the Westbahnhof. Even if you don't plan on stocking up on produce and foodstuff (the staff at your hotel might not be amused if you showed up with bushels of carrots or potatoes), the experience is colorful enough and, in some cases, kitsch enough, to be remembered as one of the highlights of your trip to Vienna.

SHOPPING CENTER

The Ringstrassen Galleries   Rental fees for shop space in central Vienna are legendarily expensive. In response to the high rents, about 70 boutiques selling everything from hosiery to key chains to evening wear have pooled their resources and moved to labyrinthine quarters near the Staatsoper, midway between the Bristol and Anna hotels. Its prominent location guarantees a certain glamour, although the cramped dimensions of many of the stores might be a turn-off. The selection is broad, and no one can deny the gallery's easy-to-find location. Each shop is operated independently, but virtually all of them conduct business Monday through Friday from 10am to 7pm and Saturday from 10am to 5pm. Two stores of particular interest to fashion hounds are Casselli and Agatha Paris, each of which is recommended separately above. In the Palais Corso and in the Kärntnerringhof, Kärntner Ring 5–13. © 01/512-51-81-11. U-Bahn: Karlsplatz.

TOYS

Kober   Kober has been a household name, especially at Christmastime in Vienna, for more than 100 years. There are old-fashioned wooden toys, teddy bears that remind you of something you might find in a Styrian forest, go-carts (parents will probably have to assemble these after purchase), building sets, and car and airplane models. The occasional set of toy soldiers might remind you more of the *Nutcracker* than anything really military. 14–15 Graben. © 01/533-6019. U-Bahn: Stephansplatz.

WINE

Wein & Co.   Since the colonization of Vindobona by the ancient Romans, the Viennese have always taken their wines seriously. Wein & Co. is Vienna's largest wine outlet, a sprawling, cellar-level testament to the joys of the grape and the bounty of Bacchus. Its shelves are loaded with Rheinrieslings, Blauburgunder, Blaufrankischer, Grüner Veltliners, Zweigelts, and a roster of obscure Austrian wines you might never have even thought about before. There's also an inventory of wines from around the world, including South Africa, Chile, and all the wine-producing countries of western Europe. Jasomirgottstrasse 3–5. ℂ **01/535-0916.** U-Bahn: Stephansplatz.

11 Vienna After Dark

Whatever nightlife scene turns you on, Vienna has a little bit of it. You can dance into the morning hours, hear a concert, attend an opera or festival, go to the theater, gamble, or simply sit and talk over a drink at a local tavern.

The best source of information about what's happening on the cultural scene is *Wien Monatsprogramm,* which is distributed free at tourist information offices and at many hotel reception desks. *Die Presse,* the Viennese daily, publishes a special magazine in its Thursday edition outlining the major cultural events for the coming week. It's in German but might still be helpful to you.

The Viennese are not known for discounting their cultural presentations. However, *Wien Monatsprogramm* lists outlets where you can purchase tickets in advance, thereby cutting down the surcharge imposed by travel agencies. These agencies routinely add about 22% to what might already be an expensive ticket.

If you're not a student and don't want to go bankrupt to see a performance at the Staatsoper or the Burgtheater, you can purchase standing-room tickets at a cost of about 5€.

Students under 27 with valid IDs are eligible for many discounts. For example, the Burgtheater, Akademietheater, and Staatsoper sell student tickets for just 8€ on the night of the performance. Theaters almost routinely grant students about 20% off the regular ticket price. Vienna is the home of four major symphony orchestras, including the world-acclaimed Vienna Symphony and the Vienna Philharmonic. In addition to the ÖRF Symphony Orchestra and the Niederöster-reichische Tonkünstler, there are literally dozens of others, ranging from smaller orchestras to chamber orchestras.

THE PERFORMING ARTS

Music is at the heart of cultural life in Vienna. This has been true for a couple of centuries or so, and the city continues to lure composers and librettists, musicians and music lovers. You can find places to enjoy everything from chamber music and waltzes to pop, rock, and jazz. There are small discos and large concert halls, as well as musical theaters. If somehow you should tire of musical entertainment, Vienna's stages present classical, modern, and avant-garde dramas. Below we describe just a few of the highlights—if you're in Vienna long enough, you'll find many other diversions on your own.

AUSTRIAN STATE THEATERS & OPERA HOUSES

Reservations and information for the four state theaters—the Weiner Staatsoper (Vienna State Opera), Volksoper, Burgtheater (National Theater), and Akademietheater—can be obtained by contacting **Österreichische Bundestheater (Austrian Federal Theatres),** the office that coordinates reservations and information for all four theaters (© **01/5144-42959;** www.bundestheater.at). Call Monday through Friday from 8am to 5pm. *Note:* The number is likely to be busy; it's easier to get information and order tickets online. The major season is September through June, with more limited presentations in summer. Many tickets are issued to subscribers before the box office opens. For all four theaters, box-office sales are made only 1 month before each performance at the Bundestheaterkasse, Goethegasse 1 (© **01/51-44-40**), open Monday through Friday from 8am to 6pm, Saturday from 9am to 2pm, and Sunday and holidays from 9am to noon. Credit- and charge-card sales can be arranged by telephone within 6 days of a performance by calling © **01/513-1513** Monday through Friday from 10am to 6pm, and Saturday and Sunday from 10am to noon. Tickets for all state theater performances, including the opera, are also available by writing to the Österreichischer Bundestheaterverband, Goethegasse 1, A-1010 Vienna, from points outside Vienna. Orders must be received at least 3 weeks in advance of the performance to be booked. No one should send money through the mail. For more information on tickets, go to the websites of the venues listed below.

Note: The single most oft-repeated complaint of music lovers in Vienna is about the lack of available tickets to many highly desirable musical performances. If the suggestions above don't produce the desired tickets, you could consult a ticket broker. Their surcharge usually won't exceed 25%, except for exceptionally rare tickets, when that surcharge might be doubled or tripled. Although at least half a dozen ticket agencies maintain offices in the city, one of the most reputable agencies is **Liener Brünn** (© **01/533-09-61**), which might make tickets available months in advance or as little as a few hours before the anticipated event.

As a final resort, remember that the concierges of virtually every upscale hotel in Vienna long ago learned sophisticated tricks for acquiring hard-to-come-by tickets. (A gratuity of at least $10 might work wonders and will be expected anyway for the phoning this task will entail. You'll pay a hefty surcharge as well.)

Akademietheater   This theater specializes in both classic and contemporary works, from Brecht to Shakespeare. The Burgtheater Company often performs here, as it's the second, smaller house of this world-famous theater (see below). Lisztstrasse 3. © 01/5144-42656. www.burgtheater.at. Tickets 4€–44€ for seats, 1.50€ for standing room. U-Bahn: Stadtpark.

Burgtheater (National Theater)   The Burgtheater produces classical and modern plays in German. Work started on the original structure in 1776. Mozart's *Marriage of Figaro* premiered here in 1786; his *Cosi fan Tutte* premiered in 1790. The theater was destroyed in World War II and was not reopened until 1955. It's the dream of every German-speaking actor to appear here. Dr.-Karl-Lueger-Ring 2. © 01/5144-4145. www.burgtheater.at. Tickets 9€–178€ for seats, 2€–3.50€ for standing room. Tram: 1, 2, or D to Burgtheater.

Volksoper   This folk opera house presents lavish productions of Viennese operettas and other musicals September through June on a daily schedule. Tickets go on sale at the Volksoper itself only 1 hour before performance. Währingerstrasse 78. © 01/5144-43318. www.volksoper.at. Tickets 7€–65€ for seats, 2.50€–4€ for standing room. U-Bahn: Volksoper.

Wiener Staatsoper (Vienna State Opera)   This is one of the three most important opera houses in the world. With the Vienna Philharmonic in the pit, some of the leading opera stars of the world perform here. In their day, Richard Strauss and Gustav Mahler worked as directors. Daily performances are given September through June. (For information on tours, see section 2, "Other Top

Attractions.") Opernring 2. © 01/5144-42250. www.wiener-staatsoper.at. Tours given almost daily year-round, often 2–5 times a day; times posted on a board outside the entrance. Tours 4.50€ per person. Tickets 10€–178€. U-Bahn: Karlsplatz.

MORE THEATER & MUSIC

If your German is halfway passable, try to see a play by Arthur Schnitzler if one is being staged during your visit. This mild-mannered playwright, who died in 1931, was the most characteristically Viennese of the Austrian writers. Through his works he gave the imperial city the charm and style more often associated with Paris. Whenever possible, we attend a revival of one of his plays, such as *Einsame Weg* (*The Solitary Path*) or *Professor Bernhardi*. Our favorite is *Reigen,* on which the film *La Ronde* was based. Schnitzler's plays are often performed at the Theater in der Josefstadt.

Konzerthaus   This major concert hall with three auditoriums was built in 1913. It's the venue for a wide cultural program, including orchestral concerts, chamber-music recitals, choir concerts, piano recitals, and opera concert stage performances. Its repertoire is classical, romantic, and folk, as well as contemporary (from recent classical music to jazz, rock, and pop). Lothringerstrasse 20. © 01/242-002. www.konzerthaus.at. Ticket prices depend on the event. Box office open Mon-Fri 9am–7:30pm; Sat 9am–1pm. U-Bahn: Stadtpark.

Musikverein   Count yourself fortunate if you get to hear a concert here. The Golden Hall is regarded as one of the four acoustically best concert halls in the world. Some 600 concerts per season (Sept–June) are presented here. Only 10 to 12 of these are played by the Vienna Philharmonic, and these are subscription concerts, so they're always sold out long in advance. Standing room is available at almost any performance, but you must line up hours before the show. Dumbastrasse 3. © 01/505-8190 for the box office. www.musikverein-wien.at. Tickets up to 120€ for seats; 3€ for standing room. Box office open Mon–Fri 9am–7:30pm; Sat 9am–5pm. U-Bahn: Karlsplatz.

Schönbrunner Palace Theater   A gem in a regal setting, this theater opened in 1749 for the entertainment of the court of Maria Theresa. The architecture is a medley of baroque and rococo, and there's a large, plush box where the imperial family sat to enjoy the shows. The theater belongs to Hochschule für Musik und Darstellende Kunst and is used for performances of the Max Reinhardt Seminar (theater productions) and for opera productions throughout the year. Operettas and comic operas are performed in July and August. A wide variety of different art groups, each responsible for its own ticket sales, performs here. There are various performances daily in July and August Tuesday through Saturday nights. At Schönbrunn Palace, Schönbrunner Schlossstrasse. © 01/512-01-00. www.schoenbrunn.at. Tickets 5€–40€. U-Bahn: Schönbrunn.

Tips **A Note on Evening Dress**

For concerts and theaters, dark suits and cocktail dresses are recommended. For especially festive occasions such as opera premieres, receptions, and balls, tails and dinner jackets are the preferred dress for men and evening dresses are recommended for women. You can rent men's evening wear, as well as carnival costumes, from several places in Vienna, which you'll find in the telephone directory classified section under *Kleiderleihanstalten*. It's a good idea to take a light topcoat when you go out in the evening, even in summer.

Theater an der Wien   This theater opened on June 13, 1801, and its opera and operetta presentations have been entertaining fans ever since. Beethoven's *Fidelio* premiered here in 1805; in fact, the composer once lived in this building. Johann Strauss Jr.'s *Die Fledermaus* premiered here in 1874, and Franz Lehár's *The Merry Widow* premiered in 1905. During the occupation after World War II, when the Staatsoper was being restored after heavy damage, the Vienna State Opera made the Theater an der Wien its home. Linke Weinzeile 6. (℃ 01/ 588-85 for tickets. www.theateranderwien.at. Tickets 30€–90€. U-Bahn: Karlsplatz.

Theater in der Josefstadt   Built in 1776, this theater prides itself on presenting comedies, dramas, and tragedies, either in their original German or in German-language translations (musical performances are almost never given here). One of the most influential theaters in the Teutonic world, it reached legendary levels of excellence under the aegis of Max Reinhardt, beginning in 1924. Josefstädterstrasse 26. (℃ 01/42700. www.josefstadt.org. Tickets 3€–46€. Box office open daily 10am–7:30pm. U-Bahn: Rathaus. Tram: J. Bus: 13.

Vienna's English Theatre   This is the major English-speaking theater in Vienna. It was established in 1963 and proved so popular that it has been around ever since. Many international celebrities and numerous British actors have appeared on the stage of this neobaroque theater. Princess Grace of Monaco played here in a performance to raise money for charity. Works by American playwrights are occasionally presented. Josefsgasse 12. (℃ 01/402-1260-0. www.english theatre.at. Tickets 20€–36€. U-Bahn: Rathaus. Tram: J. Bus: 13A.

Volkstheater   Built in 1889, this theater maintains a tradition of presenting plays from the classical repertoire of German-language theater, and it almost never schedules a purely musical performance. Some of the pieces produced here are videotaped for distribution and include original versions and translations of works by Nestroy, Raimund, and Strindberg. Modern plays and comedies are also presented. The theater's season runs September through June. Neustiftgasse 1. (℃ 01/524-7263. www.volkstheater.at. Tickets 7.50€–35€. Box office open Mon–Sat 10am–7:30pm. U-Bahn: Volkstheater. Tram: 1, 2, 49, D, or J. Bus: 48A.

THE CLUB & MUSIC SCENE
NIGHTCLUBS & CABARETS

First Floor   As its name implies, this hip and worldly nightclub is one floor above street level in an antique building in the city's historic old Jewish district. Most of the clients range in age from 25 to 45 in this metallic-looking, mostly blue environment. There's a long and very active bar area along with a vast, artfully illuminated aquarium so you can see the fish swimming around. Mixed drinks, including martinis, cost 8€ to 14€ each. There's live music—usually only a piano and bass—on Monday night. Hours are Monday through Saturday from 8pm to 4am and Sunday from 7pm to 3am. Seitenstettengasse 5. (℃ 01/533-7866. U-Bahn: Schwedenplatz.

Franco's Club   This is one of the most complete and comprehensive bar and restaurant complexes in Vienna, with touches of class and an almost guaranteed roster of available singles for anyone looking for a dance partner. It occupies the street level and cellar of what was built around 1870 as an apartment complex, just inside the Ring. Until 9:30pm on opening nights, its faux-baroque but very lavish interior is divided into a separate bar and restaurant area, but after that, very tall, very wide walnut-inset-with-leaded-glass doors slide open to interconnect them into one bustling whole. The parquet floors have been especially praised for their old-fashioned intricacies. No one will insist that you have dinner, but if you want to dine as part of your night on the town, main courses cost from 15€ to 25€. The food is Italian, and a cover charge of 40€ is added as a one-time fee to every table. Live entertainment from a five-member dance band is provided, beginning around 8:30pm. Most Thursdays through Saturdays after 11pm, Franco Andolfo, a well-known Italy-born singer (he's been referred to as "the Frank Sinatra of *Mitteleuropa*") sings, tells jokes, and entertains. There's no cover charge at the bar, and cocktails cost from 6€ to 8.50€ each. If you get tired of the scene on the street level, head to the piano bar in the basement. The complex is open Tuesday through Saturday from 3pm till 4am, with the restaurant open from 3pm until midnight, but frankly, the joint doesn't start to get interesting until around 9pm. Johannesgasse 27. ℂ 01/512-8282. AE, DC, MC, V. U-Bahn: Stadpark.

Moulin Rouge   Established long before World War II, this nightspot has survived greater changes, and more changes in venue, than many of its shorter-lived competitors. For years it functioned as a strip club, where female dancers and *artistes* amused and entertained male admirers, often in a state of complete undress and often on stage. All of that changed around the turn of the millennium, when the place was cleaned up and cleaned out, and the famous Moulin Rouge reopened as a conventional disco and supper restaurant. Many of today's patrons are under 35 and come here for set-price menus, costing from 15€ to 30€ each, and then a round of disco. The restaurant is open Tuesday through Saturday from 6pm to midnight, and the disco operates Tuesday through Saturday from 10:30pm till at least 4am. If you opt for a meal here, entrance to the disco is free. Otherwise, entrance to the disco costs from 10€ to 15€ per person, depending on the night of the week. Walfischgasse 11. ℂ 01/513-5000. U-Bahn: Karlsplatz or Stephansplatz.

U-4   Although the origins of this club go back to the 1920s, it continues to revitalize itself with every new generation of nightclubbers. Today it's always cited as one of the trendiest and most cutting-edge clubs in Vienna. Depending on that month's schedule, you're likely to experience such themes as Italian night, salsa/Latino night, and—every Thursday—gay night. Admission varies from nothing to 8€. It's open nightly from 9pm to around 5am, depending on business. Schönbrunner Strasse 222. ℂ 01/815-8307. U-4 to Pilgramgasse.

ROCK, JAZZ & BLUES CLUBS

Café Leopold   No one ever expected that the city's homage to Viennese expressionism (the Leopold Museum) would ever rock and roll with the sounds of dancing feet and high-energy music. But that's exactly what happens here three nights a week, when the museum's restaurant fills up with drinkers, wits, gossips, dancers, and people of all ilk on the make. There's a revolving cycle of DJs, each vying for local fame and approval, and a wide selection of party-colored cocktails, priced at around 8.50€ each. The cafe-and-restaurant section of this place opens daily from 9am to 2am; the disco operates only Thursday through Saturday from 9:30pm till between 2 and 3am, depending on business. There's no cover charge. In the Leopold Museum, Museumsplatz 1. ℂ 01/523-67-32. U-Bahn: Volkstheater or Babenbergstrasse/MuseumsQuartier.

Jazzland   This is the most famous jazz pub in Austria, noted for the quality of its U.S. and central European–based performers. It's in a deep 200-year-old cellar. Amid exposed brick walls and dim lighting, you can order drinks or dinner. Beer—which seems to be the thing to order here—costs 4€ for a foaming mugful. Platters of Viennese food such as *Tafelspitz,* Wiener schnitzel, and roulades of beef cost 5€ to 8€. The place is open nightly from 7pm to 1am. Music begins at 9pm, and three sets are performed. Franz-Josefs-Kai 29. ℂ 01/533-2575. Cover 11€–20€. U-Bahn: Schwedenplatz.

Papa's Tapas   This place attracts rock 'n' roll fans. It has the same location as the Atrium disco (see below). In a corner is the Würlitzer Bar, with its American-made jukebox. You get all vintage '50s stuff, including Elvis. It plays host to a changing roster of visiting rock stars, whose arrival is always noted in the Vienna newspapers. When there's no live music, Papa's operates as a bar, with a large beer costing 3€. The club is open Monday through Thursday from 8pm to 2am, and Friday and Saturday from 8pm until 3:30am. Schwarzenbergplatz 10. ℂ 01/505-0311. Cover 3.50€–10.50€, depending on the event. U-Bahn: Karlsplatz.

Rockhaus   Rockhaus is a direct competitor of the also-recommended Tunnel (see below). As such, it attracts some of the same clientele, some of the same energy, and—with perhaps a higher percentage of folk singers, reggae, soca, and new wave artists—some of the same musicians. It's also about twice as large as the Tunnel, which contributes to larger crowds and louder volumes. About half of the bands that play here are Austrian; the remainder are from other parts of Europe and, on some particularly festive nights, from such Asian music centers as the Philippines. Rockhaus rocks and rolls every Monday through Friday, with the bar drawing a heavy after-work crowd after 6pm. Live concerts can take place any day of the week, so call ahead for the live music schedule sometime after 8:30pm. Adalbert-Stifter-Strasse 73. ℂ 01/332-46-41. Cover charge 8€–30€. Tram: 33.

Tunnel   Experiences like the ones created in the 1960s and 1970s by Jimi Hendrix are alive and well, if in less dramatic form, at Tunnel. In a smoke-filled cellar near Town Hall, it showcases musical groups from virtually everywhere. You'll never know quite what to expect, as the only hint of what's on or off is a recorded German-language announcement of what's about to appear and occasional advertisements in local newspapers. But if you're willing to take potluck, you can still groove and be cool. It's open daily from 9pm to 2am, with live music beginning around 10pm. Florianigasse 39. ℂ 01/405-3465. Cover 3€–12€. U-Bahn: Rathaus.

DANCE CLUBS

Atrium   This spot is still within a 5-minute walk of its original location, where it was Vienna's first disco. Today it caters to a young crowd that gathers here Thursday and Sunday from 8:30pm to 2am, and Friday and Saturday from 8:30pm to 4am. Every Thursday and Sunday, drinks are 2-for-1 for the first hour of business. Otherwise, a large beer costs 2.80€. Schwarzenbergplatz 10 (Schwindgasse 1). ℂ 01/505-3594. Cover 3€. U-Bahn: Karlsplatz.

P1 Discothek   The leading disco of Vienna, this lively place is filled with Viennese and visitors alike, most in their mid-20s. In what used to be a film studio, the dance club has a spacious floor that can hold as many as 2,000 dancers. The club was launched on the road to fame when Tina Turner made an appearance here back in 1988. Two DJs alternate nightly. Once or twice a month, there's live music. The club is open Tuesday through Saturday from 8pm to 6am. Beer costs 3.20€ and up. Rotgasse 9. ℂ 01/535-9995. Cover 5€ Tues–Thurs; 6.50€ Fri–Sat. U-Bahn: Stephansplatz.

Queen Anne   Lots of fabulous people are attracted to this nightclub and disco. Patrons have included David Bowie, German playboy Gunther Sachs, the princess of Auersperg, and the 1970s heavy-metal band Deep Purple. The club has a big collection of the latest Stateside and Italian records, as well as occasional musical acts ranging from Mick Jagger look-alikes to imitations of Watusi dancers. The brown doors with brass trim are open daily from 10pm to 5am. A scotch and soda goes for 8.50€; beer starts at 5.50€. Johannesgasse 12. ℂ 01/ 994-8844. U-Bahn: Stadtpark.

Scotch Club   Except for the whisky, there's not much Scottish about this disco and coffeehouse in Vienna's most fashionable area, a 5-minute walk from the Hilton, Marriott, Radisson SAS, Parkring, and Imperial. It's a popular meeting place for society figures and others, and it has in the past attracted such celebrity icons as Austrian pop singer Uta Jürgens and Harry Belafonte. Furnished in a way that's plush and comfortable, it includes a hydraulic stage, an artificial waterfall, and fancy lights. Its three floors include a disco in the cellar, a bistro and supper restaurant on the street level, and a cocktail bar one floor above street level. Light snacks in the bistro are 2.30€ to 4.50€; beer anywhere on-site costs 2.50€. The disco rocks and rolls daily from 9pm to 5am; the restaurant is open daily from 11am to 4am. Parkring 10. ℂ 01/512-9417. U-Bahn: Stadtpark or Stubentor.

Titanic   A sprawling dance club that has thrived since the early 1980s, it has two different dance areas and a likable upstairs restaurant where Mexican, Italian, and international foods provide bursts of quick energy for further bouts of dancing. You'll enter a mirrored world with strobe lights, without seating areas, which encourages patrons to dance, drink, and mingle, sometimes aggressively, throughout the evening. It's popular with U.S. students and athletes. As for the music, you're likely to find everything that's playing in London or New York— soul, funk, hip-hop, house, '70s-style disco—but with the notable exception of techno and rave music, which is deliberately avoided. The restaurant serves dinners every Wednesday through Saturday from 7pm to 2am; main courses are 10€ to 17€. The dancing areas are open nightly from 10pm to around 4am, depending on business. Beer costs 2.50€ to 3.50€. Theobaldgasse 11. ℂ 01/ 587-4758. U-Bahn: Mariahilferstrasse.

THE BAR SCENE

Viennese bars range from time-honored upscale haunts to loud, trendy establishments that stay open until dawn. The most popular area (among locals and visitors) for experiencing Vienna's blossoming bar scene is the **Bermuda Triangle** (U-Bahn: Schwedenplatz). It's roughly bordered by Judengasse, Seitenstättengasse Rabensteig, and Franz-Josefs-Kai. You'll find everything from intimate watering holes to large bars with live music. Below is a sampling of bars that will appeal to a broad spectrum of tastes.

Barfly's Club   This is the most urbane and sophisticated cocktail bar in town, frequented by journalists, actors, and politicians. It's got a laissez-faire ambience that combines aspects of Vienna's *grande bourgeoisie* with its discreet avant-garde. The setting is a meticulously paneled room lined with rows of illuminated bottles, reminiscent of the bars in transatlantic ocean liners in the 1930s. A menu lists about 370 cocktails that include every kind of mixed drink imaginable, priced at 7€ to 11€. The only food served is "toast" (warm sandwiches), priced at 5€. It's open daily from 6pm to between 2 and 4am, depending on the night of the week. In the Hotel Fürst Metternich, Esterházygasse 33. ℂ 01/586-0825. U-Bahn: Kirchengasse. Tram: 5.

Esterházykeller   The ancient bricks and scarred wooden tables of this drinking spot, famous since 1683, are permeated with the aroma of endless pints of spilled beer. An outing here isn't recommended for everyone, but if you decide to chance it, choose the left entrance (facing from the street), grip the railing firmly, and begin your descent. A stroll through the endless recesses and labyrinthine passages might provide glimpses of faces like those you might have thought appeared only in movies. Wine, a specialty, starts at 1.80€ to 2.50€. Order a bottle if you plan to stay a while. The place is open Monday through Friday from 11am to 11pm, and Saturday and Sunday from 4 to 11pm. Haarhof 1. ℂ 01/ 533-3482. U-Bahn: Stephansplatz.

Kleines Café   Virtually every painter and sculptor in modern-day Vienna seems to be intimately familiar with this cramped but cozy two-room bar and cafe. In summer, tables are set up outside on Franziskanerplatz, overlooking the votive fountain dedicated to Moses. The rest of the year, people gather beneath the 18th-century vaults of an antique building that was "modernized" around 1830 with a Biedermeier facade. Few other bars depend as completely on the cult of one person, but in this case, it depends on Hammo Poeschl, a well-known entrepreneur whose interest in the arts is legendary. He's occasionally assisted by his Ohio-born wife, Kimberley. Sandwiches cost 1.50€ to 5€; main courses are 4.75€ to 6€. The place is open Monday through Saturday from 10am to 2am, and Sunday from 1pm to 2am. Franziskanerplatz. No phone. No credit cards. U-Bahn: Stephansplatz.

Krah Krah   This place is the most animated and well-known singles bar in the area. Every day an attractive, and sometimes available, after-work crowd fills this woodsy, somewhat battered space. Beer is the drink of choice here, with more than 60 kinds available, many of them on tap, from 2.50€ to 3.50€ each. Sandwiches, snacks and simple platters of food, including hefty portions of Weiner schnitzel, cost from 4.50€ to 7€ each. It's open daily from 11am to 2am. Rabensteig 8. ℂ 01/533-8193. U-Bahn: Schwedenplatz.

Loos American Bar   One of the most unusual and interesting bars in the center of Vienna, this very dark, sometimes mysterious bar was designed by the noteworthy architect Adolf Loos in 1908. At the time, it functioned as the drinking room of a private men's club, but today it's more democratic—it welcomes a crowd that tends to be bilingual and very hip singles and clients from Vienna's arts-and-media scene. Walls, floors, and ceilings sport layers of dark marble and black onyx, making this one of the most expensive small-scale decors in the city. No food is served, but the mixologist's specialties include six kinds of martinis, plus five kinds of Manhattans, each 7.20€. Just ask one of the great barhoppers of Europe, and we're sure you'll be told that Loos serves the finest martini in Vienna. Beer costs from 2.60€. It's open Sunday through Wednesday from noon to 4am and Thursday through Saturday till 5am. Kärntnerdurchgang 10. ℂ 01/512-3283. U-Bahn: Stephansplatz.

New York, New York   The decor of this place isn't as blatantly red-white-and-blue as you might have expected: In fact, it's a monochromatic study in black and white, with furniture that evokes the age of Sputnik in the 1950s. Its main link to New York, however, comes from the way it celebrates the high-octane cocktails that fueled America's rise to prominence after World War II. As such, the cocktail menu lists more than 200 kinds of drinks. Examples include all kinds of martinis (including a classic "dirty martini" made with dry gin, dry vermouth, and the brine in which the olives were stored); Manhattans (versions identified as either dry, sweet, or "perfect"), and a "guaranteed to make you stagger" roster of gimlets, daiquiris, Tom Collins's and margaritas. Don't ask for beer—as a matter of pride, "bartender of the year" (in 1998) Farhat Ellouzi simply doesn't serve it. Cocktails cost from 5€ to 8€. It's open Tuesday through Saturday from 5pm to 2am (till 3am Fri–Sat). Annagasse 8. © **01/513-8651.** U-Bahn: Stephansplatz.

Onyx Bar   One of the most appealing, though crowded, bars near the Stephensplatz is on the sixth (next-to-uppermost) floor of one of Vienna's most controversial buildings—the ultramodern, glass-fronted Haas Haus, whose facade reflects the turrets and medieval stonework of St. Stephan's. Lunch is served from noon to 3pm daily; dinner is from 6pm to midnight. The staff serves a long and varied cocktail menu from 6pm to 2am, including strawberry margaritas and caipirinhas, each priced from 3€ to 20€. Live and recorded music is presented, usually beginning after 8:30pm when some of the more exuberant folks in the crowd might actually get up and dance. In the Haas Haus, Stephansplatz 12. © **01/535-3969.** U-Bahn: Stephansplatz.

Rhiz Bar Modern   Hip, multicultural, and electronically sophisticated, with no trace at all of Hapsburg nostalgia, this bar is nested into the vaulted, century-old niches created by the trusses of the U-6 subway line, a few blocks west of the Ring. In this once-grimy industrial-age architecture, stainless-steel ventilation ducts, a green plastic bar, and a sophisticated stereo system have been installed. A TV camera constantly broadcasts images of the hipster clientele over the Internet every night from 10pm to 3am. Drinks include Austrian wine, Scottish whisky, and beer from everywhere in Europe. A large beer costs 2.90€. It's open Monday through Saturday from 6pm to 4am and Sunday from 6pm to 2am. Llerchenfeldergürtel 37–38, Stadtbahnbögen. © **01/409-2505.** www.rhiz.org. U-Bahn: Josefstädterstrasse.

GAY & LESBIAN BARS

Alfi's Goldener Spiegel   The most enduring gay restaurant in Vienna (see chapter 3) is also its most popular gay bar, attracting mostly male clients to its position near Vienna's Naschmarkt. You don't need to come here to dine, but you can patronize the bar, where almost any gay male from abroad drops in for a look-see at least once during his sojourn in Vienna. The place is very cruisy, and the bar is open Wednesday through Monday from 7pm to 2am. Linke Wienzeile 46. © **01/586-6608.** U-Bahn: Kettenbruckengasse.

Eagle Bar   This is one of the premier leather and denim bars for gay men in Vienna. There's no dancing, but virtually every gay male in town has dropped in at least once or twice for a quick look around. The bar even offers a back room where free condoms are distributed. It's open daily from 9pm to 4am. Large beers begin at 2.60€. Blümelgasse 1. © **01/587-26-61.** U-Bahn: Neubaugasse.

Frauencafé   Frauencafé is exactly what a translation of its name would imply: a politically conscious cafe for lesbian and (to a lesser degree) heterosexual women who appreciate the company of other women. Established in 1977 in cramped quarters in a century-old building, it's filled with magazines, newspapers, modern paintings, and a clientele of Austrian and foreign women. Next door is a feminist bookstore loosely affiliated with the cafe. Frauencafé is open Tuesday through Saturday from 6:30pm to 2am. Glasses of wine begin at 2€. Langegasse 11. © **01/406-37-54.** U-Bahn: Lerchenfelderstrasse.

THE *HEURIGEN*

These wine taverns on the outskirts of Vienna have long been celebrated in operetta, film, and song. Grinzing is the most visited district, but other *Heurigen* neighborhoods include Sievering, Neustift, Nussdorf, or Heiligenstadt.

Grinzing lies at the edge of the Vienna Woods, a short distance northwest of the center. Once it was a separate village, now overtaken by the ever-increasing city boundaries of Vienna. Much of Grinzing remains unchanged and looks the same as it did in the days when Beethoven lived nearby. It's a district of crooked old streets and houses, their thick walls built around inner courtyards where grape arbors shelter Viennese wine drinkers on a summer night. The sound of zithers and accordions lasts long into the night.

Which brings up another point. If you're a motorist, don't drive out to the *Heurigen*. Police patrols are very strict, and you're not allowed to be driving with more than .08% alcohol in your bloodstream. It's much better to take public transportation. Most *Heurigen* are reached in 30 to 40 minutes. Take tram 1 from to Schottentor, and change there for tram 38 to Grinzing or Sievering, or 41 to Neustift am Wald. Sievering is also reached by bus 39A. Heiligenstadt is reached by U-Bahn 4.

We'll start you off with some of our favorites.

Alter Klosterkeller im Passauerhof   One of Vienna's well-known wine taverns, this spot maintains an old-fashioned ambience little changed since the turn of the 20th century. Some of its foundations date from the 12th century. Specialties include such familiar fare as *Tafelspitz* (boiled beef), an array of roasts, and plenty of strudel. You can order wine by the glass or the bottle. Main courses range from 15€ to 25€. Drinks begin at 2.50€. It's open daily from 6pm to midnight. Live music is played from 6 to 11pm. It's closed in January and February. Cobenzigasse 9, Grinzing. ℂ 01/320-6345.

Altes Presshaus   The oldest *Heurige* in Grinzing has been open since 1527. Ask to see its authentic cellar. The wood paneling and antique furniture give the interior character. The garden terrace blossoms in summer. Meals cost 10€ to 17€; drinks begin at 3€. It's open daily from 4pm to midnight and is closed January and February. Cobenzlgasse 15, Grinzing. ℂ 01/320-0203.

Der Rudolfshof   One of the most appealing wine restaurants in Grinzing dates back to 1848, when it was little more than a shack within a garden. Its real fame came around the turn of the century, when Crown Prince Rudolf, son of Emperor Franz Josef, adopted it as his favorite watering hole. A verdant garden, scattered with tables, is favored by Viennese apartment dwellers on warm summer evenings. Inside, portraits of Rudolf decorate a setting that evokes an old-fashioned hunting lodge. Come here for pitchers of the fruity white wine *Gruner Veltliner* and a light red, *Roter Bok.* The menu lists schnitzels, roasts, and soups, but the house specialty is shish kebabs. The salad bar is very fresh. Between April and December, most nights between 7 and 9pm, informal operettas are presented in a pavilion in the garden. Access to the show, a four-course meal, and a quarter-liter of wine costs 40€ per person. It's open from mid-March to mid-January daily from 1 to 11:30pm, and from mid-January to mid-March only Friday through Sunday from 1 to 11:30pm. Cobenzlgasse 8, Grinzing. ℂ 01/320-21-08.

Grinzinger Hauermandl   Many of the guests at this rustic Grinzing inn are lively Viennese escaping the Inner City for an evening. Enter through a garden where a Gypsy wagon perches on the roof. The robust farm-style cooking includes chicken noodle soup and two kinds of schnitzels—pork schnitzels priced at 7€ and veal schnitzels priced at 10€. A quarter-liter of wine (about two glasses) costs 2.50€. The tavern is open year-round Monday through Saturday from 5:30pm to midnight. Cobenzlgasse 20, Grinzing. ℂ 01/320-3027.

Heurige Mayer   This historic house was some 130 years old when Beethoven composed sections of his *Ninth Symphony* while living here in 1817. The same kind of fruity dry wine is still sold to guests in the shady courtyard of the rose garden. Original *Heurigen* music, mainly accordions and zithers, completes the traditional atmosphere. The menu includes grilled chicken, savory pork, and a buffet of well-prepared country food. Reservations are suggested. It's open Monday through Friday from 4pm to midnight, and on Sunday and holidays from 11am to midnight. Live music is played every Sunday and Friday from 7pm to midnight. Closed on Saturday. Wine sells for 2.60€ a glass, with meals beginning at 12€. It's closed December 21 to January 15. Am Pfarrplatz 2, Heiligenstadt. ℂ 01/370-3361, or 01/370-1287 after 4pm.

Weingut Wolff   Only 20 minutes from the center of Vienna, this is one of the most enduring and beloved *Heurigen*. Although aficionados claim that the best *Heurigen* are "deep in the countryside" of lower Austria, this one comes closest to offering an authentic experience near Vienna. In summer, you're welcomed into a flower-decked garden set against a backdrop of ancient vineyards. You can fill up your platter with some of the best wursts and roast meats (especially the delectable pork), along with freshly made salads. Save room for one of the luscious and velvety-smooth Austrian cakes. Find a table under a cluster of grapes and sample the fruity young wines, especially the Chardonnay, Sylvaner, or Gruner Veltliner. The tavern is open daily from 11am to 1am with main courses ranging from 5.80€ to 10.50€. Rathstrasse 50, Neustift. ℂ 01/440-3727.

Zum Figlmüller   One of the city's most popular wine restaurants is this suburban branch of Vienna's Figlmüller. Although there's a set of indoor dining rooms, most visitors prefer the flowering terrace with its romantic garden. The restaurant prides itself on serving wines produced only under its own supervision, beginning at 2.40€ per glass. Meals include a wide array of light salads as well as more substantial food, such as enormous Wiener schnitzels for 11.50€. It's open from late April to mid-November Monday through Saturday from 4:30pm to midnight. Grinzinger Strasse 55, Grinzing. ℂ 01/320-4257.

12 More Entertainment

CASINO
Casino Wien   You'll need to show your passport to get into this casino, opened in 1968. There are gaming tables for French and American roulette, blackjack, and chemin de fer, as well as the ever-present slot machines. The casino is open daily from 11am to 4am, with the tables closing at 3pm. Esterházy Palace, Kärntnerstrasse 41. ℂ 01/512-4836.

FILMS
Filmmuseum   This cinema shows films in their original languages and presents retrospectives of such directors as Fritz Lang, Erich von Stroheim, Ernst Lubitsch, and many others. The museum presents avant-garde and experimental films as well as classics. A monthly program is available free inside the Albertina, and a copy is posted outside. The film library inside the government-funded museum includes more than 11,000 book titles, and the still collection numbers more than 100,000. Two recent retrospectives were a comprehensive survey of Jean-Luc Godard's work and an overview of Japanese art films from the 1970s. Admission costs 4€, but you must be a member. Membership for 24 hours also costs 4€; membership for a full year costs 10.90€. In the Albertina, Augustinerstrasse 1. ℂ 01/533-7054. U-Bahn: Karlsplatz.

13 Only in Vienna

We've recommended a variety of nightspots, but none seems to capture the true Viennese spirit quite like the establishments below. Each has its own atmosphere and decor, and each continues to remain uniquely Viennese.

Alt Wien   Set on one of the oldest, narrowest streets of medieval Vienna, a short walk north of the cathedral, this is the kind of smoky, mysterious, and shadowy cafe that—with a bit of imagination—evokes subversive plots, doomed romances, and revolutionary movements being hatched and plotted. During the day, it's a busy workaday restaurant patronized by virtually everybody. But as the night progresses, you're likely to rub elbows with denizens of late-night Wien who get more sentimental and schmaltzy with each beer. Foaming mugfuls sell for 2.70€ each and can be accompanied by heaping platters of goulash and schnitzels. Main courses range from 8€ to 14€. It's open daily from 10am to 4am. Bäckerstrasse 9 (1). ✆ **01/512-5222.** U-Bahn: Stephansplatz.

Kaffeehaus Drechsler   It's the best antidote for insomnia in Vienna and a worthy early-morning diversion for the jet lagged. Established around 1900, this is the largest and busiest cafe in the Naschmarkt neighborhood, that vast open-air food market that sits on what used to be a branch of the Danube. The cafe's bizarre hours reflect those of the wholesale food industry itself: Monday through Friday from 3am to 8pm and Saturday from 3am to 6pm. Platters of hearty food (concocted from very fresh ingredients procured at the stalls outside) sell for 5€ to 9€. You won't be alone if you order a beer to accompany the sunrise. And if you need a dose of caffeine, coffee pours out of urns like a Danube flood. Linke Weinzeile 22. ✆ **01/587-8580.** U-Bahn: Karlsplatz.

Karl Kolarik's Schweizerhaus   References to this old-fashioned eating house are about as old as the Prater itself. Awash with beer and central European kitsch, it sprawls across a *Biergarten* landscape that might remind you of the Hapsburg Empire at its most indulgent. *Indulgence* is indeed the word—the vastly proportioned main dishes could feed an entire 19th-century army. If you're looking for *neue Kuchen,* this isn't the place. The menu stresses old-fashioned schnitzels and its house specialty, roasted pork hocks (*Hintere Schweinsstelze*) served with dollops of mustard and horseradish. Wash it all down with mugs of Czech Budweiser. A half-liter of beer costs 3€; main courses range from 3€ to 11€. During clement weather, the action moves outside to a green area close to the entrance of one of Europe's most famous amusement park, the Prater. It's open from March 15 to October 31 only, daily from 10am to 11pm. In the Prater, Strasse des Ersten Mai 116. ✆ **01/728-01-52.** U-Bahn: Praterstern.

Möbel   Neighborhood residents perch along the long stainless-steel countertop for a glass of wine, a coffee, and light platters of food. But what makes it unusual is the hypermodern furniture that's for sale in this cafe-cum-art gallery. Everything sold is functional, utilitarian, and contemporary looking. Depending on what's being featured that month, you're likely to find coffee tables, reclining chairs, bookshelves, kitchen equipment, and even a ceramic-sided wood-burning stove priced at 1,300€. Sandwiches cost 4.50€, and glasses of wine cost from 1.50€ to 2.90€. It's open Monday through Friday from 10am to 1am, and Saturday and Sunday from 10am to 2am. Burggasse 10. ✆ **01/524-9497.** U-Bahn: Volkstheater.

Pavillion   Even the Viennese stumble when trying to describe this civic monument from the Sputnik-era of the 1950s. By general consensus, it's usually considered a summer-only music cafe. During the day, it's a cozy cafe, with a multigenerational clientele and a sweeping garden overlooking the Heldenplatz (forecourt to the Hofburg). Come here to peruse the newspapers, chat with locals, and drink coffee, wine, beer, or schnapps. The place grows much more animated after the music (funk, soul, blues, and jazz) begins around 8pm. Platters of Viennese food are priced from 4.50€ to 11€. It's open daily from 11am to 2am between October and April. Burgring 2. ℰ **01/532-0907**. U-Bahn: Volkstheater.

Schnitzelwirt Schmidt   The waitresses wear dirndls, the portions are huge, and the cuisine—only pork and some chicken—celebrates the culinary folklore of central Europe. The setting is rustic, a kind of tongue-in-cheek bucolic homage to the Old Vienna Woods, and schnitzels are almost guaranteed to hang over the sides of the plates. Regardless of what you order, it will be accompanied by french fries, salad, and copious quantities of beer and wine. The dive packs them in because of good value, an unmistakably Viennese ambience, and great people-watching. Main courses cost 5€ to 8.40€. It's open Monday through Saturday from 11am to 10pm; it's closed Sunday. Neubaugasse 52 (7). ℰ **01/523-3771**. U-Bahn: Mariahilferstrasse. Tram: 49.

Wiener Stamperl (The Viennese Dram)   Named after a medieval unit of liquid measurement, this is about as beer-soaked and as rowdy a nighttime venue as we're willing to recommend. It occupies a battered, woodsy-looking room reeking of spilled beer, stale smoke, and the unmistakable scent of hundreds of boisterous drinkers. This is about as real and colorful as it gets. At the horseshoe-shape bar, order foaming steins of Ottakinger beer or glasses of new wine from nearby vineyards served from an old-fashioned barrel. The menu consists entirely of an array of coarse bread slathered with spicy, high-cholesterol ingredients, such as various wursts and cheeses and, for anyone devoted to authentic old-time cuisine, lard specked with bits of bacon. Sidewalk tables contain the overflow from the bar, but only during nice weather. Come here for local color and a friendly and rough-and-ready kind of alcohol-soaked charm. It's open Monday through Friday from 11am to 2am, and Saturday and Sunday from 11pm to 4am. Sterngasse 1. ℰ **01/533-6230**. U-bahn: Schwedenplatz.

5

Lower Austria

Lower Austria (Niederösterreich), known as "the cradle of Austria's history," is the largest of the nine federal states that make up the country today. Although the province is located to the east of *Upper* Austria, it's named *Lower* Austria because it sits lower on the Danube, which flows through it from west to east. The 19,171 sq. km (7,402 sq. miles) of the state are bordered on the north by the Czech Republic, on the east by Slovakia, on the south by the province of Styria, and on the west by Upper Austria. It lies on Vienna's doorstep and can easily be visited from there.

This historic area was once heavily fortified, as some 550 fortresses and castles testify—many are still standing, but often in ruins. The medieval Kuenringer and Babenberger dynasties had their hereditary estates here. At the foothills of the Alps is Wiener Neustadt, the former imperial city. Along the Danube, Dürnstein, with terraced vineyards, was where Richard the Lion-Hearted was held prisoner. Many monasteries and churches, from Romanesque and Gothic structures to the much later baroque abbeys, are also found in Lower Austria. Klosterneuburg Abbey dates from 1114, and Heiligenkreuz, founded in 1133, is the country's most ancient Cistercian abbey. The province is filled with vineyards, and in summer it booms with music festivals and classical and contemporary theater.

It's relatively inexpensive to travel in Lower Austria—prices here are about 30% lower than those in Vienna, Salzburg, and Innsbruck. This price differential explains why many travelers stay in one of the neighboring towns of Lower Austria when they come to explore Vienna.

One of Lower Austria's most celebrated districts is the Waldviertel-Weinviertel (a *Viertel* is a traditional division of Lower Austria). In this case, the viertels are the woods (*Wald*) and wine (*Wein*) areas. They contain thousands of miles of marked hiking paths and many mellow old wine cellars.

Some 60% of Austria's grape harvest is produced in Lower Austria, from the rolling hillsides of the Wienerwald to the terraces of the Wachau. Many visitors like to take a "wine route" through the province, stopping often at cozy taverns to sample the local vintages of Krems, Klosterneuburg, Dürnstein, Langenlois, Retz, Gumpoldskirchen, Poysdorf, and other towns.

Lower Austria is also home to more than a dozen spa resorts, including Baden, the most frequented. Innkeepers welcome families with children at these resorts, which can be an inviting retreat from the city. Most hotels accommodate children up to 6 years old free; children ages 7 to 12 stay for half price. Many towns and villages have attractions designed especially for kids. Some hotels have only a postal code for an address, as they do not lie on a street plan. (If you're writing to them, this postal code is their complete address.) When you reach one of these small towns, finding a hotel isn't a problem because they're signposted at the various approaches to the resort or village. Parking is rarely a problem in these places, and, unless otherwise noted, you park for free.

Lower Austria & the Danube Valley

1 The Wienerwald (Vienna Woods) ★

The **Vienna Woods**—romanticized in operetta, literature, and the famous Strauss waltz—stretch all the way from Vienna's city limits to the foothills of the Alps to the south. You can hike through the woods along marked paths or take a leisurely drive, stopping off at country towns to sample the wine and the local cuisine, which is usually hearty, filling, and reasonably priced. The Viennese and a horde of foreign tourists, principally German, usually descend on the local wine taverns and cellars on weekends—we advise you to make any summer visit on a weekday. The best time of year to go is in September and October, when the grapes are harvested from the terraced hills.

ESSENTIALS

GETTING THERE You can visit the expansive and pastoral Vienna Woods by car or by public transportation. We recommend renting a car so you can stop and explore some of the villages and vineyards along the way. Public transportation will get you around, but it will take much more time. Either way, you can easily reach all of the destinations listed below within a day's trip from Vienna. If you have more time, spend the night in one or more of the quintessential Austrian towns along the way.

VISITOR INFORMATION   Before you go, visit the tourist office for **Klosterneuburg** at Niedermarkt 4, A-3400 (© **02243/32038;** fax 02243/ 26773; www.klosterneuburg.com). It is the best source of information for the Vienna Woods. It's open daily from 8am to 6pm.

ORGANIZED TOURS   Vienna Sightseeing Tours, Stelzamergasse 4, Suite 11 (© **01/712-468-30;** fax 01/714-11-41; www.viennasightseeingtours.com), runs a popular 4-hour tour called "Vienna–Mayerling." It goes through the Vienna Woods past the Castle of Liechtenstein and the old Roman city of Baden. There's an excursion to Mayerling. You'll also go to the Cistercian abbey of Heiligenkreuz-Höldrichsmühle-Seegrotte and take a boat ride on Seegrotte, the largest subterranean lake in Europe. The office is open for tours April through October daily from 6:30am to 8pm, and November through March daily from 6:30am to 5pm. It costs 30€ for adults and 15€ for children, including admission fees and a guide.

KLOSTERNEUBURG

On the northwestern outskirts of Vienna, Klosterneuburg is an old market town in the major wine-producing center of Austria. The Babenbergs founded the town in the eastern foothills of the Vienna Woods, making it an ideal spot to enjoy the countryside within easy reach of Vienna, 11km (7 miles) southeast.

Austrians and tourists gather in Klosterneuburg annually to celebrate St. Leopold's Day on November 15, with music, banquets, and a parade.

GETTING THERE   If you're driving from Vienna, take Route 14 northwest, following the south bank of the Danube to Klosterneuburg. By public transportation, take the U-Bahn to Heiligenstadt, where you can then board bus no. 239 or 341 to Klosterneuburg, or catch the S-Bahn from Franz-Josef Bahnhof to Klosterneuburg-Kierling.

KLOSTERNEUBURG ABBEY

Klosterneuburg Abbey (Stift Klosterneuburg) ⚜, Stiftsplatz 1 (© **02243/ 411212**), is the most significant abbey in Austria. It was founded in 1114 by the Babenberg margrave Leopold III and was once the residence of the famous Hapsburg emperor Charles VI.

The abbey is visited not only for its history, but also for its art treasures. The most valuable piece is the world-famous enamel altar of Nikolaus of Verdun, created in 1181. The monastery also boasts the largest private library in Austria, with more than 1,250 handwritten books and many antique paintings. Guided tours of the monastery are given daily year-round. On the tour, you visit the Cathedral of the Monastery (unless Masses are underway), the cloister, St. Leopold's Chapel (with the Verdun altar), the former well house, and the residential apartments of the emperors.

The monastery itself remains open year-round, but the museum of the monastery is closed from mid-November to April. The museum can be visited without a guide from May to mid-November Tuesday through Sunday from 10am to 5pm for 4.80€. Visits to the monastery itself, however, require participation in a guided tour. These are available at hourly intervals year-round daily from 9am to noon and 1:30 to 4:30pm. Except for a specially designated

English-language tour conducted every Sunday at 2pm, most tours are conducted in German, with occasional snippets of English if the guide is able. The price is 5.50€ for adults and 3.10€ for children. Additional English-language tours can be arranged in advance. You can purchase a cost-effective combination ticket to the monastery and museum for 6.30€ for adults and 3.90€ for children under 12.

WHERE TO STAY & DINE

The abbey has an old restaurant, the **Stiftskeller,** Albrechtsbergergasse 1 (© **02243/411212**), where you can dine well on classic Austrian specialties for 9€ to 24€ for main courses. The kitchen is especially known for its fish dishes, and the menu, which is translated into English, also features dishes low in calories and sodium. The restaurant, which is child-friendly with a playground, has one of the largest and most beautiful outdoor terraces in the vicinity, with old chestnut trees and views over Klosterneuburg. It's open year-round Monday through Saturday from 11am to 11pm and Sunday from 11:30am to 5pm.

Hotel Josef Buschenretter Built in 1970 a mile south of the town center, this hotel is white-walled with a mansard roof rising above the balcony on the fourth floor. A roof terrace and a cozy bar provide diversion for hotel guests. The well-kept medium-size bedrooms are comfortably furnished and have bathrooms equipped with shower units.

Wienerstrasse 188, A-3400 Klosterneuburg. © **02243/32385.** Fax 02243/3238-5160. 40 units. 45€–60€ double. Rates include breakfast. AE, DC, MC, V. Free parking. Closed Dec 15–Jan 15. **Amenities:** Restaurant; bar; pool; laundry; dry cleaning. *In room:* TV.

Hotel Schrannenhof Originally dating from the Middle Ages, this hotel has been completely renovated and modernized. The owners rent guest rooms with large living and sleeping rooms and small kitchens, as well as quiet and comfortable double rooms with showers. International and Austrian specialties are served in Veit, the hotel's cafe-restaurant next door. The hotel also runs the Pension Alte Mühle (see below).

Niedermarkt 17–19, A-3400 Klosterneuburg. © **02243/32072.** Fax 02243/320-7213. www.schrannenhof.at. 13 units. 80€–92€ double; 98€–118€ suite. Rates include breakfast. AE, DC, MC. Free parking. **Amenities:** Breakfast room; lounge. *In room:* TV, minibar.

Pension Alte Mühle Housed in a simple two-story building, this hotel is gracious and hospitable. The breakfast room offers a bountiful morning buffet; the comfortable restaurant-cafe, Veit, is only 690m (2,300 ft.) away. Bedrooms are furnished in a cozy, traditional style, with good beds and well-maintained, if small, private bathrooms with shower units. The Veit family owns the place, and in summer their pleasant garden lures guests.

Mühlengasse 36, A-3400 Klosterneuburg. © **02243/37788.** Fax 02243/377-8822. www.hotel-altemuehle.at. 13 units. 68€ double. Rates include breakfast. AE, DC, MC. Free parking. **Amenities:** Breakfast room; lounge; pool; laundry service. *In room:* TV, minibar, hair dryer, safe.

PERCHTOLDSDORF: A STOP ON THE WINE TOUR

This old market town with colorful buildings, referred to locally as Petersdorf, is one of the most visited spots in Lower Austria when the Viennese go on a wine tour. You'll find many *Heurigen* here, where you can sample local wines and enjoy good, hearty cuisine. Perchtoldsdorf is not as well known as Grinzing, which is actually within the city limits of Vienna, but many visitors find it less touristy. It has a Gothic church, and part of its defense tower dates from the early 16th century. A vintners' festival, held annually in early November, attracts many Viennese. Local growers make a "goat" from grapes for this festive occasion.

GETTING THERE   Perchtoldsdorf lies 18km (11 miles) from the center of Vienna (it's actually at the southwestern city limits) and 14km (9 miles) north of Baden. From Vienna's Westbahnhof, you can take the S-Bahn to Liesing. From here, Perchtoldsdorf is just a short taxi ride away (cabs are found at the train station). Bus no. 256 runs from Vienna, but it runs infrequently.

VISITOR INFORMATION   The **tourist information office,** in the center of Perchtoldsdorf (✆ **01/536100;** www.noe.co.at), is open Monday through Friday from 9am to 6pm and Saturday from 9am to 12:30pm.

WHERE TO DINE
Restaurant Jahreszeiten ✫ AUSTRIAN/FRENCH/INTERNATIONAL
Set within what was a private villa in the 1800s, this restaurant, the best in town, provides a welcome haven for escapist Viennese looking for hints of the country life. In a pair of elegantly rustic dining rooms illuminated at night with flickering candles, you can enjoy such well-crafted dishes as rare poached salmon served with herbs and truffled noodles, Chinese-style prawns in an Asiatic sauce as prepared by the kitchen's Japanese cooks, and filet of turbot with morels and asparagus-studded risotto. Try a soufflé for dessert. A tremendous effort is made to secure the freshest produce. Service is polite, hardworking, and discreet.

Hochstrasse 17. ✆ 01/86-53-129. Reservations recommended. Fixed-price lunch 24€–49€; fixed-price dinner 49€–65€. AE, DC, MC, V. Tues–Fri and Sun 11:30–2pm; Tues–Sat 6–10pm. Closed July 25–Aug 15.

HINTERBRÜHL
You'll find good accommodations and good food in this hamlet that is really no more than a cluster of bucolic homes, much favored by Viennese who like to escape the city for a long weekend. Hinterbrühl holds memories of Franz Schubert, who wrote *Der Lindenbaum* here. This tiny area is also home to Europe's largest subterranean lake (see below).

GETTING THERE   The village is 26km (16 miles) south of Vienna and 3km (2 miles) south of Mölding, the nearest large town. To reach Hinterbrühl from Vienna, take the S-Bahn from the Südbahnhof to Mölding (trip time: 15 min.) and then catch a connecting bus to Hinterbrühl, the last stop (12 min.). By car, drive southwest along the A21, exiting at the signs to Gisshubel. From there, follow the signs to Hinterbrühl and Mölding.

VISITOR INFORMATION   The **tourist information office** in Mölding (✆ **02236/26727**) is open Monday through Friday from 9am to 6pm.

AN UNDERGROUND LAKE
Seegrotte Hinterbrühl ✫ *Finds*   Ironically, some of the village of Hinterbrühl was built directly above the stalactite-covered waters of Europe's largest underground lake. From the entrance a few hundred yards from the edge of town, you'll descend a step flight of stairs before facing the extensively illuminated waters of a shallow, very still, and very cold underground lake. The famous natural marvel was the site of the construction of the world's first jet plane and other aircraft during World War II. Expect a running commentary in German and broken English during the 20-minute boat ride.

Grutschgasse 2A, Hinterbrühl. ✆ 02235/26364. Admission and boat ride 5€ adult, 3€ children under 16 and students. Daily 9am–noon and 1–3:30pm.

WHERE TO STAY
Hotel Beethoven   This hotel in the heart of the hamlet boasts one of the village's oldest buildings, a private house originally constructed around 1785. In 1992, the hotel renovated most of the interior and built a new wing. The average-size bedrooms are cozy, traditional, and well maintained, with good beds and adequate bathrooms equipped mostly with shower-tub combinations. There's no formal restaurant on the premises, although management maintains an all-day cafe where coffee, drinks, pastries, ice cream, salads, and platters of regional food are served daily.

Bahnplatz 1, A-2317 Hinterbrühl. ℂ 02236/26252. Fax 02236/277017. www.members.aon.at/hotel-beethoven. 24 units. 82€–92€ double. Rates include breakfast. AE, DC, MC, V. Free parking. **Amenities:** Cafe; bar; laundry service. *In room:* TV, minibar, hair dryer, safe (in some).

WHERE TO DINE
Restaurant Hexensitz ✿ AUSTRIAN/INTERNATIONAL   Featuring impeccable service, this restaurant celebrates the subtleties of Austrian country cooking. Its upscale setting is a century-old building whose trio of dining rooms are outfitted "in the Lower Austrian style" with wood paneling and country antiques. In summer, the restaurant expands outward into a well-kept garden with flowering shrubs and ornamental trees. It offers daily changing dishes such as asparagus-cream soup; Styrian venison with kohlrabi, wine sauce, and homemade noodles; medallions of pork with spinach and herbs; and sea bass with forest mushrooms. The traditional desserts are luscious. The kitchen personnel is devoted and professional, and the food is savory and nearly always delightful.

Johannesstrasse 35. ℂ 02236/22937. Reservations recommended. Main courses 28€–33€; fixed-price lunch 19€; fixed-price dinner 33€. AE, MC. Tues–Sun 11:30am–2pm; Tues–Sat 6–10pm.

HEILIGENKREUZ: HOME TO A CISTERCIAN ABBEY
Abbey Heiligenkreuz (Abbey of the Holy Cross) (ℂ 02258/8703) is one of the oldest Cistercian abbeys in Austria, dating from 1133. The church, founded by Leopold III, was built in the 12th century, but there has been an overlay of Gothic and baroque in subsequent centuries, with some 13th- and 14th-century stained glass still in place. Turks once ravaged the abbey, and much of the complex was reconstructed in the 17th and 18th centuries. However, the Romanesque and Gothic cloisters date from 1240. Some of the dukes of Babenberg are buried in the 1240 chapter house, including Duke Friedrich II, the last of his line, who died in 1246. Heiligenkreuz has more relics of the Holy Cross than any other site in Europe except Rome.

Today a community of 50 Cistercian monks lives here. In summer, at noon and 6pm daily, visitors can attend their solemn choir prayers. Tours are conducted daily at 10am, 11am, 2pm, and 3pm, and Easter through September also at 4pm. Visiting hours are daily from 9 to 11:30am and 1:30 to 5pm (closes at 4pm Nov–Feb). Admission is 5.20€ for adults and 2.40€ for children.

GETTING THERE   The abbey is about 16km (10 miles) north of Baden and 24km (15 miles) west of Vienna. If you're driving from Vienna, head west on the Autobahn A21, following the signs to Salzburg and Linz; then exit at the signs pointing to Heiligenkreuz. From Südtirolerplatz, you can also take bus no. 1123, 1124, or 1127 marked ALLAND (trip time: 90 min.); from Baden, hop on bus no. 1140 or 1141.

VISITOR INFORMATION   More information is available at the **Rathaus (Town Hall)** (ℂ 02258/8720; www.heiligenkreuz.at), open Monday through Friday from 8am to noon and 2 to 5pm.

2 The Spa Town of Baden bei Wien (★)

24km (15 miles) SW of Vienna; 299km (186 miles) E of Salzburg

Around A.D. 100, the Romans were drawn to Aquae, the name they gave to Baden, by its 15 thermal springs whose temperatures reach 95°F (35°C). You can still see the **Römerquelle (Roman Spring)** in the Kurpark, which is the center of **Baden bei Wien** (★) today. The resort is officially named Baden bei Wien to differentiate it from other Badens not near Vienna.

Czar Peter the Great of Russia ushered in Baden's golden age by establishing a spa there at the beginning of the 18th century. The Soviet army used the resort city as its occupation headquarters from the end of World War II to 1955. But the Russians left little mark on "the dowager empress of European health spas."

Although the spa was at its most fashionable in the early 18th century, it continued to lure royalty and their entourages, musicians, and intellectuals for much of the 19th century. This lively casino town and spa in the eastern sector of the Vienna Woods was for years the summer residence of the Hapsburg court. In 1803, Franz I began annual summer visits to Baden.

During the mid– to late 19th century, Baden became known for its Schönbrunn yellow (Maria Theresa ochre) Biedermeier buildings, which still contribute to the city's charm. The Kurpark, Baden's center, is handsomely laid out and beautifully maintained. Public concerts performed here pay tribute to great Austrian composers.

The bathing complex was constructed over more than a dozen sulfur springs. Visitors today flock to the half dozen bath establishments, as well as the four outdoor thermal springs. These springs reach temperatures ranging from 75° to 95°F (24°–35°C). The thermal complex also has a "sandy beach" and a restaurant. It lies west of the center in the Doblhoffpark, a natural park featuring a lake where you can rent sailboats. There's also a rose-petaled garden restaurant in the park.

ESSENTIALS

GETTING THERE   If you're driving from Vienna, head south on Autobahn A2, cutting west at the junction of Route 210, which leads to Baden. By train, Baden is a local rather than an express stop. Trains depart daily from 4:40am to 8pm from Vienna's Südbahnhof (trip time: 20 min.). For schedules, call (℃) **05/ 1717** or 02252/8936-2385. By bus, the Badner Bahn leaves every 15 minutes from the Staatsoper (trip time: 1 hr.).

VISITOR INFORMATION   The **tourist information office,** at Brusattiplatz 3 ((℃) **02252/22-600-600;** www.baden.at), is open Monday through Saturday from 9am to 6pm and Sunday from 9am to noon.

EXPLORING BADEN BEI WIEN

In the Hauptplatz (Main Square) is the **Trinity Column,** built in 1714, which commemorates the lifting of the plague that swept over Vienna and the Wienerwald in the Middle Ages. Also here are the **Rathaus** ((℃) **02252/86800**) and, at no. 17, the **Kaiserhaus,** Franz II's summer residence from 1813 to 1834.

Every summer between 1821 and 1823, Beethoven rented the upper floor of a modest house, above what used to be a shop on the Rathausgasse, in Baden, for about 2 weeks, hoping to find a cure for his increasing deafness. The site has been reconfigured by the city of Baden into a small museum commemorating the time he spent here, at **Beethovenhaus,** Rathausgasse 10 ((℃) **02252/858-00590**). Inside you'll find a trio of small, relatively modest rooms, furnished with one of

Beethoven's pianos, his bed, several pieces of porcelain, photographs of others of his residences around the German-speaking world, some mementos, and copies of the musical folios he completed (or at least worked on) during his time in Baden. The museum is open year-round Tuesday through Friday from 4 to 6pm, and Saturday and Sunday from 9 to 11am and 4 to 6pm. Admission costs 2.50€ for adults and 1€ for students and children under 18. Entrance is free for children under 6.

Among the other sights in Baden, there's a celebrated death mask collection at the **Stadtisches Rolletmuseum,** Weikersdorfer-Platz 1 (© **02252/48255**). The museum possesses many items of historic and artistic interest. Furniture and the art of the Biedermeier period are especially represented. It's open Monday through Wednesday and Friday through Sunday from 3 to 6pm. Admission is 2.50€ for adults and 1€ for children. To reach the museum from Hauptplatz, go south to Josefs Platz and then continue south along Vöslauer Strasse, cutting right when you come to Elisabeth Strasse, which leads directly to the square on which the museum sits.

Northeast of Hauptplatz on the Franz-Kaiser Ring is the **Stadttheater** (© **02252/48338**), built in 1909, and on nearby Pfarrgasse, the 15th-century parish church of **St. Stephan's** (© **02252/48426**). Inside there's a commemorative plaque to Mozart, who allegedly composed his "Ave Verum" here for the parish choirmaster.

The real reason to come to Baden is the sprawling and beautiful **Kurpark** 🟆. Here you can attend concerts, plays, and operas at an open-air theater or try your luck at the casino (see "Baden After Dark," below). The Römerquelle (Roman Springs) can be seen gurgling from an intricate rock basin, which is surrounded by monuments to Beethoven, Mozart, and the great playwright Grillparzer. From the park's numerous paths you can view Baden and the surrounding hills.

SPA FACILITIES

Baden bei Wien boasts 14 underground springs whose sulfurous waters are known for their health-inducing properties. They maintain a constant temperature of about 95°F (35°C) and are funneled into the resort's spa facility. Built in 1969, the spa itself isn't particularly architecturally interesting; any 19th-century charm is provided by the hotels that surround the spa. Only one hotel in town—the **Gutenbrunn,** which we recommend—has an enclosed corridor that connects it to the spa facilities.

Kurhaus, Brussatiplatz 3 (© **02252/45030**), is open daily from 10am to 10pm for the *Römertherme* (hot mineral baths). The fee is 8.20€ for 2 hours, 9.70€ for 3 hours, 10.20€ for 4 hours, and 18.60€ for a full day. No reservations are necessary. Once inside, access to the sauna is an additional 3.40€, and any massage or health/beauty regimens costs extra. Relatively wealthy clients head for the Wellness Center, which has a wide array of facilities and operates something like a medical clinic. It's open by appointment only from 7am to 8pm.

WHERE TO STAY
EXPENSIVE
Grand Hotel Sauerhof zu Rauhenstein 🟆   Although the history of this estate dates back to 1583, it became famous in 1757 when a sulfur-enriched spring bubbled up after a cataclysmic earthquake in faraway Portugal. The present building was constructed in 1810 on the site of that spring, which continues to supply water to its spa facilities today. During the 19th century, visitors included

Beethoven (who wrote his *Wellington Sieg* here and enjoyed a dinner with Karl Maria von Weber) and Mozart's archrival, Antonio Salieri. Since then, the property has served as an army rehabilitation center, a sanatorium during the two world wars, and headquarters for the Russian army. In 1978, after extravagant renovations, the Sauerhof reopened as one of the region's most upscale spa hotels.

Today the neoclassical building with a steep slate roof rambles across a wide lawn. Few of the original furnishings remain, although the management has collected a handful of vintage Biedermeier sofas and chairs to fill the elegant but somewhat underfurnished public rooms. A covered courtyard, styled on ancient Rome, has a vaulted ceiling supported by chiseled stone columns. The generous bedrooms contain beautifully kept bathrooms with shower-tub combinations and are outfitted in a contemporary decor.

There's a collection of Russian icons and a series of medieval halberds in the richly decorated, farmer-style restaurant, which serves some of the best food in town.

Weilburgstrasse 11–13, A-2500 Baden bei Wien. © 02252/41251. Fax 02252/48047. www.sauerhof.at. 88 units. 125€–215€ double; 475€–618€ suite. Rates include buffet breakfast; half-board 26€ per person extra. AE, DC, MC, V. Free parking. **Amenities:** 2 restaurants; bar; pool; 2 tennis courts; fitness center; spa; sauna; salon; room service; laundry; dry cleaning. *In room:* TV, minibar, hair dryer, safe.

MODERATE

Krainerhütte *(Kids)*   Run by Josef Dietmann and his family, this hotel stands on tree-filled grounds 5 miles west of Baden bei Wien, at Helenental. It's a large A-frame chalet with rows of wooden balconies. The interior has more detailing than you might expect in such a modern hotel. There are separate children's rooms and play areas. The medium-size bedrooms and small bathrooms with shower-tub combinations are well maintained. In the cozy restaurant or on the terrace, you can dine on international and Austrian cuisine; the fish and deer come from the hotel grounds. Hiking in the owner's forests and hunting and fishing are possible. "Postbus" service to Baden is available all day.

Helenental, A-2500 Baden bei Wien. © 02252/44511. Fax 02252/44514. www.krainerhuette.at. 113 units. 137€ double; 204€ suite. Rates include breakfast; half-board 18€ per person extra. AE, MC, V. Parking 11€. **Amenities:** Restaurant; bar; pool; tennis court; fitness center; sauna; room service; babysitting; laundry; dry cleaning. *In room:* TV, minibar, hair dryer.

Mercure Parkhotel Bader   This contemporary hotel is in the middle of an inner-city park dotted with trees and statuary. The high-ceilinged lobby has a marble floor padded with thick oriental carpets and ringed with richly grained paneling. Most of the good-size sunny bedrooms have their own loggia overlooking century-old trees; each contains a good bathroom with shower-tub combination and plenty of shelf space.

Kaiser-Franz-Ring 5, A-2500 Baden bei Wien. © 800/MERCURE in the U.S., or 02252/44386. Fax 02252/80578. www.accorhotels.at. 87 units. 126€ double; 178€ suite. Rates include breakfast. AE, DC, MC, V. Free parking. **Amenities:** 2 restaurants; bar; pool; sauna; room service; babysitting; laundry; dry cleaning. *In room:* TV, minibar, hair dryer.

Schloss Weikersdorf   The oldest part of the hotel has massive beams, arched and vaulted ceilings, an Italianate loggia stretching toward the manicured gardens, and an inner courtyard with stone arcades. Accommodations, which include 79 bedrooms in the main house plus 31 in the annex, are handsomely furnished and most comfortable. The rooms in the newer section repeat the older section's arches and high ceilings, and sport ornate chandeliers and antique or reproduction furniture. All rooms have well-maintained bathrooms with shower-tub combinations.

Schlossgasse 9–11, A-2500 Baden bei Wien. ⓒ **02252/48301.** Fax 02252/4830-1150. www.hotelschloss weikersdorf.at. 110 units. 168€ double; 239€ suite. Rates include breakfast. AE, DC, MC, V. Free parking. **Amenities:** 2 restaurants; bar; pool; 4 tennis courts; sauna; room service; massage; laundry; dry cleaning; bowling alley. *In room:* TV, minibar, hair dryer, safe.

WHERE TO DINE

Badner Stüberl AUSTRIAN   Set within a once-private house that was built in the 1860s in Baden bei Wein's oldest neighborhood, this is an old-fashioned coffeehouse and restaurant that's been impeccably run by several generations of the Ackerl family. Within an artfully antique-looking interior, you can order such Austrian staples as *Tafelspitz* (boiled beef) on Sunday, *Zwiebelrostbraten* (onion-flavored roast beef), goulash soup, very fresh salads, grilled steak, pork and veal schnitzels, and, in season, venison and pheasant. Good cooking and fresh ingredients have made this restaurant a favorite of emperors, composers, and tourists alike.

Gutenbrunnstrasse 19. ⓒ **02252/41232.** Reservations recommended. Main courses 4.50€–12€; set menus 7€–12€. AE, DC, MC, V. Daily 10am–midnight.

BADEN AFTER DARK

Casino Baden   The town's major evening attraction is the casino, where you can play roulette, blackjack, baccarat, poker (seven-card stud), money wheel, and slot machines. Many visitors from Vienna come down to Baden for a night of gambling, eating, and drinking; there are two bars and a restaurant. Guests are often fashionably dressed, and you'll feel more comfortable if you are, too (men should wear jackets and ties). It's open daily from 3pm to 3am. A less formal casino on the premises, the Casino Leger, is open daily from noon to midnight.

In the Kurpark. ⓒ **02252/444960.** Free admission; 25€ worth of chips for 21€.

3 Wiener Neustadt

45km (28 miles) S of Vienna; 309km (192 miles) E of Salzburg

Heading south from Vienna on the Südautobahn, the former imperial city of Wiener Neustadt is a good first stop. It was once the official residence of Emperor Friedrich III. Called *Allzeit Getreue* because of its loyalty to the throne, this thriving city between the foothills of the Alps and the edge of the Pannonian lowland is steeped in history.

Unfortunately, Wiener Neustadt was a target for Allied bombs during World War II, as it was the point where the routes from Vienna diverge, one toward the Semmering Pass and the other to Hungary. The 200-year-old military academy that developed officers for the Austrian army might have been an added attraction to bombers. German Gen. Erwin Rommel, "the Desert Fox," was the academy's first commandant during the Nazi era. At any rate, the Allies dropped more bombs on the city than on any other town in Austria. It's estimated that some 60% of its buildings were leveled.

The town was founded in 1192, when its castle was built by Duke Leopold V of the ruling house of Babenberg as a bulwark against Magyar attacks from the east. From 1440 to 1493, Austrian emperors lived in this fortress in the southeastern corner of the old town. Maximilian I, called "the last of the knights," was born here in 1459 and lies buried in the Church of St. George in the castle. In 1752, Maria Theresa ordered that the structures comprising the castle be turned into a military academy.

ESSENTIALS

GETTING THERE   If you're driving from Vienna, head south along Autobahn A2 until you reach the junction with Route 21, at which point you head east to Wiener Neustadt.

Trains leave for Wiener Neustadt daily from Vienna's Südbahnhof, from 5:30am to past midnight (trip time: 27–44 min.). For schedules, call © 05/1717 in Vienna or check www.oebb.at. Buses depart from the Wiener Mitte bus station throughout the day at 15- to 30-minute intervals (trip time: 1 hr.). The bus drops off passengers in the town center, at Ungargasse 2. Most visitors opt for the train.

VISITOR INFORMATION   The Wiener Neustadt **tourist information office,** at Hauptpaltz in Rathaus (© **02622/29551**), is open Monday through Friday from 8am to 6pm.

WALKING AROUND WIENER NEUSTADT

You can visit the **Church of St. George (St. Georgekirche),** Burgplatz 1 (© **02622/3810**), daily from 8am to 6pm. The gable of the church is adorned with more than 100 heraldic shields of the Hapsburgs. It's noted for its handsome interior, decorated in the late Gothic style.

Neukloster, Neuklostergasse 1 (© **02622/23102**), a Cistercian abbey, was founded in 1250 and reconstructed in the 18th century. The New Abbey Church (Neuklosterkirche), near the Hauptplatz, is Gothic and has a beautiful choir. It contains the tomb of Empress Eleanor of Portugal, wife of Friedrich III and mother of Maximilian I. Mozart's *Requiem* was first presented here in 1793. Admission is free, and it's open Monday through Friday from 9am to noon and 2 to 5pm.

Liebfrauenkirche, Domplatz (© **02622/23202**), was once the headquarters of an Episcopal see. It's graced by a 13th-century Romanesque nave, but the choir is Gothic. The west towers have been rebuilt. Admission is free, and the church is open daily from 8am to noon and 2 to 6pm.

In the town is a **Recturm,** Babenberger Ring (© **02622/279-24**), a Gothic tower said to have been built with the ransom money paid for Richard the Lion-Hearted. It's open from March to October Tuesday through Thursday from 10am to noon and 2 to 4pm, and Saturday and Sunday from 10am to noon only. Admission is free.

WHERE TO STAY

Hotel Corvinus ⭐   The best hotel in town, built in the 1970s, this place has a color scheme of white and weathered bronze. It sits in a quiet neighborhood near the city park, a 2-minute walk south of the main rail station. The good-size bedrooms have modern comforts, such as firm beds and well-maintained bathrooms equipped with shower-tub combinations. There's also an inviting bar area, a parasol-covered sun terrace, and a lightheartedly elegant restaurant serving Austrian and international dishes.

Bahngasse 29–33, A-2700 Wiener Neustadt. © **02622/24134.** Fax 02622/24139. www.hotel-corvinus.at. 68 units. 114€ double. Rates include breakfast. Children under 12 stay free in parent's room. AE, DC, MC, V. Parking free. **Amenities:** Restaurant; bar; Jacuzzi; sauna; room service; laundry; dry cleaning. *In room:* TV, minibar, hair dryer.

WHERE TO DINE

Gelbes Haus AUSTRIAN/INTERNATIONAL   Set in the historic heart of town, this long-enduring and well-respected restaurant (whose name translates as "the yellow house") takes its name from the vivid ochre color of its exterior, which is from around 1911. The Art Nouveau dining room emphasizes style and comfort. The Austrian and international cuisine is prepared with fresh ingredients, imagination, and flair. Dishes include a succulent version of *Tafelspitz* (boiled beef); an assortment of carpaccios arranged with herbs, truffle oil, goose liver, and exotic mushrooms; rump steak stuffed with goose liver, tomatoes, and onions; and filets of pork in red-wine sauce with cabbage and herbs. French and Italian dishes are added according to the whim of the chef.

Kaiserbrunnen 11. ℃ 02622/26400. Reservations recommended. Main courses 6.50€–23€; fixed-price dinners 35€–55€. DC, MC, V. Mon–Sat noon–2pm and 7–10pm. Closed Christmas, New Year's Day, and Easter.

4 The Wachau-Danube Valley ★★★

The Danube, of course, is one of the most legendary rivers in Europe, and the surrounding area is rich in scenic splendor, historic wealth, and architectural grandeur. With rolling hills and fertile soil, the Wachau, a section of the Danube Valley northwest of Vienna, is one of the most beautiful and historic parts of Austria. Throughout this part of the Danube Valley, you'll find castles, celebrated vineyards, some of the most famous medieval monasteries in central Europe, and ruins from the Stone Age, the Celts, the Romans, and the Hapsburgs. This prosperous district has won many awards for the authenticity of its historic renovations.

A great way to see the area is by paddleboat steamer, most of which operate only from April to October. You can travel by armchair, lounging on the deck along the longest river in central Europe.

If you're really "doing the Danube," you can begin your trip at Passau, Germany, and go all the way to the Black Sea and across to the Crimean Peninsula in the Ukraine. However, the Vienna–Yalta portion of the trip alone takes nearly a week. Most visitors limit themselves to a more restricted look at the Danube, taking one of the many popular trips from Vienna. If you go westward on the river, your first stop might be Klosterneuburg (see section 1, "The Wienerwald," earlier in this chapter).

ESSENTIALS

GETTING THERE   If you have only one day to explore the Danube Valley, we highly recommend one of the tours listed below. If you have more time, however, rent a car and explore this district yourself, driving inland from the river now and then to visit the towns and sights listed below. You can also take public transportation to the towns we've highlighted (see individual listings).

VISITOR INFORMATION   Before you venture into the Danube Valley, pick up maps and other helpful information at the **tourist office for Lower Austria,** Heidenschluss 2, A-1010 Vienna (℃ **01/536-100;** fax 01/513-80-2230; www.noe.co.at).

ORGANIZED TOURS   The Wachau and the rest of the Danube Valley contain some of the most impressive monuments in Austria, but because of their far-flung locations, many prefer to participate in an organized tour. The best of these are conducted by **Vienna Sightseeing Tours,** Stelzhamergasse 4, Suite 11 (℃ **01/7124-6830;** fax 01/714-1141; www.viennasightseeingtours.com), which offers guided tours by motor coach in winter and by both motor coach and boat in summer. Stops on this 8-hour trip include Krems, Dürnstein, and Melk Abbey. Prices are 60€ for adults and 30€ for children under 12, and do not include lunch. Advance reservations are required.

TULLN: THE FLOWER TOWN

Originally a naval base, Comagena, and later a center for the Babenberg dynasty, Tulln is one of the most ancient towns in Austria. Located on the right bank of the Danube, it is called "the flower town" because of the masses of blossoms you'll see in spring and summer. It's the place, according to the saga of the Nibelungen, where Kriemhild, the Burgundian princess of Worms, met Etzel, king of the Huns. A well-known "son of Tulln" was Kurt Waldheim, former secretary-general of the United Nations and president of Austria, who was plagued by his past Nazi affiliations.

GETTING THERE   Tulln lies 42km (26 miles) west of Vienna, on the south bank of the Danube, and 13km (8 miles) southwest of Stockerau, the next big town, on the north bank of the Danube. If you're driving from Vienna, head west along Route 14.

S-Bahn trains depart from the Wien Nord Station and, more frequently, from the Wien Franz-Josefs Bahnhof daily from 4:30am to 8:30pm (trip time: 27–45 min.). Tulln lies on the busy main rail lines linking Vienna with Prague, and most local timetables list Gmund, an Austrian city on the border of the Czech Republic, as the final destination. For more information, call ℰ **05/1717** or check www.oebb.at. We don't recommend taking the bus from Vienna, as it would require multiple transfers.

From mid-May to late September, river cruisers owned by the **DDSG-Blue Danube Shipping Line** (ℰ **01/588800**) depart westward from Vienna on Sunday at 8:30am en route to Passau, Germany, and arrive in Tulln around 11:45am; then they continue westward to Krems, arriving there around 2:10pm. For more information call the shipping line or the tourist office in either Tulln or Krems.

VISITOR INFORMATION   The **tourist office** in Tulln, at Albrechtsgasse 32 (ℰ **02272/65836;** www.tulln.at), is open Monday through Friday from 9am to 6pm.

EXPLORING TULLN

The twin-towered **Pfarrkirche (Parish Church)** of St. Stephan on Wiener Strasse grew out of a 12th-century Romanesque basilica dedicated to St. Stephan. Its west portal was built in the 13th century. A Gothic overlay added in its early centuries fell victim to the 18th-century baroque craze that swept the country. A 1786 altarpiece commemorates the martyrdom of St. Stephan.

Adjoining the church is the **Karner (Charnel)** ✿✿. This funereal chapel is the major sight of Tulln, the finest of its kind in the entire country. Built in the mid–13th century in the shape of a polygon, it's richly decorated with capitals and arches. The Romanesque dome is adorned with frescoes.

In a restored former prison, Tulln has opened the **Egon Schiele Museum** ✿✿, Donaulände 28 (ℰ **02272/645-70**), devoted to its other famous son, born here in 1890. Schiele is one of the greatest Austrian artists of the early 1900s. The prison setting might be appropriate, as the expressionist painter spent 24 days in jail in 1912 in the town of Neulengbach for possession of what back then was regarded as pornography. While awaiting trial, he produced 13 watercolors, most of which are now in the Albertina in Vienna. The Tulln museum has more than 90 of his oil paintings, watercolors, and designs, along with much memorabilia. It's open daily from 9am to 7pm. Admission is 4€ adults and 2€ children.

WHERE TO STAY & DINE

Hotel/Restaurant Römerhof Stoiber   Built in 1972, this hotel near the train station has a simple modern facade of white walls and unadorned windows.

THE WACHAU-DANUBE VALLEY 183

The interior is warmly outfitted with earth tones, a macramé wall hanging, and pendant lighting fixtures. The bedrooms are comfortable but utterly functional, with duvet-covered beds. Bathrooms have well-kept showers but limited storage space. A restaurant serves well-prepared meals in an attractive, rustic setting; traditional and good-tasting specialties include Wiener schnitzel and roast beef in sour-cream sauce.

Langenlebarnerstrasse 66, A-3430 Tulln an der Donau. (C) 02272-62954. www.tiscover.com/romerhof-tulln. 49 units. 70€ double. Rates include breakfast. MC, V. Closed Mon. Free parking. **Amenities:** Restaurant; beer garden; bar; sauna; laundry; dry cleaning. *In room:* TV, minibar, hair dryer.

Hotel Rossmühle   A stay at this very visible, very central hotel will almost certainly give you an insight into old-fashioned Austria at its most idiosyncratic. Rebuilt within the shells of two very old buildings in the 1970s, each within a 2-minute walk from the other, it combines many 19th-century architectural details, including wrought-iron gates, a collection of antique furniture, and crystal chandeliers. The bedrooms within the annex (about half of the total) are smaller, less grand, and cheaper than those within the main building. Regardless of their locations, however, they're outfitted in a modernized country-baroque style, with comfortable beds and vague references to the nostalgia of yesteryear. Rooms in the main core have shower-tub combinations; those within the annex have only showers. The on-site restaurant offers an all-Austrian ode to wholesome food and a faded kind of country charm. It's most frequently patronized by clients of the hotel, who arrange half-board for a supplement of 11€ per person.

Hauptplatz 12, A-03430 Tulln an der Donau. (C) 0227/62411. Fax 02272/6241113. 57 units. 66€–97€ double. Rates include breakfast. AE, MC, V. Free parking. From Vienna, drive 30 min. west along Rte. 14. **Amenities:** Restaurant; lounge. *In room:* TV.

Gasthaus zur Sonne (Gasthaus Sodoma) ⭐ AUSTRIAN   This is Tulln's finest and most famous restaurant. It's set on the town's main street, a short walk from the railway station, behind a pale blue facade of a building erected in the 1940s that looks like something midway between a chalet and a villa. Under the direction of the Sodoma family since 1968, with an English-speaking waitstaff that includes their charming daughter, Susanna, it's composed of two cozy and artfully nostalgic dining rooms, each lined with oil paintings, especially landscapes. Visitors enjoy dishes that change with the season but that invariably include well-prepared versions of dumplings stuffed with minced meat, pumpkin soup, a marvelous Weiner schnitzel, onion-studded roast beef, the boiled-beef specialty known as *Tafelspitz,* and perfectly cooked zander (a freshwater lake fish) served with potatoes and butter sauce.

Bahnhofstrasse 48. (C) 02272/64616. Reservations recommended. Main courses 7€–19€. No credit cards. Tues–Sat noon–2pm and 6–9:30pm.

HERZOGENBURG MONASTERY

Founded in the early 12th century by a German bishop from Passau, the Augustinian **Herzogenburg Monastery,** A-3130 Herzogenburg ((C) **02782/83113**), 11km (7 miles) south of Traismauer, has a long history. The present complex of buildings comprising the church and the abbey was reconstructed in the baroque style. Fischer von Erlach, a master of the style, designed some of the complex. The art painted on the high altar of the church is by Daniel Gran, and the most outstanding works owned by the abbey are a series of 16th-century paintings on wood, displayed in a room devoted to Gothic art. The monastery is well known for a library containing more than 80,000 works.

Entrance is 5€ for adults, 3€ for students, and 3.50€ for adults over 65. You can wander around alone or participate in a guided tour, departing daily at 9, 10, and 11am, and at 1, 2, 3, 4, and 5pm. The monastery is open only April through October daily from 9am to 6pm. There's a wine tavern in the complex where you can grab some Austrian fare while sampling the local grapes.

GETTING THERE   Located 16km (10 miles) south of the Danube, the monastery is reached by taking Wiener Strasse (Rte. 1) out of St. Pölten. Head east for 13km (8 miles) toward Kapelln, but turn left at the sign along a minor road to Herzogenburg.

KREMS ⊛

In the eastern part of the Wachau on the left bank of the Danube lies the 1,000-year-old city of **Krems.** The city today encompasses Stein and Mautern, once separate towns. Krems is a mellow town of courtyards, old churches, and ancient houses in the heart of vineyard country, with some partially preserved town walls. Just as the Viennese flock to Grinzing and other suburbs to sample new wine in the *Heurigen,* so the people of the Wachau come here to taste the fruit of the vine, which appears in Krems earlier in the year.

GETTING THERE   Krems is located 80km (50 miles) west of Vienna and 29km (18 miles) north of St. Pölten. If you're driving from Vienna, drive north along the A22 until it splits into three roads near the town of Stockerau. Here, drive due west along Route 3, following the signs to Krems.

Trains depart from both the Wien Nord Station and the Wien Franz-Josefs Bahnhof for Krems daily every hour or so from 5am to 8:30pm (trip time: 60–95 min.). Many are direct, although some require a transfer at Absdorf-Hippersdorf or St. Pölten. Call 𝄞 **01/1717** for schedules. Traveling by bus from Vienna to Krems is not recommended because of the many transfers required. Krems, however, is well connected by local bus lines to surrounding villages. From mid-May to late September, the **DDSG-Blue Danube Shipping Company** (𝄞 **01/588800**) runs river cruises departing Vienna on Sunday at 8:30am and arriving in Krems around 1:40pm.

VISITOR INFORMATION   The Krems **tourist office,** at Undstrasse 6 (𝄞 **02732/82676;** www.krems.at), is open Monday through Friday from 9am to 6pm, and Saturday and Sunday from 10am to noon and 1 to 6pm.

EXPLORING KREMS

The most interesting part of Krems today is what was once the little village of **Stein.** Narrow streets are terraced above the river, and the single main street, **Stein-landerstrasse,** is flanked with houses, many from the 16th century. The **Grosser Passauerhof,** Steinlanderstrasse 76 (𝄞 **02732/82188**), is a Gothic structure decorated with an oriel. Another house, at Steinlanderstrasse 84, combines Byzantine and Venetian elements among other architectural influences; it was once the imperial tollhouse. In days of yore, the aristocrats of Krems barricaded the Danube and extracted heavy tolls from the river traffic. Sometimes the tolls were more than the hapless victims could pay, so the townspeople just confiscated the cargo. In the Altstadt, the **Steiner Tor,** a 1480 gate, is a landmark.

Pfarrkirche St. Viet (𝄞 **02732/857100**), the parish church of Krems, stands in the center of town at the Rathaus, reached by going along either Untere Land-strasse or Obere Landstrasse. The overly ornate church is rich with gilt and statuary. Construction on this, one of the oldest baroque churches in the province, began in 1616. In the 18th century Martin Johann Schmidt, better known as Kremser Schmidt, painted many of the frescoes inside the church.

You'll find the **Weinstadt Museum Krems (Historical Museum of Krems),** Körnermarkt 14 (✆ **02732/801567**), in a restored Dominican monastery. The Gothic abbey is from the 13th and 14th centuries. Its gallery displays the paintings of Martin Johann Schmidt, mentioned above. The complex also has an interesting **Weinbaumuseum (Wine Museum),** exhibiting artifacts, many quite old, gathered from the vineyards along the Danube. Admission to both areas of the museum is 3.50€. It's open only from March to November Wednesday through Sunday from 1 to 6pm.

NEARBY ATTRACTIONS

Twenty-nine kilometers (18 miles) north of Krems at St. Pölten is the Museum of Lower Austria, formerly located in Vienna. Now called **Shedhalle St. Pölten,** it's at Franz-Schubert-Platz (✆ **2742/200-5011**). This museum exhibits the geology, flora, and fauna of the area surrounding Vienna. It also exhibits a collection of arts and crafts, including baroque and Biedermeier; temporary shows featuring 20th-century works are presented as well. Admission is 7€ for adults and 3.50€ for children. It's open daily from 10am to 6pm.

WHERE TO STAY

Donauhotel Krems   This large, glass-walled hotel built in the 1970s has a wooden canopy stretched over the front entrance. The bedrooms are comfortably furnished and well maintained. They are a little small for long stays but are suitable for an overnight, as the beds are fluffy and the bathrooms are spotless; most contain shower-tub combinations. Austrian fare is available in the airy cafe, on the terrace, or in the more formal restaurant.

Edmund-Hofbauer-Strasse 19, A-3500 Krems. ✆ 02732/87565. Fax 02732/875-6552. donauhotel-krems@aon.at. 60 units. 71€ double. Rates include breakfast; half-board 13€ per person extra. AE, DC, MC, V. No parking. **Amenities:** Restaurant; bar; fitness center; sauna; solarium. *In room:* TV, minibar, hair dryer, safe.

Hotel-Restaurant am Förthof   In the Stein sector of the city, this big-windowed hotel has white-stucco walls and flower-covered balconies. A rose garden surrounds the base of an al fresco cafe; inside are oriental rugs and a scattering of antiques amid newer furniture. Each of the high-ceilinged bedrooms has a foyer and a shared balcony. Most bedrooms are fairly spacious. Bathrooms, though small, have well-kept shower-tub combinations and are adequate for overnight stopovers.

Donaulände 8, A-3500 Krems. ✆ 02732/83345. Fax 02732/833-4540. hotelforthof@netway.at. 20 units. 100€–150€ double. Rates include breakfast; half-board 21€ per person extra. AE, DC, MC, V. Free parking. **Amenities:** Restaurant; bar; pool; sauna; room service; babysitting; laundry; dry cleaning. *In room:* TV, minibar, hair dryer, safe.

WHERE TO DINE

Restaurant Bacher ✆ AUSTRIAN/INTERNATIONAL   Lisl and Klaus Wagner-Bacher operate this excellent restaurant-hotel, with an elegant dining room and a well-kept garden. Lisl cooks a la Paul Bocuse, serving an imaginative array of fresh dishes. Specialties include crabmeat salad with nut oil, zucchini stuffed with fish, and two kinds of sauces. Dessert might be beignets with apricot sauce and vanilla ice cream. She has won awards for her cuisine, as her enthusiastic clientele will tell you. The wine list has more than 600 selections.

Eight double and three single rooms are offered. Rooms contain TVs, minibars, phones, and radios, and each is attractively furnished with good beds and well-maintained bathrooms. Rates are 128€ for a double with breakfast. The establishment is 4km (2½ miles) from Krems.

Südtiroler Platz 208, A-3512 Mautern. © **02732/82937.** Fax 02732/74337. Reservations required. Main courses 16€–27€; fixed-price lunch Wed–Fri 27.50€; fixed-price menus 64€. DC, MC, V. Wed–Sat 11:30am–2pm and 6:30–9:30pm; Sun 11:30am–9pm. Closed mid-Jan to mid-Feb.

DÜRNSTEIN ⭐⭐

Less than 8km (5 miles) west of Krems, Dürnstein is the loveliest town along the Danube and, accordingly, draws throngs of tour groups in summer. Terraced vineyards mark this as a Danube wine town, and the town's fortified walls are partially preserved.

GETTING THERE   The town is 80km (50 miles) west of Vienna. If you're driving, take Route 3 west. From Krems, continue driving west along Route 3 for 8km (5 miles). Train travel to Dürnstein from Vienna requires a transfer in Krems (see above). In Krems, trains depart approximately every 2 hours on river-running routes; it's a 6km (4-mile) trip to Dürnstein. Call © **05/1717** in Vienna for schedules. There's also bus service between Krems and Dürnstein (trip time: 20 min.).

VISITOR INFORMATION   A little **tourist office,** housed in a tiny shed in the east parking lot called Parkplatz Ost (© **02711/200**), is open only April through October. Hours are Monday, Thursday, and Friday from 1 to 7pm, and Saturday and Sunday from 11am to 7pm.

WHERE RICHARD THE LION-HEARTED WAS HELD PRISONER

The ruins of a **castle fortress,** 159m (520 ft.) above the town, are inextricably linked to the Crusades. Here Leopold V, the Babenberg duke ruling the country at that time, held Richard the Lion-Hearted of England prisoner in 1193. It seems that Richard had insulted the powerful Austrian duke in Palestine during the Crusades to capture the Holy Land. The story goes that when Richard was trying to get back home, his boat foundered on the rocks of the Adriatic and he tried to sneak through Austria disguised as a peasant. Somebody probably turned stool pigeon, and the English monarch was arrested and imprisoned by Leopold.

For quite some time, nobody knew exactly where in Austria Richard was incarcerated, but his loyal minstrel companion, Blondel, had a clever idea. He went from castle to castle, playing his lute and singing Richard's favorite songs. The tactic paid off, the legend says, for at Dürnstein Richard heard Blondel's singing and sang the lyrics in reply. The discovery forced Leopold to transfer Richard to a castle in the Rhineland Palatinate, but by then everybody knew where he was. So Leopold set a high ransom on the king's head, which was eventually met, and Richard was set free.

The castle was virtually demolished by the Swedes in 1645, but you can visit the ruins if you don't mind a vigorous climb (allow an hour). The castle isn't much, but the view of Dürnstein and the Wachau is more than worth the effort.

Back in the town, take in the principal artery, **Hauptstrasse** ⭐, which is flanked by richly adorned old residences. Many of these date from the 1500s and have been well maintained through the centuries. In summer, the balconies are covered with flowers.

The 15th-century **Pfarrkirche (Parish Church)** also merits a visit. The building was originally an Augustinian monastery and was reconstructed when the baroque style swept Austria. The church tower is the finest baroque example in the whole country and a prominent landmark in the Danube Valley. There is also a splendid church portal. Kremser Schmidt, the noted baroque painter, did some of the altar paintings.

WHERE TO STAY & DINE

Gartenhotel Pfeffel *Value*   This black-roofed, white-walled hotel is partially concealed by well-landscaped shrubbery. One of the best bargains in town, the hotel takes its name from its garden courtyard with flowering trees, where tasty (but not fancy) meals are served. The public rooms are furnished with traditional pieces. The bedrooms are handsomely furnished in a traditional Austrian motif, with comfortable armchairs, good beds, and medium-size bathrooms equipped with shower-tub combinations. Leopold Pfeffel, your host, serves wine from his own terraced vineyard. He has also added a swimming pool.

A-3601 Dürnstein. © 02711/206. Fax 02711/12068. www.tiscover.at/gartenhotelpfeffel. 40 units. 80€–116€ double; from 126€ suite. Rates include breakfast. MC, V. Free parking. Closed Dec–Feb. Amenities: Restaurant; bar; pool; sauna; room service; laundry; dry cleaning. *In room:* TV, minibar, hair dryer, safe.

Gasthof-Pension Sänger Blondel *Finds*   Lemon-colored and charmingly old-fashioned, with green shutters and clusters of flowers at the windows, this hotel is named after the faithful minstrel who searched the countryside for Richard the Lion-Hearted. Bedrooms are furnished in an old-fashioned, rustic style and are quite comfortable, containing small bathrooms equipped with shower units. All have good beds with fresh linens. Each Thursday, an evening of zither music is presented. If the weather is good, the music is played outside in the flowery chestnut garden near the baroque church tower. There's a good and reasonably priced restaurant serving regional cuisine.

A-3601 Dürnstein. © 02711/253. Fax 02711/2537. www.saengerblondel.at. 15 units. 82€–115€ double. Rates include breakfast. MC, V. Parking 6.50€. Closed Dec–Feb and the first week in July. Amenities: Restaurant; lounge; laundry; dry cleaning. *In room:* TV, hair dryer.

Hotel Schloss Dürnstein   The baroque tower of this Renaissance castle rises above the scenic Danube. It's one of the best-decorated hotels in Austria, with white ceramic stoves, vaulted ceilings, parquet floors, oriental rugs, gilt mirrors, and oil portraits of elaborately dressed courtiers. A beautiful shady terrace is only a stone's throw from the river. Elegantly furnished bedrooms come in a wide variety of styles, ranging from those that are large and palatial enough for an emperor to others that are rather small and modern. Modern bathrooms with shower-tub combinations are in all the bedrooms, though sometimes in cramped conditions. The restaurant serves well-prepared dishes from the kitchen of an experienced chef.

A-3601 Dürnstein. © 02711/212. Fax 02711/212-30. www.schloss.at. 39 units. 242€–280€ double; from 328€ suite. Rates include half-board. AE, DC, MC, V. Parking 7€. Closed Nov 10–Mar 25. A pickup can be arranged at the Dürnstein rail station. Amenities: Restaurant; bar; 2 pools; fitness center; sauna; gymnastics center; room service; massage; babysitting; laundry; dry cleaning. *In room:* TV, minibar, hair dryer, safe.

Romantik Hotel Richard Löwenherz   This establishment was founded as a hotel in the 1950s on the site of a 700-year-old nunnery, originally dedicated to the sisters of Santa Clara in 1289. Its richly historical interior is filled with antiques, Renaissance sculpture, elegant chandeliers, stone vaulting, and paneling that has been polished over the years to a mellow patina. An arbor-covered sun terrace with restaurant tables extends toward the Danube. The spacious bedrooms, especially those in the balconied modern section, are filled with cheerful furniture. The duvet-covered beds are the finest in the area. Each unit also has a beautifully kept bathroom with a shower-tub combination. The restaurant offers a fine selection of local wines, as well as fish from the Danube, among its many regional specialties.

A-3601 Dürnstein. 🕿 **02711/222**. Fax 02711/22218. www.richardloewenherz.at. 38 units. 139€–219€ double. Rates include breakfast. AE, DC, MC, V. Free parking. Closed Nov–Mar. **Amenities:** Restaurant; lounge; pool; room service; laundry service. *In room:* TV, hair dryer.

MELK

This is one of the greatest sites in Austria. In the words of Empress Maria Theresa, "If I had never come here, I would have regretted it." The main attraction here is the Melk Abbey, a sprawling baroque abbey that overlooks the Danube basin. Melk marks the western terminus of the Wachau and lies upstream from Krems.

GETTING THERE   Melk is 89km (55 miles) west of Vienna. **Motorists** can take Autobahn A1, exiting at the signs for Melk. If you prefer a more romantic and scenic road, try Route 3, which parallels the Danube but takes 30 to 45 minutes longer. **Trains** leave frequently from Vienna's Westbahnhof to Melk, with two brief stops en route (trip time: about 1 hr.). Between mid-May and late September, river cruisers owned by the **DDSG Blue Danube Steamship Co.** (🕿 **01/588800**; fax 01/58880-440) leave Vienna only on Sunday at 8:30am, arriving in Melk around 1:40pm.

VISITOR INFORMATION   The **Melk tourist office** at Babenbergerstrasse 1 (🕿 **02752/523-0732**; www.tiscover.com/melk), in the center of town, is open Monday through Saturday from 9am to 7pm and Sunday from 10am to 2pm.

EXPLORING MELK ABBEY

One of the finest baroque buildings in the world, **Melk Abbey** 🏛🏛, Dietmay-erstrasse 1, A-3390 Melk (🕿 **02752/555-230** or 02752/5231-2232), and the **Stiftskirche (Abbey Church)** are the major attractions today. However, Melk has been an important place in the Danube Basin ever since the Romans built a fortress on a promontory looking out onto a tiny "arm" of the Danube. Melk also figures in the *Nibelungenlied* (the German epic poem), in which it is called Medelike.

The rock-strewn bluff where the abbey now stands overlooking the river was the seat of the Babenbergs, who ruled Austria from 976 until the Hapsburgs took over. In the 11th century, Leopold II of the House of Babenberg presented Melk to the Benedictine monks, who turned it into a fortified abbey. Its influence and reputation as a center of learning and culture spread all over Austria, a fact that is familiar to readers of Umberto Eco's *The Name of the Rose*. The Reformation and the 1683 Turkish invasion took a toll on the abbey, although it was spared from direct attack when the Ottoman armies were repelled outside Vienna. The construction of the new building began in 1702, just in time to be given the full baroque treatment.

Most of the design of the present abbey was by the architect Jakob Prandtauer. Its marble hall, called the Marmorsaal, contains pilasters coated in red marble. A richly painted allegorical picture on the ceiling is the work of Paul Troger. The library, rising two floors, again with a Troger ceiling, contains some 80,000 volumes. The Kaisergang, or emperors' gallery, 198m (650 ft.) long, is decorated with portraits of Austrian rulers.

Despite all this adornment, the abbey takes second place in lavish glory to the Stiftskirche, the golden abbey church. Damaged by fire in 1947, the church is now almost completely restored, even to the gold-bullion gilding of statues and altars. Richly embellished with marble and frescoes, the church has an astonishing number of windows. Many of the paintings are by Johann Michael Rottmayr, but Troger had a hand in the decoration. The Marble Hall banquet room next to the church was also damaged by the fire but has been restored to its former ornate elegance.

Melk is still a working abbey, and you might see black-robed Benedictine monks going about their business or students rushing out of the gates. Visitors head for the terrace for a view of the river. Napoléon probably used it for a lookout when he made Melk his headquarters during the campaign against Austria.

Throughout the year, the abbey is open every day, with tours that depart at intervals of 15 to 20 minutes. The first tour begins at 9am and the last is at 5pm; guides make efforts to translate into English a running commentary that is otherwise German. Guided tours are 6.54€ for adults and 4€ for children; self-guided tours are 5.09€ for adults and 2.54€ for children.

WHERE TO STAY

Hotel Stadt Melk ☞   Just below the town's palace, a 5-minute walk from the train station, this four-story hotel has a gabled roof and stucco walls. Originally built a century ago as a private home, it was eventually converted into this cozy, family-run hotel. The simply furnished bedrooms are clean and comfortable, with sturdy beds and well-maintained bathrooms that, though small, are adequate and equipped with shower-tub combinations. Rooms in the rear open onto views of the abbey. The pleasant restaurant has leaded-glass windows in round bull's-eye patterns of greenish glass. Meals, beginning at 35€, are also served on a balcony, decorated with flowers, at the front of the hotel. The food is quite good.

Hauptplatz 1, A-3390 Melk. ☎ 02752/52475. Fax 02752/524-7519. www.tiscover.at/hotel-stadt-melk. 14 units. 72€–85€ double; 148€ suite. Rates include breakfast. AE, DC, MC, V. Parking free. **Amenities:** Restaurant; bar; sauna; laundry; dry cleaning service. *In room:* TV, minibar, hair dryer.

WHERE TO DINE

Stiftrestaurant Melk BURGENLANDER   If you're visiting Melk, this place is required dining. Don't allow the cafeterialike dimensions of this eatery to sway you from its very fine cuisine. This modernly decorated restaurant is well equipped to handle large groups—some 3,000 visitors a day frequent the establishment during peak season. From the reasonably priced fixed-price menu you might opt for the asparagus-and-ham soup with crispy dumplings; hunter's roast with mushrooms, potato croquettes, and cranberry sauce; and the famed Sacher torte for dessert.

Abt-Berthold-Dietmayrstrasse 3. ☎ 02752/525-55. Fixed-price menu 10€–14€. AE, MC, V. Daily 8am–6pm.

6

Burgenland

Austria's easternmost and newest province, Burgenland, is a little border region created in 1921 from German-speaking areas of what had formerly been Hungary. It marks the beginning of a large, flat steppe (*puszta*) that reaches almost to Budapest, but it also lies practically on Vienna's doorstep. The province shares a western border with Styria and Lower Austria, and its long eastern boundary separates it from Hungary.

Called "the vegetable garden of Vienna," Burgenland is mostly an agricultural province. It's noted for its vineyards, producing more than one third of all the wine made in Austria. The province is situated where the Hungarian puszta gradually modulates into the foothills of the eastern Alps; forests cover 29% of its area, and vineyards compose 7% of its agricultural lands. Its wonderful climate consists of hot summers with little rainfall and moderate winters. For the most part, you can enjoy sunny days from early spring until late autumn.

Burgenland's population represents a middle-Europe melting pot. Two percent of the population is Hungarian, while some 10% consists of Croats who settled here in the 16th century after fleeing their southern Slav homes before the advance of Turkish armies. For hundreds of years, the Croats, Hungarians, and German-speaking people have lived together in this area, and the groups' customs, language, dress, legends, folk songs, and folklore reflect their ethnic and religious variety. Many Burgenlanders still wear the traditional garb of their ancestors on Sunday.

This ethnic diversity has resulted in a regional cuisine that's among the best in Europe. Its eastern neighbors, especially Hungary, provide strong influences that you'll appreciate when you savor goulashes and strudels, as well as goose dishes. Much wild game lives in the wooded areas of Burgenland and is often featured on menus.

Eisenstadt, the small provincial capital of Burgenland since 1924, was for many years the home of (Franz) Joseph Haydn, and the composer is buried here. Near Eisenstadt is another composer's shrine: Franz Liszt's birthplace. Each summer there's an International Operetta Festival at Mörbisch am See, using Lake Neusiedl (Neusiedler See) as a theatrical backdrop. Neusiedl is the only steppe lake in central Europe. If you're here in summer, we suggest exploring it by motorboat. Illmitz, an old village near Lake Neusiedl, is surrounded by Seewinkel, a marshy haven for birds and rare flora. Many Viennese come to Burgenland on weekends for sailing, bird-watching, and other outdoor activities. The summer resort of Rust is famous for its stork nests and its town walls built in 1614.

Like Lower Austria, Burgenland contains numerous fortresses and castles, many in ruins. You'll see several affiliated with the Esterházy family, a great Hungarian family descended from Attila the Hun: These include Schloss Esterházy, the Eisenstadt château, as well as Forchtenstein Castle, dating from the 13th century.

Burgenland

SLOVAKIA

Vienna

Danube

Bratislava

Kitsee

9

10

Bruck

10

NIEDERÖSTERREICH
(LOWER AUSTRIA)

A2

16

Purbach

Neusiedl am See

51

Mönchhof

Podersdorf

Frauenkirchen

50

SEEWINKEL

Eisenstadt

Neusiedler See

St. Andrä

Wiener Neustadt

S31

Rust

52

Illmitz

Andau

Mattersburg

Mörbisch

Sopron

S6

A2

St. Martin

62

84

Landsee

331

Bernstein

HUNGARY

63

Bad Tatzmannsdorf

54

Oberwart

A2

STEIERMARK
(STYRIA)

0   10 mi

0   10 km

N

65

57

65

Heiligenkreuz

Vienna

Burgenland

AUSTRIA

Forchtenstein Castle 1
Franz-Liszt-Geburtshaus 2
Schloss Esterházy 3

Accommodations in this province are extremely limited, but they're among the least expensive in the country. You'll find a few romantic castle hotels. Or perhaps you'll prefer to settle into a small guesthouse. Parking is rarely a problem in these places, and, unless otherwise noted, you park for free. The touring season in Burgenland lasts April through October.

1 Eisenstadt: Haydn's Home

50km (31 miles) SE of Vienna

When Burgenland joined Austria in the 1920s, it was a province without a capital—its former seat of government, Ödenburg (now the far-western Hungarian city of Sopron) voted to remain a part of Hungary. In 1924, Burgenlanders bestowed the honor on Eisenstadt. This small town lies at the foot of the Leitha mountains, at the beginning of the steppe extending into Hungary. Surrounded by vineyards, forests, and fruit trees, it's a convenient stop for exploring Lake Neusiedl, 10km (6 miles) east.

ESSENTIALS
GETTING THERE   Board one of the many trains heading toward Budapest from the Südbahnhof (South Railway Station) in Vienna, and change trains in the railway junction of Neusiedl am See. Connections are timed to link up with the 16 or so trains that continue on to Eisenstadt (trip time: 90 min.). Call *C* **01/ 1717** in Vienna for schedules.

From the Vienna International Airport, you can take a bus to the City Air Terminal at the Vienna Hilton. From this station, buses depart for Eisenstadt every 20 minutes during the day. The sign on the bus reads EISENSTADT-DOMPLATZ (there's no number).

If you're driving from Vienna, take Route 10 east to Parndorf Ort, and then head southwest along Route 50 to Eisenstadt.

VISITOR INFORMATION   The **Eisenstadt tourist office,** Franz-Schubert-Platz 1 (*C* **02682/67390**), will make hotel reservations for you at no charge and distributes information (in English).

WHERE JOSEPH HAYDN LIVED & WORKED
Even before assuming its new role as capital, Eisenstadt was renowned as the place where the great composer (Franz) Joseph Haydn lived and worked while under the patronage of the Esterházys. For a good part of his life (1732–1809), Haydn divided his time between Eisenstadt and Esterházy Castle in Hungary. Prince Esterházy eventually gave the composer his own orchestra and a concert hall in which to perform.

In September, the **Haydn Days** festival presents an ongoing roster of the composer's works at various venues throughout town: the castle, local churches, and parks, when the weather is good.

Bergkirche (Church of the Calvary)   If you want to pay your final respects to Haydn, follow Hauptstrasse to Esterházystrasse, which leads to this church containing Haydn's white marble tomb.

Until 1954, only the composer's headless body was here. His skull was in the Vienna's Musikinstrumentensammlung (see "Neue Hofburg," p. 125), where curious spectators were actually allowed to feel it. Haydn's head had been stolen a few days after his death and wasn't reunited with his body for 145 years! In a long and complicated journey, the head traveled from one owner to another, even being sold, before finally, we hope, coming to rest with the other part of Haydn's remains at Eisenstadt.

Joseph-Haydn-Platz 1. ℂ **02682/62638**. Church free admission; Haydn's tomb 2.50€ adults, 2€ seniors, 1€ students. Daily 9am–noon and 1–5pm. Closed Nov–Mar. From Esterházy Platz at the castle, head directly W along Esterházystrasse, a slightly uphill walk.

Haydn Museum   The little home of the composer from 1766 to 1778 is now a museum honoring its former tenant. Although he appeared in court nearly every night, Haydn actually lived very modestly when he was at home. A little flower-filled courtyard is one of the few luxuries. The museum has collected mementos of Haydn's life and work.

Haydn-Gasse 21. ℂ **02682/7193900**. Admission 3€ adults; 2€ children, seniors, and students. Daily 9am–noon and 1–5pm. Closed Nov–Easter. Pass Schloss Esterházy and turn left onto Haydn-Gasse.

Schloss Esterházy 𝄞   Haydn worked in this château built on the site of a medieval castle and owned by the Esterházy princes. The Esterházy clan was a great Hungarian family with vast estates that ruled over Eisenstadt and its surrounding area. They claimed descent from Attila the Hun. The Esterházys helped the Hapsburgs gain control in Hungary. So great was their loyalty to Austria, in fact, that when Napoléon offered the crown of Hungary to Nic Esterházy in 1809, he refused it.

The castle, built around an inner courtyard, was designed by the Italian architect Carlo Antonio Carlone, who began work on it in 1663. Subsequently, many other architects have remodeled it, resulting in sweeping alterations to its appearance. In the late 17th and early 18th centuries, it was given a baroque pastel facade. On the first floor, the great baronial hall was made into the Haydnsaal, where the composer conducted the orchestra Prince Esterházy had provided for him, often performing his own works. The walls and ceilings of this concert hall are elaborately decorated, but the floor is of bare wood, which, it is claimed, is the reason for the room's acoustic perfection.

Esterházy Platz. ℂ **2682/7193000**. Admission 4.50€ adults; 3€ children, seniors, and students. Daily 8am–6pm. From the bus station at Domplatz, follow the sign to the castle (a 10-min. walk).

A SIDE TRIP TO FRANZ LISZT'S BIRTHPLACE

In Raiding, a small nearby village south of Eisenstadt, the **Franz-Liszt-Geburtshaus** contains many mementos of the composer's life, including an old church organ he used to play. Liszt's father worked as a bailiff for the princes of Esterházy, and this was his home when little Franz was born in 1811.

To get to the museum (ℂ **02619/7220**), take Route S31 south of Eisenstadt; then cut east onto a minor unmarked road at Lackenbach (follow the signs to Raiding from there). It's open only from Easter to October daily from 9am to noon and 1 to 5pm. Admission is 2.50€ for adults and 1.50€ for seniors, children, and students; a family ticket sells for 5€.

SHOPPING   Don't expect the glamour or variety of Vienna's shopping scene, but with a little effort, you might find some tempting shops tucked away in Eisenstadt's old town. In our opinion, the store that most immediately appeals to foreign visitors is **Trachten Tack,** Hauptstrasse 8 (ℂ **02682/624-28**). Within, you'll find folkloric Burgenland-derived clothing for men, women, and children, as well as the widest selection of local handcrafts in town. Don't expect everything here to have been made in Austria—some of the most interesting items might have been embroidered or crafted across the border in nearby Hungary.

Carrying an impressive inventory of wine, **Schloss Weingut Esterházy,** Schloss Esterházy (© **02682/63345**), is set on the street level of Eisenstadt's most famous building. Most of the wine is produced on the 150 acres of vineyards associated with the castle, including reds, whites (both sparkling and still), fruited liqueurs, and brandies. One part of the store is devoted to native son Joseph Haydn and, as such, sells CDs, gift items, books, and souvenirs related to his musical theories and accomplishments.

WHERE TO STAY & DINE

Hotel Burgenland   Hotel Burgenland opened in 1982 and quickly established itself as the best in Eisenstadt. A mansard roof, white stucco walls, and big windows form the exterior of this contemporary hotel located directly northeast of the bus station at Domplatz. The comfortable rooms have lots of light, comfortable beds, functional furniture, and neatly kept bathrooms with shower-tub combinations.

One of the best restaurants in Burgenland is the hotel's G'würstockl, the more formal of its two restaurants. The bright and airy restaurant serves traditional dishes such as cabbage soup and veal steak with fresh vegetables, along with some Hungarian specialties.

Schubertplatz 1, A-7000 Eisenstadt. © **02682/696.** Fax 02682/65531. www.austria-hotels.at/burgenland. 87 units. 122€ double; from 190€ suite. Rates include breakfast. AE, DC, MC, V. Parking 8€. **Amenities:** 2 restaurants; bar; pool; fitness center; sauna; room service; babysitting; laundry; dry cleaning. *In room:* TV, minibar, hair dryer, safe.

Wirtshaus zum Eder   Filled with modern furniture, deer antlers, and iron chandeliers, this family-style guesthouse also has a garden terrace surrounded by a thick wall of greenery. It's in the town center, north of the bus station at Domplatz. The simple bedrooms are clean and comfortable, with good beds but small bathrooms with shower units. The hotel's restaurant serves Austrian and Hungarian specialties at reasonable prices.

Hauptstrasse 25, A-7000 Eisenstadt. © **02682/62645.** Fax 02682/626455. www.tiscover.at/wirtshaus-zum-eder. 10 units. 47€ double. Rates include breakfast. AE, DC, MC, V. Free parking. **Amenities:** Restaurant; bar; exercise room. *In room:* No phone.

EISENSTADT AFTER DARK

Don't expect a lot, as there simply isn't much nightlife within small and sleepy Eisenstadt. You might have a quiet drink or two at such popular spots as the **Café Bauer,** Ignaz-Semmelweisse-Gasse 1 (© **02682/655-93**), or at any of the hidden bars whose clientele and flavor changes radically depending on what time of day you happen to arrive and on whoever happens to be there when you show up. One of the most appealing places is the **Piccolo Bar,** Markelgasse (© **02682/628-83**). And if you want to go dancing, head for the town's only disco, the **James Dean,** Mattesburgerstrasse (© **2682/642490**), an interesting combination of *Mitteleuropa* and 1950s America.

2 Lake Neusiedl ✦

The Lake Neusiedl region is a famous getaway for the Viennese, and North Americans will find it just as desirable. The lake offers countless diversions, making it an ideal destination for families or active travelers. You can play in and around the lake all day, and then relax over a fine meal of Burgenland cuisine. The geological anomaly of the Neusiedler (see box below) and the steppe landscape make for intriguing hikes and strolls. The towns discussed below tend to be small, sleepy hamlets offering little more than lakeside relaxation, but they are ideal bases for exploring the surrounding countryside.

NEUSIEDL AM SEE

On the northern shore of Lake Neusiedl lies this popular summer weekend spot, where watersports prevail. You can rent sailboats here and spend the day drifting around the lake. The town's Gothic parish church is noted for its "ship pulpit." A watchtower from the Middle Ages still stands guard over the town, although it's no longer occupied. Many vineyards cover the nearby fields. If you plan to be here on a summer weekend, make advance reservations.

GETTING THERE   Neusiedl am See lies 45km (28 miles) southeast of Vienna, 359km (223 miles) east of Salzburg, and 34km (21 miles) northeast of Eisenstadt. This town is your gateway to the lake, as it's less than an hour by express train from Vienna. If you're driving from Vienna, take the A-4 or Route 10 east. If you're in Eisenstadt, head northeast along Route 50, cutting east along Route 51 for a short distance. It's better to have a car if you're exploring Lake Neusiedl, although there are bus connections that depart several times daily from the Domplatz bus station at Eisenstadt.

VISITOR INFORMATION   The **Neusiedl am See tourist office,** in the Rathaus (town hall), Hauptplatz 1 (✆ **02167/2229**), distributes information about accommodations and boat rentals. It's open Monday through Friday from 8am to 7pm, Saturday from 10am to 3pm, and Sunday from noon to 4pm.

WHERE TO STAY & DINE

Gasthof zur Traube   This small hotel stands on the town's bustling main street. The pleasant ground-floor restaurant is filled with country trim and wrought-iron table dividers. You can stop in for a meal from 11am to 10pm or book one of the cozy upstairs rooms (you have to register at the bar in back of the restaurant). Both the rooms and shower-only bathrooms are a bit on the small size. In summer, guests can relax in the garden. Franz Rittsteuer and his family are the owners.

Hauptplatz 9, A-7100 Neusiedl am See. ✆ **02167/2423.** Fax 02167/24236. traube@netway.at. 7 units. 51€ double. Rates include breakfast. AE, DC, MC, V. **Amenities:** Restaurant; bar. *In room:* TV.

Hotel Wende ✿   This place is actually a complex of three sprawling buildings interconnected by rambling corridors. Set at the edge of town on the road leading to the water, the hotel is almost a village unto itself. The aura here is one of clean but slightly sterile propriety. The bedrooms are well furnished, with well-maintained bathrooms containing shower-tub combinations.

The best food and best service, as well as the most formal setting, are found in the hotel's restaurant. Under a wood-beamed ceiling, the rich and bountiful table of Burgenland is set to perfection. In summer, tables are placed outside overlooking the grounds. Because Burgenland is a border state, the menu reflects the cuisines of Hungary and Austria. The menu includes a savory soup made with fresh carp from nearby lakes; pork cutlets with homemade noodles, bacon-flavored rösti, baby carrots, and fresh herbs; breast of chicken with polenta and fresh herbs; filet of zander in a potato crust with a sherry-cream sauce and wild rice; Hungarian crepes stuffed with minced veal and covered with paprika-cream sauce; and, for dessert, iced honey parfait with seasonal fresh fruits, or perhaps a strudel studded with fresh dates and topped with marzipan-flavored whipped cream.

Seestrasse 40-50, A-7100 Neusiedl am See. ✆ **02167/8111.** Fax 02167/811-1649. anfrage@hotelwende.at. 106 units. 120€–144€ double; 284€ suite. Rates include half-board. AE, DC, MC, V. Parking garage 9€.

Closed last week in Jan and first 2 weeks in Feb. Free pickup at the train station. **Amenities:** Restaurant; bar; pool; 3 tennis courts; fitness center; Jacuzzi; sauna; salon; room service; massage; babysitting; laundry; dry cleaning. *In room:* TV, minibar, hair dryer.

PURBACH AM SEE

If you take Route 50 south from the northern tip of Lake Neusiedl, your first stop might be in this little resort village, which has some decent accommodations. Purbach is also a market town, and you can buy Burgenland wine in the shops. Some of the town walls, built against invading Turks, still stand.

GETTING THERE   Purbach is 50km (31 miles) southeast of Vienna and 18km (11 miles) northeast of Eisenstadt. From Eisenstadt, you can take a daily bus that leaves from the station at Domplatz. If you're driving from Eisenstadt, head northeast along Route 50; if you're coming from Vienna, cut southeast along Route 10.

VISITOR INFORMATION   Contact the **Neusiedler See tourist office** in Neusiedl am See, Hauptplatz 1 (✆ **02167/2229**). It's open Monday through Friday from 8am to 7pm, Saturday from 10am to 3pm, and Sunday from noon to 4pm.

WHERE TO STAY

Am Spitz   The main building of this hotel has a gable trimmed with baroque embellishments. The Holzl-Schwarz family is your host here, where a hotel has

 The Capricious Lake

Lake Neusiedl (Neusiedler See) is a popular steppe lake lying in the northern part of Burgenland. But this strange lake should never be taken for granted—in fact, from 1868 to 1872, it completely dried up, as it has done periodically throughout its known history. Such behavior has led to some confusing real-estate disputes among bordering landowners. The lake was once part of a body of water that blanketed all of the Pannonian Plain. Today its greatest depth is about 1.8m (6 ft.), and the wind can shift the water dramatically, even causing parts of the lake to dry up. The lake is between 7km and 15km (4¼ and 9¼ miles) wide and about 35km (22 miles) long.

A broad belt of reeds encircles the huge expanse. This thicket is an ideal habitat for many varieties of waterfowl. In all, some 250 different species of birds inhabit the lake, including the usual collection of storks, geese, duck, and herons. If you're tall enough, you could walk through the thicket, but we're not recommending that! The plant and animal life in the lake is unique in Europe. Within its slightly salty waters, alpine, Baltic, and Pannonian flora and fauna meet.

Viennese flock to the lake throughout the year, in summer to fish, sail, and windsurf, and in winter to skate. Nearly every lakeside village has a beach (although on any given day it might be swallowed up by the sea or be miles from the shore, depending on which way the wind blows). The temperate climate and fertile soil surrounding the west bank are ideal for vineyards. Washed in sun, the orchards in Rust produce famous award-winning vintages.

stood for more than 600 years. The current incarnation includes accommodations with wonderful views of the lake. The hotel staff takes care and pride in the maintenance of its average-size rooms and small but quite serviceable shower-only bathrooms. The hotel is well directed, conservative, and deserving of its three-star government rating. The adjoining restaurant, rustically decorated and cozy, is one of the best places in the region for Burgenland cuisine.

A-7083 Purbach am See. ℂ 02683/5519. Fax 02683/551920. amspitz@aon.at. 15 units. 64€–78€ double; 100€ apt. Rates include breakfast. MC, V. Free parking. Closed Christmas–Easter. The hotel will pick up guests at the bus station. **Amenities:** Restaurant; lounge; room service; laundry; dry cleaning. *In room:* TV, minibar, hair dryer.

WHERE TO DINE
Romantik-Restaurant Nikolauszeche ⚐ AUSTRIAN   This upscale restaurant is housed in what was 5 centuries ago a cloister for monks. The authentically regional menu changes every 2 weeks. Diners can order the rich bouillon or cabbage soup, the *Fogosch* (a white fish), and the chef's special ham crepes. The wine list is well chosen. Accordion or organ music is played. If you want privacy and calm, you can find a quiet corner in the interior courtyard.

Bodenzeile 3. ℂ 02683/5514. Reservations recommended. Main courses 9.50€–21€; fixed-price menu (including wine) 25€–36€. AE, DC, MC, V. May–Sept Mon–Fri 11:30am–2pm and 6–10pm; Sat–Sun 11:30am–10pm. Oct–Apr Mon–Tues 11:30am–2pm and 6–10pm; Sat–Sun 11:30am–10pm. Closed Wed–Fri in winter and Jan 3 to mid-Mar.

RUST
Leaving Purbach, head south toward Rust, a small resort village with limited accommodations. It's famous for its stork nests, which are perched on chimneys throughout the town. The antiquated charming town center is well preserved and clean. Its walls were built in 1614 for protection against the Turks.

Rust is the capital of the Burgenland lake district, lying in a rich setting of vineyards famed for the Burgenlander grape. If it's available, try the *Blaufränkisch,* a red wine that seems to be entirely consumed by the locals and visiting Viennese who flock to the area. Sometimes you can go right up to the door of a vintner's farmhouse, especially if a green bough is displayed, to sample and buy wine on the spot.

The little lakeshore resort has a warm and friendly atmosphere, especially on weekends. Summers are often hot, and the lake water is surprisingly tepid. Sailboats and windsurfers can be rented on the banks of the shallow Neusiedler See.

GETTING THERE   The village is 18km (11 miles) northeast of Eisenstadt, 71km (44 miles) southeast of Vienna, and 349km (217 miles) east of Salzburg. There's no train station, but buses connect Eisenstadt with Rust. For information, call the bus station in Eisenstadt (ℂ 02682/6236011). From Eisenstadt by car, head east on Route 52. From Purbach, take Route 50 south toward Eisenstadt. At Seehof, take a left fork to Oggau and Rust.

VISITOR INFORMATION   The **Rust tourist office,** in the Rathaus (town hall) in the center of the village (ℂ 02685/502), can arrange inexpensive stays with English-speaking families. It's open Monday through Friday from 9am to noon and 2 to 6pm, Saturday from 9am to noon, and Sunday from 10am to noon.

WHERE TO STAY & DINE
Hotel-Restaurant Sifkovitz ⚐   Attracting summer visitors from Vienna and Hungary, this hotel consists of an older building with a new wing. The facade is concrete and stucco, and the older building has a red-tile roof and big windows.

Rooms get a lot of sun and are comfortably furnished, if rather functional. There's no great style here, but the beds are firm and the bathrooms, although not large, are well maintained and equipped with shower-tub combinations. Singles are very hard to get during the busy summer season. There is access to tennis courts, but they're on the grounds of another hotel nearby (the staff will make arrangements). Food, both Austrian and Hungarian, is served daily.

Am Seekanal 8, A-7071 Rust. (🕿) **02685/276.** Fax 02685/36012. 35 units. 64€–116€ double. Rates include breakfast. AE, DC, MC, V. Closed Dec–Mar. **Amenities:** Restaurant; bar; fitness center; sauna; room service; laundry; dry cleaning service. *In room:* TV, minibar, hair dryer, safe.

Seehotel Rust 𝒜 Seehotel Rust is one of the most attractive hotels in the lake district. Set on a grassy lawn at the edge of the lake, this well-designed hotel remains open year-round. It has an appealing series of connected balconies, rounded towers that look vaguely medieval, and a series of recessed loggias. The hotel offers pleasantly furnished bedrooms and clean bathrooms equipped with a shower unit. The rooms are a little too "peas-in-the-pod" for most tastes; however, an overnight stopover can be just fine.

Offerings in the restaurant include *Tafelspitz* (boiled beef) with chive sauce, calves' brains with a honey vinegar, watercress soup, and sole meunière. A Gypsy band provides entertainment.

A-7071 Rust. (🕿) **02685/381419.** Fax 02685/381419. www.trendhotels.at. 110 units. 148€ double. Rates include breakfast. AE, DC, MC, V. Free parking. **Amenities:** Restaurant; bar; pool; 4 tennis courts; squash court; sauna; boat rental; room service; babysitting; laundry; dry cleaning. *In room:* TV, minibar, hair dryer.

ILLMITZ: A STEPPE VILLAGE

This old puszta (steppe) village on the east side of the lake has grown into a town with a moderate tourist business in summer. From Eisenstadt, take Route 50 northeast, through Purbach, cutting southeast on Route 51, via Pordersdorf, to Illmitz. It's a 61km (38-mile) drive, which seems long because traffic must swing around the lake's northern perimeter before heading south to Illmitz.

NEARBY OFFBEAT ATTRACTIONS

Leaving Illmitz, head east on the main route and then cut north at the junction with Route 51. From Route 51, the little villages of St. Andrä bei Frauenkirchen and Andau are both signposted.

Near the Hungarian border, the tiny village of **St. Andrä bei Frauenkirchen** is filled with thatch houses. The town is known for its basket weaving, so you might want to drive here for a shopping expedition.

A short drive farther will take you to **Andau,** which became the focus of world attention in 1956 during the Hungarian uprising. It was through this point that hundreds of Hungarians dashed to freedom in the west, fleeing the grim Soviet invasion of Budapest.

Starting in the late 1940s, the border with Hungary was closely guarded, and people who tried to escape into Austria were shot from the Communist-controlled watchtowers. But now all that has changed. In 1989, the fortifications were rendered obsolete as hundreds fled across the frontier to the west. Before the year was out, the once fortified border was completely opened.

The surrounding marshy area of this remote sector of Austria, called **Seewinkel,** is a large natural wildlife sanctuary. The area, dotted with windmills and reed thickets, is a haven for birds, many small puszta animals, and some rare flora.

Seewinkel is very different from Austria's celebrated Alps and thick forests, and is little known to North Americans or even to most Europeans. In other words, it's a great place to get off the beaten track and add a little adventure to your travels.

WHERE TO STAY & DINE

Weingut-Weingasthof Rosenhof 🌟 A block from the main highway running through the center of town, this charming baroque hotel stands in a gardenlike setting. Through the arched gateway, framed by a gold-and-white facade, is a rose-laden courtyard filled with arbors. The tile-roofed building, capped with platforms for storks' nests, contains cozy, perfectly maintained bedrooms. Bathrooms have good-size towels and shower units.

In an older section, you'll find a wine restaurant whose star attraction is the recent vintage produced by the Haider family's wine presses. The restaurant serves Hungarian and Burgenland specialties to its guests and much of the neighborhood. Dishes might be as exotic as wild boar cooked in a marinade and thickened with regional walnuts. Local fish, such as carp and the meaty zander from the Danube, are available. In autumn, the inn serves *Traubensaft*—delectable grape juice made from freshly harvested grapes that is consumed before it becomes alcoholic. In the evening, musicians fill the air with Gypsy music.

Florianigasse 1, A-7142 Illmitz. 🕻 02175/2232. Fax 02175/22324. www.rosenhof.cc. 15 units. 64€–88€ double. Rates include breakfast. MC, V. Closed Nov to Easter. **Amenities:** Restaurant; bar; room service; laundry; dry cleaning. *In room:* TV, hair dryer.

PODERSDORF: BEST IN SWIMMING

Podersdorf am See is one of the best places to go swimming in the lake, as the shoreline here is relatively free of reeds. Over the years, the little town has become a modest summer resort. The parish church in the village dates from the late 18th century. Check out the thatched-roof cottages where you might see storks nesting in the chimneys. The Viennese like to drive out here during the summer to go for a swim and to purchase wine from the local vintners.

GETTING THERE Podersdorf lies 14km (9 miles) south of the major center along the lake, Neusiedl am See (see above). It's easiest to drive here, although buses run throughout the day from Eisenstadt, going via Neusiedl am See. If you're driving from Eisenstadt, head northeast along Route 50, via Purbach, cutting southeast at the junction with Route 51; you'll go via Neusiedl am See before cutting south along the lake to Podersdorf.

VISITOR INFORMATION In summer, a little **tourist office** at Hauptstrasse 2 (🕻 **02177/2227**) dispenses information Monday through Friday from 8am to noon and 1 to 4pm.

WHERE TO STAY

Gasthof Seewirt This hotel sits at the edge of the lake, within a short walk of a great swath of marshland. It charges the same prices and shares the same owners as the roughly equivalent but newer Haus Attila, with which it is frequently compared. Rooms are clean, comfortable, and utilitarian, but only medium in size. Duvets cover the comfortable beds, and the shower-only bathrooms are a bit cramped but spotlessly kept. Public areas bear the owners' personal touch and include one of the best restaurants in town (see below).

Strandplatz 1, A-7141 Podersdorf. 🕻 02177/2415. Fax 02177/246530. 35 units. 72€–115€ double. Rates include half-board. No credit cards. Closed Dec 1–Feb 15. **Amenities:** Restaurant; lounge; pool; Jacuzzi; sauna; room service. *In room:* TV, hair dryer, safe.

Haus Attila Newer and more recently renovated than its sibling, the Seewirt, this hotel was renovated and enlarged in 1992. The light-grained balconies are partially shielded by a row of trees, and many overlook the lake. Rooms are clean and comfortable, and the tiny shower-only bathrooms are well maintained.

Many visitors who check in for a couple of days of lakeside relaxation never move too far, consuming their meals in the dining room of the Seewirt, less than 100 yards away. In the basement of a nearby annex is a well-stocked wine cellar, where a member of the Karner family can take you for a wine tasting. Some of the vintages are produced from their own vineyards.

Strandplatz 8, A-7141 Podersdorf. ℂ **02177/2415.** Fax 02177/246530. 36 units. 72€–115€ double. Rates include breakfast. AE, MC, V. Closed Nov 1–Mar 30. **Amenities:** Restaurant; lounge; pool; sauna; room service. *In room:* TV, hair dryer, safe.

Seehotel Herlinde   An excellent government-rated two-star choice, this vacation spot is on the beach of Lake Neusiedl away from the main highway. All the functionally furnished rooms have their own balconies; the best have views of the lake. Room size is only adequate; the beds nothing special, though the mattresses are firm. The shower-only bathrooms are small but are polished brightly every day. The food and wine are plentiful, the latter often enjoyed on a 200-seat terrace.

Strandplatz 17, A-7141 Podersdorf. ℂ **02177/2273.** Fax 02177/2430. 40 units. 70€–90€ double. Rates include breakfast and lunch. No credit cards. **Amenities:** Restaurant; bar; sauna; room service; laundry service. *In room:* TV, minibar, hair dryer.

WHERE TO DINE

Gasthof Seewirt Café Restaurant 𝒢 BURGENLANDER/INTERNA-TIONAL   The preferred place for dining at the resort is this likable and unpretentious hotel restaurant that prepares bountiful dishes served by formally dressed waiters who are eager to describe the nuances of the local cuisine. The Karner family, well-known vintners whose excellent Rieslings, red and white Pinots, and *Weisserburgundens* are available for consumption, are proud of their long-established traditions and a local cuisine that in some ways resembles that of neighboring Hungary. A house specialty is *Palatschinken Marmaladen,* consisting of tender roast beef glazed with apricot jam, and a dessert called *Somloer Nockerl,* concocted from vanilla pudding, whipped cream, raisins, and nuts encased in a biscuit shell.

Strandplatz 1. ℂ **02177/2415.** Main courses 6€–17€. MC, V. Daily 11am–9pm. Closed Dec 1–Feb 15. Closed Mon–Tues Feb 16–April 30 and Sept 15–Nov 30.

3 Forchtenstein Castle

8km (5 miles) SW of Mattersburg; 71km (44 miles) S of Vienna

After exploring the lake district, head south from Eisenstadt toward the narrow waistline of the province, a small corridor between north and south Burgenland created when Ödenburg, then the capital (now the Hungarian frontier city of Sopron), voted to remain under Budapest's rule. The castle is the main attraction in Forchtenstein, an area inhabited by fruit growers.

ESSENTIALS

GETTING THERE   From Eisenstadt, take Route S31 southwest to Mattersburg, and from there follow the signs along a very minor road southwest to Forchtenstein. Three buses per day (only one on Sun) run from Vienna to Forchtenstein. There are no direct trains; the nearest railway station is 10km (6 miles) away, in Mattersburg. From here, take a taxi or one of the three buses a day that go to Forchtenstein.

VISITOR INFORMATION   In lieu of a tourist office, the **town council** in the mayor's office at Hauptstrasse 54 (ℂ **02626/63467**) provides information Monday through Friday from 9am to 2pm.

BURG FORCHTENSTEIN

Visitors come here chiefly to see the castle, **Burg Forchtenstein,** Burgplatz 1
(✆ **02626/81212**), 14km (9 miles) southeast of Wiener Neustadt in Lower
Austria. The castle was constructed on a rocky base by order of the counts of
Mattersdorf in the 13th century. The Esterházy family had it greatly expanded
around 1636. From its belvedere, you can see as far as the Great Hungarian
Plain.

The castle saw action in the Turkish sieges of Austria in 1529 and in 1683. A
museum since 1815, it now holds the Prince Esterházy collections, which consist
of family memorabilia, a portrait gallery, large battle paintings, historical banners,
and Turkish war booty and hunting arms. It's the largest private collection of
historical arms in Austria. Legend has it that Turkish prisoners carved the castle
cistern out of the rock, more than 137m (450 ft.) deep.

Admission is 5.50€ for adults and 3.10€ for children, and the castle is open
April through October daily from 9am to 5pm; November through March,
tours are offered only when requested in advance. A guide shows you through.

WHERE TO STAY

Gasthof Sauerzapf   A long, farmlike building, this hotel has two stories of
weathered stucco, renovated windows, and a roofline that's red on one side and
black on the other. The updated interior is cozy and attractive, albeit simple, and
is kept immaculate. Anna Daskalakis-Sauerzapf, the owner, rents modestly furnished rooms that are reasonably comfortable for the price. Their style is reminiscent of your great-aunt's house—comfortable beds and just-adequate
shower-only bathrooms, but an inviting place nonetheless. The restaurant serves
good food and an array of local wines.

Rosalienstrasse 39, A-7212 Forchtenstein. ✆ and fax **02626/81217**. 12 units. 40€–48€ double. Rates include
breakfast. No credit cards. Free parking. Closed Wed. **Amenities:** Restaurant; lounge. *In room:* No phone.

Gasthof Wutzlhofer   The core of this hotel was built in the 1660s as a private house. Greatly enlarged and improved over the years, it has been a hotel
since 1955. The view from the rooms of this family-run guesthouse encompasses
the whole valley and miles of forested hills. Don't expect luxury or frills here.
What you get are comfort, good food, and well-kept but small bathrooms with
shower stalls. Herbert Wutzlhofer, the owner, offers one of the best bargains in
the area. The hotel's restaurant, which has a reputation among locals for hearty
cuisine, unfortunately closes with the hotel in winter.

Rosalia 50, A-7212 Forchtenstein. ✆ **02626/81253**. 9 units. 40€–48€ double. Rates include breakfast. No
credit cards. Closed Nov–Mar. **Amenities:** Restaurant; lounge. *In room:* No phone.

WHERE TO DINE

Reisner AUSTRIAN   This well-managed restaurant, the area's best, has
expanded over the years from its original century-old core. Here you'll find good
food, particularly the regional specialties and Burgenland wines. The main dining
room is perfectly acceptable, but our favorite area is the cozy, rustic, smaller room,
which the locals prefer as well. Besides the especially good steaks, you might enjoy
trout filet served with a savory ragout of tomatoes, zucchini, potatoes, and basil.
The five-course fixed-price meal is gargantuan.

Haupstrasse 141. ✆ **02626/63139**. Reservations recommended. Main courses 7€–18€; 5-course fixed-
price menu 40€; 4-course fixed-price menu 32€; 3-course fixed-price menu 21€. No credit cards. Wed–Sun
9am–2:30pm and 6–10pm. Closed 3 weeks in Feb.

7

Salzburg: City of Mozart

A baroque city on the banks of the Salzach River, Salzburg is the beautiful capital of Land Salzburg. This former site of the Roman town of Juvavum is set against a pristine mountain backdrop. The city and the river were named after the early residents who earned their living in the region's salt mines.

This "heart of the heart of Europe" is the city of Mozart, who was born here in 1756. And the composer's association with the city continues to draw loads of tourists and tourist revenue. You can visit this favorite son's birthplace, the Gerburtshaus, an old burgher's house.

The Old Town lies on the left bank of the river, where a monastery and bishopric were founded in A.D. 700. From that simple start, Salzburg grew in power and prestige, becoming an archbishopric see in 798. At the height of the prince-archbishop's power, the city was known as the "German Rome." On medieval maps, the little province of Land Salzburg was titled "church lands." Long a part of the Holy Roman Empire, Land Salzburg was joined to Austria in 1816 following the Congress of Vienna.

Salzburg, a city of 17th- and 18th-century houses, is internationally known for its architectural grandeur. Much of the work was done by the masters of the baroque, Fischer von Erlach and Johann Lukas von Hildebrandt. The Salzburg Cathedral (Dom) is the first deliberately Italian-style church to be built north of the Alps. Several beautiful castles and palaces dot the city: Hohensalzburg Fortress, the former stronghold of the prince-archbishops of Salzburg; Residenz, an opulent palace and seat of the Salzburg prince-archbishops after they abandoned the gloomy Hohensalzburg; and Schloss Hellbrunn, 5km (3 miles) south of the city, summer residence of the prince-archbishops. The beautifully baroque Mirabell Gardens were laid out by the famous Fischer von Erlack.

The city is the setting for The Salzburg Festival, a world-renowned annual event that attracts music lovers, especially Mozart fans, from all over the globe. Salzburg was also the setting for *The Sound of Music;* yes, the hills are alive with music—and reachable by tour.

Ever since the end of World War II, Salzburg has had a strong American connection. While the Soviets occupied a section of Vienna and Lower Austria, Salzburg was a part of the American zone. The real postwar economy didn't develop in Eastern Austria until 1955 when the Russians pulled out. However, economic development began in Salzburg right at the end of the war, giving the city a 10-year head start and cementing its friendship with the United States.

1 Orientation

Salzburg is only a short distance from the Austrian-German frontier, so it's convenient for exploring many of the nearby attractions in Bavaria (see *Frommer's Germany* or *Frommer's Munich & the Bavarian Alps*). On the northern slopes of the Alps, the city is at the intersection of traditional European trade routes and is well served today by air, autobahn, and rail.

GETTING THERE

BY PLANE   The **Salzburg Airport–W. A. Mozart,** Innsbrucker Bundesstrasse 95 (✆ **0662/8580;** www.salzburg-airport.com), lies 3km (2 miles) southwest of the city center. It has regularly scheduled air service to all Austrian airports, as well as to Frankfurt, Amsterdam, Brussels, Berlin, Dresden, Düsseldorf, Hamburg, London, Paris, and Zurich. Major airlines serving the Salzburg airport are Austrian Airlines (✆ **0662/85-45-11**), Air France (✆ **01/50-2222-403**), Lufthansa (✆ **081010/258-080**), and Tyrolean (✆ **0662/85-45-33**).

Bus 77 runs between the airport and Salzburg's main rail station. Departures are frequent, and the 20-minute trip costs 2.80€ one-way. By taxi it's only about 15 minutes, but you'll pay at least 10€ to 15€.

BY TRAIN   Salzburg's main rail station, the **Salzburg Hauptbahnhof,** Südtirolerplatz (✆ **05/1717**), is on the major rail lines of Europe, with frequent arrivals not only from all the main cities of Austria, but also from other European cities such as Munich. Between 5:05am and 8:05pm, trains arrive every 30 minutes from Vienna (trip time: 3½ hr.). A one-way fare costs 32€. There are eight daily trains from Innsbruck (trip time: 2 hr.). A one-way fare costs 25€. Trains also arrive every 30 minutes from Munich (trip time: 2½ hr.), with a one-way ticket costing 22€.

From the train station, buses depart to various parts of the city, including the Altstadt (Old Town). Or, you can walk from the rail station to the Old Town in about 20 minutes.

The rail station has a currency exchange, storage lockers, and ticket-selling windows.

BY CAR   Salzburg is 336km (209 miles) southwest of Vienna and 153km (95 miles) east of Munich. It's reached from all directions by good roads, including Autobahn A8 from the west (Munich), A1 from the east (Vienna), and A10 from the south. Route 20 comes into Salzburg from points north and west, and Route 159 serves towns and cities from the southeast.

VISITOR INFORMATION

The **Salzburg Information Office,** Mozartplatz 5 (✆ **0662/88987-330;** www.salzburginfo.at; bus: 5, 6, or 51), is open in summer daily from 9am to 8pm and off-season Monday through Saturday from 9am to 6pm. In addition to dispensing information, the office can book tour guides for you or make hotel reservations for a deposit of 7.2% of your total hotel bill (which will be credited), plus a 2.20€ booking fee.

There's also a tourist information office on Platform 2A of the Hauptbahnhof, Südtirolerplatz (✆ **0662/88887-340**).

CITY LAYOUT

Most of what visitors come to see lies on the left bank of the Salzach River in the **Altstadt (Old Town).** If you're driving, you must leave your car in the modern part of town—the right bank of the Salzach—and enter the Old Town on foot, as most of it is for pedestrians only.

The heart of the inner city is **Residenzplatz,** which has the largest and finest baroque fountain this side of the Alps. On the western side of the square stands the **Residenz,** palace of the prince-archbishops, and on the southern side of the square is the **Salzburg Cathedral** (or Dom). To the west of the Dom lies

Domplatz, linked by archways dating from 1658. Squares to the north and south appear totally enclosed.

On the southern side of Max-Reinhardt-Platz and Hofstallgasse, edging toward **Mönchsberg,** stands the **Festspielhaus (Festival Theater),** built on the foundations of the 17th-century court stables.

STREET MAPS   The best map is published by **Falk** (the words *Falk plan* appear on the distinctive yellow-and-blue cover). You'll find these handy pocket-size maps, with street indexes, all over the city at bookstores, newsstands, and hotels. A special insert map contains a blowup of the heart of Salzburg.

NEIGHBORHOODS IN BRIEF

ALTSTADT   Most visitors head for the Altstadt, or Old Town, on the left bank of the Salzach, that part stretching from the river to Mönchsberg. This is a section of narrow streets (many from the Middle Ages) and slender houses, in complete contrast to the town constructed by the prince-archbishops across the river. The Old Town contains many of Salzburg's top attractions, including the cathedral, Mozart's birthplace, and St. Peter's Cemetery.

NONNBERG   The eastern hill occupied by the Hohensalzburg Fortress, Nonnberg rises to 455m (1,493 ft.). Some of the scenes from *The Sound of Music* were shot here. Nonnberg stands to the south of Kajetanerplatz. Stift Nonnberg is a Benedictine nunnery founded

about A.D. 700 by St. Rupert. Dominating the entire district, however, is the towering Hohensalzburg Fortress, lying south of the Old Town on the southwestern summit of Mönchsberg.

MÖNCHSBERG   To the west of the Hohensalzburg, this area is a mountain ridge slightly less than 3km (2 miles) long. It rises over the Old Town to a height of 542m (1,778 ft.). Fortifications atop it are from the 15th through the 17th centuries.

RIGHT BANK   The newer part of town is on the right bank of the Salzach, below Kapuzinerberg, the right-bank counterpart of Mönchsberg. This peak rises 637m (2,090 ft.) and is a lovely woodland area.

2 Getting Around

BY PUBLIC TRANSPORTATION

Information about local public transportation is available at the local tourist office.

BY BUS/TRAM   The city buses and trams provide quick, comfortable service through the city center from the Nonntal parking lot to Sigsmundsplatz, the city-center parking lot. The one-ride fare is 1.45€ for adults and .85€ for children 6 to 15; those 5 and under travel free. Note that buses stop running at 11pm.

Discount Passes   The **Salzburg Card** not only lets you use unlimited public transportation, but it also acts as an admission ticket to the city's most important cultural sights. With the card you can visit Mozart's birthplace, the Hohensalzburg fortress, the Residenz gallery, the world-famous water fountain gardens at Hellbrunn, the Baroque Museum in the Mirabell Gardens, and the gala rooms in the Archbishop's Residence. The card is also good for sights outside of town, including the Hellbrunn Zoo, the open-air museum in Grossingmain, the salt mines of the Dürnberg, and the gondola trip at Untersberg. The card, approximately the size of a credit card, comes with a brochure with maps and sightseeing hints.

Cards are valid for 24, 48, and 72 hours and cost 19€, 27€, and 33€, respectively. Children up to 15 years of age receive a 50% discount. You can buy the pass from Salzburg travel agencies, hotels, tobacconists, and municipal offices.

BY CAR

Driving a car in Salzburg is definitely *not* recommended. In most places it's impossible, since the monumental landmark center is for pedestrians only. Public parking lots—designated with a large P—are conveniently located throughout the city. If you're driving into Salzburg, leave your car on the left bank of the Salzach River. You'll find convenient underground parking lots like the one at Mönchsberg, from which it's an easy walk to the center and Domplatz.

However, we do recommend a car for touring around Land Salzburg (see chapter 8); relying on public transportation means a lot of travel time.

RENTALS   Arrangements for car rentals are always best if made in advance (see chapter 2). If not, then try **Avis** (© **0662/877278**) or **Hertz** (© **0662/876674**), both located at Ferdinand-Porsche-Strasse 7. Both are open Monday through Friday from 8:30am to 6pm and Saturday from 8am to 1pm.

REPAIRS   Try **ÖAMTC (Austrian Automobile Service),** Alpenstrasse 102 (© **0662/639-9-90**), or **ARBÖ (Austrian Motorists Association),** Münchner Bundesstrasse 9 (© **0662/433-6-01**), day or night. The emergency number, in case of automobile breakdowns, is © **120** for ÖAMTC and © **123** for ARBÖ.

BY TAXI & HORSE-DRAWN CAB

You'll find taxi stands scattered at key points all over the city center and in the suburbs. The Salzburg Funktaxi–Vereinigung (radio taxis) office is at Rainerstrasse 2 (© **0662/8111** to order a taxi in advance). Fares start at 2.90€.

A "traditional taxi"—a horse-drawn cab—will provide you with not only a ride, but a bit of history of the region as well. You can also rent a horse-drawn cab (called a *Fiaker* in German) at Residenplatz. Four people usually pay 22€ for 20 minutes and 45€ for 50 minutes. But all fares are subject to negotiation.

BY BICYCLE

In an effort to keep cars out of the center, Salzburg officials have developed a network of bicycle paths, which are indicated on city maps. One bike path goes along the Salzach River for 14km (9 miles) or so to Hallein, the second-largest town in Land Salzburg (see "Side Trips from Salzburg," later in this chapter).

May through September, you can rent bicycles at **Topbike,** at the Staatsbrücke (Main Bridge) (© **0662/6764-76-7259**), daily from 9am to 7pm. Rentals cost about 13€ per day, with a 10% discount for Salzburg card holders.

 FAST FACTS: Salzburg

American Express The office, located at Mozartplatz 5–7 (© **0662/8080;** bus: 5 or 6), adjacent to Residenzplatz, is open Monday through Friday from 9am to 5:30pm and Saturday from 9am to noon.

Babysitters English-speaking students at the University of Salzburg often earn extra money by babysitting, usually at various hotels in the city. Call

© **0662/8044-6001** to make arrangements; be sure to book as far in advance as possible.

Business Hours Most shops and stores are open Monday through Friday from 9am to 6pm. Some smaller shops shut down at noon for a lunch break, which can last 1 or 2 hours. Saturday hours in general are 9am to noon. Salzburg observes *langer Samstag*, which means that on the first Saturday of every month, most stores stay open 9am to 5pm. Banks are open Monday through Friday from 8am to noon and 2 to 4:30pm.

Currency Exchange You can exchange money at the Hauptbahnhof on Südtirolerplatz daily from 7am to 10pm, and at the airport daily from 9am to 4pm.

Dentists For information on how to find an English-speaking dentist, call Dentistenkammer, Faberstrasse 2 (© **0662/87-34-66**).

Doctors If you suddenly fall ill, your best source of information for finding a doctor is the reception desk of your hotel. If you want a comprehensive list of doctors and their respective specialties, which you can acquire in Salzburg or even before your arrival, contact **Ärztekammer für Salzburg,** Bergstrasse 14, A-5020 Salzburg (© **0662/87-13-27**). And if your troubles flare up over a weekend, the **Medical Emergency Center of the Austrian Red Cross** maintains a hot line (© **141**), which you can use to describe your problem. A staff member here will either ask you to visit their headquarters at Karl Renner Strasse 7 or send a medical expert to wherever you're staying. This service is available from 5pm on Friday to 8am on Monday, and on public holidays. For more information on medical emergencies, refer to "Hospitals," below.

Drugstores Larger pharmacies, especially those in the city center, tend to remain open without a break Monday through Friday from 8am to 6pm and Saturday from 8am to noon. Pharmacies in small towns near Salzburg and in the suburbs have similar hours but close for lunch, usually from 12:30 to 2:30pm Monday through Friday. For night service, and service on Saturday afternoon and Sunday, pharmacies display a sign giving the address of the nearest pharmacy that has agreed to remain open over the weekend or throughout the night. A pharmacy that's particularly convenient to Salzburg's commercial center is **Elisabeth-Apotheke,** Elisabethstrasse 1 (© **0662/87-14-84**), north of Rainerstrasse toward the train station.

Embassies & Consulates The **Consular Agency of the United States,** at Alter Markt 1 (© **0662/84-87-76**), is open Monday through Thursday from 9am to noon to assist U.S. citizens with emergencies. The **Consulate of Great Britain,** at Alter Markt 4 (© **0662/84-81-33**), is open Monday through Friday from 9am to noon.

Emergencies For emergencies, call the following numbers: police © **133**, fire © **122**, and ambulance © **144.**

Hospitals Salzburg is well equipped with medical facilities, including **Unfahl Hospital,** on Dr.-Franz-Rehrl-Platz 5 (© **0662/65-80-0**); and **Krankenhaus und Konvent der Barmherzigen Brüder,** Kajetanerplatz 1 (© **0662/80-88-0**).

Internet Access The most convenient cafe with Internet capability is the **Internet Café,** Mozartplatz (© **0662/84-48-22;** bus: 5 or 6), across from the tourist office. It's open daily from 9am to 11pm and charges 9€ per hour of Internet access.

Luggage Storage & Lockers Both are available at the Hauptbahnhof, Südtirolerplatz (📞 **0662/888-73-163**), open 24 hours daily. For 2 days, you can rent a large locker for 3€ or a small locker for 2€. The luggage storage counter is open from 4am to midnight and costs 3€ per day.

Police For the police, call 📞 **133**.

Post Offices The main post office is at Residenzplatz 9 (📞 **0662/844-1210**; bus: 5 or 6). The post office at the main railway station is open daily from 7am to 10pm. The postal code for Salzburg is A-5020; for Anif, A-5081; and for Bergheim, A-5101.

Restrooms Toilets are identified by the wc signs and are found throughout the city in museums and at sightseeing attractions, the rail station, and the airport. You can stop at a cafe, but these establishments prefer you to be a customer, even if it's for only some small purchase.

Safety Salzburg has a low crime rate compared with most European cities, but there is crime here. Take the usual precautions here as you would elsewhere. Use discretion, of course, and common sense.

Taxes The government value-added tax (VAT) and the service charge are included in restaurant and hotel bills presented to you. For a VAT refund, see "Fast Facts: Austria," in chapter 2. Other than this blanket tax mentioned above, Salzburg imposes no special city taxes.

Transit Information For information about local buses and trams, go to the city transport office at Alpenstrasse 91; even better, call 📞 **0662/ 62-05-51-552**.

Useful Telephone Numbers For the airport, call 📞 **0662/8580**; for train information, 📞 **05/1717**.

3 Where to Stay

Some of the best places to stay, particularly the castle hotels, converted farmhouse pensions, and boardinghouses, lie on the outskirts of Salzburg, within an easy drive of the city. But if you don't have a car, you'll probably want to stay right in the city, within walking distance of all the major sightseeing attractions.

If you have access to a car, check chapter 8 before selecting a hotel. Since Salzburg hotels are often very crowded in summer (and are impossibly booked during the Salzburg Festival in August), you might want to reserve less expensive accommodations in Land Salzburg and drive into Salzburg.

A pension or guesthouse in Salzburg does not necessarily mean a less expensive rate. These places can be luxurious, with a five-star rating, or of a more modest class, comparable to (but often better than) a third-class hotel.

Many hotels in the Old City must be reached on foot because of the pedestrian-only streets. However, taxis are allowed to take passengers from the airport or the rail and bus stations and deliver them to the door of a hotel. Many hotels away from the city center can be reached by public transportation.

ON THE LEFT BANK (OLD TOWN)
VERY EXPENSIVE

Altstadt SAS Radisson ⭐⭐   This is not your typical Radisson property—in fact, its style and charm are a rather radical departure for the chain. Dating from

1377, this is a luxuriously and elegantly converted Altstadt inn. Its closest rival in town is the old-world Goldener Hirsch, to which it comes in second. The old and new are blended in perfect harmony here, with the historic facade concealing top-rate comforts and luxuries. The cozy, antiques-filled lobby sets the tone, while a flower-lined, sky-lit atrium adds cheer even on the darkest of days. Stone arches from the medieval structure still remain. Most guests are housed in the main building. Rooms vary greatly in size but have a certain charm and sparkle, with some of the city's best beds, complemented by elegant bathrooms equipped with shower-tub combinations. Overlooking the river, the Restaurant Symphonie is one of the best hotel dining rooms in the city. The cuisine is good and the ambience is inviting, with a stained-glass ceiling and walls of windows.

Rudolfskai 28/Judengasse 15, A-5020 Salzburg. © 800/333-3333 in the U.S., or 0662/848-571. Fax 0662/848-571-6. www.austria-trend.at. 62 units. 215€–495€ double; 470€–610€ suite. Rates include buffet breakfast. AE, DC, MC, V. Parking 25€. Bus: 5, 6, or 55. **Amenities:** Restaurant; bar; room service; babysitting; laundry; dry cleaning. *In room:* TV, minibar, hair dryer, safe.

Goldener Hirsch 🏨🏨🏨   Goldener Hirsch wins the award for the finest hotel in Salzburg; this establishment is so steeped in legend and history that any Austrian will instantly recognize its name. The hotel is built on a small scale, yet it absolutely reeks of aristocratic elegance, which is enhanced by the superb staff. Sitting in an enviable position in the Old Town, a few doors from Mozart's birthplace, it's composed of three medieval town houses joined together in a labyrinth of rustic hallways and staircases. A fourth, called "The Coppersmith's House," is across the street and has 17 charming and elegant rooms. Street-side units have double-glazed windows. All are beautifully furnished and maintained. Bathrooms are generous in size, with shower-tub combinations and robes.

The formal Goldener Hirsch and the more casual Herzl Tavern are two of the more distinguished restaurants in Salzburg (see "Where to Dine," later in this chapter).

Getreidegasse 37, A-5020 Salzburg. © 800/325-3535 in the U.S., or 0662/8084. Fax 0662/8485-178-45. www.goldenerhirsch.com. 69 units. 331€–650€ double; 593€–1,090€ suite. Higher rates at festival time (the first week of Apr and mid-July to Aug). AE, DC, MC, V. You can double-park in front of the Getreidegasse entrance or at the Karajanplatz entrance, and a staff member will take your vehicle to the hotel's garage for 28€. Bus: 55. **Amenities:** 2 restaurants; bar; room service; babysitting; laundry; dry cleaning. *In room:* TV, minibar, hair dryer, safe.

MODERATE

Altstadthotel Weisse Taube   The hotel is in the pedestrian area of the Old Town a few steps from Mozartplatz, but you can drive up to it to unload baggage. Constructed in 1365, the Weisse Taube has been owned by the Haubner family since 1904. Rooms are, for the most part, renovated and comfortably streamlined, with traditional furnishings, frequently renewed beds, plus small but efficiently laid out bathrooms with shower-tub combinations. Housekeeping is spotless.

Kaigasse 9, A-5020 Salzburg. © 0662/84-24-04. Fax 0662/84-17-83. www.weissetaube.at. 31 units. 93€–125€ double. Rates include breakfast. AE, DC, MC, V. Garage 9€. Bus: 5, 51, or 55. **Amenities:** Breakfast room; bar; lounge. *In room:* TV, minibar, hair dryer, safe.

Cordial Theater Hotel   Set within a short walk of Salzburg's medieval core, this establishment contains both time-sharing units and some conventional hotel accommodations. Most of the theatrical-looking design you'll see today derives from a radical renovation that occurred in the late 1980s, when a 19th-century shell was gutted and reconfigured into the vaguely Jugendstil-style setting you see

Salzburg Accommodations

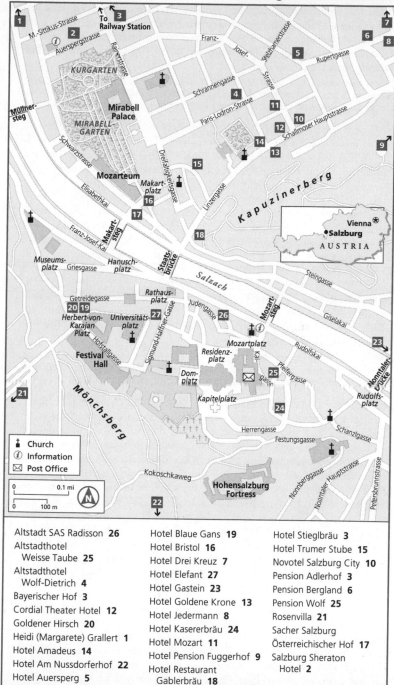

Altstadt SAS Radisson **26**

Altstadthotel
   Weisse Taube **25**

Altstadthotel
   Wolf-Dietrich **4**

Bayerischer Hof **3**

Cordial Theater Hotel **12**

Goldener Hirsch **20**

Heidi (Margarete) Grallert **1**

Hotel Amadeus **14**

Hotel Am Nussdorferhof **22**

Hotel Auersperg **5**

Hotel Blaue Gans **19**

Hotel Bristol **16**

Hotel Drei Kreuz **7**

Hotel Elefant **27**

Hotel Gastein **23**

Hotel Goldene Krone **13**

Hotel Jedermann **8**

Hotel Kasererbräu **24**

Hotel Mozart **11**

Hotel Pension Fuggerhof **9**

Hotel Restaurant
   Gablerbräu **18**

Hotel Stieglbräu **3**

Hotel Trumer Stube **15**

Novotel Salzburg City **10**

Pension Adlerhof **3**

Pension Bergland **6**

Pension Wolf **25**

Rosenvilla **21**

Sacher Salzburg

Österreichischer Hof **17**

Salzburg Sheraton
   Hotel **2**

today. Accommodations are scattered over three floors; each is painted a pale yellow and named after a composer or a writer. All rooms are comfortable, neatly maintained, and equipped with well-kept shower-only bathrooms. As a result of its artistic theme, the hotel's clientele includes lots of singers and composers. The Barcarole restaurant serves dinner only.

Schallmooser Hauptstrasse 13, A-5020 Salzburg. ℂ **0662/8816-810.** Fax 0662/8816-8692. chsalzburg@ cordial.co.at. 58 units. 95€–180€ double. Rates include breakfast. AE, DC, MC, V. Bus: 29. **Amenities:** Restaurant; bar; sauna; room service; massage; babysitting; laundry; dry cleaning. *In room:* TV, minibar, hair dryer.

Hotel Am Nussdorferhof   The only drawback to this hotel is its location in a quiet residential suburb, within a 20-minute walk south of Salzburg's historic core. If that isn't a problem for you (and many readers have greatly appreciated its clean air and the ability to sleep at night with the windows open, enjoying an absolute lack of noise), it might make a safe and happy refuge for you during your time in Salzburg. Its congenial owners, Herbert and Ilse Kronegger, know the cultural and geographical features of their city in intricate detail and are eager to help newcomers with the city's logistics. Expect a solid, 70-year-old stucco-covered building that's been much renovated over the years. About half the bedrooms are outfitted in old-fashioned Teutonic patterns, with touches of wood and alpine references. The other half are conservatively international, with bland 1970s-era furnishings and enough modern comforts to ensure a comfortable overnight stay. Bathrooms are trimmed in tile, in most cases with shower-tub combinations. On-site is a bar and a cozy Italian restaurant (La Fontana), with a menu that features well-prepared versions of pizza, pasta, and (usually) tried-and-true northern Italian cuisine.

Moosstrasse 36, A-5020 Salzburg. ℂ **0662/824838.** Fax 0662/824-8389. www.nussdorferhof.at. 30 units. High season 130€ double; winter 98€–115€ double. Rates include breakfast and parking. AE, DC, MC, V. Bus: 15 or 16. **Amenities:** Restaurant; bar; room service; babysitting. *In room:* TV, hair dryer.

Hotel Blaue Gans   "The Blue Goose" lies in the historic core of Salzburg, near the underground garages of the Mönchsberg, a few doors away from hotels that charge almost twice as much. The building that contains it is probably 700 years old, but the rooms were renovated extensively between 1998 and 2000. Each has modern furniture and a bit more space than you might have expected. Rooms facing the courtyard are quieter than those facing the street; nos. 332 and 336 are probably the biggest. All units have well-kept bathrooms with shower-tub combinations. You'll register in an understated lobby, one that's so discreetly tucked away that it might be hard to identify. Within the same building is a historic restaurant and beer hall, "Stadtgasthof Blaue Gans" (see "Where to Dine," later in this chapter).

Getreidegasse 43, A-5020 Salzburg. ℂ **0662/84-13-17.** Fax 0662/84-13-179. www.blauegans.at. 38 units. 129€–179€ double. Rates include buffet breakfast. AE, DC, MC, V. Parking 14€. Bus: 1 or 2. **Amenities:** Restaurant; bar; babysitting; laundry; dry cleaning. *In room:* TV, minibar, hair dryer, safe.

Hotel Elefant   Near the Old Town Rathaus, in a quiet alley off Getreidegasse, is this well-established, family-run hotel. It, too, is in one of Salzburg's most ancient buildings—it's more than 700 years old. The well-furnished and high-ceilinged rooms have small bathrooms with shower-tub combinations. Within the hotel are two restaurants serving Austrian and international cuisine. One of our favorites is the vaulted Bürgerstüberl, where high wooden banquettes separate the tables. You can also dine in the historic Ratsherrnkeller, which was known as the wine cellar of Salzburg in the 17th century.

Sigmund-Haffner-Gasse 4, A-5020 Salzburg. © 0662/84-33-97. Fax 0662/84-01-0928. www.elefant.at. 31 units. 122€–176€ double. Rates include buffet breakfast. AE, DC, MC, V. Parking 7.30€. Bus: 1, 2, 5, 6, or 51. **Amenities:** 2 restaurants; bar; room service; babysitting; laundry; dry cleaning. *In room:* TV, minibar, hair dryer, safe.

Hotel Kasererbräu   In one of the Old Town's most colorful neighborhoods, a few blocks from the cathedral, the Kasererbräu has baroque and Biedermeier furniture that goes well with the oriental rugs and embellished plaster ceilings. Most double rooms are spacious and all are cozy. Rooms are equipped with double beds or paired twins. Many bathrooms had to be squeezed into small spaces, but even so, doubles have bidets, along with shower-tub combinations and thick towels. The small singles have half-tubs or shower stalls. Breakfast is the only meal served, but dozens of restaurants and taverns are close by.

Kaigasse 33, A-5020 Salzburg. © 0662/84-24-45. Fax 0662/842-44-551. www.kasererbraeu.at. 43 units. 109€–202€ double; 217€ apt accommodating up to 4 persons. Rates include breakfast. AE, DC, MC, V. Parking 6€. Bus: 55. **Amenities:** Restaurant; lounge; sauna; laundry; dry cleaning. *In room:* TV, minibar.

Pension Wolf *Value*   Ideally located near Mozartplatz, this place dates from 1429. A stucco exterior with big shutters hides the rustic and inviting interior that is decorated with a few baroque touches and often sunny rooms. Some have recently been renovated, and many new bathrooms have been installed, making this a more inviting choice than ever. The rooms are a bit cramped, as are the shower-only bathrooms. Still, this pension represents very good value for high-priced Salzburg. Since the hotel is usually full, reservations are imperative.

Kaigasse 7, A-5020 Salzburg. © 0662/84-34-530. Fax 0662/84-24-234. www.hotelwolf.com. 15 units. 100€–145€ double. Rates include breakfast. AE, MC, V. Tram: 5, 6, 51, or 55. **Amenities:** Breakfast room; lounge; babysitting. *In room:* TV.

ON THE RIGHT BANK
EXPENSIVE

Hotel Bristol ★   Built in 1890, this traditional government-rated five-star hotel lies near the Mirabell Gardens and opposite Mozart's former home, encompassing a view of the Hohensalzburg Fortress. Compared with the noble courtliness of the Goldener Hirsch, this hotel appears a bit frumpy, although improvements have been made. And despite its rather blatant commercialism, the hotel is often fully booked. Rooms range from upper-class functional to opulently baroque, with decorated ceilings and crystal chandeliers. Most have been redecorated with antiques, chandeliers, oriental rugs, often half-canopied beds, and spacious closets. Bathrooms are small and lacking in shelf space, but have shower-tub combinations. Try for a front room for a view of Mirabell Palace.

Restaurants include the Polo Lounge, seating 40, and the Crystal Room, seating 80. High-standard Austrian and international cuisine is served. The piano bar has terrazzo floors, oriental rugs, and discreet music.

Makartplatz 4, A-5020 Salzburg. © 800/457-4000 in the U.S. and Canada, or 0662/87-35-57. Fax 0662/873-55-76. www.salzburginfo.at/Bristol. 61 units. 189€–392€ double; 327€–581€ suite. Rates include breakfast. AE, DC, MC, V. Self-parking 17€; valet parking 24€. Closed Feb 1–Mar 26. Bus: 1, 5, 29, or 51. **Amenities:** 2 restaurants; bar; lounge; room service; massage; babysitting; laundry; dry cleaning. *In room:* A/C, TV, minibar, hair dryer, safe.

Rosenvilla ★ *Finds*   The setting is a gracefully proportioned 100-year-old villa, located in a residential suburb within a 20-minute walk southwest of Salzburg's historic core, across the Salzach River from the city's center. Sheathed with ocher-colored stucco and flanked with roses that climb over wrought-iron supports and a small garden, it's small-scale, personalized, conservative, and a bit sleepy. Bedrooms are more lavish than you'd expect, with wooden floors, theatrical draperies, deep upholsteries, and a decor that you might have expected in a conservative and well-mannered private home. Some have four-poster beds draped with fabric, and in some cases, the bathrooms are unusually plush. Regardless of the category of the room you opt for, all bathrooms have shower-tub combinations. Other than breakfast, no meals are served here, but the hotel is associated with the also-recommended Hotel Pfefferschiff, several miles away. Be warned in advance that the reception facilities of this quiet hotel are completely closed after 9pm, so time your arrival accordingly.

Höfelgasse 4, A-5020 Salzburg. © 0662/621765. Fax 0662/625-2308. www.rosenvilla.sbg.at. 14 units. High season 146€–255€ double, 291€ junior suite; winter 110€–165€ double, 197€ suite. Rates include breakfast. AE, DC, MC, V. Bus: 49. **Amenities:** Laundry; dry cleaning. *In room:* TV.

Sacher Salzburg Österreichischer Hof ★★★
Built originally as the Hotel d'Autriche in 1866, this popular hotel was soon attracting guests from all over the world. It has survived the ravages of war, always keeping up with the times through renovations and expansions. A new era began when the Gürtler family, owners of the Hotel Sacher in Vienna, took over in 1988. After a year of renovating, the ÖH, as its guests fondly call it, has become a jewel of the riverbank. However, it still lacks the charm and personal service of the Goldener Hirsch. Inside are big windows with panoramic views of the Old Town. The cheerful and comfortable rooms are well furnished, with excellent beds. Try to reserve a room overlooking the river. Most doubles are large; singles tend to be small. Bathrooms, medium in size, have shower-tub combinations.

A host of drinking and dining facilities is available, including the Wintergarden, a cozy bar with piano music in the evening; the Roter Salon, an elegant dining room facing the river; the Zirbelzimmer, an award-winning restaurant; the Salzachgrill, offering everything from a snack to a steak, with a riverside terrace; the ÖH-Café, a traditional Austrian cafe, also with a riverside terrace; and a pastry shop that sells the famous Sacher torte.

Schwarzstrasse 5–7, A-5020 Salzburg. © 800/223-6800 in the U.S. and Canada, or 0662/889-77. Fax 0662/889-77-551. www.sacher.com. 127 units. 205€–800€ double; 555€–1,890€ suite. Rates include buffet breakfast. AE, DC, MC, V. Parking 25€. Bus: 1, 5, 6, 29, or 51. **Amenities:** 2 restaurants; 2 bars; cafe; lounge; fitness center; sauna; room service; laundry; dry cleaning. *In room:* TV, minibar, hair dryer, safe.

Salzburg Sheraton Hotel ★★
One of the crown jewels of the Sheraton chain, this government-rated five-star seven-story hotel opened in 1984 in a desirable location about a 10-minute walk from Mozartplatz. The Austrian architect who designed this place took great pains to incorporate it into its 19th-century neighborhood. The exterior is capped with a mansard roof, and the casement windows are ringed with elaborate trim. As you enter, the lobby opens to reveal sun-flooded views of the garden. Rooms have thick wall-to-wall carpeting and contain beds with built-in headboards. Bathrooms have makeup mirrors and hair dryers. The exclusive junior, queen, and president suites are filled with elegant Biedermeier furniture. Half the rooms look out over Mirabell Park.

The cream-and-crystal Restaurant Mirabell serves a good-value luncheon buffet Monday through Friday and a dressed-up version on Saturday and Sunday. A less formal dining area, the Bistro, offers daily specials, wine, and beer. A piano bar is outfitted with burnished brass, richly grained wood, and Art Nouveau decor.

Auerspergstrasse 4, A-5020 Salzburg. © 800/325-3535 in the U.S., or 0662/88-99-90. Fax 0662/88-17-76. www.sheraton.at. 184 units. 130€–287€ double; 321€–535€ suite. AE, DC, MC, V. Parking 12€. Bus: 1. **Amenities:** 2 restaurants; bar; pool; sauna; room service; babysitting; laundry; dry cleaning. *In room:* TV, minibar, hair dryer, safe.

MODERATE

Bayrischer Hof   A 2-block walk from the railway station close to the Mirabell Gardens, this streamlined hotel often hosts groups of central Europeans. The attractive, modern lobby is paneled with light-grained oak and is carpeted. Rooms are well-insulated refuges from the surrounding commercial neighborhood. The beds are comfortable and the bathrooms are moderate in size with shower-tub combinations. Housekeeping is a definite plus here. The hotel's thriving trio of dining rooms feature Austrian specialties.

Kaiserschützenstrasse 1, A-5020 Salzburg. (C) **0662/46-97-00.** Fax 0662/46-970-25. www.bayrischerhof.com. 34 units. 118.50€–192€ double. Rates include breakfast. AE, DC, MC, V. Free parking outdoors. **Amenities:** Restaurant; bar; room service; babysitting; laundry; dry cleaning. *In room:* TV, minibar, hair dryer.

Hotel Auersperg ⭐   A traditional family-run hotel near the right bank of the Salzach, this hotel lies only a 5-minute walk from the Altstadt, former stamping ground of Mozart. With its own sunny gardens, it consists of two buildings, a main structure and a less expensive annex. The inviting rooms are warm, large, and cozy, with big windows, excellent beds, and well-equipped bathrooms, moderate in size, with shower-tub combinations. There's an old-fashioned charm to the place, from the reception hall with its 19th-century molded ceilings to the antiques-filled drawing room. The library bar is not only convivial and informal, but also one of our favorite spots for drinking and conversation in Salzburg. The hotel also has a good restaurant. On the top floor, you'll find a roof terrace offering nice views of Salzburg.

Auerspergstrasse 61, A-5027 Salzburg. (C) **0662/889-44-0.** Fax 0662/88-944-55. www.auersperg.at. 51 units. 129€–176€ double; 173€–227€ suite. Rates include breakfast. AE, DC, MC, V. Free parking. Bus: 15 from the train station. **Amenities:** Breakfast room; bar; fitness center; sauna; laundry; dry cleaning. *In room:* TV, minibar, hair dryer, safe.

Hotel Mozart *(Kids (Value*   The six-story Hotel Mozart is a comfortable family-run hotel located in the city center. It is known for its unpretentious charm and its welcoming hospitality. Everything is homey and traditional in this breakfast-only hotel filled with oriental rugs, local paintings, and an attractive TV lounge. It's a 10-minute walk from the train station and only 5 minutes from the pedestrian area of Linzergasse and the famous Mirabell Gardens. Rooms are often sunny and come with all the standard extras. Most are quite spacious, with built-in furniture and twin beds. Bathrooms are medium in size, with shower-tub combinations. The accommodations facing the street are soundproof. Some of the guest rooms are big enough to sleep four comfortably. The courteously attentive staff provides careful service and thoughtful touches.

Franz-Josef-Strasse 27, A-5020, Salzburg. (C) **0662/87-22-74.** Fax 0662/87-00-79. www.hotel-mozart.at. 33 units. 85€–150€ double. Rates include breakfast. AE, DC, MC, V. Free parking. Bus: 5, 6, 27, 29, or 55. **Amenities:** Breakfast room; lounge; room service; babysitting; laundry; dry cleaning. *In room:* TV, minibar, hair dryer, safe.

Hotel Stieglbräu   Located in the Mirabell district, this hotel provides comfortable and contemporary accommodations within a 10-minute walk of Salzburg's historic core and a 5-minute walk from the railway station. The clean rooms have big windows and simple furniture, including comfortable beds. Bathrooms are spotless and equipped with shower-tub combinations. Two pleasant restaurants, serving international cuisine, offer at least half a dozen cozy dining rooms and a spacious outdoor garden-style terrace for warm-weather drinking and dining.

Rainerstrasse 14, A-5020 Salzburg. (C) **0662/88-992.** Fax 0662/88-99-271. www.imlauer.com. 77 units. 143€–176€ double; 156€–198€ suite. Rates include breakfast. AE, DC, MC, V. Free parking in the hotel's own parking lot. Bus: 1. **Amenities:** Restaurant; bar; room service; massage; laundry; dry cleaning. *In room:* A/C, TV, minibar, hair dryer.

Novotel Salzburg City *Kids*   This welcome addition brings a successful chain format to Salzburg, although it lacks the style of the Sheraton. Unlike most Novotels (which tend to be on the outskirts of cities), this one is centrally located, within walking distance of many major sights. Rooms, although no style-setters, are well maintained, with good beds and medium-size bathrooms with shower-tub combinations. Nevertheless, for families this is a favorite and by Salzburg standards, its prices are reasonable. Geared to early or late arrivals, the mediocre restaurant, bar, and cafe are open daily from 6am to midnight.

Franz-Josef-Strasse 26, A-5020 Salzburg. ⓒ **800/221-4542** in the U.S., or 0662/88-20-41. Fax 0662/874-240. www.astron-hotels.com. 140 units. 128€–178€ double. Rates include breakfast. AE, DC, MC, V. Free parking. Bus: 29. **Amenities:** Restaurant; bar; cafe; pool; sauna; room service; laundry; dry cleaning. *In room:* TV, minibar, hair dryer, safe.

INEXPENSIVE

Altstadthotel Wolf-Dietrich *Kids*   Two 19th-century town houses were joined together to make this select little hotel. The lobby and ground floor reception area have a friendly and elegant atmosphere and bright, classical furnishings. The smallish rooms are comfortably furnished, appealing, and cozy, with excellent beds and tiny bathrooms with shower-tub combinations. Many rooms were renovated in the late 1990s. The ground-floor cafe, Weiner Kaffeehaus, is reminiscent of the large extravagant coffeehouses built in the former century in Vienna, Budapest, and Prague. Alpine carvings and graceful pine detailing adorn one of the two restaurants. Decorating the indoor swimming pool are mirrors and unusual murals of Neptune chasing a sea nymph.

Wolf-Dietrich-Strasse 7, A-5020 Salzburg. ⓒ **0662/87-12-75.** Fax 0662/88-23-20. www.salzburg-hotel.at. 27 units. 109€–179€ double. Rates include breakfast. AE, DC, MC, V. Parking 11€. Closed Feb–Mar 15. Bus: 1, 2, 5, 6, or 51. **Amenities:** 2 restaurants; bar; cafe; pool; sauna; solarium; room service; babysitting; laundry; dry cleaning. *In room:* TV, minibar, hair dryer.

Heidi (Margarete) Grallert *Finds*   Emotionally and psychologically, this small-scale bed and breakfast couldn't be more different from the mass-market chain hotels that are sometimes recommended. The venue is an intensely personalized private home set within a well-maintained and rather large garden, dotted with roses, venerable trees, stone statues of bunnies, and live squirrels. Your hostess is the congenial and hard-working matron Heidi Grallert, whose ochre-colored chalet-style home is open to overnight guests. You'll occupy cozy, family-style bedrooms, each conservatively decorated in a well-scrubbed but not at all flamboyant style, each on the ground floor of a 15-year-old house whose upper floors are devoted to the personal life of the Grallert family. Ms. Grallert has been very helpful in assisting readers of this guide with information about Salzburg—some have maintained Christmas card exchanges with her years after their departure from her premises. Some visitors prefer walking for a brisk 25-minute trek beside the river to get here; others simply take the bus.

Fasaneriestrasse 17, A-5020 Salzburg. ⓒ and fax **0662/424860.** 3 units. 23€ single; 44€ double. Rates include breakfast. No credit cards. Bus: 49 or 95.

Hotel Amadeus   The walls and foundations of this government-rated three-star, four-story hotel date from the 15th century, but much of what you'll experience today is a mid-20th-century improvement. The quietest rooms are those overlooking the rear, with views of the graveyard where the wife of Mozart is buried. Rooms are pleasant, accessible via a cramped elevator, and decorated with reproductions of country-Austrian furniture. Bathrooms are cramped but contain shower-tub combinations and are well organized. Breakfasts are generous; the staff is helpful. The building's ground-floor cafe, the Amadeus, serves drinks and bistro-style food throughout the day and evening.

Linzer Gasse 43–45, A-5020 Salzburg. ✆ **0662/87-14-01** or 0662/87-61-63. Fax 0662/87-61-63-7. walkets@ salzburg.co.at. 30 units, 27 with bathroom. 30€ double without bathroom; 93€–130€ double with bathroom. Rates include breakfast. AE, DC, MC, V. Parking 15€. Bus: 1, 2, 5, 6, or 51 to Makartplatz. **Amenities:** Breakfast room; cafe; lounge. *In room:* TV, hair dryer, safe.

Hotel Drei Kreuz   The name *Drei Kreuz* refers to the three crosses of the nearby Kapuzinerberg, which was the site of public executions centuries ago. Once you get past the dreary bunkerlike facade, you'll find a warmly decorated and inviting interior. The restaurant has some of the most massive beams we've ever seen in Austria, and a cozy bar with rustic decor. The often small rooms are tasteful and well furnished. Bathrooms are also small but comfortable, with shower-tub combinations and spotless maintenance. It's about a 10-minute walk from the historic center.

Vogelweiderstrasse 9, A-5020 Salzburg. ✆ **0662/872-79-00.** Fax 0662/87-27-906. www.hoteldreikreuz.at. 24 units. 69€–115€ double. Rates include breakfast. AE, DC, MC, V. Free parking. Bus: 27 or 29. **Amenities:** Restaurant; bar; laundry; dry cleaning. *In room:* TV, hair dryer.

Hotel Gastein 🖈   This prosperous-looking Teutonic villa was built as a private home in 1953. It lies amid calm green scenery on the bank of the Salzach River. Only a few minutes from the center of the town's oldest boroughs, the house offers true Salzburg atmosphere. Although it's officially classified as a hotel, you'll feel like you're staying in an upper-class private home. During the annual music festival, the place is filled with musicians, who love the spacious flowering garden for breakfast or afternoon tea. You can spot colonies of ducks paddling behind a screen of riverside saplings. The large rooms have furniture crafted by well-known Salzburg artists, firm beds, and private balconies. Bathrooms, though often small, are exceedingly well maintained and equipped with shower-tub combinations.

Ignaz-Rieder-Kai 25, A-5020 Salzburg. ✆ **0662/62-25-65.** Fax 0662/62-25-659. www.hotel-gastein.at. 16 units. 105€–156€ double; 156€–248€ suite. Rates include breakfast. AE, DC, MC, V. Free parking. Bus: 49. **Amenities:** Breakfast room; lounge. *In room:* TV, minibar.

Hotel Goldene Krone   Our favorite part of this family-run guesthouse is the big sun terrace with ivy-covered walls, where a family member will serve you coffee after a tiring day in the city. The hotel is only a few minutes from the Staatsbrücke. Rooms range from small to medium, but furnishings, including the beds, are comfortable. Bathrooms aren't large, but they have neatly kept shower units and adequate shelf space. A breakfast buffet is the only meal served.

Linzer Gasse 48, A-5020 Salzburg. ✆ **0662/872-300.** www.hotel-goldenekrone.com. 26 units. 80€–90€ double. Rates include breakfast. AE, DC, MC, V. Parking 13€. Bus: 1 or 2. **Amenities:** Breakfast room; lounge. *In room:* TV.

Hotel Jedermann   Set within a quiet, tree-lined residential neighborhood about a half mile north of Salzburg's medieval core, this is a respectable and decent pension that has received favorable recommendations from Frommer's readers. The building was constructed as a spacious private home in the 1930s, and today it remains home to the Gmachl family, its owners and managers. Public areas contain soothingly old or old-fashioned furnishings that create a comfortable, if kitschy, 1950s atmosphere. Rooms have modern furniture and good beds. Bathrooms, though small, are equipped with shower units, scrubbed clean, and constantly supplied with freshly laundered towels. Breakfast is the only meal served.

Rupertgasse 25, A-5020 Salzburg. ℂ 0662/873-241-0. Fax 0662/873-241-0. www.salzburginfo.at/jedermann. 16 units. 75€–105€ double. Rates includes breakfast. AE, DC, MC, V. Bus: 27, 29. Amenities: Breakfast room; lounge. In room: TV, minibar.

Hotel Pension Fuggerhof This family-run boardinghouse stands on the south slope of the Kapuzinerberg. From the outside, it looks like a secluded mountain home. The furnishings are comfortably rustic and often painted in regional designs. Each guest room has a fridge, good beds, and a small bathroom equipped with a shower-tub combination. Herta Kammerhofer is your congenial hostess. The hotel has an elevator.

Eberhard-Fugger-Strasse 9, A-5020 Salzburg. ℂ 0662/641-290-0. Fax 0662/64-12-904. 22 units. 87€–116€ double; 146€ suite. Rates include breakfast buffet. No credit cards. Free parking. Closed Dec 20–Jan 26. Bus: 6. Amenities: Breakfast room; bar; lounge; pool; sauna; laundry; dry cleaning. In room: TV, minibar, hair dryer, safe.

Hotel Restaurant Gablerbräu This inviting hotel is near the Makartplatz. Rooms are furnished in a simple, modern style: an utter functionalism that deters lingering or long stays. Nonetheless, beds are frequently renewed, housekeeping is good, and the tiny shower-only bathrooms are well kept. Inside are three restaurants: one with vaulted ceilings and murals, another covered with wrought-iron detailing, and the third—the least formal—a beer hall.

Linzergasse 9, A-5020 Salzburg. ℂ 0662/88-965. Fax 0662/88-965-55. www.gablerbrau.com. 52 units. 104€–152€ double. Rates include breakfast. AE, DC, MC, V. Parking 14€. Bus: 51. Amenities: 2 restaurants; bar; room service. In room: TV, hair dryer, safe.

Hotel Trumer Stube Originally built in 1869 as a private home, this pink-fronted town house rises six floors above a desirable location that's midway between the Mirabellplatz and the Stadsbrüke, about a 6-minute stroll from Mozart's birthplace, and across the river from the Altstadt. For years, it thrived as a restaurant, but when meals were discontinued in the 1970s, it retained its original name (Trumer Stube), a fact that sometimes causes confusion since visitors assume that it's still a restaurant. The ground floor, presided over by the kindly manager, Silvia Rettenbacher, is devoted to the reception and breakfast rooms. Upstairs, an elevator carries you to a collection of cozily rustic, country-baroque rooms, each with smallish but well-designed bathrooms with shower units and a sense of calm and good order.

Bergstrasse 6, A-5020 Salzburg. ℂ 0662/87-47-76 or 0662/87-51-68. Fax 0662/87-43-26. http://members. eunet.at/hotel.trumer-stube.sbg. 22 units. 86€–132€ double; 86€–140€ triple; 125€–154€ quad. Rates include breakfast. AE, MC, V. Bus: 1, 2, 5, 6, or 51 to Mirabellplatz. Amenities: Breakfast room; lounge. In room: TV.

Pension Adlerhof Only the second and third floors of this guesthouse near the train station retain their original baroque embellishments. The high-ceilinged but cozy interior has wooden furniture with occasional painted designs, plus many folksy touches. Rooms, frequently renovated, are *very* snug and cozy, suitable for an overnight stay—not a long vacation. Bathrooms with shower units are a bit cramped, but housekeeping is exemplary. The Pregartbauer family is the owner.

Elisabethstrasse 25, A-5020 Salzburg. ℂ 0662/87-52-36. Fax 0662/873-66-36. www.pension-adlerhof.com. 35 units, 28 with bathroom. 56€–64€ double without bathroom; 69€–80€ double with bathroom. Rates include continental breakfast. No credit cards. Bus: 1, 51, 6, or 55. Amenities: Breakfast room; lounge. In room: TV.

Pension Bergland ⚡ *Finds*   Cozy, personalized, and substantial, this guesthouse sits within a quiet residential neighborhood. It was bought by the grandfather of the present owner in 1912, rebuilt after its destruction during World War II, and then renovated and enlarged in 1999. Today it welcomes visitors in a "music room" where there's a beer, wine, and coffee bar and a collection of guitars and lutes displayed on the walls. There's an on-site computer with an Internet connection so guests can check their e-mail, a green *Kachelofen* (tiled stove), and a decor that might remind you of a ski lodge high in the Alps. Rooms are comfortable, minimalist, and modern-looking, with larger-than-expected bathrooms containing shower-tub combinations and, in many cases, a piece of furniture hand-made by members of the Kuhn family, your hosts. The pension will rent you a bike and dispense information about where to ride.

15 Rupertsgasse, A-5020 Salzburg. © **0662/872318.** Fax 0662/872318-8. www.berglandhotel.at. 18 units. 80€ double. Rate includes buffet breakfast. AE, DC, MC, V. Free parking. Closed Nov. Bus 29. **Amenities:** Breakfast room; lounge. *In room:* TV, hair dryer.

AT MÖNCHSTEIN
VERY EXPENSIVE

Hotel Schloss Mönchstein ⚡⚡   This Teutonic-style manor house, really a small castle, stands on top of a hill above the center of Salzburg. Be warned in advance that the hotel is glacially snobby, attracting a so-called "exclusive" clientele that is socially secure, many of whom return year after year. From its elegant salons, guests can enjoy panoramic views of the city. The site was constructed as a fortified tower in 1350 and wasn't transformed into a hotel until 1950. In late 2002 and early 2003, it underwent a complete transformation. It is easy to see why the hotel has claimed the motto "urban sanctuary of the world." On the premises are a wedding chapel and a garden terrace overlooking a statue of Apollo in the private park. Rooms come in varying sizes and styles, but are all uniformly comfortable, with roomy closets. Some are rather elegant, with oriental rugs resting on parquet floors, king beds, and CD players. Average-size bathrooms contain tub and shower combinations; some even have antique stoves. The suites are some of the most spectacularly decorated rooms in Salzburg. The restaurant and bar, Paris Lodron, serves first-rate Austrian and international dishes at elegant, candlelit tables. Harp concerts are regularly featured. The hotel also has a garden terrace, Apollo; a cocktail bar, P. L.; and a cafe, Maria Theresia.

Mönchsberg Park 26, A-5020 Salzburg. © **800/44-UTELL** in the U.S., or 0662/84-855-50. Fax 0662/84-85-59. www.monchstein.at. 15 units. 320€–475€ double; from 625€ suite. Rates include breakfast. AE, DC, MC, V. Parking 18€. **Amenities:** Restaurant; bar; cafe; tennis court; access to nearby health club; tour desk; secretarial services; room service; in-room massage; babysitting; laundry; dry cleaning. *In room:* TV, minibar, hair dryer, safe.

AT PARSCH
INEXPENSIVE

Haus Arenberg   Staying in a place like this gives you the chance to enjoy the best of the Austrian countryside while only a short bus ride from the Old Town. On a fieldstone foundation, the two balconied stories feature white stucco and wood detailing. Parts of the interior are completely covered in blond paneling, while the scenic breakfast room is accented with hunting trophies and oriental rugs. Rooms are rather small, but the staff works hard to ensure comfort by providing well-managed bathrooms with shower-tub combinations and spotless housekeeping. Views usually encompass the nearby city. Don't expect a lot of style, but count on a tranquil retreat. Breakfast is the only meal served.

Blumensteinstrasse 8, A-5020 Salzburg. ℂ **0662/64-00-97.** Fax 0662/64-00-973. 20 units. 110€–140€ double. Rates include breakfast. AE, MC, V. Free parking. Bus: 6 or 49. Take Westautobahn toward Graz, exit at Salzburg Süd. Follow signs to Salzburg, then Anif. Make left at first light in Anif, then left on Blumenstein-strasse. **Amenities:** Breakfast room; lounge. *In room:* TV.

AT HELLBRUNN
MODERATE
Maria Theresien Schlössl ✿ *(Finds)* An archbishop ordered this castle built in the early 17th century, and there's still a vaguely ecclesiastical feeling to it. The place became a hotel in 1896, with a lemon-colored baroque facade and curved gables. Lying on the town's southern outskirts, 4km (2½ miles) from the center, it's more a manorial home than an actual castle; in fact, it was once an out-building of the neighboring Hellbrunn palace. You won't find any royalty today, but you'll get good-size, well-maintained rooms with frequently renewed bath-rooms that are equipped with shower-tub combinations. Guests are welcome to wander freely through the hotel's spacious, parklike grounds and well-manicured gardens. In the hotel dining room, the helpful staff serves good food, including Austrian, German, and French specialties.

Morzgerstrasse 87, A-5020 Salzburg-Hellbrunn. ℂ **0662/82-01-91.** Fax 0662/82-01-91-13. 12 units. 110€–170€ double. Rates include breakfast. AE, DC, MC, V. Free parking. Restaurant closed Jan–Feb. Bus: 55. Take Westautobahn toward Graz, exiting at Salzburg Süd. Follow signs to Salzburg, then Anif. In Anif, make left at first traffic light. Go straight until Morzgerstrasse. **Amenities:** Restaurant; bar; room service; babysit-ting; laundry; dry cleaning. *In room:* TV, minibar, hair dryer.

AT ROTT
INEXPENSIVE
Pension Helmhof *(Value)* On the western outskirts, Pension Helmhof is an appealingly rustic stucco chalet with flower-bedecked balconies and a stone-trimmed sun terrace. Rooms are comfortably furnished and well kept. Recent improvements have led to small bathrooms equipped with shower-tub combi-nations being added to all units. There is old-fashioned chalet-style comfort to this snug nest.

Lieferinger Hauptstrasse (Kirchengasse 29), A-5020 Salzburg-Liefering. ℂ **0662/43-30-79.** Fax 0662/43-30-79. helmhof@salzburginfo.at. 16 units. 55€–65€ double. Rates include breakfast. AE, MC, V. Free parking. Bus: 1 or 2 and 29. Adjacent to the SALZBURG-MITTE exit off A1 Autobahn. **Amenities:** Breakfast room; lounge; pool. *In room:* TV.

IN ANIF
MODERATE
Hotel Friesacher ✿ This elegant chalet has a hipped roof, a long expanse of gables, and natural-grained wooden balconies covered with flowers. An older building a few steps away across the flowering lawn serves as a well-furnished annex. Rooms are generally spacious and well furnished, with good beds and ample bathrooms equipped with shower-tub combinations. Service is provided by the Friesacher family. There's a country-style dining room, one of the finest in the area. In summer, guests can eat on the open-air terrace. Food is served Thursday through Tuesday from 11:30am to 2:30pm and 6 to 9:30pm, so you might want to drive out for an evening here even if you aren't staying in Anif. Specialties are typically Austrian, including *Tafelspitz* and dumpling soups, along with such classic sweets as *Topfenstrudel* (made with cottage cheese) and *Palatschinken* (dessert crepes).

Hellbrunnerstrasse 17, A-5081 Anif. ℂ 06246/8977. Fax 06246/897749. www.hotelfriesacher.com. 52 units. 113€–182€ double. Rates include breakfast. AE, DC, MC, V. Free parking. Closed 3 weeks in Jan. Bus: 55.

Take Westautobahn toward Graz and exit at Salzburg Süd. Follow signs to Salzburg and then Anif. In Anif, make a left at first traffic light. **Amenities:** Restaurant; 2 bars; exercise room; sauna. *In room:* TV, minibar, hair dryer, safe.

Romantik Hotel Schlosswirt 🎿 This country inn on the outskirts of Anif, 6km (4 miles) south of the center of Salzburg, was founded in 1607; with its flagstone floors, thick walls, and collection of local artifacts and hunting trophies, it has done a thriving business ever since. It's so well known that Austrians sometimes drive all the way from Innsbruck to dine here. Rooms have Biedermeier furniture, good beds, and modern bathrooms equipped with shower-tub combinations. If you're a late riser, be warned that beginning at 7am, traffic might disturb you if you're housed in the annex, which is right on the highway. There's a generous breakfast buffet of wurst, cheese, and poached eggs. Dinner is an elegant experience. Menu items include matjes herring with dill, wild game (in season), duckling in rosemary sauce, and many traditional fish dishes. A kind English-speaking hostess in regional dress will help you with translations.

Salwachtalvumess 7, A-5081 Anif. © 06246/72175. Fax 06246/721758. www.schlosswirt-anif.com. 28 units. 127€–166€ double; 215€–258€ suite. Rates include buffet breakfast. AE, DC, MC, V. Free parking. Closed Feb. Take the Salzburg-Süd exit from Autobahn A10 and drive for a half mile. Bus: 55. **Amenities:** 2 restaurants; bar; room service; laundry; dry cleaning. *In room:* TV, minibar, hair dryer.

IN AIGEN
INEXPENSIVE

Gasthof-Hotel Doktorwirt *Kids* On the southern edge of Salzburg, 10 minutes by bus from the Old Town, this chalet has prominent gables, a red-tile roof, and white stucco walls. The adjoining restaurant produces many of the sausages it serves, as well as a collection of tempting pastries. The decor is rustic, sunny, and pleasant, with wood detailing. The cozy rooms come in sizes ranging from singles to junior suites. The triple rooms and the family units are extremely popular, as the Schnöll clan prides itself on running a family hotel. The best rooms are the two tower units. The small bathrooms have shower-tub combinations.

Glaserstrasse 9, A-5026 Salzburg-Aigen. © 0662/62-29-73. Fax 0662/622-97-324. www.doktorwirt.co.at. 39 units. 105€–160€ double. Rates include breakfast. AE, DC, MC, V. Parking 5€. Exit from Autobahn A10 at Salzburg-Süd. Bus: 49 from Salzburg. **Amenities:** Restaurant; bar; pool; fitness center; sauna; room service; babysitting; laundry; dry cleaning. *In room:* TV, hair dryer, safe.

IN BERGHEIM
INEXPENSIVE

Hotel Gasthof Gmachl Six kilometers (4 miles) north of the center of Salzburg, this place looks like an affluent private chalet. The *Gasthof* was originally built as a farmhouse 250 years ago and has been gradually enlarged and improved to achieve the well-maintained aura of prosperous, unhurried leisure you see today. In one of the public areas, a massive hearth burns under a stone-and-stucco overhang. The cozy rooms have homey personal touches and average-size bathrooms equipped with shower-tub combinations. Most have a balcony. A *Tagesmenu* (daily menu) in the dining room features fresh local cuisine. A distance of 4km (2½ miles) away from the hotel is a riding stable.

Dorfstrasse 35, A-5101 Bergheim. © 0662/452-124. Fax 0662/452-12468. www.gmachl.at. 58 units. 130€–192€ double; 206€–250€ suite. Rates include breakfast. AE, MC, V. Free parking. Take the Bergheim local train from Salzburg's main station. By car, you must follow 1 boulevard from the center that changes names. Take the Imbergstrasse to Schwartzstrasse, to Haunspergstrasse, to Schillerstrasse, to Lamprechts Hausener Strasse, and then to Dorfstrasse. **Amenities:** Restaurant; bar; pool; sauna; room service; laundry; dry cleaning. *In room:* TV, minibar (in some), hair dryer, safe.

A CASTLE HOTEL IN OBERALM

The main reason for visiting Oberalm, directly north of Hallein and also north of Golling, is to stay at the castle hotel recommended below, which lies 16km (10 miles) south of Salzburg. From Salzburg, take the A10 south; from Golling, take the A10 north. However, if you're nearby, you might want to stop to see the Romanesque **Pfarrkirche (Parish Church),** with Gothic extensions. It has a magnificent high altar from 1707 by J. G. Mohr. The church is embellished with baroque furnishings and heraldic tombstones. See the funereal shield from 1671.

Schloss Haunsperg *(Finds)* Signposted at the approach to town, this early-14th-century castle is decorated with towers and interior ornamentation. A small but ornate baroque chapel adjoins the hotel. The public areas include a series of vaulted corridors furnished with antiques and rustic chandeliers, several salons with parquet or flagstone floors, and a collection of antiques. Our favorite is the second-floor music salon. Many of the accommodations, which contain period furniture, are divided into suites of two or three rooms, along with some doubles, each with medium-size bathrooms containing neatly kept shower units. The von Gernerth-Mautner Markhof family is the owner.

A-5411 Oberalm bei Hallein. ℂ **06245/80662.** Fax 06245/85680. www.schlosshaunsperg.com. 8 units. 134€–160€ double; 150€–200€ suite. Rates include breakfast. AE, DC, MC, V. Free parking. **Amenities:** Breakfast room; lounge; tennis court. *In room:* TV, hair dryer.

4 Where to Dine

Two special desserts you'll want to sample while in Salzburg are the famous *Salzburger Nockerln*, a light mixture of stiff egg whites, and *Mozart-Kugeln*, with bittersweet chocolate, hazelnut nougat, and marzipan. You should also try a beer in one of the numerous Salzburg breweries.

If you want to picnic, the city has a number of delis where you can stock up on supplies. The best place to eat your picnic goodies is Mirabell Gardens, on the right bank (see section 5, "Seeing the Sights," later in this chapter).

While Salzburg is not a late-night dining town in the way that New York, Los Angeles, and some European cities are, many restaurants stay open late, often to accommodate concert- or theater-goers. But "late" in this sense rarely means beyond 11pm. Local favorites for late-night dining include Alt-Salzburg, Zum Eulenspiegel, Purzelbaum, and Spaghetti & Co., all reviewed below.

ON THE LEFT BANK (OLD TOWN)
VERY EXPENSIVE

Goldener Hirsch *(★★★)* AUSTRIAN/VIENNESE   Fans of this place are willing to travel long distances just to enjoy the authentic ambience of this renovated inn, established in 1407. Don't be fooled by the relatively simple decor of this place, a kind of well-scrubbed and decent simplicity that's emulated by dozens of other restaurants in resorts throughout Austria. Cuisine is superb, and the wine list is virtually unsurpassed. The venue is chic, top-notch, impeccable, and charming, richly sought after during peak season. The restaurant is staffed with a superb team of chefs and waiters. The food is so tasty and beautifully served that the kitchen ranks among the top two or three in Salzburg. Specialties include saddle of farm-raised venison with red cabbage, king prawns in an okra-curry ragout served with perfumed Thai rice, and tenderloin of beef and veal on morel cream sauce with cream potatoes. In season, expect a dish devoted to game, such as venison or roast duckling.

Salzburg Dining

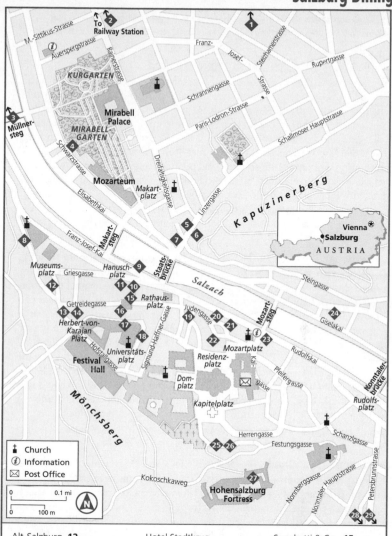

Alt-Salzburg **12**
BIO Wirtshaus Hirschenwirt **1**
Café Bazar **4**
Café Riverside **9**
Café Tomaselli **19**
Café-Restaurant
  Glockenspiel **23**
Fasties **23**
Festungsrestaurant **27**
Goldener Hirsch **13**
Hagenauerstuben **17**
Herzl Tavern **14**

Hotel Stadtkrug
  Restaurant **5**
Konditorei Ratzka **24**
Krimpelstätter **3**
Mundenhamer Bräu **2**
Purzelbaum **28**
Restaurant Bristol **6**
Restaurant K & K **22**
Restaurant
  Petersbrunnhof **29**
Restaurant Symphonie **21**
Ristorante/Pizzeria Il Sole **8**

Spaghetti & Co. **15**
Stadtgasthof
  Blaue Gans **14**
Sternbräu **11**
Stiftskeller St. Peter **25**
Weisses Kreuz
  Balkan Restaurant **26**
Yuen **16**
Zipfer Bierhaus **18**
Zum Eulenspiegel **10**
Zum Fidelen Affen **7**
Zum Mohren **20**

Getreidegasse 37. ℂ **0662/80-84-0.** Reservations required. Main courses 20€–26€; 3-course fixed-price lunch or dinner 36€; 5-course fixed-price dinner 52€. AE, MC, V. Daily noon–2:30pm and 6:30–9:30pm. Bus: 55.

EXPENSIVE

Alt-Salzburg 🍴 AUSTRIAN/INTERNATIONAL   A retreat into old-world elegance, Alt-Salzburg is one of the most venerated restaurants in the city, a bastion of formal service, snobbism, and refined cuisine. The restaurant, which often gives you a glacial reception unless they know you, occupies a building constructed into the side of the steep and rocky cliffs of Mönchsberg. The wood-ceilinged room is crafted to reveal part of the chiseled rock of the Mönchsberg. The menu features main dishes such as filet of river char sautéed with tomatoes, mushrooms and capers, leaf spinach, and potatoes; and lamb chops sautéed in a herb crust and thyme sauce with zucchini and potato cakes. In August, the restaurant is also open on Sunday and Monday for lunch.

Bürgerspitalgasse 2. ℂ **0662/84-14-76.** Reservations required. Main courses 12€–24€; fixed-price menu 38€–45€. AE, DC, MC, V. Mon 6–10:30pm; Tues–Sat 11:30am–2pm and 6–10:30pm (to midnight in Aug). Closed 1 week in Feb. Bus: 1, 15, or 49.

Purzelbaum 🍴 AUSTRIAN/VIENNESE   During the Salzburg Festival, you're likely to see the most dedicated music lovers in Europe congregating around the tables of this sophisticated bistro. Located in a residential neighborhood not often frequented by tourists, it's near a duck pond at the bottom of a steep incline leading up to Salzburg Castle. A cramped corner of the bar is reserved for visitors who want to drop in for only a drink. Most guests, however, reserve a table in one of the trio of rooms containing an Art Nouveau ceiling and marble buffets from a French buttery. Menu items change according to the whim of the chef and include well-prepared dishes such as turbot-and-olive casserole, lamb in white-wine sauce with beans and polenta, and the house specialty, scampi Grüstl, composed of fresh shrimp with sliced potatoes baked with herbs in a casserole. In August, the restaurant is also open on Sunday.

Zugallistrasse 7. ℂ **0662/84-88-43.** Reservations required. Main courses 20€–28€; 4-course fixed-price menu 45€. AE, DC, MC, V. Mon–Sat noon–2pm and 6–11pm. Closed July 1–14. Bus: 55.

Restaurant Symphonie 🍴 INTERNATIONAL   Set within a riverfront building whose origins go back to the 15th century, this restaurant evokes the kind of 18th-century country-baroque setting where a young Mozart might have given a concert. Most menu items focus on traditional Austrian specialties, including marinated fried chicken, Viennese-style *Tafelspitz* (boiled beef), and a vegetarian specialty consisting of creamed mushrooms with rosemary and herbs. Fish dishes include filet of sole with a zucchini crust and olive puree, and crispy-roasted filet of char with parsley potatoes and salad. For dessert, consider buttermilk dumplings with marinated cherries.

In the Hotel Altstadt SAS Radisson, Rudolfskai 28. ℂ **0662/848571-55.** Reservations recommended. Main courses 18€–25€; fixed-price menus 28€–32€ for 3 courses; 34€–42€ for 4 courses. AE, DC, MC, V. Mon–Sat noon–2pm and 6:30–10pm.

MODERATE

Herzl Tavern 🍴🍴 *Value* AUSTRIAN/VIENNESE   With an entrance on the landmark Karajanplatz, Herzl Tavern lies next door to the glamorous Goldener Hirsch, of which it's a part. Good value attracts both visitors and locals to its pair of cozy rooms, one paneled and timbered. You'll see photos of musicians who have dined here while performing at the Salzburg Festival, including Leonard

Bernstein, Herbert von Karajan, Helmut Luhner, and actor Curt Jurgens. Waitresses in dirndls serve appetizing entrees, which are likely to include roast pork with dumplings, various grills, game stew (in season), and, for the heartiest eaters, a farmer's plate of boiled pork, roast pork, grilled sausages, dumplings, and sauerkraut.

Karajanplatz 7. (C) **0662/808-4889.** Reservations recommended. Main courses 10€–15€; fixed-price menu 12€. AE, DC, MC, V. Daily 11:30am–11pm. Bus: 55.

Restaurant K & K AUSTRIAN/INTERNATIONAL   Separated into about half a dozen intimate dining rooms on four floors, the K & K is decorated with wood paneling, slabs of salmon-colored marble, flickering candles, antique accessories, and a well-dressed clientele. An elaborate wrought-iron and gilt bracket holds a sign marking the location above a giant plaza near the cathedral. The menu contains a medley of well-crafted dishes, ranging from the traditional to the innovative, including roast filet of beef in a cognac-cream sauce with fresh mushrooms and green peppercorns, *Tafelspitz* (boiled beef), breast of chicken in a curry-cream sauce, and several kinds of shellfish. If you'd like to check out a cool informal hangout and witness a marvel of masonry, head down the massive stone staircase to reach the *Bierkeller*, a beer cellar that serves drinks and snack food to a sometimes rowdy crowd.

Waagplatz 2. (C) **0662/84-21-56.** Reservations required. Main courses 10€–18€; fixed-price menu 30€–42€. AE, DC, MC, V. Daily 11am–2:30pm and 6–11:30pm; drinks and snacks daily 11:30am–midnight. Bus: 55.

Stiftskeller St. Peter (Peterskeller) ☞ AUSTRIAN/VIENNESE   Legend has it that Mephistopheles met with Faust in this tavern, which was established by Benedictine monks in A.D. 803. In fact, it's the oldest restaurant in Europe, housed in the abbey of the church that supposedly brought Christianity to Austria. Aside from a collection of baroque banquet rooms, there's an inner courtyard with vaults cut from the living rock, a handful of dignified wood-paneled rooms, and a brick-vaulted cellar with a tile floor and rustic chandeliers. In addition to wine from the abbey's own vineyards, the tavern serves good home-style Austrian cooking, including roast pork in gravy with sauerkraut and bread dumplings, braised oxtail with mushrooms and fried polenta, and loin of lamb with asparagus. Vegetarian dishes, such as semolina dumplings on noodles in a parsley sauce, are also featured. They are especially known here for their desserts. Try the apple strudel or sweet curd strudel with vanilla sauce or ice cream, and, most definitely, the famed *Salzburger Nockerln.*

St.-Peter-Bezirk 1–4. (C) **0662/84-12-680.** Reservations recommended. Main courses 14€–15€; fixed-price menus 18€–46€. AE, MC, V. Daily 11:30am–2:30pm and 6–10pm. Closed Sept 24. Bus: 29.

Weisses Kreuzbalkan Restaurant BALKAN   Just south of the cathedral, this restaurant's stone facade is almost hidden on a small villagelike street. A grape arbor shelters the front terrace, where in summer tables are set out for relaxed eating and drinking. The cuisine includes Balkan bean soup, boiled beef, mutton chops, and roast beef in a cream-and-onion sauce. More exotic specialties include moussaka, fried mincemeat loaf with pickled peppers, and Dalmatian steak with rice and stuffed cabbage. Stuffed eggplant and venison steak are other popular dishes, along with a catchall specialty called the Balkan platter. The staff speaks very little English.

In the Hotel Weisses Kreuz, Bierjodlgasse 6. (C) **0662/84-56-41.** Reservations recommended. Main courses 11€–20€. AE, DC, MC, V. Daily 11:30am–2:45pm and 5–11pm. Closed 2 weeks in Feb. Bus: 5, 6, or 51.

Cafes

Café Bazar, Schwarzstrasse 3 (℗ 0662/87-42-78; bus: 1, 5, or 29), is deeply entrenched in Salzburg's social life and has been so since 1906. Its regular clientele comes from all walks of life. Housed in a palatial pink-stucco building with many baroque features, it's located across the river from the main section of the Old Town. The interior is high-ceilinged and vaguely Art Deco. You'll still occasionally see someone with a Franz Josef mustache wearing a gray flannel Styrian suit with loden trim, but a growing number of the patrons are young and stylish. You can order salads, sandwiches, and omelets. It's open Monday from 8am to 6pm and Tuesday through Saturday from 7:30am to 11pm.

Its location on one of Salzburg's most colorful squares has made **Café-Restaurant Glockenspiel** ✿, Mozartplatz 2 (℗ 0662/84-14-03-0; bus: 55), the most popular in the city. About 100 tables with armchairs in front of the cafe are perfect for people-watching. If the day is warm enough, you might want to spend an afternoon here, particularly when there's live chamber music. The inside is dominated by a wonderful sight, a glass case filled with every highly caloric delight west of Vienna. The rooms on either side contain big arched windows overlooking the statue in the square. The restaurant upstairs is tastefully decorated in brown and beige, with a big balcony. Lunch specials include veal goulash with dumplings and roast sausages with sauerkraut. For dinner, you can sit on the balcony and look over Salzburg's famous buildings while enjoying regional and international specialties. Many people, however, come just for the drinks and pastries. Try the Maria Theresia, which contains orange liqueur. In summer, the cafe is open daily from 9am to midnight (food served to 11pm); the rest of the year, it's open daily from 9am to 8pm (food served to 6pm). It's closed the second and third weeks of November and January.

Established in 1705, **Café Tomaselli** ✿, Alter Markt 9 (℗ 0662/84-44-88; bus: 5, 6, or 55), opens onto one of the most charming cobblestone squares of the Altstadt. Aside from the summer chairs placed outdoors, you'll find a high-ceilinged room with many tables. It's a great place to just sit and talk. Another more formal room to the right of the entrance with oil portraits of well-known 19th-century Salzburgers attracts a haute bourgeois crowd. A waiter will show you a pastry tray filled with 40

Zum Eulenspiegel ✿ AUSTRIAN/VIENNESE   Housed in a white-and-peach building opposite Mozart's birthplace, Zum Eulenspiegel sits at one end of a quiet cobblestone square in the Old Town. Inside, guests have a choice of five rooms on three different levels, all rustically but elegantly decorated. You really can pick where you want to sit, so feel free to look around if all the tables aren't full. A small and rustic bar area on the ground floor is a pleasant place for predinner drinks. Traditional Austrian cuisine is meticulously adhered to here. The menu features such classic dishes as *Tafelspitz* (boiled beef), Wiener schnitzel, braised trout with dill-flavored potatoes, filet of pork with warm cabbage salad and bacon, and *Salzburger Nockerln,* or peaches with hot fudge and different kinds of cakes, which you're free to order or wave away. Other menu items include omelets, wursts, ice cream, and a wide range of drinks. Of course, the pastries and ice cream are all homemade. The cafe is open Monday through Saturday from 7am to midnight and Sunday from 8am to 9pm.

A melody by Mozart, who was born next door, might accompany your before-dinner drink at **Hagenauerstuben,** Universitätsplatz 14 (✆ **0662/84-26-57**; tram: 2, 49, or 95). Many visitors never get beyond the street-level bar, where snacks (such as salads and goulash) and drinks are served in a 14th-century room with stone floors and a vaulted ceiling, highlighted by a changing exhibition of modern lithographs and watercolors. At the top of a narrow flight of stone steps, you'll discover an austere trio of thick-walled rooms decorated with a ceramic stove and wooden armoires. A central serving table holds an array of salads and hors d'oeuvres. The cafe is open Monday through Saturday from 8:30am to 6pm.

The small **Konditorei Ratzka,** Imbergstrasse 45 (✆ **0662/64-00-24**; bus: 5, 6, or 55), 10 minutes from the center of town, is owned by its pastry chef, Herwig Ratzka. A master at his craft, he uses the freshest ingredients to produce about 30 different pastries. Since the cakes are made fresh every day, much of the selection is gone by late afternoon, so go early. It's open Tuesday through Friday from 8am to 5pm and Saturday from 8am to 12:30pm and 1:30 to 6pm. Closed 2 weeks in January, June, and September. Mr. Ratzka requests that patrons don't smoke in the shop.

Almost every item sold at the old-time Austrian confectionery **Schatz-Konditorei,** Getreidegasse 3 (✆ **0662/84-27-92**; bus: 55), is made from traditional recipes. Our favorite treat is the well-known *Mozart-Kugeln,* a cookie of pistachio, marzipan, and hazelnut nougat, all dipped in chocolate. You can enjoy the pastries and coffees at a table inside the cafe or take them away. Some varieties of pastry, including the *Mozart-Kugeln,* can be shipped around the world. It's open Monday through Friday from 8:30am to 6:30pm and Saturday from 8am to 5pm, with extended hours during the summer Salzburg Festival.

vanilla ice cream, for dessert. Walter and Gabi Ritzberger-Wimmer are the polite owners of this place.

Hagenauerplatz 2. ✆ **0662/84-31-80**. Reservations required. Main courses 12€–20€. AE, MC, V. Mon–Sat 11am–2pm and 6–10:30pm. Closed Feb 1–Mar 15. Tram: 2. Bus: 2.

INEXPENSIVE

Café Riverside AUSTRIAN   Cozy, rustic, and warm, this bar, cafe, and bistro occupies a wood-sided chalet that's set directly beside the pedestrian walkway that parallels the edge of the Salzach River, a 5-minute walk from the monumental heart of town. Part of its appeal derives from a gemütlichkeit ambience that's a refreshing change from the rococo splendor of other parts of Salzburg. Head for the paneled interior, or if the weather is clement, to any of the tables and chairs set outside. Don't expect culinary finesse: What you get are generous portions and a cozy sense of old-fashioned alpine warmth. Good-tasting menu items include soups, especially homemade tomato; pork cutlets with french fries; meal-size salads; and pastries that feature strudels and yogurt tortes. The beer of choice here is Wieninger Bräu.

Müllner Hauptstrasse 4. ☎ **0664/102-3842.** Reservations not necessary. Main courses 4€–10€. No credit cards. Wed–Mon 9am–9pm (to 11pm in Aug).

Fasties INTERNATIONAL   This is an inexpensive, unpretentious restaurant that doesn't take itself too seriously. It specializes in "fasties," but, unlike most fast food, the fasties actually contain flavor and nutrients. Set at the corner of the Papagenoplatz, in one of the most historic neighborhoods of Salzburg, the restaurant has a stand-up counter where you place your order and three large communal wooden tables where a staff member will serve you. When the weather cooperates, additional tables are set up on the square outside. The menu, written on a blackboard, changes daily but invariably includes at least two soups, salads, and sandwiches. Platters are more substantial, consisting of assorted patés and cheeses, goulashes, roasts, and at least one vegetarian special. A second branch of this restaurant that's even more cramped is in an inconvenient location across the river from the historic core, about a half mile north of the center at Lasserstrasse 19 (☎ **0662/873-876;** bus: 5).

Pfeifergasse 3. ☎ **0662/844-774.** Reservations not accepted. Main courses 4€–9€. AE, DC, MC, V. Mon–Sat 8am–10pm. Bus: 1.

Festungsrestaurant ★ *Kids* SALZBURG/AUSTRIAN   Come here and you'll be dining at the former stronghold of the prince-archbishops of Salzburg. The restaurants and gardens are actually in the castle, perched on a huge rock 122m (400 ft.) above the Old Town and the Salzach. The restaurant commands a panoramic view of the city and the surrounding countryside. From Easter to October, classical concerts are held nightly in the *Fürstenzimmer,* often featuring the work of Mozart. The kitchen offers local specialties such as a Salzburger *Bauernschmaus,* Salzburger *Bierfleisch,* and Salzburger schnitzel, along with many other dishes. This is good old-fashioned Austrian cooking. In winter, when the restaurant is closed, the *Burgtaverne* inside the castle serves food and drink.

Hohensalzburg, Mönchsberg 34. ☎ **0662/84-17-80.** Reservations required July–Aug. Main courses 7.50€–13.50€. MC, V. Apr–Oct daily 10am–9pm; Dec–Mar daily 10am–5pm. Closed Nov. Funicular from the Old Town.

Krimpelstätter SALZBURGIAN/AUSTRIAN   This restaurant has been an enduring favorite in Salzburg, with a history dating from 1548. Originally designed and constructed as an inn, it retains chiseled stone columns that support the vaulted ceilings and heavy timbers. In summer, the beer garden, full of roses and trellises, attracts up to 300 visitors at a time. If you want a snack, a beer, or a glass of wine, head for the paneled door marked GASTZIMMER in the entry corridor. If you're looking for a more formal, less visited area, a trio of cozy antique dining rooms sits atop a flight of narrow stone steps. Each room serves the same menu, tasty and high-quality Land Salzburg regional cuisine featuring wild game dishes. Start with the cream of goose soup or else homemade chamois sausage. Traditional main courses include roast pork with dumplings, and fried sausages with sauerkraut and potatoes. Spinach dumplings are topped with a cheese sauce, and marinated beef stew comes with noodles in butter. From its blood sausages to its pork lights (lungs) with dumplings, this is definitely not the place to watch the calories or the cholesterol.

Müllner Hauptstrasse 31. ⓒ **0662/43-22-74.** Reservations recommended. Main courses 5.60€–14€. No credit cards. Tues–Sat 11am–2pm and 6pm–midnight (and Mon May–Sept). Closed 3 weeks in Jan. Bus: 49 or 95.

Restaurant Petersbrunnhof INTERNATIONAL   Established in 1997 within the Theater Elizabethbühne Salzburg, this restaurant's historical overtones are partially masked by bright colors of red and blue, but conservatively modern furnishings and an emphasis on the artistic and theatrical create a pleasant atmosphere. The emphasis is on lighthearted, light-textured cuisine, a gratefully noted contrast to the more copious portions and recipes served at many of its competitors. Menu items include watercress soup with strips of smoked salmon, prosciutto with slices of fresh melon, a vegetarian platter containing grilled fresh vegetables in garlic-flavored vinaigrette sauce, and sautéed filet of lamb with tomatoes, leeks, zucchini, and mushrooms. When the weather is good, additional seating is set up in the garden.

Erzabt Klotz Strasse 22. ⓒ **0662/845-664.** Reservations recommended. Main courses 7.30€–16€. AE, DC, MC, V. Mon–Fri 11am–3pm and 5pm–midnight; Sat–Sun 5pm–midnight. AE, DC, MC, V. Bus: 5 or 55.

Ristorante/Pizzeria Il Sole ITALIAN   The venue is charming and convivial, and the prices are relatively modest at this well-managed Italian restaurant that sits immediately adjacent to the lower stage of the Mönchsberg elevator. The Austrian-born owners, the Rauzenberger brothers, are "Italian by adoption," thanks to the dozens of business and holiday trips they've made south of the border during the acquisition of the Italy-derived foodstuffs and decorative objects that are showcased within this restaurant. The street level is less formal and more animated than the dining room upstairs, but regardless of where you opt to sit, the menu is the same. With dining companions, we recently enjoyed a tantalizing fettuccine with shrimp as well as vegetable tortellini stuffed with blue cheese and spinach. Equally vibrant was a platter of chicken Il Sole, with fresh Parmesan, a zesty tomato sauce, and pesto. The lemon-flavored chicken with fresh tagliatelle was a delight, as was a selection of grilled or sautéed fresh fish. Pizzas come in 15 different flavors, with the house brand (Il Sole, made with ham, salami, artichoke hearts, and mozzarella) being the most consistently popular.

Gstättengasse 15. ⓒ **0662/843284.** Reservations not necessary. Pizzas and pastas 7€–9€; main courses 10€–13€. AE, DC, MC, V. Daily 11:30am–2pm and 5:30pm–midnight. Bus: 1, 27, or 49.

Spaghetti & Co. (Kids) ITALIAN/INTERNATIONAL   This simple, efficient, and unpretentious establishment offers a welcome relief from the more expensive restaurants in the historic center. Within four cheerfully rustic dining rooms, you can order pizzas, pastas, or gnocchi, and serve yourself from a fresh and well-stocked salad bar. Known for its reasonable prices, the place attracts families with children, students, backpackers, and employees of the neighborhood's many shops. Set close to Mozart's birthplace, on a pedestrian-only historic street, it also serves beer, wine, and drinks.

Getreidegasse 14. ⓒ **0662/841-400.** Pizzas, pastas, salads, and gnocchi 5€–12€. AE, DC, MC, V. Daily 11am–1am. Bus: 1, 2, 5, 6, or 51.

Stadtgasthof Blaue Gans AUSTRIAN   This restaurant that consistently attracts local residents, some of whom plan their week around a meal here, is an old-fashioned testimonial to *gutbürgerlich* (home-style) cooking. Within a timeless-looking setting that includes vaulted ceilings that were originally designed in 1432, and a scattering of antique oil paintings, you can order such dishes as Wiener schnitzel, one of the best in town; *Tafelspitz* (boiled beef); and osso buco of lamb with polenta. Pink-roasted lamb is an enduring favorite. Don't overlook this establishment's newest addition, a stone-built cellar, 500 years old, some of which is visible from above via a tempered glass plate set directly into the floor of the upstairs bar.

Getreidegasse 43. ℂ 0662/84-24-91. Reservations recommended. Main courses 6.90€–14€; 3-course set menu 20€. AE, DC, MC, V. Wed–Mon 11am–11pm (last order 10pm).

Sternbräu AUSTRIAN   The entrance to this establishment is through an arched cobblestone passageway leading off a street in the Old Town. The place seems big enough to have fed half the Austro-Hungarian army, with a series of eight rooms in varying degrees of formality. The Hofbräustübl is a rustic fantasy combining masonry columns with hand-hewn beams and wood paneling. Other rooms have such accessories as sea-green tile stoves, marble columns, and oil paintings. You can also eat in the chestnut tree–shaded beer garden, which is usually packed on summer nights, or under the weathered arcades of an inner courtyard. Drinks are served in the restaurant's bar, Grünstern. Daily specials include typically Austrian dishes such as Wiener and chicken schnitzels, trout, cold marinated herring, Hungarian goulash, hearty regional soups, and many other solid selections. Come here for the hearty, filling portions—not for refined cuisine.

Griesgasse 23. ℂ 0662/84-21-40. Reservations not accepted. Main courses 5.50€–15€; fixed-price menu 11€–15€. AE, MC, V. Daily 10am–11:30pm. Bus: 2, 5, 12, 49, or 51.

Yuen CANTONESE/SZECHUAN   This restaurant is located in a courtyard off the main shopping street of Salzburg. Yuen is not only the first Chinese restaurant in Salzburg, established in 1973, but it's also one of the better ones. The Austrians call this *Ausländische Küche*, or foreign cooking, but its offerings will be familiar to most North Americans. Its owners and staff come from both Malaysia and Hong Kong. You might begin with a spring roll or Chinese fish soup and proceed to crispy duck Szechuan style or chicken with mango. The chef also caters to vegetarians and prepares several kinds of chop suey. Under a wood ceiling, Chinese lamps provide soft lighting, and the service is polite and efficient.

Getreidegasse 24 ℂ 0662/84-37-70. Main courses 8€–13€; fixed-price meal 8€ at lunch, 13€ at dinner. AE, DC, MC, V. Daily 11:30am–11pm. Bus: 1 or 2.

Zipfer Bierhaus AUSTRIAN   This long-time favorite is especially popular with the after-concert crowd. In a building dating from the 1400s, the establishment, in spite of its name, is more of a restaurant than a beer hall, although the decor is definitely in the beer-house tradition. The good food is familiar if you've been in Austria for a while: noodle casserole with ham in a cream sauce, breaded and fried filet of plaice or trout, veal goulash, and a spicy paprika salad with wurst and cheese. The food is well prepared and the portions are generous.

Sigmund-Haffner-Gasse 12. ℂ 0662/840-745. Reservations recommended. Main courses 7.60€–27€. DC, MC, V. Mon–Sat 10am–midnight (kitchen closes at 10pm). Bus: 1, 2, or 55.

Zum Mohren 🐾 AUSTRIAN   A statue of an exotic-looking Moor sits atop the wrought-iron sign at the entrance to this restaurant, in a house built in 1423. You'll have to descend a flight of stone steps to reach the three distinctly different eating areas, the best of which is on the right as you enter. Replicas of Moors, gold earrings and all, in either bas-relief or full-rounded sculpture, provide an offbeat decor. A third area, on the left as you enter, is more cavelike, with an orange ceramic stove and a low ceiling. Meals might include entrecôte Parisian style, sirloin steak with herb butter, grilled lamb chops, a good selection of cheese, and many rich desserts. It's great to eat here in autumn and midwinter, when the restaurant emphasizes game, usually from the mountains near Salzburg, including fresh venison from the Unterberg (a mountain visible from the center of town); fresh local mushrooms (*Eier Schwammel*) in herb sauce, a dish favored by regional gourmets; and breast of duckling with apple and red-cabbage dressing and homemade dumplings.

Judengasse 9. ℂ 0662/84-23-87. Reservations recommended. Main courses 8.30€–19€. AE, DC, MC, V. Mon–Sat noon–3pm and 6pm–midnight. Bus: 5, 6, or 55.

ON THE RIGHT BANK
EXPENSIVE

Restaurant Bristol CONTINENTAL   This is the dining counterpart of the upscale restaurant within Salzburg's other topnotch hotel, the Goldener Hirsch. In this case, the venue is a stately, baronial-looking area outfitted in tones of pale orange and accented with large-scale oil paintings. A well-trained staff organizes meals, the best of which include scampi with arugula salad and tomatoes; carpaccio of beef or (in season) venison; Arctic char served with homemade noodles, saffron sauce, and goose liver; roasted lamb served with a gratin of polenta and spinach; and all-vegetarian casseroles. Expect the kind of pomp and circumstance that comes almost automatically with a hotel of this stature, and some extremely well-prepared food. Immediately adjacent to the restaurant is a club-style bar with the requisite leather upholsteries and well-oiled paneling.

In the Hotel Bristol, Makartplatz 4. ℂ 0662/873-5577. Reservations recommended. Main courses 18€–25€. AE, DC, MC, V. Mon–Sat 11am–2pm and 6–10pm. Bus: 1, 5, 29, or 51.

INEXPENSIVE

BIO Wirtshaus Hirschenwirt ⭐ (*Finds*) AUSTRIAN   This is a hotel dining room, but a hotel dining room with a difference: All of the ingredients used in its cuisine derive from organically grown ingredients, raised in Austria without chemical fertilizers or insecticides. The setting is a quartet of cozy and traditional-looking dining rooms, each with a name that evokes a chalet high in the mountains. There's the *Stüberl*, strictly reserved for nonsmokers; the *Schank* (a bar area, with a handful of dining tables as well); the *Speisesaal* (the richly paneled main dining room); and *Hirsch Saal* (Deer Room, with lots of memorabilia related to hunting). Menu items change with the season but might include a creamy pumpkin soup, carpaccio of Austrian beef, *Tafelspitz* (boiled beef), several versions of Wiener schnitzel, and about five different vegetarian dishes, the best example of which is small spaetzle in a cheese-flavored onion sauce.

In the Hotel zum Hirschen, St. Julien Strasse 23. ℂ 0662/88-13-35. Reservations recommended. Main courses 7.90€–17€. AE, DC, MC, V. Mon–Sat 12:30–3pm and 6–10pm. Tram 3 or 6.

Hotel Stadtkrug Restaurant AUSTRIAN/INTERNATIONAL   Across the river from the Old Town, on the site of what used to be a 14th-century farm, this restaurant occupies a structure that was rebuilt from an older core in 1458. In the 1960s, a hotel was added in back of the old-fashioned dining rooms, which now serve as one of the neighborhood's most popular restaurants. In an artfully rustic setting, illuminated by gilded wooden chandeliers, you can enjoy conservative and flavorful Austrian cuisine. Good, hearty dishes include cream of potato soup "Old Vienna" style, braised beef with burgundy sauce, grilled trout or catfish, and glazed cutlet of pork with caraway seeds, deep-fried potatoes, and French beans with bacon. A dessert specialty is a honey parfait with raspberry sauce.

Linzer Gasse 20. ℭ 0662/87-35-45. Reservations recommended. Main courses 18€–25€. AE, DC, MC, V. Wed–Mon noon–2pm and 6–11pm. Bus: 27 or 29.

Mundenhamer Bräu SALZBURGIAN/INTERNATIONAL   This warm-hued restaurant near the main train station has been serving copious portions of food to Salzburgers since the 1930s. There are several different seating areas—our favorite is the big-windowed section with a view of a city park. In season, game is a specialty; otherwise, menu items might include Salzburger cream schnitzel, paprika cutlets, mushroom ragout, and a house specialty called Mundenhamer potpourri, a mixed grill for two. The menu is in English and the portions are large.

Rainerstrasse 2. ℭ 0662/875-693. Reservations recommended. Main courses 7€–15€; fixed-price menu 10€. AE, DC, MC, V. Mon–Sat 11:30am–2pm and 5:30–11:30pm. Bus: 5, 6, 49, 51, 55, or 95.

Zum Fidelen Affen AUSTRIAN   Set on the eastern edge of the river near the Staatsbrücke, this restaurant is the closest thing in Salzburg to a loud, animated, and jovial pub with food service. Its circular bar is great for those who just stop in for a drink, although many patrons eventually wander into dinner, too. Management's policy on reservations allows only three tables on any particular evening to be reserved; the remainder are given to whomever happens to show up. It's best to give your name to the maître d'hôtel and then wait at the bar.

Menu items are simple, inexpensive, and based on regional culinary traditions. A house specialty is a gratin of green (spinach-flavored) noodles in cream sauce with strips of ham. Also popular are Wiener schnitzels, ham goulash with dumplings, casseroles of seasonal meats and mushrooms, and at least three different kinds of main-course dumplings flavored with meats, cheeses, herbs, and various sauces. Dessert might be a cheese dumpling or one of several kinds of pastries. True to the establishment's name, translated as "The Funny Monkey," its interior depicts simians, both painted and sculpted, cavorting across the walls.

Priesterhausgasse 8. ℭ 0662/877-361. Reservations not accepted. Main courses 8€–13€. DC, MC, V. Mon–Sat 5–11:30pm.

ON THE OUTSKIRTS
VERY EXPENSIVE

Pfefferschiff ✦ *Finds* CONTINENTAL   Its setting is a country-baroque rectory, originally built about 300 years ago as a home for the village priest, immediately adjacent to a church and a domed 17th-century chapel in the suburb of Hallwang, 2 miles northeast of Salzburg's center. Inside, a trio of high-ceilinged, rather stiffly formal dining rooms, each evoking a sense of solidly upper-class bourgeois values, showcases the cuisine of owner and chef Klaus Fleishhaker. His wife, Petra, oversees the dining rooms, where fine china, silver, and crystal contribute to the hushed and somewhat restrained sense of propriety. The menu changes frequently, with an emphasis on whatever is fresh within the region at the time. The finest dishes include monkfish in an olive-based crust with pesto-laced polenta, pan-fried foie gras with gingerbread and spinach salad, roasted veal in an herb-flavored cream sauce, and a ragout of scallops and seafood in a saffron-flavored cream sauce. Roasted rack of lamb is always a good choice, as is the shrimp tempura served with braised arugula and asparagus. Desserts are sublime—especially the rhubarb tart served with buttermilk-flavored ice cream.

Take a cab or else drive along the north edge of the Kapuzinerberg in the direction to Hallwang; then follow the signposts into Söllheim.

Sollheim 3, in the suburb of Hallwang. (C) 0662/661242. Reservations required. Main courses 20€–30€; set-price menus 50€–60€. AE, DC, MC, V. Tues–Sat noon–1:30pm and 6:30–9pm.

Restaurant Paris Lodron 🎯🎯🎯 INTERNATIONAL   This is the most glamorous and prestigious restaurant in Salzburg, thanks to a historic pedigree and cuisine that defines it as one of the most appealing Relais & Château members in Austria. Named after the medieval archbishop of Salzburg who commissioned the construction of the Schloss Mönchstein in which it's housed, the establishment is composed of two separate dining rooms, both elegantly outfitted. There's also an outdoor terrace open in good weather. Menu items change with the seasons and the whims of the chefs, but might include delectable king prawns with sesame oil and fresh ginger; butter-fried filets of pike perch nestled on a puree of celery; filet of sole in an herb-enriched crust with a mild mustard sauce; and a roasted loin of lamb dredged in pumpkin seeds and served with sage sauce. In autumn and early winter, savory game dishes include medallions of venison with rosemary sauce.

In the Hotel Schloss Mönchstein, Mönchsberg 26. (C) 0662/848-555-0. Reservations recommended. Main courses 25€–47€. AE, DC, MC, V. Daily noon–2pm and 6–10pm. Limited menu available daily 2–6pm.

EXPENSIVE

Brandstätter 🎯 AUSTRIAN   One of the best restaurants in Salzburg is actually right outside the city limits in Liefering, lying just off the motorway (*Autobahn-Mitte*). It's northwest of the city, about 30 minutes by bus, or 20 minutes if you prefer to take a taxi. Brandstätter is an intimate, cozy choice for a special meal. Diners like this friendly place so much that they often linger long after their meal is finished.

The daily menus are seasonal so that the best and freshest produce and game and meat dishes are always available. We recommend beginning with the terrine of goose liver with an apple-and-celery salad and proceeding to the salmon trout with white-wine sauce. Some dishes might be only for the adventurous—for example, veal lungs with dumplings—but others are quite elegant, including a perfectly cooked roast pheasant breast with a bacon-and-cranberry sauce. Finish your meal with one of the homemade desserts, such as a hazelnut parfait. The wine list contains Austrian, Italian, and French vintages.

Münchner Bundesstrasse 69, Liefering. (C) 0662/43-45-35. Reservations required. Main courses 8€–25€. AE, MC, V. Mon–Sat 11:30am–2pm and 6–9:30pm. Closed 2 weeks in late June and early July (dates vary). Bus: 29 from the center of Salzburg to the Fischergasse stop.

MODERATE

Gasthof Riedenburg 🎯 CONTINENTAL   One of the best restaurants in and around Salzburg occupies a substantial-looking white-sided villa in the suburb of Reidenburg, about 2 miles south of the city's historic core. Elegant and well-respected by virtually everyone in town, it attracts well-groomed and well-heeled members of the local bourgeoisie. Enter a trio of paneled dining rooms, each with an elegantly rustic motif of Land Salzburgundian charm. Menu items are urbane, sophisticated, and delicious—some of the best in town. Examples include carpaccio of goose liver with truffled vinaigrette; lamb cutlets with couscous and chives; marinated brook trout with sweet-and-sour vegetables and fresh herbs; cream of crabmeat soup with aged port; turbot with lobster mousse, spinach, and fennel; breast of hen with mushroom polenta and Madeira sauce; and filet of venison with white pepper sauce, noodles, and artichokes. Dessert might be a white chocolate mousse with mandarin oranges. Let the house pick a glass of whatever the wine steward thinks will be appropriate with each course of your meal—the results can be surprisingly delectable.

Neutorstrasse 31. ℂ 0662/83-08-15. Reservations recommended. Main courses 17€–28€; fixed-price menus without wine 35€–50€; fixed-price menus with wine 50€–75€. AE, DC, MC, V. Mon–Sat noon–2pm and 6pm–midnight. Bus: 15.

5 Seeing the Sights

The Old Town lies between the left bank of the Salzach River and the ridge known as the Mönchsberg, which rises to a height of 503m (1,650 ft.) and is the site of Salzburg's casino. The main street of the Old Town is Getreidegasse, a narrow little thoroughfare lined with five- and six-story burghers' buildings. Most of the houses along the street date from the 17th and 18th centuries. Mozart was born at no. 9 (see below). Many of the houses display lacy-looking wrought-iron signs over carved windows.

You might begin your explorations at **Mozartplatz,** with its outdoor cafes. From here you can walk to the even more expansive **Residenzplatz,** where torchlight dancing is staged every year, along with outdoor performances.

SIGHTSEEING SUGGESTIONS

If You Have 1 Day

Even on a short day visit, Salzburg is to be savored. Start slowly with a cup of coffee at the Café-Restaurant Glockenspiel on Mozartplatz. Then from the Old Town, take the funicular to the Hohensalzburg Fortress for a tour. After lunch, visit Mozart's birthplace on Getreidegasse and stroll along the narrow street. Later, visit the Residenz.

If You Have 2 Days

Spend Day 1 as above. In the morning of your second day, visit the Dom (cathedral) and the cemetery of St. Peter's, and wander through the Altstadt. In the afternoon, explore Hellbrunn Palace, 5km (3 miles) south of the city.

If You Have 3 Days

Spend Days 1 and 2 as above. On Day 3, in the morning, visit other attractions of Salzburg, such as the Mönchsberg, the Mozart Wohnhaus, and the museum Carolino Augusteum in the morning. In the afternoon, tour the Mirabell Gardens and Mirabell Palace and at least look at the famous Festspielhaus (Festival Hall), dating from 1607; tours are sometimes possible.

If You Have 4 or 5 Days

Spend Days 1 to 3 as above. On Day 4, head for some of the fascinating sights in the environs of Salzburg. In the morning, go to Gaisberg, which, at 1,296m (4,250 ft.), offers one of the most panoramic views of the Salzburg Alps. After a visit here and lunch, head for Hallein, the second-largest town in Land Salzburg, for its salt mines.

On Day 5, take the "*Sound of Music* Tour" (see section 6, "Organized Tours," later in this chapter) and visit the places where this world-famous musical with Julie Andrews was filmed. Return to Salzburg in time to hear a Mozart concert, if one is featured (as it often is). If you can spend more time in the area, the vast attractions of Land Salzburg (see chapter 8) await you.

Salzburg Attractions

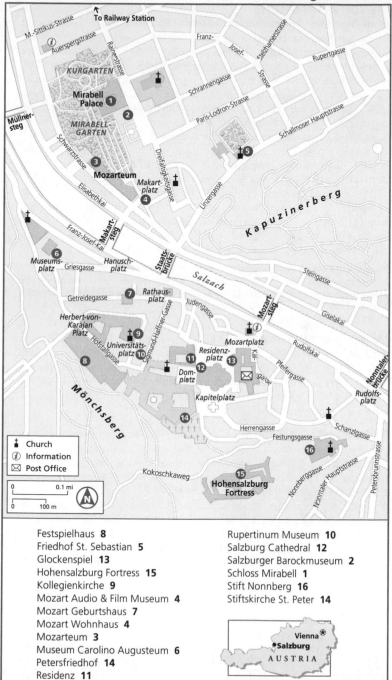

Festspielhaus **8**
Friedhof St. Sebastian **5**
Glockenspiel **13**
Hohensalzburg Fortress **15**
Kollegienkirche **9**
Mozart Audio & Film Museum **4**
Mozart Geburtshaus **7**
Mozart Wohnhaus **4**
Mozarteum **3**
Museum Carolino Augusteum **6**
Petersfriedhof **14**
Residenz **11**

Rupertinum Museum **10**
Salzburg Cathedral **12**
Salzburger Barockmuseum **2**
Schloss Mirabell **1**
Stift Nonnberg **16**
Stiftskirche St. Peter **14**

THE TOP ATTRACTIONS

Residenz State Rooms/Residenzgalerie Salzburg ✮✮   This opulent palace, just north of Domplatz in the pedestrian zone, was the seat of the Salzburg prince-archbishops after they no longer needed the protection of the gloomy Hohensalzburg Fortress of Mönchsberg. The Residenz dates from 1120, but work on a series of palaces, which comprised the ecclesiastical complex of the ruling church princes, began in the late 1500s and continued until about 1796. The lavish rebuilding was originally ordered by Archbishop Wolfgang (usually called "Wolf") Dietrich. The Residenz fountain, from the 17th century, is one of the largest and most impressive baroque fountains north of the Alps.

The child prodigy Mozart often played here in the Conference Room for guests. In 1867, Emperor Franz Joseph received Napoléon III here. More than a dozen state rooms, each richly decorated, are open to the public via guided tour.

On the second floor, you can visit the **Residenzgalerie Salzburg** (✆ **0662/ 84-04-51**), an art gallery founded in 1923, which now contains European paintings from the 16th to the 19th century, displayed in 15 historic rooms. Paintings from the Dutch, Flemish, French, Italian, Austrian baroque, and Austrian 19th-century schools are exhibited. Self-guided audio tours are included in the admission.

Residenzplatz 1. ✆ **0662/80-42-26-90** or 0662/84-04-51. Admission to Residenz state rooms 5€ adults, 4€ students 16–18 and seniors, 2€ children 6–15, free for children 5 and under. Combined ticket to state rooms and gallery 7.25€. Residenz Gallery 4.70€ adults, 3.60€ students 16–18 and seniors, 1.80€ children 6–16. Jan–Apr and Nov Mon–Fri 10am–5pm; May–Oct and Dec daily 10am–4:30pm. Bus: 5 or 6.

Glockenspiel (Carillon) ✮ *Kids*   The celebrated glockenspiel with its 35 bells stands across from the Residenz. You can hear this 18th-century carillon at 7am, 11am, and 6pm. At press time, actual visitation of the interior was not allowed. The ideal way to hear the chimes is from one of the cafes lining the edges of the Mozartplatz while sipping your favorite coffee or drink.

Mozartplatz 1. ✆ 0662/80-42-27-84. Bus: 1.

Salzburg Cathedral (Dom) ✮   Located where Residenzplatz flows into Domplatz (where you'll see a 1771 statue of the Virgin), this cathedral is world-renowned for its 4,000-pipe organ. The original building from A.D. 774 was superseded by a late-Romanesque structure erected from 1181 to 1200. When this edifice was destroyed by fire in 1598, Prince-Archbishop Wolf Dietrich commissioned construction of a new cathedral, but his overthrow prevented the completion of this project. His successor, Archbishop Markus Sittikus Count Hohenems, commissioned the Italian architect Santino Solari to build the present cathedral, which was consecrated in 1628 by Archbishop Paris Count Lodron.

Hailed by some critics as the "most perfect" Renaissance building in the Germanic countries, the cathedral has a marble facade and twin symmetrical towers. The mighty bronze doors were created in 1959. The themes are Faith, Hope, and Love. The interior has a rich baroque style with elaborate frescoes, the most important of which, along with the altarpieces, were designed by Mascagni of Florence. In the cathedral, you can see the Romanesque font at which Mozart was baptized. The dome was damaged during World War II but was restored by 1959. In the crypt, traces of the old Romanesque cathedral that once stood on this spot have been unearthed.

The treasure of the cathedral, and the "arts and wonders" the archbishops collected in the 17th century, are displayed in the **Dom Museum** (✆ **0662/ 84-41-89**), entered through the cathedral.

The **cathedral excavations** (℃ **0662/84-52-95**) are entered around the corner (left of the Dom entrance). This exhibition of excavation work shows ruins of the original foundation.

The allegorical play *Everyman*, adapted by Hugo von Hofmannsthal, is performed near the cathedral in Domplatz during the Salzburg Festival.

South side of Residenzplatz. ℃ **0662/84-41-89**. Free admission to cathedral; excavations 1.80€ adults, .70€ children 6–15, free for children 5 and under; museum 4.50€ adults, 1.50€ children. Cathedral daily 8am–7pm (to 6pm in winter); excavations Easter to mid-Oct Wed–Sun 9am–5pm (closed mid-Oct to Easter); museum Wed–Sun 9am–5pm, Sun 1–6pm. Closed Nov–Apr. Bus: 1, 3, or 5.

Stiftskirche St. Peter ⭐⭐   Founded in A.D. 696 by St. Rupert, whose tomb is here, this is the church of St. Peter's Abbey and Benedictine Monastery. Once a Romanesque basilica with three aisles, the church was completely overhauled in the 17th and 18th centuries in an elegant baroque style. The west door dates from 1240. The church is richly adorned with art treasures, including some altar paintings by Kremser Schmidt. The Salzburg Madonna in the left chancel is from the early 15th century.

St.-Peter-Bezirk. ℃ **0662/844-578**. Free admission. Daily 9am–6pm. Bus: 5, 6, or 55.

Petersfriedhof (St. Peter's Cemetery) ⭐⭐   This cemetery lies at the stone wall that merges into the rock called the Mönchsberg. Many of the aristocratic families of Salzburg lie buried here along with many other noted persons, including Nannerl Mozart, sister of Wolfgang Amadeus (4 years older than her better-known brother, Nannerl was also an exceptionally gifted musician). You can also see the Romanesque Chapel of the Holy Cross and St. Margaret's Chapel, dating from the 15th century. The cemetery and its chapels are rich in blue-blooded history, monuments to a way of life long vanished.

You can also take a self-guided tour through the early Christian catacombs in the rock above the church cemetery.

St.-Peter-Bezirk. ℃ **0662/84-45-78-0**. Free admission to Cemetery. Catacombs 1€ adults, .60€ children. May–Sept daily 10:30am–5pm; Oct–Apr daily 10:30am–3:30pm. Bus: 1.

Hohensalzburg Fortress ⭐⭐ *(Kids)*   The stronghold of the ruling prince-archbishops before they moved "downtown" to the Residenz, this fortress towers 122m (400 ft.) above the Salzach River on a rocky dolomite ledge. The massive fortress crowns the Festungsberg and literally dominates Salzburg. Guided tours are available, purchased with a combined ticket of admission and tour, 6€ for adults and 3.50€ for children. To get here, you can hike up one of the paths or lanes leading to the fortress, or you can walk from Kapitelplatz by way of Festungsgasse or from the Mönchsberg via the Schartentor. You can also take the funicular from Festungsgasse (℃ **0662/84-26-82**) at the station behind the cathedral. You can purchase an advance ticket to the museum, including the funicular ride, for 5.50€ for adults and 3€ for children; or a ticket that includes admission, the funicular ride, and a guided tour for 8€ for adults and 4€ for children. Call the museum or the Festungsgasse telephone number in advance for ticket availability.

Work on Hohensalzburg began in 1077 and was not finished until 1681, during which time many builders of widely different tastes and purposes had a hand in the construction. This is the largest completely preserved castle left in central Europe. Functions of defense and state were combined in this fortress for 6 centuries.

The elegant state apartments, once the dwellings of the prince-archbishops and their courts, are on display. Note the coffered ceilings and intricate ironwork, and check out the early-16th-century porcelain stove in the Golden Room.

In Mozart's Footsteps

Wolfgang Amadeus Mozart was born in Salzburg on January 27, 1756, son of an overmanagerial father, Leopold Mozart, whose controlling power he eventually fled. Amadeus was a child prodigy, writing musical notes at the age of 4, before he could even shape the letters of the alphabet. By the time he'd reached the ripe old age of 6, he was performing at the Schönbrunn Palace in Vienna before assembled royalty and aristocrats.

Although for a time at least he pleased the audiences of Vienna, he once complained that the audiences in his hometown of Salzburg were rather wooden and no more responsive than "tables and chairs." Ironically, while Salzburg today pays great tribute to Mozart—many merchants live solely off his reputation—he was not appreciated here in his lifetime and often struggled to make ends meet. In spite of the success of *The Magic Flute* in 1791, his career ended in obscurity, with his 1790 *Cosí fan Tutte* meeting a cool reception.

Since Mozart's death in 1791, his image is everywhere in Salzburg. In the heart of town, **Mozartplatz** bears his name, with a statue of the composer erected in 1842, the first recognition of his birth he'd received in the town since his death.

A music academy in Salzburg is named after Mozart, and, of course, his music dominates the Salzburg Festival. Too bad he couldn't have been more honored during his lifetime. He died in Vienna on December 5, 1791, and the body of the 35-year-old musical genius was carried in a pauper's hearse to a common grave in the cemetery of Vienna's St. Marx. Today, if his grave site had been better marked, it would be a world-class memorial.

You can visit **Mozart Geburtshaus (Birthplace)** , Getreidegasse 9 (© **0662/84-43-13**). He lived here until he was 17—that is, when he was in Salzburg at all and wasn't touring such cities as Prague or Vienna. There are three floors of exhibition rooms, which includes the Mozart family apartment. The main treasures are the valuable paintings (such as the well-known oil painting *Mozart and the Piano,* left unfinished by Joseph Lange) and the original instruments: the violin Mozart used as a child, his concert violin, and his viola, fortepiano, and clavichord. It's open daily from 9am to 5pm. Admission is 5.50€ for adults, 4.50€ for students, and 1.50€ for children.

The **Burgmuseum** is distinguished mainly by its collection of medieval art. Plans and prints tracing the growth of Salzburg are on display, as are instruments of torture and many Gothic artifacts. The Salzburger Stier (Salzburg Bull), an open-air barrel organ built in 1502, plays melodies by Mozart and his friend Haydn in daily concerts following the glockenspiel chimes. The **Rainermuseum** has arms and armor exhibits. The beautiful late Gothic St. George's Chapel, dating from 1501, has marble reliefs of the Apostles.

Visit Hohensalzburg even if you're not interested in the fortress, just for the view from the terrace. From the Reck watchtower, you get a panoramic sweep of the Alps. The Kuenberg bastion has a fine view of Salzburg's domes and towers.

You can also visit the restored **Mozart Wohnhaus** ✿, Makartplatz 8 (✆ **0662/84-43-13**), where the composer lived from 1773 to 1780. Damaged in World War II air raids, the house reopened in 1996, honoring the year of Mozart's 240th birthday. In 1773, the Mozart family vacated the cramped quarters of Mozart's birthplace for this haunt on Makartplatz. In the rooms of these former apartments, a museum documents the history of the house, life, and work of Wolfgang Amadeus Mozart. There's a mechanized audio tour in six languages with musical samples. The museum is open June through September daily from 9am to 5pm and October through May daily from 10am to 5pm. Admission is 5.50€ for adults, 4.50€ for students, and 1.50€ for children. Mozart aficionados will want to stop by the International Mozarteum Foundation's **Mozart Audio and Film Museum,** Makartplatz 8 (✆ **0662/88-34-54**). Here is a collection of 11,000 audio and 1,000 video titles, all concerned with Mozart's compositions. There are also sections devoted to the work of contemporary Salzburg composers. You can watch and listen to 8 video and 10 audio stations; plus, there's a large-scale screen for groups. The museum, which is free, is open Monday, Tuesday, and Friday from 9am to 1pm and Wednesday and Thursday from 1 to 5pm.

You have to make an appointment to visit the **Mozarteum,** Schwarzstrasse 26 (✆ **0662/88-940**). This is the center of the International Mozarteum Foundation, an edifice in Munich Jugensdstil architecture built from 1910 to 1914. The jewel on the second floor is the library—a *Bibliotheca Mozartiana* with approximately 12,000 titles devoted to Mozart. The Viennese Hall seats 200 people and provides an intimate atmosphere for concerts and conferences. The wing at Schwarzstrasse 28 houses the larger concert hall where up to 800 guests enjoy concerts throughout the year. The highlight is the celebratory festival *Mozartwoche,* which commemorates Mozart's birthday (Jan 27) with 10 days of concerts and operas. It's open Monday through Friday from 10am to 5pm.

In the garden stands the **Magic Flute House,** a little wooden structure in which Mozart composed *The Magic Flute* in 1791. It was shipped here from the Naschmarkt in Vienna. In 1971, the Mozarteum was designated as the College of Music and the Performing Arts.

You can see the fortress grounds on your own or take a tour of the interior. Conducted 40- to 50-minute tours go through the fortress daily, but hours and departure times depend on the season: November through March from 10am to 4:30pm, April through June from 9:30am to 5pm, July through August from 9am to 6pm, and September through October from 9:30am to 5pm. The conducted tour of the fortress and the Rainier Museum costs 3€ for adults and 1.50€ for children 6 to 15; it's free for children under 6.

Mönchsberg 34. ✆ **0662/84-24-30-11.** Admission (excluding guided tour but including museum) 7.10€ adults, 4€ children 6–19, free for children 5 and under. Family ticket 8.70€. Fortress and museums, Oct–Mar daily 9:30am–5pm; Apr–Sept daily 9am–6pm.

Schloss Mirabell (Mirabell Palace) ⚘   This palace and its gardens (see "Parks & Gardens," below) were originally built as a luxurious private residence called Altenau. Prince-Archbishop Wolf Dietrich had it constructed in 1606 for his mistress and the mother of his children, Salome Alt. Unfortunately, not much remains of the original grand structure. Johann Lukas von Hildebrandt rebuilt the *Schloss* in the first quarter of the 18th century, and it was modified after a great fire in 1818. The official residence of the mayor of Salzburg is now in the palace, which is like a smaller rendition of the Tuileries in Paris. The ceremonial marble Barockstiege-Englesstiege (angel staircase), with sculptured cherubs, carved by Raphael Donner in 1726, leads to the Marmorsaal, a marble-and-gold hall used for concerts and weddings. Chamber music concerts are staged here.

Rainerstrasse. ℭ **0662/8072-0.** Free admission. Staircase: daily, 8am–6pm. Marmorsaal: Mon, Wed, and Thurs 8am–4pm; Tues and Fri 9am–4pm. Bus: 1, 5, 6, or 51.

Festpielhaus (Festival Hall)   Designed by Wolf Dietrich and built in 1607, this was once the court stables. Today it's the center for the major musical events of Salzburg, its cultural activity peaking during the August festival. The modern hall seats 2,300 spectators, and most major concerts and big operas are performed here. Many outstanding Austrian artists contributed to the decoration of the modern Festival Hall. *Note:* Tours are canceled if there is a rehearsal or performance of virtually anything—so this is no longer a major stop on the Salzburg tourist scene, but a grace note fitted in for music buffs when more pressing musical or theatrical events don't override it.

Hofstallgasse 1. ℭ **0662/849-097.** Admission to tours 5€. June–Sept tours daily at 9:30am, 2pm, and 3:30pm. The rest of the year daily at 2pm. Reservations are necessary. Bus: 1.

MORE ATTRACTIONS

For the many sites and attractions focusing on Salzburg's favorite son, Mozart, see the box "In Mozart's Footsteps," above.

CHURCHES

Friedhof St. Sebastian (St. Sebastian Cemetery)   Prince-Archbishop Wolf Dietrich commissioned this cemetery in 1595 to be laid out like an Italian *campo santo.* The tombs of Mozart's wife and his father, Leopold, are here. In the middle of the cemetery is St. Gabriel's Chapel, containing the mausoleum of Dietrich. The mausoleum's interior is lined with multicolored porcelain.

To reach the cemetery, walk down the Italian-style steps from St. Sebastian's Church. The original late Gothic edifice dated from the early 16th century. It was rebuilt and enlarged in 1749, in the rococo style. Destroyed by fire in 1818, it was later reconstructed. Only the 1752 rococo doorway remains from the old church building. Paracelsus, the Renaissance doctor and philosopher who died in 1541, is entombed here. According to ancient Roman Catholic tradition, ceremonies here are carried out entirely in Latin.

ℭ **0662/88-887-330.** Linzergasse. Free admission. Daily 7am–7pm (until dusk in winter). Bus: 1 or 5.

Kollegienkirche (Collegiate Church)   Opening onto an open-air marketplace, this church was built between 1694 and 1707 for the local (Benedictine) university founded in 1622 and designed by the great baroque architect Fischer von Erlach. The university, disbanded in 1810, was reopened in 1962 as part of the University of Salzburg (the main campus is in the suburb of Nonntal). There are a few other old university buildings in the area, including a fine library and reading room. This, von Erlach's greatest and largest Salzburg church, is one of the most celebrated baroque churches in all of Austria (and that's saying a lot). Altar paintings are by Rottmayr.

Universitätsplatz. ℂ **0662/841-327-72.** Free admission. Daily 9am–6pm. Bus: 2.

MUSEUMS

Museum Carolino Augusteum This museum details Salzburg's cultural history through a variety of collections and exhibits. The one devoted to archaeology contains a few well-known pieces, including the Dürnberg beaked pitcher, as well as some Roman mosaics. Examples of Salzburg's 15th-century art world are on view, including a rich trove of Gothic panel painting and many paintings from the Romantic period. Works by Hans Makart, who was born in Salzburg in 1840, are also on display. Founded in 1834 and destroyed by a 1944 bombing, the present building was reconstructed in 1966.

Museumsplatz 1. ℂ **0662/6208-08-111.** Admission 3.20€ adults, 2€ seniors over 60, 1€ children 6–19, free for children 5 and under. Daily 9am–5pm. Bus: 1, 49, or 95.

Rupertinum Museum of Modern Art Salzburg This gallery, housed in a 17th-century building, is known for its wide variety of temporary exhibits, plus a permanent collection of works by Klimt, Kokoschka, and lesser-known artists. There is also a display of photography and graphic arts. Although it's a fairly minor attraction, it's a nice stop for those interested in 20th-century art.

Wiener Philharmonikergasse 9. ℂ **0662/8042-2541.** Admission 8€ adults, 4.50€ students, free for children 15 and under. Apr–Sept Thurs–Tues 10am–6pm (Wed 9pm); Oct–Mar Tues–Sun 10am–5pm (Wed 9pm). Bus: 29.

Salzburger Barockmuseum The museum in the orangerie of the Mirabell Gardens (see "Parks & Gardens," below) displays 17th- and 18th-century European art, with works by Giordano, Rottmayr, Bernini, Straub, and other artists.

Mirabellgarten 3. ℂ **0662/87-74-32.** Admission 3€ adults, 1.50€ students 15–18 and seniors, free for children 14 and under. Tues–Sat 9am–noon and 2–5pm; Sun and holidays 10am–1pm. Bus: 1, 5, or 6.

PANORAMIC VIEWS
KAPUZINERBERG

This forested area on the right bank of the Salzach River rises more than 610m (2,000 ft.) above the city and is today a landscaped park. To get here, cross the Staatsbrücke spanning the Salzach to the right bank, continue walking for 2 minutes until you come to Steingasse, and cut right; after exploring Steingasse, walk through the Steintor, then climb an adjoining stone stairway, and follow the signs to Kapuzinerberg.

A Capuchin friary was built here at the very end of the 16th century, constructed inside an old medieval fortification. On the south side of the hill is Steingasse, a pretty street from medieval times, and the Steintor, which was once a gate in the walls of Salzburg. From vantage points on the Kapuzinerberg, you can see into Bavaria, in Germany.

The birthplace of Josef Mohr (1792–1848), who penned the lyrics to "Silent Night," is now the **Silent Night Museum,** Steingasse 9 (ℂ **662/87-83-74;** www.silentnightmuseum.org), open Thursday through Sunday from 11am to 5pm. Admission is 2€ for adults and 1€ for children. You can see the original 1816 autograph copy of the song.

MÖNCHSBERG

West of the Hohensalzburg Fortress, this heavily forested ridge extends for some 2km (1½ miles) above the Old Town and has fortifications dating from the 15th century. From several vantage points, including the Mönchsberg Terrace just in front of the Grand Café Winkler, you can see Salzburg.

You can get up here by taking the express elevators leaving from Gstättengasse 13 (© **0662/448-06-285**). The elevators leave daily from 9am to 11pm. Round-trip fare is 2.40€ for adults and 1.25€ for children 6 to 15; it's free for children 5 and under.

PARKS & GARDENS

On the right bank of the river, laid out by Fischer von Erlach, the baroque **Mirabell Gardens** ☆, off Makartplatz, are the finest in Salzburg. Now a public park, they're studded with statues and reflecting pools. Von Erlach also designed some of the marble balustrades and urns. There's a natural theater as well. For the best view of the gardens and also of Salzburg, pause at the top of the steps where Julie Andrews and her seven charges showed off their singing voices in *The Sound of Music.* As you wander in the gardens, be sure to visit Zwerglgarten, the bastion with fantastic marble baroque dwarfs and other figures. It's located by the Pegasus Fountains in the lavish garden west of Schloss Mirabell. From the garden, you have an excellent view of the Hohensalzburg Fortress. The marble statues make Mirabell Gardens virtually an open-air museum. The gardens are open daily from 7am to 8pm. In summer, free brass band concerts are held Wednesday at 8:30pm and Sunday at 10:30am.

ESPECIALLY FOR KIDS

Of the attractions already reviewed, those that children will most like include the **Glockenspiel, Hohensalzburg Fortress, Mönchsberg,** and, on the outskirts, the **Hellbrunn Zoo** (see "Side Trips from Salzburg," later in this chapter). Kids will also enjoy the **Salzburger Marionetten Theater** (see section 8, "Salzburg After Dark," later in this chapter).

Spielzeugmuseum (Toy Museum) *(Kids* In what used to be the Salzburg City Hospital, this museum is a toy wonderland—from the toys that kids played with in the 1500s to those that are popular today. The vintage model trains, the early carousels, the old musical instruments, and the large collection of arts and crafts delight children and adults alike.

Burgerspitalgasse 2. © 0662/84-75-60. Admission (including entrance to the Punch and Judy shows) 2.54€ adults, .70€ children 6–15, free for children 5 and under. Daily 9am–5pm; Punch and Judy shows Tues–Wed at 3pm. Bus: 1, 2, 27, or 29.

SPECIAL-INTEREST SIGHTSEEING FOR THE ARCHITECTURE BUFF

All of the **Altstadt** and much of **baroque Salzburg** will interest students of architecture. It's the whole left bank of the city, not just one particular building, that makes Salzburg world renowned for its beauty.

Much of the celebrated architecture was created in the reign of prince-archbishop Johann Ernst von Thun (1687–1709). He secured the services of one of Austria's greatest architects, Johann Bernhard Fischer von Erlach, who created a harmonious collection of baroque structures in the center of town. Von Erlach designed at least a dozen buildings in and around Salzburg, most notably the **Kollegienkirche.**

Thun's successor, prince-archbishop Franz Anton von Harrach (1709–27), wasn't all that enthusiastic about von Erlach and replaced him with his chief competitor, Johann Lukas von Hildebrandt, best known for the Belvedere Palace in Vienna. Von Hildebrandt proceeded to design the **Residenz** and **Schloss Mirabell,** the latter famous for its Marble Hall and grand staircase.

Both these architects, although deadly rivals, are credited with changing the face of Salzburg. Fortunately for us, the architectural treasures were spared the fury of Allied bombing raids in World War II.

6 Organized Tours

The best organized tours are offered by **Salzburg Panorama Tours,** Mirabellplatz (✆ **0662/88-32-11-0;** www.panoramatours.at), which is the Gray Line company for Salzburg.

The original *"Sound of Music* Tour" combines the Salzburg city tour with an excursion to the lake district and other places where the 1965 film with Julie Andrews was shot. The English-speaking guide shows you not only the highlights from the film, but also historical and architectural landmarks in Salzburg and parts of the Salzkammergut countryside. The 4½-hour tour departs daily at 2pm and costs 33€.

You must take your passport along for any of the three trips into Bavaria in Germany. One of these—called the "Eagle's Nest Tour"—takes visitors to Berchtesgaden and on to Obersalzburg, where Hitler and his inner circle had a vacation retreat. The 4½-hour tour departs daily at 9am from May 15 to October 20 and costs 45€.

"The City & Country Highlights" tour takes in historic castles and the surrounding Land Salzburg landscape. This 5-hour tour departs daily at 1pm and costs 45€. Coffee and pastry at the Castle Fuschl are an added treat.

You can book these tours at the bus terminal at Mirabellplatz/St. Andrä Kirche (✆ **0662/87-40-29**). Tour prices are the same for all ages.

7 Shopping

While Salzburg doesn't have Vienna's wide range of merchandise, there's still plenty of shopping here. Good buys in Salzburg include souvenirs of Land Salzburg (dirndls, lederhosen, and petit point) and all types of sports gear. **Getreidegasse** is a main shopping thoroughfare, but you'll also find some intriguing little shops on **Residenzplatz.**

Most stores are open Monday through Friday from 9am to 6pm, but note that many stores, especially smaller shops, take a 1- or 2-hour break for lunch. On weekends, stores are generally open only Saturday mornings.

SHOPPING A TO Z
BOOKS & PRINTS
Eduard Höllrigl   This is the oldest bookstore in the country, dating from 1594. It sells more than books. You'll find an array of maps, sheet music, and the most interesting postcards in town. Sigmund-Haffner-Gasse 10. ✆ **0662/84-11-46.** Bus: 5, 6, or 55.

CHINA & CRYSTAL
Lobmeyr   Lobmeyr is the Salzburg branch of the famous store in Vienna's Kaerntnerstrase. Lobmeyr offers a wide range of crystal drinking sets and elegant Herendchina, as well as some of the prettiest breakfast services one can find, many made in Hungary. Schwarzstrasse 20. ✆ **0662/873-181.** Bus: 5, 6, or 55.

CRAFTS

Drechslerei Lackner   If you like wood crafts, there's no better place in Salzburg. It offers both antique and modern country furniture, especially chairs. Among the newly made items are chests, chessboards, angels, cupboards, crèches, and candlesticks. Badergasse 2. ℂ 0662/84-23-85. Bus: 68 or 81.

Salzburger Heimatwerk   In a dignified stone building in the least-crowded section of Residenzplatz, with a discreet sign announcing its location, this is one of the best places in town to buy local Austrian handcrafts and original *Tracht,* or costumes. Items include Austrian silver and garnet jewelry, painted boxes, candles, wood carvings, copper and brass ceramics, tablecloths, and alpine designs for cross-stitched samplers. A special section sells dressmaking materials such as cotton and silk, with dressmaker patterns. Another section sells Austrian *Tracht* like dirndls, capes, and the rest of the regalia that's still actually worn during commemorative ceremonies and festivals. Wherever you go in this curious store, you're bound to find little treasures, so keep exploring. Am Residenzplatz 9. ℂ 0662/84-41-10. Bus: 5, 6, or 55.

Wiener Porzellanmanufaktur Augarten Gesellschaft   This is the premier shop in Salzburg for Austrian porcelain, specializing in Augarten porcelain. Patterns like Viennese Rose and Maria Theresia are still very popular, but its most famous item is the black-and-white coffee set created by architect/designer Josef Hoffmann. Alter Markt 11. ℂ 0662/84-07-14. Bus: 68 or 81.

FASHION

Brigitte Kinder-Trachten   Children up to age 14 are dressed here in plain or embroidered knit jackets, dirndls, and folk dresses that are the longtime favorite apparel of Land Salzburg. Lederhosen for boys come in full or short lengths with all the appropriate accompaniments. Although American kids often prefer their jeans, Austrian and German children (or at least their parents) sometimes like these looks. Universitätsplatz 7. ℂ 0662/84-11-93. Bus: 5, 6, or 55.

Jahn-Markl   This small and elegant clothing store in Old Town has been in the same family for four generations, although its origins date from 1408. It carries lederhosen, leather skirts, and traditional Austrian coats and blazers. Leather for both women and men is also sold, including jackets, pants, and gloves. Some children's clothing is available. Less expensive items can be bought off the racks, but more expensive pieces are usually made to order in 4 weeks and can be mailed anywhere in the world for an additional charge. Residenzplatz 3. ℂ 0662/84-26-10. Bus: 5, 6, or 55.

Lanz   At this well-stocked store across the river from the Old Town, you'll find one of the widest collections of long-skirted dirndls in town, in dozens of different fabrics and colors. Men's clothing includes loden-colored overcoats. The store also sells dirndls for little girls and hand-knitted sweaters. There's another branch along the main shopping street of Salzburg at Kranzlmarkt 1, Getreidegasse (ℂ 0662/84-03-00). Schwarzstrasse 4. ℂ 0662/87-42-72. Bus: 68 or 81.

LIQUOR

Petersporer   Specializing in exotic schnapps and liqueurs, this is our favorite shop in all of Salzburg, partly because what it sells are one-of-a-kind libations and partly because it doubles as a cramped but convivial bar. It was established in 1903 by the grandfather of the present owner, in a desirable location adjacent to the Goldener Hirsch Hotel. Everything sold is distilled in Austria, usually from medleys of local herbs and high-altitude berries that lend each product a distinctive aroma and flavor. Bottles include liqueurs distilled from apricots, black currants, sour cherries, pears, elderberries, or herbs and flowers. Some clients come here at regular intervals with their own flasks, bottles, and/or decanters, which a staff member will fill for them, saving them the cost of a container. What's the most popular liqueur sold here? It's a homemade version of schnapps distilled from herbs and marketed under the name Hausmisching. You can taste any of the brands sold here at the bar and then opt to buy a bottle or two of whatever you fancy as a conversation stimulus for after your return home. It's open Monday through Saturday from 9am to 12:30pm and 2:30 to 6pm, and Sunday from 8:30am to 5pm. MasterCard and Visa are accepted. Getreidegasse 39. © 0662/84-54-31. Bus: 5, 6, or 55.

MUSIC
Musikhaus Pühringer   Established in 1910, this store sells all kinds of classical musical instruments, as well as a large selection of electronics (including synthesizers and amplifiers). You'll find classical and folk-music CDs and tapes, plus many classical recordings, especially those by Mozart. The store is only a few buildings away from the composer's birthplace. Getreildegasse 13. © 0662/ 84-32-67. Bus: 5, 6, or 55.

PASTRIES
Schatz-Konditorei (Kids)   This excellent pastry shop (reviewed above in the "Cafes" box in "Where to Dine") is one of the few in Salzburg that will mail cakes around the world. The store's specialty is the highly acclaimed *Mozart Kugeln,* a cookie of pistachio, marzipan, and hazelnut nougat dipped in chocolate. Packages of this gourmet delight can be airmailed to North America. Getreidegasse 3. © 0662/84-27-92. Bus: 68 or 81.

SPORTING GOODS
Sporting Goods Dschulnigg   Queen Elizabeth II and Prince Philip have been photographed on a shopping expedition at this upper-crust emporium for clothes and sporting goods. Among the items sold are many kinds of sporting goods, including guns, as well as children's outfits, overcoats for both men and women, intricately patterned sweaters, and fur-lined hats. You can get hunting rifles (but not pistols or revolvers) in Austria without a license, although the Customs officers back home might present a problem. Griesgasse 8. © 0662/ 842-376-0. Bus: 5, 6, or 55.

TOYS & SOUVENIRS
Neumüller Spielwaren   In winter, this store sells children's toys. In summer, the stock changes with the tourist influx, and the shelves fill up with handcrafted souvenirs such as mugs, cowbells, and rustic art objects. Rathausplatz 3. © 0662/ 84-14-29. Bus: 5, 6, or 55.

8 Salzburg After Dark

The annual cultural events, which reach their peak at the Salzburg Festival, overshadow any after-dark amusements such as dance clubs and beer halls. Clubs come and go in Salzburg fairly rapidly.

It's said that there's a musical event—often a Mozart concert—staged virtually every night in Salzburg. To find out what's playing, visit the **Salzburg**

tourist office, Mozartplatz 5 (📞 **0662/88987-330**), where you can get a free copy of *Offizieller Wochenspiegel,* a monthly pamphlet listing all major and many minor local cultural events. The annual Mozart Week is in January.

FREE CONCERTS & SPECIAL EVENTS   Free concerts are frequently presented by students in the **Mozarteum,** Schwarzstrasse 26 (📞 **0662/88-94-0; bus: 1, 5, 6, or 51**). In summer, free brass band concerts are performed in the Mirabell Gardens on Wednesday at 8:30pm and, depending on the venue, either Saturday or Sunday at 10:30am; Sunday chamber-music concerts are held throughout the city at major landmarks such as the Residenz.

The second-most famous music festival in Salzburg is the **Osterfestspiele (Easter Festival),** which features high-quality operas and concerts performed in the Festspielhaus. Some, but not all, of the music focuses on works associated with the resurrection of Christ as interpreted by the great 18th- and 19th-century composers. Established by Herbert von Karajan in the 1960s, the festival requires that spectators purchase tickets to the opera and each of the three concerts associated with the event. Prices for the series are anything but cheap: They range, per person, from 300€ to 570€, plus an annual membership fee of 300€. For information and ticket purchases, contact the **Osterfestspiele,** Herbert von Karajan Platz 9, A-5020 Salzburg (📞 **0662/804-5361; bus: 1**).

Christmas Eve in Salzburg is unforgettable. Traditionally, in the little chapel of Oberndorf, north of Salzburg, "Silent Night" is performed. Franz Gruber wrote the melody to that song here when he was an organist in the early 19th century.

BUYING TICKETS   If you don't want to pay a ticket agent's commission, you can go directly to the box office of a theater or concert hall. However, many of the best seats might have already been sold, especially those at the Salzburg Festival. Despite the availability of ticket outlets in any of the below-mentioned theaters, many visitors head for the larger umbrella ticket agency that is affiliated with the city of Salzburg. Located adjacent to Salzburg's main tourist office, at Mozartplatz 5, it's called the **Salzburger Ticket Office** (📞 **0662/84-03-10**). Open Monday through Friday from 9am to 6pm (to 7pm in midsummer) and Saturday from 9am to noon, it's the single best source for cultural information and ticket sales in town, usually with tickets to virtually every musical event in the city on sale—except, of course, to those events that are sold out long in advance.

Curiously, though Salzburg is well known as a city of music and culture, it has no famed local troupes. It does, however, attract visiting guest artists with blue-chip credentials in the world of performing arts.

THE PERFORMING ARTS
OPERA, DANCE & MUSIC
Festspielhaus   All the premier ballet, opera, and musical concerts are performed at this world-famous citadel of Salzburg culture. The *Grosses Haus* (Big House), the larger venue, seats 2,170. The *Kleines Haus* (Small House) seats 1,323, which isn't that small. Instead of going directly to the Festspielhaus, you can purchase tickets in advance at the box office at Waagplatz 1A (📞 **0662/ 84-53-46**), close to the tourist office, Monday through Friday from 9:30am to 4:30pm. Most performances begin at 7:30pm, although there are matinees from time to time at 11am and 3pm. Hofstallgasse 1. 📞 **0662/8045**. Tickets 8€–200€ (the higher cost for the best seats at the Salzburg Festival); average but good seats run 35€–80€. Bus: 1, 5, or 6.

The Salzburg Festival

One of the premier music attractions of Europe, the Salzburg Festival celebrates its 83rd season in 2003. Composer Richard Strauss founded the festival, aided by director Max Reinhardt and writer Hugo von Hofmannsthal.

An annual event is Hofmannsthal's adaptation of the morality play *Everyman,* performed in German and staged outside the cathedral in Domplatz. Concerts are usually conducted in the Rittersaal of the Residenz Palace (Mozart conducted here) and in the marble salon of Mirabell Palace (Mozart's father, Leopold, conducted here). The Salzburger Marionetten Theater (see below) also presents performances. Ballet performances are usually given by the Vienna State Opera Ballet with the Vienna State Opera Chorus and the Vienna Philharmonic. International soloists—such big names as Luciano Pavarotti—are invited annually, and the London Symphony or the Berlin Philharmonic is also likely to be invited.

Festival tickets, however, are in great demand, and there never are enough of them. Don't arrive expecting to get into any of the major events unless you've already purchased tickets. Travel agents can often get tickets for you, and you can also go to branches of the Austrian National Tourist Office at home or abroad. Hotel concierges, particularly at the deluxe and first-class hotels of Salzburg, always have some tickets on hand, but expect to pay outrageous prices for them, depending on the particular performance you want to attend. At first-night performances of the major productions, remember that evening dress is de rigueur.

Subject to many exceptions and variations, and without agent commissions, drama tickets generally run 25€ to 180€. Opera tickets can begin as low as 40€, ranging upward to 285€.

For festival details, contact the Salzburg Festival box office, Hofstallgasse 1, A-5020 Salzburg, Austria (✆ **0662/8045-579**; www.salzburg festival.at).

Festung Hohensalzburg   If your visit to Salzburg doesn't happen to coincide with any of the city's annual music festivals, you can always attend the concerts that are presented within the Hohensalzburg Fortress. Here, in historic and dramatic settings, you're likely to hear heavy doses of Mozart and, to a lesser degree, works by Schubert, Brahms, and Beethoven. From mid-May to mid-October, performances are likely to be held at 8 or 8:30pm every night of the week. The rest of the year, they're presented most (but not all) nights, with occasional week-long breaks, usually at 7:30pm. The box office for the events is at Adlgasser Weg 22 (✆ **0662/82-58-58**). Mönchsberg 34. ✆ **0662/84-24-30-11.** Tickets cost 9€ families, 4 € adults, and 2€ children 4–15. To reach the fortress, take the funicular from Festungsgasse.

Mozarteum   On the right bank of the Salzach River, near Mirabell Gardens, is the Mozarteum, Salzburg's major music and concert hall. All the big orchestra concerts, as well as organ recitals and chamber-music evenings, are presented here.

In the old building at Schwarzstrasse, there are two concert halls, the Grosser Saal and the Wiener Saal. In the newer building on Mirabellplatz, concert halls include the Grosses Studio, the Leopold-Mozart Saal, and the Paumgartner Studio. Make sure to find out which hall your musical event is in. It's also a music school, and you can ask about free events staged by the students. The box office is open Monday through Thursday from 9am to 2pm and Friday from 9am to 4pm. Performances are at 11am or 7:30pm. Schwarzstrasse 26 and Mirabellplatz 1. © 0662/ 87-31-54. Tickets 8€–185€; the best seats run 90€–185€. Bus 1, 5, 6, or 51.

Salzburger Schlosskonzerte   The Salzburger Schlosskonzerte (Palace Concerts) are privately owned by the Salzburg violinist Luz Leskowitz, who carries on the 44-year-old tradition of presenting the best ensembles. The carefully chosen programs combine with the beautiful, historic venues (the Marmorsaal, where Mozart himself played) to create an atmosphere of perfect harmony. Mozart's music is heavily featured, but the famed music of classical Austria and Italy are also included in the repertoire. Beethoven, Mendelssohn, Schubert, Bach, Brahms, Vivaldi, Hadyn—the list seems endless. Unchanged since the days of Mozart, concerts are staged in the richly decorated baroque chambers. Go to the box office at Schloss Mirabell 1 hour before the concert begins (8pm in winter, 8:30pm in summer), or book in advance at Griesgasse 6, from 9am to noon and 2 to 5pm. Schloss Mirabell, Mirabellplatz. Booking office, Theatergasse 2. © 0662/84-85-86. Tickets 26€–31€ adults, 14€ students. Bus: 1, 5, 6, or 51.

THEATER

Although the **Salzburger Landestheater,** Schwarzstrasse 22 (© 0662/87-15-120; www.theater.co.at; bus: 68 or 81), doesn't always play for summer visitors, you can see its regular repertoire of operas (not just Mozart) and operettas if you're in Salzburg from September to mid-June. You might see a thrilling performance of Verdi's *Traviata.* Opera tickets usually range from 25€ to 46€. In July and August, Salzburg Festival performances are held here.

   Salzburger Marionetten Theater, Schwarzstrasse 24 (© 0662/87-24-06; www.marionetten.at; bus: 5, 6, or 55), presents shows from Easter to September, as well as special shows at Christmas and during Mozart Week, the last week of January. The puppets perform both opera (usually Mozart) and ballet, to the delight of both adults and children. Founded in 1913, the theater continues to be one of the most unusual and enjoyable theatrical experiences in Salzburg. You might forget that marionettes are onstage; it's that realistic. Tickets are 22€ to 35€.

THE CLUB & MUSIC SCENE

To hear some good jazz, head to the **Jazzclub Live Salzburg,** Schallmooser Hauptstrasse 50 (© 0662/87-08-94; bus: 68 or 81), the most popular jazz spot in town. Sets on Friday nights go from 8pm to midnight from September to May. Cover is 15€. Once you're inside, half a liter of beer costs 3€ to 5€. It's open Monday through Saturday from 5am to midnight.

   The best alternative music spot is **Rockhouse,** Schallmooser Hauptstrasse 46 (© 0662/88-49-14; bus: 68 or 81), which also has a cafe. Local and European bands are booked to play this tunnel-like venue, which offers everything from blues, funk, and jazz to techno pop. Sometimes groups from the United States or even Africa appear here. The structure itself is from the 1840s, having once been a wine cellar and ice storage depot. Cover is 7€ to 20€, depending on the act. Call to see what's happening at the time of your visit.

There's something disheveled and disorganized about the **Republic Cafe,** Anton Neymayr Platz 2 (℗ **0664/41-30-668;** bus: 5, 6, or 55), but it's a hotbed of countercultural activities in Salzburg. It defines itself as a cross between a bar and a cafe, with a "radical performance space." Its nerve center is a battered street-level bar and cafe, open daily from 9am to 2am. You can hang out at the bar, chatting with hard-rock music fans, rave participants, and all kinds of grunge musicians, and ordering simple platters of food priced at 5€ to 8€ each. Radiating from the cafe are several performance spaces which might or might not be booked by local jazz ensembles, avant-garde theater groups, performance artists, and nihilist poets, depending on the week's schedule. Frankly, there's a lot that's slipshod and disorganized about this place, but part of its charm derives from a haphazard schedule and its own sense that it's a cauldron for artistic-statements-in-the-making.

Entrance is free to **Jexx,** Gstättengasse 7 (℗ **0662/844181**), a three-tiered nightlife emporium combining a bar and a restaurant on its street level and a dance club upstairs. The decor is vaguely Mexican, the cuisine is completely Mexican, and the bar is a rollicking, animated kind of place where meeting and making new friends is the order of the night. Dance before or after dinner is in the stone-walled disco area upstairs. Music includes the kind of thing you might have expected at a hip dance club in Berlin or Paris. Reservations for the restaurant are recommended, with small and large platters costing 3.50€ to 11€. It's open Monday through Tuesday from 6pm to 1am and Wednesday through Saturday from 6pm to 4am. Music and dancing begin at 9:30pm.

BEER GARDENS & CELLARS

Augustiner Bräustübl   For an enjoyable, authentic evening in Salzburg, we recommend paying a visit to this famous beer garden. (The place got its name from an old Augustinian monastery.) The *Bierstube* has served suds of one kind of another since 1622, although over the years it has expanded massively. In winter, guests retreat inside to one of several large beer halls, but in fair weather the beer-drinking fraternity spills into the leafy chestnut garden. The brew, incidentally, is excellent. The activity gets louder and rowdier as the night wears on, especially when young men on summer tours from Munich invade from neighboring Bavaria. To get here, you climb a steep, narrow cobblestone street and go through a stone entranceway, passing statues of saints and cherubs.

After descending a baroque staircase, you'll find about a dozen kiosks, where you can buy takeout portions of salads, wursts, sandwiches, and pretzels. Farther on, you choose a thick stoneware mug from the racks and carry it to the beer tap, paying the cashier as you go. Take your own mug to one of the trio of cavernous rooms (*Saals*) nearby. This place has been known to squeeze in some 2,200 drinkers (the busiest night on record). A full liter begins at 4€; a half liter costs 2€ depending on the type of beer. It's open Monday through Friday from 3 to 11pm and Saturday and Sunday from 2:30 to 11pm. Augustinergasse 46. ℗ **0662/43-12-46.** Bus: 27.

Salzburger Altstadtkeller   No one in Salzburg is really sure of whether to classify this place as a restaurant, an inn, a pub, or a nightclub, since it combines so gracefully elements of all of them. The result is a witty and sometimes exuberant after-dark retreat that welcomes everyone from high-brow musicians at the Salzburg Festival to factory workers who might not be overly concerned about the nuances of classical music. The result is fun and convivial, thanks partly to the tone established by its entrepreneurial owners, Adi and Margot Jüstel. The setting is a medieval cellar set beneath the Altstadt Radisson Hotel, immediately adjacent to the banks of the river. Don't come here expecting fine dining: What you'll get is a short list of Austrian-style platters—Wiener schnitzel, *Tafelspitz* (boiled beef), turkey schnitzels with gravy, rice, and salad—and a reverberating roster of musical acts that include swing, Latino, jazz, and blues. Every Thursday, the acts get more nostalgic and folkloric, as the stage is turned over to bands specializing in Austrian or Bavarian "evergreen" music. Music plays from around 9:15pm to 1am, with guests then lingering over their drinks for at least another hour. There's no cover charge, but a half-liter mug of beer costs 3.10€. Main courses cost from 8€ to 12€, and service is Tuesday through Sunday from 7pm to 2:30am. Rudolfskai 27. ℂ 0662/849688. Bus: 5, 6, or 55.

Stiegelkeller   To reach this place, you'll have to negotiate a steep cobblestone street that drops off on one side to reveal a panoramic view of Salzburg. Part of the establishment is carved into the rocks of Mönchsberg mountain, so all that's visible from the outside is a gilded iron gate and a short stone stairway. The cavernous interior is open only in summer, when you can join hundreds of others in drinking beer and eating sausages, schnitzels, and other *Bierkeller* food.

   Sound of Music dinner shows, featuring music from the film, are presented May through September daily from 7:30 to 10pm. A three-course meal and show costs 40€. Or, you can arrive at 8:15pm to see the show and just have *Apfelstrudel* and coffee for 25€. On the first Sunday of the month, a *Fruhschoppen*—a traditional Salzburger music fest—is presented from 10:30pm to midnight. No ticket is necessary—you pay for what you eat and drink. Likewise, no ticket is necessary to attend another musical evening, a *Happing*, staged from May to September every Thursday from 6 to 8pm. Festungsgasse 10. ℂ 0662/84-26-81. Bus: 5, 6, or 55.

THE BEST BARS

Bar Saitensprung   This very hip bar spins the most recent music in a cave that's partially natural, partly dug by hand several centuries ago into the rock of the Kapuzinerberg. The bar serves a full menu of cocktails, including American-style martinis at 4.30€ each, and the even more popular roster of Austrian wine by the glass, priced at 4€. There's a limited food menu, in case you get hungry. Prosciutto with melon and cheese and paté platters are priced at around 7€ each. The crowd tends to be young, 20 to 25. It's open nightly from 9pm to at least 4am. Steingasse 11. ℂ 0662/881-377. Bus: 5, 6, or 55.

Chez Roland   Roland Kübler and his sister, Elizabeth Gessmer, have maintained this stylish, unusual cocktail bar since the mid-1970s. In the process, they've entertained some of the biggest names of the Salzburg festival and nurtured an arts-conscious crowd ranging from 25 to 75. The bar is set within an old salt storage cellar with a vaulted ceiling that allows natural illumination. You can always order a martini, but the large majority of drinkers here opt for glasses of Austrian wine. Priced at 2.90€ to 3.70€, they include many vintages of Styrian Chardonnays and Sauvignons. There's also Warsteiner beer selling for 2.20€ and a limited menu, priced at 3€ to 6.20€, that includes spaghetti carbonara and goulash soup. It's open daily from 7pm to at least 4am and usually later, depending on business. Giselakai 15. ℂ 0662/874-335. Bus: 1 or 51.

Maestro Bar   Everything about this place honors the memory of Salzburg's most important maestro, Herbert von Karajan, legendary conductor and promoter of the Salzburg Festival. Stylish, hip, and insider-ish, it's a cubbyhole-size bar that's entirely sheathed in slabs of Brazilian white onyx illuminated from behind with concealed lighting, all of which casts a flattering glow over whomever happens to be sipping beer or champagne at the time. In the cellar, beneath an 800-year-old ceiling vault that reeks of medieval spookiness, is an additional gathering spot for prearranged parties. Thomas Lochmann, son of the dentist of the late conductor, is the very hip owner. With his wife, he's likely to appear entirely in leather for a style-setting evening that's sure to attract a lot of musicians. It's open Monday through Saturday from 4pm to 1am. 1 Herbert von Karajan Platz. © 0662/840628. Bus: 1.

Shamrock Irish Pub   The crowds tend to be young, gregarious, sudsy, flirtatious, and sometimes rowdy, but if you're in the mood for such a thing, it can be a lot of fun. Set within an interconnected network of stone-vaulted cellars in the heart of the old town, it rocks and rolls with live music (Australian, Scottish, Irish, or Welsh) every night 9pm to 1am. Most folks come here just to drink: Tequila costs from 2.50€, and Austrian or Irish beers range from 2.25€ to 3.50€. But if you're hungry, you can order up to seven kinds of pizza for 5€ to 8€ or baguette sandwiches for 3.50€. Hours are daily from 3pm to between 2 and 4am, depending on the night of the week. The Judengasse entrance, incidentally, closes every night at 8:30pm. Rudolfskai 12 or Judengasse 1. © 0662/841-610. Bus: 5, 6, or 55.

2 Stein   Campy, friendly, and counterculture, this is the most recent newcomer to Salzburg's extremely limited gay nightlife scene. The bar lies within a not-very-large modern club setting, with a prominent bar and a clientele that knows just about every other openly gay person in and around Salzburg. On selected, widely preannounced evenings, a small stage area is devoted to drag acts, most of which begin around 10pm and for which there might be a cover charge of 8€. It's open daily from 6pm to 4am. Giselakai 9. No phone. Bus: 1 or 51.

A CASINO

Casino Salzburg Schloss Klessheim   The only year-round casino in Land Salzburg is a landmark to the gamblers who come here from hamlets throughout the province. It occupies the soaring Schloss Klessheim, a baroque palace designed by one of the most influential architects of Austria's baroque age, Fischer von Erlach, in 1745 for one of the archbishops of Salzburg.

The minimum bet is 5€ at both the roulette and blackjack tables. Monday night is poker night, and if you want to play, a staff member will organize groups of four from whomever happens to be interested. To enter the casino, you must present some form of identification, either a driver's license or a passport. There's also a dress code: Except during the hottest months of summer, men are encouraged to wear jackets and ties. The complex is open daily from 3pm to 3am.

On the premises is a stylish restaurant, charging 10€ to 15€ for a main course and 18€ to 30€ for a full meal. A bar overlooks the casino.

To get here, drive west along highway A1, exiting at the SCHLOSS KLESSHEIM exit, about a mile west of the center of Salzburg. The casino also runs red-sided shuttle buses that depart, without charge, from the rocky base of the Mönchsberg every hour on the half-hour daily from 2:30pm to midnight. A-5071 Walzsezenheim. © 0662/854-4550. Cover 21€; includes 25€ worth of casino chips.

9 Side Trips from Salzburg

The environs of Salzburg are incredibly scenic; to explore them fully, refer to chapter 8, "Land Salzburg." The area is a setting of old castles, charming villages, glacial lakes, salt mines, ice caves, and some of the most panoramic alpine scenery in Europe. But before going on to Land Salzburg, we'll describe a few attractions right on the city's doorstep.

A PALACE, ZOO & MUSEUM IN HELLBRUNN

Schloss Hellbrunn (Hellbrunn Palace) 🎯   A popular spot for outings from Salzburg, this palace dates from the early 17th century and was built as a hunting lodge and summer residence for Prince-Archbishop Markus Sittikus. The Hellbrunn Zoo, also here, was formerly the palace deer park. It's a 20-minute drive from Salzburg; turn off Alpenstrasse at the Mobil gas station.

The palace **gardens,** one of the oldest baroque formal gardens in all Europe, are known for their trick fountains. As you walk through, take care—you might be showered from a surprise source, such as a set of antlers, when you least expect it. Set to organ music, some 265 figures in a mechanical theater are set in motion hydraulically.

The rooms of the *Schloss* are furnished and decorated in 18th-century style. See, in particular, the banquet hall with its trompe l'oeil painting. There's also a domed octagonal room that was used as a music and reception hall.

On the grounds, a natural gorge forms the **Stone Theater,** where the first opera in the German-speaking world was presented in 1617. This attraction (signposted) is reached on foot, about a 20-minute walk from the castle. A Hellbrunn Festival is held in the gardens, palace, and theater in August.

Fürstenweg 37, Hellbrunn. © 0662/820-372. www.hellbrunn.at. Admission 7.50€ adults, 3.50€ children. July–Aug daily 9am–10pm; Sept–June daily 9am–5:30pm. Tours given July–Aug daily 6–10pm on the hour. Closed Nov–Mar. Bus: 55.

Salzburger Tiergarten Hellbrunn *(Kids)*   The beautiful landscape provides a wonderful setting for viewing the diverse animals of the Zoo Hellbrunn, located just south of Salzburg. Chamois, otter, white rhinoceros, and antelope share large outdoor enclosures. You can also see free-flying griffin vultures and cheetahs. There's a children's zoo as well.

Schloss Hellbrunn, Morzgerstrasse. © 0662/82-01-76. Admission 6.50€ adults, 4.70€ students, 3.30€ youths 4–14, free for children 3 and under. Oct–Mar daily 8:30am–5pm; Apr–Sept Mon–Thurs and Sun 8:30am–7:30pm, Fri–Sat 8:30am–10:30pm. Bus: 55.

Carolino Augusteum-Volkskundemuseum   Overlooking Hellbrunn Park, the Volkskunde Museum offers a folk collection assembled by Prince-Archbishop Markus Sittikus in 1615. The displays, spread over three floors, reflect a cross-section of local folk art and depict popular religious beliefs, folk medicine, and the traditional costumes of Land Salzburg.

Monatsschlösschen, Hellbrunn. © 0662/62-08-08-300. Admission 2.50€ adults, .70€ under age 20. Daily 9am–5pm. Closed Nov–Mar. Bus: 55.

HALLEIN & THE DÜRRNBERG SALT MINES

The second-largest town in Land Salzburg, Hallein, once a center for processing the salt from the mines of Dürrnberg, was a prize possession of the prince-archbishops of Salzburg. Today you pass through this interesting industrial town on the Salzach River on the way to the Dürrnberg mines. The **tourist office** at Unterer Markt 1, A-5400 Hallein (© **0662/889-87-330**), is open Monday through Friday from 9am to 6pm and Saturday from 10am to 1pm.

On the north side of the Hallein parish church are the former home and tomb of the man who composed the music for Mohr's Christmas carol, Franz-Xaver Gruber, a schoolteacher who died in 1863.

The **Dürrnberg salt mines** (Salzbergwerk Hallein) (© **06245/83511-0**) are the big draw. This popular attraction is easily visited on a day trip from Salzburg. On guided tours, visitors walk downhill from the ticket office to the mine entrance, and then board an electric mine train that goes deep into the caverns. From here, tourists go on foot through galleries, changing levels by sliding down polished wooden slides before exiting the mine on the train that brought them in. An underground museum traces the history of salt mining back to ancient times.

Hallein is connected to Salzburg, 16km (10 miles) away, by both train and bus. From here there's a cable railway to Dürrnberg, although many Germans and Austrians prefer to walk to the mines; the trip takes about an hour.

Tours last 1½ hours and are conducted April through October daily from 9am to 5pm and November through March daily from 11am to 3pm. Admission is 16€ for adults, 9.30€ for children 6 to 15, and 4€ for children 4 to 6. Children under 3 are not admitted. There's a modern road from Hallein directly to a large parking lot near the ticket office to the mines.

THE ICE CAVES OF EISRIESENWELT ★★

Some 48km (30 miles) south of Salzburg by train is the "World of the Ice Giants," the largest known **ice caves** in the world. The caves, opening at some 1,678m (5,500 ft.), stretch for about 42km (26 miles), although only a portion of that length is open to the public. Fantastic ice formations at the entrance extend for half a mile. Like an ice queen's kingdom, this underground wonderland is lined with amazing ice figures and frozen waterfalls. The climax of this chill underworld tour is the spectacular "Ice Palace."

Please keep in mind that a visit to this spelunking oddity is recommended only for those who are quite fit and hardy, and is not suggested for elderly travelers or small children. You'll be walking down narrow, slippery passages.

To reach the Eisriesenwelt, head for Werfen, a village that's the center for exploring the ice caves. The village is also home to Castle Hohenwerfen, founded in the 11th century and frequently reconstructed. It's one of the most important castles in Land Salzburg and is visible for miles around.

If you come by train from Salzburg, you can take a taxi-bus from Werfen's Hauptplatz (Main Square) along a mountain road that rises from 488m to 915m (1,600 ft.–3,000 ft.). After 6km (3½ miles), you'll see a parking lot. Unless you choose to climb (and some very fit visitors do), you'll have to take a cable car to the entrance of the caves. Even this involves a 15-minute walk along a shady path with alpine views from Werfen's parking lot to the cable car's lower station. The round-trip cable car ride costs 8.80€ for adults and 4.40€ for children.

Tours begin at a mountain outpost with its own cafe/restaurant, the Dr.-Friedrich-Oedl-Haus, 1,568m (5,141 ft.) above sea level. From here, you walk to the nearby entrance to the caves. Supervised tours take about 2 hours and cost 7.20€ for adults and 3.60€ for children. Tours are conducted May through October daily each hour on the half-hour from 8:30am to 4:30pm. This schedule is accelerated whenever demand justifies it, especially during July and August. For more information, call © **06468/5248.**

Allow about 5½ hours for the entire trip from Werfen and back. Dress warmly and wear shoes appropriate for hiking. Even if you don't want to go underground, we recommend making the drive up to the cave, as the scenery and views are gorgeous.

8

Land Salzburg

The geographic borders of this lofty province in the high Alps might appear to be the work of a mapmaker gone haywire, but actually they follow the dictates of nature over those of man. Craggy mountains, deep valleys, winding rivers, lakes, and rolling foothills, plus a little political expediency, all affected the cartographer's pen. Within this *Bundesland* (state or province) of some 7,154 sq. km (2,762 sq. miles) are some of the most beautiful waterfalls in Austria. The spectacular Krimml Falls are the highest in Europe.

Land Salzburg is an outdoor playground, perfect for those seeking Austria's clear alpine air and blue mountain lakes, the country made famous in *The Sound of Music*. You can begin by exploring the Salzkammergut lake country, a narrow corridor in Land Salzburg between Bavaria and Upper Austria. (Parts of it are covered in other chapters.) Many parts of Salzkammergut, which means "domain of the salt office," grew rich from mining salt—and also gold.

Although there are often Land Salzburg excursions leaving from Salzburg, we think it's much more fun and less expensive to do it on your own. Most people involved in tourist services speak English, and you can travel in relative security and comfort.

This is a land of summer and winter sports, with such celebrated spas as Badgastein and renowned ski resorts like Zell am See, Kaprun, Saalbach, and Hinterglemm. Relax at a lakeside resort, such as St. Gilgen, or stay at a mountain hotel where the air is crisp and the stars are clear.

Of course, Land Salzburg is a skier's paradise. The season begins about 10 days before Christmas and usually lasts until Easter or beyond, depending on snow conditions. Skiing on some of the lofty plateaus is possible year-round. Kaprun, Saalbach, and Zell am See are long-established *and* expensive resorts. However, in the true spirit of the Frommer's guides, we've sought less familiar and even undiscovered places—many known only to the Austrians and an occasional German tourist.

The terrain directly around Salzburg is flat, but most of Land Salzburg is mountainous. Always inquire about local weather conditions before embarking on a day's sightseeing, particularly if you're going to be traversing one of those lofty alpine highways. The highest mountain range in Austria, the Hohe Tauern, lies on the southern fringe of Land Salzburg. The Hohe Tauern national park encompasses one of the most beautiful areas of the eastern Alps and remains mainly undeveloped. The park's core is formed of mighty mountains, steep rock faces, glaciers, and glacial streams, one of which feeds the Krimml Falls. Mountain meadows, alpine pastures, and protective woods comprise the park's periphery. Other natural attractions are Liechtensteinklamm, south of St. Johann in Pongau, the most dramatic gorge in the eastern Alps; Gollinger Wasserfall (the Golling Waterfall), between the Valley of Kaprun and its powerful dams; and an ascent to the Kitzsteinhorn at 2,931m (9,612 ft.).

Land Salzburg

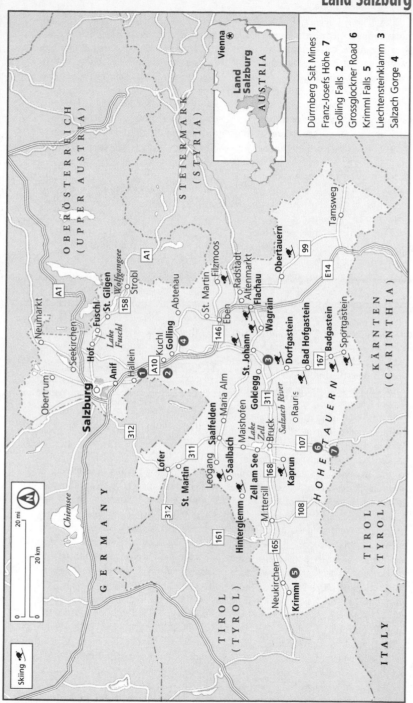

Dürrnberg Salt Mines **1**
Franz-Josefs Höhe **7**
Golling Falls **2**
Grossglockner Road **6**
Krimml Falls **5**
Liechtensteinklamm **3**
Salzach Gorge **4**

Skiing

20 mi
20 km

OBERÖSTERREICH
(UPPER AUSTRIA)

STEIERMARK
(STYRIA)

Vienna ✴
Land Salzburg
AUSTRIA

GERMANY

Chiemsee

Neumarkt
Obertrum
Seekirchen
Salzburg
Anif
Hallein
Hof
Fuschl
St. Gilgen
Lake Fuschl
Wolfgangsee
Strobl
Kuchl
Golling
Abtenau
St. Martin
Eben
Filzmoos
Radstadt
Altenmarkt
Flachau
Wagrain
St. Johann
Dorfgastein
Bad Hofgastein
Badgastein
Sportgastein
Obertauern
Maria Alm
Golcegg
Saalfelden
Maishofen
Bruck
Rauris
Salzach River
Leogang
Lake Zell
Zell am See
Kaprun
Saalbach
Hinterglemm
Mittersill
Neukirchen
Krimml
St. Martin
Lofer

HOHE TAUERN

KÄRNTEN
(CARINTHIA)

Tamsweg

TIROL
(TYROL)

TIROL
(TYROL)

ITALY

A1
A1
A10
158
146
312
311
311
167
168
165
161
312
312
107
108
99
E14

1 2 4 3
5 6 7

The Tauern Highway is one of the most important north-south roads over the Alps. Vehicles pass through two tunnels while traversing the highway. The Tauerntunnel is 6km (4 miles) long, and the Katschbergtunnel is 5km (3¼ miles) long. Because many of the alpine highways require extensive upkeep, tolls are charged, but they're not excessive. The Grossglockner Road, with hairpin turns and bends, is Europe's longest and prettiest alpine highway.

Unlike regions of Austria more devoted to serious skiing, Land Salzburg derives a good percentage of its income from midwinter vacationers who appreciate the region's accessibility from the major (snow-free) highways and rail routes of Austria. Prices in midsummer (Aug) tend to be roughly equivalent to prices in January and February, and cheaper in off-season months, such as June and October. (Resort hotels in Land Salzburg often close completely during the gray meltdown days of early spring and the rainy days of late autumn.)

Instead of staying in Salzburg, especially crowded during the Salzburg Festival months, reserve a room at a resort described below and commute to the province's capital city. You'll find the prices often lower and the atmosphere more laid back.

Accommodations are wide-ranging, from deluxe resorts to a mountain hut or just a *Zimmer* (room) in one of the local houses, usually perched in some idyllic spot. There are a few castle hotels in Land Salzburg to suit those who have traditional and romantic tastes and don't always demand the latest in plumbing fixtures.

Most hotels in the district automatically price your accommodation with half-board included. Although you can always request a bed-and-breakfast rate and take your meals elsewhere, the supplement for half-board usually represents a good value, sometimes allowing you to eat your main meal of the day for between 10€ and 18€ per person. You could try out the local restaurants at lunch. Hotels here almost always have the best restaurants anyway, so we suggest selecting a hotel dining room for dinner. Most hotels listed in this chapter are priced with half-board included in their rates. Parking is rarely a problem in these places, and, unless otherwise noted, you park for free.

Long cut off from the rest of the world but now accessible because of modern engineering achievements, some sections of Land Salzburg still cling tenaciously to their traditions. Old costumes and folklore still flourish in the province.

For information on Land Salzburg, contact the **Salzburg State Tourist Board,** P.O. Box 1, Wiener Bundesstrasse 23, A-5300 Hallwang (© **0662/6688-0;** fax 0662/6688-66; www.salzburgerland.com).

TIPS FOR ACTIVE TRAVELERS

The district of Land Salzburg seems like one vast outdoor playland—from skiing in winter to canoeing, fishing, golfing, hiking, and much more in summer.

CANOEING & RAFTING In summer, many visitors head for either the Salzkammergut or the Pinzgau, regions of Land Salzburg known for their beautiful lakes and roaring white-water streams. Lakes here are ideal for canoeing, rafting, or kayaking because the waters aren't polluted and the government limits powerboats, making the waters safer.

One of the best outfitters is **Club Zwilling,** Waldhof 64, Abtenau (© **06243/3069**), and well recommended is **Motion Center,** Andreas Voglastätter, Lofer (© **06588/7524**), located at the edge of Lake Sallachsee.

Other centers for watersports include **Sportschedule Saalachtal,** Almer Strasse 19, at Saalfelden (© **06582/74926**), at the edge of the

Ritzensee; and **Rafting Center Taxen-bach,** Höf 59 (℡ **06543/5352**), at the edge of the Salzach River. You can also call **Adventure Service,** Steinergrasse 9, in Zell am See (℡ **06542/73525**), a cheerful and well-managed outfit that offers guided excursions, with instruction, in rafting, white-water kayaking, sailing, and canoeing, as well as in paragliding, hiking, and mountain climbing.

CROSS-COUNTRY SKIING & DOWNHILL SKIING We've previewed in this chapter the most important ski resorts. For more options, contact one of the 120 local tourist offices for details on the dozens of ski schools in the province that provide instruction to novice and experienced skiers. For complete skiing data, write

or call the Salzburg State Tourist Board (see above).

FISHING You'll find some wonderful places to fish, but you'll need a license, which you can obtain at the local tourist office where you're staying. For more information about where to fish in the province, call the Salzburg State Tourist Board (see above).

GOLF If you'd like to play a round of alpine golf, you can get a complete listing of the provincial courses from the Salzburg State Tourist Board (see above).

HIKING This is a great place to hike. The Salzburg State Tourist Board (see above) stocks a very helpful brochure called "Walking and Trekking." It surveys the many trails in the province.

1 The Tennengau

The Tennengau, named for the Tennen massif, is a division of the Salzach Valley south of Salzburg, characterized by rolling hills and woodlands. Waterfalls dot the landscape—those outside the town of Golling are the most visited. Much of the Tennengau area, especially the houses with their gables and window boxes full of geraniums, will remind visitors of neighboring Bavaria.

As you leave Salzburg, going south on the left bank of the Salzach River, you'll pass through Anif, on the outskirts of Salzburg. You'll find some excellent old romantic accommodations in Anif (reviewed in chapter 7), if you'd like to stay near the provincial capital.

If you don't want to stay in the Tennengau region, you might consider it a day trip from Salzburg. Its chief sight is the Dürrnberg Salt Mines outside Hallein (see "Side Trips from Salzburg," in chapter 7). However, if you'd like to stay in the district, you'll find good accommodations in Golling.

GOLLING

Golling was first mentioned in historical sources as a farm hamlet in the 9th century. Today residents of this quietly stylish outlying burg tend to commute to work in Salzburg. Many visitors use Golling as a base for various outdoor activities in the nearby mountains.

GETTING THERE It's on the rail lines for local trains that head south to Villach and Klagenfurt in Carinthia. Trains depart from Salzburg for the 31km (19-mile) journey at 1- to 2-hour intervals; the trip takes 20 minutes. Railway officials refer to the village station as Golling-Abtenau. For rail information in Salzburg, call ℡ **0662/1717.**

Buses depart approximately every hour throughout the day from Salzburg's main railway station (with a subsequent stop at Mirabellplatz). The trip to Golling takes about 65 minutes. For information about buses from Salzburg to the outlying regions, call ℡ **06243/2229.**

VISITOR INFORMATION   For **tourist information,** go to Verkehrsverein, Am Marktplatz 51 (just follow the signs), in the center of town. The office (✆ **06244/4356**) is open in winter Monday through Friday from 8:15am to noon, and in summer Monday through Friday from 8:15am to noon and 1:30 to 6pm.

THE GOLLING WATERFALL 🐾🐾 & SALZACH GORGE

What draws visitors to Golling, 12km (7½ miles) south of Hallein via the A10, is the **Gollinger Wasserfall (Golling Waterfall).** It's 2km (1½ miles) west of the little resort along an unnumbered local road (look for signs saying GOLLINGER WASSERFALL), followed by a 20-minute walk from the parking lot to the falls. The waterfall—between Golling and Kuchl, 27km (17 miles) south of Salzburg—tumbles down more than 153m (500 ft.) over a rock wall.

You can also visit the **Salzach Gorge** near Golling. It's an hour's walk from Golling up to Pass Lueg. It lies 3km (2 miles) south of Golling and is accessible by following Highway B159. The entrance is not strictly regulated. You might arrive before the park attendants do (as local climbers are known to do). Admission is 2€ per person. In winter, snow and ice block access and the gorge is unsafe except for experienced rock and ice climbers. Visits to both the falls and the gorge are possible from May to October daily from 9am to 6pm; or if you're a bit adventurous, you can visit year-round at your own risk. It's best to go while attendants are on hand.

Heimatmuseum Burg Golling (✆ **06244/4356**) has a chapel and an interesting folklore collection. You'll see remains of cave bears, fossils, and copies of rock drawings, plus old pictures of the village. There's also a hunting room, exhibits of regional costumes, and a chamber of torture. It's open from June to mid-September Tuesday through Sunday from 10am to noon. Admission is 2€.

WHERE TO STAY & DINE

Goldener Stern   Built in the 12th century but given its present antique look in 1925, Goldener Stern sits amid a row of picture-book houses in the center of the village. Rustic yet modern furniture fills the interior. Rooms are cozy and comfortable, with spotless bathrooms equipped with shower-tub combinations. The hotel even has a sauna and a solarium.

Many of the region's gourmets frequent the in-house restaurant, the Döllerer, serving Austrian, French, and Italian food. Its specialties include dried alpine beef, sliced wafer-thin and served with pearl onions and pickles; beef Stroganoff; an Austrian version of the Italian saltimbocca (veal with ham); and a number of seafood dishes. A la carte menus cost 14€ to 30€. The distinguished wine list includes mainly Austrian and Italian vintages. The dining room is open Tuesday through Sunday from 8am to midnight; reservations are suggested. On the premises are a deli and a wine store.

Am Marktplatz 56, A-5440 Golling. ✆ **06244/42200.** Fax 06244/691242. www.doellerer.at. 20 units. 72€–135€ double. Half-board 13€ per person. Minimum 5-day stay. Rates include breakfast. DC, MC, V. **Amenities:** 2 restaurants, bar; sauna; solarium; room service; babysitting; laundry; dry cleaning service. *In room:* TV, minibar, hair dryer, safe.

2 The Pongau

Badgastein and Bad Hofgastein, covered in greater detail later in this chapter, are part of an area of Land Salzburg known as the Pongau—one of several sections of an alpine valley called Salzach. The Pinzgau section (also later in this chapter) of the Salzach Valley is to the southwest.

Visitors to the Pongau most frequently go through the **Gastein Valley,** of which Badgastein and Bad Hofgastein are a part. For many centuries, the Gastein Valley has been known for its hot springs, but since World War II it has also become a winter-sports center. As a consequence, many old spas such as Badgastein suddenly find themselves overrun with skiers in winter.

The **Radstädter Tauern** region is the second most popular section of the Pongau. It sprawls across five mountains and four valleys, with a mammoth expanse of terrain from St. Johann to Obertauern. In between, you'll find that Wagrain, Flachau, Altenmarkt, and Radstadt have many places to stay. It's helpful to have a car here, although most of Radstädter Tauern can be reached by lifts and runs.

DORFGASTEIN

This alpine village (839m/2,750 ft.) in the Gastein Valley is both a winter and a summer resort, its tranquil ambience attracting many who shun the more commercial Badgastein and Bad Hofgastein. Dorfgastein lies 53 miles (85km) south of Salzburg, 248 miles (399km) southwest of Vienna, and 5 miles (8km) north of Bad Hofgastein. It has an assortment of hotels and guesthouses, as well as an open-air swimming pool heated by solar energy. Note that this tiny hamlet doesn't use street addresses.

Dorfgastein is popular with Austrian families who, in winter, can park the small fry at a ski kindergarten and go off to enjoy the ski runs and slopes. In fact, the resort has many faithful regulars who resent its increasing popularity. The ski circus comprising Dorfgastein and Grossarl offers four chairlifts and 15 T-bar lifts to slopes of varying skill levels. There's also a natural toboggan run and a curling rink. A Gastein ski pass is valid for all cable cars and lifts in the Gastein Valley, and the ski bus is free.

GETTING THERE   Getting to Dorfgastein by train usually requires taking an express train from Salzburg to Schwarzach–St. Veit, 68km (42 miles) south of Salzburg, and transferring to a local train to Dorfgastein (trip time: 74–84 min.). For rail information in Salzburg, call ℂ **0662/1717.**

There's one daily bus that stops at Dorfgastein on its route between Salzburg's Mirabellplatz and its final destination in Badgastein.

If you're driving from Salzburg, take the A10 south to the junction with Route 311. Follow 311 southwest to the junction with Route 167 and take 167 south toward Badgastein.

VISITOR INFORMATION   Dorfgastein's **tourist office,** in the center of town (ℂ **06433/7277**), is open Monday through Friday from 9 to noon and 3 to 5pm.

SIGHTS IN & AROUND DORFGASTEIN

The village has a **Pfarrkirche (Parish Church)** "updated" in the baroque style but originally built in the 14th century.

You can take a bus from the heart of the village to the lower station of the chairlift; the trip takes less than an hour. The lift takes you to Wengeralm, and from here you can go by another lift to Kreuzkogel (2,040m/6,690 ft.).

Another popular attraction is in the stalactite cavern, **Entrische Kirche** (ℂ **0643/37695**), 77km (48 miles) from Salzburg. This cave was first recorded in 1428. It takes more than half an hour of walking from the town of Klamstein to reach these alternately water-bearing stalactite and dry caves. Total length is 3km (2 miles) on three levels. The caves are open from the end of April to October Tuesday through Sunday from 10am to 6pm. Conducted tours last 50 minutes. Admission is 7€ for adults and 4.50€ for children. The cave is signposted from the center of town.

WHERE TO STAY & DINE

Hotel/Restaurant Römerhof   Signposted at the approach to town, this chalet-style establishment has four floors of well-built wood and stucco. Constructed in 1966, it's run by the Hasenauer family, who maintain the comfortable accommodations. Bathrooms are small but well maintained and are equipped with shower-tub combinations. The interior is decorated with wood beams, wrought-iron embellishments, and rustic furniture.

Painted floral designs cover the exterior walls of the wood-paneled restaurant, which serves Austrian and Land Salzburg cuisine and, it is generally conceded, is the resort's finest. Fixed-price menus are 16€ to 27€, and a la carte meals cost 12€ to 20€.

A-5632 Dorfgastein. (℗ **06433/7209.** Fax 06433/7209-12. www.roemerhof.com. 45 units in Stadlergud annex. 70€–110€ double; from 110€ apts and suites. Rates include half-board. DC, MC, V. Closed for 3 weeks after Easter and Oct 20–Dec 1. **Amenities:** Restaurant, bar; pool; fitness center; Jacuzzi; sauna; room service; babysitting; laundry; dry cleaning. *In room:* TV, minibar, hair dryer, safe.

DORFGASTEIN AFTER DARK

When darkness falls on the slopes, weary skiers like to rest their legs and grab a drink. Nightlife is fairly restrained, taking place for the most part in hotel lounges and bars, many of which have open blazing fires.

The town's busiest and most interesting nightspot lies within the previously recommended Hotel Römerhof (℗ **06433/7209**), which shelters the **Pub im Turm (Tower Pub).** Originally built 900 years ago, it contains a busy bar area, and although no one ever really goes here to dance, it's still the resort's most active and boisterous bar. It's open in winter every day from 4pm to 1am, and from June 15 to September 15 Friday and Saturday only, from 8pm to 1am. Beer costs from 2.50€.

GOLDEGG

Goldegg lies on a small lake dominated by a 14th-century castle. This winter- and summer-sports resort is reached by going through Schwarzach–St. Veit at the western end of the Pongau. A nine-hole golf course is nearby.

Don't expect crystal-clear waters from the shallow lake, Goldeggersee, whose waters abut the town center: Years of percolating through the surrounding moors have infused the waters with organic matter, mostly peat, and transformed them into a greenish-brown brew, resembling weak tea. Locals claim that the waters are healthy and beneficial, but only one hotel, the Hotel Gesinger Zur Post (see below), pipes the water into its in-house spa. Incidentally, the brown color of the water absorbs sunlight faster than clear water, so in summer, the water actually becomes tepid.

GETTING THERE   Goldegg is 71km (44 miles) south of Salzburg and 389km (242 miles) southwest of Vienna. No rail lines go directly to Goldegg. Trains run from Salzburg to the nearby railway station at Schwarzach–St. Veit; call ℗ **0662/1717** in Salzburg for schedules. From here, buses make the 15-minute run at intervals of between 45 minutes and 2 hours throughout the day.

If you're driving from Salzburg, take the A10 south to the junction with Route 311. Continue west until you see the signposted turnoff to Goldegg. Then head northwest along an unmarked road.

VISITOR INFORMATION   Goldegg's **tourist information office** is at Hofmarkt (℗ **06415/81-31**), in the town center. It's open in winter Monday through Friday from 8:15am to noon, and in summer Monday through Friday from 8:15am to noon and 1:30 to 6pm.

THE OLD CASTLE OF GOLDEGG

Count Christoph of Schernberg bought the old castle of Goldegg in the 16th century and added the Rittersaal, a big hall now decorated with paintings of the Roman-German Empire, Renaissance ornaments, Christian images, and depictions of ancient myths. In 1973, the local municipality bought the building and began renovating it. The Count of Galen still lives in the village.

In the castle is the **Pongau Folk Museum,** Hofmarkt 1 (© **06415/81-31,** the number of the tourist office). It displays old tools used in the everyday lives of those who once lived here, as well as local sports equipment from the past 300 years. Guided tours are conducted in May, June, and September on Thursday and Sunday at 3 and 4pm; July and August Tuesday, Thursday, and Sunday at 3 and 4pm; and October through April Thursday at 2pm. Adults pay 3.50€, children 1€.

WHERE TO STAY & DINE

Hotel Gesinger Zur Post ✰   This lakeside hotel with a mountain view consists of two interconnected country-style buildings, both with flowered balconies and window boxes. The oldest part of the building was erected in 1890. The interior is outfitted with painted regional furniture, polished pine paneling, and homey details. The congenial hosts, Raimund and Hertha Gesinger, do everything they can to make guests comfortable. The cozy rooms are equipped with spacious private bathrooms with shower-tub combinations, and usually have enclosed sleeping compartments behind full-length curtains.

Under the rafters of what was a barn, the hotel has installed a pub complete with hanging lanterns and intimate corners. The Hotel Zur Post Restaurant serves Austrian and international cuisine. You might want to dine here even if you're not a guest of the hotel.

Hofmarkt 9, A-5622 Goldegg. © **06415/81-0-30.** Fax 06415/81-04-59. www.tiscover.at/hotelpost-goldegg. 38 units. 96€–172€ double; 146€–202€ suite. Rates include breakfast. Half-board 11€ per person extra. V. Free parking outside; 8€ in the garage. Closed Apr and Nov. **Amenities:** 3 restaurants; bar; pool; health spa; sauna; game room; room service; massage; babysitting; laundry; dry cleaning service. *In room:* TV, hair dryer, safe.

Hotel Seehof ✰   Hotel Seehof is filled with the kind of rustic artifacts and local painted furniture that many of us spend weeks looking for in antiques shops. This hotel dates from 1449 and sits on the lake, which reflects the chalet's forest-green shutters and the flowerpots on the hotel's balconies. An outdoor terrace sports sun umbrellas. In summer, guests can enjoy the private lakeside beach, and in winter the hotel rents ski equipment for the nearby slopes. Rooms are contemporary and warm, with good beds, modern private bathrooms with shower-tub combinations, and often private balconies and sloped, paneled ceilings.

The owner, Mr. Schellhorn, is director of the cross-country ski school of Goldegg, where you can find 58km (36 miles) of the best groomed cross-country ski trails in Land Salzburg. He's also the director of the resort's golf course and offers hotel residents discounts on greens fees.

Hofmarkt 8, A-5622 Goldegg. © **06415/8137.** Fax 06415/8276. seehof@salzburg.co.at. 30 units. 146€ double; 166€ suite. Rates include half-board. AE, DC, MC, V. Closed Apr and Nov. **Amenities:** Restaurant; bar; 18-hole golf course; sauna; room service; babysitting; laundry; dry cleaning. *In room:* TV, hair dryer, safe.

ST. JOHANN IM PONGAU

St. Johann im Pongau (there's a larger St. Johann in Tyrol) is 61km (38 miles) south of Salzburg on a sun-drenched terrace on the right bank of the river.

The winter-sports season here lasts December through April, and there are more than 52 lifts and cable cars in the tri-resort area, plus some 97km (60 miles)

The Most Spectacular Gorge in the Eastern Alps

Just 3km (2 miles) south of St. Johann in Pongau is the most spectacular gorge of the eastern Alps, the **Liechtensteinklamm** *⚘*, which attracts more visitors than any other such site. A path has been blasted through to the 1km-long (¾-mile) gorge, and during a 25-minute trek you can climb up the mammoth gorge with rock walls some 305m (1,000 ft.) high. At its tiny waist, the gorge is only 4m (12½ ft.) wide. A tunnel leads to the waterfall, with a drop of about 61m (200 ft.) at the gorge's end.

The wooden bridges and the footpath that runs along the bottom of the gorge were paid for by the prince of Liechtenstein, who supposedly lent his name to the site. In some areas the ravine is so narrow that the sky is barely visible from the bottom. Roaring waterfalls and swiftly flowing waters add to the site's allure.

To reach the Liechtensteinklamm, go a mile by road to Grossarl. The road to the gorge is marked. From here, count on about an hour by foot. The gorge can be visited from May 10 to the first Sunday in October daily from 8am to 5pm. Admission is 3€ for adults and 1.80€ for children 6 to 18.

of prepared runs. This well-known ski-lift network in the Salzburg mountains is called Drei-Taler-Skischaukel (Three-Valley Ski Swing).

If you're a nature lover, St. Johann is a good base for visiting the **Grossarilbach Valley** to the south of the town and the mouth of **Wagrainer Tal** to the north.

The town's twin-towered **Pfarrkirche (Parish Church)** was built in 1855, but a house of worship has stood on this site since A.D. 924.

GETTING THERE   St. Johann lies directly on the main rail line connecting Munich and Salzburg with Klagenfurt, Venice, and Trieste. Between 5:40am and 9pm, these trains depart from Salzburg's Hauptbahnhof no more than 2 hours apart (trip time: just under 1 hr.). If the delay between trains poses an inconvenience, consider taking one of the more frequent trains between Salzburg and the important railway junction of Schwarzach–St. Veit, and then backtrack, taking a taxi or bus the 5km (3 miles) to St. Johann. For rail information in Salzburg, call © **0662/1717.**

Unless you're coming in from one of the neighboring villages, arriving by bus in St. Johann isn't practical because of the multiple transfers required from such cities as Salzburg and Innsbruck.

If you're driving, head south from Salzburg on the A10; then cut southwest at the junction with Route 311.

VISITOR INFORMATION   St. Johann's **tourist office** is at Hauptstrasse 16 (© **06412/6036-0**). It's open in winter Monday through Friday from 8am to 6pm, Saturday from 9am to noon and 2 to 5pm, Sunday from 9am to noon; in summer Monday through Friday from 8am to 6pm, Saturday from 9am to noon.

WHERE TO STAY & DINE

Alpenland *⚘*   Set in the heart of the village, this is the largest hotel in St. Johann and one of the largest time-sharing resorts in Land Salzburg. Built in the

1980s and designed like a big interconnected series of alpine chalets, it contains an excellent set of facilities and comfortable accommodations that are among the best in town. Each is furnished with vaguely chalet-style decor, a bit functional but with excellent beds and good-size bathrooms equipped with shower-tub combinations. On the premises are two restaurants (Italian and Austrian), with an attentive and helpful staff. Throughout, you'll find burnished pine and regional accessories. Meals in the most formal of the restaurants begin at 24€, although many less expensive options are available on-site. The hotel rents bicycles to anyone interested in exploring the nearby region for 12€ per day.

Hans-Kappacher-Strasse 7, A-5600 St. Johann im Pongau. ℗ 06412/70210. Fax 06412/702151. www.alpen land.at. 144 units. 106€–175€ double; 247€–297€ suite. Half-board 16€ per person. AE, DC, MC, V. Garage parking 5.80€. **Amenities:** 2 restaurants; 2 bars; nightclub; lounge; pool; 2 tennis courts; fitness center; Jacuzzi; sauna; boutiques; room service; massage; babysitting; laundry; dry cleaning. *In room:* TV, minibar, hair dryer.

WAGRAIN

At 839m (2,750 ft.), Wagrain sits in a sunny valley amid green meadows and forests in summer and fine ski runs in winter. This tiny resort is in the three-valley ski network of Flachau–Wagrain–St. Johann. It's 71km (44 miles) south of Salzburg and 380km (236 miles) southwest of Vienna.

Wagrain is the hometown of poet Karl-Heinrich Waggerl, whose memory is honored in the **Wagrainer Heimatmuseumsverein,** Markt 14 (℗ **06413-8213**). The museum also has exhibits on the history of Wagrain. It's open from June 1 to June 30 and from September 1 to October 26 Tuesday, Thursday, and Friday from 2 to 6pm; from July 1 to August 31 Tuesday through Saturday from 2 to 6pm; from December 22 to April 4 Tuesday, Thursday, and Friday from 2 to 6pm; and from April 5 to May 30 Tuesday through Saturday from 2 to 6pm. It's closed from October 27 to December 21. Admission is 4€ for adults and 2€ for children.

From mid-December to mid-April, some 97km (60 miles) of groomed downhill runs are open, suitable for everybody from beginners to intermediates; they are served by three ski schools in the area. Three chairlifts, two cable cars, and 11 surface lifts are available. The top station is at 2,013m (6,600 ft.). You can get to the neighboring resorts of Flachau and St. Johann by cable car.

For nonskiers, Wagrain offers rambling trails, tobogganing, folk evenings, Austrian curling, and horse-drawn sleigh rides in winter. Summer visitors can use the cable cars for sightseeing, swim in a heated outdoor pool, or take advantage of the four tennis courts.

GETTING THERE   Trains run from Salzburg to the nearby railway station at St. Johann im Pongau. From here, buses depart at intervals of 1 to 2 hours for the 25-minute run up the valley to Wagrain. Alternately, you can reach Wagrain by taking the train from Salzburg to Radstadt, and then connecting at Radstadt's railway station with one of the five daily buses that make the 30-minute run into Wagrain. From St. Johann, drive 5 minutes east on Route 163 to Wagrain.

VISITOR INFORMATION   The **tourist information office** (℗ **06413/ 8265**) in the town center is open in winter Monday through Saturday from 8:30am to 6pm, Sunday from 10 am to noon and 2 to 5pm; in summer Monday through Friday from 8:30am to 5pm, Saturday from 10am to noon and 2 to 5pm.

WHERE TO STAY & DINE

Alpengasthof Kirchboden ✬   This chalet has cutout patterns on its three tiers of balconies, arched windows on its ground floor, and a flowered sun terrace dotted with umbrellas. Inside, a timbered mantelpiece caps a fieldstone fireplace.

The view encompasses most of the village of Wagrain. Rooms are furnished in a cozy alpine style; although not large, they contain excellent beds and ample bathrooms with shower-tub combinations. The adjoining restaurant is excellent. The well-prepared specialties tend to be regional (Palatschinken, Pariser schnitzel), along with good appetizers and a fine selection of cheeses and fresh fish. Meals begin at 12€.

Kirchboden 61, A-5602 Wagrain. ℂ 06413/8202. Fax 06413/8696. info@kirchboden.at. 49 units. 64€–140€ double. Rates include half-board. AE, MC, V. Closed Apr 15–June 15 and Sept 15–Dec 15. **Amenities:** Restaurant; lounge; Jacuzzi; sauna; laundry; dry cleaning. *In room:* TV, safe.

Gasthof Grafenwirt   Ivy covers the outside of this three-story villa, and the walled garden is a good place for a summer drink. The interior is designed with paneling, rustic artifacts, and brightly contrasting patterns. The smallish rooms have minimal decor but are comfortable nevertheless, with well-kept bathrooms equipped with shower-tub combinations. The in-house restaurant is one of the best in the region. Colorfully decorated with wrought iron and pretty chandeliers, it serves standard Austrian specialties such as beef goulash and Tyrolean-style liver. Set-price menus begin at 11€ in winter, and daily specials are offered for 8€ in summer.

Markt 92, A-5602 Wagrain. ℂ 06413/8230. Fax 06413/7162. www.grafenwirt.com. 15 units. 81€–139€ double. Rates include half-board. No credit cards. Closed June and Nov. **Amenities:** Restaurant; bar; room service; babysitting. *In room:* TV, hair dryer, safe.

FLACHAU

This third member of a group of resorts that also includes Wagrain and St. Johann im Pongau is just 8km (5 miles) southwest of Altenmarkt, in a lovely setting in the Enns Valley, on the A10 south from Salzburg. From the village, you can take a cable car to Griesskareck at 1,992m (6,530 ft.).

Flachau, previously known only to Europeans, is just beginning to attract more international skiers. Hence, the prices are fairly reasonable. The site has almost a mile of floodlit downhill runs, modern lift facilities that include the world's first six-seat bubble-encased chairlift, and buses that haul the easily bored from one ski area to another. Snowfall here is practically guaranteed, plus there are four ski schools, 161km (100 miles) of cross-country ski trails, toboggan runs, and ice-skating facilities

GETTING THERE   Take the train to either Radstadt or the village immediately adjacent to it, Altenmarkt. From the stations of either town, eight buses depart daily on the 11km (7-mile) drive southwest into Flachau.

WHERE TO STAY & DINE

Hotel Pongauerhof   This stucco-and-wood chalet is small and intimate. The cheerful, well-furnished rooms are more spacious than those in other local hotels. Housekeeping here is impeccable, and the beds are comfortable. Bathrooms, though small, are equipped with adequate shelf space and shower units. Local residents like the in-house restaurant. Snails are a specialty of the chef, who also prepares a full line of snacks, including pizzas and various salads. Full meals might include pork Wiener schnitzel and marinated roast pork. Full meals cost 11€ to 17€. A wide variety of Austrian beer is on tap as well.

Flachauerstrasse 138, A-5542 Flachau. ℂ 06457/2242. Fax 06457/224225. www.pongauerhof.at. 36 units. Winter 68€ per person; summer 46€ per person. Rates include half-board. No credit cards. Closed Apr 15–May 15 and Nov 1–Dec 10. **Amenities:** Restaurant; bar; room service; pool; sauna; laundry; dry cleaning. *In room:* TV, hair dryer, safe.

Tauernhof Hotel & Appartements ☝ The finest hotel in this mountain resort area, Tauernhof is a government-rated four-star base camp for those who come to Austria for sports and the outdoors. Run by the Schmid-Harml family, this unique hotel has its own mountain biking guide service. Free use of a bike comes with your room. In winter, the hotel is situated near some of the region's finest skiing and snowboarding. The all-inclusive hotel will even arrange for a host of other outdoor activities, from paragliding to rafting. Rooms are well furnished in a rustic decor. The beds are comfortable, and the medium-size bathrooms have well-kept shower units. Both the buffet breakfast and the four-course dinner included in the double rates are excellent. The well-decorated apartments include use of a kitchen.

Flachauerstrasse 163, A-5542 Flachau. ℂ **06457/23110.** Fax 06457/231182. www.tauernhof.at. 70 units. Winter 80€–100€ double, 105€–125€ apt; summer 62€–85€ double, 85€–98€ apt. Rates include half-board. MC, V. Closed Oct 26–Nov 1. **Amenities:** Dining room; bar; pool; 2 tennis courts; fitness center; sauna; solarium; game room; laundry; dry cleaning. *In room:* TV, minibar, hair dryer, safe.

OBERTAUERN

An unspoiled winter and summer resort at 1,809m (5,930 ft.), Obertauern lies at the top of an old Roman road dividing Land Salzburg from Carinthia (see chapter 12), about 97km (60 miles) southeast of Salzburg. A car isn't really necessary here, as you can easily get around on skis in winter and on foot in summer.

One of the newest ski resorts in Land Salzburg, Obertauern has become an international sports center, with ski lifts and a cable car. The ski school has state-qualified instructors, and there are children's ski courses, plus a ski kindergarten.

The high elevation ensures that the snow is good and the season is long. You can ski November through May at this "snow-proof" resort. You can ski all around the village, but it's easier on one side and steeper on the other.

GETTING THERE   Most visitors take the train from Salzburg or Innsbruck to Radstadt, and then transfer to one of the seven daily buses that depart from Radstadt's railway station for the 40-minute overland trek to Obertauern. The bus from Radstadt traverses a mountainous route, originally developed by the ancient Romans, that eventually terminates near the railway station at the remote town of Tamsweg (Carinthia) to the south.

If you're driving from Salzburg, head south on the A10 to Radstadt; then cut southeast along Route 99 to Obertauern.

WHERE TO STAY & DINE

Hotel Kohlmayr ☝ As you approach this well-run government-rated four-star hotel built in 1965, it appears to be a pleasantly situated chalet with stucco walls and several rows of wooden balconies with matching shutters. You'll soon realize, however, that the entire construction rests on top of a glass-walled foundation with a view of the mountains. The rest of the hotel is tastefully filled with bric-a-brac. The spacious, sunny rooms look out over the Alps, and can sometimes be divided into two sections by a full-length curtain (which you can close if you plan to sleep late). The hotel is rightly proud of its good beds and ample bathrooms with shower-tub combinations.

Kressestrasse 102, A-5562 Obertauern. ℂ **06456/7272.** Fax 06456/7406. www.hotel-kohlmayr.at. 60 units. Winter 75€–110€ per person; summer 55€–82€ per person. Rates include half-board. AE, DC, MC, V. Closed May and Nov. **Amenities:** Restaurant; bar; pool; exercise room; sauna; room service; laundry; dry cleaning. *In room:* TV, minibar, hair dryer, safe.

3 Bad Hofgastein ⟨⋆

88km (55 miles) S of Salzburg; 8km (5 miles) NW of Badgastein; 42km (26 miles) SE of Zell am See

The old, established spa of **Bad Hofgastein** (869m/2,850 ft.) has long been a rival of Badgastein for the tourist euro. It's smaller than Badgastein but almost as charming. The little resort is actually almost a satellite of the larger spa, as the radioactive waters of Badgastein are pumped to its neighbor. Some hardy visitors like to follow a marked footpath on the 2½-hour walk between the two towns. The two resorts welcome almost as many visitors as Salzburg.

ESSENTIALS

GETTING THERE   Bad Hofgastein is a major stop on the main rail lines connecting Munich and Salzburg with Klagenfurt and Venice. Most efficient are the express trains from Salzburg, which depart about once an hour throughout the day (trip time: 1¼ hr.). Night trains might require a transfer at Schwarzach–St. Veit, 68km (42 miles) south of Salzburg. Dozens of trains traveling from Innsbruck also stop in Schwarzach–St. Veit. Call 🕿 **06432/71100** for more information.

One daily bus runs in both directions between Salzburg's Mirabellplatz and the railway station in Bad Hofgastein. (This bus continues on to Badgastein.)

If you're driving, take the A10 south of Salzburg, cut right onto Route 311, and continue west to the junction with Route 167, where you head south to Badgastein.

VISITOR INFORMATION   The **tourist information office** in the town center (🕿 **06432/71100**) is open Monday through Saturday from 8am to 6pm.

SPA FACILITIES

The thermally heated waters of Bad Hofgastein originate in the same high-altitude springs that feed the spa facilities of Badgastein, 8km (5 miles) away. Bad Hofgastein is a newer resort than Badgastein, and a bit more upscale and glamorous as well. The waters are rich in radon, a controversial element that doctors once dismissed as harmful but now say is beneficial in small doses of no more than 20 minutes of immersion per day.

There are no public facilities here as in Badgastein; instead, three local hotels have built full spa facilities on their premises. You won't have to move between buildings for treatments, a bonus during cold or snowy weather.

The most complete Bad Hofgastein spa lies within the Grand Park Hotel (see below). The spa treatments are great for the foot-sore (and leg, and back, and more) traveler. You can get all types of massages, electrotherapy, aromatherapy, saunas, steam baths, and mud packs, or take part in aerobic classes or gymnastics. Less scientific "cures" include lying prone on plastic bags filled with dried flowers, or being partially buried in tubs of wet straw that have been soaked in the hot thermal waters.

SEEING THE SIGHTS

The **Pfarrkirche (Parish Church)** of this tiny village is late Gothic, dating from the late 15th century, although it has a baroque altar. Some sights, such as old houses with turrets, are reminders of the gold-mining days of the Gastein Valley. In the 16th century, the nearby gold mines made Bad Hofgastein rival even Salzburg in wealth. A rich mining family lived at the 15th-century Weitmoserchlössl, which has now been turned into a cafe.

The Gastein Valley and Bad Hofgastein are attracting more and more winter-sports fans. Some 50 gondolas and ski lifts provide access to more than 241km (150 miles) of well-marked and well-groomed ski runs. Thanks to the high capacity of an updated funicular, a mono-cable rotation gondola lift with cabins for six passengers, two quadruple chairlifts, and a triple chairlift, skiers don't have to wait in long lines. The Dorfgastein–Grossarl connection and the lift network from Schlossalm via the Angertal and Jungeralm ski center up to the Stubnerkogel (the largest lift interconnection in Land Salzburg) provide some of the most enjoyable ski runs in the valley.

Also available are cross-country skiing on well-maintained tracks, tobogganing, skating, and riding in horse-drawn sleighs.

WHERE TO STAY & DINE
VERY EXPENSIVE

Grand Park Hotel ★★ Originally constructed in the 1920s, this government-rated five-star hotel was completely rebuilt in the early 1990s and reopened in 1994 under a new administration. It's a majestic, classically styled building set in its own birch-filled park, with a swimming pool and lawn chairs on the grassy lawns around it. The elegant interior is filled with stone and polished wood, plush carpets, and shining brass. Rooms are handsomely furnished and beautifully maintained, with excellent beds and ample bathrooms with shower-tub combinations.

The hotel restaurant, open to nonguests, is one of the area's finest, serving Austrian and international cuisine. A pianist entertains every evening.

Kurgartenstrasse 26, A-5630 Bad Hofgastein. © 06432/63560. Fax 06432/8454. www.grandparkhotel.at. 89 units. Winter 185€–308€ double, 318€–452€ suite; summer 181€–212€ double, 312€–342€ suite. Rates include half-board. MC, V. **Amenities:** Restaurant; bar; pool; fitness center; health spa; Jacuzzi; sauna; room service; massage; babysitting; laundry; dry cleaning service. *In room:* TV, minibar, hair dryer, safe.

EXPENSIVE

Kurhotel Palace ★ Situated in a quiet, sunny spot, this first-class hotel is a few minutes' walk from the resort center. This is a surprisingly snug and cozy retreat in spite of its large size. The well-furnished rooms all have radios and balconies. Beds are about the finest in the resort, so comfortable that you might not want to get out of them; bathrooms are generous in size and well maintained, and each has a shower-tub combination. There's an elevator.

A daily program of entertainment and activities includes fashion shows, a lively nightclub, a Vienna coffeehouse, and bars. The Salzburger Stuberl serves Austrian, international, and vegetarian cuisine, and the Wiener Café offers homemade cakes and tarts.

Alexander-Moser-Allee 13, A-5630 Bad Hofgastein. © 06432/67150. Fax 06432/6715-567. www.kurhotel palace.at. 90 units. Winter 182€ double; summer 170€ double. Rates include half-board. AE, DC, MC, V. Closed Oct 25–Dec 15. **Amenities:** Restaurant; 2 bars; nightclub; cafe; pool; 4 tennis courts; fitness center; spa treatment; sauna; solarium; salon; room service; babysitting; laundry; dry cleaning service. *In room:* TV, radio, minibar, hair dryer, safe.

Hotel Sendlhof ★ The six floors here are surrounded by balconies and potted flowers, and an outdoor heated swimming pool lies across the lawn. The interior has large windows, cozy fireplaces, and extra touches such as ceramic stoves. Management sometimes provides live zither music in the evening. The elegant, cozy rooms have exposed wood, and most have private balconies. Bathrooms, although neatly kept with shower-tub combinations, might be a bit cramped.

Pyrkerstrasse 34, A-5630 Bad Hofgastein. © 06432/63-51-0. Fax 06432/635160. 60 units. Winter 130€–175€ double; summer 125€–150€ double. Rates include half-board. No credit cards. Parking 4.50€.

Closed Apr–May 15 and Oct 15–Dec 18. **Amenities:** Restaurant; bar; pool; fitness center; sauna; room service; babysitting; laundry; dry cleaning service. *In room:* TV, hair dryer, safe.

Hotel St. Georg ✿   An elegant country-house atmosphere prevails at this hotel offering attractive and well-furnished rooms and family suites designed for discerning guests. The manager and hotel staff make sure rooms are well maintained with medium-size bathrooms, equipped with shower-tub combinations. Half-board includes a buffet breakfast and a four-course dinner. Tempting Austrian cuisine is served in the country-style restaurant, and special diets can be accommodated. Although it's not as well known as the previously recommended hotel, it has its devotees.

Dr.-Zimmermann-Strasse 7, A-5630 Bad Hofgastein. ✆ 06432/6100-0. Fax 06432/610061. www.stgeorg.com. 50 units. Winter 200€ double, 231€ suite for 2; summer 154€ double, 188€ suite for 2. Rates include half-board. MC, V. Parking 3€. Closed Nov 10–Dec 19. **Amenities:** Restaurant; bar; pool; fitness center; sauna; solarium; room service; massage; babysitting; laundry; dry cleaning service. *In room:* TV, hair dryer, safe.

MODERATE
Kurhotel Germania ✿   Beautiful Victorian antiques (including an exquisite collection of armchairs) fill some of the big-windowed public areas of this four-star hotel, which dates from around 1900. If your guest room has a balcony—and many of the pleasant and sunny rooms do—you'll have a view of the houses and barns of the valley below. Traditional alpine furnishings are somewhat functional but retain a bit of charm. Rooms have small bathrooms with shower-tub combinations.

Kurpromenade 4, A-5630 Bad Hofgastein. ✆ 06432/6232. Fax 06432/623265. www.gasteinertal.com/germania. 70 units. Winter 74€–105€ per person double, 103€ per person suite; summer 64€–86€ per person double, 86€ per person suite. Rates include half-board. MC, V. Parking 10€. Closed Nov–Dec 16 and Apr 16–May 13. **Amenities:** Restaurant; lounge; pool; fitness center; health spa; sauna; room service; laundry; dry cleaning. *In room:* TV.

Kur-Sport-Hotel Astoria ✿   This government-rated four-star hotel, built in the 1950s, is a generously proportioned five-story building with a simple wood-balconied facade. The interior has been renovated in a contemporary design of streamlined furniture and warm, inviting colors. Rooms are only standard in size, but each is quite comfortable, with good beds and small bathrooms with shower-tub combinations. Austrian regional specialties are served, and a country buffet is offered once a week.

Salzburger Strasse 24, A-5630 Bad Hofgastein. ✆ 06432/62770. Fax 06432/627777. www.kur-sporthotel-astoria.com. 73 units. Winter 85€–130€ per person; summer 60€–80€ per person. Rates include half-board. AE, DC, MC, V. Closed Oct 10–Dec 20. **Amenities:** Restaurant; bar; pool; fitness center; spa treatments; sauna; room service; babysitting; laundry; dry cleaning. *In room:* TV, minibar, hair dryer, safe.

INEXPENSIVE
Hotel Carinthia ✿   This large, solid-looking chalet has flower-filled balconies on all sides. The interior has elegant and unusual touches, such as the tucked-away corner bar and modern chandeliers in the high-ceilinged dining room. The spacious rooms have a contemporary decor; each is well equipped with excellent beds and a medium-size bathroom with a shower-tub combination.

Dr. Zimmermann-Strasse 2, A-5630 Bad Hofgastein. ✆ 06432/83740. Fax 06432/837475. www.hotel-carinthia.com. 35 units. Winter 116€–176€ double; summer 110€–124€ double. Rates include half-board. No credit cards. Closed Easter–May 10 and Oct 20–Dec 20. **Amenities:** Dining room; bar; pool; fitness center; sauna; babysitting; laundry; dry cleaning. *In room:* TV, minibar, hair dryer, safe.

Kur- und Sporthotel Moser ✿ *Value*   On the main town square, this hotel has sections dating from the 12th century. You'd never know it from the facade, which is pleasantly balconied above the street-level awnings. The interior, however, is vaulted and cozy, with old exposed wood, heavy beams, and oriental rugs. The furnishings are rustic and regional, with homey touches such as racks of pewter in the dining room. When the weather is good, the rooms are often flooded with sunlight. Although the hotel might date from the Middle Ages, the emphasis is on comfort, as reflected by the traditional furniture and duvet-covered beds. Bathrooms are just adequate for the job, but each comes with a shower-tub combination. There's an intimate lounge and terrace dining, as well as a cozy cellar for dining and dancing in winter.

Kaiser-Franz-Platz 2, A-5630 Bad Hofgastein. (€ 06432/6209. Fax 06432/620988. www.gourmethotel-moser. com. 54 units. 60€–76€ per person. Rates include half-board. DC. Closed Apr and Nov 1–Dec 15. **Amenities:** Restaurant; bar; fitness center; sauna; room service; massage; babysitting. *In room:* TV, hair dryer, safe.

Kurhotel Völserhof   Built in the 1960s, this hotel rises five balconied stories above a flowering garden near the edge of town. In summer, masses of red flowers bloom above the windows of the second-floor restaurant. Rooms are rather small and don't have much charm, but each is comfortably equipped with good beds. The adjoining bathrooms with shower-tub combinations are also small but spotless. The city's recreation center is within a 5-minute walk, and the terminus of the funicular is 10 minutes away. The Lang family, your host, is very helpful in providing information about the area. One of the best times to book here is during the last 3 weeks of January, when rates are even lower than they are in the discounted summer season.

Pyrkerstrasse 28, A-5630 Bad Hofgastein. (€ 06432/8288. Fax 06432/828810. www.voelserhof.com. 30 units. Winter 140€–154€ double; summer 100€–116€ double. Rates include half-board. No credit cards. Closed Apr and Sept 13–Dec 15. **Amenities:** Dining room; bar; sauna; babysitting; laundry; dry cleaning. *In room:* TV, minibar, hair dryer.

BAD HOFGASTEIN AFTER DARK

For your big night on the town, take a taxi from Bad Hofgastein to Badgastein to gamble at the casino (see below). In Bad Hofgastein itself, you can go clubbing, sit in a tavern beside an open fire, or dance to the music of a live band at one of the hotels in the winter season. The tourist office will give you the latest information on which hotels or clubs are likely to have nightlife at any given time.

One of Bad Hofgastein's busiest nightspots is the **Norica Bar,** just off the lobby of the Hotel Norica, Kaiser-Franz-Platz 3 ((€ **06432/8391**). Open every day from 3pm, it offers some kind of music act, from evergreen oompah to rock 'n' roll, in both winter and summer. There's no cover charge, and beer costs 3€ to 4€. Closing time varies, depending on business.

4 Badgastein ★★: Austria's Premier Spa

100km (62 miles) S of Salzburg; 410km (255 miles) SW of Vienna

Badgastein is not only Austria's premier spa, but it's also one of the great spa towns of Europe. The local tourist industry began when Frederick, Duke of Styria, came here in the 15th century for treatment of a gangrenous wound. The duke was healed, and word spread. Badgastein had made its way onto the medieval tourist map. Royalty and aristocrats flocked here around the turn of the 19th century to "take the waters." And good waters they are—radioactive springs with healing properties.

Badgastein lies on the north slope of the Tauern massif in one of the most scenic spots in Austria. The spa town is spread across steep hillsides split by the waters of the tumbling Gasteiner Ache. Hotels, many with water piped in directly from the Ache, adorn the steep slopes formed by the cascading waterfall. The spa's indoor swimming pool is carved into a rock filled with the radon waters.

Although Badgastein was first a summer retreat, it's now also a center for winter sports. With its pristine alpine air, skiing equal to that of St. Moritz in Switzerland, the finest hotels in Land Salzburg, 18 hot springs for thermal hydrotherapy, and a mountain tunnel that has been called "the world's only natural giant sauna," Badgastein is the pinnacle of mountain spa resorts.

ESSENTIALS

GETTING THERE   Badgastein is a major stop on the main rail line connecting Munich and Salzburg with Klagenfurt and Venice. Express trains from Salzburg depart every hour throughout the day (trip time: 1½ hr.). Certain trains, especially night trains from Salzburg, might require a transfer in the railway junction of Schwarzach–St. Veit, 68km (42 miles) south of Salzburg. Dozens of trains traveling from Innsbruck also stop in Schwarzach–St. Veit. Call ℂ **0662/1717** in Salzburg for schedules.

One daily bus makes a 2-hour run in both directions between Salzburg's Mirabellplatz and the railway station in Badgastein. Buses from Badgastein make frequent runs into the surrounding villages.

If you're driving, take the A10 south of Salzburg and cut west at the junction with Route 311. At the junction with Route 167, head south.

VISITOR INFORMATION   The **tourist office** (ℂ **06434/25-3-10**) in the center of town is open year-round Monday through Friday from 8am to 6pm, Saturday from 10am to 6pm. In winter, it's also open Sunday from 10am to 6pm.

WHAT TO SEE & DO

Along with the natural scenery of the town and the surrounding area, you can see the **Nikolauskirche,** a 15th-century church with well-preserved Gothic frescoes, a late-Gothic stone pulpit, and baroque altars and tombs.

In summer, besides swimming in thermal baths, the spa offers a host of saunas, massages, and solariums. There's also an 18-hole course, tennis courts, horseback riding, hiking, and a variety of excursions, perhaps in a *Fiaker* (horse-drawn carriage). Cable cars and chairlifts (see below) are not only for winter-sports crowds; in summer, take one up to the top and get a panoramic view of the Hohe Tauern.

In winter, most visitors are drawn to this region for the great skiing. In 1958, Graukogel, one of the main ski areas, was the site of the world championships.

NEARBY ATTRACTIONS

One of the region's most quirky attractions is the **Gasteiner Heilsollen,** A-5645 Bergstein (ℂ **06434/3753**), a labyrinth of underground tunnels carved out of the **Böckstein** during the 18th and 19th centuries as a gold mine. It has been transformed into a small-scale health spa, where tiny cars carrying six patients are shuttled through the tunnels on a narrow-gauge railway. The 15-minute trip through the heated and mildly radioactive air (local doctors claim the effects are dispersed from the body within an hour) is cited as a cure for arthritis.

Between mid-January and October, you can ride through the tunnels Monday through Saturday from 8am to 4pm for 50.50€. The tunnels are 3km (2 miles) from Badgastein. Follow the signs from Bergsteinerstrasse, or take one of the hourly blue-and-gray Lackner buses.

Graukogel (2,508m/8,224 ft.), to the east of the valley, is reached by bus from Badgastein. Expert European skiers crowd these slopes in the afternoon.

A chairlift takes skiers to the halfway station, and a double chairlift or surface lift takes them to the top. A round-trip ticket costs 13.50€ to 32€, depending on the season. A mountain restaurant stands at the halfway station. This is also a favorite starting point for alpine walking tours. Call © 06434/2322 for ticket information. Service is daily from 9am to 4pm.

On the west side of the valley rises **Stubnerkogel** (2,230m/7,310 ft.). A six-seat gondola takes you most of the way; however, it takes a chairlift and a couple of surface lifts to reach the top. There's also a mountain restaurant with a panoramic view. The gondola and the chairlift (© 06434/2322) are in service from late May to mid-October daily from 8:30am to 4pm; a round-trip ticket costs 13.50€ to 32€.

Kreuzkogel (2,684m/8,800 ft.) is at **Sportgastein,** 8km (5 miles) up the valley to the south of the village of Böckstein, site of the tunnel sauna mentioned above. This is a great place to come for high-altitude bowl skiing. It's about a 20-minute bus ride from Badgastein. A chairlift will take you to the halfway station, with a surface lift pulling you to Kreuzkogel's top station. Besides the well-equipped skiing facilities here, including cross-country trails, you can enjoy hiking, indoor horseback riding, indoor tennis, curling, and ice-skating.

You can drive from Badgastein to Sportgastein along Gasteiner Alpenstrasse at elevations ranging from 900m to 1,454m (3,000 ft.–4,766 ft.). The toll charge is 3€ per person; it's free for children 4 and under. In winter, the ski-season ticket includes the road toll.

WHERE TO STAY & DINE

Hotels are signposted at the approach to town.

EXPENSIVE

Arcotel Elisabethpark ✹✹   This is Badgastein's premier address. The four-star hotel has a ceiling covered with heavily textured knotty pine and rooms crowned with Moorish patterns of geometric greens and reds. The public areas stretch on and on—not surprising, since the hotel is a vast, sprawling collection of buildings with a white exterior, many balconies, and a series of hallways that are decorated with unusual paintings, hunting trophies, and regional antiques. Available in a wide variety of sizes, the rooms are traditionally furnished, often with antiques. Each is equipped with a larger than average bathroom, with a shower-tub combination. The hotel restaurant is one of the best at the spa, offering both Austrian and international dishes.

Franz-Josef-Strasse 5, A-5640 Badgastein. © 06434/25-5-10. Fax 06434/2551-10. www.arcotel.at. 120 units. 98€–310€ double; 262€–420€ suite. Rates include half-board. AE, DC, MC, V. Parking 10.50€. **Amenities:** Restaurant; bar; pool; fitness center; sauna; room service; massage; babysitting; laundry; dry cleaning service. *In room:* TV, minibar, hair dryer.

Hotel Grüner-Baum ✹✹   This hotel is a complex of five chalets surrounding a grassy area in the Kötschach Valley on the outskirts of Badgastein. During its long history, the establishment has offered hospitality to Kaiser Wilhelm, the shah of Iran, conductor Arturo Toscanini, and actor Charles Laughton. The oldest parts of the building are exquisitely crafted of local woods, sometimes with elaborate regional carvings, and decorated with hunting trophies beneath the beamed ceilings. Rooms are cozy and rustic, with wood paneling and a recessed sleeping alcove in some of the singles. The beds and mattresses ensure a good night's sleep. Bathrooms are more than ample, with shower-tub combinations and enough room to spread out your stuff.

Organized weekly activities and a bar with dancing provide the entertainment. The hotel's restaurants, Gunghoferstüberl, Rösslstube, and Hochzeitsstube, are open from 6pm to midnight in winter and from 6 to 11pm in summer, serving excellently prepared Austrian and international specialties. There's also a garden restaurant in summer.

Kötschachtalstrasse 25, A-5640 Badgastein. ℂ **06434/2516-0.** Fax 06434/251625. www.grunerbaum.com. 100 units. Winter 110€–140€ per person double; 114€–160€ per person suite. Summer 126€–144€ per person double; from 140€ per person suite. Rates include half-board. AE, DC, MC, V. Parking 8€. Closed Oct 26–Dec 6. **Amenities:** 3 restaurants; bar; lounge; 2 pools; 2 tennis courts; bowling alley; fitness center; sauna; room service; massage; babysitting; laundry; dry cleaning. *In room:* TV, hair dryer.

Hotel Weismayr ☆   Situated prominently in the town center between the congress hall and the casino, the Hotel Weismayr has been one of the leading hotels in the Gastein Valley since 1832. Surrounded by the soaring Alps, the hotel makes an ideal starting point for outdoor activities in the valley: golfing, horseback riding, skiing, swimming, hiking, climbing, and relaxing, to name just a few. At this cozy abode, rooms are well furnished with especially good beds. Adjoining bathrooms are medium in size, each with a shower-tub combination. Parasols and plants dot the terrace cafe, and the elegant, high-ceilinged dining room is beautifully decorated. Austrian and international dishes are prepared with the freshest ingredients.

Franz-Josef-Strasse 2, A-5640 Badgastein. ℂ **06434/2594.** Fax 06434/2594-14. www.weismayr.com. 89 units. Winter 188€–256€ double; 204€–276€ suite for 2. Winter rates include half-board. Summer 101€–108€ double; 108€–120€ suite for 2. Summer rates include buffet breakfast. AE, DC, MC, V. Parking 10.20€. Closed Oct 15–Dec 15. **Amenities:** Restaurant; bar; cafe; pool; fitness center; sauna; beauty treatments; room service; massage; babysitting; laundry; dry cleaning service. *In room:* TV, minibar, hair dryer, safe.

MODERATE

Hotel and Spa Haus Hirt ☆   Originally built in 1930 and completely renovated in 1997, this hotel retains touches of folkloric and old-fashioned charm that some newer hotels have a hard time matching. It's a 20-minute walk downhill from the center of town. All rooms have comfortable furnishings and neatly maintained bathrooms with shower-tub combinations. There's a bar, sweeping views over the Gastein Valley, and a sense of family-run thrift and virtue, thanks to the on-site presence of the owners. The hotel's cozily paneled dining room serves Austrian specialties that taste particularly good after a day in the great outdoors. There's even a sunny, wind-sheltered terrace that attracts many sunbathers.

An der Kaiserpromenade, A-5640 Badgastein. ℂ **06434/2797.** Fax 06434/2787-48. www.haus-hirt.com. 30 units. Summer 79€–176€ double; winter 90€–198€ double. Rates include breakfast. MC, V. Closed mid-Oct to Nov and mid-Apr to May. **Amenities:** Restaurant; bar; pool; fitness center; sauna; room service; massage; babysitting; laundry; dry cleaning. *In room:* TV, minibar, hair dryer, safe.

Hotel Wildbad *Value*   With its dark-yellow facade, big windows, and prominent balconies, Hotel Wildbad, in the center of the village near the indoor thermal pools and the ski lifts, stands out from the buildings around it. The medium-size rooms have much comfort. Most offer panoramic valley views; some have a sitting area. Bathrooms are a bit small but beautifully maintained and equipped mostly with shower-tub combinations. There's also a terrace sun deck with chaise longues and cafe tables. Gerhard Hörtnagl, owner and manager, sees to it that excellent food is provided, with a superb salad bar and a buffet breakfast.

K. H. Waggerlstrasse 20, A-5640 Badgastein. ℂ **06434/3761.** Fax 06434/376170. www.hotel-wildbad.com. 40 units. Winter 102€–186€ double; summer 88€–128€ double. Rates include buffet breakfast. MC, V. Closed Apr 15–May 15 and Oct 15–Dec 15. **Amenities:** Restaurant; bar; lounge; fitness center; health spa; sauna; room service; massage; babysitting; laundry; dry cleaning. *In room:* TV, hair dryer, safe.

Kurhotel Miramonte   On the landscaped side of an alpine hill, the Miramonte offers a panoramic view of the valley. A big terrace with sun umbrellas provides a nice spot to sit and relax. The comfortable and traditionally furnished rooms make for a snug retreat. Although the hotel dates from the 1950s, its accommodations have been renovated many times. Today each room contains an adjoining bathroom that, though small, is adequate, with spotless maintenance and shower-tub combinations. The public areas are elegant yet simple.

Reitelpromenade 3, A-5640 Badgastein. (C) **06434/2577.** Fax 06434/25779. www.gasteinertal.com/miramonte. 36 units. 54€–77€ per person. Rates include half-board. AE, DC, MC, V. Parking 3.60€. Closed May–June 15 and Oct 15–Dec 15. **Amenities:** Restaurant; bar; sauna; room service; massage; babysitting; laundry; dry cleaning. *In room:* TV, minibar, hair dryer, safe.

INEXPENSIVE

Alpenblick   This chalet has a side wing containing comfortable rooms with balconies and big windows offering mountain views. Beds are good, and the bathrooms, although tiny, are tidily kept and equipped with shower-tub combinations. Well-prepared and rather hearty meals are served in the timbered and beamed dining room.

Kötschachtalerstrasse 17, A-5640 Badgastein. (C) **06434/2062.** Fax 06434/206258. 38 units. Winter 39€–54€ per person; summer 39€–53€ per person. Rates include half-board. AE, MC, V. Closed Easter–May 8 and Nov 1–Dec 12. **Amenities:** Restaurant; bar; pool; fitness center; sauna; room service; babysitting; laundry; dry cleaning service. *In room:* TV, hair dryer.

Hotel Mozart *(Value*   This unusual hotel, designed in the 19th century, has a long veranda on the ground floor and a gabled mansard roof. Inside, beautifully patterned oriental rugs cover the floor of the wood-paneled lobby area, and crystal chandeliers hang from the detailed plaster ceiling. All the comfortably furnished rooms have private, immaculate bathrooms with shower-tub combinations, in addition to the thermally heated baths on each floor. Rooms aren't large, but the beds are comfortable and housekeeping is first rate. Both traditional and innovative cuisine are served in the hotel's restaurant, the Mozartstuben.

Kaiser-Franz-Joseph-Strasse 25, A-5640 Badgastein. (C) **06434/26-86-0.** Fax 06434/268662. www.hotel mozart.at. 60 units. 67€–76€ double. DC, MC, V. **Amenities:** Restaurant; bar; pool; fitness center; sauna. *In room:* TV.

Villa Hubertus   Simple, unpretentious, and evocative of old-time Badgastein, this government-rated two-star hotel, a 5-minute walk from the center of town, was built as a Jugendstil-inspired villa in 1908. Two rooms have private balconies; the others are simply but comfortably outfitted. All units have neatly kept bathrooms with shower units. Other than breakfast, no meals are served, but the kindly staff (some of whom speak very little, if any, English) will direct you to any of several restaurants nearby.

Kaiser-Franz-Josef-Strasse 24, A-5640 Badgastein. (C) **06434/2607.** Fax 06434/4014. 6 units. Winter 60€–80€ double; summer 54€–60€ double. Rates include breakfast. No credit cards. **Amenities:** Breakfast room; lounge. *In room:* No phone.

AFTER DARK IN BADGASTEIN

There's actually a lot to do at night in Badgastein, with cabaret, theater, folk events, and other activities. The center of nightlife—and the place to be seen—is the **Casino Badgastein** ((C) **06434/2465**). Here you can play roulette, baccarat, poker, and blackjack, but you'll need a passport to get in. The entrance fee is 17€, which entitles you to 20€ worth of chips. The casino is open Christmas through April 30 and July 1 through September 3 daily from 7pm to 2am.

At **Schaflinger Schi-Alm,** Böcksteiner Bundesstrasse 27 (© **06434/2036**), by the light of a blazing open fireplace, young and old enjoy dance music and the romantic alpine atmosphere of this popular hall. Nightly themes range from a cheese-and-knockwurst evening (Mon) to a re-creation of a *Heurige,* complete with Austrian wines and music (Wed), to a candlelit dance (Sat). Drinks begin at 5€, and full meals are served daily from 6 to 9pm.

If you want more conventional dancing, head for the **Arcotel Elisabethpark** (see "Where to Stay & Dine," above). This elegant nightspot is the place to go if you want to get all dolled up.

5 The Pinzgau

The Pinzgau section of Land Salzburg stretches east from the Gerlos Pass to the Gastein Valley, with the Salzach River flowing through. To the south lies Hohe Tauern, and to the north is the Kitzbühel alpine region.

For visitors, skiing is the reason to come. The twin villages of **Saalbach** and **Hinterglemm** lie at the end of a valley ringed by a horseshoe of mountains laced with more than 40 ski lifts. The chief resort of the Pinzgau is **Zell am See** (see section 7 later in this chapter). Another outstanding ski resort in the Upper Pinzgau region is **Kaprun.** The **Grossglockner Road** also begins in Pinzgau (see section 6 later in this chapter).

LOFER ⊛

Ideally situated among forests, valleys, and mountain rivers is the old market town of Lofer. This is a good base for exploring much of Land Salzburg, including Salzburg itself, the Grossglockner alpine road, Krimml Falls, the dams at Kaprun, Kitzbühel, and Innsbruck, as well as Lake Chiemsee and Berchtesgaden in Germany. Within an hour's drive are three 18-hole golf courses.

GETTING THERE   The nearest railway stations are at St. Johann in Tyrol and at Saalfelden. From Saalfelden, nine buses depart every day for the 39km (24-mile) trek to the northwest. From St. Johann, 10 buses depart daily for the 43km (27-mile) ride northeast to Lofer. Note that some bus routes, traversing the strip of Germany that juts into Austria at this point, travel directly from Salzburg's railway station about five times a day; the trip takes about an hour. If you choose this route, you might be asked to show your passport.

Motorists can take Route 305 southwest of Salzburg through Germany, and then continue southwest at the junction with Route 312.

EXPLORING LOFER

Lofer has a **Bauerntheater (Peasant Theater)** and a Gothic-style **Pfarrkirche (Parish Church),** whose tower dominates the town with its two onion-shape domes. Many houses are decorated with oriels, an architectural style inspired by nearby Bavaria.

Lofer is both a health resort and a ski center, offering hospitality, tradition, and rural charm. It's known for its peat-water and mud baths, as well as its Kneipp cures. The area around Lofer is nice for walking or hiking in both summer and winter. Sports facilities include a tennis court, skating rink, miniature golf course, and enclosed swimming pool.

A ski school operates here, and there are nine T-bar lifts. A chairlift will deliver you to the Sonnegg-Loderbühel at 1,003m (3,290 ft.) and the upper station of the Loferer Alm at 1,403m (4,600 ft.). Rising in the background of the town are the Loferer Steinberge and the Reiter Steinberge.

You can visit **Lamprechtshöhle** (© **06582/8343**), Austria's deepest water-bearing cave, on the road from Lofer to Weissbach (Rte. 311), about 60km (37 miles) from Salzburg by bus. A guided tour takes about 40 minutes. The cavern is open daily from 8:30am to 6pm; admission is 3€ for adults and 1.50€ for children. It's closed from March to April 15 and from October 20 to December 15.

WHERE TO STAY & DINE

Das Bräu ⚑ Situated in the village center, this hotel has a lemon-colored facade and curved wrought-iron balconies on the second floor. You'll recognize it by the ornate bracket (shaped like the head of a mythical bird) extending out over the pavement. Parts of the hotel were constructed in 1639, and the antiques inside add to the historic atmosphere. There's a warm, cozy alpine feeling to the rooms, which have small but efficient bathrooms with shower-tub combinations.

At the upscale restaurant, the Salzburger Stube, meals cost 26€ to 85€ for a fixed-price menu. A more rustic pair of dining rooms, the Braustube and the Tirolerstube, serve traditional Austrian meals for around 25€ for *Tagesmenus*, the day's menu. Specialties include a delectable smoked trout soup, venison and mushrooms, roast pork in a Gorgonzola-cream sauce served with green spätzle, and *Tafelspitz* (boiled beef). Desserts might feature fresh strudels.

Centrum 28, A-5090 Lofer. © **06588/82070.** Fax 06588/820771. 28 units. 80€ double or suite. Rate includes breakfast. AE, DC, MC, V. **Amenities:** 3 restaurants; bar; lounge; sauna; room service; babysitting; laundry; dry cleaning. *In room:* TV, hair dryer, safe.

Hotel St. Hubertus ⚑⚑ This hotel, the largest and best in Lofer, was originally built in the mid-1960s. The chalet windows provide great views over the Saalach River and the Loferer Steinberge mountain ranges. Rooms are well furnished, and most have balconies. The doubles are large enough to be rented as triples, and the suites (without kitchen) are big enough to house two to four guests. Bathrooms are not large, but they are well planned and equipped with shower-tub combinations. In summer, guests enjoy the garden with its sunny terrace. About a 5-minute walk from the village center and the cableways, it's near several walking paths and promenades. For cross-country skiers, tracks begin only 2 minutes from the hotel. Half-board includes a buffet breakfast followed that evening by a four-course meal with a large choice of desserts and cheeses. The hotel bar provides a cozy retreat.

Fam. Grisseman, A-5090 Lofer 180. © **06588/8266.** Fax 06588/7465. hubertusk@netway.at. 56 units. 62.50€–67.50€ per person double. Rates include half-board. AE, DC, MC, V. Closed late Apr to mid-May and Nov 1–Dec 15. **Amenities:** Dining room; bar; pool; sauna; room service; massage; laundry; dry cleaning service. *In room:* TV, hair dryer, safe.

ST. MARTIN BEI LOFER

This tiny, quaint village, about 2km (1½ miles) south of Lofer, is visited for its pilgrimage church, a large baroque edifice called **Maria Kirchenthal.** The building was designed by the renowned baroque master J. B. Fischer von Erlach. The church's museum displays votive pictures from the 17th to the 19th centuries. A mile west of the village, the church is reached by a toll road open only in summer, or by an hour's walk from Lofer.

Vorderkaser Gorge (© **06588/8520,** the tourist office in St. Martin bei Lofer) can be visited from St. Martin. A 2.4km (1½-mile) road connects the gorge with the Mittelpinzgau road near the Vorderkaser bus stop. It's open to the public from the second weekend in May to October 20 daily from 9am to 5pm. Admission is 2.50€ for adults and 1.20€ for children.

A restaurant at Prommer Rudolf, open daily in summer from 9am to 8pm (but closed in winter), provides a good place to eat and drink.

GETTING THERE   Getting to St. Martin is similar to getting to Lofer. The buses that originate in Saalfelden and Salzburg also stop in St. Martin. If you take a bus in St. Johann, however, you'll have to transfer to another bus in Lofer or call a taxi for the short continuation to St. Martin. If you're driving, continue south of Lofer along Route 311.

SAALBACH & HINTERGLEMM ⍟

This internationally known tourist resort, at an elevation of 1,003m (3,290 ft.), emphasizes relaxation, recreation, and sports—both summer and winter. It's located 64km (40 miles) southwest of Salzburg, 399km (248 miles) southwest of Vienna, and 185km (115 miles) southwest of Linz.

Saalbach has seen rapid growth as a winter-sports resort in recent years. Hinterglemm, its twin, is about an 8-minute drive west on an unclassified road that's signposted at the head of the valley. Often the region is spoken of as a unit—the Saalbach-Hinterglemm ski area. The resorts are linked by a lift system and ski bus.

Saalbach has numerous lifts near the center of town. There's one cable car big enough to carry 100 passengers, along with 40 tows and chairlifts that provide access to a variety of well-groomed slopes and deep-powder runs. The major lift, the Schattberg cableway, leaves from the heart of Saalbach, taking skiers to the top station (2,001m/6,560 ft.), where an excellent restaurant boasts a sunny terrace with a panoramic view. Of course, summer visitors can also take the cableway to enjoy the scenery.

The Glenntal Ski Pass, valid for the 60 lifts and the 193km (120 miles) of downhill runs of the Obertauern region (Saalbach, Hinterglemm, and Leogang), costs 33.50€ for 1 day and 91.60€ for 3 days. It's sold at the bottom of the biggest ski lift as well as the **Schi-Pass Kasenbureau** on Dorfstrasse (© **06541/6271**).

The Saalbach-Hinterglemm visitors' racing course is open Tuesday through Sunday from 10am to noon and 2 to 4pm, with slaloms, giant slaloms, and parallel slaloms being held. Both resorts have ski schools and provide ski-circus runs. In the winter, tobogganing is also popular, as are ski-bobbing, sleigh rides, and curling. Many cross-country ski tracks start from here.

From spring until late in the autumn, you can take quiet walks or extended hikes along some 257km (160 miles) of well-laid-out footpaths, as well as go mountain climbing, horseback riding, or bowling, or play minigolf and tennis. A nearby lake is great for swimming and sailing. A kindergarten caters exclusively to vacationers' children.

Saalbach can be a good base for exploring the neighboring resorts of Kaprun and Zell am See (see below).

GETTING THERE   The nearest railway line is at Zell am See (see section 7). Here, you'll have to transfer to one of the many buses that travel up the winding valley road. Buses depart from the railway station at Zell am See about every hour throughout the day, stopping first at Saalbach (trip time: 30 min.) and then continuing on to Hinterglemm (40 min.).

If you're driving, take Route 312 southwest from Salzburg to Lofer, and then cut south at the junction with Route 311.

VISITOR INFORMATION   The **tourist office** (© **06541/680-068**) is in the center of Saalbach but also provides information for Hinterglemm. It's open in winter Monday through Saturday from 9am to 6pm, and Sunday from 9am to noon; in summer Monday through Friday from 8:15am to noon and 1:30 to 6pm, Saturday from 8:15am to noon and 3 to 6pm, Sunday from 9am to noon.

WHERE TO STAY & DINE

Most visitors dine at their hotels.

Expensive

Alpenhotel Saalbach 🐪   Built in 1968, this fairly large chalet-style hotel is renovated in part every 2 years. Its convenient location in the center of Saalbach is near the cable car, chairlifts, and tennis courts. The cozy, well-furnished interior includes a collection of country artifacts and several fireplaces. Your host, the Thomas family, rents comfortable rooms plus a series of suites or apartments sleeping two to six guests, suitable for extended stays. Rooms feature spotless bathrooms with shower-tub combinations. Those opening onto private balconies are the most requested.

Part of the hotel's draw is that it's a major gathering spot for the whole resort. It has a trio of restaurants, including the Alpenstube, the Vitrine, and the Saloon. For a drink, there's Thomas' Pub, which also serves food, and the Kuhstall bar. The Pipamex offers live music.

Dorfstrasse 212, A-5753 Saalbach. (℡) **06541/6666.** Fax 06541/6666888. www.alpenhotel.at. 96 units. 128€–174€ double; from 178€ per person suite. Rates include half-board. AE, DC, MC, V. Parking 7€. Closed Apr 15–May 20 and Oct 15–Dec 19. **Amenities:** 3 restaurants; 2 bars; pool; sauna; room service; babysitting; laundry; dry cleaning. *In room:* TV, minibar, hair dryer, safe.

Hotel Glemmtalerhof   This chalet-style hotel rises six stories above the village's central street. Built in 1951, it was completely renovated and partially rebuilt in 1992. The street level contains a few small shops. Inside, the hotel offers cozy public areas, some with fireplaces. There are public tennis courts only a few buildings away. Rooms, covered with mellow pine and invitingly lit, are medium size and exceedingly comfortable, with fine beds and ample bathrooms, each with a neatly kept shower unit. A *Tagesmenu* (daily menu) is offered at lunch and dinner. The hotel staff can also organize mountain or biking excursions for you.

Glemmtalerlaudstrasse 150, A-5754 Hinterglemm. (℡) **06541/7135.** Fax 06541/713563. www.glemmtalerhof.at. 85 units. Winter 148€–244€ double, 178€–244€ suite; summer 123€–142€ double, 129€–163€ suite. Rates include half-board. AE, DC, MC, V. Parking 6€. Closed Apr 15–May 15 and Nov 1–Dec 15. **Amenities:** Restaurant; 3 bars; cafe; nightclub; pool; 3 tennis courts (nearby); fitness center; sauna; room service; massage; babysitting; laundry; dry cleaning service. *In room:* TV, hair dryer, safe.

Hotel Ingonda 🐪🐪   This hotel restaurant exudes an aura of well-established, even antique, prosperity. In 1999, it was dramatically upgraded and now enjoys a status as the finest of the government-rated four-star hotels in town. In the center of Saalbach in a traffic-free zone, it's named for the charming wife of the owner. The hotel contains well-furnished rooms, each with a balcony, armchairs, and desk space. Bathrooms are well maintained and come with shower-tub combinations.

Skiers appreciate the hotel's proximity to the village's three ski lifts, a 1-minute trek from the entrance on skis. In the well-recommended restaurant, guests enjoy such specialties as scampi flambéed in gin, filet of beef jambalaya, tender cuts of well-seasoned beef, and homemade strudels. If you're dropping in to dine in season, reserve a table. Aside from the Ingonda's five-star restaurant, the social center is a rambling pine-covered bar with an intricately crafted wood ceiling and comfortable leather chairs.

Dorfstrasse 218, A-5753 Saalbach. (℡) **06541/6262.** Fax 06541/7334-62. www.ingonda.at. 73 units. Winter 90€–136€ per person double, 119€–165€ per person suite; summer 34€–49€ per person double,

60€–74€ per person suite. Rates include half-board. AE, DC, MC, V. Parking 11€. Closed Apr and Nov. **Amenities:** Restaurant; bar; pool; fitness center; Jacuzzi; sauna; solarium; room service; massage; babysitting; laundry; dry cleaning. *In room:* TV, minibar, hair dryer, safe.

Moderate

Gasthof Unterwirt   Built in 1973 as a modern interpretation of a traditional chalet, this pleasant and relaxed establishment, with its rustic decor of ceiling beams and ceramic tile stoves, is owned by the Kroll family. Rooms range from small to medium and have traditional alpine furnishings. Bathrooms are equipped mostly with shower-tub combinations and are beautifully maintained. The international and regional cuisine is hearty and plentiful.

Unterdorf 31, A-5753 Saalbach. ℭ **06541/6274.** Fax 06541/73-47-55. www.saalbach.at. 53 units. Winter 130€–190€ double; summer 84€–104€ double. Rates include half-board. MC, V. Closed Mar 30–May 15 and Nov 1–Dec 10. **Amenities:** Restaurant; bar; sauna; laundry; dry cleaning service. *In room:* TV, hair dryer.

Hotel Haus Wolf   If you're interested in ski lessons, this might be an ideal place to stay, since the local ski school is headquartered here. The hotel, right beside the Reiterkogel cable car, has wooden balconies and a first-floor sun terrace. In winter, fires burn beneath copper-sheathed chimneys, and guests often congregate in one of the several bars or restaurants. A smaller annex provides comfortable but less inspired accommodations. The alpine-style rooms have good, firm beds, and small but efficient bathrooms equipped with shower-tub combinations.

Reiterkogelweg 169, A-5754 Hinterglemm. ℭ **06541/6346.** Fax 06541/634669. www.wolf-hotels.at. 40 units. Winter 126€–220€ double; summer 104€–218€ double. Rates include half-board. MC, V. Closed Apr 15–May 15 and Oct 15–Dec 20. **Amenities:** Restaurant; bar; pool; sauna; babysitting; laundry; dry cleaning. *In room:* TV, hair dryer, safe.

Hotel Kristiana ⭐ (Value)   A local favorite since it was built in 1979, this well-managed hotel lies a short walk uphill from the village center. Balconies adorn its facade, and in one corner, just above the sun terrace, an artist has executed a series of etched panels depicting the seasons. The interior is a rustic fantasy of carved beams and well-polished paneling, open fireplaces, and comfortable, well-planned rooms. Most rooms have fine views and individual character, but all are equipped with good beds and spotless bathrooms with shower-tub combinations. Johann Breitfuss and his family serve tasty meals only to hotel guests and maintain a pleasant bar.

Dorfstrasse 40, A-5753 Saalbach. ℭ **06541/6253.** Fax 06541/828999. www.kristiana.at. 34 units. Winter 168€–218€ double. Summer 110€–130€ double. Rates include half-board. MC, V. Closed Apr–May 15 and Oct–Dec 10. **Amenities:** Restaurant; bar; room service; sauna; babysitting; laundry; dry cleaning service. *In room:* TV, hair dryer, safe.

THE RESORTS AFTER DARK

Saalbach is one of the liveliest centers in Land Salzburg for nightlife. The after-skiing crowd shuttles back and forth between Saalbach and Hinterglemm, and after a few drinks, the resorts seem to merge into one.

Hexenhäusl, Zwolferkogelbahnweg 122 (ℭ **06541/6334**), is one of the busiest and most consistently popular après-ski venues in Hinterglemm. Positioned at the bottom of the Zwolferkogelbahn gondola, it combines the functions of a bar, pub, and cafe into a rowdy, sudsy, beery, schnapps-permeated mountain hut. Cozy, dark, candlelit, and moderately claustrophobic, it's a place where English and French skiers mingle with locals, some of whom aren't particularly interested in skiing at all. Beer sells for 2€ to 5.50€; snacks such as strudels, pizzas, and baguettes sell for 1.50€ to 4.50€. You'll recognize the place by the carved effigies of witches (*Hexen*) that decorate the outside and inside of this folkloric but very hip place. From May to October, it's open Tuesday through Saturday from 3pm to 6am; from November to April, it's open daily from 3pm to 6am—so late that anyone who actually remains on-site till closing will probably not venture onto the ski slopes the following day.

Since its opening in the 1950s, **Hotel Glemmtalerhof,** Glemmtalerlaudstrasse 150, Hinterglemm (℃ **06541/7135**), has always maintained an active nightlife for both vacationers and local residents. The folksy Glemmerkeller Nightclub hosts a series of live bands performing everything from Bavarian oompah music to more modern (and highly danceable) tunes. It's open every night 9pm to 1:30am, although during ski season it's also open every afternoon for post-slopes revelry 4 to 6pm. A small but energetic disco, the **Almbar,** plays high-volume sounds from New York, London, and Los Angeles. There's no cover to get into either bar, and beer costs 3€ in summer and 4€ in winter.

In winter, live dance music is usually featured at **Knappenhof Knappenkeller,** Knappenhof Tirolerhof, Haupstrasse 222, Hinterglemm (℃ **06541/6497**), while the adjacent disco plays recorded tunes. Sometimes Tyrolean music is interspersed with more modern sounds. Grilled specialties are offered as well as Wiener schnitzel, pizza, and Italian food, with meals beginning at 7€. A beer costs 3€. The cover charge of 5€ includes your first drink. It's open daily from 9pm to 4am; it's closed in October.

The cellar at **Saalbacher Hof,** Dorfstrasse 27, Saalbach (℃ **06541/7111**), is devoted every Wednesday to drinking, dancing, and alpine folk music. On other nights of the week, the theme is more modern. The music begins around 8:30pm in summer and winter. There's no cover; beer costs 3€.

Club Discoteque Club, in Berger's Sporthotel, Dorfstrasse 33, Saalbach (℃ **06541/6577**), offers good bands and good drinks (often many good drinks) to a young crowd energized by a day on the slopes. A beer begins at 3€. It's open December through March only, daily from 9pm to 3am.

SAALFELDEN ❦

An old market town lying in a broad valley formed by the Saalbach River, Saalfelden is set against a background of towering mountains in the Middle Pinzgau. This is a good center for exploring the **Steinernes Meer,** or Sea of Stone, a limestone plateau with underground rivers and caverns that the Austrian government has turned into a nature reserve. Saalfelden lies 64km (40 miles) south of Salzburg and 399km (248 miles) southwest of Vienna.

Although Saalfelden is primarily a summer resort, winter-sports areas in the mountains are within easy reach. The town has a **Pfarrkirche (Parish Church)** with a Gothic crypt beneath the choir and a late-Gothic triptych in the presbytery.

At **Ritzen Castle** (℃ **06582/72759**), which dates from 1563, a local museum (Heimatmuseum) is devoted to life in the Pinzgau region. Here you'll see a rich collection of Christmas cribs by artist Xandl Schläffer. Another hall displays pictures and ecclesiastic art along with exhibits tracing the geology of Saalfelden, a peasant's room from the 1700s, an open-hearth kitchen, native handicrafts, and various documents on the history of the area. Admission is 3.30€ for adults and 1€ for children. It's open from June 16 to September 15 Tuesday through Friday from 10am to noon and 2 to 5pm, and Saturday and Sunday from 2 to 5pm; off-season, it's open Wednesday, Saturday, and Sunday from 2 to 4pm and is closed in November.

GETTING THERE Saalfelden is a major stop on express and local trains from both Innsbruck and Salzburg. Trains from Innsbruck are usually direct, while trains from Salzburg sometimes require a change in Schwarzach–St. Veit. With transfers included, the trip from both cities to Saalfelden takes about 1⅔ hours. Trains arrive there about once an hour throughout the day.

Although Saalfelden is the transfer point for many bus routes heading into the surrounding mountains, few visitors would consider reaching Saalfelden by bus from any large Austrian city, with the possible exception of Salzburg. These buses depart from Salzburg's main railway station about six times a day, making many stops en route (trip time: about 95 min.).

If you're driving from Zell am See, head north along Route 311. From Salzburg, head southwest on Route 312. At Lofer, continue south on Route 311.

VISITOR INFORMATION   The **tourist office** is at Bahnhofstrasse 3 (© 06582/72513). It's open in winter Monday through Friday from 8am to 6pm, and Saturday from 9am to noon; in summer Monday through Friday from 8am to 5pm, Saturday from 9am to noon.

WHERE TO STAY
Hotel Gasthof Hindenburg ★★   Set in the heart of Saalfelden, this hotel is one of the oldest in the region, with foundations and a reputation for hospitality that date back more than 500 years, and an alpine design that looks a lot older than the 1992 renovation that transformed it into the hip-roofed, many-gabled design you'll see today. Rooms are cozily outfitted with mostly contemporary furniture. Bathrooms are up-to-date and contain mostly shower-tub combinations. There's a trio of restaurants, the most formal of which is the richly paneled Gastestube. Overall, it's a worthy government-rated four-star choice with as many luxuries and conveniences as any of its competitors in Saalfelden.

Bahnhofstrasse 6, A-5760 Saalfelden. © 06582/7930. Fax 06582/793-78. www.hotel-hindenburg.at. 45 units. 94€–164€ double. Rates include breakfast. AE, DC, MC, V. **Amenities:** 3 restaurants; bar; fitness center; sauna; solarium; room service; babysitting; laundry; dry cleaning service. *In room:* TV, minibar, hair dryer, safe.

WHERE TO DINE
Restaurant Schatzbichl AUSTRIAN   At this alpine country house, waitresses wearing regional garb serve time-honored recipes. Specialties are often brought to your table in a copper pan for members of your party to dig into with forks and spoons. You might enjoy *Kasfarfeln* (thick consommé with cheese, onions, chives, and dumplings) or our favorite, *Erdäpfelgröstl* (a big pot with potatoes, broth, sausages, onions, and chives).

Ramseiden 82. © 06582/73281. Reservations recommended. Main courses 5€–6€. AE, DC, MC, V. Wed–Mon noon–2pm and 6–10pm. Closed Nov.

KAPRUN & ITS DAMS
A summer resort and a winter ski center, Kaprun is known for its high glacier skiing. The town is hardly the most attractive or the most atmospheric in Land Salzburg, but serious skiers don't seem to mind.

GETTING THERE   The nearest railway station is in Zell am See, 8km (5 miles) north. From here, about 14 buses a day depart for the 15-minute uphill run to Kaprun. (*Note:* Don't confuse the village of Kaprun with the more southerly and much more isolated ski hamlet of Kaprun Heidnische Kirche, which requires an additional transfer.) Motorists in Zell am See should head west on Route 168 to Fürth, at which point they can cut south on an unclassified road to Kaprun.

VISITOR INFORMATION   The **tourist office** (© 06547/8643) is in the town center. It's open Monday through Saturday from 9am to 6pm and Sunday from 10am to noon.

EXPLORING THE VALLEY OF KAPRUN

The area takes in the Valley of Kaprun and its powerful dams, as well as the surrounding heights. An ascent to the **Kitzsteinhorn** (2,931m/9,612 ft.) can be quite complicated, involving postal buses, funiculars, and cableways, but it's equally rewarding. Always have your routes outlined at the tourist office with a detailed area map before you set forth. An English-speaking staff member will supply the best possible routes and provide you with the most up-to-date information on hours, costs, types of services likely to be available at the time of your visit, and weather conditions. For example, after mid-October, tours to the valley of the dams might not be possible. However, a visit to the Kitzsteinhorn is an attraction in both summer and winter.

To reach the Kitzsteinhorn, you can take either a cable car, transferring to the Langweidbahn (a chairlift), or the glacier railway, an underground funicular, to the Restaurant Alpincenter (2,446m/8,020 ft.), where you can enjoy lunch with a view halfway up Kitzsteinhorn. At Alpincenter, change to a cable car, which swings west, coming to a stop near the summit of the Kitzsteinhorn.

A little below the summit, you'll find the 305m (1,000-ft.) **Panoramatunnel** cut through the mountain and opening onto an incredible view of Nationalpark Hohe Tauern. On clear days, you'll be able to see Grossglockner, the highest peak in Austria, at 3,764m (12,340 ft.). You can also eat at the Aussichtsrestaurant (talk about dining with a view!), or if you want to feel snow in summer, you can take a short cable car down to the glacier.

It's best to purchase a day ticket—round-trip, naturally—for both the cable railway and the glacier lift; it costs 34€ for adults and 17€ for children under 15. It's open daily from 8am to 4pm.

THE DAMS

The **Kapruner Tal** ⚘, or the Valley of Kaprun, is visited in summer for its dams, one of the more dramatic alpine sights. Constructed in tiers, the dams were originally built as part of the U.S.-financed Marshall Plan. Experts from all over the world come here to study these hydroelectric constructions, which are brilliant feats of engineering.

Visit the hydroelectric plant, Turbinenhaus, inside the **Tauernkraftwerke** (© 06547/7151-527). Its shafts, tunnels, turbines, and bulwarks are an interesting change of pace for most visitors. A small museum, filled with technical drawings and photographs, conveys the magnitude of the project.

If you want to explore the region and see how the dams manage to hold back up to 19 billion gallons of alpine water, the staff at Kaprun's tourist information office offers a self-guided full-day tour (16€) that encompasses overviews of the three lakes formed by the dams, and transportation. The ascent up to the dams, including the **Limsbergsperre,** the **Moosersperre** ⚘⚘, and the **Drossensperre,** is via yellow post buses and a funicular. You can visit daily from 8am to 4pm from mid-March to mid-October, depending on weather conditions.

WHERE TO STAY

Hotel Orgler _(Kids_   This cream-colored house is in the middle of the village. Slightly isolated from its neighbors, it offers peace, quiet, and a rustic interior of high ceilings, heavy beams, and chalet furniture. Each room has a balcony and a medium-size bathroom containing a shower-tub combination. Apartments with three or four beds are available for families. The hotel's dining room and restaurant are furnished in traditional Austrian style, as are the cozy lounges and the bar with an open fireplace.

Schlosstrasse 22, A-5710 Kaprun. © **06547/8205.** Fax 06547/7567. www.hotel-orgler.at. 37 units. Winter 142€ double, 110€ per person apt; summer 110€ double, 65€ per person apt. Rates include half-board. DC, MC, V. **Amenities:** Restaurant; bar; 36-hole golf course; tennis court; fitness center; Jacuzzi; sauna; solarium; room service; babysitting; laundry; dry cleaning. *In room:* TV, minibar, hair dryer, safe.

Sporthotel Kaprun   On the village's outskirts, this large chalet has a sloping roof and flowered balconies. Built in 1977, it has paneled ceilings, big windows, and spacious public areas. The good-size rooms are modern and comfortable, and most have a balcony. Bathrooms are carefully maintained and equipped mostly with shower-tub combinations. There's a restaurant for half-board diners, plus a pizzeria.

A-5710 Kaprun. © **06547/8625-0.** Fax 06547/862519. www.sporthotel-kaprun.at. 60 units. Winter 118€–162€ double; summer 101€–113€ double. Rates include half-board. AE, MC, V. Take the cable lift to the stations at the southern exit of Kaprun. **Amenities:** Restaurant; bar; fitness center; game room; sauna; solarium; room service; babysitting; laundry; dry cleaning. *In room:* TV, minibar, hair dryer, safe.

WHERE TO DINE

Restaurant "Take Two" AUSTRIAN/ITALIAN   Its battered paneling and its general sudsiness might remind you of an Irish pub, but inside, with the falling snow and a clientele that might be dressed in ski attire, the venue is purely alpine. The atmosphere is friendly and informal, without much emphasis on a rigid protocol and with a great focus on good food. Menu items include the most popular dishes from the Austrian and Italian repertoire, including Wiener schnitzels, *Rostbratens,* and lasagnes, as well as local dishes from the Pinzgau.

In the Hotel Hubertushof, Nikolas Gassnar Strasse 460. © 06547/8504. Reservations recommended in winter. Main courses 6€–16€. AE, DC, MC, V. Daily 4pm–midnight. Closed mid-Mar to mid-June and mid-Sept to mid-Dec.

KAPRUN AFTER DARK

Kaprun has its own relatively modest nightlife, but should you ever get bored, take the shuttle bus over to Zell am See for much more excitement. Nightlife reaches its modest peak in Kaprun on Friday and Saturday nights. On other nights you might like to turn in with a good book or sit and drink around an open fire. Nearly all hotels and pensions welcome outside guests.

One of the most popular spots in town is the coffee shop, **Morokutti,** Nicolaus-Gassner-Strasse 572 (© **06547/8424**). It's open daily from 9:30am to 11pm but is closed Tuesday in April and June. A glass of wine costs 1.50€, and hot coffee starts at 2€.

Café Baum Bar (© **06547/8216**) is about a mile north of Kaprun's center, far enough from all the hotels that the noisy crowd won't disturb anyone's sleep. This is the largest, most crowded, and most sociable watering hole in town. Although a part of it is devoted to serving pizzas, Wiener schnitzels, pastas, salads, and sandwiches, it's best known as a disco that thumps every night of the week, summer and winter, from 9pm to 3am. Kitchen hours vary according to demand but usually last to midnight. Management runs minivans between Kaprun's center and the Baum at frequent intervals, although some visitors opt for a midnight walk (or crawl) to and from the site. The place was built, incidentally, as an outbuilding for a local cattle farm in the 1930s. Pizzas cost 6€ to 10€. The disco's cover charge is 2€ to 7€, depending on the live act; it's free when there's recorded music. Beer begins at 2€ in the early afternoon but increases in price to 3€ after 9pm.

There's also dancing at the **Nindl Café,** Nicolaus-Gassner-Strasse 380 (© **06547/8259**). In winter, folk shows are presented along with live and recorded music. There's no cover. Call to find out what's happening at the time of your visit. It's open daily from 11am to 1am but is closed 2 weeks in June and September. Beer costs 2.75€. Snacks, such as salads, pizzas, and hamburgers, are served at Nindl's cafe daily from 4pm to 2am.

KRIMML

Krimml is the best base for exploring the Krimml Falls. The village is in a heavily forested valley called Krimmler Ache, between the Kitzbühel Alps and the Hohe Tauern. Although it is mostly a summer resort, there's also good skiing at **Gerlos-platte** (1,708m/5,600 ft.), 11km (7 miles) away.

GETTING THERE   A slow local train, making more than 50 stops en route, travels from Zell am See to Krimml. Trains depart every 2 to 3 hours (trip time: about 90 min.). About a dozen buses depart every day from the railway station at Zell am See for Krimml (trip time: about 75 min.). If you're driving from Zell am See, take Route 168 west to Mittersill, and there continue west along Route 165.

VISITOR INFORMATION   The **tourist office** (© 06564/7239) in the town center is open Monday through Friday from 8:30am to noon and 2:30 to 5:30pm, Sunday from 8:30 to 10:30am and 4:30 to 6pm. Krimml lies 153km (95 miles) southwest of Salzburg.

KRIMML FALLS ✵✵✵

This village in the far-western extremity of Land Salzburg is visited mainly for the iridescent **Krimml Falls (Krimmler Wasserfalle).** The highest in Europe, these spectacular falls drop 381m (1,250 ft.) in three stages. They lie to the south of the Gerlos Pass, which connects the Salzach Valley in Land Salzburg to the Siller Valley in the Tyrol.

If you drive here, you can either leave your car at the parking lot at the south of the village and walk 30 minutes to the lower falls, or take the Gerlos Pass toll road, open from June 1 to September 30. If you don't have a car, you can take one of the frequent buses marked KRIMML from the center of town. Get off at Maustelle Ort, where the path to the falls begins. The falls are open daily from 8am to 6pm; it costs 1.50€ for adults and .50€ for children.

Visitors should allow about 3½ hours to explore the entire falls area. On a sunny day, try to visit around noon when the falls are at their most dramatic. In summer, the waterfalls are likely to be floodlit on Wednesday nights, depending on weather conditions. Wear good, sturdy shoes and, if you don't want to get sprayed, a raincoat.

After you've checked out the lower falls, if you want to see the second stage, count on another 12-minute walk. From here it's only another 5 minutes to the third and final stage for viewing the cataracts. There are paths leading to two more viewing points. The middle part of the falls can be seen at the sixth and seventh lookouts. At the Bergerblick, you'll have your greatest view of the water-falls, reached by continuing another 20 minutes from the seventh viewing point. If you want, you can go on to the Schettbrücke (1,464m/4,800 ft.) for a look at the upper cascades.

The waterfalls lie under a deep ice layer during the winter.

WHERE TO STAY & DINE

Hotel Klockerhaus (Value)   This peaceful two-story chalet has wooden balconies from which you can view the Krimml Falls. Located on the border of the Hohe Tauern National Park, the family hotel has well-furnished lounges. Rooms range from small to medium, each tastefully decorated and immaculately kept with good beds, ample bathrooms with mostly shower-tub combinations, and balconies. The kitchen serves Austrian and international specialties. The proprietors, Bruno and Margarethe Czerny, see to the well-being of their customers.

Wasserfallstrasse 10, A-5743 Krimml. © 06564/7208. Fax 06564/7208-46. klockerhaus@netway.at. 43 units. Winter 67€–84€ double; summer 48€–52€ double. Rates include breakfast. MC, V. Closed Nov. **Amenities:** Restaurant; lounge; fitness center; sauna; room service. *In room:* TV, hair dryer.

Hotel Krimmlerfälle   Sea-green shutters and wood siding cover the third and fourth floors of this pretty four-story house, built a century ago but renovated in the 1990s. Your congenial hosts, the Schöppl family, rent tasteful and comfortable rooms with balconies covered in pink and red flowers in summer. Some rooms are in a less desirable annex nearby. These are rather bland and only functionally furnished, but they're still comfortable. Rooms in the main building tend to be more spacious, but all are equipped with comfortable beds and small but spotless bathrooms that, for the most part, contain shower-tub combinations.

Wasserfallstrasse 42, A-5743 Krimml. © 06564/7203. Fax 06564/7473. krimmlerfaelle@netwing.at. 58 units. Winter 50€–100€ per person; summer 52€–67€ per person. Rates include half-board. AE, DC, MC, V. Closed Oct 19–Dec 12. **Amenities:** Restaurant; bar; pool; sauna. *In room:* TV, hair dryer.

6 The Grossglockner Road ✦✦✦

The longest and most splendid alpine highway in Europe, and one of the outstanding tourist attractions on the continent, **Grossglocknerstrasse** (Route 107) will afford you one of the greatest drives of your life.

The hairpin turns and bends would challenge even Grand Prix drivers. It's believed that this was the same route through the Alps used by the Romans, although this was forgotten until 1930, when engineers building the highway discovered remains of the work their road-building predecessors did some 19 centuries earlier. This engineering feat was finished in 1935. Switzerland and France copied it years later when they built their own alpine highways.

The highway runs for nearly 48km (30 miles), beginning at Bruck an der Grossglocknerstrasse at 757m (2,483 ft.), via Fusch/Grossglocknerstrasse; and heading toward Ferleiten, Hochmais, and Fuschtörl through the Hochtortunnel, where the highest point is 2,507m (8,220 ft.); to Guttal and Heiligenblut (1,301m/4,267 ft.) in Carinthia. The actual mountain part of the road stretches for some 22km (13½ miles), usually at about 1,983m (6,500 ft.). It has a maximum gradient of 12%.

Many visitors opt to drive this spectacular stretch. But because of the high altitudes, the road is passable only from mid-May to mid-November, depending on weather conditions. Always check with some authority about the road conditions before considering such a drive, especially in spring and autumn. The passenger car toll for a round-trip is 26€, collected at either Ferleiten or Heiligenblut.

You can also take a yellow-sided Austrian Postal Bus from Zell am See. From May to October, the buses depart from in front of the main railway station twice daily at 8:50 and 9:50am. Stopping at about a dozen small villages en route, the buses meander up Grossglockner to its most panoramic point, the Franz-Josefs-Höhe, where passengers can get out and explore for about 2½ hours before boarding the same buses (at 2:45 and 3:45pm, respectively) and returning to Zell am See. A round-trip costs 16.70€. For information, call either the tourist office in Zell am See (© **06542/7700**) or the local bus station (© **06542/544-412**).

Going south from Bruck, you enter the Foscher Valley, where the road winds through beautiful alpine scenery. Six kilometers (4 miles) from the Hochtor-tunnel on the north side, you can branch off onto Edelweiss-Strasse, going along for about 2km (1½ miles) to the parking lot at the Edelweiss-Spitze (2,572m/8,433 ft.). The stunning view from here encompasses 37 3,050m (10,000-ft.) peaks. This is the best vantage point to take in the tremendous mountain and alpine lakes of the **Hohe Tauern** National Park. Really a massive mountain range, the Hohe Tauren covers 29 towns, 304 separate mountains, and nearly 250 glaciers. At Edelweiss-Spitze is an observation tower, going up to more than 2,577m (8,450 ft.).

One of the interesting detours along the road is to the stone terrace of the **Franz-Josefs-Höhe** ✹✹✹. It's named for the emperor who once had a mansion constructed here in the foothills of the Pasterze Glacier. The stretch from Gletscherstrasse to Franz-Josefs-Höhe (2,370m/7,770 ft.) is some 8km (5 miles) long, branching off near Guttal. This road lies above the Pasterze Glacier, oppo-site the Grossglockner (3,791m/12,430 ft.). The Pasterze, incidentally, is the largest glacier in the eastern Alps, 9km (5½ miles) long.

If you're traveling in spring and autumn, it might not be possible to take detours to the Edelweiss-Spitze or the Franz-Josefs-Höhe if heavy snow falls. If you do take the side trip to the latter site, avoid arriving there around midday. On a bright, sunny day in summer, the place is literally mobbed. It has an out-standing view of the majestic Grossglockner.

From May to September it's possible to descend from Freiwandeck to Pasterze Glacier by funicular. Service is available every hour daily from 8am to 4pm.

7 Zell am See ✭

389km (242 miles) SW of Vienna; 85km (53 miles) SW of Salzburg

Founded by monks around the middle of the 8th century, the old part of Zell am See lies on the shore of the Zeller See (Lake Zell), under a backdrop of mountains. The Zeller See is a deep glacial lake filled with clear blue alpine water. The town today is the most popular resort in the Middle Pinzgau, a dis-trict that has already been previewed in this chapter. Zell is crowded and fash-ionable in both summer and winter. It's also a center for those who'd like to get an early start and travel the Grossglockner alpine highway, described above.

ESSENTIALS

GETTING THERE   Zell am See is one of the most important stops astride the rail lines carrying passengers between Salzburg and Innsbruck. Conse-quently, express trains arrive from Innsbruck about once an hour, after the under-2-hour trip. Trains from Salzburg take about 90 minutes and depart about once an hour as well. Frequent connections are also possible to and from Klagenfurt, although a transfer is required at the nearby railway junction of Schwarzach–St. Veit, about 34km (21 miles) to the east.

Zell am See is the junction for several bus routes heading upward into the surrounding mountains. Because of the many transfers required for passengers coming from outside the immediate region, however, most visitors arrive by train.

If you're driving from Salzburg, cut south on the A10 to the junction with Route 311, at which point you head west.

VISITOR INFORMATION   The **tourist office** on Bruckner Bundesstrasse (© **06542/7700**) is open Monday through Friday from 9am to 6pm, Saturday from 10am to noon.

SEEING THE SIGHTS

Unlike most resorts in Land Salzburg, Zell am See has some old buildings worth exploring. These include the **Kastnerturm,** or Constable's Tower, the oldest building in town, dating from the 12th century. It was once used as a grain silo. The town's **Pfarrkirche (Parish Church)** is an 11th-century Romanesque structure. Inside is a late Gothic choir from the 16th century. **Castle Rosenberg,** also from the 16th century, was once an elegant residence of the free state of Salzburg, built in the southern Bavarian style. Today it houses the Rathaus (town hall), with a gallery.

The **folklore museum** is in the old tower, the Vogtturm, near the town square. The tower itself is about 1,200 years old. In the museum, old costumes are displayed, and exhibited artifacts show the traditional way of life in old Land Salzburg. From June to October, the museum is open Monday through Friday from 2 to 5pm. Admission is 2€ for adults and 1.10€ children ages 6 to 15.

WINTER & SUMMER SPORTS

For winter visitors, snow conditions in the Zell area are usually ideal from December to the end of April. Zell am See attracts beginner and intermediate skiers, plus many nonskiers—people who like the bustling life of the winter resort even if they never take to the slopes. Even if skiing isn't your thing, take the chairlift (shoes are fine) for the alpine scenery. Skiing is possible at elevations ranging from 915m to 2,745m (3,000 ft.–9,000 ft.).

There is a Zell/Kaprun Ski Pass that covers both Zell am See and Kaprun. A 2-day pass costs 58€ to 61.50€ and is sold at the tourist office in Zell am See and often at the lifts. A free shuttle bus runs between the two resorts during the day from December 20 to April 13 every 15 minutes. If you are coming to Land Salzburg to ski, we recommend purchasing a ski package from your travel agent. A package will include the cost of all lifts and ski passes, and will be more economical than paying for each activity separately.

Sports fans gravitate to the **Kur-und-Sportzentrum,** an arena northwest of the resort housing a mammoth indoor swimming pool as well as saunas and an ice rink. Sometimes in cold weather the lake is frozen over.

Zell am See also attracts visitors in the peak summer months. **Lake Zell,** which has been called the cleanest lake in Europe, is warm, maintaining an average temperature of some 70°F (21°C) in summer. The lake is 4km (2½ miles) long and 2km (1 mile) wide. Motorboats can be rented. You can go along a footpath from the town to the bathing station at Seespitz, a half-hour walk.

GOING UP THE SCHMITTENHÖHE ★★

Schmittenhöhe, at 1,967m (6,450 ft.), towers to the west of Zell am See. There are four different ways to ascend the mountain, with even more options for getting down. In summer, the hardy have been known to climb it in 4 hours. We suggest, however, that you take the cableway. The view from here is one of the finest in the Kitzbühel Alps, the majestic glacial peaks of the Grossglockner range. You can have lunch at the *Berghotel* at the upper station. From the west side of Zell am See, you can also take a four-seat cableway to the middle station. From here you can connect with several lifts that will take you to the upper platform. A sun terrace at the upper station is popular in both summer and winter.

(Don't be surprised to see bare breasts, even in February.) It's about a mile up Schmittenhöhe. Figure on at least 1¾ hours for your round-trip, plus another 18 minutes by cable car. In summer, service is every half-hour.

You can also take the Sonnalm cableway (entrance near the Schmittenhöhe terminus) to Sonnalm at 1,385m (4,540 ft.). Another restaurant is perched here. From Sonnalm, it's possible to go by chairlift to Sonnkogel (1,836m/6,020 ft.) and by surface lift to Hochmais (1,728m/5,665 ft.). From the eastern part of Lake Zell, you can take the chairlift up to Ronachkopf (1,487m/4,875 ft.).

From Zell am See, you can also take a funicular to Kaprun (see section 5, earlier in this chapter), at the foot of the Kitzteinhorn, for glacier and year-round skiing. In fact, some of the most spectacular excursions possible from Kaprun can be made easily from Zell am See (refer to the Kaprun section for more details).

WHERE TO STAY & DINE
EXPENSIVE
Hotel Salzburger Hof 🌟🌟   Just a glimpse of the handcrafted interior of this government-rated five-star chalet-style hotel near the lake, and you know you're in for a treat. Inside a fire blazes in an unusual stucco fireplace in the salon. The Holleis family maintains the pleasant outdoor garden with its sun terrace for summer barbecues. Evening programs include dancing, playing the zither, and telling folk tales. Accommodations include suites with private saunas and open fireplaces. Rooms are carpeted and well maintained, if lacking in style; they have generous storage space and balconies with a nice view. The small bathrooms come with robes and shower-tub combinations.

The hotel's restaurant serves some of the area's finest regional specialties. A fixed-price menu costs 30€ and might include such classic dishes as cream of sauerkraut with smoked-meat dumplings, cream of black salsify (oyster plant) with truffled dumplings, and filet of jack salmon in a potato crust. Many of the chef's best dishes are fish from either the lake or the sea.

Auerspergstrasse 11, A-5700 Zell am See. © **06542/765**. Fax 06542/765-66. www.salzburgerhof.at. 70 units. Winter 220€–430€ double, 250€–510€ suite for 2; summer 190€–260€ double, 220€–460€ suite for 2. Rates include half-board. AE, DC, MC, V. Free parking outside. Closed Nov. **Amenities:** Restaurant; bar; pool; fitness center; Jacuzzi; sauna; salon; room service; massage; babysitting; laundry; dry cleaning. *In room:* TV, minibar, hair dryer, safe.

Sporthotel Alpin 🌟   This is a 1970s chalet encircled almost completely by balconies. The elegant and sporty interior has big sunny windows. The well-proportioned and comfortably furnished rooms open onto balconies and have excellent bathrooms with shower-tub combinations. The hotel is just outside the village, giving it both an excellent view of the lake and easy accessibility to the ski lifts. The restaurant's specialties are both Austrian and international, ranging from wild game to innovative modern dishes. If you're lucky, your visit will coincide with one of the suckling pig banquets or one of the elaborate farmer's buffets.

Gartenstrasse 11, A-5700 Zell am See. © **06542/769**. Fax 06542/76971. www.sporthotelalpin.com. 42 units. Winter 170€–200€ double; summer 180€ double; year-round from 220€–294€ apt for 2. Rates include half-board. Stays of 1–3 days subject to 20% supplement. AE, DC, MC, V. Closed Apr 15–June 1 and Oct 15–Dec 15. **Amenities:** Restaurant; bar; pool; sauna; room service; babysitting; laundry; dry cleaning. *In room:* TV, minibar, hair dryer.

MODERATE
Grand Hotel 🌟   This is the third "grand hotel" that has stood on this site over the years, with the present structure dating from 1986. Based on a late Victorian model, it's a wedding cake of mansard roofs and cream-colored stonework whose

elaborate cornices and moldings are reflected in the cold waters of the lake. Centrally located on its own peninsula, it has a private beach and sun terrace. Although there are other four-star hotels in town of comparable range, this one enjoys the most desirable location, jutting onto the lake. Most of the suites are in the main (Grand Hotel) building; the single and double rooms are in a more lackluster annex. Accommodations come in a wide range of sizes and designs, and some have kitchenettes. Sofa beds are most comfortable, and the bathrooms are superb, with stall showers, tubs, and dual sinks.

The Seerestaurant offers fresh fish daily; equally appealing are the Imperial, a cozy bar, and the Wüder bar, which is housed in a glass dome near the lobby. Recreation instructors offer special programs on such sports as parasailing, river rafting, and glacier skiing.

Esplanade 4, A-5700 Zell am See. ℂ 06542/788. Fax 06542/788-305. www.grandhotel-zellamsee.at. 121 units. 52€–100€ per person double; 85€–112€ per person suite. Rates include half-board. AE, DC, MC, V. Parking 10€. Closed mid-Oct to mid-Nov and 2 weeks around Easter. **Amenities:** Restaurant; 2 bars; room service; babysitting; laundry; dry cleaning. *In room:* TV, minibar, hair dryer, safe.

Hotel St. Georg ⓆkidⓈ
Hotel St. Georg, the stylish country hotel of Zell am See, is graced with flowery balconies and curved awnings. The interior has beamed ceilings, antique wrought iron, and old painted chests. Rooms are medium size, well kept, and nicely decorated, with bathrooms equipped with shower-tub combinations. The hotel also rents five two-bedroom apartments, a favorite with families. Depending on the season, these apartments rent for 90€ to 125€ per person. Apartments are suitable for up to five guests.

The restaurant has vaulted ceilings and a circular open fireplace. A la carte meals are 12€ to 30€. The Austrian cuisine is highly recommended. Try the marinated slices of ox with corn salad and tomato vinaigrette, or perhaps smoked salmon tartar. Main dishes might include medallions of deer in a juniper-cream sauce flavored with cinnamon, or filet of lamb in a thyme sauce with spinach.

Schillerstrasse 32, A-5700 Zell am See. ℂ 06542/768. Fax 06542/768300. st.georg@zell-am-see.at. 36 units. Winter 70€–110€ per person; summer 60€–90€ per person. Rates include half-board. AE, DC, MC, V. Free parking. Closed Apr and Nov. **Amenities:** Restaurant; bar; pool; fitness center; sauna; room service; babysitting; laundry; dry cleaning. *In room:* TV, minibar, hair dryer, safe.

Hotel St. Hubertushof Ⓠ ꝩalue
This large, sprawling hotel is designed like a collection of balconied chalets clustered into a single unit. The sober, elegant decor attracts many repeat visitors, and the flat-roofed dance bar ranks as one of the area's top nightspots. Run by owner Josef Hollaus, the hotel is located in one of the resort's sunniest spots. The large, comfortable, and rustic rooms are a bit cramped if you have a lot of ski equipment, but they contain fine beds. Housekeeping is good, and the small bathrooms are well maintained and contain mostly shower-tub combinations. The menu in the adjoining restaurant includes international specialties as well as a few regional recipes. Meals are well prepared and beautifully served.

Seeuferstrasse 7, Thumersbach, A-5700 Zell am See. ℂ 06542/767. Fax 06542/767-71. www.zellamsee. at/hubertushof. 110 units. Winter 49€–65€ per person double; summer 49€–53€ per person double. Rates include half-board. AE, DC, MC, V. Closed Nov 1 to mid-Dec. **Amenities:** Restaurant; bar; sauna. *In room:* TV.

Hotel Zum Hirschen
Members of the Pacalt family are the congenial, hard-working owners of this balconied hotel with a central location across from the post office. The snug and comfortable rooms are traditionally furnished; bathrooms are

moderate in size with shower-tub combinations and spotless housekeeping. Guests can use the golf course for reduced fees.

Restaurant Zum Hirschen has a rustic setting of light-grained paneling. Specialties include fresh lavarits from the nearby lake, mountain game, and homemade paté. There's also creamed chipped veal or entrecôte Café de Paris. A la carte meals run 8€ to 26€.

Dreifaltigkeitsstrasse 1, A-5700 Zell am See. (℗ 06542/774. Fax 06542/774-0. www.zumhirschen.at. 45 units. Winter 148€–188€ double; summer 76€–104€ double. Rates include half-board. MC, V. Parking 8€. Closed mid-Apr to mid-May and mid-Oct to Dec 1. **Amenities:** Restaurant; bar; pool; fitness center; sauna; solarium; room service; massage; babysitting; laundry; dry cleaning. *In room:* TV, minibar, hair dryer, safe.

ZELL AM SEE AFTER DARK

Zell am See has one of the liveliest after-ski scenes in Land Salzburg. All the clubs and taverns are very informal and, unlike some other resorts, are unpretentious. In addition to the establishments below, there are countless taverns where you can sit around an open fire and enjoy a cold pint of beer or warm wine.

Bacchuskeller, in the Hotel Waldhof, Schmittenstrasse 47 (℗ **06542/775**), is a rustic alpine tavern that often has a local musician, attired in lederhosen and red stockings, play for skiers, who like to dance on the small floor. A beer costs 2€, and a four-course supper goes for 15€ to 25€. It's open daily from 6:30 to 9pm; it's closed April 15 through 30 and October 15 through December 15.

Gasthof Alpenblick, Alte Landersstrasse 6 (℗ **06542/5433**), is a typical Austrian Bierstüberl in the satellite hamlet of Schüttdorf on the road to Kaprun. Zither music is usually played every evening in winter. There's a restaurant on the premises, popular with hikers in summer and skiers in winter. It serves food daily from noon to 9pm in summer and from noon to 10:30pm in winter. Meals here cost 11€ to 20€, and beer goes for 3€. The Gasthof is closed April 5 through May 5 and November 28 through December 28.

8 The Flachgau

So far, we've been exploring sections of Land Salzburg south and southwest of Salzburg; now we'll introduce you to resorts northeast of Salzburg, on our way to Linz in Upper Austria (see chapter 9). One of the chief attractions of the Flachgau district is **Wolfgangsee (Lake Wolfgang),** which lies mainly in Land Salzburg, although its major center, St. Wolfgang, is in Upper Austria. The best-known lake in the Salzkammergut, the Wolfgangsee is 10km (6 miles) long and 2km (1¼ miles) wide. The northwestern shores are fairly inaccessible. The major Land Salzburg resort on the lake is St. Gilgen. Many people visit Lake Wolfgang on day trips from Salzburg, as it's within easy commuting distance.

The Flachgau is a relatively flat area, dividing the Austrian province of Styria from Bavaria in Germany. Unlike the other areas of Land Salzburg discussed above, the Flachgau is primarily a summer resort area for those who enjoy lakeside retreats.

HOF BEI SALZBURG

About 15 minutes from Salzburg on Lake Fuschl is this resort, once popular with Salzburg aristocrats who came for its private hunting and fishing preserves set among mountains, woods, and alpine waters.

There's a nine-hole golf course here, and you can lazily spend the day fishing for trout on the lake. From here it's easy to explore not only the Fuschlsee, but also the Wolfgangsee and the Mondsee.

Like the suburb of Anif (see chapter 7), Hof bei Salzburg is an ideal spot for traditional accommodations, especially come festival time in August, when hotel rooms are virtually impossible to obtain in Salzburg.

GETTING THERE   There are no railway lines running into Hof bei Salzburg, but buses run frequently to and from the nearest railway junctions, at Salzburg and at Bad Ischl. From the railway station at Bad Ischl, about a dozen buses depart every day, each of which stops in Fuschl (trip time: 1 hr.). An equal number of buses departs from the railway station at Salzburg (trip time: 30 min.). If you're driving, take Route 158 east of Salzburg for 18km (trip time: 11 miles). Hof bei Salzburg lies 299km (186 miles) southwest of Vienna.

VISITOR INFORMATION   The **tourist office** in the town center (℡ 06457/ 2214) is open in winter Monday through Saturday from 8am to 7pm, Sunday from 9am to noon and 3 to 5pm; in summer Monday through Saturday from 8am to 6pm, Sunday from 10am to noon.

WHERE TO STAY & DINE
Gasthof Nussbaumer   This 1970s country hotel is set next to an alpine meadow, with outdoor tennis courts and a grassy children's playground. Many of the cozy rooms have balconies, and all have comfortable beds and medium-size bathrooms with tub-and-shower combinations. Everything was completely restored in 2002. On the premises are an indoor heated pool, a sauna, a solarium, a steam bath, and comfortable public areas with sunny windows. The hotel sits just beside a ski lift and offers rentals and lessons for wintertime guests.

Gitzen 13, A-5322 Hof bei Salzburg. ℡ **06229/2275.** Fax 06229/227572. info@nussbaumer.at. 59 units. 75€ double. Rates include half-board. No credit cards. Closed Oct 18–Nov 19. **Amenities:** Dining room; pool; sauna; solarium; steam bath. *In room:* TV.

Hotel Jagdhof ★★   This well-managed four-star hotel is owned and operated by the same group that manages the nearby (and recommended, below) Hotel Schloss Fuschl. Providing less expensive accommodations than those at its grander (five-star) neighbor, it was originally built in the 1500s as a farmhouse and has an authentic style that many 20th-century Austrian hotels have tried to emulate. Rooms vary in size and design, but each is cozily furnished and inviting with excellent beds. Good-size bathrooms are equipped with shower-tub combinations. The hotel is well maintained and tasteful, with an accommodating staff and an excellent restaurant. A la carte meals begin at around 14€ to 18€ each. Specialties include pike terrine with green sauce, and a wide choice of fish and game dishes.

A-5322 Hof bei Salzburg. ℡ **800/528-1243** in the U.S., or 06229/2372. Fax 06229/2372-413. 140 units. 116€–261€ double. Rates include breakfast. AE, DC, MC, V. **Amenities:** Restaurant; bar; pool; 18-hole golf course; tennis court; fitness center; health spa; Jacuzzi; sauna; game room; room service; massage; babysitting; laundry; dry cleaning. *In room:* TV, minibar, hair dryer, safe.

Hotel Schloss Fuschl ★★★   The main section of this castle built in 1450 has a simple facade of unadorned windows. Its former guests have included Jawaharlal Nehru, Eleanor Roosevelt, and Nikita Khrushchev. In World War II, von Ribbentrop selected the *Schloss* as his headquarters; later, Mussolini came here to meet with Nazi leaders. It was the former hunting lodge of the prince-archbishops of Salzburg, who cultivated the peninsula garden jutting onto Lake Fuschl. The interior is decorated with elegant fireplaces, along with timbered ceilings, stone columns, and handcrafted stonework. The swimming pool is dedicated to the Roman goddess Diana.

You can rent either a modern, well-furnished room inside the hotel or a luxurious suite fit for a prince and studded with valuable antiques. From the ample bathrooms with shower-tub combinations to the luxurious beds, each room is inviting and warmly and individually decorated.

The wonderful food at Schloss Restaurant makes it one of the most popular restaurants in Land Salzburg. Patrons may dine in the winter garden or, in summer, on the terrace overlooking the lake. Inside are several elegant rooms, all decorated with antiques and paintings. The view encompasses much of the lake and sometimes a peek of Salzburg. On the menu are lobster terrine with caviar, summer truffles, and a host of seasonal specialties. Reservations are needed. A *Tagesmenu* (daily fixed-price menu) costs 48€ for four courses and 76€ for six courses. The dining room is open daily from 12:15 to 2pm and 7 to 9pm.

A-5322 Hof bei Salzburg. © **06229/22530**. Fax 06229/2253-1531. www.arabellasheraton.com. 84 units. 294€ double; from 494€ suite. Half-board 68€ per person extra. AE, DC, MC, V. **Amenities:** Restaurant; bar; pool; 18-hole golf course; fitness center; health spa; sauna; room service; babysitting; laundry; dry cleaning. *In room:* TV, minibar, hair dryer, safe.

FUSCHL AM SEE

Fuschlsee, the Land Salzburg lake closest to Salzburg, lies 31km (19 miles) east of the festival city, reached by Route 158. The fact that there isn't much to do in Fuschl is the very reason it's so crowded with Salzburgers on weekends, who come to relax by the beautiful lake, and eat and drink in the taverns. Lake Fuschl is ringed by woodland, some of which comprises a nature reserve. The lake, lying to the northwest of the larger Lake Wolfgang, is only 4km (2½ miles) long and less than a mile wide. Fuschl, strictly a summer resort, is on the eastern strip of the lake, across from Hof Bei Salzburg.

You might choose to stay in Fuschl am See as an alternative to Salzburg at any time of the year, but it is especially worth considering during the festival season. From here you can also explore Wolfgangsee.

GETTING THERE   There are no railway lines running into Fuschl, but buses run frequently to and from the nearest railway junctions, at Salzburg and at Bad Ischl. From the railway station at Bad Ischl, about a dozen buses depart every day, each of which stops in Fuschl (trip time: 1 hr.). An equal number of buses departs from the railway station at Salzburg (trip time: 35 min.).

VISITOR INFORMATION   The **tourist office** in the town center (© **06226/ 8250**) is open in winter Monday through Friday from 9am to noon and 3 to 5pm; in summer Monday through Friday from 8am to noon and 3 to 6pm, Saturday from 9am to noon.

WHERE TO STAY

Ebner's Waldhof, Silencehotel ⋨   Opened in the late 1950s as a small inn, this first-class chalet hotel has expanded to become the largest and one of the most prestigious in the village. The interior has a crackling open fireplace. Opening onto geranium-lined balconies, each of the individually decorated rooms is warm and inviting. Beds are comfortable, and bathrooms, which have shower-tub combinations, are spotless. Guests can sign up for guided nature walks, which often end up at the local tavern.

Seepromenade, A-5330 Fuschl am See. © **06226/8264**. Fax 06226/8644. 75 units. 160€–169€ double; 93€ per person apt. Rates include half-board. DC, MC, V. Closed Mar and Nov–Dec 15. **Amenities:** Restaurant; bar; pool; fitness center; sauna; salon; room service; massage; babysitting; laundry; dry cleaning service; shooting gallery. *In room:* TV, minibar, hair dryer, safe.

WHERE TO DINE

Brunnwirt ♣ AUSTRIAN   Brunnwirt is one of the region's leading restaurants, serving light and well-prepared meals to vacationing gourmets from as far away as Vienna. Housed in a 15th-century building thick with atmosphere, the restaurant serves cuisine inspired by regional recipes. The kitchen staff is directed by Frau Brandstätter, who insists on strictly fresh ingredients. Specialties include game dishes, veal, and lamb. The daily menu changes frequently, and portions are generous. Main dishes include roast venison with an herb-flavored cream sauce, mushrooms, and dumplings; marinated char with asparagus mousse; and breast of duckling with orange sauce. Herr Brandstätter will help you select a wine.

Wolfgangseestrasse 11, A-5330 Fuschl am See. ℂ **06226/8236.** Reservations recommended. Main courses 16€–25€. AE, DC, MC, V. Tues–Sat 6–11pm; Sun noon–1:30pm and 6–11pm; July–Aug daily noon–2pm and 6–11pm. Closed Jan.

ST. GILGEN

This leading lakeside resort lies at the western edge of the Wolfgangsee. It's easily accessible from Salzburg, just 29km (18 miles) away. Once a stronghold of the prince-archbishops of Salzburg, St. Gilgen today is the playground for the city's new aristocracy: the fashionable and wealthy who maintain mountain villas here. Parties at festival time tend to be lavish, and you're lucky if you get an invitation. In summer the resort attracts mainly Austrians and Germans to the indoor swimming pool and bathing beach.

The town has many Mozart connections. In the vicinity of the Rathaus (Town Hall) is the house in which Mozart's mother, Anna Maria Pertl, was born in 1720. After the composer's sister, Nannerl, married Baron Berchtold zu Sonnenberg, she also settled in St. Gilgen. The Mozart Fountain, built in 1927, stands on the main square in front of the Rathaus.

GETTING THERE   There are no railway lines running into St. Gilgen, but buses (the same line serving Fuschl am See and Hof bei Salzburg) run frequently to and from the nearest railway junctions, stopping in St. Gilgen after a ride from Salzburg (trip time: 50 min.) or Bad Ischl (trip time: 40 min.). Motorists should head east of Salzburg for 34km (21 miles) on Route 158.

VISITOR INFORMATION   The **tourist office** (ℂ **06227/23480**) in the town center is open in winter Monday, Tuesday, Thursday, and Friday from 9am to noon and 2 to 5pm, Saturday from 9am to noon; in summer Monday through Saturday from 9am to 7pm, Sunday from 10am to noon.

WHERE TO STAY & DINE

Parkhotel Billroth ♣ *(Finds*   A mile from the resort, this hotel, standing on its own spacious grounds, was built in the 1890s but was vastly revamped and enlarged in the 1960s. One wing was designed in a white-walled villa style, while the main section looks more like an overblown chalet. The view from the rooms and from the parasol-dotted sun terrace takes in the lake and the mountains beyond. Most rooms are well furnished, with oriental carpets and often several windows. All have spotlessly maintained bathrooms with a tub and shower. The hotel has its own lakeside beach, with a floating raft ideal for sunbathing. It also allows easy access to the ski lifts.

Billrothstrasse 2, A-5340 St. Gilgen. ℂ **06227/2217.** Fax 06227/221825. www.billroth.at. 48 units. 72€–150€ double. Rates include breakfast. No credit cards. Closed Sept 26–May 1. **Amenities:** Restaurant; bar; tennis court; sauna; massage; babysitting. *In room:* TV.

9

Upper Austria

Too often neglected by North Americans unaware of its charms, Upper Austria contains some of the country's most beautiful scenery. It's a land of mountains, lakes, and picturesque valleys, with Styria and Land Salzburg to its south and Bavaria to the west. To the north it borders the Bohemian forest in the Czech Republic. Its eastern neighbor is Lower Austria. The Austrian name of this province is Bundesland–Ober Österreiche—*Ober*, or upper, because it's closer to the source of the Danube than its twin, Lower Austria.

Upper Austria has three different landscapes. In the north are granite- and gneiss-laden hills, separated in the center of the province by the Valley of the Danube. There are also the limestone Alps and the Salzkammergut lake district, about a 30-minute drive from Linz, which crosses into Upper Austria. Here you'll find the area's most idyllic settings. You can center your activities at the Mondsee or Attersee, Austria's largest lake. Other possible bases are the Traunsee, one of the biggest lakes in the Salzkammergut, or the Wolfgangsee, Austria's most romantic lake.

These lakes (*Seen*) are all great for boating, but if you like to swim, know that the *See* water here is not as warm as you'll find in Carinthia (see chapter 12). The lake district is dotted with farms and fruit trees, from which an excellent cider is produced that actually competes with wine for popularity among the locals.

Upper Austria is a choice location for nature lovers. Most of its towns are small, and although there's a lot of industry, it doesn't blight the province with grime. Industrial installations are often discreetly hidden away, much as they are in Switzerland. Linz, the provincial capital, harbors many historic treasures. Near Linz, the former Nazi concentration camp at Mauthausen is a tragic reminder of the horrors of World War II. Bad Ischl, once a retreat of the imperial court, is the area's most fashionable spa. Emperor Franz Joseph summered here for 60 years. From the beautiful village of Hallstatt, you can tour still-active salt mines at Salt Mountain.

Historic abbeys abound in the province: Abbey of St. Florian, outside Linz, the province's largest abbey and an outstanding example of baroque architecture; Lambach Abbey, outside Wels, a Benedictine abbey founded in 1056; and Kremsmünster Abbey, near Bad Hall, a Benedictine abbey from 777, noted for its famed fish pond and Hall of the Emperors.

You'll find most hotels in the Salzkammergut region, but in every town and village are one or two moderately priced to inexpensive inns. There are few deluxe accommodations here, although several old castles have been turned into romantic lodges. Most hotels around the lakes are open only in the summer. Parking is rarely a problem in these places, and, unless otherwise noted, you park for free.

May is an ideal time to visit. These areas tend to be overrun with visitors, especially Germans, in the peak months of July and August.

Many North Americans aren't familiar with the ski areas of Upper Austria, as they lie for the most part in the southeastern corner. The **Dachstein** is a major ski area—and the **Dachstein Caves** are a spectacular natural attraction. If you like to ski and don't demand massive facilities and a big night scene, you'll find Upper Austria's emerging ski resorts far less expensive than the more popular and frequented resorts in Tyrol and Land Salzburg.

1 Linz: The Provincial Capital ✶

187km (116 miles) NW of Vienna; 130km (81 miles) NE of Salzburg; 269km (167 miles) E of Munich

Linz, the provincial capital of Upper Austria, is the third-largest city in the country after Vienna and Graz. It's the biggest port on the Danube, which widens out considerably here to become a majestic thoroughfare. Three bridges connect Linz with the suburb of Urfahr, on the left bank of the river. If you enter the country from Passau, Germany, Linz will be your gateway to Austria.

Linz was the site of a Roman castle and settlement, Lentia, in the 1st century A.D. By the Middle Ages it had become a thriving center of trade because of its position on the river. Emperor Friedrich III lived here from 1489 to 1493. Now the city sits on a direct rail route linking the Adriatic and Baltic seas. It was here that Austria's first railroad terminated. Because of these factors, Linz became an industrial and manufacturing center, with blast furnaces and steel factories. Its industrial capacity was rapidly built up after Hitler seized Austria in 1938, and the Nazis later established chemical plants here. Unfortunately, Linz's industrial boom made it a frequent target of Allied bombing; it took years to repair the destruction rained upon the city.

Linz today is one of the leading cultural centers of Austria, although it doesn't rival Vienna or Salzburg. The city's name appears in numerous Germanic songs, and many notable figures have been connected with Linz, including native son and composer Anton Bruckner. Mozart dedicated a symphony to the city, and Beethoven wrote his *Eighth Symphony* here. Franz Schubert described with pleasure his holidays in Linz. Goethe, who had a romance with a Linz *Fräulein,* dedicated one of his most lyrical works "to the beautiful girls of Linz."

ESSENTIALS

GETTING THERE   By Plane   Austrian Airlines and its subsidiary, Tyrolean Airways, are the major connections into Linz, especially if you're flying in from another Austrian city. Foreign airlines serving Linz include Lufthansa and Swissair; connections are possible from Düsseldorf, Frankfurt, London, Paris, and Zurich. **Flughafen Linz,** or Blue Danube Airport (✆ **07221/6000;** www.flughafen-linz.at), is 12km (7½ miles) southwest of the city, near the hamlet of Hörsching. There's no bus that runs all the way into Linz, although the airport maintains a 24-hour shuttle bus from the airport to the railway station at Hörsching; from here, you can take one of the commuter trains into Linz—there's one about every hour from early morning to midnight. It's more convenient to take a taxi, which will cost about 25€ one-way to virtually anywhere in Linz.

By Train   Linz sits directly astride the rail lines that connect Salzburg with Vienna, and on those that connect Prague to Graz and the major cities of Slovenia and Croatia. Trains, many of them express, depart at hourly intervals throughout the day and night from Vienna's Westbahnhof (trip time: 2 hr.) and from Salzburg's main station (1¼ hr.). One train every 2 hours throughout the day departs from Graz for Linz (3½ hr.). For rail information, call ✆ **0732/ 1717.** The train station is located south of the city center at Bahnhofplatz.

Upper Austria

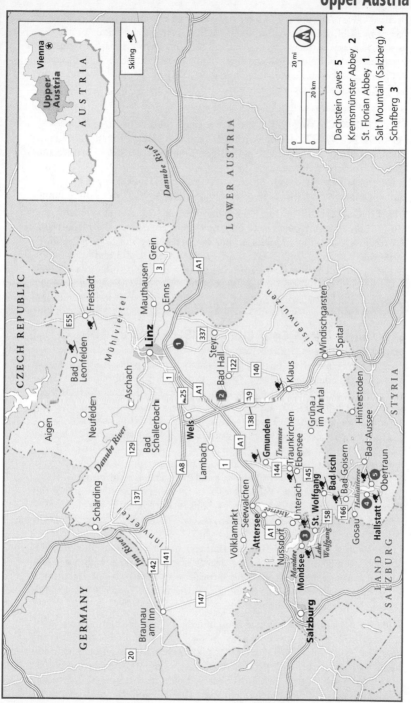

Skiing

Legend:
Dachstein Caves **5**
Kremsmünster Abbey **2**
St. Florian Abbey **1**
Salt Mountain (Salzberg) **4**
Schafberg **3**

20 mi
20 km

AUSTRIA

Upper Austria

Vienna ✳

CZECH REPUBLIC

GERMANY

LOWER AUSTRIA

STYRIA

LAND SALZBURG

Danube River

Inn River

Mühlviertel

Innviertel

Eisenwurzen

Freistadt
Bad Leonfelden
Aigen
Neufelden
Schärding
Braunau am Inn
Aschach
Bad Schallerbach
Lambach
Wels
Linz
Mauthausen
Grein
Enns
Steyr
Bad Hall
Klaus
Windischgarsten
Spital
Grünau im Almtal
Hinterstoden
Bad Aussee
Gmunden
Traunkirchen
Ebensee
Bad Ischl
Bad Goisern
Obertraun
Hallstatt
Gosau
St. Wolfgang
Unterach
Seewalchen
Attersee
Völklamarkt
Nussdorf
Mondsee
Salzburg

Traunsee
Attersee
Mondsee
Lake Wolfgang
Hallstätter

E55
A1
3
337
122
140
19
138
144
145
158
166
1
A1
A8
25
129
137
141
142
147
20

① ② ③ ④ ⑤

293

By Bus   Linz is the center of an extensive network of bus lines carrying passengers from its busy railway station to the outlying villages and hamlets of Upper Austria. However, because of its frequent rail connections to Vienna, Salzburg, and the major cities of Europe, few passengers would consider traveling long distances to Linz by bus. For bus information, call © **0732/1671.**

By Car   If you're driving from Salzburg, head northeast along the Autobahn A-1; from Vienna, take the A-1 autobahn west.

VISITOR INFORMATION   The **Linz tourist office** is at Hauptplatz 1 (© **0732/7070-1777**). It's open Monday through Friday from 8am to 7pm (6pm in winter), Saturday from 9am to 7pm (6pm in winter), and Sunday from 10am to 7pm (6pm in winter).

American Express has an office at Bürgerstrasse 14 (© **66-90-13**), open Monday through Friday from 9am to 5:30pm and Saturday from 9am to noon.

GETTING AROUND   Most visitors limit their exposure in Linz to the city's historic core, most of which is a pedestrian zone centered on the Hauptplatz. Expect lots of shopping possibilities, lots of cafes serving the city's best-known confection (the linzer torte), and access via tram nos. 1 and 3 and bus nos. 19 and 19A, any of which make access to the center from the periphery easy. Buses and trams operate daily from 5am to midnight and cost 1.60€ per ride, for access between any points in Greater Linz. For more information, contact the city tourist office.

EXPLORING LINZ'S CHURCHES & HISTORICAL BUILDINGS

Among the four major cities of Austria, Linz is the least publicized and the least visited by foreign tourists, but its charms are many and its history as a Danube port is long and illustrious. The best way to explore the town is to hire one of the officially sanctioned English-speaking guides provided by the **Linz tourist office,** Hauptplatz 1 (© **0732/7070-2926**). Do-it-yourselfers can request the brochure "A Walk Through the Old Quarter," which highlights the city's main attractions.

The most popular shopping district in the city is **Landstrasse,** which is filled with a variety of boutiques.

Hauptplatz was the original marketplace and is now one of Europe's biggest and most beautiful squares, with baroque and rococo facades surrounding it. On the east side is the **Rathaus (Town Hall).** In the heart of the square stands the **Trinity Column (Dreifaltigkeitssaule),** built in 1723 to mark the city's deliverance from plague, fire, and Turkish invasions. This marble column rises 26m (85 ft.).

The concert hall, named **Brucknerhaus** in honor of Anton Bruckner, the Linz-born composer, has an elliptical facade of glass and steel with a wooden interior. Concerts presented in this acoustically perfect hall have been transmitted throughout the world. The building was constructed from 1969 to 1973 as a cultural and conference center.

Alter Dom   The largest baroque church in the city and formerly the cathedral of Linz, the Alter Dom was constructed by the Jesuits at the end of the 17th century. You mustn't judge this church by its relatively simple exterior. The inside warms up considerably with pink marble columns, an intricately carved pulpit, and lots of statues. The high altar is bedecked with marble images. Native son Anton Bruckner was the church organist for 12 years, and the annual Bruckner Festival is centered here. Two other composers are honored at the same time—

Linz

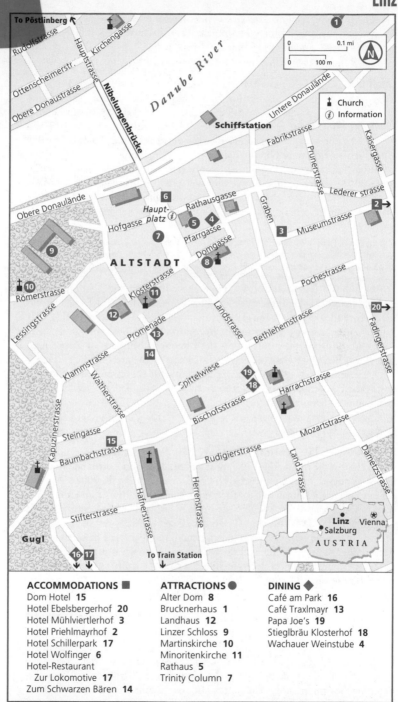

To Pöstlinberg

Rudolfstrasse
Hauptstrasse
Kirchengasse
Ottenscheimerstr.
Obere Donaustrasse
Nibelungenbrücke

Danube River

Schiffstation

Untere Donaulände
Fabrikstrasse
Prunerstrasse
Kaisergasse

Church
ⓘ **Information**

0   0.1 mi
0   100 m

Obere Donaulände

Haupt-platz
Hofgasse ⓘ
Rathausgasse
Lederer strasse
Graben
Museumstrasse

6
5 **4**
7
Pfarrgasse
3
2 →

ALTSTADT
Domgasse
8
Pochestrasse

10
Römerstrasse
Klosterstrasse
11
20 →

Lessingstrasse
12
Promenade
13
Landstrasse
Bethlehemstrasse
Fadingerstrasse

14
Klammstrasse
Walthierstrasse
Spittelwiese
19
18
Harrachstrasse
Mozartstrasse

Kapuzinerstrasse
Steingasse
15
Baumbachstrasse
Bischofsstrasse
Rudigierstrasse
Landstrasse
Dametzstrasse

Stifterstrasse
Hafnerstrasse
Herrenstrasse

Gugl
16 **17**
↓ ↓
To Train Station
↓

Linz ⊛ Vienna
● Salzburg
AUSTRIA

Mozart, who composed his *Linz Symphony* (no. 36) at the building now designated as the city tourist office (Hauptplatz 1), and Beethoven, who composed part of his *Eighth Symphony* in Linz.

Domgasse. ℂ **0732/76-10-31-51.** Free admission. Daily 7am–noon and 3–7pm. Bus: 33.

Landhaus   One of the most important historic buildings in Linz, the Landhaus today serves as the headquarters for Upper Austria's government. The original structure was built around 1570 with a gracefully arcaded courtyard surrounding a fountain. The complex served as the city's university during the 1600s and is still celebrated as the site where Johann Kepler, the noted astronomer and mathematician, taught and developed his theories of planetary motion.

Within the Landhaus's labyrinthine confines are the Church of the Minorite Brothers (see below) and the richly furnished apartments used by Empress Elisabeth ("Sissi") on the night she spent en route from her childhood home in Bavaria to the Hapsburg court in Vienna just before her marriage to Franz Joseph in 1854.

Klosterstrasse 7. ℂ **0732/65-84-0.** Free admission for views of the courtyard and the Minorite church; for more extensive visits, join one of the tourist office's organized tours. Summer daily 8am–4pm; off-season daily 8–11am. (Hours extended for tourist office's organized tours.) Bus: 33.

Linzer Schloss (Linz Castle) ⚶   High above the river and a 5-minute walk west of Hauptplatz stands the castle used by Emperor Friedrich III when he and his court resided in Linz (1486–89). At the turn of the 17th century, Rudolf II erected a new building. A catastrophic fire destroyed the south wing in the early 19th century. Today the castle houses the **Provincial Museum of Upper Austria.** Its exhibits range from medieval art to works by the great moderns. There's an extensive arts-and-crafts department and a folklore collection. During the last few years, the permanent exhibitions have been expanded to include special exhibitions on cultural history.

Tummelplatz 10. ℂ **0732/77-44-19.** Admission 3€ adults, 1.50€ students and seniors. Tues–Fri 9am–5pm; Sat–Sun and holidays 10am–4pm. Bus: 27.

Martinskirche (St. Martin's Church)   The finest example of Carolingian architecture in the region, this is the most ancient church in Austria still (more or less) in its original form. Constructed by Charlemagne during the 700s, it used the ruins of an ancient Roman wall for parts of its foundation. Its interior is decorated with frescoes, several fine examples of baroque art, and a 15th-century Gothic choir. Restored in 1948, the church stands a 10-minute walk west of Hauptplatz, in a neighborhood filled with commercial buildings. A covered passageway connects it directly to the Linzer Schloss (see above). Although it is not open to the public, the church is almost always included as part of the official tours sponsored by the Linz tourist office (ℂ **0732/7070-1777**).

Römerstrasse. Free admission as part of tourist office's official guided tours. Bus: 33.

Minoritenkirche (Landhauskirche, or Church of the Minorite Brothers) Originally built during the 1200s in the early Gothic style, this building was for some time the seat of the city's municipal government until the larger Landhaus was built around it in the late 1500s. The interior was given a baroque overlay in 1758. The building's masterpiece is the high altar by Bartolomeo Altomonte, depicting the Annunciation. The church also contains three red marble side altars.

Klosterstrasse. ℂ **0732/77-20-13-64.** Free admission. Summer daily 8am–4pm; off-season daily 8–11am. (Hours extended for tourist office's organized tours.) Bus: 33.

The Silicon Valley of Mitteleuropa

Linz is not as preoccupied with its baroque and imperial past as many visitors believe. It's also home to a new generation of computer-industry whiz kids, who are transforming prosperous but staid Upper Austria into the Silicon Valley of Mitteleuropa (central Europe). Their ambitions are celebrated at Linz's **Ars Electronica** festival, held annually over a 5- or 6-day period during mid-June. Originating in 1979, it awards the coveted Nika Prize to whichever entrepreneur or developer has created the previous year's most memorable electronic product. The festival has been called "The Oscar Awards Ceremony of the European Computer World." Previous awards have gone to the developer of the best international Web site and the developers of the most realistic computer game.

To house this beehive of computer-driven energy and creativity, and to mark Linz's leading role in Austrian computer development, the **Ars Electronica Center,** Hauptstrasse 2 (✆ **0732/72-720**), was inaugurated in 1995. Its five floors of concrete and glass contain an exhibition hall and a convention center, which, when not in use, are the site of a "museum of the future." Exhibitions here are based on the most recent trends and inventions in the computer world. When conventions and awards ceremonies are not underway, the museum is open Wednesday through Sunday from 10am to 6pm. Admission is 6€ for adults and 3€ for children 14 and under.

SIDE TRIPS FROM LINZ
PÖSTLINGBERG
The most popular day trip from Linz is to Pöstlingberg, 5km (3 miles) northwest of the city on the north bank of the Danube. You can drive here via Rudolfstrasse on the left bank of the river, taking a right turn onto Hagensstrasse; or, you can take the electric railway.

Pöstlingberg has a **botanical garden** with exotic tropical plants, and the summit terrace is a riot of blooming flowers in summer. A defensive tower now houses a grotto with a miniature railway, a favorite with children. The **pilgrimage church** is worth a visit for its 18th-century carved wood Pietà, but most tourists make the ascent mainly to take in the view over the Danube Valley, with Linz spread out below. The panorama stretches all the way to the foothills of the Alps and to the Bohemian forest in the Czech Republic.

MAUTHAUSEN: THE CONCENTRATION CAMP
You can make a sobering outing from Linz to Mauthausen, 29km (18 miles) down the Danube (southeast) from the provincial capital. The village is very beautiful in its own right and is often visited for its medieval architecture. Overshadowing its attractiveness is the fact that during World War II, the Nazis operated a concentration camp and extermination center about 3km (2 miles) northwest of the village. Austria's Jews were slaughtered in great numbers, and the camp remains a horrifying testament to the evils of Nazism. Thousands of other so-called undesirables were also annihilated here, including homosexuals and Gypsies.

A Baroque Masterpiece: The Abbey of St. Florian

The **Abbey of St. Florian** ⚔⚔, the largest in Upper Austria, is an outstanding example of baroque architecture. Augustinians have occupied this site since the 11th century, although the baroque structures you see today were built between 1686 and 1751. St. Florian was a Christian martyr who was drowned in the Enns River around A.D. 304. He is often called upon by the faithful to protect their homes against flood and fire. The abbey was constructed over his grave.

The greatest composer of church music in 19th-century Austria, Anton Bruckner (1824–96), became the organist at St. Florian as a young man and composed many of his masterpieces here. Although he went on to greater fame in Vienna, he was granted his wish and buried at the abbey church underneath the organ he loved so dearly. You can visit the crypt as well as the room where the composer lived for about a decade.

The western exterior of the abbey is crowned with a trio of towers. The doorway is especially striking. As you enter the inner court, you'll see the **Fountain of the Eagle.** In the library, which contains some 140,000 books and manuscripts, are allegorical ceiling frescoes by Bartolomeo Altomonte. The marble salon honors Prince Eugene of Savoy for his heroic defense of Vienna against a major siege by the Turks. The ceiling paintings here depict the Austrian victory over the "infidels."

The **Altdorfer Gallery** is the most outstanding part of the abbey, surpassing even the Imperial Apartments. Well-known works by Albrecht Altdorfer, a 16th-century master of the Danube school of painting, are displayed. Altdorfer was a warm, romantic contemporary of Dürer, to whom he is often compared. He painted more than a dozen panels for the abbey's Gothic church, depicting, among other scenes, the martyrdom of St. Sebastian.

The **Imperial Apartments,** the Kaiserzimmer, are reached by climbing a splendid staircase. Pope Pius VI once stayed here, and a whole host of royalty have occupied these richly decorated quarters. You're allowed to visit the bedrooms of the emperors and empresses.

The **abbey church** has twin towers reaching 79m (260 ft.). The church is distinguished by columns of pink marble, quarried near Salzburg. Lavish stucco decoration was used in the interior, and the pulpit is in black marble. The choir stalls are heavily gilded and adorned with ornamentation and carving. You should allow about an hour for a tour.

Visitors can enter the church free, but guided tours of the monastery are 5€ for adults and 1.30€ for children. Tours are conducted April through October daily at 10 and 11am and at 2, 3, and 4pm. Otherwise, you must write to the abbey for permission to visit.

The abbey, Stiftstrasse 1, St. Florian (© **07224/89020**), lies 19km (12 miles) southeast of Linz. It has its own exit (St. Florian) from the autobahn linking Linz and Vienna. In addition, bus nos. 2040 and 2042 run throughout the day from Linz to St. Florian.

The Austrian government doesn't try to hide the site of so many atrocities. The camp was declared a national monument in 1949, and often schoolchildren are brought here and taught what went on in this notorious camp. Various countries that lost citizens here have erected memorials outside the camp to honor their dead. It's believed that the Nazis killed some 200,000 victims here, although exact figures are not known.

You can visit the huts where the condemned, most of whom almost surely knew their fate, were kept. You are also led down the infamous "Stairway of Death," which the prisoners took on their last walk. To visit the ghastly site is a shattering experience, but still people come here to be painfully reminded of a cruel and savage era.

To reach Mauthausen from Linz, take one of the dozen or so local buses departing from Linz's main railway station for Mauthausen (trip time: 1 hr.).

It takes about 1½ hours to take a tour of the camp. The camp is open February through April and October through December 15 daily from 8am to 4pm, and May through October daily from 8am to 6pm; it's closed November through January. For more information, call © **07238/2269.** Admission is 2€ for adults and 1€ for children.

SHOPPING

Quietly prosperous Linz is the regional center of the antiques trade, so if you're interested in adding a piece or two to your collection, consider dropping into any of the following shops, including **Richard Kirchmayr Antiquitäten,** Bethlehemstrasse 5 (© **0732/77-01-17).**

Linz is home to a branch of Vienna-based **Dorotheum,** Fabrikstrasse 26 (© **0732/77-31-320),** an auction house that has allowed many socially prominent but impoverished families to keep their bills paid during hard times by means of discreet auctions of the family heirlooms. Auctions take place every Wednesday at 1:30pm, but there's plenty of time for viewing the objects during normal business hours in the week preceding the sale.

Less desirable objects are scattered randomly among the display tables at the **Linzer Flohmarkt (Linz Flea Market),** which takes place on the Hauptplatz every Saturday from March to mid-November from 7am to around 2pm, or until the inventories are depleted. Amid lots of junk and debris from estate sales throughout the region, it's still possible to find something charming and handcrafted.

At **O. Ö. Heimatwerk,** Landstrasse 31 (© **0732/7733760),** you can buy local handcrafts such as pewter, intricately patterned silver, rustic ceramic pots, slippers, dresses, and dressmaking fabrics in regional patterns (lots of polka dots). The entrance to the airy, sunny store is under an arcade, although the shop windows face the busy pedestrian walkway of Linz's main shopping district.

WHERE TO STAY
EXPENSIVE
Hotel Schillerpark ☆☆   The finest and most prestigious hotel in town, this mirror-covered structure was built around 1980 at the edge of the city's pedestrian zone, a 5-minute walk north of the railway station. A center of nightlife in Linz, the government-rated five-star hotel contains three comfortable restaurants, two bars, and a gambling casino, open daily from 3pm to 3am. Rooms are airy, sunny, and filled with tastefully streamlined furniture. The beds are very comfortable, and the bathrooms are well equipped with robes and shower-tub

combinations. Two rooms are furnished with waterbeds, which must be specially requested when reservations are made.

Of the three restaurants within the hotel, the Rouge et Noir, serving French and Austrian cuisine, is the best; the Rotisserie am Schillerpark offers upscale dining, serving regional cuisine; and the Café am Pair serves small meals plus snacks, pastries, and coffees.

Rainerstrasse 2–4, A-4020 Linz. © **0732/6950.** Fax 0732/69509. www.austria-trend.at. 111 units. 176€–206€ double; 240€–446€ suite. Rates include breakfast. AE, DC, MC, V. Parking 12€. Tram 1 or 3. **Amenities:** 3 restaurants; 2 bars; casino; fitness center; sauna; room service; babysitting; laundry; dry cleaning. *In room:* A/C, TV, minibar, hair dryer, safe.

MODERATE
Dom Hotel ⚑   Ideally located in a quiet area in the center of town, this hotel is only a few minutes' walk from the main rail station. It was built in the 1970s and renovated in the late 1980s, and today it provides five floors of subdued decor a few steps from the cathedral. The owners maintain the hotel as a cozy stopping place. The comfortably furnished rooms have private (though small) bathrooms, with adequate shelf space and mostly shower-tub combinations. On the ground floor is a cocktail bar, and the hotel restaurant serves international specialties and Austrian dishes.

Baumbachstrasse 17, A-4020 Linz. © **0732/778441.** Fax 0732/775432. 44 units. 100€ double; 120€ suite. Rates include breakfast. AE, DC, MC, V. Tram: 1 or 3. **Amenities:** Restaurant; bar; fitness center; sauna; solarium; room service; babysitting; laundry; dry cleaning service. *In room:* TV, minibar, hair dryer.

Hotel Ebelsbergerhof   Located in the leafy suburb of Ebelsberg, 3 miles (5km) east of the center of Linz, this government-rated four-star hotel built around 1990 is easy to find because of its vivid yellow-and-green facade. The interior is woodsy and elegant, with lush curtains and thick beams. Rooms are well furnished, with small but spotless bathrooms containing shower-tub combinations.

Wiener Strasse 485, A-4020 Linz. © **0732/311-733.** Fax 0732/31-17-33-402. www.tiscover.com/ebels bergerhof. 43 units. 102€ double; 170€ suite. Rates include breakfast. AE, DC, MC, V. Tram: 1, then bus 11. **Amenities:** Restaurant; bar; sauna; solarium; room service; babysitting; laundry; dry cleaning. *In room:* TV, minibar, hair dryer, safe.

Hotel Prielmayrhof ⚑   This government-rated four-star hotel is housed in a distinguished-looking five-story structure, one of the few privately owned buildings constructed in Linz during World War II (in 1942); a new wing was added in 1994. Between 1945 and 1955, the hotel housed American occupation troops, who faced their Soviet counterparts across the Danube during the early days of the Cold War. Today the hotel is owned by Franz Zihitner, the English-speaking son of the original builders. It contains efficiently modern and comfortable rooms, with bathrooms that leave much to be desired; about half contain shower-tub combinations. In the restaurant, Prielmayrhof, a *Tagesmenu* (daily menu) depends on the chef's whims and market availability.

Weissenwolfstrasse 33, A-4020 Linz. © **0732/77-41-31.** Fax 0732/77-15-69. 64 units. 105€ double; 130€ apt. Rates include buffet breakfast. AE, DC, MC, V. Half a mile east of Hauptplatz. Bus: 21. **Amenities:** Restaurant, lounge; sauna; laundry; dry cleaning. *In room:* TV, minibar, hair dryer, safe.

Hotel Wolfinger   Hotel Wolfinger is housed in a 500-year-old building on what is the largest and best preserved baroque square in Europe. The entrance is through an arcade, a short distance from the Danube, in the middle of a pedestrian zone. A new wing was added to the hotel in 1992. Since 1975, the Dangl family, with the help of an enthusiastic staff, has run the hotel. With a respect for tradition, they have added modern comforts. Rooms are furnished with antiques. The beds are comfortable, and the small, well-maintained bathrooms contain shower-tub combinations.

Hauptplatz 19, A-4020 Linz. © 0732/773291. Fax 0732/77329155. wolfinger@austria-classic-hotels.at. 46 units. 110€ double. Rate includes buffet breakfast. AE, DC, MC, V. Bus: 26 or 27. **Amenities:** Restaurant; bar; lounge. *In room:* TV.

INEXPENSIVE
Hotel Muhlviertlerhof *(Value)*   This three-story town house, originally built in the 1740s, is maintained by the Lumpi family. Cozy and comfortable, with a convenient location about 100 yards from Hauptplatz, the hotel offers well-scrubbed accommodations designed with both charm and efficiency. The small rooms have good beds and well-organized bathrooms with shower-tub combinations. About half the rooms offer views of a small garden in back. The Klosterhof Restaurant, under different management, occupies part of the building's street level. Parking is usually available free after 6pm on nearby streets.

Graben 24–25, A-4020 Linz. © 0732/77-22-68. Fax 0732/77-22-68-34. 23 units. 67€ double. Rate includes breakfast. AE, DC, MC, V. Tram: 3. **Amenities:** Restaurant; bar. *In room:* TV.

Hotel-Restaurant Zur Lokomotive   This simple, unpretentious, and comfortable place is a family-operated hostelry in a five-story building erected just before World War I. Its interior has been efficiently renovated. Rooms as well as the bathrooms are a bit small but have shower-tub combinations. A restaurant on the premises serves traditional Austrian food to many business workers throughout the day, as well as passengers departing from or arriving at the railway station, which is about a minute's walk away.

Weingartshofstrasse 40, A-4020 Linz. © 0732/65-45-54. Fax 0732/65-83-37. www.hotel-lokomotive.at. 46 units. 72€ double. Rate includes breakfast. AE, DC, MC, V. Tram: 3. **Amenities:** Restaurant; bar; room service; babysitting. *In room:* TV.

Zum Schwarzen Bären *(Value)*   Set within a block of the main, all-pedestrian shopping street of Linz, this is a substantial-looking stucco-covered building that offers a traditional-looking restaurant and *Weinstube* (wine tavern); a sense of solid, somewhat unimaginative tradition; and well-scrubbed but not overly large bedrooms. Each of them has touches of wooden paneling, or at least varnished wooden trim, a mixture of alpine and blandly contemporary furniture, and a tile-sheathed bathroom with a shower (in rare instances, there's a shower-tub combination). A plaque in front identifies the building as the birthplace of one of Linz's most renowned native sons, Richard Tauber (1891–1948), an opera singer who was born here long before the many architectural alterations enlarged and revised the original design of the house.

Herrenstrasse 9-11, A-4020 Linz. © 0732/772477-0. Fax 0732/772477-47. www.linz-hotel.at. 30 units. 72€–96€ double. Rates include breakfast. AE, DC, MC, V. Bus: 33. **Amenities:** Restaurant; wine tavern; laundry service. *In room:* TV.

WHERE TO DINE
EXPENSIVE
Restaurant Verdi and Restaurant Einkeher ★★ MODERN CONTINENTAL/AUSTRIAN   The core of this house, whose panoramic view sweeps out over and above Linz, was built about a century ago, but because of frequent alterations, very little of it is still recognizable. Many Linzers come here for the view, the fresh high-altitude air, and a cuisine that includes both conservative

time-tested folkloric dishes (in Einkeher) and more experimental modern cuisine in Verdi. Frankly, the main allure that attracts residents as a destination in its own right is Verdi, where rich-looking earth tones and leather-covered chairs create the kind of place where you can hang out for a prolonged evening meal. Menu items reflect the changing seasons and a willingness to experiment on the part of the kitchen staff. The best examples include cannelloni stuffed with a purée of celeriac, served with king prawns and lobster sauce; roasted rack of lamb with gnocchi, thyme, and antipasti-style roasted peppers; and—in season—filet of venison with apple-studded cabbage, two different sauces, and bread dumplings. Previous diners have included the captains and coaches of some of Austria's most venerated soccer teams, politicians, and discreetly rich local residents.

Pachmayrstrasse 137, in Lichtenberg. (✆) **0732/733005.** Reservations recommended for Verdi, not necessary at Einkeher. In Verdi, main courses 17.50€–22€, set-course menu 58€. In Einkeher, main courses 12€–17€. DC, MC, V. Tues–Sat 5pm–midnight. Directions: There's no public bus to this place. Either take a taxi or drive north from Linz, following the Leonfelder Strasse for 3km (2 miles). On the outskirts of the village of Lichtenberg, you'll see a sign pointing to the Restaurant Verdi.

INEXPENSIVE

Papa Joe's 🅐 *Finds* CAJUN/CREOLE/CARIBBEAN   Between the mid-1400s and 1975, this dignified-looking building was an Ursuline convent. In 1999, one of the town's newest restaurants opened within its historic premises. Today you'll find a busy American-style bar area near the entrance, with margaritas selling for 7€ each and a trio of New Orleans–inspired dining rooms filled with chattering diners and the smell of spicy Cajun and Creole cuisine. Come here for a reminder of some of the restaurant themes you left behind in the U.S. and for the possibility of meeting a local at the bar. Savory menu items include jambalaya, gumbos and stews, jerk chicken and pork, and, when it's available, spicy preparations of fish that include catfish. There's live music virtually every night—pianos, guitars, and jazz trios—beginning between 7 and 10pm, depending on the night's schedule.

Landstrasse 31. (✆) **0732/774686.** Reservations not necessary. Main courses 4€–17€. MC, V. Daily 10am–1am. Tram: 1 or 5.

Stieglbräu Klosterhof AUSTRIAN   In some rooms of this large homelike restaurant, formally dressed waiters serve food under high ceilings, with 18th-century paintings by local artists on the walls; in others, youths in jeans and leather jackets, along with a scattering of older people, fill the air with smoke and loud talk. A quick tour of the variety of rooms might help you decide where you feel most comfortable. (The most sedate areas tend to be one floor above street level.)

Centuries ago, this building served as one of the outposts of Kremsmünster Abbey, several days' horseback ride away. Today, from a position on the edge of Linz, it functions as the town's most likable beer garden, with a sprawling outdoor terrace and a cavernous interior. An old-fashioned, overworked staff serves copious portions of traditional Austrian food throughout. Menu items include Wiener schnitzels, pork schnitzels, paprika goulash, salads, and braised beef served with mushrooms. Desserts include a linzer torte covered with apricot jam. Many people come for just a drink.

Landstrasse 30. (✆) **0732/77-33-73.** Reservations recommended. Main courses 5€–15€. DC, MC. Daily 9am–midnight. Tram: 1 or 3.

Wachauer Weinstube AUSTRIAN   A baroque bas-relief of an ecstatic saint adorns the corner of this historic building on a cobblestone sidewalk near the old cathedral. The smallest portion of any wine sold here is a quarter liter, about two full glasses. Wines from the Wachau region are featured, including five whites, four reds, and one rosé, each priced from 1.60€ per glass. The establishment serves a limited menu of standard fare, including bean or goulash soup, bratwurst, and half a grilled chicken, plus a self-service buffet with salads, vegetables, and pasta. Pfarrgasse 20. (**C**) **0732/774-618.** Reservations recommended. Main courses 5.50€–12€. AE, MC, V. Mon–Fri 11am–1am. Bus: 33.

CAFES

Linz is world famous for the linzer torte, which looks like an open jam pie. The torte is filled mainly with raspberry jam or preserves, while the batter, made in part from ground unblanched almonds, is flavored with cinnamon, cloves, and cocoa. The treat is cut in thin wedges and sprinkled with confectioners' sugar. You shouldn't leave Linz without trying a piece.

Café am Park, in the Hotel Schillerpark, Rainerstrasse 2–4 (**C** **0732/6950;** tram: 1 or 3), is the hottest and most popular place to go on a Sunday afternoon in Linz. It's a big L-shape room redecorated in 1994 in a streamlined modern style. You can get all the beverages and light snacks you'd expect, as well as wholesome meals priced from 7€ to 15€. It's open daily from 6:30am to 11pm.

Café Traxlmayr, Promenade 16 (**C** **0732/773353;** bus: 26 or 27), has an amazing pre–World War I mystique. This 150-year-old coffeehouse is next to a baroque palace on a wide ornamental boulevard, in a beige-and-brown building. Its outdoor sun terrace is lined with thick privets and geraniums. It even has a fountain in front, designed to resemble a little boy playing with two gurgling fish. Inside, the formally dressed staff scurry around with trays of coffee and cakes. The decor includes 1890s-style round marble tables, big mirrors, and crystal-and-gilt chandeliers. A rack of Austrian and foreign-language newspapers gives this place all the trappings of a Viennese coffeehouse. During cold weather, hot dishes such as goulash soup are served. Elaborate pastries are priced from 2€; coffee starts at 2€. It's open Monday through Saturday from 8am to 11pm.

LINZ AFTER DARK

Although the nightlife here isn't as trendy or as edgy as what you will find in Vienna, Linz offers reputable theater and music venues, and enough nocturnal diversions to keep you amused during your stay.

CULTURAL LINZ

The city's most prestigious and visible theater is the historic **Landestheater,** Promenade 39 (**C** **0732/76-11-100;** bus: 26 or 27). Originally built in 1670 and home to the local opera company, it's the city's all-purpose venue for theater, dance, and music of all kinds. Part of its interior is devoted to the smaller **Kammerspiele** (same address and phone), which tends to put on more contemporary and, in many cases, more experimental theater. A more modern concert venue is the one within the **Brucknerhaus,** Untere Donaulände 7 (**C** **0732/77-52-30;** bus: 19 or 19A). Originally built in the 1970s, it presents concerts every year from mid-September to early October as part of the city's annual Bruckner Festival. Although most of the performances are devoted to the symphonies of Linz's native son, Anton Bruckner, works by Beethoven and Mozart are also included.

Tickets to performances within any of the theaters mentioned above can be obtained directly at their box offices (Brucknerhaus box office is open Mon–Fri 10am–6pm) or by contacting the ticket agency that represents virtually everything in Upper Austria, **Kartenbüro,** Herrenstrasse 4 (**C** **0732/77-88-00;** tram: 1 or 3).

For a rundown on what's doing within Upper Austria, ask for a copy of the monthly pamphlet "Was Ist Los in Linz und Oberösterreich" ("What's Happening in Linz and Upper Austria"). The tourist office will usually give you a copy for free; it will cost you 2€ if you buy it at a local newsstand.

THE BAR & CLUB SCENE

At night, Linz becomes a little more lively than you might have expected, judging from its daytime pace. There are a number of decent bars worth checking out, including the **Nachtschwärmer Bar,** Hofberg 4 (© **0732/79-60-50;** tram: 1 or 3). With a name that translates from German as the "Nightcruiser Bar," how can you possibly go wrong? A cellar-level spot described by virtually everyone under 25 as the coolest place in Linz is the **Alex Bar,** Hofberg 4 (© **0732/77-12-62;** tram: 1 or 3). And a cozy site that's as friendly as anywhere else in town, aside from the odd habit of playing bouts of heavy metal, is **Ostbahn Bar,** Obere Dunaulände 13 (© **0732/77-24-22;** bus: 19 or 19A).

Looking to linger over a glass of wine in Old Austria? Head for the **Alte Welt Weinkeller,** Hauptplatz 4 (© **0732/77-00-53;** tram: 1 or 3), where a choice of mostly Austrian and Hungarian wines are sold by the glass or the bottle in a very old, very traditional setting that, judging by the state of the wood, has been here virtually forever. At least once a week, based on an iffy schedule, live bands perform or poets and writers read from their works, usually in German.

DANCING

If you want to go dancing, head to Linz's biggest disco, **Funky Town,** Wegscheider Strasse 3 (© **0732/37-13-34;** tram: 1 or 3), where one huge floor is divided into several bars with several different sound systems. A completely separate area, with its own music, is **Filou** (same address and phone). A cover charge of 5€ buys you your first drink and unrestricted access between both areas. Filou tends to have a little older crowd, but frankly, the boundaries seem to be more fluid every year. Both sites are open Wednesday through Saturday from 9pm till around 4am.

CASINO ACTION

Yes, there's a **casino** in Linz, within the Hotel Schillerpark (see above), Rainerstrasse 2–4 (© **0732/65-44-870;** tram: 1 or 3), but nothing so scintillating that it will tempt you to mortgage your house or spend the children's college fund. The casino contains two separate sections of different degrees of formality. The **Casino Léger,** open daily from noon to midnight, has no dress code and houses most of the establishment's slot machines. A step away, the **Linzer Casino,** open daily from 3pm to 4am, is more formal and grander. A ticket that grants admission to both sections costs 21€ but is accompanied by gaming tokens for an equivalent amount. You must be over 18 and present a valid passport to enter either area.

2 Lakes Attersee & Mondsee

ATTERSEE 🏵🏵

The largest lake in the Austrian Alps, Attersee comes alive in summer when a sports-loving crowd flocks to the resort town that bears the lake's name. In our opinion, the lake is too cold for swimming almost all the time (although Polar Bear Club members might disagree), but it's a great draw for boaters in summer. Attersee is 50km (31 miles) east of Salzburg and 69km (43 miles) west of Linz.

Those interested in fishing will appreciate the lake's clear alpine waters, with trout, char, and, in little tributaries, brook trout beneath the surface. At many guesthouses along the shore you can have the fish you caught for dinner.

The blue-green *See* is 20km (12½ miles) long and about 2km (1½ miles) wide, with many orchards growing on its uplands. There's a road around the entire body of water. From the southern part of the lake to the west of Burgau, you can take a 12-minute walk to a beautiful gorge, the **Burggrabenklamm,** with a waterfall, one of the most scenic sights along the Attersee.

GETTING THERE   Attersee lies at the terminus of a small railway running from the junction of Vöcklamarkt, just under 14km (9 miles) to the north (about a dozen trains make the short run from Vöcklamarkt to Attersee every day). Reaching Vöcklamarkt is easy, as rapid trains stop there every 2 hours or less from both Salzburg and Linz. Attersee is not served by bus lines. If you're driving from Linz, head west along the A-1; from Salzburg, go east on the A-1.

VISITOR INFORMATION   The **tourist office,** A-4864 Attersee (© **07666/ 7719**), is in the town center. It's open in winter Monday through Friday from 9am to noon and 2 to 5pm; in summer Monday through Friday from 9am to 6pm, Saturday from 9am to noon, Sunday from 9am to 11am.

WHERE TO STAY & DINE IN TOWN
Hotel Seegasthof Oberndorfer   This well-established, traditional family-owned hotel sits on the shores of the Attersee. The sunny, carpeted, and comfortable medium-size rooms have balconies. Bathrooms have plenty of shelf space and shower-tub combinations. From the rooms there's a good view over the lake to the Höllengebirge. Gertrude Oberndorfer serves excellent Austrian cuisine, and in warm weather, meals are served on a terrace next to the lake, which is shaded by old chestnut trees.

Hauptstrasse 18, A-4864 Attersee. © **07666/786491.** Fax 07666/364-91. www.tiscover.com. 29 units. 112€–124€ double; 149€–180€ suite. Rates include buffet breakfast. Notify desk at reservations if you intend to use a credit card. AE, MC, V. Free parking in a lot next to the hotel, 8€ in the garage. Closed Nov. **Amenities:** Restaurant; bar; swimming lake; fitness center; sauna; room service; massage; babysitting; laundry; dry cleaning. *In room:* TV, minibar, hair dryer.

WHERE TO STAY & DINE AROUND THE LAKE
At the northern extremity of the Attersee is the small village and holiday resort of **Seewachen am Attersee.** It offers sailing and other watersports, but the main reason we recommend it is the Gasthof Häupl (see below).

You could also base yourself at the lakeside hamlet of **Unterach am Attersee.** It's so small it doesn't appear on most maps, but it occupies one of the loveliest positions on the lake. It's on the right bank, across from Weissenbach, and from here you can explore either the Attersee or Mondsee.

Gasthof Häupl 🟊🟊   One of the region's most elegant hotels, with some of its finest food, too, this establishment began its life as a simple inn during the 1600s. Today, it stays open year-round, unusual for these parts. It sits in the center of the village, across the street from the lakeshore. From the street side, it has a pleasant facade and a steeply sloped series of interconnected gables. From the lakeside, masses of flowers hang from boxes on handcrafted balconies. The interior looks like a tastefully opulent private house. Rooms are well furnished, beautifully maintained, and often quite large. Bathrooms, among the finest in the area, are equipped with shower-tub combinations and are spotlessly maintained.

In the rustic dining room, one of the region's best, the chef prepares such delicacies as grilled char from the lake with baby vegetables in a savory sauce, perhaps followed by a dessert of curd-paste dumplings with stewed plums. Frau Häupl, whose family has run this place for the past seven generations, inspires the culinary

The Great Outdoors in the Salzkammergut

The **Salzkammergut** is one of the summer playgrounds of Europe, centered on the towns of **Bad Ischl, St. Wolfgang,** and **Hallstatt.** Soaring mountains with needlelike peaks and shimmering lakes along forested valleys are the backdrop for any number of outdoor activities, including boating, fishing, swimming, and hiking. The best known of all the Salzkammergut's 27 lakes lie to the west of Bad Ischl: the **Mondsee,** the **Attersee,** and the **Wolfgangsee.**

BIKING   While most of the province's terrain is too hilly for biking, you'll find great places to bike in the districts around the lakes, particularly around the Attersee or the Traunsee. The best cycling path is the 14km (9 miles) from Bad Ischl to St. Wolfgang; of course, biking on the back roads is more scenic. Tourist offices in either town will help you plan routes. You can rent bikes from the most visible gas station in Attersee, **Petrol Schweiger** (② 07666/7821), for around 10€ per day. If you'd like to join a local bicycle tour through and around the region, consider **Eurobike Eurofun Touristik,** Mühlstrasse 20, Obertraum am See (② 06219/7444).

BOATING   Most of the lakes scattered amid the forests of Upper Austria are deep, cold, and clear, and as such, boaters love them. If you want to rent a boat, the local tourist offices of every lakefront resort covered within this chapter can recommend local outfitters, one of the most visible of which is **Wolfgangseeschiffahrt,** A-5360 St. Wolfgang (② 06138/2232-0).

If you're interested in exploring one of the lakes while someone else worries about navigation and maintenance of the equipment, consider one of the Attersee tours offered by **Stern Schiffahrt,** A-4863 Attersee (② 07666/7806). From June to mid-September, a 2-hour cruise along the south shore of the Attersee is 11€; cruises depart every 2 hours from 9am to 5pm. During the same time period, a 1-hour tour along the lake's north shore costs 7€ and departs at hourly intervals every day from 10am to 5pm.

CANOEING   Some of Upper Austria's best white water lies along the swift-flowing Traun River. An excellent outfitter of kayak expeditions is **Daxner,** A-4853 Steinbach (② 07663/268), headquartered in a village across the lake from Attersee. A half-day expedition is 30€, a full-day expedition is 50€, and a 3-day outing is 132€.

techniques of an able group of chefs. Except for December 24, the restaurant is open daily from 11:30am to 2pm and 6 to 9:45pm.

Hauptstrasse 20, A-4863 Seewachen am Attersee. ② **07662/6363.** Fax 07662/6363-62. www.oberoester reich.at/haeupl. 33 units. 90€–100€ double; 135€–200€ suite. Rates include buffet breakfast. AE, DC, MC, V. **Amenities:** Restaurant; bar; sauna; room service; babysitting; laundry; dry cleaning. *In room:* TV, minibar.

Hotel Georgshof *Value*   Built in the early 1980s of well-preserved wood and cream-colored stucco, this cozy chalet (one of the town's two hotels) is set on a hillside about a 5-minute uphill walk from the center; it's 183m (600 ft.) higher than the town itself. Windows are embellished with regional designs and look out onto

FISHING The Salzkammergut is one of the best places to fish in all of Austria—or Europe, for that matter. You'll need a license, though. For information, ask at a local tourist office, especially those at Attersee, Hallstatt, Mondsee, and St. Wolfgang.

GOLF The best course is the **Salzkammergut Golfclub** at Bad Ischl (© 06132/26340). This 18-hole, par-71 course charges greens fees of 40€ to 50€ daily.

HIKING The Salzkammergut is great hiking country, and local tourist offices not only suggest hikes, but also provide route maps. The Bad Ischl area, for example, has more than 100km (62 miles) of trails. In the Attersee area, one 35km (22-mile) hike takes 8 hours to finish. One of the best hiking trips involves circumnavigating Austria's largest lake (Attersee), which can take anywhere from 3 to 5 days, depending on your fitness level and how extensive an itinerary you want to pursue. Depending on your route, you can hike between 50km and 97km (31 and 60 miles), and choose paths of varying degrees of difficulty. For more details about possible outings, the tourist office in Attersee (© 07666/7719) will send you a booklet indicating the hiking possibilities and their estimated times.

TENNIS Your best bet is the **Tennisclub Bad Ischl** in the heart of the resort (© 06132/24432 or 06132/23926). The club offers both indoor and outdoor courts along with ball-throwing machines. You can also rent rackets.

WATERSPORTS Because of their proximity to such cities as Linz and Salzburg, the lakes of Upper Austria are popular spots for water-skiing and scuba diving. If you want to go water-skiing, the reception desk at lakeside hotels can provide names and addresses of suitable establishments. A well-recommended company on the Attersee, however, is **Häuplhof,** which operates out of the hamlet of Muhlbach, near Attersee (© 07666/7788). And if you want to scuba-dive in waters that originated high in the Alps, head for **Reiter,** in the town of Unterach (© 07665/8524), which specializes in year-round dives into the cold, dark waters of lakes whose depths sometimes exceed 168m (550 ft.).

a backyard with a sun terrace. Inside is a timber-and-stucco bar area. The Hollerweger family, your host, offers spacious and tastefully furnished bedrooms. Beds are comfortable, and the well-kept bathrooms contain shower-tub combinations.

A-4866 Unterach am Attersee. © 07665/8501. Fax 07665/85018. 25 units. 54€–76€ double. Rates include half-board. AE, DC, MC, V. Closed the last week of Nov–Dec 20. **Amenities:** Dining room; lounge; pool; sauna; laundry; dry cleaning. In room: TV.

MONDSEE ⚓

"Moon Lake," or **Mondsee,** is one of the warmest lakes in the Salzkammergut. Since Roman times, this crescent-shape lake has been named for the celestial body it resembles. The Salzburg–Vienna autobahn runs along the south shores of this, the third-largest lake in the Salzkammergut district. In the background you can see the **Drachenwand** and the **Schafberg** mountains. The lake is sparsely settled, so if you want to find accommodations, you should head to the northwest corner for the village of Mondsee. A popular summer resort, with sailing schools and beaches, Mondsee is 270km (168 miles) southwest of Vienna, 27km (17 miles) east of Salzburg, and 100km (62 miles) southwest of Linz.

GETTING THERE   No rail lines extend to Mondsee. Most visitors travel by train to either Salzburg or Strasswalchen, a town conveniently on the main line between Salzburg and Vienna. Buses depart from the railway station in Salzburg every hour throughout the day (trip time: 50 min.). From Strasswalchen, about half a dozen buses head south every day for Mondsee (trip time: 35 min.). From Salzburg, drivers head east on the A-1; from Linz, they go west on the A-1.

VISITOR INFORMATION   The **tourist office** (© **06232/2270**) is in the town center at Dr. Franz Müllerstrasse 3. It's open year round Monday through Friday from 8am to noon and 1 to 5pm. It's also open Saturday from 9am to noon and 3 to 6pm in summer, and Sunday from 9am to 7pm in July and August.

EXPLORING MONDSEE

A Benedictine abbey was once situated in Mondsee, dating from A.D. 748. However, when Emperor Joseph II ordered the abbey dissolved in 1791, the abbey church became the **Pfarrkirche (Parish Church),** still a point of interest in the village. It's a 15th-century structure with an added baroque exterior, but its crypt dates from the 11th century. The church was richly decorated by Meinrad Guggenbichler, a sculptor born in 1649. He designed seven of the more than a dozen altars.

Part of the abbey is now the **Schloss Mondsee.** The castle, where the wedding scene in *The Sound of Music* was filmed, is adjacent to the church.

Heimatmuseum und Pfahlbaumuseum   This museum is in the former cloisters of the abbey. Local artifacts related to the province's earlier eras are displayed in the Heimatmuseum. The Pfahlbaumuseum is dedicated to prehistoric archaeology; its exhibits trace local habitation from the time Neolithic humans constructed dwellings on pilings in the lake. Discoveries from as far back as 3000 B.C., up to the disappearance of prehistoric people in 1800 B.C., include Mondsee-Keramik pottery.

Hilfbergstrasse. © 06323/2270. Admission 3€ adults, 1.50€ children. May to mid-Sept Tues–Sun 10am–6pm; mid-Sept to mid-Oct Tues–Sun 10am–5pm; mid-Oct to Oct 31 Sat–Sun only, 10am–5pm. Closed Nov–Apr.

Mondseer Rauchhaus   This rustic wood chalet flanked by outbuildings was once a smokehouse used by farmers from the district. There's no chimney above the vaulted hearth.

Hilfbergstrasse. Admission 2.20€ adults, 1.10€ children. May–Sept daily 10am–6pm; Apr and Oct 15–31 Sat and Sun 10am–5pm. Closed Nov–Mar.

WHERE TO STAY

Austria Classic Hotel Leitnerbräu ⚲   Back in the 17th century, this site was a popular brewery, which closed in 1904. Since then, the place has functioned as a hotel, run by many generations of the Marschallinger family. Their house stands in the center of Mondsee opposite the famous Pfarrkirche. Rooms are usually generous in size. Some have sitting areas and private balconies. Bathrooms are spacious and excellent, with mostly shower-tub combinations. Bikes are available free of charge. Guests enjoy good, hearty Austrian cuisine.

Steinerbachstrasse 6, A-5310 Mondsee. ✆ 06232/6500. Fax 06232/6500-22. www.leitnerbraeu.at. 30 units. 117€–150€ double. AE, DC, MC, V. **Amenities:** Restaurant; bar; fitness center; Jacuzzi; sauna; room service; massage; babysitting; laundry; dry cleaning. *In room:* TV, minibar, hair dryer, safe.

WHERE TO DINE

Café Frauenschuh ✰   This famous establishment, which has flourished since the 1950s, is known by sweet tooths throughout the region for its delectable pastries and chocolates. Set in the middle of the village, it offers racks of fruited and chocolate-covered confections, which you can eat on the spot or buy by the dozen. In midsummer, rows of tables are set up amid flowerpots outdoors. One of the most popular items, a piece of strudel with ice cream or whipped cream, costs 4.20€. Other pastries begin at 2.40€, with a coffee going for 2.15€. The cafe also offers sandwiches and salads.

Marktplatz. ✆ 06232/2312. Daily 7am–7pm. Closed Wed off-season.

La Farandole FRENCH   An outdoor terrace, used during good weather, provides a view of the nearby forest. Specialties change with the seasons and include a delectable tartare of lake fish from the Mondsee, duck confit salad with fresh seasonal greens, roast rack of lamb with garlic, roebuck with chanterelle sauce, and marinated filets of salmon. Dessert might be a heavenly symphony of black- and white-chocolate mousses or artfully arranged truffles.

Schossl 150. ✆ 06232/3475. Reservations recommended. Main courses 12€–20€. MC, V. July–Aug Tues–Sun noon–2pm and 7–9:30pm; Sept–June Tues–Sat noon–2pm and 7–9:30pm. Many guests walk the ½ mile north from the center, but the bus marked MONDSEE–ZELL AM MOOS passes nearby as well.

3 St. Wolfgang & Bad Ischl

These two resorts, though only a short distance apart in the Salzkammergut, are quite different in character.

St. Wolfgang lies on the Wolfgangsee (see section 8, "The Flachgau," in chapter 8). The boundary between Land Salzburg and Upper Austria crosses the lake. St. Wolfgang is 50km (31 miles) east of Salzburg, 114km (71 miles) southwest of Linz, and 13km (8 miles) west of Bad Ischl.

ST. WOLFGANG ✰

In the mountains of the Salzkammergut, the **Wolfgangsee** is one of the most romantic lakes in Austria. St. Wolfgang, a little holiday resort on the northeastern side of the lake below the Schafberg (see below), is set among all this natural beauty. In summer, the resort is overrun with visitors.

If you drive here, there are two parking lots at the entrance to the town. You can park your car and then explore the town on foot. Late spring to early fall, it's better to go to St. Wolfgang by boat, leaving from the landing stage at Gschwendt, on the southern rim of the lake. Departures from mid-May to mid-October are usually hourly.

Other than a cog railway, which extends from St. Wolfgang to the top of the Schafbergspitz, St. Wolfgang is not serviced by any rail lines. Its only access is by bus, taxi, or car.

GETTING THERE   Buses depart from the railway station of Bad Ischl about a dozen times a day, making stops at both the marketplace (St. Wolfgang Markt- platz) and the base of the Schafbergbahn (St. Wolfgang Schafberg Rack Railway). Trip time to either is about 40 minutes.

If you're driving from Salzburg, take Route 158 east. From Linz, head southwest on the A-1; then cut southwest at the junction with Route 145 to Bad Ischl. From Bad Ischl, continue west on Route 158.

VISITOR INFORMATION   The St. Wolfgang **tourist office** (© **06138/ 22-39**) is in the town center. It's open in winter Monday through Friday from 9am to noon and 2 to 5pm; in summer Monday through Friday from 9am to 9pm, Saturday from noon to 2pm.

SWIMMING, HIKING, SKIING & MORE
In summer, swimming, playing watersports, and just sitting at a beach cafe are all highly regarded activities at this resort. Hiking is also possible in almost any direction.

There's skiing in the hills, usually December to mid-March, and you'll also find facilities here for skating, curling, and horse-drawn sleigh rides.

St. Wolfgang is the site of the celebrated **White Horse Inn** (see below); the landscape provided the perfect setting for Ralph Benatzky's operetta *White Horse Inn,* which brought glory to the town.

Pfarrkirche St. Wolfgang (Pilgrimage Church Of St. Wolfgang)   Since the
12th century, long before it was a vacation resort, St. Wolfgang was a renowned pilgrimage center. This church is said to stand on the same rocky spur of land above the lake where St. Wolfgang built a hermitage (signs from the center point the way). The church contains a magnificent Michael Pacher altarpiece (1481), pictured in many Gothic art books. Pacher's altarpiece is luxuriantly adorned with panel paintings and masterfully carved figures. The main panel depicts the *Coronation of the Virgin.* A new museum recently opened within the tower of the church; however, at press time, visitation at the museum was restricted to summer only, by appointment, Tuesday through Saturday from 2 to 4pm.

A-5360, St. Wolfgang im Salzkammergut. © **06138/2321.** Free admission. Church May–Sept daily 9am–6pm; Oct–Apr Mon–Sat 10am–4pm, Sun 11am–4pm. Museum July–Aug by request Tues–Sun 2–4pm.

A SIDE TRIP TO SCHAFBERG
The most popular excursion from St. Wolfgang is to **Schafberg** ★★, which offers the most stunning view in Upper Austria. Legend has it that you can see 13 lakes of the Salzkammergut from here, but we've never been able to do so. However, you're almost sure to have a good view of the Mondsee and the Attersee, and, of course, the entire Wolfgangsee. On a clear day, you can see as far as the Berchtesgaden Alps. You can also gaze at the wonderful backdrop to the lakes, the peaks of the Höllengebirge, and the glacier-capped Dachstein.

The whole trip to Schafberg takes about 4½ hours, nearly half by rack rail called **Schafbergbahn,** which operates from early May to late October. Once you're here, allow for about 30 minutes of walking. Departures are hourly: from mid-May to mid-June daily from 8:30am to 4:30pm; from mid-June to mid-September daily from 8:05am to 6:40pm; and from mid-September to mid-October daily from 8:30am to 6:20pm. Round-trip fare is 20€ for adults and 10€ for children. For more information, call © **06138/2232.** There's a hotel on the summit of the mountain, which rises to 1,784m (5,850 ft.).

WHERE TO STAY & DINE
Moderate
Gasthof/Pension Zimmerbräu *Value*   This 400-year-old house was once a local beer brewery, and for more than a century it has been a guesthouse run by

the Scharf family. Set in the center of town, it doesn't open onto the lake; however, it has its own private beach cabin with a sun terrace on the lake. The traditionally furnished rooms have balconies, good beds, and ample bathrooms equipped with shower-tub combinations. Consider dining here, as the food is reasonably priced and the chef is known for his Austrian specialties, including homemade beef goulash, braised beef in red wine, deer stew, and a selection of fish. One section of the menu, called "healthy and light," has vegetarian dishes.

Im Stöcki 89, A-5360 St. Wolfgang. ℂ 06138/2204. Fax 06138/242745. www.zimmerbraeu.com. 26 units. 87€ double. Rate includes half-board. No credit cards. Free parking at hotel, 7€ garage parking. Closed Nov. Amenities: Restaurant; bar, lounge. In room: TV.

Hotel Landhaus zu Appesbach 𝒜   Set within a 5-minute walk downhill from the center of St. Wolfgang, this gracefully proportioned lakefront inn was originally built as a private home in the late 19th century. Sometime during its tenure as a private home, the Duke of Windsor spent several weeks here, a visit that added immeasurably to the building's social gloss. Today it's a socially correct address with a scattering of antique and contemporary furnishings and frequent but vague references to the building's illustrious past. Rooms are well furnished, in a wide range of sizes, as befits a former private home. The bathrooms in each unit are well maintained and equipped mostly with shower-tub combinations. Staff is polite, charming, and inexperienced. There's a bar and a restaurant on the premises, but both are open only to residents of the hotel and their guests.

Au Promenade 18, A-5360 Wolfgang. ℂ 06138/2209-0. Fax 06138/2209-14. www.appesbach.com. 25 units. 75€–130€ double; 84€–158€ suite. Rates include breakfast buffet and dinner. AE, DC, MC, V. Amenities: Restaurant; bar; tennis court; exercise room; sauna; room service; massage; laundry; dry cleaning. In room: TV, minibar, hair dryer, safe.

Im Weissen Rössl (White Horse Inn) 𝒜𝒜   This hotel was the setting used for a popular play (*Im Weissen Rossl am Wolfgangsee*) written in 1896 and adapted for the Berlin stage by a group of actors and directors who returned here to rewrite it in 1930. Actually, there has been an inn on this site since 1474, with continuous ownership by the Peter family since 1912. Much of the hotel you see today dates from 1955, when the historic core was enlarged and expanded in a style true to the original design.

This scene of the famous operetta absolutely exudes a romantic atmosphere. Its stippled yellow facade conceals a collection of carved antiques. The public areas are large and sunny, usually wood-paneled and upholstered in cheerful colors. Rooms come in a variety of sizes, but all have the finest beds with firm mattresses. Bathrooms are spotless, with shower-tub combinations. There is a wide lakeside sun terrace within view of the village church and sailing, water-skiing, and windsurfing facilities along their private beach. In the evening the management usually provides live piano or zither music.

The inn's two restaurants serve both Austrian and international specialties, and are among the finest in the area—but overly touristy. Meals range from 14€ to 24€.

Markt 74, A-5360 St. Wolfgang. ℂ 06138/2306-0. Fax 06138/2306-41. www.weissesroessl.at. 72 units. 136€–216€ double; 186€–236€ suite. Rates include buffet breakfast. Half-board (3-day minimum) 20€ per person supplement. AE, DC, MC, V. Parking 8€. Closed Nov 1–Dec 19. Amenities: 2 restaurants; bar; pool; 2 tennis courts; fitness center; Jacuzzi; sauna; solarium; room service; massage; babysitting; laundry; dry cleaning service. In room: TV, minibar, hair dryer, safe.

THE SPA OF BAD ISCHL ⊛

Bad Ischl is one of the country's most fashionable spas and was the summer seat of Emperor Franz Joseph for more than 60 years. The town, constructed on a peninsula between the Traun River and its tributary, the Ischl, still reflects a certain imperial conceit in its architecture, much of it left over from the heyday of the Austro-Hungarian Empire. The spa establishments provide relaxing brine-sulfur mud baths, which might not be the most aromatic of experiences but supposedly are beneficial for a variety of ailments.

GETTING THERE   Bad Ischl sits astride a secondary rail line that runs north to the major rail junction of Attnang-Puchheim and south to the equally important junction of Stainach-Irdning. At these junctions, trains connect frequently with those traveling from Salzburg, Vienna, Linz, and Graz. The trip from Vienna, with connections, takes 3¾ hours; from Graz, it's around 4½ hours.

Many travelers opt for one of the buses that depart every hour from Salzburg's main railway station for Bad Ischl. The trip takes about 90 minutes, and transfers are usually not required. By car, Bad Ischl can be reached from Salzburg or Munich by taking Route 158 east from Salzburg.

VISITOR INFORMATION   The **tourist office,** at Bahnhofstrasse 6 (② 06132/27-757), will give you complete directions and information about all the sights in the immediate vicinity if you'd like to make some day trips from the spa. It's open in winter Monday through Friday from 8am to 5pm, Saturday from 9am to noon; in summer Monday through Friday from 8:30am to 6pm, Saturday from 9am to 3pm, Sunday from 10am to 1pm.

EXPLORING BAD ISCHL

Bad Ischl has chic shopping even today, as you'll note if you go along **Pfarrgasse.** This street comes to an end at the **Esplanade,** a shaded promenade where the most famous figures in Europe once strolled. Wealthy salt merchants lived along this promenade, and Maximilian, ill-fated emperor of Mexico, was born in a royal dwelling here in 1832.

The former pump room, **Trinkhalle,** where the fashionable have eaten and drunk since 1831, is in the middle of town on Ferdinand-Auböck-Platz. Many of the buildings on the square are in Biedermeier style. The 1753 **Pfarrkirche (Parish Church)** was rebuilt when Maria Theresa was empress.

Kaiservilla (Imperial Villa) ⊛⊛   The most important attraction in town is this villa close to the center. Emperor Franz Joseph used this Biedermeier palace for 60 summers as a residence and recreation center. Highlights include the Gray Salon, where Empress Elisabeth lived and from which she left on July 16, 1898, for Switzerland, a trip that ended with her assassination. In the emperor's study, Franz Joseph signed the Manifest, a declaration of war that led to World War I.

In the Kaiserpark. ② 06132/232-41. Admission 9.50€ adults, 4€ children. May to mid-Oct daily 9am–noon and 1–5pm. Closed off-season.

Marmorschlössl   Surrounded by the Kaiserpark, this structure, dating from the mid-1800s, houses a photo-historic collection (Sammlung Frank) documenting the history of the spa. The tiny place was once used by Empress Elisabeth as a tea pavilion.

In the Kaiserpark. ② 06132/24422. Admission to museum 1.50€ adults, .70€ children. Apr–Oct daily 9:30am–5pm. Closed Nov–Mar.

Museum der Stadt Bad Ischl   This is the house where Emperor Franz Joseph announced his engagement to the Bavarian princess Elisabeth von Wittelsbach, nicknamed "Sissi." Today it's a city museum devoted to the spa's history and culture, with memorabilia not only about the emperor, but also from famous composers who vacationed or lived here.

Esplanade 10. (C) 06132/25476. Admission 4€ adults, 1.90€ children. Tues and Thurs–Sun 10am–5pm; Wed 2–7pm. Closed Nov.

Villa Lehár   This lovely villa, now a museum, stands on the opposite bank of the Tauern River. Franz Lehár (1870–1948), the composer best known for his operetta *The Merry Widow,* lived here from 1912 until his death.

Traunkai. (C) 06132/26992. Admission 4.40€ adults, 1.90€ children. May–Sept daily 10am–noon and 2–5pm. Closed Oct–Apr.

WHERE TO STAY

Austria Classic Hotel Goldenen Schiff 🏨   This hotel has a great location—central but quiet—plus a garden overlooking the Traun River and the Villa Lehár. Rooms are generally spacious and offer tiny but well-kept bathrooms equipped mostly with shower-tub combinations. The riverfront rooms contain balconies and anterooms, and all are well furnished with radios and wall safes. Christine Gruber, son Edwin, and family try to satisfy all guests in this snug retreat. In the cozy dining rooms, you'll enjoy excellent cuisine. There is a personal computer with Internet access in the lobby for hotel guests.

Stifterkai 3, A-4820 Bad Ischl. (C) 06132/24241. Fax 06132/24-24-158. www.goldenes-schiff.at. 53 units. 85€–150€ double. Rates include buffet breakfast. AE, DC, MC, V. **Amenities:** Restaurant; bar; fitness center; sauna; solarium; room service; massage; laundry service. *In room:* TV, minibar, hair dryer, safe.

Hotel Schenner/Hotel Goldener Stern 🏨   These two charming hotels are a minute's walk from one another on a quiet street in the center of the resort. Both have comfortably rustic decor, with stone detailing, plenty of exposed wood, and wrought-iron accents plus a handful of hunting trophies. Regardless of which hotel you stay in, you'll register and eat breakfasts and (if you opt for half-board) meals at the Schenner. There's an outdoor solar-heated swimming pool with a view over the rooftops of Bad Ischl. The Schenner has 27 units; the Goldener Stern has 13 units. Each is comfortably furnished, containing comfortable beds and bathrooms, mostly with shower-tub combinations. The most desirable rooms, and usually the first to go, are those with private balconies.

Schulgasse 9, A-4820 Bad Ischl. (C) 06132/24600. Fax 06132/246007. www.hotel-schenner.at. 40 units. 64€–104€ double. Rates include buffet breakfast. AE, DC, MC, V. Parking 9€. **Amenities:** Restaurant; bar; pool; sauna; room service; laundry; dry cleaning service. *In room:* TV, minibar, hair dryer.

WHERE TO DINE

Villa Schratt 🏨🏨 AUSTRIAN   During the heyday of Bad Ischl, when the aristocracy of the Hapsburg Empire descended on the town every summer with Emperor Franz Joseph, one of the town's brightest inhabitants was the actress Katharina Schratt. Famous throughout the German-speaking world, she rose to a discreet kind of stardom as the mistress of the emperor, a relationship that lasted many years with the tacit approval of Franz Joseph's estranged wife, the Empress Elisabeth ("Sissi").

Today the villa that Katharina occupied is a touristy but rather upscale restaurant. Set about 4km (2½ miles) west of town, beside the highway leading to Salzburg, the house was originally built in 1610 and was acquired by Ms. Schratt in 1889. She occupied it every summer until the death of Franz Joseph in 1916.

In the restaurant's dining rooms, where all the references to Ms. Schratt seem vague and ever-so-polite, you can order such menu items as a terrine of duck *en gelée,* carpaccio of salmon-trout with salad, neck of lamb with garlic sauce, filet of venison with elderberry sauce, and, for dessert, cheese dumplings with cinnamon and fruit sauce. The extensive wine list contains selections from Austrian, Italian, and French vineyards.

Steinbrüch 43. ℂ 06132/27647. Reservations required. Main courses 14€–31€. AE, MC. Thurs–Mon 11:30am–2pm and 6–9pm. Closed Nov 2–20.

Weinhaus Attwenger 🏤 AUSTRIAN   This is one of the region's best-known restaurants, with strong connections to musical prodigies Bruckner, who dined here frequently, and Lehár, who lived next door and shared a garden and many glasses of fine wine with the owners. The restaurant's central section was originally built in 1540, and its old-style decor is much imitated. In summer, you can dine, or just savor a glass of wine or coffee, on the sun terrace over the Traun River. If you want a full meal, the delicious menu includes medallions of veal chef's style, paprika schnitzel or pork schnitzel, *Tafelspitz* (boiled beef), and several kinds of fresh lake fish.

Lehárkai 12. ℂ 06132/23327. Reservations recommended. Main courses 6.90€–17.80€. DC, MC, V. Daily 11:30am–2pm; Mon–Sat 6pm–midnight. Closed 1 month around Christmas.

A CAFE: OLDEST IN AUSTRIA
After viewing the summer playgrounds of the Hapsburg monarchs, anyone with a love of history should head to **Konditorei-Kaffee Zauner Gesellschaft mbH & Co KG,** Pfarrgasse 7 (ℂ **06132/233100**), the oldest pastry shop and coffee-house in Austria. The imperial court used to order pastries here, and it was said that the easiest way to tap into the pulse of the empire was to eavesdrop on a nearby table during July and August. The cafe's guest book shows a clientele as rich and diverse as the pastry offerings.

You can buy the exquisite pastries from the gold-and-white rococo showroom (which has been renovated to handle the flood of summer tourists) or eat at the small tables in a series of elegant inner rooms. Many items can be mailed as gifts. Sandwiches and salads are also on the menu. Coffee costs 2.15€, with pastries starting at 3€. It's open from April to September daily from 8:30am to 6pm, and from October to March Wednesday through Monday from 8:30am to 6pm.

BAD ISCHL AFTER DARK
Most of the year, Bad Ischl seems trapped in its imperial past, a nostalgia that can be relaxing at best and soporific at worst. During July and August, however, the spa livens up a bit and presents a well-rehearsed operetta in whichever public building can accommodate it. In the past, *The Merry Widow* or Johann Strauss's *Der Tzigeunerbaron* have been presented 3 nights a week, usually at 8pm. Tickets cost 21€ to 35€. For reservations and information, call ℂ **06132/23839.**

4 Hallstatt

88km (55 miles) SE of Salzburg; 19km (12 miles) S of Bad Ischl

Hallstatt, a small market town south of Bad Ischl, is a beautiful Austrian village. It stands on the left bank of the dark, brooding Hallstättersee in the Salzkammergut, at the province's southernmost tip, bordering Land Salzburg (see chapter 8) and Styria (see chapter 13). Many people drive to the lake through Styria, via Bad Aussee.

The Hallstättersee is a narrow lake, about 8km (5 miles) long and 2km (1½ miles) at its widest, almost completely surrounded by mountains. Its waters are so dark they're often called black.

Now a modern town, Hallstatt is the oldest still-inhabited village in Europe, owing its longevity to the local deposits of salt. Its perch against a mountain on a rocky terrace overlooking the Hallstättersee seems like a curious place to build a town, but this was the site of an early Iron Age culture dating from 800 to 400 B.C. Many Iron Age relics have been unearthed in the area. The mining of salt from the mountain behind Hallstatt was known among pre-Celtic tribes of 1000 B.C. It died out in medieval times but was revived by the Hapsburgs and continues to flourish today.

ESSENTIALS

GETTING THERE   Hallstatt is serviced by the same rail lines that go to Bad Ischl, which lies two stops to the north. (For more information, see "St. Wolfgang & Bad Ischl," above.) Hallstatt is 43km (26½ miles) north of the rail junction at Stainach-Irdning and 64km (40 miles) south of the rail junction at Attnang-Puchheim. The trip to Hallstatt from Linz, with connections, takes 2 hours; from Vienna, it takes 4 hours.

Around eight buses per day depart from the railway station at Bad Ischl, through Bad Goisern, and continue on to Hallstatt (trip time: about 35 min.).

If you're driving, go to Bad Ischl, continue south along Route 145 until you reach Route 166, and then head south via Steeg to Hallstatt.

VISITOR INFORMATION   The **tourist office** is in the Kultur- und Kongresshaus, Seestrasse 169 (© **06134/8208**). It's open Monday through Saturday from 8am to 6pm.

EXPLORING THE VILLAGE

The village of Hallstatt gave its name to one of the most important eras of prehistory. Some 2,000 graves of prehistoric people, half of them cremated, have been excavated in the area, which Austrians refer to as a "cradle of civilization." Many of the artifacts excavated here dating from Neolithic times are displayed in the **Prähistorisches Museum,** Seestrasse 56 (© **06134/8208,** the tourist office). The cremation graves have revealed artifacts that indicated the existence of a ruling class. Apparently the burials continued to about 350 B.C., the late Iron Age. The museum is open June through August daily from 10am to 6pm, May and September through October daily from 10am to 4pm, and November through April Wednesday from 2 to 4pm (Dec 22–Jan 6 daily 10am–4pm). Admission is 7€ for adults and 3€ for children.

The center of this beautifully situated village, with views of the Dachstein mountain massif, is the **Market Square,** which contains some 16th-century buildings. The lakeside terrace is from the 18th century. Hallstatt's streets are narrow and often steep.

You can visit the **Pfarrkirche (Parish Church),** which is situated within a churchyard bordering the dark waters of the lake. The house of worship is a large structure from the latter part of the 15th century. Visitors can also go to the **Chapel of St. Michael,** a Gothic church next to the parish church. The cemetery was so small that this *Karner* (charnel house or bone house) had to be used as a burial site starting in the 17th century.

OUTDOOR ACTIVITIES

Numerous cable cars and lifts are found in the town and surrounding area that can take you up into the mountains for a panoramic view of the area. If you'd like a little exercise, there are many walking paths or hiking trails as well. Mountain climbing is also possible on the nearby **Dachstein** massif (2,995m/9,820 ft.), and you can explore the **Dachstein Giant Ice Caves,** although the mountain is more easily reached from nearby Obertraun than from Hallstatt. For a great way to spend a morning, fish in the Hallstättersee and the Traun River, or try sailing, rowing, motorboating, swimming, or tennis. In winter, Hallstatt is also a sports center, with snow from November to April. You can go skiing, sledding, curling, and ice-skating, or hike along pleasant winter footpaths. The tourist office (see above) will provide complete details about which of these activities will be available at the time of your visit.

THE SALT MINES IN SALZBERG

Northwest of Hallstatt is one of the most distinctive geological formations in the region, **Salzberg (Salt Mountain)** ✦ (✆ **06134/8251**), which is not to be confused with Salzburg, the city. Miners have been hauling vast quantities of salt out of the mountain for centuries; the mines are still active and can be toured for an insight into the vast amounts of work that is needed to create and run a modern mine. Teams of archaeologists have accumulated many rare objects from the debris left by former miners.

To reach Salt Mountain from Hallstatt, take an uphill ride on the cable car that departs from the western suburb of Lahn, a 5-minute walk from Hallstatt's railway station. In May and from mid-September to mid-October, the funicular runs daily from 9am to 4:30pm; from June to mid-September, it runs daily from 9am to 6pm. The only way you can visit the mines is as part of a guided tour, which is 19.50€ for adults and 11.70€ for children ages 4 to 14. (Children under 4 are not admitted.) The price includes round-trip transfers on the funicular. From May 1 to May 24 and from mid-September to late October, tours are conducted daily at frequent intervals, from 9:30am to 3pm. From May 25 to September 13, tours are conducted daily from 9:30am to 4:30pm. The mines are closed from late October to April 13. Although tours of the mines themselves take only 50 minutes, you should allow 2½ hours for the full experience.

There's a restaurant and snack bar with a terrace and a belvedere for taking in the view. Hikers can go all the way from here to the **Iron Age cemetery,** an approximately 1½-hour trip. If you ask, the tourist office will outline a series of hikes in the area. One that goes along the Echerntal to **Waldbachstrub,** at the top of the valley, has lovely waterfalls along the way. You can also climb to the **Tiergartenhütte,** which has a small inn, and on to the **Wiesberghaus,** 1,885m (6,180 ft.). After that, only the hardy continue to the **Simony-Hüttee** at 2,205m (7,230 ft.), where there's another small inn lying at the foot of the Hallstatt Glacier. From Simony-Hüttee, mountain climbers can summit the **Hoher Dachstein,** the loftiest peak in the massif (2,995m/9,820 ft.); the climb takes 3½ hours.

DACHSTEIN CAVES ✦

The Dachstein Ice Caves, Dachstein Bahn, A-4831 Obertraun, are among the most spectacular natural sights of Upper Austria. To reach them, drive to Obertraun, 6km (3¾ miles) east of Hallstatt, where a sign in the vicinity will direct you to the lower station of the cableway that takes you to the caves. The cableway deposits you at the intermediate platform (1,351m/4,430 ft.) on the Schönbergalm. From here, it's about a 20-minute walk to the entrance to the caves. A round-trip ticket costs 13€ for adults and 7.50€ for children.

Among the many attractions is the **Giant Ice Cave (Rieseneishöhle),** where even in summer the temperature is about 30°F (–1°C). Be sure to dress for the cold. Among the ice cave's breathtaking features are the frozen waterfalls. You'll also see the so-called King Arthur's Cave and the Great Ice Chapel. The ice cave is open from the first of May until mid- to late October daily from 9am to 4pm; a guided tour is 8€ for adults and 4.80€ for children. If you also want to visit Mammoth Cave, a combined ticket is 21€ for adults and 13.30€ for children. Mammoth Cave has large galleries (subterranean passageways) cut through the rock by some ancient underground torrent. It takes about 1½ hours to go on a guided tour of these caves. You're allowed to visit only a small part of the cave network, which totals 37km (23 miles) in length, with a drop of 1,180m (3,870 ft.). For information, call © 06131/362 or 06131/273.

From the Schönbergalm station, you can go by cableway to the upper platform at a height of 2,111m (6,920 ft.). This is the **Hoher Krippenstein** ★★, which offers a panoramic view of the Dachstein massif. A chapel erected in the 1950s commemorates the accidental deaths here of 13 teachers and students. The cableway operates every 15 minutes daily from 9am to 4pm. In summer, don't be surprised if there's a line. From Krippenstein you can take a cable car down to **Gjaidalm** (1,793m/5,880 ft.).

OTHER NATURAL ATTRACTIONS

The region around Hallstatt is riddled with geological oddities, including caves, caverns, and glaciers whose ice never melts. A local cavern that's particularly easy to visit is **Koppenbrüllerhöhle (Koppenbrüller Cave).** Within its bowels, there's a raging underground stream whose activity causes continual erosion (and enlargement) of the cavern. The local municipality views it as a natural wonder and, as such, maintains a series of underground catwalks and galleries that you can walk along.

The easiest way to reach the cave is by car or taxi, but it's also accessible via trains, about three a day, that pull into the local station, Koppenbrüllerhöhle, after a 15-minute ride from Hallstatt or a 5-minute ride from Obertraun. There's a hotel, the Gasthaus Koppenrast, nearly adjacent to the railway station, which serves as an additional landmark for motorists. From here, you have to walk for about 15 minutes across well-marked trails to reach the cave. One-hour guided tours are conducted from early May to late September daily from 9am to 4pm for 6.80€ for adults and 4.10€ for children.

A final option for natural sightseeing is to check out the view over the steep and foreboding south wall of the Dachstein. For the best outlook, take the **Gletscherbahn** cable car uphill to an alpine plateau known as **Hunerkogel,** site of a hotel with its own cafe and restaurant. To reach the base of the Gletscherbahn cable car, drive for 16km (10 miles) along Route 166, following the signs to Ramsau (which you'll pass through) and Schladming, which lies across the border from Upper Austria, in Styria. The 12-minute cable car ride operates year-round daily from 8am to 5pm, with the exception of annual closings between November and Christmas and from early April to mid-May. At the upper belvedere (the above-mentioned Hunerkogel, 2,696m/8,840 ft. above sea level), you'll enjoy a panoramic view that includes the Grossglockner Pass and the Salzkammergut Alps, and a sweep of the Schladminger Gletscher, where some hardy locals sometimes ski on rock-strewn, granular snow even in midsummer.

WHERE TO STAY & DINE

Gasthof Zauner ★ *(Value)*   In the center of the town's historic market square stands this century-old inn where you are welcomed by its mountaineering owner bedecked in traditional lederhosen. A long-enduring family-run hotel, the guesthouse is often visited by nonresidents who know that it serves the freshest fish specialties direct from Hallstatt Lake. The wine cellar also enjoys local renown. The wooden chalet is a cliché of Austrian folkloric charm, with balconies overlooking the village and a lake where a delectable white fish, the mild *Reinanke,* is caught and made ready for the grill. The pine-paneled rooms are rustically but comfortably furnished with carved headboards. Each is immaculately kept, with a small bathroom with a shower.

Marktplatz, A-4830 Hallstatt. ℂ **06134/8246.** Fax 06134/8246-8. 12 units. 122€ double. DC, MC, V. Closed mid-Nov to mid-Dec. **Amenities:** Restaurant. *In room:* TV, hair dryer.

Seehotel Grüner Baum   This historic and rustically elegant hotel was originally established around 200 years ago as a lakeside inn and was amply enlarged around 1900. Capped with a hipped roof of hammered copper, it has an ochre-colored facade with white, heavily bordered windows. Prices for the comfortable rooms are determined almost exclusively by the views, of either Marktplatz (the town's main square), the lake, or the street. Rooms come in a variety of sizes but all are equipped with comfortable beds. Bathrooms tend to be small but are well maintained and equipped with shower-tub combinations. The hotel's sun terrace extends out over the water on a pier, where you can go swimming or simply relax with a drink on a chaise lounge. The hotel contains a restaurant that specializes in fish from the nearby lake, when available. The hotel maintains an apartment for larger parties.

Marktplatz 104, A-4830 Hallstatt. ℂ **06134/8263.** Fax 06134/420. www.hallstatt.net/gruenerbaum. 19 units. 85€–145€ double; 150€–160€ apt. Rates include breakfast. Half-board 16€ per person extra. AE, DC, MC, V. Closed Oct 26–May 1. **Amenities:** Restaurant; bar, lounge; exercise room; sauna; solarium; room service; babysitting; laundry; dry cleaning service. *In room:* TV.

5 The Traunsee (★(★

One of the biggest lakes in the Salzkammergut, the Traunsee is about 12km (7½ miles) long and some 3km (2 miles) wide at its broadest. It lies east of the two major lakes already explored: the Attersee and the Mondsee. Three mountain peaks—Traunstein, Hochkogel, and Eriakogel—form a silhouette that Austrians call Schlafende Griechin (Sleeping Greek Girl). Some sections of the Salzkammergut road (Route 145) run along the western edge of the lake.

The most dramatic part of this road is from the Ebensee, at the lake's southwestern tip, to Trauenkirchen. A feat of engineering, this corniche had to be hewn out of rock. The Traunsee is ringed with a number of resorts, the chief town being Gmunden. There's lake steamer service in summer. To reach this lake from Bad Ischl (see section 3, above), you drive northeast along the Traun River (Route 145), following the signs.

GMUNDEN ⊕★

This is one of the most popular summer resorts in the Salzkammergut, perched on the northern rim of the Traunsee with pine-green mountains forming the backdrop. Gmunden is located 169km (105 miles) southwest of Vienna, 40km (25 miles) southwest of Linz, and 76km (47 miles) northeast of Salzburg.

GETTING THERE   All train passengers to Gmunden must transfer in the railway junction of either Attnang-Puchheim (the more convenient) or Lambach. Both sit directly on the main rail line between Linz and Salzburg, handling many express trains throughout the day.

From Attnang-Puchheim, about 64km (40 miles) to the north, about a dozen trains continue on to Gmunden's Hauptbahnhof (Main Railway Station). From Lambach, only around three trains per day run to Gmunden's Seebahnhof (Lakeside Railway Station). Taxis are readily available for the short trip between these two stations, although the Hauptbahnhof is more convenient to most hotels. Gmunden is the starting point for many buses heading out into the surrounding valleys. Most visitors arrive in Gmunden by train, however.

To reach Gmunden from Linz by car, take the A-1 southwest to the junction with Route 144, at which point you head south.

VISITOR INFORMATION   The **tourist office** is at Am Graben 2 (© **07612/ 64305**). It's open in winter Monday through Thursday from 8am to 1pm and 2 to 6pm, Friday from 8am to 1pm and 2 to 5pm, Saturday from 9am to 1pm; in summer Monday through Friday from 8am to 7pm, Saturday from 9am to 1pm and 4 to 7pm, Sunday from 10am to noon.

WALKING AROUND GMUNDEN

Chestnut trees line the mile-long, traffic-free **Esplanade** &, the town's chief attraction. You can walk from **Rathausplatz (Town Hall Square)** to the **Strandbad (Lakeside Beach),** watching the many majestic swans glide serenely along the lake. In days of yore, emperors, kings, and members of the aristocracy strolled along the Esplanade and in the town's park, just as you can do today. The Welfen from Hannover, Württembergs, Bourbons, and archdukes of Austria favored Gmunden as a pleasure ground, as did Franz Schubert, Friedrich Hebbel, and Johannes Brahms, among others.

The lake beaches are some of the best in the whole area, and in summer you can enjoy a wide variety of lakeside activities, from swimming and sailing to windsurfing and water-skiing, as well as tennis and horseback riding. For the experienced, it's also possible to do a little mountain climbing. For those in the mood for less strenuous activity, there are folkloric performances and discos, or you can just relax in a wine tavern or an outdoor cafe. The tourist office will supply details.

Gmunden, former center of the salt trade, has long produced Gmundner ceramics, and you'll see artistic work in faience (opaque colored glazes) and green-flamed pottery.

One of the more evocative curiosities of Gmunden is the **Schloss Ort (Ort Castle)** &, now a ruined jumble of stones built on ancient Roman foundations that's set on a small island a few yards offshore from Gmunden's town center, at the far end of the Esplanade. Visitors are free to wander among the ruins or stop at a nearby restaurant, the Orther Stuben (© **07612/62499**), a short distance from the ruins. Guided tours can be arranged with several days' advance notice through the tourist office (see above), although most visitors to Gmunden opt to wander around on their own.

The region around Gmunden is rich with sweeping panoramas. From a well-marked spot close to the town center, you can take a cable car, the **Grünberg Seilbahn** (© **07612/66014**), to the top of the town's nearest mountain, the Grünberg, where you'll be able to see out over the Traunsee and the Dachstein. The cable car, hauling four persons up and downhill within each of its *Cabines,* operates only May through October; it charges 10€ for adults and 6€ for children round-trip from Gmunden to the top, a 12-minute ride each way. May, June, and October, it operates daily from 8:30am to 4:30pm; July, August, and September, hours are daily from 8:30am to 5pm.

In winter, ski lifts, runs, and slopes on the Grünberg are easily reached from Gmunden. Other winter activities in Gmunden are curling, ice-skating, and walking along the lake.

WHERE TO STAY & DINE

Pension Haus Magerl   These premises were originally built in the 1600s and were converted to a farmhouse around 1900. In the 1950s, members of the Magerl family transformed it into a pleasant hotel, with a new annex added in 1991. The establishment you see today sits in a grassy meadow about half a mile east of Gmunden, with a view overlooking the nearby lake. Each floor contains a residents' lounge, and rooms are simple yet comfortable. Beds are adequate, not spectacular, and the bathrooms are a bit small but equipped with shower-tub combinations. Housekeeping, however, is excellent.

Ackerweg 18, A-4810 Gmunden. © 07612/63675. Fax 07612/63675-220. 70 units. 84€ double. Rate includes breakfast. DC, MC, V. **Amenities:** Breakfast room; lounge; pool; fitness center; sauna. *In room:* TV, hair dryer, safe.

Schlosshotel Freisitz Roith 🏰🏰   On foundations dating from the 15th century, this castle was built as a summer house by the Hapsburg emperor Rudolf II in 1597. After centuries of private ownership, it was transformed into a hotel in 1965. One mile east of the town center, it's set amid a garden on a forested hillside, overlooking the lake. It looks like a combination baroque private house and a Victorian-style hotel. Dozens of architectural oddities include a crenellated tower with tall arched windows, wrought-iron window bars, jutting parapets over many of the balconied windows, and a stone terrace—site of a well-recommended restaurant—built into the slope of the grass-covered hill. On the grounds, a private footpath leads downhill to a beach at the edge of the lake.

The interior today incorporates modern building materials with the older stone-accented design of vaulted ceilings. Rooms range from old-fashioned and dignified to contemporary yet conservatively furnished. As befits such an old castle, rooms come in a variety of sizes, but all have comfortable beds. Bathrooms have been equipped with spotlessly maintained shower-tub combinations.

Traunsteinstrasse 87, A-4810 Gmunden. © 07612/64905. Fax 07612/4905-17. www.tiscover.com/schlosshotel. 24 units. 58€–79€ double; 110€–114€ suite. Rates include breakfast. AE, DC, MC, V. **Amenities:** Restaurant; bar; fitness center; sauna; room service; babysitting; laundry; dry cleaning. *In room:* TV, minibar, hair dryer, safe.

6 Wels ★

200km (124 miles) W of Vienna; 32km (20 miles) SW of Linz; 105km (65 miles) NE of Salzburg

A flourishing town in Roman times, **Wels** lies on the left bank of the Traun River in the center of a large farm belt known today for its agricultural fairs. Wels is most often used as a base for exploring the hinterlands, although it has some attractions of its own. In about 1½ hours, you can walk through the town and see all the major sights.

ESSENTIALS

GETTING THERE   Wels sits astride the main rail line connecting Salzburg with Linz and Vienna's Westbahnhof (West Railway Station). From both directions, at least three trains per hour pull into Wels, many of them express. The trip from Vienna takes about 2 hours; from Salzburg, about 1 hour; and from Linz, only 15 minutes.

Because of the frequency of trains, few local residents would consider taking the bus from most other large cities of Austria. Wels is, however, the point of origin of many bus lines heading into the surrounding hills and valleys. There's also bus service from Linz's main railway station to Wels around four times a day. Compared to the train, the trip is slow, taking about 50 minutes.

If you're driving from Linz, head southwest on Autobahn A-1, but cut west onto Autobahn A-25 for the final run to Wels. From Salzburg, head east on Autobahn A-1 before turning north on Route 138.

VISITOR INFORMATION   The **tourist office** is at Kaiser-Josef-Platz (© **07242/43495**). It's open Monday through Friday from 9am to 6pm.

WALKING AROUND WELS

Beautifully decorated facades of old houses, an intricately carved fountain, and a broad, cobbled pavement make **Stadtplatz** one of the most architecturally harmonious town squares in Austria. Most of the houses date from the 16th to the 18th centuries. The baroque **Rathaus,** built in 1748, is one of the most ornate buildings in the Old Town. The **Ledererturm,** dating from 1618, is the only tower remaining of those that once studded the town walls. Many homes or shops in the Old Town are supported by arches and passageways with vaulted ceilings.

Emperor Maximilian I died in Wels in 1519, stricken as he was traveling from the Tyrolean country to Wiener Neustadt. The house in which he died is called the **Kaiserliche Burg.** On Burggasse, it has been turned into a museum of minor importance. You can see the room in which the emperor took his last breath.

The **Stadtpfarrkirche (Town Parish Church)** has a 14th-century Gothic chancel and three stained-glass windows from that same century. The entire church was once Gothic until baroque architects went to work on it. The Romanesque inner doorway is surmounted by a tower with a bulbous dome, dating from 1732.

Across from the church stands the privately owned **Salome Alt House.** Salome Alt was the mistress of Prince-Archbishop Wolf Dietrich, so frequently encountered in Salzburg history, and mother of 15 of his children. Following Wolf Dietrich's disgrace and overthrow, she retired to Wels.

On Ringstrasse, you can see what's left of **Schloss Pollheim,** where, the story goes, the shoemaker-poet Hans Sachs lived. Wagner is said to have based his character in *Die Meistersinger von Nürnberg* on Sachs.

NEARBY ABBEYS

Benediktinerstift Lambach (Lambach Abbey) ⚿   Founded in 1056, this Benedictine abbey lies in Lambach, 16km (10 miles) southwest of Wels and about 24km (15 miles) north of the Traunsee, where the Traun River meets its tributary, the Ager. Drive southwest for 16km (10 miles) along Highway 1 (referred to on some maps as Hwy. 144), following signs to Lambach.

The once Romanesque monastery, which stands on Marktplatz (Market Square) of the old market town, now sports a baroque exterior. A towering marble gateway from 1693 leads into the first courtyard.

In the so-called ringing chamber, you can see one of the abbey's major attractions, 11th-century Romanesque frescoes. These works of art were once hidden but later discovered. They were restored in 1967 and put on public view, an event hailed by the Austrian press.

The abbey's other attractions include a richly decorated library and a rather sumptuous refectory from the 18th century. The abbey church was built in the

1650s, and its main altar is believed to have been designed by the celebrated baroque architect J. B. Fischer von Erlach. The only surviving monastic theater in Austria, built in 1770, is reached by a stairway.

Marktplatz, in Lambach. (℃) **07245/28355,** Lambach tourist office. Admission 7€ adults, 4€ children. Mon–Sat 10–11am; Sun 2:30–5pm.

Stiftskremsmünster (Kremsmünster Abbey) ✰   Near Bad Hall, between the emerging hills of the Alps and the Danube River, overlooking the Valley of Krems, this Benedictine abbey was founded in A.D. 777. Two domed towers of the abbey church dominate the local skyline. According to a 14th-century legend, Tassilo III, a Bavarian duke, had the abbey built to honor his son Gunther, who was killed by a wild boar during a hunt. The abbey's design was Romanesque, but in the 17th and 18th centuries it was given the baroque treatment.

The most outstanding feature of a tour through Kremsmünster is the **Fischbehalter,** a fish pond made by the noted architect Carlo Antonio Carlone. It has five basins, each encircled by arcades, with statues that spout water. Figures depict everybody from Samson to Neptune.

In the cluster of abbey buildings, the **Kaisersaal (Hall of the Emperors)** has a portrait collection of the Holy Roman emperors, painted by Altomonte at the end of the 17th century. One of the most outstanding works of art is the *Crucifixion,* by Quentin Massys. The abbey still owns the chalice of Tassilo that was presented to the monks by the founding duke. It's the most ancient piece of goldsmith's work in either Austria or Bavaria, the duke's home. In the library is the priceless *Codex Millenarius,* an 8th-century translation of the Gospels.

An observatory tower, called the first skyscraper in Europe, rises nearly 61m (200 ft.) and has an exhibition on astronomy and other sciences. Many noted men have been pupils at the abbey school, including novelist Adalbert Stifter. The observatory tour (more about natural science) lasts 1½ hours and includes the fish pond.

To reach the abbey, take a train departing from the Linz Hauptbahnhof (Main Railway Station) for Graz, which leaves every 40 to 60 minutes (trip time: 45 min.). The train stops at either Kremsmünster Markt or Kremsmünster Bahnhof, which are very close to one another. Once you exit, you'll see many signs pointing toward the Stift Kremsmünster. It's a well-marked ramble eastward for 20 minutes. From Bad Hall, buses depart from Bad Hall's railway station approximately every 90 minutes throughout the day for the 15-minute ride to Kremsmünster. From Wels, take Route 138 south and then Route 122 east to Kremsmünster.

In Kremsmünster. (℃) **07583/52-75-216,** Kremsmünster tourist office. Admission 5€, plus another 4.80€ for the observatory tour. Abbey: Easter to late Oct daily 10am–4pm; Nov–Easter daily 11am–2pm. Observatory open for tours only May–Oct daily at 10am, 2pm, and 4pm. Tours in German, or in English if reserved in advance. An English-language pamphlet explaining the tour is available. The observatory is closed Nov–Apr. The abbey is located 32km (20 miles) southwest of Linz and 26km (16 miles) west of Bad Hall.

WHERE TO STAY

Avalon Hotel Greif   The Greif's simple exterior hides a nicely decorated, cozy interior with origins dating from 1561. This hotel is one of the best members of an Austrian hotel chain. Rooms are equipped with neatly kept bathrooms containing shower-tub combinations. The atmosphere is richly traditional, and if you stay here you'll be following in the footsteps of politicians, artists, kings, and emperors. After a beer in the Greif Café and Bar, you can enjoy American food in the Restaurant Steak.

Kaiser-Josef-Platz 50–51, A-4600 Wels. ℭ 07242/45361-0. Fax 07242/44629. 56 units. 122€ double. Rate includes breakfast. AE, DC, MC, V. **Amenities:** Breakfast room; bar; lounge; room service. *In room:* TV, mini-bar, hair dryer.

WHERE TO DINE

Cafe-Konditorei Urbann PASTRIES/SNACKS   Offering a shady summer garden, this cafe near the train station is the best-known in town. You'll see all kinds of people here, including the many local residents who show up every day for their usual cup of coffee and favorite pastry. The cafe prepares freshly made specialties such as handmade chocolate truffles, marzipan and nut *Kugeln* (balls), homemade gingerbread (winter only), and homemade jams and ice creams.

The Urbann family has owned this place since 1853, and there was a candle and gingerbread shop on the premises from as early as 1630. The place prefers not to be classified as a restaurant, but nonetheless it serves sandwiches, toast, and eggs. Coffee costs 2€, with pastries going for 2€.

Schmidtgasse 20. ℭ 07242/46051. Mon–Fri 8:30am–6:30pm; Sat 8am–11pm.

Restaurant Wirt am Berg 𝒦 *(Finds* AUSTRIAN/INTERNATIONAL Established in 1630, this restaurant, about 4km (2½ miles) outside Wels, has been owned by the same family since 1881. Follow the signs toward Salzburg. Prominent diners have included the royal family of Monaco. The three-story restaurant, painted a deep yellow-orange, opens into a series of rustically decorated dining rooms with hunting trophies. On warm days you might prefer to dine under the chestnut trees on the brick-covered terrace. Wild game is the most popular item on the menu in hunting season, although at any time of year you can enjoy an appetizer of carpaccio (raw slices) of venison with fresh fine herbs and a special salad marinated in walnut oil, or consommé of pheasant. This could be followed by venison ragout or *Tafelspitz* (boiled beef). Dessert might be curd dumplings with buttered bread crumbs and stewed plums. The restaurant also offers more than 3,000 kinds of wine.

Salzburgestrasse 227. ℭ 07242/45059. Reservations recommended. Main courses 12€–25€; fixed-price menu 32€ for 4 courses; 53€ for 7 courses at dinner. AE, DC. Tues–Sat noon–2pm and 6–10pm.

Innsbruck & Tyrol: The Best of Scenic Austria

Land of ice and mountains, dark forests and alpine meadows full of spring wildflowers, Hansel and Gretel villages, summer holidays, and winter sports—that's Tyrol. One of the greatest sightseeing attractions in Europe is the Tyrolean Alps, and the mountain scenery is beautiful and panoramic at any time of year. In addition to being famous for its skiing, this spectacular alpine region offers travelers a host of other outdoor activities year-round, such as wonderful hiking and mountain climbing, glacier tours, and trout fishing. July and August bring the most visitors to the province, many of them North Americans, so reservations are essential.

If you're heading for Tyrol and want to travel around the region, Innsbruck is the best place to situate yourself. Several major roads (A12, A13, and 171) merge at Innsbruck, and you can easily reach most of the major ski resorts, as well as the Ötz Valley, Arlberg, and the Kitzbühel area. Parking is rarely a problem in these places, and, unless otherwise noted, you park for free. In addition to offering visitors a great location, Innsbruck has a great deal to offer, including a wonderful Alpenzoo, home only to animals indigenous to the Alps, and several great palaces, Hofburg and Schloss Ambras.

Tyrol and its capital, Innsbruck, were centers of power at the end of the Middle Ages, when the Hapsburg Holy Roman Emperor, Maximilian I,

ruled from here. Many of the wonderful castles that were scattered across the medieval countryside are only ruins today.

With a population of about half a million Austrians occupying some 12,489 sq. km (4,822 sq. miles), Tyrol was a much larger district until South Tyrol was lost to Italy in 1919. South Tyrol was a large wine-producing area and the wealthiest part of Tyrol; its loss was a great blow for the Tyrolean people who remained in Austria, as it separated many of them from relatives, friends, and sometimes livelihood.

By the same post–World War I treaty, East Tyrol, whose capital is Lienz, was divided from North Tyrol, where Innsbruck is the capital. The two are separated by the portion of Tyrol given to Italy, which connects with a strip of Land Salzburg border. East of North Tyrol, the larger portion of the split province, lies Land Salzburg. To its west is the Austrian province of Vorarlberg (covered in chapter 11), to the north is Germany, and to the south are Italy and a small part of Switzerland. East Tyrol is bordered by Carinthia on the east, Land Salzburg on the north, and Italy.

Tyrol lies at the junction of several transcontinental links. The Valley of the Inn River cuts across the northern part of the province, and there are many other valleys connecting with that major artery. In addition to its famous mountains, the province is

Tyrol

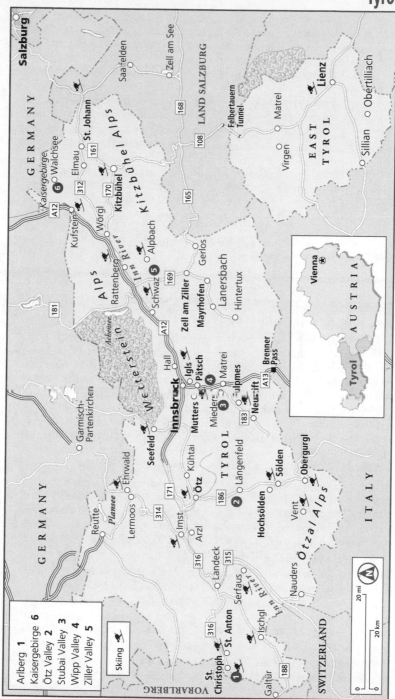

Skiing key:
- Arlberg 1
- Kaisergebirge 6
- Ötz Valley 2
- Stubai Valley 3
- Wipp Valley 4
- Ziller Valley 5

Salzburg

GERMANY

Saalfelden · Zell am See

LAND SALZBURG

Kaisergebirge
Walchsee 6
Elmau
St. Johann 161

Kufstein A12
312

Wörgl
170 Kitzbühel

Kitzbühel Alps

168

108

Felbertauern Tunnel
Lienz
Obertilliach
Sillian

EAST TYROL

Matrei
Virgen

Rattenberg
Schwaz
Alpbach 5
169
Gerlos
Zell am Ziller
Mayrhofen
Lanersbach
Hintertux

165

Alps

Achensee

Wetterstein

181

Hall
Igls Pätsch
Innsbruck
Seefeld
Mutters
Matrei
Mieders 3
Fulpmes 4
183 Neustift
Brenner Pass
A13

Garmisch-Partenkirchen

Ehrwald

Kühtai
Längenfeld 2
186
Ötz
171

Sölden
Obergurgl

Reutte
Plansee
Lermoos
314
Imst
Arzl

Hochsölden
Vent

Ötzal Alps

ITALY

GERMANY

316
Landeck
315

Serfaus
Nauders

St. Anton
St. Christoph 316
1
Galtür 188
Ischgl

Inn River

SWITZERLAND

VORARLBERG

TYROL

AUSTRIA
Vienna ⊛

Tyrol

20 mi

20 km

known for its deep-blue alpine lakes, such as the Achensee and the Walchsee. The Drau River, rising in the Höhe Tauern Alps, runs through East Tyrol. The Kaisergebirge is a nature reserve of Tyrol, with coniferous forests and meadowlands. And the Ötz Valley extends for 56km (35 miles) from the south bank of the Upper Inn.

Tyrol is a province of colorful folklore and customs, including *Schuhplatter* dancing, brass bands, and yodeling. Today Tyrol is a popular tourist spot, especially favored by Americans, who have, to an extent, supplanted the once firmly entrenched British vacation crowds. It didn't become a mecca for American tourists until shortly before World War I, when rail magnate J. Pierpont Morgan spent time in Innsbruck and publicized the area upon returning home. Since World War II, the province's resorts have made it a popular destination.

Tyrol is Austria's most frequented winter playground, and many prefer its ski slopes to those of Switzerland. Skiers and snowboarders flock here from mid-December until the end of March (when reservations at the most fashionable resorts are tight). And Seefeld, near Innsbruck, is one of Austria's "Big Three" rendezvous points for the international ski crowd. Kitzbühel ranks as one of the world's most fashionable ski resorts, and at the Kitzbühel Ski Circus, it's possible to ski downhill for 80km (50 miles). Serious skiers also head for St. Anton am Arlberg, the birthplace of modern skiing techniques.

TIPS FOR ACTIVE TRAVELERS

There's plenty to do outdoors in the dramatic high-altitude landscapes in Tyrol. If you don't want to make plans until you arrive, that's fine: Every hotel, inn, and pension in the region is well versed in where, when, and how you can fish, swim, ski, play tennis, or work out at a local spa. But if you want to plan in advance, here's a list of specialists who can help you plan your outdoor adventure and, in some cases, link you with specialized tours.

The best outfitter for arranging specialized tours, such as mountain climbing and hiking vacations, is **David Zwilling,** Waldhof 64, A-5441 Abtenau (© **06243/306-90**). This outfitter will also arrange any number of other tours, including white-water rafting, biking tours, and even paragliding.

BIKING   During your attempts to cycle through Tyrol, be warned that many areas of the territory are simply too rocky and steep for cycling. With a bit of planning, however, you can usually limit your cycling to trips up and down valleys that separate the region's many mountains. You can arrange rentals at **Sport Kaserer,** Bilgeriestrasse 18, Innsbruck (© **0512/37-72-47**), and at **Schönherr,** Dorf 105, at Neustift (© **05226/35-30**).

BOATING   If you'd like to explore one of Tyrol's lakes by boat, the best outfitter is **Segelschule Tirol,** A-6213 Pertisam (© **05243/20123**), in Maurach, a town that lies 48km (30 miles) east of Innsbruck. This company arranges boating activities on the Achensee, a long and narrow glacial lake 10km (6 miles) from end to end. The Achensee is 35km (22 miles) east of Innsbruck via the A12 superhighway.

CANOEING & RAFTING   For canoeing and white-water rafting, contact either branch of **Sportschule Fankhauser,** a specialist in maintaining boats that seem at home on the streams and lakes of the Tyrol, and a specialist in conducting waterborne excursions. The company's branches consist of one at A-6382 Kirchdorf (© **05352/625-87**), 35km (22 miles) from Innsbruck, and one at A-6425 Haiming (© **05266/886-06**), 40km (25 miles) from Innsbruck.

CROSS-COUNTRY SKIING In winter, you can check with the tourist offices to find out about snow conditions. The staff will also tell you how to get to the major ski areas. One of the top three outfitters includes **Skischule Nordisch,** 6100 Seefeld (© **05212/30-60**). The other two are in the nearby alpine hamlet of Igls: **Igls 2000,** Eichlerstrasse 16 (© **0512/37-73-77**), and **Schischule Schigls,** Bilgeristrasse 18 (© **0512/37-73-83**).

FISHING Some of the best trout and carp fishing in Austria is in the streams and lakes near the town of **Kössen,** about a 30-minute drive north of Kutzbühel. A social and fishing club that's willing to share ideas and camaraderie with well-meaning newcomers is **Fischerverein Kössen,** Bichlach 18, A-6345 Kössen (© **05375/22-70**). Its spokesperson is Gerhard Baumgart. Before you cast your lines into the water, you'll have to buy a fishing license, priced at 26€ per day for the Kolhbach or Weissenbach Rivers, or 10€ to 15€ per day for the Taubensee. Licenses are for sale at the **Kössen Tourist Office** (© **05375/ 62-87**), open daily from 8am to 6:30pm.

GOLF Many of the golf courses in Tyrol are private, but at some, you can call in advance to reserve a tee-off time. Well-respected courses that welcome new-comers include the **Golfplatz Rinn,** A-6074 Rinn (© **05223/781-77**), 10km (6 miles) south of Innsbruck, and **Golfplatz Lans,** A-6072 Lans (© **0512/ 37-71-65**), 8km (5 miles) south of Innsbruck. A bit farther afield, in the vicinity of Seefeld, is **Golfacademy Seefeld,** Reitherspitzstrasse, A-6100 Seefeld (© **05212/37-97**).

MOUNTAIN CLIMBING Austria's most dramatic mountain climbing occurs on the rocky (and sometimes icebound) slopes of Tyrol, particularly at **St. Anton, Mayrhofen, Kitzbühel,** and **Saalbach/Hinterglemm.** One of the best outfitters is Martin Ripfl-Marx, owner of **Bergsportzentrum Tirol,** Seewald 11, A-6105 Leutasch (© **05214/51-52**). Set in an alpine hamlet 5km (3 miles) northwest of Seefeld, this outfitter offers physically fit adventurers a series of climbing excursions in the Tyrolean Alps. The trips range from a half-day initiation course for beginners, priced at 30€ per person, to weeklong, high-endurance exposures to such alpine activities as rock and ice climbing, and "canyoning" down streambeds deeply eroded into layered bedrock. A worthy competitor closer to Innsbruck is the **Alpine Schule,** In der Stille, A-6161 Natters (© **0512/54-60-00**).

SNOWBOARDING & SKIING Your best bet for snowboarding is to call **Austro Tours/Austria Ski** (© **800/333-5533** in the U.S., or 0664/200-4655). This organization also arranges ski trips and winter hiking tours.

TENNIS There are many tennis courts in Innsbruck, but since they are so popular, you should reserve court time in advance. The best courts are at **Tennishalle West,** Fürstenweg 172 (© **0512/28-43-64**).

1 Innsbruck ★★★: The Capital of Tyrol

489km (304 miles) SW of Vienna; 159km (99 miles) S of Munich; 360km (224 miles) SW of Linz; 190km (118 miles) SW of Salzburg; 204km (127 miles) SE of Bregenz

The capital of Tyrol, Innsbruck (elevation 573m/1,880 ft.), is one of Europe's most beautiful cities. It has long been a center of commerce and traffic, as it lies at the junction of two important routes across the central Alps. In the eastern Alps, Innsbruck is about 30 minutes from the Italian border and 45 minutes from the German border.

Today Innsbruck's beauty is protected by town planners who ensure that any new structures built in the inner city harmonize with the pre-existing Gothic, Renaissance, and baroque buildings. Modern urban development exists, spreading along the Inn River to the east and west, away from the historic areas.

The name Innsbruck means "bridge over the Inn," the river that flows through the city. The city lies at a meeting place of the Valley of the Inn and the Sill Gorge. As long ago as 1180, a little settlement on the river was moved from the northern bank to the site of the present Old Town (Altstadt). In 1239, as a part of Swabia Bavaria, it was granted its own "rights and privileges," and in 1420, Innsbruck became the capital of Austria.

The city was celebrated throughout Europe under the Hapsburg Holy Roman Emperor Maximilian I. Under Maximilian, whose reign (1490–1519) signaled the end of the Middle Ages, Innsbruck reached the height of its cultural and political importance (it's still the cultural center of Tyrol). The city had a second imperial heyday some 300 years later, during the 40-year reign of Maria Theresa. Much later, in 1945, Innsbruck became the headquarters of the French zone of occupation.

Twice in a dozen years—in 1964 and 1976—the eyes of the world turned to Innsbruck when it hosted the Winter Olympics. It's now a winter sports center with modern facilities. Skiers who come to Innsbruck benefit twice: They stay in a cosmopolitan city called the jewel of the Alps, and they ski on some of the world's choicest slopes. Nonskiers and summer visitors can enjoy the sights of the medieval Old Town, the shops with Tyrolean specialties, and the many other outdoor activities that Tyrol offers.

ESSENTIALS
GETTING THERE
BY PLANE   Innsbruck's airport, **Flughafen Innsbruck-Kranebitten,** Fürstenweg 180 (© 0512/22525; www.Innsbruck-airport.com), is 3km (2 miles) west of the city. It offers regularly scheduled air service from all major Austrian airports, as well as from Amsterdam, Frankfurt, London, Paris, and Zurich. **Tyrolean Airlines** (© 0512/2222) serves the airport exclusively, although some foreign carriers will charter flights.

The best gateways from New York are Frankfurt and Vienna (from there to Innsbruck on Tyrolean Airways). Flying time from Zurich and Frankfurt is 50 to 70 minutes. From the airport, bus F leads to the city center. Tickets cost 1.50€. A taxi ride takes about 10 minutes and costs 8€ or more.

There are only two car-rental kiosks at the Innsbruck Airport: **Budget** (© 0512/58-84-68), the more popular and better organized of the two, and **Exclusiv Autovermietung** (© 0512/29-12-79). If you are renting a car, to get from the airport to downtown Innsbruck take the Fürstenweg (which becomes Mariahilfstrasse) for 2km (1¼ miles), following the signs to Innsbruck Centrum.

BY TRAIN   Innsbruck is connected with all parts of Europe by international railway links. Trains arrive at the main railway station, the **Hauptbahnhof,** Südtiroler Platz (© 05/1717 for all rail information). There are at least five daily trains from Munich (trip time: 3 hr.) and eight daily trains from Salzburg (1 hr.).

BY BUS   Bus service to all Austrian cities is provided by both **Postal Buses** and **Federal Railway Buses.** You can take a bus from Salzburg, although the train is quicker. For information about various bus routings through Tyrol, call © 0512/58-51-55.

Innsbruck

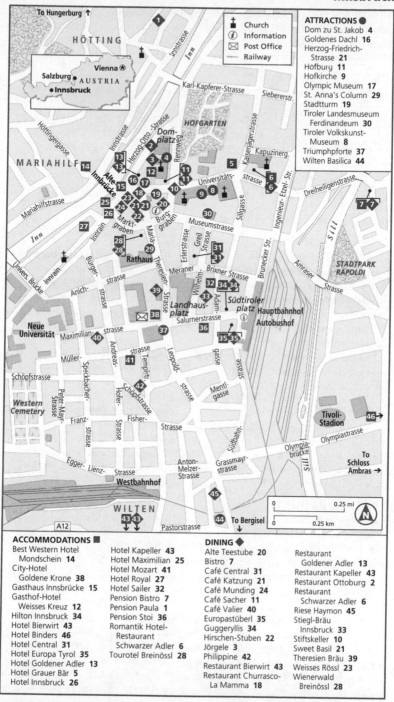

LEGEND
- ✝ Church
- ⓘ Information
- ✉ Post Office
- ---- Railway

Map labels: To Hungerburg ↑, HÖTTING, Salzburg, Vienna ❂, AUSTRIA, Innsbruck, MARIAHILF, Höttingergasse, Innstrasse, Herzog-Otto-Strasse, Dom-platz, HOFGARTEN, Karl-Kapferer-Strasse, Siebererstr., Kaiserjägerstrasse, Kapuzinerg., Rennweg, Alte Innbrücke, Mariahilfstrasse, Markt-graben, Burg-graben, Universitäts-strasse, Siligasse, Ingenieur-Etzel-Str., Dreiheiligenstrasse, Innrain, Inn, Marktgraben, Maria Theresien-Strasse, Museumstrasse, Erlerstrasse, Greil-Strasse, Brunecker Str., Amraser Strasse, STADTPARK RAPOLDI, Sill, Univers. Brücke, Innrain, Rathaus, Meraner, Brixner Strasse, Südtiroler platz, Hauptbahnhof, Autobushof, Neue Universität, Maximilian-strasse, Andreas-strasse, Tempelstr., Leopold-strasse, Landhaus-platz, Salurnerstrasse, Müller-strasse, Schöpfstrasse, Speckbacher-Strasse, Hofer-, Schöpfstrasse, Fisher-Strasse, Peter-Mayr-Strasse, Franz-Strasse, Western Cemetery, Egger-Lienz-Strasse, Anton-Melzer-Strasse, Grassmayr-strasse, Südbahn-strasse, Menl-gasse, Tivoli-Stadion, Olympiastrasse, Olympia-brücke, Sill, To Schloss Ambras →, Westbahnhof, WILTEN, A12, Pastorstrasse, To Bergisel

Scale: 0 — 0.25 mi / 0 — 0.25 km, N

BY CAR   If you're **driving** down from Salzburg in the northeast, take Auto-bahn A8 west, which joins Autobahn A93 (later it becomes the A12), heading southwest to Innsbruck. This latter autobahn (A93/A12) is the main artery from Munich. From the south, you can take the Brenner toll motorway.

VISITOR INFORMATION
Innsbruck-Information, Burggraben 3 (© **0512/56-20-00** or 0512/53-56-30), is open Monday through Saturday from 8am to 6pm and Sunday from 9am to 6pm. You can stock up on printed information about Innsbruck (and other parts of Tyrol) and ask questions about virtually any touristic feature of the town. Staff members can also arrange city tours, sell tickets to concerts and cultural events, and make hotel reservations.

In the same building, two floors above street level, a somewhat more exclusive network of services, **Innsbruck Tourism** (© **0512/59850**), is available for tour operators, travel industry pros, and journalists. Its services are available Monday through Friday from 8am to 6pm and Saturday from 8am to noon.

CITY LAYOUT
The main street of the **Old Town (Altstadt)** historic district is Herzog-Friedrich-Strasse, which becomes Maria-Theresien-Strasse, the main axis of the postmedieval **New Town.** Altstadt developed on the right bank of the River Inn, site of the baroque and medieval buildings that give the city its architectural flair. To the south, Altstadt's boundaries end at Burggraben and Marktgrabben. After 10:30am, it becomes strictly pedestrian, but that's all right, since the best way to see that part of Innsbruck is on foot.

Most of your explorations will be in Altstadt because (with a few exceptions) the New Town contains mostly residential neighborhoods. The dividing line between the Old and New Towns is Egger Lienz Strasse.

The Inn River divides this historic city into left- and right-bank districts, and many of the attractions, including the Hofkirche and the Goldenes Dachl, are on the right bank (in Altstadt). There are two major crossing points over the river: the **Universitätssbrücke** and the **Alte Innsbrücke (Old Inn Bridge).**

If you arrive at the **Hauptbahnhof (Main Railway Station),** take Salurner Strasse and Brixener Strasse to Maria-Theresien-Strasse, which will take you into the very heart of Innsbruck.

GETTING AROUND
A network of 3 **tram** and 25 **bus lines** covers all of Innsbruck and its close environs, and buses and trams use the same tickets. Single tickets in the central area cost 1.50€, and a booklet of four tickets goes for 3.20€. The tram is called either *Strassenbahn* or *Trambahn.* On the left bank of the Inn, the main tram and bus arteries are Museumstrasse and Mariahilfstrasse. On the right bank, trams and buses aren't routed into the pedestrian zone, but to their main stop in Marktgraben.

For information about various routes, call the **Innsbrucker Verkehrsbetriebe** (© **0512/530-7102**). Most tickets can be purchased at the Innsbruck tourist office, tobacco shops, and automated vending machines. A *Tageskarte* **(day pass)** is available only from the tourist information office, tobacco shops, and cafes.

Postal Buses leave from the Central Bus Station (Autobushof), adjacent to the Hauptbahnhof on Sterzinger Strasse. Here buses head for all parts of Tyrol. The station is open Monday through Friday from 7:30am to 6pm and Saturday from 7am to 1pm. For information about bus schedules, call © **0512/58-51-55.**

Taxi stands are scattered at strategic points throughout the city, or you can call a radio car (© **0512/5311**). For a nostalgic ride, you can hire a horse-drawn carriage (*Fiaker*) from a spot adjacent to the **Tiroler Landestheater,** Rennweg. Clip-clopping along the cobble-covered pavements costs around 25€ for 30 minutes.

If neither the tram nor the carriage option appeals to you, you might consider renting a **bike** at the Hauptbahnhof. Rentals cost 20€ per day. You can return these bikes to any rail station in Austria if you don't plan on returning to Innsbruck. Rentals are available from April to early November only. For more information, call **Sport Neuner** (© **0512/561-501**).

Although you can make a better deal renting a car before leaving North America, it's also possible to rent cars in Innsbruck. You might try **Avis,** Salurner Strasse 15 (© **0512/57-17-54**), or **Hertz,** Südtirolerplatz 1 (© **0512/58-29-51**), across from the Hauptbahnhof. Although paperwork and billing errors are harder to resolve whenever you rent from a non-U.S.-based car-rental outfit, you might also check the rates at a local car outfitter, **Ajax,** Amrasserstrasse 6 (© **0512/583-232**).

The center of Innsbruck is peppered with covered parking lots, many concealed underground. One of the largest and best positioned is at the **Tourist Center,** Salurnerstrasse 15 (© **0512/57-23-53**). It charges 2.20€ per hour day and night. Otherwise, parking in the city center's short-term parking zones (marked by special signs) is 1.10€ for each 30 minutes. Parking within these zones is limited to a maximum of 90 to 120 minutes. If you're parking in a limited parking zone, you must purchase a voucher. Write down the time you parked the car, and place the voucher on the dashboard inside the windshield. Vouchers can be purchased at banks, gas stations, or tobacconists.

 FAST FACTS: Innsbruck

Babysitters For an English-speaking babysitter, most hotel concierges will make arrangements for you.

Consulates U.S., Canadian, New Zealand, and Australian visitors have to use their respective consulates in Vienna. There's also an **American Consulate** in Salzburg. British citizens can go to the **British Consulate,** Mathias-Schmidt-Strasse 12 (© **0512/58-83-20**), open Monday through Friday from 9am to noon.

Currency Exchange You can exchange money at any of the dozens of banks that line Innsbruck's commercial areas. Banks are usually open Monday through Thursday from 7:45am to 12:30pm and 2:30 to 4pm, and Friday from 7:45am to 3pm. There are also exchange facilities at Innsbruck's tourist office (see above) and at the Hauptbahnhof. The branch at the Hauptbahnhof maintains automated currency exchange facilities available 24 hours a day. They accept American dollars in denominations of $20, $50, and $100.

Dentists & Doctors Check with the tourist office for a list of private English-speaking dentists and doctors, or contact the **University Clinic,** Anichstrasse 35 (© **0512/504**).

Drugstores In the heart of Innsbruck, **St.-Anna Apotheke**, Maria-Theresien-Strasse 4 (© 0512/58-58-47), is open Monday through Friday from 8am to 12:30pm and 2:30 to 6pm, and Saturday from 8am to noon. As required by law, the pharmacy posts addresses of other pharmacies open on weekends or at night.

Emergencies Call © **133** for the police, **122** for the fire department, or **144** for an ambulance.

Hospitals Try the **University Clinic,** located at Anichstrasse 35 (© 0512/504).

Internet Access You can check e-mail or access the Internet at the **Modern Internet Café,** Maria-Theresien-Strasse 16 (© 0512/58-48-48; tram 3). For a fee of 1.20€ an hour, you can Web-surf to your heart's content. Platters of simple food and drinks are available. It's open Monday through Saturday from 7:30am to 1am.

Luggage Storage & Lockers At the Hauptbahnhof, on Südtirolerplatz (© 0512/1717), you can rent small lockers for 2€, or larger ones for 3€, for 48 hours. You can also store luggage here for 2€ per item. The office is open May through October 24 hours daily and November through April daily from 7am to midnight.

Police Call © **133** for the police.

Post Offices The **Hauptpostamt (Central Post Office),** Maximilianstrasse 2 (© 0512/5000), is open daily from 8am to 9pm. The post office at the **Hauptbahnhof,** Bruneckstrasse 1–3 (© 0512/5000), is open Monday through Saturday from 6:30am to 9pm.

Restrooms These are found at the airport, at the bus and rail stations, and at various cafes and museums scattered throughout the city. Public restrooms in the city center are labeled WC: Some require a .50€ coin for access to a sit-down toilet.

Safety Innsbruck has a low crime rate, but that doesn't mean you should-n't take the usual precautions.

Taxes Innsbruck levies no special city taxes other than the value-added tax imposed on all goods and services in Austria.

Transit Information For information about local buses and trams, call the **Innsbrucker Verkehrsbetriebe** (© 0512/530-7102).

Useful Telephone Numbers For the airport, call © **0512/22525,** for train information, © **05/1717.**

EXPLORING THE TOWN

Maria-Theresien-Strasse ★★, Innsbruck's main street, cuts through the heart of the city from north to south, and it is a good place to begin your exploration. It's fascinating just to watch the passersby, especially when they're attired in Tyrolean regional dress. Once this street was traversed by wayfarers heading over the Brenner Pass from Italy and on to Germany. Today many 17th- and 18th-century houses line the street.

On the south end of this wide street, a **Triumphpforte (Triumphal Arch),** modeled after those in Rome, spans the shopping street. Maria Theresa ordered it built in 1765 with a twofold purpose: to honor the marriage of her son, the Duke of Tuscany (later Emperor Leopold II), to a Spanish princess, and to mourn the death of her beloved husband, Emperor Franz I. From this arch southward, the street is called Leopoldstrasse.

Traveling north from the arch along Maria-Theresien-Strasse you'll see **St. Anna's Column (Annasäule),** a much photographed attraction. It enjoys the same renown in Innsbruck as the Eros statue does in London's Piccadilly Circus. A statue of the Virgin Mary stands on a crescent moon atop this Corinthian column, which has statues of saints Cassianus, Virgilius, George, and Anna surrounding the base. Standing in front of the 19th-century **Rathaus (Town Hall),** the column was erected in 1706 to celebrate the withdrawal, in 1703, of invading Bavarian armies during the War of the Spanish Succession.

Not far north of the Annasäule, the wide street narrows and becomes **Herzog-Friedrich-Strasse,** running through the heart of the Altstadt. This street is arcaded and flanked by a number of well-maintained burghers' houses with their jumble of turrets and gables. Look for the multitude of dormer windows and oriels. Most buildings here are overhung with protective roofs to guard them against snowfalls.

MORE SIGHTS

Alpenzoo ✪ *(Kids)*   From this zoo, lying on the southern slope of the Hungerburg plateau, you'll get a panoramic view of Innsbruck and the surrounding mountains. The zoo contains only those mammals indigenous to the Alps, plus alpine birds, reptiles, and fish. Sheltered within are more than 800 animals, belonging to more than 140 different and sometimes rare species, including otters, eagles, elk, rabbits, vultures, wildcats, bison, and wolves.

Weiherburggasse 37. ✆ 0512/29-23-23. Admission 5.80€ adults, 4€ students, 2.90€ children 6–15, 1.80€ children 4–5, free for children 3 and under. Winter daily 9am–5pm; other seasons daily 9am–6pm. Bus: 2 (May 15–Sept only) or 4, C, D, or E. Tram: Hungerburgbahn (cog railway).

Dom zu St. Jakob (Cathedral of St. James)   Based on designs by the baroque architect Johann Jakob Herkommer, this church was rebuilt between 1717 and 1724. It is roofed with domes and has a lavish baroque interior, part of which was executed by the Asam brothers. Unfortunately, the church was heavily damaged during World War II. One of its chief treasures is the *Maria Hilf* (Mary of Succor), painted by Lucas Cranach the Elder, on the main altar. In the north aisle, look for a 1620 monument honoring Archduke Maximilian III, who died in 1618.

Domplatz 6. ✆ 0512/58-39-02. Free admission. Winter daily 6:30am–6pm; summer daily 7am–7pm. Closed Fri noon–3pm. Tram: 1 or 3.

Goldenes Dachl (Golden Roof) & Maximilianeum ✪   The Golden Roof is Innsbruck's greatest tourist attraction, certainly its most characteristic landmark. It's a three-story balcony on a house in the Old Town; the late Gothic oriels are capped with 2,657 gold-plated tiles. It was constructed for Emperor Maximilian I to serve as a royal box where he could sit in luxury and enjoy tournaments in the square below. Completed at the dawn of the 16th century, the Golden Roof was built in honor of Maximilian's second marriage, to Bianca Maria Sforza of Milan (Maximilian was a ruler who expanded his territory through marriage, not conquest). Not wishing to alienate the allies gained by his first marriage, to Maria of Burgundy, he had an image of himself between the two women painted on his balcony. He is, however, looking at his new wife, Bianca.

In 1996, the city of Innsbruck added a small museum, the **Maximilianeum,** to the second floor of the municipal building that's attached to the Goldenes Dachl. Inside you'll find exhibits that celebrate the life and accomplishments of the Innsbruck-based Hapsburg emperor, Maximilian I, who bridged the gap between the Middle Ages and the Northern Renaissance. Look for costumes, silver chalices and coins, portraits, and a video that depicts his era and personality.

You can also visit the **Stadtturm (City Tower),** Herzog-Friedrich-Strasse 21 (℡ 0512/561-5003), nearby. Formerly a prison cell, the tower dates from the mid-1400s and stands adjacent to the Rathaus. From the top, there's a panoramic view of the city rooftops and the mountains beyond. It's open daily from 10am to 5pm (8pm July–Aug). Admission is 2.50€ for adults and 1.25€ for children.

While you're here, take a look at the **Helblinghaus,** Herzog-Friedrich-Strasse, opposite the Goldenes Dachl. It's a Gothic structure to which a rococo facade was added.

Herzog-Friedrich-Strasse 15. ℡ 0512/581-111. Admission to the Maximilianeum 3.60€ adults, 2.70€ seniors and students, 1.40€ children 17 and under. No charge for views of the Goldenes Dachl, and no restrictions on when it can be viewed. Summer daily 10am–6pm; winter Tues–Sun 10am–12:30pm and 2–5pm. Tram: 1 or 3.

Hofburg 🎯

The 15th-century imperial palace of Emperor Maximilian I was rebuilt in the baroque style (but with rococo detailing) during the 18th century on orders of Maria Theresa. Later it would hold sad memories for the empress, as her husband died here in 1765. The palace, flanked by a set of domed towers, is a fine example of baroque secular architecture. The structure has four wings and a two-story *Riesensaal* (Giant's Hall) painted in white and gold and filled with portraits of the Hapsburgs.

Also of compelling interest within the Hofburg are the State Rooms, the chapel, and a scattering of private apartments. You can wander at will through the rooms, but if you want to participate in a guided tour, management conducts two a day, at 11am and 2pm, in a multilingual format that includes English. Each tour lasts 30 to 45 minutes and costs 2€.

Rennweg 1. ℡ 0512/58-71-86. Admission 5.45€ adults, 2.54€ students, 1.09€ children under 12. Daily 9am–4:30pm. Tram: 1 or 3.

Hofkirche

Ferdinand I built this Gothic royal court church and tomb in 1553. Its most important treasure is the cenotaph of Maximilian I, although his remains are not in this elegant marble sarcophagus glorifying the Holy Roman Empire. He was never brought here from Wiener Neustadt, where he was entombed in 1519. This tomb, a great feat of the German Renaissance style of sculpture, has 28 bronze 16th-century statues of Maximilian's real and legendary ancestors and relatives surrounding the kneeling emperor on the cenotaph, with 24 marble reliefs on the sides depicting scenes from his life. Three of the statues are based on designs by Dürer. Tyrol's national hero, Andreas Hofer, is entombed here.

The Hofkirche has a lovely Renaissance porch, plus a nave and a trio of aisles in the Gothic style. One gallery contains nearly two dozen small statues of the saint protectors of the House of Hapsburg. The wooden organ, dating from 1560, is still operational.

Another chapel, the **Silberne Kapell (Silver Chapel),** was constructed between the church and the palace in 1578. Archduke Ferdinand II of Tyrol had it constructed as the final resting place for him and his wife, Philippine Welser.

The chapel takes its name from a large embossed silver Madonna in the center of the altarpiece (made of rare wood). The silver reliefs surrounding the Madonna symbolize the Laurentanian Litany. Alexander Colin designed the sarcophagi of Ferdinand and Philippine. The Tiroler Volkskunst-Museum (see below) is reached through the same entranceway. You can purchase a combined ticket to the church and the museum for 5.45€ for adults and 2.55€ for children.

Universitätsstrasse 2. ✆ 0512/58-43-02. Admission 4.35€ adults, 1.45€ students or children, free for children 5 and under. Mon–Sat 9am–5pm. Tram: 1 or 3.

Swarovski Kristallwelten (Crystal Worlds) ✦✦✦ *Kids*   If Disney had ever created a magical Kingdom of Crystal, he would surely have used this fabled attraction as his role model. In just 15 minutes (by taking the Wattens bus from the Busbahnhof, next to the Hauptbahnhof), you are delivered to a fantasy world, a man-made hill where you'll see a giant face spouting a waterfall. This bizarre fantasy sets the theatrical stage for what's hidden inside and below. Deep inside the hill is a wonder world of crystal—an underground fantasy with seven linked chambers. Designed by the Viennese multimedia artist Andrew Heller, the kingdom is dedicated to the vision of Daniel Swarovski, founder of the world's leading producer of full crystal. Since it opened in 1995, millions of visitors have descended on the site.

After entering the giant head with its glittering eyes and waterfall, you'll immediately see a long wall of crystal with 12 tons of the finest cut stones in the world. In other chambers, you can wander into the "Planet of the Crystals," with a 3D light show. Crystalline works of art on display were designed by everybody from Andy Warhol to Salvador Dalí. In the Crystal Dome, you get an idea of what it's like being inside a giant crystal, and in the Crystal Theater, a fairy-tale world of color, mystery, and graceful movement unfolds.

After your visit, purchases can be made from the mammoth range of Swarovski products at the on-site shop. These range from detailed crystal items such as tiny musical instruments to depictions of animals in crystal. There is also a wide selection of crystal jewelry such as necklaces and earrings. The Crystal World also contains an alpine garden with rare and indigenous plants, plus an adventure playground for children. You can easily spend 2 hours at this attraction.

Kristallweltenstrasse 1. ✆ 05224/51080. Admission 5.45€; free for children under 12. Daily 9am–6pm.

Tiroler Landesmuseum Ferdinandeum (Ferdinandeum Tyrol Museum) ✦   This celebrated gallery of Flemish and Dutch masters also traces the development of popular art in Tyrol, with highlights from the Gothic period. You'll also see the original bas-reliefs used in designing the Goldenes Dachl.

Museumstrasse 15. ✆ 0512/59-489. Admission 4.50€ adults, 3€ students, 1.50€ children. May–Sept daily 10am–5pm, Thurs 10am–5pm and 7–9pm; Oct–Apr Tues–Sat 10am–noon and 2–5pm, Sun 10am–1pm. Tram: 1 or 3.

Tiroler Volkskunst-Museum (Tyrol Museum of Popular Art) ✦✦   This museum is in the **Neues Stift (New Abbey),** which dates from the 16th and 18th centuries, and it adjoins the Hofkirche on its eastern side. The museum contains one of the largest and most impressive collections of Tyrolean artifacts, ranging from handicrafts to religious and profane popular art, furniture, and national costumes. The three floors house a collection of Tyrolean mangers, or Christmas cribs, some from the 18th century. The *Stuben* (the finest rooms) are on the upper floors. Displays include styles ranging from Gothic to Renaissance to baroque, as well as a collection of models of typical Tyrolean houses.

Universitätsstrasse 2. © 0512/58-43-02. Admission 4.35€ adults, 1.45€ children and students. Mon–Sat 9am–5:30pm; Sun 9am–noon. Tram: 1 or 3.

OUTDOOR ACTIVITIES

Ski areas around Innsbruck are excellent for winter activity or for summer mountain walks. Five cableways, 44 chairlifts, and surface lifts allow access to the five sunny, snow-covered areas around Innsbruck. In winter, the city is also known for bobsled and toboggan runs and ice-skating rinks.

In summer, you can enjoy tennis at a number of courts, golf on either a 9- or an 18-hole course, and go horseback riding, mountaineering, gliding, swimming, hiking, and shooting.

The **Hofgarten,** a public park containing lakes and many shade trees, lies north of Rennweg. Concerts are often presented at the Kunstpavillon in the garden in summer.

NEARBY ATTRACTIONS

Many satellite resorts, such as Igls (see section 2, later in this chapter), are good for day trips from Innsbruck. Below we've offered highlights of those attractions on the outskirts of the city.

HUNGERBURG 🕊🕊

The Hungerburg mountain plateau (872m/2,860 ft.) is the most beautiful spot in Tyrol, affording the best view of Innsbruck, especially on summer nights when much of the city, including fountains and historic buildings, is brightly lit. Some of the most scenic hotels in the Innsbruck area are here.

You can **drive** to the plateau or take the **cable railway (Hungerburgbahn),** which departs about four times an hour from 8am to 6pm and then about every 30 minutes until 10:30pm; one also departs at 11pm on Friday and Saturday night. The departure point lies about half a mile east of the center of Innsbruck, at the corner of Rennweg and Kettenbrücke. (It's accessible from Innsbruck's center via tram no. 1 or bus no. C.) Round-trip fares are 4.20€ for adults and 2.10€ for children. For schedules and information, call © 0512/58-61-58.

Once you reach the plateau, you can progress even further into the alpine wilds via the **Nordkette Cable Railway (Nordkettenbahn)** (© 0512/29-33-44). It takes you up to the Seegrube and the Hafelekar (2,335m/7,655 ft.) for a sweeping view of alpine peaks and glaciers. This is the starting point of high mountain walks and climbing expeditions. The cable railway runs daily (except Apr and Nov, when it's closed) every hour from 8am to 6pm. A round-trip from Innsbruck to Hafelekar costs 20€ for adults and 10€ for children.

SCHLOSS AMBRAS 🕊🕊

This Renaissance palace, 3km (2 miles) southeast of the heart of Innsbruck on the edge of the Mittelgebirgsterrace, was built by Archduke Ferdinand II of Austria, Count of Tyrol, in the 16th century. It's divided into a **lower** and an **upper castle** set in the remains of a medieval fortress. This was Ferdinand's favorite residence and the center of his court's cultural life. The lower castle was planned and constructed by the archduke as a museum for his various collections, including arms and armor, art, and books, all of which can be seen today. The **Spanish Hall,** one of the first German Renaissance halls, was built to house the portraits of the counts of Tyrol.

The upper castle has a small but fine collection of medieval sculpture, black-and-white frescoes on the wall of the inner courtyard, and a portrait gallery hung with dynastic paintings from the 14th to the 18th centuries. In some of the living rooms, you can see 16th-century frescoes, late 16th-century wooden ceilings, and 17th-century furniture.

After viewing the interior, walk through the castle grounds. April through October, Schloss Ambras, Schloss Strasse 20 (© **0512/348-446**), is open daily from 10am to 5pm. December through March, it's open daily from 2 to 5pm. It's closed in November. Admission is 4.50€ for adults and 3€ for students and children. A guided tour costs an extra 2€. To reach it, you can take tram 3 or 6 from Innsbruck's Hauptbahnhof. The castle also maintains its own shuttle bus, a white-sided vehicle with the words SCHLOSS AMBRAS written on its sides, which departs from a point adjacent to the Landhaus on the Maria-Theresien-Strasse every hour during the palace's open hours. Service runs less frequently December through April. Round-trip costs 2€ adults and 1€ children.

THE WILTENER BASILICA ⊛
In the southern district of Innsbruck where the Sill River emerges from a gorge, Wilten is one of the most dramatic landscapes around the city. This ancient spot was once the Roman town of Veldidena.

Wilten's parish church, the **Wiltener Basilica,** Haymongasse 6 (© **0512/ 58-33-85**), is one of the most splendid houses of worship in the Tyrolean country. Built between 1751 and 1755 in a rich rococo style with twin towers, the church did not became a basilica until 1957. Wiltener Basilica is noted for its stuccowork by Franz Xaver Feichtmayr. The ceiling frescos are by Matthaus Gunther. A sandstone figure depicting Our Lady Under the Four Columns has been the subject of pilgrimage since the Middle Ages. Both the church and the basilica are open daily from 9am to dusk.

Across from the basilica is a cluster of baroque buildings that belonged to an abbey founded here in 1138. The abbey church, the **Stift Wilten,** Haymongasse 1 (© **0512/58-30-480**), merits a visit. Dating from the 1650s, the church has two stone giants guarding the porch and a grille from 1707 in the narthex (entranceway). This church was damaged by World War II bombings. To reach the site, take tram no. 1 to Stubaitalbahnhof/Bergisel.

BERGISEL
If you're driving, head out the Brenner road to **Bergisel** (747m/2,450 ft.), a lovely wooded section just outside Innsbruck that's ideal for leisurely strolls in warmer weather. It lies near the gorge of the Sill River on the southern outskirts of Innsbruck, about a 20-minute walk from the Wiltener Basilica. Here you'll see the ski jumps built for the 1964 and 1976 Olympic Winter Games, and there's a great panoramic view from the top of the jumps.

The hill is a historic site, scene of the 1809 battles in which Andreas Hofer led some Tyrolean peasants against French and Bavarian forces (he was later shot to death in Mantua on orders of Napoléon). Below the ski jump, on the north side, is the Andreas Hofer monument erected in 1893 to commemorate the battle. Tyroleans speak of this as their "field of remembrance," and it's filled with memorials and visitors. Heroic though the local deeds might be, they might not interest North Americans. Visit this place simply for the views and the relaxing walks.

SHOPPING
In Innsbruck, you can buy Tyrolean specialties such as lederhosen, dirndls, leather clothing, wood carvings, loden cloth, and all sorts of skiing and mountain-climbing equipment. Stroll around **Maria-Theresien-Strasse, Herzog-Friedrich-Strasse,** and **Museumstrasse,** ducking in and making discoveries of

your own. Stores are generally open from 9am to 6pm on weekdays and from 9am to noon on Saturday. Here are a few recommendations to get you going.

Lodenbaur   Lodenbaur, similar to a department store, is devoted to regional Tyrolean dress. Most goods are made in Austria, including lederhosen, coats, dresses, dirndls, and accessories for men, women, and children. Be sure to check out the basement. Brixner Strasse 4. ℂ 0512/58-09-11. Tram: 1 or 3.

Tiroler Heimatwerk   This is one of Innsbruck's best stores for handcrafted Tyrolean items such as sculpture, pewter, textiles, woolen goods, hand-knit sweaters, and lace. Do-it-yourselfers can buy regionally inspired fabrics and dress patterns, and whip them into a dirndl (or whatever). Also for sale are carved chests, mirror frames, and furniture. The store's elegant decor includes ancient stone columns and vaulted ceilings. Meraner Strasse 2. ℂ 0512/58-23-20. Tram: 1 or 3.

WHERE TO STAY

Always arrive with a reservation, as Innsbruck is never out of season. Accommodations are particularly scarce from June until the end of summer and from mid-December to mid-April. Hotel information is available at the tourist office (see "Visitor Information," p. 330).

VERY EXPENSIVE

Hotel Europa Tyrol 𝒢𝒢   Opposite Innsbruck's railway station, in the heart of the city, the Europa is the best hotel in Innsbruck (it's also part of the Steigenberger Reservations System). Dating from 1869, this very formal but friendly hotel has hosted Queen Elizabeth II, the shah of Iran, General Patton, and the crew of *Apollo 14*. Rooms and suites are handsomely furnished with modern conveniences and Tyrolean or Biedermeier-style decorations. Each room offers a comfortable bed and a bathroom with a neatly kept shower-tub combination. The uniformed staff is helpful in every way and will usually be willing to show you the ornate yellow-and-white Barock Saal, which the Tyrolean government uses for its most important functions. The ballroom was constructed by King Ludwig's Bavarian architects and builders. The restaurant, Europastüberl (p. 344), is the finest in Tyrol.

Südtirolerplatz 2, A-6020 Innsbruck. ℂ 800/223-5652 in the U.S. and Canada, or 0512/5931. Fax 0512/ 58-78-00. www.europatyrol.com. 122 units. 152€–246€ double; 268€–374€ suite. Rates include breakfast. AE, DC, MC, V. Parking 11€. **Amenities:** Restaurant; bar; sauna; solarium; room service; babysitting; laundry; dry cleaning. *In room:* TV, minibar, hair dryer, safe.

EXPENSIVE

Hilton Innsbruck 𝒢   Erected in the mid-1980s and located 2 blocks from the railway station, this is the largest hotel and the tallest building (14 stories) in Innsbruck. Its contemporary comfort and capacity for large-scale conferences have made it very popular as well. Rooms, especially those on the upper floors, provide a view over the baroque spires of Innsbruck and its mountains. All contain built-in furniture and extras you'd expect of a government-rated four-star hotel. Bathrooms tend to be small, with showers and tiny tubs. The **Jackpot Bar** provides slot fixes and drinks, depending on your whim and the time of day. Its restaurant, **Guggeryllis,** is well-recommended (see "Where to Dine," later in this chapter).

Salurner Strasse 15, A-6010 Innsbruck. ℂ 0512/5935-0. Fax 0512/5935-220. www.hilton.com. 176 units. 190€–210€ double; 230€–250€ suite. Rates include buffet breakfast. AE, DC, MC, V. Parking 10€. Tram: 1 or 3. **Amenities:** Restaurant; bar; pool; fitness center; sauna; room service; babysitting; laundry; dry cleaning. *In room:* A/C, TV, minibar, hair dryer, safe.

Hotel Grauer Bär ⭐ This hotel, located in the center of Innsbruck, is next to the Imperial Gardens, the most interesting sights, and the shopping area. "The Gray Bear" (its English name) has long been a family favorite. The good-size rooms are well maintained and traditionally furnished, with thick carpeting and built-in furnishings. Bathrooms have showers and tubs. Front rooms are the most comfortable and the best appointed, but they also suffer from the most traffic noise. To the side of the large lobby is the dining room, **Bärenstube,** with an ornate ribbed and vaulted white ceiling supported by a central stone column. Well-prepared international and Austrian and Tyrolean specialties are served.

Universitätsstrasse 7, A-6021 Innsbruck. © 0512/59240. Fax 0512/574535. www.innsbruck-hotels.at. 199 units. 118€–155€ double. Rates include breakfast. AE, DC, MC, V. Parking 12€. **Amenities:** Restaurant; bar; fitness center; sauna; room service; massage; babysitting; laundry; dry cleaning. *In room:* TV, minibar, hair dryer, safe.

Hotel Innsbruck ⭐ This modern, streamlined, and comfortable hotel facing the Inn River is favored by upscale tourists and international business travelers. The staff is hardworking and multilingual. The furnishings in the rooms aren't remarkable, but all the beds are firm and the neatly kept bathrooms contain shower-tub combinations. A few guest rooms have been remodeled, and these are brighter and more inviting. The best rooms are on an upper floor and have small balconies; the dormer rooms on each floor are also superior. If you're stuck in one of the accommodations in the back, you'll do fine—in some respects, these are the coziest and most romantic rooms, opening onto vistas of the Altstadt.

The hotel contains two restaurants, one outfitted in a woodsy Tyrolean style with plenty of paneling, rustic accessories, and dirndl-clad waitresses. Unfortunately, most of the year, the restaurants cater to groups by reservation only. In such times, the hotel staff will recommend a nearby dining choice, even offering car service upon request. There's also a glassed-in winter garden for drinks, light meals, and coffee.

Innrain 3, A-6020 Innsbruck. © **0512/59-868.** Fax 0512/57-22-80. www.hotelinnsbruck.com. 114 units. 108€–119€ double. Rates include buffet breakfast. Half-board in winter only 12€ per person extra. AE, DC, MC, V. Parking 12€. Tram: 1 or 3. **Amenities:** 2 restaurants; bar; winter garden; lounge; pool; sauna; room service; babysitting; laundry; dry cleaning. *In room:* TV, hair dryer, safe.

Hotel Maximilian ⭐ Built in 1982 and renovated in 1992, this inner-city hotel rates as one of the most attractive and up-to-date in Innsbruck. Possessing an antique charm, it offers modern and convenient accommodations. Rooms are rather small yet exceedingly up-to-date, with very firm beds. The most desirable ones look out over the back, where you'll have a close-up view of the shingled onion dome of the oldest church in Innsbruck (now used as the headquarters of a company that makes keys). Bathrooms are small but well maintained, with shower-tub combinations. Parking is sometimes available for free on the street; otherwise, it costs 14€ per day in a nearby public garage. The hotel's restaurant, serving mainly Austrian dishes, is open only to hotel guests.

Marktgraben 7–9, A-6020 Innsbruck. © **0512/59-967.** Fax 0512/57-74-50. 40 units. 110€–130€ double. Rates include breakfast. AE, DC, MC, V. Tram: 1. **Amenities:** Restaurant; bar; room service; babysitting; laundry; dry cleaning. *In room:* TV, safe.

Romantik Hotel-Restaurant Schwarzer Adler ⭐⭐ An appealing alternative to Innsbruck's modern hotels, the Schwarzer Adler lies behind an antique facade of stucco, shutters, and a big-windowed tower. The Ultsch family, the owners, furnished the interior in an authentic style with aged paneling, hand-painted regional furniture, antiques, and gemütlich clutter that make for a cozy and inviting ambience. Rooms are virtually one of a kind, each with its special character and period decor. Persian carpets cover parquet floors, and the bathrooms have dual basins, powerful showerheads, and large tubs. We prefer the older accommodations, which are more spacious and have more Tyrolean character. Some of the best rooms also contain private safes. The two suites are even more luxurious.

Kaiserjägerstrasse 2, A-6020 Innsbruck. ℂ 0512/58-71-09. Fax 0512/56-16-97. www.deradler.com. 39 units. 141€–202€ double; 255€–470€ suite. Additional person 46€. Rates include breakfast. AE, DC, MC, V. Parking 9€. Tram: 1 or 3. **Amenities:** Restaurant; bar; fitness center; health spa; room service; massage; laundry; dry cleaning. *In room:* A/C, TV, minibar, hair dryer, safe.

MODERATE

Best Western Hotel Mondschein *Value*   This is one of four Best Western hotels in Innsbruck and possibly one of our favorites of the four. It occupies a pink-fronted antique building that was originally erected in 1473 and that later functioned as a relay station for the Austrian (then horse-drawn) postal service. The antique integrity of its exterior has been carefully preserved, complete with its bay windows and solid proportions. Inside, however, it has been thoroughly modernized, with sturdy furniture and decor, and bedrooms that correspond to a modern international aesthetic of smooth lines, wood-grained furniture, and standardized comforts. Each of the rooms has a shower-tub combination and toilets set within small rooms that are otherwise separate from the bathrooms. Most have views of the river Inn or of Innsbruck's Old Town, whose northern edge lies within about 200 yards of the hotel.

Mariahilfstrasse 6, A-6010 Innsbruck. ℂ 0512/22784. Fax 0512/22784-90. www.mondschein.at. 103€ double; 180€ triple. Rates include breakfast. Free parking. AE, DC, MC, V. Tram: 1. **Amenities:** Bar; babysitting; laundry; dry cleaning. *In room:* TV, minibar; hair dryer; safe.

Hotel Central   One of the most unusual hotels in Innsbruck, Hotel Central was originally built in the 1860s, but from its very modern exterior you might not realize it. Throughout, you'll see a high-tech composition of textured concrete and angular windows. The comfortable rooms have an Art Deco design that evokes an almost Japanese sense of simplicity. Most are quite spacious, with excellent beds. Bathrooms are small, with shower-tub combinations. In total contrast to the simplicity of the rest of the hotel, the ground floor contains a grand Viennese cafe with marble columns, sculpted ceilings, and large gilt-and-crystal chandeliers.

Gilmstrasse 5, A-6020 Innsbruck. ℂ 0512/59-20. Fax 0512/58-03-10. www.central.co.at/central. 85 units. 122€–144€ double. Rates include breakfast. Additional person 21€ extra. AE, DC, MC, V. Parking 12€. Tram: 1 or 3. **Amenities:** Restaurant; bar; fitness center; sauna; room service; laundry; dry cleaning. *In room:* TV, minibar, hair dryer.

Hotel Goldener Adler   Even the phone booth near the reception desk of this 600-year-old family-run hotel is outfitted in antique style. Famous guests have included Goethe, Mozart, and the violinist Paganini, who cut his name into the windowpane of his room. Rooms are handsomely furnished and vary in size and decor. Some have decorative Tyrolean architectural features such as beamed ceilings. Others are furnished more modernly. The size of bathrooms depends on your room assignment, everything from spacious combination models to cramped rooms with shower stalls.

Herzog-Friedrich-Strasse 6, A-6020 Innsbruck. ℂ 0512/57-11-11. Fax 0512/58-44-09. www.goldeneradler. com. 35 units. 128€–168€ double; from 198€ suite. Rates include breakfast. AE, DC, MC, V. Parking 11€. Tram: 1 or 3. **Amenities:** 5 restaurants; bar; room service; babysitting; laundry; dry cleaning. *In room:* TV, minibar, hair dryer, safe.

Hotel Kapeller   Set within a 5-minute drive east of Innsbruck's historic core, this establishment is centered on a 500-year-old house and a 1960s four-story hotel. They're interconnected with a greenhouse-style reception area and bar. Rooms are outfitted in artfully rustic reproductions of Tyrolean-style furniture and have largish bathrooms with shower-tub combinations. Many overlook the mountains and the hotel's well-manicured garden. Staff is attentive, English-speaking, and cooperative. The restaurant is recommended under "Where to Dine," later in this chapter. The hotel derives its name, incidentally, from a small Romanesque-era chapel that lies within a short walk.

Philippine-Welser-Strasse 96, A-6020 Innsbruck. ℂ **0512/34-31-06.** Fax 0512/34-31-06-68. www.kapeller. at. 36 units. 110€–140€ double; 120€ suite for 2–4 occupants. Rates include breakfast. AE, DC, MC, V. Tram 3. **Amenities:** Restaurant; bar; room service; laundry; dry cleaning. *In room:* TV, minibar, hair dryer, safe.

Hotel Royal   Set beside the river, this efficient and convenient hotel is a very short walk from most of the historic treasures of Innsbruck. Renovated in the 1970s, it has a light-gray exterior; a sunny, cheerful breakfast room; and comfortable, contemporary rooms with firm beds and small bathrooms with shower-tub combinations. There's no restaurant on the premises, but the staff will direct you to many nearby choices.

Innrain 16, A-6020 Innsbruck. ℂ **0512/58-63-85.** Fax 0512/58-63-85-10. www.royal-hotel.at. 20 units. 95€–104€ double. Rates include breakfast. AE, DC, MC, V. Free parking. Tram: 1. **Amenities:** Breakfast room; bar; lounge. *In room:* TV, hair dryer.

Hotel Sailer ⓡ   Now into a family management that has stretched over five generations, this is one of the best and more affordable hotels of Innsbruck, lying a short walk west of the Hauptbahnhof. A trio of antique buildings were joined together to form this welcoming hotel. Even though in the city, you get the feel of an alpine retreat here because of the use of woodwork on every floor. The public rooms are warm and inviting, often filled with red tile floors and throw rugs. Guest rooms are small to medium in size and lack the character and taste of the public rooms, but they're well maintained and beautifully kept with mainly built-in pieces. All of them come with tiny modular bathrooms—half with tubs, the others with showers. The best views, as would be expected, are on the upper floors. In a series of rustically decorated restaurants, Tyrolean specialties are served, and the intimate and wood-paneled bar is a retreat after you return from the slopes. In winter, folkloric shows are often presented.

Adamgasse 6. ℂ **0512/53630.** Fax 0512/53637. www.sailer-innsbruck.at. 86 units. 110€ double, 130€–140€ suite. AE, DC, MC, V. Tram: Hauptbahnhof. **Amenities:** Restaurant; bar; sauna; laundry; dry cleaning. *In room:* TV.

Tourotel Breinössl   Constructed about a century ago and recently renovated, this building was originally erected as an oversize private home with enough bedrooms to double as a boardinghouse. Flowered loggias and bay windows protrude from the ochre-colored facade. The inside is tastefully woodsy, with touches of wrought iron and regional sculpture in the public areas. The comfortable rooms have attractively modern furniture and good beds. Bathrooms are small but well maintained and equipped with shower-tub combinations. The hotel is owned and operated by a nationwide restaurant chain, Wienerwald, which also operates a restaurant on the hotel's ground floor.

Maria-Theresien-Strasse 12, A-6020 Innsbruck. ℂ **0512/58-41-65.** Fax 0512/58-41-65-26. www.tourotel.at. 41 units. 109€–139€ double; 149€ suite. Rates include breakfast. AE, DC, MC, V. Bus: R, O. **Amenities:** Restaurant; bar; room service; babysitting; laundry; dry cleaning. *In room:* TV.

INEXPENSIVE

City-Hotel Goldene Krone   Near the Triumphal Arch on Innsbruck's main street, this baroque house has a green-and-white facade. Rooms are modern, comfortable, well maintained, and, for the most part, spacious with plenty of light filtering through the many windows. Most have a table with chairs, and all have firm mattresses and triple-glazed windows to cut down on noise. Bathrooms are small with shower stalls but are spotless. The hotel offers good comfort: an elevator, soundproof windows, and a Viennese-inspired coffeehouse/restaurant, the **Art Gallery-Café.**

Maria-Theresien-Strasse 46, A-6020. Innsbruck. ℂ **0512/58-61-60.** Fax 0512/580-18-96. www.city-crown hotel-innsbruck.com. 37 units. 74€–103€ double; 108€–139€ suite. Rates include breakfast. AE, MC, V. Parking 7.50€. Tram: 1. Bus: A, H, K, or N. **Amenities:** Restaurant; cafe; lounge; babysitting. *In room:* TV.

Gasthaus Innsbrücke   This three-story hotel sits directly beside the Inn River, on the northern fringes of the Altstadt, about a 3-minute walk to the center of Innsbruck's historic core. Each room was upgraded and modernized in 1999 and boasts contemporary, angular, no-nonsense furniture. Ten units have well-kept bathrooms with shower units. Rooms facing the river have better views, but accommodations facing the back tend to be a bit quieter. The owners, the Winkler family, maintain a simple restaurant on the building's street level that's open Monday through Saturday for both lunch and dinner.

Innstrasse 1, A-6020 Innsbruck. ℂ **0512/28-19-34.** Fax 0512/27-84-10. 27 units, 10 with bathroom. 44€ double without bathroom; 59€ double with bathroom; 64€ triple without bathroom; 85€ triple with bathroom. AE, MC, V. Bus: A. **Amenities:** Restaurant; bar. *In room:* TV, no phone.

Gasthof-Hotel Weisses Kreuz 🅖 *Value*   This atmospheric inn, located in the center of Innsbruck, has not changed much during its lifetime, with the exception of the elevator that now carries newcomers up two flights to the reception area. In 1769, 13-year-old Wolfgang Mozart and his father, Leopold, stayed here, and in recent times, locally famous German-speaking actors and actresses have made it their temporary home. If you choose to avoid the elevator, you'll have to climb up a stairway before arriving at the reception area. Here you'll be pleasantly surprised by the carved stone columns, a TV room with an arched, wood-covered ceiling, a collection of massive Tyrolean chests, and a carved balustrade worn smooth by the palms of countless visitors. Rooms are cozy and atmospheric, either small or medium in size, with comfortable furnishings. Some have private bathrooms with neatly kept shower units. Hallway bathrooms are adequate and well maintained.

Herzog-Friedrich-Strasse 31, A-6020 Innsbruck. ℂ **0512/594790.** Fax 0512/59-47-990. www.weisseskreuz. at. 40 units, 31 with bathroom. 63€–66€ double without bathroom; 83€–95€ double with bathroom. Rates include breakfast. AE, MC, V. Parking 9€. Tram: 3. **Amenities:** 2 restaurants; bar; room service. *In room:* TV.

Hotel Bierwirt   This hotel consists of a pair of buildings that face each other across a busy street on the southern outskirts of town, about a 15-minute walk from the historic core. The older section dates from 1615 and benefits from a 1998 renovation that brought the cozy interior up to modern standards. The restaurant and all but a dozen of the rooms are in the original building, but regardless of their location, each room has a modern bathroom with a shower-tub combination and many contemporary comforts. Its restaurant is recommended separately in "Where to Dine," below.

Bichlweg 2. A-6020 Innsbruck. ℂ **0512/34-21-43.** Fax 0512/34-21-435. www.bierwirt.com. 50 units. 106€ double. MC, V. Tram 3 or Bus K. **Amenities:** Restaurant; bar; sauna. *In room:* TV, hair dryer.

Hotel Binders *Value*   This is an unusual hotel, crafted and managed with a bit more imagination that equivalently priced inns within its immediate, somewhat remote, neighborhood. It presents a utilitarian, white-stucco facade to a suburban neighborhood southwest of Innsbruck's center, near the town's Olympic stadium, about a 20-minute walk from the center. Inside you'll find a carefully organized and thrifty interior, wherein a bar and cafe near the reception area function as the hotel's social center. Members of the Binder family recently installed an elevator in this older building and have renovated its public areas so frequently that not many traces remain to hint at the building's original construction. In distinct opposition to this, bedrooms run the gamut of stylishness. Most desirable are the recently rebuilt space-age modern rooms, with names like Maple, Aluminum, Pink, and Turquoise. Older rooms still retain a dark-paneled, somewhat dowdy version of an Alpine-rustic decor that hasn't been much changed since the 1970s. Ten of the units, the cheapest of all, don't have private baths, but share toilet and shower facilities set off the hallways. The higher you climb within this place, the better accessorized and more modern the bedrooms become. At the very top, just under the eaves, are a pair of stylish "loft-rooms," with high ceilings and waterbeds.

Dr.-Glatz-Strasse 20, A-6020 Innsbruck. © 0512/334360. Fax 0512/334-3699. www.arthotel.at. 50 units, 40 with bathroom. 49€ double without bathroom; 64€–99€ double with bathroom. Rates include breakfast. AE, DC, MC, V. Tram: 3. **Amenities:** Bar; sauna. *In room:* TV, minibar.

Hotel Mozart   This renovated hotel has a central location and offers small rooms, especially those family rooms with three or four beds. The beds aren't the town's most comfortable, but the price is right. Bathrooms are exceedingly small but do contain shower-tub combinations. You don't get a lot of frills here, but you do receive good, solid comfort at a reasonable price. From the railway station, walk down Salurner Strasse, crossing Leopoldstrasse, which leads you to Müllerstrasse and the hotel in about 10 minutes.

Müllerstrasse 15, A-6010 Innsbruck. © 0512/59-538. Fax 0512/59-53-86. hotel.mozart@aon.at. 42 units. 80€–84€ double. Rates include breakfast. AE, DC, MC, V. Parking 5.60€; parking garage 9€. Closed Nov 30–Dec 26. Tram: 1. **Amenities:** Breakfast room; lounge. *In room:* TV, hair dryer, safe.

Pension Bistro   This is a simple but engaging government-rated two-star hotel that occupies a building from around 1955 located within a 15-minute walk of the center. Rooms are relatively spacious, albeit blandly decorated in an internationalist modern style. Double-paned windows block out most of the noise from the busy street outside, and some have views of the nearby mountains. The well-scrubbed bathrooms contain shower-tub combinations. The restaurant is recommended separately in "Where to Dine."

Pradler Strasse 2, A-6020 Innsbruck. © 0512/34-63-19. Fax 0512/360-252-52. bistro@eunet.at. 11 units. 63€–67€ double. Rates include breakfast. Bus O and R. **Amenities:** Restaurant; bar. *In room:* TV, hair dryer.

Pension Paula *Finds*   Set on a hillside above Innsbruck and surrounded with greenery, this hotel evolved during the 1950s from the core of a 17th-century farmhouse. Today it's still maintained by the grandson (Wolfgang Gunsch) of the matriarch (Paula) who founded the place, and still retains reminders on the ground floor of the building's original function. Rooms are cozy but simple, with a bare-boned but comfortable ambience that's permeated with personalized attention. Half of the rooms contain well-kept private bathrooms with shower units. The pair of rooms (especially no. 15) under the sloping eaves of the third floor is among the most sought-after, partially because of the sense of privacy and romance. Panoramic views are available from the porch and terrace that extend out from the two lower floors of the building, and overall there's a sense of cordiality and friendliness.

Weiherburggasse 15, A-6020 Innsbruck. ℂ 0512/29-22-62. Fax 0512/29-30-17. www.pensionpaula.at. 14 units, 7 with bathroom. 45€–49€ double without bathroom; 54€ double with bathroom. No credit cards. Bus D. **Amenities:** Lounge. *In room:* No phone.

Pension Stoi *(Kids)* This pension is 3 minutes from the train station. The rooms are comfortable, with good beds and hallway showers. Because some rooms have three or four beds, this pension has long been a favorite of families on a budget. No breakfast is served, but there are several cafes nearby.

Salurner Strasse 7, A-6020 Innsbruck. ℂ 0512/58-54-34. Fax 05238/87-282. 18 units, 7 with bathroom. 56€ double without bathroom; 49€ double with bathroom; 56€ triple without bathroom; 63€ triple with bathroom; 63€ quad without bathroom; 75€ quad with bathroom. No credit cards. Tram: 1 or 3. **Amenities:** Lounge. *In room:* No phone.

WHERE TO DINE

Dining is never a problem in Innsbruck, as this alpine town has more than 200 restaurants, inns, and cafes, some of which offer evening entertainment. If you're going to be in Austria for only a short time, we suggest that you stick to original Tyrolean specialties. However, if that doesn't suit you, there are restaurants serving international cuisine.

EXPENSIVE

Europastüberl *(★★* AUSTRIAN/INTERNATIONAL This distinguished restaurant, with a delightful Tyrolean ambience, is in a hotel that's the finest address in Innsbruck. Traditional regional and creative cooking is the chef's goal, and he achieves this exceedingly well. Diners can choose from both warm and cold appetizers, ranging from iced angler fish with Chinese tree morels to a small ragout of crayfish in a spicy biscuit with kohlrabi, to a warm salad with cabbage and bacon. Soups might include lobster minestrone with basil oil or cream of spinach and potato. Some dishes are served only for two people, such as roast pike perch with vegetables and buttery potatoes, and Bresse guinea hen roasted and presented with an herb sauce. Fresh Tyrolean trout almost always appears on the menu, or you might prefer the meat dishes, ranging from red deer ragout to saddle of venison, to fried jelly of calves' head Vienna style with a lamb's tongue salad. Many dishes, including *Tafelspitz* (boiled beef), represent traditional Austrian cuisine. Desserts are often lavish, or you can settle for a Tyrolean apple strudel.

In the Hotel Europa Tyrol, Brixnerstrasse 6. ℂ 0512/5931. Reservations required. Main courses 10€–25€; fixed-price 4-course menu 36€–40€. AE, DC, MC, V. Daily 11am–2:30pm and 6:30–11pm.

Guggeryllis SCANDINAVIAN/INTERNATIONAL Located one flight above the lobby level of this government-rated four-star hotel, this popular restaurant is a favorite of the international business community, and it's romantic enough for intimate celebrations as well. In an attractive setting with potted palms, the restaurant is named for Emperor Maximilian's best-known and most popular court jester. Menu items emphasize a combination of Scandinavian, Austrian, and international foods, some of the best examples of which appear at the lunchtime buffet. We consider it, with its trio of meats and large array of salads, one of the most appealing in town. A la carte items include such Nordic specialties as noisettes of reindeer with forest mushrooms and braised red cabbage, and such Austrian dishes as Wiener schnitzels, *Tafelspitz,* saddle of veal steak in a morel-studded cream sauce, and a perfectly prepared version of grilled sole with lemon butter.

In the Hilton Innsbruck, Salurner Strasse 15. ✆ 0512/593-5308. Reservations recommended. Main courses 13€–22€; lunch buffet 12€. AE, DC, MC, V. Daily 11:30am–2:30pm and 6–10:30pm. Tram: 1 or 3.

Restaurant Goldener Adler ✿ AUSTRIAN/TYROLEAN/INTERNA-TIONAL
Richly Teutonic and steeped in the decorative traditions of alpine Tyrol, this beautifully decorated restaurant has a deeply entrenched reputation and a loyal following among local residents. The menu includes good, hearty fare based on cold-weather outdoor life—the chefs aren't into delicate subtleties. Examples include Tyrolean bacon served with horseradish and farmer's bread, cream of cheese soup with croutons, and Tyroler *Zopfebraten*, a flavorful age-old specialty consisting of strips of veal steak served with herb-enriched cream sauce and spinach dumplings. A well-regarded specialty is a platter known as *Adler Tres*. It contains spinach dumplings, stuffed noodles, and cheese dumplings, all flavorfully tied together with a brown butter sauce and a gratin of mountain cheese.

Herzog-Friedrich-Strasse 6. ✆ 0512/57-11-11. Reservations recommended. Main courses 12€–22€; set menus 12€–18€. AE, DC, MC, V. Daily 11:30am–10:30pm. Tram: 1 or 3.

Restaurant Schwarzer Adler ✿✿ AUSTRIAN
Even if you're not a guest at the richly atmospheric Romantik Hotel Schwarzer Adler (separately recommended in "Where to Stay"), you might appreciate a meal within its historic premises. If you do, you'll follow in the footsteps of the 18th-century Kaiser Maximilian, who housed one of his mistresses in one of the lodgings within this building and who used to entertain her in one or another of these dining rooms. You'll have the option of dining within one of three cozily wood-paneled *Stube* near the reception desk, on the hotel's ground floor, or within the more stately looking cellar, beneath the soaring vaulted ceilings of a dining room (Spiesesaal K&K—*Kaiser und Königlich*) that honors its long-ago associations with royalty. Cuisine is elaborate and intricate, the product of a management that's proud of the hotel's status as a member of Europe's Romantik Hotel chain. The finest examples include a salad of wild quail served with lentils, strips of braised goose liver, and a sauce that's enhanced with apple liqueur. There's also a divine smoked venison with a terrine of wild grouse and black bread; grilled filets of wild boar served with butter, roasted potatoes; a gratin of wild mushrooms; and a salad of wild and mixed baby greens. Dessert might include a selection of sorbets flavored with wild alpine berries. As you'd expect, the wine list is long, broad, and impressive, with lots of wines from relatively obscure regions of Austria.

In the Hotel Schwarzer Adler, Kaiserjägerstrasse 2. ✆ 0512/587-109. Reservations recommended. Main courses 17€–22€. AE, DC, MC, V. Mon–Sat 11am–2pm and 6–10:30pm. Tram: 1 or 3.

MODERATE
Hirschen-Stuben ✿✿ AUSTRIAN/ITALIAN
Beneath a vaulted ceiling in a house built in 1631, this restaurant is charming, well established, and well recommended. You'll see hand-chiseled stone columns, brocade chairs, and a short flight of stairs leading down from the historic pavement of the street outside. The establishment, by its own admission, is at its best in spring, autumn, and winter, since it lacks a garden or outdoor terrace for outdoor summer dining. The food is well prepared, the staff is charming, and the ambience is appropriately welcoming. Menu items include steaming platters of pasta, fish soup, trout meunière, sliced veal in cream sauce Zurich style, beef Stroganoff, pepper steak,

stewed deer with vegetables, and filet of flounder with parsley and potatoes. The kitchen staff is equally familiar with the cuisine of both Austria and Italy.

Kiebachgasse 5. © 0512/58-29-79. Reservations recommended. Main courses 8.80€–19€. DC, MC, V. Mon–Sat 11am–2pm and 6–11pm. Tram: 1 or 3.

Jörgele (*Value* AUSTRIAN/TYROLEAN   Set in the historic core of town, on two floors of a half-timbered house first mentioned in local records as a wine house (Weinhaus Jörgele) in 1580, this restaurant celebrates the old-fashioned traditions of Tyrolean cuisine. Its trio of dining rooms (the Weingartner Stube, the Bienerstube, and the Steinbok Stube, each of them elegantly rustic and intricately paneled) lie on the second and third floors of the building, requiring an upstairs hike from the busy sidewalk below. Once here, you'll be exposed to all the alpine accessories of old-fashioned Tyrol and grandmother-style food that some locals remember fondly from their childhoods. The best example of this is Tyrolean *Gröstel,* consisting of a spicy version of boiled beef capped with a fried egg and served with roasted potatoes and a cabbage salad. A bit less two-fisted might be game stew with wild mushrooms and spinach dumplings; braised calves' liver with tomatoes, bacon, and onions; roasted rumpsteak with onions and wine sauce; and tasty schnitzels. The wine list is extensive and worldly.

> **Impressions**
>
> The chief crop of provincial Austria is scenery.
>
> —John Gunther, *Inside Europe* (1938)

Herzog-Friedrich-Strasse 13. © 0512/582217. Reservations recommended. Main courses 8€–26€. AE, DC, MC, V. Tues–Sun 11:30am–2pm and 6–10pm. Tram: 1 or 3.

Sweet Basil INTERNATIONAL   The venue is pan-European, the staff is young and more or less hip, and the cuisine is relatively sophisticated. Even better, it's an affordable alternative to some of the grander and more expensive restaurants nearby. You'll get a sense of somewhat monastic simplicity in the decor here, with very old stone walls, a color scheme of mostly yellow, and at least a hundred framed photographs, artworks, and etchings, each of which evokes the personal and eclectic tastes of the owners. Menu items include fresh salads (some of them meals in themselves) and some that rely heavily on sweet basil, an herb that, in our opinion, is hard to use too much of. The best dishes include a saffron-laced version of bouillabaisse that uses local and Atlantic fish instead of the more traditional Mediterranean versions; a savory teriyaki chicken with a sweet-and-sour peach chutney; several kinds of pasta, including a version of linguini with—guess what—a simple pesto (basil) sauce; and grilled steaks. Every month, the menu is revised in favor of a different culinary theme, with a new set of daily specials based on, among others, cuisines from Mexico, Thailand, Spain, or Japan.

Herzog-Friedrich-Strasse 31. © 0512/584996. Reservations recommended. Main courses 14€–19€. AE, DC, MC, V. Tues–Sun 11am–1am. Tram: 1 or 3.

INEXPENSIVE

Bistro AUSTRIAN/INTERNATIONAL   Within one large and paneled dining room, you'll find hints of folkloric charm, a loyal lunchtime clientele from surrounding office buildings, and a well-prepared menu that reflects the changing seasons. During springtime, expect creative use of asparagus; during autumn and early winter, look for venison prepared in a variety of different ways. There's a year-round emphasis on fish that include Atlantic versions of turbot and sole, and such local freshwater varieties as *Saibling,* pike perch, zander, and trout. As its name suggests, this is an unpretentious affair, with solid, generous portions.

Pradler Strasse 2. (✆ **0512/34-63-19**. Reservations not necessary. Main courses 9€–18€. AE, DC, MC, V. Tues–Sun noon–3pm; daily 6–11pm (last order). Bus O or R.

Philippine VEGETARIAN/FISH/INTERNATIONAL   The inspiration for the mostly vegetarian food here derives from around the world, including India and Mexico, but the origins of its name are purely Austrian: It refers to Philippine Welser, wife of the 16th-century overlord of the Tyrol, Ferdinand II, and author of a book on the healing power of herbs. Positioned one floor above street level, with somewhat anonymous-looking decor that might remind you of a contemporary-looking airport waiting lounge, it was established as a public works project about a decade ago as a means of feeding and employing the city's homeless. All of that changed, however, in 2000, when members of the Puffing family took over its administration and whipped it into cracking good shape as a privately operated restaurant. Cuisine is tasty and flavorful, most of it focusing on all-vegetarian presentations of salads, lasagnas, vegetarian curries, polenta with Gorgonzola, cannelloni with tofu, and pumpkin risotto with ginger and Parmesan cheese. There is a limited array of fish dishes, including stir-fries of shrimp with vegetables, braised salmon with a wine-flavored herb sauce, and zander (pike perch) with an herb-flavored butter sauce. Since lunches here are more popular than evening meals, lunch is served both on the street level and in the upstairs dining room. Dinners, however, are served only in the somewhat more formal dining room upstairs.

Templstrasse 2 at Müllerstrasse. (✆ **0512/589157**. Reservations recommended. Main courses 8€–15€. AE, DC, MC, V. Mon–Sat 11:30am–2pm and 6–10pm. Tram: 1.

Restaurant Bierwirt *(Value* AUSTRIAN   Antique-looking, with an architectural pedigree that goes back 300 years, this cozy alpine-style restaurant has lots of Tyrolean artifacts, carefully oiled paneling, and an excellent reputation for good food. Menu items include most of the traditional Tyrolean specialties, ribsticking fare that goes down well in chilly weather. Examples include ragout of venison in a port wine sauce, a savory version of *Kasfarfeln* (thick consommé with cheese, onions, chives, and dumplings), savory stews, Wiener schnitzels, *Tafelspitz* (boiled beef with horseradish), and a medley of roasts and sausages.

Bichlweg 2. (✆ **0512/34-21-43**. Reservations recommended. Main courses 9€–17€. Mon–Fri noon–2pm; Mon–Sat 5–11pm. MC, V. Tram 3 or Bus K.

Restaurant Churrasco–La Mamma ITALIAN/INTERNATIONAL   Informal and likable, this warmly decorated restaurant offers a copious bar and two floors of dining areas. Located in a much-modernized pre–World War I building beside the river, it offers an international menu on the street level, which is served amid modern copper sculptures and plants. A flight of antique stairs leads up to a dining room (La Mamma) with decor and menu options more intensely Italian than those of its street-level counterpart. Menu items in either area include pizzas, pastas, salads, baked fish, seasonal game dishes, and grilled meats such as steak and chicken. In summertime, tables are placed outside at the edge of the river.

Innrain 2. (✆ **0512/58-63-98**. Main courses 7€–18€; pizzas 5€–10€. AE, DC, MC, V. Daily 8:30am–midnight; warm food available daily 11:30am–11:30pm. Tram: 1 or 3.

Restaurant Kapeller AUSTRIAN/CONTINENTAL   This restaurant occupies a 500-year-old house that was expanded into a hotel in the 1960s. Cozy and welcoming, it includes three paneled dining rooms, an attentive staff, and plenty of Tyrolean artifacts and charm. Savory menu items vary with the season but are likely to include braised lamb with vegetables and a gratin of potatoes, duck with honey-flavored croutons and potato croquettes, and filets of sole with salmon mousse served with grape sauce and asparagus-flavored risotto. Die-hard regionalists sometimes appreciate an age-old Tyrolean dish, *Peuscherl*, composed of the tongue, hearts, and offal of beef and sheep, served with an herb-flavored sauce, that some Tyroleans remember from their childhoods.

Philippine-Welser-Strasse 96. ✆ 0512/34-31-06. Reservations recommended. Main courses 14.60€–28€. AE, DC, MC, V. Tues–Sat 11:30am–2pm; Mon–Sat 6–10pm. Tram 3.

Restaurant Ottoburg ☆ AUSTRIAN/INTERNATIONAL
This historic restaurant, established around 1745, occupies a 13th-century building that some historians say is the oldest in Innsbruck. Inside, four intimate and atmospheric dining rooms with "19th-century neo-Gothic decor" lie scattered over two different floors. Hearty dishes include venison stew, "grandmother's mixed grill," pork chops with rice and carrots, and fried trout. The international menu emphasizes Tyrolean specialties, best seen in the dessert list, which offers two kinds of strudel and several other pastries. In summer, a beer garden operates in the rear, open daily from 10:30am to 11:30pm. A large beer costs 2.50€, with a glass of wine going for 3€. Sometime during the lifetime of this edition, management will change—there could be some alterations in policies and cuisine.

Herzog-Friedrich-Strasse 1. ✆ 0512/58-43-38. Reservations recommended. Main courses 7.27€–22€. AE, DC, MC, V. Tues–Sun 11am–3pm and 5:30pm–midnight. Tram: 1 or 3.

Riese Haymon TYROLEAN/AUSTRIAN
Inside this 400-year-old building in the heart of the old city, you'll find an intensely Tyrolean ambience that includes four separate dining rooms, each paneled and accessorized with old-time artifacts, plus an attentive staff. Menu items include old-fashioned but flavor-filled dishes that rely on the seasonality of the ingredients and that often come with one of the restaurant's specialties, dumplings. Look for a changing menu that usually includes such local freshwater fish as *Saibling,* pike perch, salmon, and trout; veal and chicken dishes in wine sauce or brown stocks; Wiener schnitzel; braised liver; herb-flavored terrines of freshwater crayfish; and an especially savory version of braised oxtail.

Haymongasse 4. ✆ 0512/56-68-00. Reservations recommended. Main courses 7€–16€; set-price lunch 6.50€–8.50€. DC, MC, V. Daily noon–2pm and 6–10pm. Tram 1 or 3.

Stiegl-Bräu Innsbruck AUSTRIAN/INTERNATIONAL
One of the most reliable and atmospheric of Innsbruck's budget restaurants, this Tyrolean-style restaurant, an animated beer hall since 1935, serves well-prepared platters of food and copious amounts of wine and beer. Three different dining rooms are scattered over two floors, and, in summer, there's an outdoor beer garden. Salads, roasts, schnitzels, sausages, and stews are the straightforward fare here, often followed by the preferred dessert of Salzburg, a *Nockerl* prepared for two or more diners. The waitstaff here refers to the cuisine as "the people's food."

Wilhelm-Greil-Strasse 25. ✆ 0512/58-43-88. Reservations accepted. Main courses 10€–22€. No credit cards. Mon–Sat 11am–midnight. Tram: 1 or 3.

Stiftskeller AUSTRIAN/INTERNATIONAL
The baroque detailing on this 18th-century yellow-and-white palace-turned-restaurant across from the Hofburg can be admired from the street-side beer garden: At night, lights illuminate the garden. In cold weather, you can, of course, dine inside, where there

are several dining rooms. Meals are posted on a blackboard, and typical menu items include spaghetti carbonara and venison schnitzel in a pheasant-flavored cream sauce, followed by fresh homemade apple strudel. This place can get rowdy at night.

Burggraben 31. (℃) **0512/58-34-90.** Reservations required. Main courses 14€–25€. AE, DC, MC, V. Daily 10am–11pm. Closed 3 weeks in Nov and Jan 8–Feb 20. Tram: 1 or 3.

Theresien Bräu AUSTRIAN/INTERNATIONAL   There's a lot of energy, ambience, and goodwill associated with this place, which is reflected in the fact that it has become one of its neighborhood's most popular dining and drinking venues since it was established in 1996. As such, it's the newest brewery in Tyrol and the only one that's based within the city limits of Innsbruck. The setting is on two floors of what was originally built in the 1940s as a movie theater. Today, in lieu of a big screen, you'll find all the apparatus and paraphernalia of a brewery (including big copper and stainless steel vats), artfully positioned in full view of the bar and the dining tables. The theme of the place doesn't evoke alpine Austria, as so many other restaurants in Innsbruck rather shamelessly do. Instead, you can expect a nautical motif of fish nets, brass and mahogany navigational instruments, rowboats, and old-fashioned steamer trunks. All of this is peripheral, of course, to the beer, which comes in as many as four different varieties that vary with the season and the whims of the brewmaster. Regardless of the color and flavor of the brew you select, it costs about 3€ for a foaming (half-liter) mugful, or 7.80€ for an American-style 1.4-liter pitcher. Menu items might include everything from a small platter of beer-compatible sausages (a snack that management prices at 5€) to more substantial platters of meat, potatoes, or noodle-based dishes. Noodles are savory: One of the best versions is garnished with ham, cheese, and an herb-flavored cream sauce.

Maria-Theresien-Strasse 51–53. (℃) 0512/587580. Reservations not necessary. Main courses 7€–20€. AE, DC, MC, V. Daily 10am–midnight. Tram: 3.

Weisses Rössl ⍟ AUSTRIAN/TYROLEAN   You'll enter this time-honored place through a stone archway opening onto one of Old Town's most famous streets. At the end of a flight of stairs, marked with a very old crucifix, you'll find a trio of dining rooms with red-tile floors and a history of welcoming guests that stretches from 1590. One of the dining rooms (the Nebenstube) has what might be the most extensive set of stag horns (complete with the initials of the hunter and the date of the shooting) in Innsbruck. At first glance, the menu appears simple, listing such dishes as a Tiroler *Grüstl* (a kind of hash composed of sautéed onions, sliced beef, alpine herbs, and potatoes cooked and served in a frying pan), *Saftgoulash* with polenta, several kinds of schnitzels, and a grilled platter *Alt Insprugg* for two diners. A dish the restaurant is especially proud of is served only in midwinter and usually evokes vivid childhood memories for many of this restaurant's Tyrolean clients—fresh blood and liver sausages with sauerkraut. In summer, the establishment expands onto an outdoor terrace. They also rent rooms; a double costs 100€, including breakfast.

Kiebachgasse 8. (℃) **0512/58-30-57.** Reservations recommended. Main courses 9€–160€. AE, MC, V. Mon–Sat 11:30am–2pm and 6–10pm. Closed 2 weeks after Easter and 2 weeks in Nov. Tram: 1 or 3.

CAFES

Within a Bordeaux-red decor that closely emulates the rich cafe life of its mother-lode original in Vienna, you can visit the Innsbruck branch of the **Café Sacher,** Rennweg 1 (℃) **0512/565626**). Make no mistake: Rip-offs and unauthorized copies of this chain's most famous pastry, the Sacher torte, have cost contestants millions in litigation over the years, and the holders of the original 19th-century recipes (the owners of the Hotel Sacher in Vienna) have clung ferociously to their property. You can order coffee, priced at from around 2.10€, and the famous pastry, at 4.30€ per slice. And if you're in the gift-giving motif, you can haul a Sacher torte, attractively boxed in a wooden container, away with you for between 8.90€ and 33€, depending on the size. Any of these carries "certificates of authenticity," adding to the experience's somewhat pompous charm. The place is open daily from 8:30am to midnight. Tram: 1 or 3. Bus: H or Y.

If you're tired of too constant a diet of Austrian pastries, or if you want an insight into the way other countries create fattening between-meal treats, head for the **Café Valier,** Maximilianstrasse 27 (© **0512/586180**). Here, within a pink, mostly Jugendstil decor, you'll choose from French and Italian (not Austrian) pastries that—according to the owners—are unique in Innsbruck. Forget about *Apfelstrudels* and *Salzburger Nockerl* here, since they simply don't exist. Instead, look for French-inspired *tarte aux framboises;* a *tarte tatin,* a *mousse à l'orange,* or a *mousse au chocolat;* a light and airy *gâteau au chocolate avec mousse à l'orange;* and chestnut creams and chestnut sauces that, while all the rage in France, aren't really understood (except here) within the rest of Austria. There's been a bakery on-site here for at least a century, but the sit-down cafe part didn't get set up till around 1964. Don't expect full-fledged meals here, since most of the menu is devoted to pastries, most of which sell for around 3€ each, and sandwiches, toasted or otherwise. It's open Monday through Friday from 8am to 7pm and Saturday from 8am to 1pm. Tram: 1.

One of the best views of the exterior of the Goldenes Dachl is available from the front terrace of the **Café Katzung,** Herzog-Friedrich-Strasse 16 (© **0521/586183**), a time-tested cafe whose interior was ripped apart and rebuilt during a 5-month period in 2002. The decor today is more streamlined and a bit more modern-looking than the cranky, faux-baroque decor it replaced, but the medley of international newspapers (at least 10 of them) is still available, suspended vertically on rods, in a style you'd have expected in a library. Within a decor of wooden floors and a color scheme of pale green and cream with touches of red, you'll select from a full range of whiskies, coffees, Austrian wine, and light platters that consist mostly of sandwiches, soups, and salads. More impressively, there's an in-house pastry chef who concocts tray after tray of strudels and tortes, all the Austrian staples, priced at 1€ to 2.80€ each. It's open Monday through Saturday from 8am to midnight and Sunday from 9am to midnight. Tram: 1 or 3.

Although they're commonplace in such cities as London, **Alte Teestube** ⚐, Riesengasse 6 (© **0512/58-23-09;** tram: 1 or 3), is the only teahouse in Tyrol. It was established in 1978 by the present owner, a Hamburg-born authority on the origins of tea. Elaborately renovated in 1994, the Teestube offers at least 70 kinds of tea imported from India, China, Kenya, Indonesia, Russia, and Japan. A steaming pot for one person costs from 2.20€. (Listed on the menu is one of the world's most esoteric teas, Darjeeling First Flush, which is increasingly rare both within and outside of India.) A wide range of sandwiches and pastries (including Sacher torte and homemade *Apfelstrudel*), available as an accompaniment, are priced from 3€ to 5€. The Teestube lies one floor above street level, in the heart of the Old Town. It's open Monday through Saturday from 9am to 11pm.

On a quiet corner in the Old Town, **Café Munding** ⓖ, Kiebachgasse 16 (ⓒ **0512/58-41-18;** tram: 1 or 3), is in a comfortable-looking house built in 1720 that has baroque frescoes, carved bay windows, and Tyrolean detailing. Although it's the oldest cafe in Tyrol, the interior has been modernized, offering an interconnected series of rooms, one of which has an ornate plaster ceiling and an abstract mural. The first thing you'll see when you enter is a pastry and chocolate shop. Food is served in the inner rooms; in addition to coffee priced from 2.30€, the menu includes typical Tyrolean dishes, pizza, and toast, plus a vast selection of wine by the glass. Hours are daily from 8am to 10pm in summer and daily from 8am to 8pm in winter.

INNSBRUCK AFTER DARK

Innsbruck is more lighthearted about its nightlife than Vienna is. If you're in luck, you'll get to attend a summer concert in the park or perhaps take in an operetta at the theater. You might retire to a beer hall to listen to brass bands and yodeling or be lulled by zither music at a restaurant. Best of all, you can attend a Tyrolean folkloric evening or retreat to a local wine tavern offering entertainment. Many restaurants offer Tyrolean evenings (featuring evergreen music and dancing) in addition to food.

Ask the tourist office about current theatrical and folkloric events. In summer, a Tyrolean brass band often parades in costume, with a concert at the Goldenes Dachl. There are also often concerts at Schloss Ambras, ecclesiastical music at Wilten Basilica, and organ concerts at the Igls parish church.

In the center of the Altstadt, across from the Hofburg, the 150-year-old **Landestheater,** Rennweg 2 (ⓒ **0512/52-074**), is the major venue for theatrical or operatic presentations. The box office is open daily from 9:30am to 7pm, and performances usually begin at 7:30 or 8pm. Ticket prices are 7€ to 36€ for most operas or operettas, and 7€ to 40€ for theater seats. It's also the showcase for musicals and light operetta. For tickets, call ⓒ **0512/53-56-30.**

Concerts are presented at the Kunstpavillon in the Hofgarten in summer.

If you want to gamble, you have to drive to the resort of Seefeld, where the **Spiel-Casino** offers roulette, baccarat, and blackjack daily from 5pm. Or, you can try your luck on the slot machines at the **Holiday Inn Innsbruck.**

THE BAR & CLUB SCENE

Blue Chip   One of Innsbruck's best organized and most whimsical discos, Blue Chip is set within a modern building in the center of town, adjacent to the casino. It contains two bars, a busy dance floor, and a clientele ages 25 to 40. Music includes an appealing mixture of funk, soul, "black beat" (their term), and clubhouse music. Entrance is free, and hours are Wednesday through Saturday from 11pm to 4am. Wednesday is the cheapest night, when beers cost only 2.80€, and, as such, it's packed with university students. Other nights, beer sells for 3€ each. *Note:* If you happen to arrive a bit early, before too many other clients pack the dance floor, consider a drink at this establishment's competitor, **Jimmy's Bar,** one flight up within the same building (ⓒ **0512/57-04-73**). There's no dance floor and no live music, but it's something of an Innsbruck cliché that you should begin your evening at Jimmy's with a drink or two before proceeding downstairs to the Blue Chip for more drinks and a round of dancing. The bar is open daily from 11am to 2am. Wilhelm-Greil-Strasse 17. ⓒ **0512/56-50-00. Tram: 1 or 3.**

Club Filou   In the heart of the Old Town, this is the best bar and nightclub in Innsbruck. In summer, the tiny square in front blossoms with ivy-covered trellises, recorded music, and quadruplicate umbrellas, which shade the copper-covered outdoor bar. If you venture inside, past the antique cash register (whose zinc-plated drawers contain candy), you'll find an intimate hangout filled with Victorian settees and pop art. The bar is usually patronized by visiting musicians, athletes, and local residents. Food is available until 3am every night, and you can enjoy it at the bar or at a tiny table. The house specialty is spareribs, although salads, soups, schnitzels, scampi, smoked salmon, and desserts are also available. A main course begins at around 6€, but no one will mind if you order a snack or just a drink. In a separate, very old room, the high ceiling of a disco is supported by medieval stone columns and ringed with a high-tech steel balcony. Tall drinks (such as a Tom Collins) in both the cafe and the disco begin at around 5€; beer starts at 2.70€. The cafe is open daily from 6pm to 4am; the disco is open daily from 8pm to 2am. Stiftsgasse 12. ✆ 0512/58-02-56. Tram: 1 or 3.

Hofgartencafe   Just north of Alstadt (Old Town), this is perhaps the most popular place in Innsbruck. Lying in Hofgarten, it is especially packed in summer; it offers not only live music, but also seating indoors or outdoors. A lively crowd of young people, mostly in their 20s and 30s, is attracted to these precincts where more beer is consumed than anywhere else in town. You can opt for the home-brewed beer or else a wide selection of wines, many from such South American countries as Chile and Argentina. Long drinks cost from 6.50€, and you can also order from platters for 8€ and up. It's open in summer daily from 10am to 2am. In winter, hours are Tuesday through Thursday from 6pm to 2am, and Friday and Saturday from 6pm to 4am. Hofgarten, Rennweg 6. ✆ 0512/588871. Tram: 1 or 3.

Jackpot Bar   The attractive bar near the hotel lobby is one of the best places in Innsbruck to meet for a drink. Beer costs 2€ and up, and there are slot machines. It's open daily from noon to 1am. In the Holiday Inn Innsbruck, Salurner Strasse 15. ✆ 0512/59-350. Tram: 3.

Limerick Bill's   There are a handful of other pubs in Innsbruck, but this is the only one owned outright by Irish-born investors—in this case, most of whom come from southwestern Ireland. Dark and cavelike, thanks to a location in a building without windows, it sprawls over three floors, a short walk north of Old Town, on a busy commercial street lined with restaurants, banks, shops, and office buildings. As such, it draws a thirsty after-work crowd of genuine Irish people and Celtic wannabes. The cellar is the place most likely to attract a crowd that likes to dance, usually on Friday and Saturday nights, especially between December and March, when there's live music every Friday and Saturday from 8pm to midnight. Both the street level and the second floor contain their own bars, each as dark and cozy and, on some evenings, as raucous and uninhibited as the cellar. Guinness and Kilkenny sell for 4.25€ per half-liter mug; Irish whiskey costs from 4.50€ a shot. There isn't a lot of emphasis on food here, other than simple platters of fish and chips, priced at about 6.50€ each. It's open daily from 4pm to 3am. Maria-Theresia-Strasse 9. ✆ 0512/5820111. Tram: 1 or 3. Bus: O.

Nightclub Lady-O   Opposite the post office and near the train station, this is the only real nightclub in Innsbruck, featuring strip shows. Drinks begin at 10€, and the club also has an X-rated bar. It's open daily from 9pm to 5am, with shows beginning at 10:30pm and continuing until 5am. Bruneckerstrasse 2. ✆ 0512/58-64-32. Cover 2€. Tram: 1 or 3.

Restaurant Fischerhausel Bar   Although a lot of its business derives from its busy first-floor restaurant, the street-level bar also adds appeal. Rustically outfitted in a modernized version of the Tyrolean style, it's open daily from 10am to 2am. No one will mind if you remain in the bar, quaffing schnapps or suds or whatever, but if you opt to eventually migrate up to the dining room, a *Tagesmenu* (fixed-price menu) will cost 8.50€. During warm weather, drinkers and diners tend to move out to the verdant garden in back, soaking up the sunlight and the brisk alpine air. Herrengasse 8. © 0512/58-35-35. Tram: 1 or 3.

Sparkling Cocktails   Pubs and nightclubs come and go, even in such stable cities as Innsbruck, but this remains one of the most fashionable watering holes in town. Virtually any kind of mixed drink or cocktail, including an award-winning martini or an almost lethal zombie, can be crafted by the highly experienced staff. Drinks are 5€ to 10€. It's open Monday through Saturday from 7pm to at least 2am. Innstrasse 45. © 0512/28-78-80. Tram: 1 or 3.

Treibhaus   Young people interpret this comprehensive and flexible gathering place as a combination of daytime cafe, snackish restaurant, concert hall, and dance club. Within its battered walls, you can attend a changing roster of art exhibits, cabaret shows, and protest rallies, all from a location within an alleyway about a block from Burggraben. A large beer costs 2.80€; snacks are priced from 2.11€. It's open Monday through Saturday from 10am to 1am, with live music presented at erratic intervals. Angerzellgasse 8. © 0512/58-68-74. Cover for live performances 10€–17€. Tram: 1 or 3.

FOLK MUSIC

Throughout the Christmas season, Easter, and the high season, from 6 to 11pm, you can visit the **Goethe Stube,** in the Restaurant Goldener Adler, Herzog-Friedrich-Strasse 6 (© 0512/57-11-11; tram: 1 or 3), to hear authentic Tyrolean melodies, including the zither and "jodlers." There's a one-drink minimum, and a large beer costs 3€. Meals start at 9.10€.

Another evening of authentic Tyrolean folk entertainment can be experienced courtesy of the shows of **Tiroler Alpenbühne/Geschwister Gundolf** (© 0512/26-22-63), who have been performing in Innsbruck for nearly 4 decades. While you have dinner, a brass band plays along with traditional Tyrolean instruments such as an alphorn, zither, singing saw, and Tyrolean folk harp. It's big, boisterous, and definitely unique. Shows are presented daily at 8:40pm at two locations (the **Gasthaus Sandwirt,** Reichenauerstrasse 151; bus: O or R; and **Messe-Saal,** Ing., Etzel-Strasse 35; tram: 1) in Innsbruck April through October. Tickets for the shows cost from 15€. Dinner is optional but does complete the experience of the sounds of the region with the tastes of the region; it usually costs an additional 14€. For tickets and information, contact Tiroler Alpenbühne/Geschwister Gundolf daily from 8am to 11pm, or ask your hotel concierge if tickets are available. Tickets can be purchased on-site at both venues, but it's highly recommended that you secure a reservation. Scheduled performances are not held in November; from December to March, however, special shows will take place once a week for groups by request. If you're traveling alone or in a *small* group, call ahead to see if a show has been booked.

GAY CLUBS

Bacchus   Located across the street from Innsbruck's Holiday Inn, this is a cellar-level disco that attracts a clientele composed of about 70% gay men, 25% gay women, and 5% interested and usually well-intentioned straight people. It's open nightly 9pm to 2am or later, depending on the crowd and the night of the week. Salunerstrasse 18. © 0512/57-08-94. Tram: 1 or 3.

Piccolo   Although it wasn't openly gay after it was founded in 1948, today's owner, Beata, claims that it has always functioned as a "meeting point" for gay people in Innsbruck. Today its cozy, pine-paneled interior is the leading gay bar in the Tyrol, with a busy trade in drinks and a location in the heart of Old Town. There's no dance floor (it corresponds to a beer-hall format rather than a dance club), but locals and visitors have a good time here nonetheless. *Toasts* (sandwiches), priced at 2.50€ each, are the only food served, and beer costs 3€ a glass. It's open Thursday through Tuesday from 9pm to 4am. Seilergasse 2. ℂ 0512/58-21-63. Tram: 1 or 3.

2 Igls & the Environs

This area, where many events of the Olympic Winter Games of 1964 and 1976 were held, might be called "Olympic Innsbruck." The cluster of resorts, the best known of which is Igls, are all within easy reach of the Tyrol capital, some just a half-hour away. A complete system of lifts opens up alpine scenery to everybody, from the beginner to the most advanced skier—or to the sightseer in warm weather. You might consider staying in one of these resorts instead of at an Innsbruck hotel.

IGLS ✿

Lying on a sunny plateau in the alpine foothills at an elevation of 877m (2,875 ft.), Igls is the resort choice of many travelers who prefer staying here and driving into Innsbruck, which is 5km (3 miles) north (take Rte. 82). Although its number swells greatly with winter and summer visitors, the town has a population of fewer than 2,000. Long known as the "sun terrace" of Innsbruck, Igls is never likely to be too hot, even on the hottest day in Austria. Because it's so popular, Igls is certainly not the cheapest resort in Tyrol.

GETTING THERE   A streetcar from the **Berg Isel** station in Innsbruck will deliver you to Igls, 305m (1,000 ft.) higher than the capital, in about 30 minutes. Bus J leaves on the hour and the half-hour from the Innsbruck Hauptbahnhof. Tram 6 leaves Innsbruck at a quarter past each hour, and it leaves Igls at a quarter to each hour. For transportation information, call ℂ **0512/58-51-55.**

VISITOR INFORMATION   The **Igls tourist office** is on Hilberstrasse 15 (ℂ **0512/37-71-01**; www.tiscover.com/igls). It's open Monday through Friday from 8:30am to 6pm and Saturday from 9am to noon.

EXPLORING "THE OLYMPIC INNSBRUCK"

Although much of its world renown has been based on winter sports, Igls is also a popular summer resort where you can wander along alpine trails, play golf, or enjoy tennis.

This is also Innsbruckers' favorite place to ski, and they're joined by throngs of visitors. Igls shared the Winter Olympics festivities and sporting competition with Innsbruck, and boasts a bobsled and toboggan run.

WHERE TO STAY

Aegidihof   This solidly built chalet-style hotel first opened its doors in 1953. Rooms are cozy and traditional, with alpine furnishings and good, firm beds. Some open onto balconies with mountain vistas. Bathrooms are small but well maintained; all units contain shower-tub combinations. The food, both Austrian and international cuisine, also wins praise, starting with the plentiful buffet breakfast and ending with the wide choice of menus at the hotel's dining facilities, which include the **Tiroler Stube.**

Bilgeristrasse 1, A-6080 Igls. ℂ **0512/37-71-08.** Fax 0512/37-71-086. 23 units. Winter 81€–137€ double; summer 80€–95€ double. Rates include breakfast. AE, DC, MC, V. Free parking outdoors, 8€ in the garage. Bus: 3. **Amenities:** Restaurant; bar; sauna; room service; babysitting; laundry; dry cleaning. *In room:* TV, minibar, hair dryer.

Hotel Batzenhäusl ⌖   Only a 2-minute walk from the center, this traditional hotel/inn began as a winery in 1893. Its name derives from the Austrian word *Batzen*, a silver coin commonly used in the late 19th century. The tavern's ornate paneling is carved from what the locals call "stone pine," the glow from which beautifully complements the flowered carpets, leaded windows, and hand-worked lamps. Other sections of this comfortable hotel are crafted in a more modern style. Rooms are medium in size and well furnished with alpine styling and wooden bed frames. The maids keep the small bathrooms with shower-tub combinations spotlessly clean. Even if you don't stay here, you might want to consider having dinner in the restaurant (see "Where to Dine," below); it's great.

Lanserstrasse 12, A-6080 Igls. ℂ **0512/38-618.** Fax 0512/38-61-87. www.batzenhaeusl.at. 38 units. 88€–124€ double; 141€–186€ apt for 2. Rates include half-board. AE, MC, V. Closed late Oct to Dec 15. **Amenities:** Restaurant; bar; fitness center; Jacuzzi; sauna; room service; babysitting; laundry; dry cleaning. *In room:* TV, minibar, hair dryer, safe.

Schlosshotel Igls ⌖⌖   The town's most historic and glamorous hotel, this baroque monument was built as a private castle in 1880 and converted into a small and plush hotel in the 1970s. It sits on its own grass-covered plateau at the end of a narrow street. Many famous guests to Tyrol have stayed here. Rooms are spacious and individually decorated with luxurious beds, and bathrooms have shower-tub combinations. Some rooms offer panoramic mountain views. The most renowned of the accommodations is the Rubino Suite, with a fireplace, terrace, and sauna. The hotel's excellent restaurant serves both traditional and international food in turn-of-the-19th-century surroundings. Guests also have access to the two tennis courts at the Schlosshotel's jointly owned hotel, the Sporthotel (see below).

Viller Steig 2, A-6080 Igls. ℂ **0512/37-72-17.** Fax 0512/37-72-17. www.schlosshotel-igls.com. 18 units. 300€–400€ double; 240€–440€ suite for 2. Rates include half-board. AE, DC, MC, V. Free parking outdoors, 9€ inside. Closed Mar 30–May 1 and mid-Oct to Christmas. **Amenities:** Restaurant; bar; pool; fitness center; sauna; room service; babysitting; laundry; dry cleaning. *In room:* TV, minibar, hair dryer, safe.

Sporthotel Igls ⌖   Built in 1900, the Sporthotel is a fancifully designed establishment that's a cross between a baroque castle and a mountain chalet. Its details include jutting bay windows, at least three ornate hexagonal towers, and rows of flower-covered balconies. The spacious interior is dotted with antiques and conservative furniture, with plenty of gemütlich corners and sunny areas, both indoors and out. An annex handles the overflow. Rooms, which come in a variety of sizes, are cozily outfitted in the Tyrolean style, with lots of varnished pine and regional knickknacks. Bathrooms have shower-tub combinations with new plumbing and are kept spotlessly clean. The owners also own an 18-unit Relais & Châteaux property, the Schlosshotel Igls (see above).

The hotel has a large dining room where dinner is served to guests on the half-board plan. It also has an attractive a la carte restaurant for nonguests. Non-smoking areas are provided. Tyrolean/Austrian cuisine is served, along with international and diet menus. In the evening, a one-man band plays in the hotel bar, and Tyrolean folkloric evenings are sometimes staged.

Hilberstrasse 17, A-6080 Igls. ⓒ 800/528-1234 in the U.S., or 0512/37-72-41. Fax 0512/37-86-79. www.sporthotel-igls.com. 91 units. 160€–344€ double; 214€–404€ suite for 2. Rates include half-board. AE, DC, MC, V. Parking 10€. Bus: J. Closed Oct 10–Dec 21 and 3 weeks after Easter. **Amenities:** Restaurant; bar; pool; 2 tennis courts; fitness center; health spa; sauna; room service; massage; babysitting; laundry; dry cleaning. *In room:* TV, minibar, hair dryer, safe.

WHERE TO DINE

Gasthof Wilder Mann AUSTRIAN   This place offers a breath of the Tyrolean mountains and country life in the Innsbruck suburb of Igls. Originally built in the 1600s, the building has been enlarged and modified over the years. If you appreciate architecture, you'll enjoy studying the stucco tower attached to the corner of this elongated building with a half-timbered triangular section just under the sloping roofline. The interior is spacious and rustic, with good service and a series of well-prepared traditional specialties such as wine soup, venison paté with Cumberland sauce, and filet steak in a pepper-cream sauce. Dessert could be a *Salzburger Nockerl.*

Römerstrasse 12. ⓒ 0512/37-73-87. Reservations recommended. Main courses 10€–30€. AE, DC, MC, V. Daily 11:30am–2:30pm and 5:30–10:30pm.

Restaurant Batzenhäusl AUSTRIAN   In this carefully paneled antique-style dining room, the chalet chairs are intricately carved and the service is good. A house specialty is flambé filet steak "Didi," a popular creation prepared at your table. Other well-prepared Austrian dishes include three kinds of meat on the same platter (covered in a mushroom-cream sauce), *Apfelstrudel,* and a series of savory meat-flavored soups. You might prefer the outdoor veranda or the garden in summer, although the dining room inside is most attractive.

In the Hotel Batzenhäusl, Lanserstrasse 12. ⓒ 0512/38618. Main courses 7€–19€; fixed-price menu 11€–15€. AE, MC, V. Daily 11am–2pm and 6–9pm. Closed Nov–Dec 15.

PÄTSCH

This small village above Igls stands on the sunny western slope of the Pätscherkofel, with a panoramic view of the Stubai Glaciers. Lying on the old Roman road below the peak, Pätsch is only a short distance from the mountain's Olympics slopes.

In winter, Pätsch attracts visitors with its skiing facilities (including cross-country runs), ice-skating, and curling; the resorts offer a ski school. Horse-drawn sleighs take you along snow trails. In summer, you can go on hikes, swim, or play golf and tennis. Summer skiing is also possible on the Stubai Glacier.

The most dramatic way to spend time in Pätsch involves taking a cable car, the **Patscherkofelbahn** (ⓒ 0512/37-72-34 for information), up to the top of the Patscherkofel, a panoramic site at an elevation of 1,961m (6,430 ft.). From here, you'll have access to a cafe, a restaurant, and a network of hiking and ski trails. The cable car ride covers a distance of 4km (2½ miles) and takes about 18 minutes. Round-trip passage costs 15€ for adults and 8€ for children. Except for a closing during November, it operates year-round daily from 9am to 4pm.

GETTING THERE   There is no **train service** to Pätsch, but buses depart from Innsbruck's Hauptbahnhof for Pätsch usually once an hour (trip time: 20 min.). For **bus information,** call ⓒ 0512/58-51-55. If you're **driving,** you can reach Pätsch by the Brennerbahn, via the Europabrücke; there's a 4.70€ toll. An alternate route is the road from Innsbruck going up through Vill and Igls.

VISITOR INFORMATION   For information in Pätsch, call ⓒ 0512/377-332.

WHERE TO STAY & DINE

Hotel Bär Sections of this amply proportioned hotel, specifically the reception area and the well-recommended Bauernstube, date from the 1200s, when they functioned as part of a simple inn. In 1970, a modern addition was built around the original core, turning the place into an unpretentious but worthwhile three-star hotel noted for its relatively reasonable rates. Today, you'll find public areas sheathed in pinewood paneling and stone. Big panoramic windows and an antique ceramic stove add to the cozy atmosphere. The cozy and traditionally furnished rooms offer plenty of comfort, from the excellent beds to the well-polished bathrooms equipped with shower-tub combinations. Maintenance and housekeeping are first rate, and Farbmacher family members are your hosts. Meals in the Bauernstube are served daily from noon to 2pm and 6 to 10pm. Main courses are 10€ to 16€.

A-6082 Pätsch. © 0512/38-611. Fax 0512/38-611-41. baer@patsch.netway.at. 39 units. Winter 86€–124€ double; summer 86€–104€ double. Rates include half-board. AE, DC, MC, V. Closed Oct 25–Dec 18 and Apr 10–May 8. **Amenities:** 2 restaurants; bar; lounge; pool; sauna; room service; babysitting. *In room:* TV, hair dryer.

Hotel Grünwalderhof 🎿 Once the private hunting lodge of the counts of Thurn and Taxis, members of the Seiler-Wanner family now operate this hotel. Standing on the site of an ancient Roman road, the hotel is in one of the town's prettiest chalets, with a natural-grained lattice relief under the slope of its gabled roof, striped shutters, and a modern extension stretching out the back toward the secluded outdoor swimming pool. Inside, the decor includes a scattering of antiques, paneling, and leather-upholstered chairs in the spacious and comfortable dining room. With their alpine coziness and good housekeeping, the rooms, which come in several sizes, are among the finest at the resort; some open onto private balconies with mountain vistas. Bathrooms are small but adequate with shower-tub combinations

Römerstrasse 1, A-6082 Pätsch. © 0512/37-73-04. Fax 0512/37-80-78. www.tiscover.com/gruenwalderhof. 26 units. Winter 104€ double; summer 94€ double; year-round from 138€ suite. Half-board 18€ per person extra. AE, DC, MC, V. Closed Apr and Nov. **Amenities:** Dining room; lounge; pool; tennis court; fitness center; sauna; room service; babysitting; laundry; dry cleaning. *In room:* TV, hair dryer.

MUTTERS 🎿

On a sunny southern plateau above Innsbruck, Mutters—often called "the most beautiful village in Tyrol"—is just 10km (6½ miles) southwest from Innsbruck. You can drive to the center of the city from here in about 15 minutes along Mutters Strasse.

Mutters is in the skiing and recreation area of the Mutterer Alm and the Axamer Lizum, which were the central bases for the 1964 and 1976 Olympic Winter Games. Mutterer Alm is the place for easygoing skiers. It can be reached by cableway.

GETTING THERE The **Stubaitalbahn tram** (© 0512/53-07-12 for information) departs from Innsbruck's Hauptbahnhof 18 times a day, bound for Fulpmes and stopping at Mutters en route (trip time: 28 min.).

Buses from Innsbruck are infrequent (one or two per day) and usually require a change in Götzens, Natters, and/or Axam. Transfers, however, tend to be so complicated that many people opt for the train. For **bus information,** call © 0512/58-51-55. The village is separated from Innsbruck by a wide green section of forest lying above the city and the Inn Valley.

VISITOR INFORMATION   For **tourist information** in Mutters, call
© **0512/548-410.** The office is open Monday through Friday from 8:30am to
noon and 3 to 6pm and Saturday from 8:30 to 11am.

WHERE TO STAY & DINE

Hotel Altenburg ⚜   Local archives refer to a restaurant on this site in 1622.
Later it became a farmhouse and then an annex of the nearby church. In 1910,
it was transformed into a flower-bedecked chalet hotel. The ground floor is sheltered by a three-arched arcade, which serves as an attractive backdrop for the
nearby greenhouse-style cafe. Each snugly furnished, comfortable room has a
small but spotlessly clean bathroom with a shower-tub combination. The hotel's
elegant restaurant is filled with upholstered banquettes and conservative furniture, with big windows overlooking the mountains. The **Restaurant Altenburg**
serves first-rate Tyrolean and international cuisine, with a fixed-price menu
priced from 11€ to 15€. Occasionally, only hotel guests can dine here, so it's
best to check. Evening entertainment is sometimes provided. The Wishaber
family is your host.

Kirchplatz 4–6, A-6162 Mutters. © **0512/54-85-24.** Fax 0512/54-85-24-6. www.tiscover.com/hotel-
altenburg. 34 units. 55€–75€ double. Rates include buffet breakfast. Half-board 12€ per person extra. AE,
DC, MC, V. Closed Apr 1 to mid-May and Oct 10–Dec 10. **Amenities:** Restaurant; bar; sauna; solarium; room
service; babysitting; laundry; dry cleaning. *In room:* TV, minibar, hair dryer, safe.

Muttererhof ⚜   This hotel, only a short walk from the village center, has a
gabled roof and a dignified chalet facade—in season, its balconies are covered
with flowers. The snug and comfortable rooms, in a variety of sizes, are furnished in a Tyrolean style: The best open onto private balconies with mountain
vistas. The small bathrooms are well equipped, including shower-tub combinations. The hotel has an elegantly paneled restaurant filled with carved chairs,
leaded windows, and antiques; and a verdant lawn with cafe tables in summer.
Fixed-price menus in the hotel restaurant cost 14€ to 19€.

Natterersttrasse 20, A-6162 Mutters. © **0512/54-84-91.** Fax 0512/54-84-915. muttererhof@tirol.com. 20
units. Winter 98€–174€ double; summer 86€–94€ double. Rates include breakfast. Half-board (minimum
3-day stay) 14€ per person extra. AE, DC, MC, V. Closed Apr and Nov. Tram: STB from Innsbruck. **Amenities:**
Restaurant; bar; pool; sauna; room service; babysitting; laundry; dry cleaning. *In room:* TV, minibar, hair dryer,
safe.

3 The Stubai & Wipp Valleys ✦

Two of the most beautiful valleys in Tyrol are the Stubai and Wipp valleys, their
alpine peaks some 16km (10 miles) west of Innsbruck. From the Brenner Road,
you can fork off at Schönberg into the Stubaital, which has little villages such as
Fulpmes and neighboring Neustift along the way, both summer and winter playgrounds. One of the first hamlets you'll encounter, and one of the most charming, is **Mieders** (952m/3,120 ft.). From Mieders, there's a chairlift that goes up
to Kopeneck at 1,632m (5,350 ft.).

If you decide to stay in one of these little resorts, you'll find that prices will
please your checkbook. (Note that hotels are often signposted at the entrance of
their respective resorts; not all are on street plans.) However, you could also stay
in Innsbruck and drive through the valley, either by private car or on a bus, in a
day. Or, you could take a narrow-gauge electric train. If you travel by rail, you
can go only as far as Fulpmes. After that, you must continue by bus.

The **Wipp Valley,** or Wipptal, is the valley of the Sill River, stretching from
Innsbruck to the Brenner Pass. An autobahn, a great engineering feat, pierces the

valley right on the outskirts of Innsbruck, going over the **Europabrücke** (Europe Bridge, on the A13), 191m (625 ft.) high and 824m (2,700 ft.) long. As you travel over it, you'll feel as though you're driving on a highway in the sky.

Brenner Pass, which marks the boundary between Italy and Austria, is known as the lowest gap in the major alpine chain and has been used since Roman times—and probably before.

FULPMES

Your first stop in this area might be Fulpmes, reached along Route 183, southwest of Innsbruck. High mountains surround this major resort, which lies about halfway up the valley, the most ancient hamlet in the Stubai Valley: A document dating from 1344 refers to a village here. **Serles Mountain,** to the south of Fulpmes, rises to a height of 2,715m (8,900 ft.). You might enjoy an excursion up to **Telfes,** slightly more than a mile by road above Fulpmes.

Most visitors see the Stubaital on day trips from Innsbruck, but the resort, a spot to visit in both summer and winter, offers a range of excellent hotels charging moderate prices—a winning combination. In summer, an indoor heated swimming pool between Fulpmes and Telfes is open. Chairlifts operate in both summer and winter, one going from Fulpmes to Froneben, at 1,351m (4,430 ft.), and one to Kreuzjoch, at 2,105m (6,900 ft.).

If you're here at the right time, you might enjoy a historical play presented about Tyrol's hero, Andreas Hofer, who led Bavarian and Tyrolean peasants against Napoléon and freed Tyrol from the French emperor's domination.

GETTING THERE   Fulpmes is the final destination on the well-known tram **Stubaitalbahn,** which departs from Innsbruck's railway station around 18 times a day. The trip, with many stops at small panoramic villages en route, takes about an hour. In addition, buses depart from Innsbruck's **Hauptbahnhof** at intervals of 60 to 90 minutes throughout the day (trip times 35 min.) For bus **information,** call © **0512/58-51-55.**

VISITOR INFORMATION   The **tourist office** in the town center (© **05225/ 62-235;** www.tirol.at/stubai) is open Monday through Friday from 8am to 5pm and Saturday from 9am to noon and 4 to 6pm.

WHERE TO STAY & DINE

Alpenhotel Tirolerhof   Built in 1966 and renovated at least three times since, this well-managed, government-rated four-star hotel is a 7-minute walk west of the town center. Our favorite part of this double chalet is the central fireplace near the reception desk. Its design of roughly applied stucco is curved around a widely splayed grate and fanciful andirons, and in winter it's usually kept burning most of the day. Rooms, which come in a variety of sizes, are well furnished and decorated in a cozy Tyrolean style, with small but tidy bathrooms equipped with shower-tub combinations. There's access to many nearby sports facilities.

Clemens-Holzmeister-Strasse 38, A-6166 Fulpmes. © **05225/62-422.** Fax 05225/62022. 38 units. Winter 128€–150€ double, 158€ suite; summer 98€–100€ double, 140€ suite. Rates include half-board. No credit cards. Closed mid-Nov to mid-Dec. **Amenities:** Restaurant; bar; pool; fitness center; Jacuzzi; sauna; babysitting; laundry; dry cleaning. *In room:* TV, hair dryer, safe.

Hotel-Restaurant Holzmeister   Originally conceived as a farmhouse during the 1600s and enlarged later, this hotel/restaurant about 600 feet north of the village center has dozens of unique architectural details. Many of the vaulted ceilings are embellished with painted regional designs, and woodwork on the walls and ceilings is painstakingly polished and ornate. Most of the rooms are spacious, and many are wood paneled with cozy sitting areas. Beds, often made of wood, are among the neatest we've inspected in the area. Bathrooms, although not large, are well maintained and, for the most part, equipped with shower-tub combinations. Under family ownership for many years, the hotel also offers a cozy Tyrolean *Stube* (tavern). Half-board consists of a tasty breakfast buffet and a flavorful and nourishing evening meal.

A-6166 Fulpmes. ✆ 05225/62-26-00. Fax 05225/62-36-724. holzmeister@fulpmes.netwing.at. 27 units. 100€–120€ double. Rates include half-board. AE, DC, MC, V. **Amenities:** Restaurant; bar; lounge; sauna; solarium. *In room:* Hair dryer.

NEUSTIFT

The name of this village means "new monastery" or "new church," and, in fact, it's a few centuries more recent than, say, the 12th-century New Forest in England. But Neustift dates from 1505, when Emperor Maximilian I did some hunting here and had a chapel built, called *das neue Stift.* This village and others in the Stubai Valley have been in the tourist business since the 19th century, when mountain climbers discovered the area and made it accessible. Neustift lies 27km (17 miles) southwest of Innsbruck and 6km (4 miles) south of Fulpmes.

There are two well-defined districts to Neustift. They include Neustift-Dorf, the more northerly and more populous of the two, and a satellite hamlet about 2km (1½ miles) to the south called Neustift-Kreuz. When locating things, it makes a big difference.

Neustift, about 915m (3,000 ft.) above sea level, is surrounded by extensive hiking trails for summer visitors, leading up to the glaciers of the **Stubai Alps** ⟨ℜ⟩. The Stubai Glacier lift will take you to a dizzying 3,065m (10,050-ft.) height, where year-round skiing is pursued.

There are baby slopes here, served by T-bars, or you can take a chairlift from Neustift to Elferberg, a favorite with advanced skiers. Elferberg is also known for its panoramic view and long toboggan runs.

GETTING THERE   **Buses** to Neustift leave from the Innsbruck Hauptbahnhof every 60 to 90 minutes. Some passengers opt to take one of these buses all the way to Neustift (trip time: 1⅓ hr.). Most visitors, however, opt to take the previously recommended Stubaitalbahn to Fulpmes and then board one of the buses that continues for the 12-minute ride on to Neustift. These buses depart every 50 to 90 minutes. For **bus information,** call ✆ 0512/58-51-55. If you're driving from Innsbruck, head southwest along Route 183.

WHERE TO STAY

Alpenhof Neustifterhof   This hotel links a pair of Tyrolean chalets with an underground passage. They lie a few steps from the most modern indoor tennis courts in the region, in an outlying hamlet (Neder Neustift) less than a mile east of the center of the resort. The sprawling interiors contain public areas paneled in full-grained softwoods and filled with comfortable nooks and crannies. Each balconied room is decorated with a modernized Tyrolean charm. The owners take justifiable pride in offering some of the region's best comfort, as reflected by their exceedingly good beds and their medium-size bathrooms with shower-tub combinations. There are a pair of restaurants, along with an alpine bar with an adjacent cubbyhole of a firelit Stüberl.

Neder 406, A-6167 Neder Neustift. ✆ 05226/2711. Fax 05226/2711-308. 60 units. Winter 110€–145€ double; summer 105€–135€ double. Rates include half-board. AE, DC, MC, V. **Amenities:** 2 restaurants; bar; pool; fitness center; sauna; room service; massage; babysitting. *In room:* TV, hair dryer, safe.

Sporthotel Neustift ⭐ A wood-and-stucco facade, with ornamental eaves and painted country baroque patterns around the windows, conceals one of the most glamorous interiors in the area. The hotel owners say they want to surround their guests with luxury and beautiful things, and they have done just that, combining art with crafts and many carved-wood accents, evoking a feeling of warmth and coziness. From the grand comfortable public areas to the elegant bar, this is not rustic alpine charm, but style, taste, and sophistication.

The wood-paneled, medium-size Tyrolean rooms are beautifully maintained, comfortable, and inviting. All rooms have neatly kept bathrooms with shower-tub combinations. The hotel's cuisine is widely praised in the area, beginning with a generous buffet breakfast and ending with a "nouvelle cuisine tyrolienne" four-course multiple-choice menu. Buffets are presented throughout the week, along with a gala dinner 1 night a week.

Dorf 703, A-6167 Neustift. ℂ **05226/25-09.** Fax 05226/25-09-19. www.sporthotelneustift.at. 67 units. Winter 167€–250€ double, 182€–268€ suite for 2; summer 158€–172€ double, 174€–188€ suite for 2. Rates include half-board. MC, V. Closed Apr 24–May 22. **Amenities:** Restaurant; bar; pool; fitness center; Jacuzzi; sauna; solarium; room service; massage; babysitting; laundry; dry cleaning. *In room:* TV, minibar, hair dryer, safe.

WHERE TO DINE

Hotel Hoferwirt AUSTRIAN   This hotel restaurant, with two adjacent dining rooms, is one of the most consistently reliable in town. Its tradition of feeding visitors was established more than 300 years ago. (The hotel is housed in what was originally built as a farmhouse with a pair of rooms rented to boarders.) In addition to serving the usual array of grilled steaks, stews, fondues, and fresh salads, the kitchen is known for its large and succulent Wiener schnitzels and for its sauté of venison with *Spätzle* and fresh vegetables.

In addition, the hotel rents 30 well-furnished rooms, each with a bathroom, TV, and phone. Half-board, which includes both a buffet breakfast and a four-course evening dinner, ranges from 42€ to 55€ per person.

A-6167 Neustift-Dorf. ℂ **05226/22-01.** Fax 05226/22-01-22. Reservations recommended. Main courses 10€–21€. AE, DC, MC, V. Wed–Mon 11am–10pm. Closed Dec 8–19 and for a month after Easter.

Silberdistel ⭐ *Finds* FONDUE   Owned and operated by the nearby Jagdhof hotel, this is the only restaurant in Neustift that specializes in fondues, the steaming, rib-sticking stews that are hauled from the kitchen in bubbling pots. Here they come in a half dozen varieties. As such, you're likely to get heavy doses of Tyrolean nostalgia—a dining room that's mostly sheathed in varnished pine and enough alpine knickknacks to make you begin yodeling the moment you enter its gemütlich premises. Your only choice is fondue, which might contain meat, fish, cheese, or vegetables, depending on what you order. The only dessert option is (surprise) chocolate fondue. The cuisine goes especially well with cold weather, bottles of wine, and dark nights. You'll find the restaurant within a modern, Tyrolean-style house a few yards from the hotel. Regrettably, it's open only in winter.

Scheibe 124, Neustift-Dorf. ℂ **05226/3171.** Reservations recommended. Main courses 11€–35€. MC, V. Wed–Mon 6–10pm. Closed May–Nov.

4 The Ötz Valley ⭐⭐

This next excursion into the Ötz Valley is one of the most scenic in Tyrol. Following the Valley of the Inn, you head west from Innsbruck, but before reaching Irnst you take a good but winding road (Rte. 186) south toward the Italian border. Along the way are many worthy places to stop, as each town or village offers good food and hotels, again at reasonable prices.

Ötztaler Ache flows through the valley, which extends for about 56km (35 miles) from the south bank of the Upper Inn. The mouth of the valley is at Ötz (spelled "Öetz" on some maps). Along the road, you'll see many waterfalls as you ascend. Arrive on a sunny day, and you'll marvel at the glaciers and peaks of the Ötztal Alps 🌟🌟 spreading before you. The valley cuts deep into the heart of some of the highest peaks in the eastern alpine range and leads into the midst of what has been called the "Tyrolean Arctic," a glacier region of ethereal beauty. The mountain villages have glacier lifts for extensive skiing. Glacier skiing is possible from spring through fall on the gigantic **Rettenbachferner.**

This long valley has good skiing in its lower and outer reaches, but if it's summer and you're here just for the sightseeing, the inner or middle part of the valley is the most spectacular.

ÖTZ

Our first stop is Ötz, which can be reached by going 5km (3 miles) south from the junction of the Inn River and the Ötztaler, 47km (29 miles) west of Innsbruck. A holiday center in both winter and summer, the resort, noted for its mild climate, is perched 822m (2,695 ft.) high on a sunny slope.

GETTING THERE   Trains from Innsbruck stop at **Ötztal Bahnhof (Ötz Valley Railway Station),** 7km (4½ miles) downhill from Ötz (trip time: 40 min.). There are two or three trains per hour in both directions.

Once travelers reach Ötztal Bahnhof, several **buses** (at least one per hour) make the short uphill ride to Ötz. Rather than waiting for the bus, most visitors opt to take a taxi to their hotel from the station. In addition, about four daily buses travel from Innsbruck's Hauptbahnhof to Ötz. For **bus information,** call 📞 **0512/58-51-55.**

If you are **driving** to Ötz from Innsbruck, head west along Route 171 to the junction with Route 186, at which point you go south.

VISITOR INFORMATION   The tourist office in the town center (📞 05252/ 66-69; www.oetz.com) is open Monday through Friday from 8:30am to noon and 2:30 to 6:30pm, and Saturday from 8:30am to noon and 5 to 6pm.

IN & AROUND ÖTZ

Ötz has many old buildings, often with traditional oriels and painted facades. A Gothic **Pfarrkirche (Parish Church)** dates from the 14th century, although it was enlarged centuries later.

Just 3km (2 miles) southwest of the town is a warm body of water, **Piburger Lake** (915m/3,000 ft.), which is popular in summer. From Ötz, you can also make a 9km (5½-mile) trek south to the hamlet of **Umhausen,** the oldest village in the valley, now a holiday resort.

WHERE TO STAY

Gasthof Zum Stern (Value)   Parts of this inn predate the year of its first mention in local archives, 1611, and it served at least part of its life as the local courthouse. Today the facade is opulently covered with bay windows painted with country-baroque designs. You'll recognize the hotel by the gilt and wrought-iron bracket hanging over the sidewalk, just below the cascades of summer geraniums. The paneled interior is filled with rustic details, including a ceramic stove. The Griesser family offers comfortable rooms furnished in Tyrolean style, and staying here is almost like staying at a family boardinghouse rather than a formal hotel. Rooms come in a variety of sizes, housekeeping is excellent, and the comfort level is high, as reflected by the small but adequate bathrooms equipped with shower-tub combinations. The Gasthof, in the town center close to the church, is one of the few to remain open year-round.

Kirchweg 6, A-6433 Ötz. Ⓒ and fax **05252/63-23.** 12 units. 66€ double. Rates include half-board. No credit cards. **Amenities:** Restaurant; bar. *In room:* TV.

Hotel Habicherhof   This hotel began its life as an alpine restaurant with two rustic bedrooms in the 1930s. In 1959, the parents of the present managers bought it and, over the years, enlarged it into its present six-story form, which sits on the main road less than a mile south of Ötz in the agrarian hamlet of Habichen. Today you'll see a strikingly designed establishment whose lines are based on an alpine chalet with many different extensions. The high-ceilinged interior contains a bar area with Tyrolean stools, several cozy dining areas, and sitting rooms. The multilingual staff, directed by members of the Haslwanter family, creates a homelike informal atmosphere. It is obvious that the owners planned the rooms and tidy bathrooms with shower-tub combinations for the comfort of their guests.

Habichen 46 (at Habichen), A-6433 Ötz. Ⓒ **05252/62-48.** Fax 05252/62-48-66. www.habicherhof.at. 45 units. Winter 134€–188€ double; summer 120€–140€ double. Rates include half-board. AE, MC, V. Free parking outside, 4€ in the garage. Closed 1 week after Easter and Oct 25–Dec 19. **Amenities:** Restaurant; bar; pool; exercise room; sauna; laundry; dry cleaning. *In room:* TV, hair dryer, safe.

WHERE TO DINE
Café-Restaurant Heiner AUSTRIAN/INTERNATIONAL This is the most deeply entrenched restaurant and cafe in Ötz, a family-run bastion of highly caloric pastries and dairy products that skiers and outdoor enthusiasts appreciate for their bursts of quick energy. The family that runs it is so well known that some of the locals refer to the place by their family name, Haid. Stop in for whatever you fancy, be it a wide collection of coffees and teas, yogurt, eggnog, or pastries from the family-owned bakery that's attached to the place. If you're in the mood for a full-fledged meal, you'll find steaming bowls of oxtail soup with sherry; omelets; veal, beef, and pork dishes; and seasonal availability of wild game (especially venison), usually served with port or red-wine sauces.

Hauptstrasse 58. Ⓒ **05252/63-09.** Main courses 8€–25€; fixed-price menu 9€–20€. AE, DC, MC, V. Daily 8:30am–midnight.

SÖLDEN ⟨⟨
The capital of the inner Ötz Valley, Sölden, about 1,342m (4,400 ft.) above sea level, draws visitors to this valley in summer, to the woods in spring and autumn, and to the heights in winter. This old-fashioned village is full of folkloric interest. It's 60km (37 miles) south of Ötz, 69km (43 miles) southeast of Imst, and 90km (56 miles) southwest of Innsbruck.

Sölden is linked by road, cable car, and ski lift to the part-time winter resort of **Hochsölden** (2,074m/6,800 ft.), 9km (5½ miles) away, via the **Giggjochbahn** (Ⓒ **05254/508**), a cable car that charges 10€ round-trip for adults and 6€ for children. Although Hochsölden won't provide as many amenities or diversions as the larger community of Sölden, some skiers prefer it for its isolation and small scale. Newly established as a reaction to winter-season alpine tourism, it contains only about five hotels and can also be reached via car after a 20-minute drive from Sölden.

One of the best-known cable cars in Austria is the **Geislachkogelbahn** (© **05254/23-61**), which connects Sölden to the top of the Geislachkogel peak, 3,031m (9,940 ft.) above sea level. Here you'll be rewarded with a panoramic sweep of the Ötzal Alps and a view of a cross jutting skyward from a point near the summit. En route, the cable car travels above glacial fields and savage-looking rocks to one of the most isolated regions of Austria. Round-trip passage on the cable car costs 20€ to 30€. Children under 8 travel free. It operates from mid-June to mid-September every day from 9am to 5:30pm and from December to Easter daily from 9am to 4pm.

Sölden is also the start of the **Otztaler Gletscherstrasse (Ötzal Glacier Road)** 🟊🟊, an 18km (11-mile) stretch through the Rettenbachtal that showcases some of the loftiest pieces of road engineering in Europe, rising to a height of some 2,821m (9,250 ft.). Accessible only from April to November, it ends at a point near the Ötzal Glacier, where a panoramic view stretches out over a year-round river of ice. At a point near the road's summit, a mile-long tunnel connects the hamlet of Rettenbachferner with a small-scale resort of Tiefenbachferner.

GETTING THERE   You can reach Sölden, which doesn't have a train station of its own, via the same **buses** that service Ötz (see above), most of which continue uphill from Ötz into Sölden. The nearest **railway station** to Sölden is **Ötzal Bahnhof,** a distance of 40km (25 miles). To reach Sölden from Innsbruck, **drive** west along Route 171; then cut south at the junction of Route 186.

VISITOR INFORMATION   The **tourist information office** in the town center (© **05254/5100;** www.soelden.com) is open Monday through Saturday from 8am to 6pm and Sunday from 9am to noon and 3 to 6pm.

WHERE TO STAY & DINE

Gasthof Waldcafe 🟊   Although it's a 20-minute walk uphill from the center of Sölden, this hotel is the best of the resort's government-rated three-star hotels. Built in 1964, it's less expensive and, in some ways, more personalized than many of its competitors. The alpine-style rooms are comfortable, clean, and warm, but not overly large. Each unit has a neatly kept bathroom with shower-tub combination. Although residents are always assured of meal service, the Waldcafe Restaurant, out of which the hotel originally developed, is open only in winter. Offering cozy refuge against the sometimes brutal weather outside, it features platters of Austrian and Tyrolean food priced from 7€ to 14€ throughout the day and early evening, whenever business seems to justify its opening. The hotel's location, high above the town center, is particularly convenient to skiers, who can arrive and depart from the hotel's front door every day on skis.

Innerwald, A-6450 Sölden. © **05254/23-19.** Fax 05254/24-60-46. 27 units. Winter 118€–130€ double; summer 70€ double. Rates include half-board. No credit cards. Restaurant daily Dec–Apr. Hotel closed May–June, and Oct–Dec 20. **Amenities:** Restaurant; bar; sauna; babysitting. *In room:* TV.

Hotel Bergland   Set adjacent to the village church on the main street, this government-rated four-star hotel includes an upper-level sun terrace with umbrellas that is always crowded on sunny days. The family-run hotel contains elegant, well-crafted interiors. Rooms, in a variety of sizes, are warmly inviting, intimate, and accented with exposed wood. All are recommended for their cleanliness and comfort, including the small but efficient bathrooms with shower-tub combinations. They must be doing something right because the staff often greets returning guests. There's a separate dining room for residents on half-board plans, as well as a beautifully appointed a la carte restaurant open to outsiders, with main courses 14€ to 21€.

Hauptstrasse, A-6450 Sölden. ℂ 05254/22-34. Fax 05254/22-40-150. 87 units. Winter 121€–151€ double; summer 114€–140€ double. Rates include half-board. AE, DC, MC, V. Amenities: Restaurant; bar; pool; fitness center; sauna; room service; laundry; dry cleaning. In room: TV, hair dryer.

Hotel Central 🏵🏵   This likable family-run riverside chalet in the village center is the only government-rated five-star hotel in the area. The interior features beautifully grained timbers, stucco arches, glowing wooden floors, and regional details. The spacious rooms are tasteful, with well-kept bathrooms with shower-tub combinations; the most desirable open onto balconies with mountain views. There's a piano bar and a rustic, intimate restaurant with excellent service and specialties including international dishes like calves' liver in a chanterelle-cream sauce. Garnishes for some main courses are unusual—ginger crepes, for example, or a sweet chestnut parfait in a calvados-and-grape sauce. Meals are 17€ to 45€.

Postfach 70, A-6450 Sölden. ℂ 05254/22-60. Fax 05254/22-60-511. www.central-soelden.com. 118 units. Winter 276€–392€ double, 172€–225€ per person suite; summer 196€–272€ double, 141€–165€ per person suite. Rates include half-board. AE, DC, MC, V. Free parking outdoors, 7€ in the garage. Closed May–June 23. Amenities: 2 restaurants; bar; pool; health spa; Jacuzzi; room service; massage; babysitting; laundry; dry cleaning. In room: TV, minibar, hair dryer, safe.

HOCHSÖLDEN

Lying on a sunny alpine plateau 40km (25 miles) west of Innsbruck, this resort (2,074m/6,800 ft.) towers over Sölden and attracts visitors in both summer and winter. At first Hochsölden might not seem like a village at all, but rather a cluster of modern hotels. It's connected to Sölden by road, cable car, and ski lift. Because of the easy communication between the two resorts, Sölden's much larger facilities, including the après-ski life, are available to guests at the Hochsölden hotels.

Its higher elevation makes it possible to ski at Hochsölden later in the season than at Sölden. **Rettenbachferner** and **Tiefenbachferner,** summer glacier skiing areas, are easily accessible to both resorts (see above).

GETTING THERE   Hochsölden does not have a train station. A few **buses** originating in Innsbruck and traveling to Sölden also continue the remaining 7km (4½ miles) to Hochsölden. In view of the short distance between the villages, however, many travelers get to Sölden and then take a taxi to Hochsölden. In addition, about five buses run every day, summer and winter, from many of the Sölden hotels up to the Hochsölden's ski lifts. Although Sölden and Hochsölden's most distant points lie 7km (4½ miles) apart, their facilities are broadly scattered along the road between them.

WHERE TO STAY & DINE

Alpenhotel Enzian   On sunny days in late winter, you're likely to see dozens of visitors stretched out on chaise longues on the big sun terrace. Designed with curved corners, gables, and honey-colored exterior planking, the elegant Enzian contains a modern interior with exposed wood. The Riml family, the owners, rent well-furnished, well-maintained rooms, exceedingly comfortable because of the good beds and the spotless bathrooms with mostly shower-tub combinations. The restaurant serves Austrian and international specialties such as goulash, and a mixed grill of three meats served with an onion-and-herb sauce.

A-6452 Hochsölden. ℂ 05254/22-52. Fax 05254/2846. www.hotel-enzian.at. 45 units. Winter 138€–260€ double; summer 84€–109€ double. Rates include half-board. AE, DC, MC, V. Free parking. Closed May–June and Nov. **Amenities:** Restaurant; bar; sauna; game room; massage; laundry; dry cleaning. *In room:* TV, mini-bar, hair dryer, safe.

Hotel Alpenfriede   In recent years, this government-rated four-star hotel has shortened its opening season to only those months when it can be ensured a relatively full house. If it's open when you're visiting, the Langler family will extend access to clean and comfortable rooms and a cozy setting that evokes alpine Austria. Each well-furnished room has a balcony. Bathrooms are medium in size and have shower-tub combinations along with adequate shelf space. There's a paneled sitting room and a warmly decorated bar area with heavy ceiling timbers and an open fireplace. The Italian National Ski Team members are frequent patrons here.

A-6452 Hochsölden. ✆ **05254/23-08.** Fax 05254/23-08-56. 54 units. Winter 160€–240€ double. Rates include half-board. AE, DC, MC, V. Closed late Mar to mid-July and Sept to mid-Dec. **Amenities:** Restaurant; bar; fitness center; sauna; solarium; room service; babysitting; laundry; dry cleaning. *In room:* TV, minibar, hair dryer, safe.

OBERGURGL ✦

This village with the funny-sounding name is part of a three-resort complex that includes **Hochgurgl** (see below) and **Untergurgl.** Obergurgl, lying less than 3km (2 miles) upstream from Untergurgl, is one of Austria's loftiest villages at 1,928m (6,322 ft.) and the second-highest parish in Europe. This is where the Swiss physicist and aeronaut Dr. Auguste Piccard landed in his celebrated balloon.

This district is one of the major ski centers of the Tyrolean country. It's not well known among American skiers, although if you stay here, you'll be virtually on the doorstep of the Ötztal Alps, surrounded by towering peaks and glistening glaciers. All the ski runs end right in the village. A two-stage chair lift, leaving from the center of Obergurgl, services the principal ski area, the **Gaisberg-Hohe-Mutt.**

GETTING THERE   Obergurgl has no direct train connections. Most travelers take a train to the railway station at Ötztal Bahnhof and then board one of the dozen or so daily buses that travel the 54km (33½ miles) up the Ötz Valley to Obergurgl (trip time: 90 min.). Four daily buses make the 101km (63-mile) trip west from Innsbruck's Hauptbahnhof to Obergurgl (2⅓ hr.). For **bus information,** call ✆ **0512/58-51-55** in Innsbruck.

If you're **driving** from Innsbruck, head west on Route 171 to the junction with Route 186, where you should cut south.

VISITOR INFORMATION   The **tourist office** in the town center (✆ **05256/6466;** www.obergurgl.com) is open Monday through Friday from 9am to 5:30pm, Saturday from 9am to 4pm, and Sunday from 9:30am to noon.

WHERE TO STAY & DINE

Hotel Edelweiss & Gurgl ✦   Close to the village church in the resort's center, this is the best-equipped and most lavishly decorated hotel at Obergurgl. The hotel rises imposingly, a massive bulk of chalet-inspired balconies and wood trim. The Scheiber family has run this famous old hostelry, which dates from 1889, for many years. Facilities include bars for entertainment and après-ski possibilities, as well as restaurants and blazing fireplaces, and cozy nooks and crannies. Rooms contain comfortable beds and big windows looking out over the nearby ski lifts. The small bathrooms are adequate, with shower-tub combinations. For reliable comfort and genuine hospitality, this is one of the finest places to stay in the valley. The hotel is a good choice for lunch or dinner, even if you're not staying here. Main courses are 9€ to 18€.

Obergurgl 19, A-6456 Obergurgl. © **05256/62-23.** Fax 05256/64-49. www.edelweiss-gurgl.com. 97 units. 134€–180€ double. Rates include half-board. AE, DC, MC, V. Parking 9€. Closed Sept 25–Nov 17. **Amenities:** 2 restaurants; 2 bars; pool; sauna; room service; babysitting; laundry; dry cleaning. *In room:* TV, minibar, hair dryer, safe.

Hotel Gotthard Zeit ★★ Built in 1971, reconstructed in 1987, and radically renovated in the 1990s, this is our favorite government-rated four-star hotel in Obergurgl. Located a few hundred yards above the village, this attractive eight-story hotel prides itself on the fact that guests can ski down from the hotel to the lifts in the morning and ski directly to the hotel's front door after a day on the slopes. The interior has carefully crafted wooden walls and ceilings, a ceramic stove surrounded by a warming bench and a well-rated restaurant with panoramic views over the countryside. The cozy rooms, in a variety of sizes, are rustic but sport modern bathrooms with shower-tub combinations and excellent beds. Many open onto private balconies.

A-6456 Obergurgl. © **05256/62-92.** Fax 05256/63-75-26. www.gotthard-zeit.com. 49 units. Winter 156€–314€ double, 170€–314€ suite; summer 100€–130€ double, 130€ suite. Rates include half-board. MC, V. Free parking outdoors, 5€ indoors. Closed mid-Apr to late June and mid-Sept to late Nov. **Amenities:** Restaurant; bar; pool; fitness center; sauna; room service; laundry; dry cleaning. *In room:* TV, minibar, hair dryer, safe.

Hotel Josl A minute's walk from the village center, this chalet has a big sun terrace and a gently sloping alpine roof. Its rustic interior welcomes guests in both summer and winter—the Sport Café is popular with skiers and other lovers of the outdoors. The cozy, comfortable rooms have neatly kept bathrooms with shower-tub combinations; some have a south-facing balcony. Guests can relax in the sauna and later meet for drinks in the fireside lounge. The Josl-Keller is a lively après-ski rendezvous. The restaurant is known for its good food, featuring Tyrolean specialties including deer, chamois, and fresh fish. Vegetarian food and fondues are also featured. Dinner, served nightly from 6:30 to 9pm, costs 9€ to 15€.

A-6456 Obergurgl. © **05256/62-05.** Fax 05256/64-60. www.hoteljosl.com. 18 units. Winter 52€–103€ per person; summer 20€–35€ per person. Rates include half-board. AE, DC, MC, V. Closed May and Nov. **Amenities:** Restaurant; bar; sauna; room service. *In room:* TV, hair dryer, safe.

HOCHGURGL

If Hochgurgl (2,150m/7,050 ft.) were actually a village, it would take the "loftiest village in Austria" title away from other claimants. However, Hochgurgl is really little more than a cluster of hotels, whose owners anxiously await the first snowfall each year.

Getting to Hochgurgl, 5km (3 miles) east of Obergurgl, requires a steep uphill transit that you can approach from the **Timmelsjoch Alpine Road.** Hochgurgl is so obscure that it doesn't even appear on the country's bus map. A bus provided by the hotel chairlift authority (a ski bus) makes two or three daily round-trips from Obergurgl to Hochgurgl. Round-trip fare for the 5km (3-mile) run is 4€, although if anyone buys a ski pass giving access to the local lift system, the bus ride is free. Most new arrivals avoid this bus because of their luggage, preferring instead to take one of the many taxis that make the run frequently from Obergurgl.

Consider Hochgurgl mainly a choice for a winter visit, as nearly everything closes in summer when it becomes a sleepy little hamlet with not much happening. In winter, however, it comes out of hibernation and can get quite lively if the crowd is right.

This is an area for dedicated skiers who want access to some of Europe's highest peaks. A three-section chairlift, leaving from Untergurgl, just outside Obergurgl, will transport you to **Wurmkogl** at some 3,050m (10,000 ft.). At this lofty elevation, skiing is possible year-round. From a restaurant at Wurmkogl, you have a panoramic view of the **Italian Alps.**

WHERE TO STAY & DINE

Hochgurgl Hotel ⟨⟩ This is the region's finest hotel, its government-rated five-star rating challenged only by a handful of others within the entire valley. Conceived in 1961 as the first hotel in what later became a thriving winter colony (it's in the resort's center, adjacent to the chairlifts), it glows at night from the many lights illuminating its rustic yet contemporary facade. The interior contains handsomely appointed rooms filled with comfortable furniture, including the area's finest beds and medium-size bathrooms with shower-tub combinations. The Tyrolean *Weinstube* (tavern) inside is adorned with old paneling and rustic accessories and has about the coziest ambience in town.

A-6456 Hochgurgl. ⓒ **05256/62-65.** Fax 05256/62-65-10. 60 units. 130€–205€ double per person. Rates include half-board. AE, DC, MC, V. Closed May 2–Nov 14. **Amenities:** 2 restaurants; 2 bars; pool; fitness center; sauna; boutiques; room service; babysitting; laundry; dry cleaning. *In room:* TV, minibar, hair dryer, safe.

Sporthotel Ideal Built in 1970 and renovated several times since, this hotel is set in a slightly isolated, sunny position just west of the village center. One of the very few hotels in town that opens its doors in summer, it has a woodsy decor that features horizontal planking, paneled and coffered ceilings, and comfortable furniture. All units contain well-kept bathrooms with shower-tub combinations. There is an alpine warmth to the place, and its excellent beds will give you a good night's sleep. The restaurant serves Austrian and regional cuisine, with main courses 8€ to 20€.

A-6456 Hochgurgl. ⓒ **05256/62-90.** Fax 05256/63-02. 38 units. Winter 105€–135€ double; summer 73€–99€ double. Rates include half-board. AE, MC, V. Closed May–June and Sept 16–Nov 20. **Amenities:** Restaurant; bar; pool; fitness center; sauna; room service; babysitting; laundry; dry cleaning. *In room:* TV, minibar, hair dryer, safe.

5 The Eastern Side of the Arlberg: A Skiing Mecca

There's no such thing as a sacred ski (and snowboarding) mountain—as far as we know—but if there were, it would have to be the **Arlberg.** This is where alpine skiing began its conquest of the world. On the east side of the Arlberg, 114km (71 miles) west of Innsbruck, is what's known as the cradle of alpine skiing. Here the legends and stars known to all dedicated skiers were born: the Ski Club Arlberg, the early Kandahar races, and Hannes Schneider and his Arlberg method. (The west side of the Arlberg is covered in chapter 11.)

The Arlberg, with peaks that top the 2,745m (9,000-ft.) mark, lures skiers with its vast network of cableways, lifts, runs stretching for miles, a world-renowned ski school, and numerous sporting amenities. Runs begin at the intermediate level, reaching all the way to the nearly impossible.

The Arlberg, the loftiest mountain in the **Lechtral range,** marks the boundary between the settlers of the Tyrolean country and the **Vorarlbergers,** who live in the extreme western province of Austria. One of the Arlberg's most celebrated peaks is the **Valluga,** at 2,812m (9,220 ft.).

In 1825, a road was opened allowing traffic to travel to the **Arlberg Pass.** A 10km-long (6-mile) rail tunnel was opened in 1884, linking Tyrol and Vorarlberg. Finally, in 1978, a new road tunnel, Europe's third-longest, linked the two provinces. The toll for the highway tunnel is 11€. If you're not driving, you'll find the area serviced by the well-known **Arlberg Express rail link.**

ST. ANTON AM ARLBERG ✦✦✦

A modern resort has grown out of this old village on the **Arlberg Pass,** a place where ski history began. Here is some of the finest skiing in the Alps.

It was at St. Anton (1,289m/4,225 ft.) that Hannes Schneider developed modern skiing techniques and began teaching tourists how to ski in 1907. The Ski Club Arlberg was born here in 1901. In 1911, the first Arlberg-Kandahar Cup competition was held, with the best alpine skier winning a valuable trophy. Before his death in 1955, Schneider saw his ski school rated as the world's finest. Today the ski school, still at St. Anton, is one of the world's largest and best, with about 300 instructors, the majority of whom speak English.

The little town is a compact resort village with a five-story limit on buildings. No cars are allowed in the business area, but sleds and skis are plentiful.

GETTING THERE   St. Anton is an express stop on the main **rail lines** crossing over the Arlberg Pass between Innsbruck and Bregenz. Just to the west of St. Anton, trains disappear into the Arlberg tunnel, emerging almost 11km (7 miles) later on the opposite side of the mountain range. About one train per hour arrives in St. Anton from Innsbruck (trip time: 75–85 min.) and from Bregenz (trip time: 85 min.).

Because of St. Anton's good rail connections to eastern and western Austria, most visitors arrive by train. From the city, however, many travelers take the **bus** on to other resorts such as **Zürs** and **Lech.**

St. Anton is 599km (372 miles) west of Vienna and 100km (62 miles) west of Innsbruck. If you're **driving** from Innsbruck, take Route 171 west.

VISITOR INFORMATION   The **tourist office** in the **Arlberghaus** in the town center (✆ **05446/22-690;** www.stantonamarlberg.com) is open Monday through Friday from 8am to noon and 2 to 6pm, Saturday from 9am to noon, and Sunday from 10am to noon.

SKIING & MORE

The snow in this area is perfect for skiers, and the total lack of trees on the slopes makes the situation ideal. The ski fields of St. Anton stretch over some 16 sq. km (6 sq. miles). Beginners stick to the slopes down below, and for the more experienced skiers there are the runs from the **Galzig** and **Valluga** peaks. A cableway will take you to Galzig (2,092m/6,860 ft.), where there's a self-service restaurant. You go from here to Vallugagrat (2,649m/8,685 ft.), the highest station. The peak of the Valluga, at 2,812m (9,220 ft.), commands a panoramic view. **St. Christoph** (see later in this chapter) is the mountain annex of St. Anton.

In addition to the major ski areas we just mentioned, there are two other important sites. The **Gampen/Kapall** area is an advanced-intermediate network of slopes, whose lifts start just behind St. Anton's railway station. Also noteworthy is the **Rendl,** a relatively new labyrinth of runs to the south of St. Anton that offers many novice and intermediate slopes.

In winter, St. Anton am Arlberg is quite fashionable, popular with the wealthy and (occasionally) royalty—there's a more conservative segment of the rich and famous here than you'll see at other posh ski resorts. There are many other cold-weather pursuits besides skiing, including ski jumping, mountain tours, curling, skating, tobogganing, and sleigh rides, plus après-ski on the quiet side.

There's so much emphasis on skiing here that there's little talk of the summertime attractions. In warm weather, St. Anton is tranquil and bucolic, surrounded by meadowland. A riot of wildflowers blooming in the fields announces the beginning of spring.

At any time of the year, you can visit the **Ski und Heimat Museum (Skiing and Local Museum),** in the Arlberg-Kandahar House (© **05446/24-75**), where displays trace the development of skiing in the Arlberg, as well as the region's history from the days of tribal migrations in and around Roman times. The museum, in the imposing structure at the center of the Holiday Park in St. Anton, is open in summer Tuesday through Sunday from 11am to 5pm, and in winter Sunday through Friday from 3:30pm to midnight. Admission is 3€ for adults and 1€ for children.

The local library is also housed in the Arlberg-Kandahar House, and the park provides a variety of leisure activities, including minigolf, a woodland playground, a fishing pond, table tennis, open-air chess, and a curling rink.

WHERE TO STAY
Expensive
Hotel Alte Post ⓐ   Designed long ago, this rambling four-story building with ochre-colored walls, green shutters, and jutting gables can easily be reached from the town's rail station. It was originally built in the 17th century as a postal station. Renovations retained most of the thick-timbered beauty. Recently renovated rooms combine old-fashioned paneling with tiled and timbered private bathrooms that have shower-tub combinations and sometimes very elegant accessories. Members of the Tandl family are your hosts.

Since it became a hotel in the 1920s, some prominent skiers and show-business personalities have relaxed with lesser-known clients in the hotel's cozy niches, some of which are warmed with crackling fires. The hotel contains an excellent restaurant (see "Where to Dine," below).

A-6580 St. Anton am Arlberg. © **05446/25-530.** Fax 05446/25-53-41. www.hotel-alte-post.at. 56 units. Winter 232€–367€ double, 276€–382€ junior suite for 2; summer 184€–246€ double, 208€–236€ junior suite for 2. Rates include half-board. AE, DC, MC, V. Closed late Apr to late May and late Oct to Dec 1. **Amenities:** Restaurant; bar; pool; fitness center; Jacuzzi; sauna; room service; babysitting; laundry; dry cleaning. *In room:* TV, minibar, hair dryer, safe.

Hotel Neue Post ⓐ   In the 1990s, a large and sprawling hotel complex was divided into two smaller (and adjacent) properties, the Hotel Alte Post (see above) and the Hotel Neue Post. The Neue Post is not as new as its name would imply. Built in 1896 and noteworthy because of its sprawling dimensions and wood-and-stucco facade, it has established a reputation as one of the resort's most sports-oriented hotels. It offers appealing rooms comfortably equipped with medium-size bathrooms with shower-tub combinations. Housekeeping and general maintenance here are state-of-the-art.

The hotel contains a dimly lit and woodsy series of spacious public rooms, two dining rooms, and two of the most popular nightlife facilities in St. Anton, the Postkeller and Piccadilly Pub (see "St. Anton am Arlberg After Dark," later in this chapter).

A-6580 St. Anton am Arlberg. © **05446/22-130.** Fax 05446/23-43. www.st-anton.co.at. 66 units. Winter 210€–404€ double; summer 106€–132€ double. Rates include half-board. AE, DC, MC, V. Free parking. Closed mid-Oct to Dec 4 and late Apr to early July. **Amenities:** 2 restaurants; bar; 2 nightclubs; room service; laundry; dry cleaning. *In room:* TV, minibar, hair dryer, safe.

Hotel St. Antoner Hof ⚡⚡   The only government-rated five-star hotel in St. Anton, the St. Antoner Hof is a bit more posh and a bit more attentive than other hotels in town. Built in the early 1980s and run by a group of enthusiastic skiers (the Raffl family), it rises in severe dignity about a block from the resort's historic center. Rooms, in a variety of sizes, are plush and fastidiously maintained, all with thick carpeting, fireplaces, and the most comfortable beds at the resort (often canopied). Bathrooms are medium in size and spotless, with shower-tub combinations and ample shelf space. The atmosphere is considerably enhanced by the hotel's charming director, Maggie Raffl (frequent winner of local ski contests), who imbues the place with the sense of an elegant house party.

Guests enjoy the public rooms, each of which seems awash in Tyrolean accessories, thick timbers, and collections of rustic implements. Blazing fireplaces and good cuisine are all part of the experience here; the restaurant, **Raffl Stube,** is recommended below.

A-6580 St. Anton am Arlberg. © **05446/29-10.** Fax 05446/35-51. www.antonerhof.at. 37 units. Winter 120€–245€ double, 220€–425€ suite for 2; summer 120€–185€ double, 140€–265€ suite for 2. Rates include half-board. DC, MC, V. Closed May and Nov–Dec 1. **Amenities:** Restaurant; bar; pool; fitness center; Jacuzzi; sauna; solarium; room service; babysitting; laundry; dry cleaning. *In room:* TV, minibar, hair dryer, safe.

Hotel Schwarzer Adler ⚡⚡   In the center of St. Anton, this hotel has been owned and operated by the Tschol family since 1885. The beautiful fresco-covered building was constructed as an inn in 1570. The inn became known for its hospitality to pilgrims crossing the treacherous Arlberg Pass and was eventually declared an "officially registered" hotel by Empress Maria Theresa. The hotel's interior contains several blazing fireplaces, painted Tyrolean baroque armoires, and oriental rugs. There are handsomely furnished and well-equipped rooms in the main hotel, plus 13 slightly less well-furnished (but also less expensive) rooms in the annex, across the street and above the Café Aquila (see "Cafes & Stubes," below). All rooms have exceedingly comfortable beds. Nearly all bathrooms have big bathtubs, although a few singles offer only showers.

A-6580 St. Anton am Arlberg. © **800/528-1234** in the U.S., or 05446/22-440. Fax 05446/22-44-62. www. tiscover.com/adler.stanton. 50 units. Winter 131€–297€ double; summer 112€–176€ double. Rates include half-board. AE, DC, MC, V. Closed May–June and Sept–Dec 5. **Amenities:** Restaurant; bar; pool; fitness center; sauna; room service; massage; babysitting; laundry; dry cleaning. *In room:* TV, hair dryer, safe.

Sporthotel St. Anton ⚡   This sprawling government-rated four-star 1974 hotel sits on the main pedestrian thoroughfare of St. Anton. Ideal for shopping, it's a good choice for skiers too, since it's a 3-minute walk from the chairlifts. In winter, you're greeted at the entrance with the sight of a bar and the music of a full-time organist, whose melodies add to the feeling that a happy ski vacation involves at least several cocktails per day. Rooms are medium-size, comfortable, and contemporary, each with a balcony. Bathrooms are small but well laid out, with shower-tub combinations and adequate shelf space. Many patrons come to this hotel just to enjoy its food and drink (see "Where to Dine," below).

A-6580 St. Anton am Arlberg. © **05446/31-11.** Fax 05446/31-11-70. www.tiscover.com/sporthotel.st.anton. 53 units. Winter (including half-board) 178€–272€ double; summer 52€ per person (including breakfast), half-board 14€ per person extra. AE, DC, MC, V. Free parking outside; 10€ garage. Closed May and Oct–Nov. **Amenities:** Restaurant; bar; pool; sauna; solarium; room service; babysitting; laundry; dry cleaning. *In room:* TV, minibar, hair dryer, safe.

Moderate

Hotel Kertess ⚡ *(finds)*   Located in a quiet residential section named Oberdorf, this hotel is an address jealously guarded by its devotees. It lies on a hillside above the main tourist district of St. Anton, a steep 12-minute climb up the hill (and then only if you're hale and hearty). As you approach, you'll recognize the hotel by its country-baroque window trim. The hotel is family run, owned by Maria Kertess, a former ski instructor. In winter, you register near a blazing corner fireplace whose cheer permeates even the stylish Tyrolean bar a few steps away. Each snug and cozy room offers plenty of exposed wooden trim, functional if not stylish furniture, and, if you're lucky, a view of the Rendl ski slope. The bathrooms are well maintained with shower-tub combinations. Even if you're not a guest here, consider the hotel's restaurant (see "Where to Dine," below). Because it's located in a residential neighborhood away from the town center, the hotel runs a shuttle bus service to St. Anton and its ski areas.

A-6580 St. Anton am Arlberg. ℭ 05446/20-05. Fax 05446/20-06-56. www.kertess.com. 56 units. Winter 120€–150€ double; summer 60€–85€ per person double. Rates include half-board. AE, DC, MC, V. Closed May–June and Nov. **Amenities:** Restaurant; bar; pool; fitness center; sauna; massage. *In room:* TV, safe.

Hotel Montjola   Lying half a mile west of the resort's center, about a 10-minute uphill walk, this hotel is rustically appealing. Most rooms are in a comfortable annex built in 1991, although the reception desk, restaurant, and bar are in the original core—a carefully preserved wood-and-stone structure dating from the 1930s. Rooms come in a variety of sizes, and decor ranges from traditional to contemporary; each has a good bed plus a small but efficient bathroom with a shower-tub combination. Throughout both sections, you'll see heavy ceiling beams, a stone-rimmed fireplace, rustic knickknacks, and immaculately set dining room tables. Fondue is a specialty in the in-house restaurant.

A-6580 St. Anton am Arlberg. ℭ 05446/23-02. Fax 05446/23-029. www.montjola.com. 42 units. Winter 136€–296€ double; summer 94€–124€ double. Rates include half-board. AE, DC, MC, V. Closed Apr 21–June 4 and Oct 2–Dec 5. **Amenities:** Restaurant; bar; fitness center; solarium; sauna; room service; massage; babysitting; laundry; dry cleaning. *In room:* TV, hair dryer, safe.

WHERE TO DINE
Expensive
Raffl-Stube ⍟ AUSTRIAN   This restaurant didn't exist until 1982, when members of the Raffl family enclosed a corner of their lobby. The place contains only eight tables, and in the peak of the season, reservations are imperative, especially if you're not staying here. Overflow diners are offered a seat in a spacious but less special dining room across the hall. The hotel has long enjoyed a favored reputation for its cuisine, but somehow the food in the stube tastes even better. Quality ingredients are always used, and the kitchen prepares such tempting specialties as roast goose liver with salad, cream of parsley soup with sautéed quail eggs, filet of salmon with wild rice, trout "as you like it," and roast filet of pork, along with the ever-popular fondue bourguignonne.

In the Hotel St. Antoner Hof, St. Anton am Arlberg. ℭ 05446/29-10. Reservations required. Main courses 14€–28€; fixed-price menu 35€–52€. AE, DC, MC, V. Daily 11:30am–2pm and 6–10:30pm. Closed mid-Oct to mid-Dec and mid-Apr to mid-June.

Restaurant Brunnenhof ⍟ *(Finds* AUSTRIAN/INTERNATIONAL   In the neighboring resort of St. Jakob, this restaurant is tucked in an Arlberg farmhouse dating from 1752. Its owners, members of the Wolfram family, are known for their well-prepared Tyrolean and international dishes. Dinner might begin with a cheese-noodle soup, followed by *Tafelspitz* with spinach and *Rösti* or lamb in a rosemary sauce. Any of these dishes will verify what skilled cooks the chefs are. We are always especially pleased with the fresh taste of the dishes served here. The service is courteous and polite, and the house has a good wine list.

Brunnenhof 47, St. Jakob. ℂ **05446/22-93**. Reservations required. Main courses 16€–23€; 5-course fixed-price menu 53€. MC, V. Daily 7–10pm. Closed Apr 15–Dec 15.

Steakhouse 🐟 STEAKHOUSE   The Steakhouse occupies part of the street level of the Sporthotel St. Anton on the resort's main pedestrian thoroughfare. Here you can watch your steak sizzling as you sip a drink in warm comfort. Some guests prefer to sit on a barstool; perched here, you can talk directly to the chef at the nearby grill about the preferred degree of doneness of your dish. The steaks are just as good at a table in the wood-trimmed dining room. Menu selections include Lyons-style onion soup, small and "giant" salads, grilled crayfish, filet of veal in mushroom sauce, filet of pepper steak, and, if cholesterol is a problem, sliced roast turkey with pineapple on toast. Beer comes in foam-covered mugs, and wine is served in bottles as well as less expensive carafes.

In the Sporthotel St. Anton, St. Anton am Arlberg. ℂ **05446/31-11**. Main courses 16€–28€. AE, DC, MC, V. Daily 11:30am–2pm and 5–9:30pm. Closed May and Oct–Nov.

Moderate

Hotel Alte Post Restaurant 🐟 AUSTRIAN   Outsiders are welcomed into this historic establishment's five small antique dining rooms, where green ceramic stoves and intricately crafted wrought iron lend a mellow and graceful accent. The chefs cook with flair, turning out such classic dishes as rack of lamb, filet of beef, sweetbreads (in delightful ways), venison goulash, fresh duckling, and fondue Bacchus. Although traditional, the chefs are quite skillful. They might be using old recipes, but they give you lots of flavor and first-rate ingredients. You'll be guided through the menu by an attentive staff.

St. Anton am Arlberg. ℂ **05446/25-530**. Reservations recommended. Main courses 10€–20€. AE, DC, MC, V. Daily 11:30am–2pm and 7–9:30pm. Closed late Apr to June and late Oct to Dec 1.

Hotel Kertess Restaurant 🐟🐟 AUSTRIAN   Some of the area's finest food—some say the best in St. Anton—is served at this restaurant. It lies in the suburb of Oberdorf, high on a slope. Guests dine in one of a trio of alpine rooms, with ceramic tile stoves, oriental rugs, and views of a snow-covered ski slope. Specialties include filet of venison in port-wine sauce, stuffed squab, salmon in Riesling sauce, and, for dessert, apple fritters in beer-flavored pastry with cinnamon. The cooking is delicious, sometimes even inspired. The hotel's bar, warmed by a blazing fire in the nearby reception area, is open throughout the afternoon. The restaurant is known to serve only hotel guests—check when you make table reservations.

St. Anton am Arlberg. ℂ **05446/20-05**. Reservations required. Main courses 11€–22€. AE, DC, MC, V. Winter daily 11am–10pm; summer daily 11am–10pm (but hot food only 6–9pm). Closed May–June and Nov.

Hotel Schwarzer Adler Restaurant 🐟🐟 AUSTRIAN/INTERNATIONAL This restaurant prides itself on its Tyrolean authenticity, which reaches its zenith in one of its two wood-paneled stubes, the preferred place to dine here. The darker of the stubes boasts paneling said to be 4 centuries old. Here, the lighting fixtures are especially noteworthy, each designed from raw horns and fashioned into some mythical or allegorical figure from a Teutonic legend. Atmosphere aside, the real reason patrons come here is the food. The kitchen brigade displays outstanding skills, which are best shown at one of the buffets. The menu tempts at every turn with such dishes as homemade salmon ravioli with a chervil-flavored cream sauce or medallions of anglerfish with ratatouille. The *Tafelspitz* (boiled beef) is another favorite. Deer and local fish are served in season.

St. Anton am Arlberg. © **05446/22-440**. Reservations required. Main courses 10€–18€; fixed-price menu 17€–30€. AE, DC, MC, V. Daily 6:30–10pm. Closed May–June and Oct–Nov.

Restaurant Ferwall ★★ AUSTRIAN/INTERNATIONAL   Set in the high-altitude region approaching the Arlberg Pass, this restaurant is isolated, rustic and very, very famous. Ideal for a snowy night, it has entertained guests from the royal families of both Britain and the Netherlands, such musical luminaries as the late Herbert von Karajan, and scores of local residents who appreciate its romantic nostalgia for the Tyrol of myth and legend. The restaurant was established in 1972 in what was then an 11-year-old chalet. Some of the dining areas rely exclusively on candlelight—romance seems rampant, especially on cold winter nights. Menu items are based on traditional recipes that management considers a closely guarded secret. Venison frequently appears on the menu, often grilled and served with any of a wide choice of sauces, or baked into casseroles, or ground and pressed into sausages and served with sauces and sauerkraut. The entire experience is a celebration of the virtues of Tyrolean country life and high-altitude high spirits.

Most visitors reach the restaurant by car or taxi, although in winter many opt for a ride here in a horse-drawn sleigh, which costs about 55€ each way for four occupants. (If this is your intention, inform the restaurant when you book a table, and they'll make the arrangements for you.) Sleighs depart from the base of the three-star Mooserkreuz hotel, which lies on a very steep hillside about a mile west of St. Anton.

An der Ferwall-Loipe. © **05446/32-49**. Reservations required. Main courses 10€–25€. AE, DC, MC, V. Winter daily 10am–midnight; summer daily 10am–6pm. Closed Apr to late May and Nov–Dec 15. Take Rte. 197 to St. Christoph and the Arlberg Pass 5km (3 miles) west of the center of St. Anton.

CAFES & STUBES

The popular **Café Aquila** (© **05446/22-45**) achieved a certain kind of fame in the ski world as the Café Tschol. Now under another name, it lies just across the street from its founder, the Hotel Schwarzer Adler. Light meals, pastries, beer, wine, tea, and several varieties of coffee are served here. Dishes include spaghetti, goulash soup, spinach-stuffed ravioli, and a serve-yourself buffet of appetizers. Simple, uncomplicated meals begin at 12€, although a wide choice of snack food is also available. It's open daily from 9am to 6pm.

Our favorite cafe in St. Anton, **Café Haeferl** (© **05446/39-8**), seems more animated and more folkloric than any of its competitors, thanks to a decor that's rich with Tyrolean artifacts and the glow of varnished pine. Inside you'll find a crowd that includes dedicated hipsters as well as long-time seniors looking for a caffeine fix and a midmorning pastry. Don't expect full meal service—only salads, platters, and small portions of such foods as goulash soup and *Toasts* (sandwiches) are served. It's open daily from 8am to 10pm. You might want to drink or eat all day at **Fuhrmannstube** (© **05446/29-21**). Conveniently located near the town church on the main street, this rustic cafe and restaurant serves reasonably priced meals starting at 9€. It has a predictable but well-prepared array of such Teutonic specialties as *Rösti, Spätzle,* goulash, and venison (in season). It's open daily from 10am to 11pm; it's closed in May, June, October, and November.

ST. ANTON AM ALBERG AFTER DARK

St. Anton's after-dark spots are among the most frequented in Tyrol. It'll be best if you like your fellow skiers; in season you're likely to be knocking elbows (or whatever) in most places.

Cartouche   Hidden behind this hotel's 400-year-old exterior frescoes lies a bar where holiday-makers dance the night away after a day on the slopes. A large beer begins at 3.20€. It's open daily from 9pm to 2am, but in winter only. In the Hotel Schwarzer Adler. ℂ 05446/22-44-606. Cover 5€.

Drop-In Disco   This place is the most popular and energetic dance club in town. The bar is round, allowing drinkers to casually check out their fellow imbibers. The dance music is imported, and its decor makes absolutely no concessions to Tyrolean gemütlichkeit: Instead, it's international. Although the Drop-In is on the premises of the Sporthotel St. Anton (described above), it's no longer managed or controlled by the hotel. The professional staff adeptly handles "fancy drinks"; January, March, and April feature live entertainment twice weekly. Access is directly from Hauptstrasse, not from inside the hotel. It's open from December to April daily from 9pm to 2am. In the Sporthotel St. Anton. ℂ 05446/3111. Cover 10€.

Krazy Kanguruh   This restaurant/disco, originally built as a stable, attracts the resort's restless and reckless. To reach it, you'll have to either ski from the resort's uppermost slopes, walk breathlessly up the steep hill from the village, or drive your car via the suburb of Moos along a winding and treacherously narrow road. A phone call in advance will apprise you of driving conditions and directions, whose complexity you'll appreciate only after you get here.

Owned and operated by a dashing Swede, Gunnar Munthe, the place serves different functions depending on the hour of the day. From 11am to 2pm, lunches consisting of hamburgers, Wiener schnitzels, and such are served by some of the most attractive employees in Tyrol. Happy hour is raucous, rowdy, and loud. Be sure to ask for a shot of the pear-and-plum schnapps that a local farmer distills especially for the Krazy Kanguruh. Lunches begin at 6€. No dinner is served.

The basement disco is predictably energetic and the most fun in town, but it functions only in the afternoon, closing around 7pm. Some more adventurous patrons have dared slide back to town on a slippery plastic bag—and ended up in the hospital as a result. Beer costs 2.70€ and up. It's closed from April 15 to December 10. Moos 113. ℂ 05446/26-33.

Picadilly Pub   As its name suggests, this is an English-style pub. Lined with photos of happy revelers enjoying snow and suds, the place offers rowdy fun and loud music. Special tongue-in-cheek events such as Australia Day feature icons made of stuffed koala bears. The place is off the main pedestrian thoroughfare behind etched-glass swinging doors. A large beer begins at 3.50€. It's open from December to March daily from 9am to "very early the next morning." In the Hotel Neue Post. ℂ 05446/22-13.

Platz'l Bar   Set in the heart of town, adjacent to the Hotel Alte Post, this warm and rustic hangout features a live pianist whose soothing tones create an ambience more sophisticated than the rock 'n' roll mode of other bars nearby. Later in the evening, it usually offers recorded disco music as the town's nightlife begins to heat up. Beer costs 2.70€ for a large mugful. The bar's open only during the ski season, when fires inside burn brightly, December through April daily from 4pm to 3am. In the Hotel Alte Post, St. Anton. ℂ 05446/25-530.

Postkeller   This energetic and bubbly winter-only nightspot is in the basement of the Hotel Neue Post, with a decor of pinewood paneling, unbreakable chairs and banquettes, and a long bar area. Live music is occasionally offered.

The management creates an array of midwinter theme parties from time to time, including toga contests, beach parties, and carnival Rio parties. A large beer begins at 3.50€. The only food offered is an array of simple platters and snacks. November through April, it's open daily from 4:30 to 7pm for après-ski fun; then it reopens as a nightclub and disco from 9pm to 3am. In the Hotel Neue Post. ℂ 05446/22-13. Cover 5€.

Rodelhütte Open only in winter, this après-ski hangout offers the chance to combine a drink or two beside a blazing fire and finish with a flourish—with a zesty downhill run by toboggan. You can reach the place only after a brisk 20-minute uphill climb from St. Anton, as it lies about a half mile from the center. It's open daily November through April from 9am to around 9pm, depending on business; it's at its most convivial and crowded beginning around 5pm, as night falls over the nearby mountains. It is also open in July and August daily from 9am to 9pm. At the top of the town's toboggan run. ℂ 069910/858855.

Sennhütte Cozy, charming, and artfully rustic, this wood-sided structure is most appropriately reached by ski or snowboard from higher elevations along the Galzig ski slope. As shadows lengthen on winter afternoons, skiers gravitate toward the blazing fireplace and the stiff drinks that make après-ski here unusually convivial. It's an event only during ski season and doesn't last as long as some other bar venues at lower altitudes that rock on into the wee hours. (It's at its peak only around 4–7:30pm.) Know in advance that after a day on the slopes and after some drinks here around dusk, maneuvering your way downhill on skis might break a leg, as has often happened. It's open in winter when the skiers descend daily from 10am to 8:30pm. It is also open from late June to late September, keeping the same hours. On the lower elevations of the Galzig ski slopes. ℂ 0663/20-48.

Underground In the square at the end of the pedestrian zone, this bistro/piano bar/club combination offers a happy hour and tea dance from 4 to 6pm, a cocktail hour from 6 to 8pm, and bistro specialties including a salad bar and fondues, plus *raclette,* vegetarian dishes, and fish and chips, served from 7pm to midnight daily. Meals begin at 10€. In the piano bar, from 9pm to 3am daily you can listen to live jazz, blues, rock, and ballads, as well as dance to recorded music during the breaks. Hot snacks are available. It's open January through March daily from 4pm to 3am. St. Anton. ℂ 05446/20-00.

ST. CHRISTOPH ✶✶

The mountain way station of St. Anton, **St. Christoph** (1,784m/5,850 ft.) is linked to the St. Anton terrain by a cableway at Galzig. It's on the road to the Arlberg Pass and has essentially the same ski facilities available as St. Anton, only here you're closer to the action. If you're not driving your own car, take the train to St. Anton and then go by either bus or taxi to St. Christoph.

A hospice was originally established here in 1386 by a now-legendary saint-like mountain man, Heinrich of Kempten, whose self-imposed duty was to bury the remains of pilgrims who froze to death in the treacherous snowdrifts of one of the world's most unpredictable and temperamental mountain passes.

Because the Arlberg was the single most important route for commerce between northern Italy and the Teutonic world throughout the Middle Ages, literally hundreds of pilgrims froze to death at the pass or died of hunger, exposure, or avalanches. Kempten single-handedly founded the Order of Saint Christopher, a church-related society and monastery that has evolved into one

of the most beneficent monastic orders of Europe. The monastery has accumulated some famous artistic treasures, many donated by grateful merchants whose
caravans were sheltered and saved.

Appropriately, the monastery was built on the uppermost heights of the frequently snowbound pass, on the Tyrolean side. The land the monastery was
built on was so hostile that after the surrounding trees were felled for fuel, large
carts were required to bring all the basic necessities into the community.

Throughout the Age of Enlightenment, the hospice continued to recruit new
members, who would patrol the pass every morning and evening. The members
searched for frozen bodies, assisted wayfarers in trouble, and provided desper-
ately needed accommodations for the thousands of caravans carrying goods
across the pass.

By the late 19th century, honorary membership in the Order of St. Christopher was granted to VIPs and charitably minded individuals around the world,
frequently by request of the Austrian government. Today members are initiated
with pomp, ceremony, and good humor; they include such personalities as King
Juan Carlos of Spain, the village postman, and Queen Juliana and Prince Bernhard of the Netherlands.

As roads, phone lines, and helicopter rescue teams made passage over the Arlberg less treacherous, the Arlberg Pass developed into one of the world's leading
ski resorts. In the 1950s, the monastery, which had had difficulty recruiting new
members, sold the complex to members of the Werner family. Under the guid-
ance of the family patriarch, the monastery was brought into the 20th century
with the addition of electricity and many of the era's creature comforts.

Tragically, only a few weeks after the completion of the improvements, a dev-
astating fire destroyed all but a portion of the ancient monastery. The fire provided the opportunity to rebuild the Arlberg Hospiz hotel, recommended below.

GETTING THERE   Few commercial rail lines could negotiate the steep and
winding slopes leading up to the Arlberg Pass and St. Christoph. Passengers
usually take the **train** to St. Anton and then board one of the five daily **buses**
traveling north over the mountain passes to St. Christoph (trip time: 15 min.).
Contact **St. Anton's tourist office** (*©* **05446/22-690**) for bus and train
schedules.

Motorists can continue west from St. Anton am Arlberg (see above), following Route 316. The location is 8km (5 miles) west of St. Anton and 35km (22
miles) west of Landeck.

VISITOR INFORMATION   The **tourist office** in the village center
(*©* **05446/22-690;** www.stantonamarlberg.com) is open Monday through
Friday from 8am to noon and 2 to 6pm, Saturday from 9am to noon and 1 to
6pm, and Sunday from 9am to noon and 2 to 5pm.

WHERE TO STAY & DINE

Arlberg Hospiz 𝒢𝒢𝒢   This world-class winter-only hotel contains as much
mystery, legend, and romance as any Austrian hotel. Many of its most charming
touches were painstakingly re-created from old photographs. Visitors are welcomed into a luxurious world with more style and plush antique comfort than
the medieval monks could have imagined. An equally luxurious annex is connected to the main building by an underground passageway. The plush accommodations are well furnished, with a host of extras and the finest service in
Tyrol. Rooms are beautifully maintained and have double-glazed windows,
working fireplaces, walk-in dressing areas, and balconies. The beds are some of

the most luxurious in the area, and the spacious bathrooms have big tubs, powerful showerheads, and robes.

The Arlberg Hospiz offers superb food and an array of in-house entertainment. The party room changes its decor from year to year: Once it was transformed into an ancient Roman tavern.

Even if you don't stay here, consider having a meal in the hotel's "farmhouse"— but reserve in advance.

A-6580 St. Christoph. ⓒ **05446/26-11**. Fax 05446/3545. www.hospiz.com. 99 units. 390€–545€ double; from 940€ suite for 2. Rates include half-board. AE, DC, MC, V. Parking 11€. Closed May–Nov. **Amenities:** Restaurant; bar; nightclub; pool; Jacuzzi; sauna; game room; room service; massage; babysitting; laundry; dry cleaning. *In room:* TV, minibar, hair dryer, safe.

Gasthof Valluga   This is the least expensive hotel on the Arlberg Pass, a simple chalet-style guesthouse with cramped but clean rooms and impressive views from the windows of its dining room and bar. The German-speaking owner, Lydia Haueis, maintains impeccably proper rooms, two suitable for up to four occupants. Each has thick carpeting, good beds, and cozy charm, although the bathrooms with shower-tub combinations are a bit cramped. The restaurant is warmly accommodating, serving reasonably priced meals. Meals range from 12€ to 20€. It's open in winter daily from 8am to 10pm. Menu items include Tyroler crusted dumplings with bacon and cream sauce.

A-6580 St. Christoph. ⓒ **05446/28-23**. Fax 05446/28-23-160. www.arlberg.com/gasthof-valluga. 10 units. 190€–232€ double. Rates include half-board. MC, V. Closed June to late Nov. **Amenities:** Restaurant; bar; sauna; room service; babysitting; laundry; dry cleaning. *In room:* TV, minibar, hair dryer, safe.

Hotel Arlberghöhe   Simple and unpretentious to the point of being almost bare-boned, this hotel stands across from the more glamorous, prestigious, and expensive Arlberg Hospiz. It was built around 1940 but has been modernized several times since. Its rustic interior and heavy ceiling beams give the impression of far greater age. Skiers take warm refuge here, enjoying the well-scrubbed comfort as the gales blow around the chalet's dark-stained balconies. Many guests come here year after year, requesting a favorite chamber. Many rooms are quite spacious and heavy on wood tones, and they have beautiful tile bathrooms with shower-tub combinations. The wooden beds are exceedingly comfortable and cozy, especially on a wintry alpine night. The food is good and there's plenty of it, a combination of classic Austrian dishes, Tyrolean specialties, and international offerings.

A-6580 St. Christoph. ⓒ **05446/26-35**. Fax 05446/26-35-44. 17 units. 216€–274€ double (half-board included). MC, V. Closed Oct 15–Nov 30 and late May to Aug 15. **Amenities:** Restaurant; bar. *In room:* TV.

6 Seefeld (★/★)

24km (15 miles) NW of Innsbruck

Seefeld, a member of Austria's "Big Three" international rendezvous points for winter-sports crowds, lies on a sunny plateau some 1,052m (3,450 ft.) above sea level. This is the town that hosted the Nordic events for the 1964 and 1976 Olympic Winter Games and the 1985 Nordic Ski World Championships.

ESSENTIALS

GETTING THERE   More than a dozen **trains** per day depart from Innsbruck for the 40-minute trip to Seefeld. Other trains leave from Munich and pass through the Bavarian resort of Garmisch-Partenkirchen before arriving in Seefeld.

Despite its position on several different bus routes heading up into the nearby valleys, most visitors arrive here by train. You can, however, take one of the dozen or so buses departing daily from Innsbruck's Hauptbahnhof for the 45-minute trip. For **bus information,** call ℂ **0512/58-51-55** in Innsbruck.

If you're **driving** from Innsbruck, head west along Route 171 until you reach the junction with Route 313, at which point you go north.

VISITOR INFORMATION   The Seefeld **tourist office,** Klosterstrasse 43 (ℂ **05212/23-13;** www.seefeld-tirol.com), is open Monday through Saturday from 8:30am to 6:30pm and Sunday from 10am to noon.

WINTER & SUMMER SPORTS

The slopes are served by one cable car railway, two cable cars, three chairlifts, and 14 drag lifts. The beginner slopes lie directly in the village center, and the base stations for ski lifts leading to Seefeld's main skiing areas lie a half mile north of the resort (for the **Gschwandtkopf runs**) and a half mile south of the resort (for the **Rosshütte/Seefelder Joch runs**). They, and virtually everything else in town, are served throughout the winter by the free shuttle buses that operate at 20- to 30-minute intervals during daylight hours. In addition to its downhill runs, Seefeld has more than 200km (124 miles) of well-maintained cross-country tracks.

Other winter activities offered here include curling, horse-drawn sleigh rides, ice-skating (**Ice Skating School;** ℂ 05212/30-50) on artificial and natural ice rinks, horseback riding, indoor tennis (**Swedish Tennis School;** ℂ 05212/45-15), tube sliding (you slide on rubber inner tire tubes), indoor golf, parasailing, bowling, squash, hiking (97km/60 miles of cleared paths), fitness workouts, swimming, and sauna sessions.

Summer visitors can enjoy swimming in three lakes, a heated open-air swimming pool near Seefeld Lake, or the Olympia indoor and outdoor pools. Other summer sports include tennis on 18 open-air and 8 indoor courts (Swedish Tennis School), riding (two stables with indoor schools), and golf on the 18-hole course, which has been rated by golf insiders as one of the 100 most beautiful courses in the world. There are 200km (124 miles) of walks and mountain paths to hike, as well as cycling, minigolf, parasailing, and rafting.

Whatever time of year it is, you can try your luck at the casino (**Bahnhofstrasse;** ℂ 05212/23-40), where roulette, baccarat, blackjack, seven-card stud poker, and slot machines are played.

While based in Seefeld, you'll find it relatively easy to explore part of Bavaria, in Germany (see our companion guide, *Frommer's Germany*). You might or might not get to see little Wildmoos Lake. It can, and sometimes does, vanish all in a day or so, and then there may be cows grazing on what has become meadowland. However, the lake will suddenly come back again, and if conditions are right, it will become deep enough for swimmers. Wildmoos Lake comes and goes a lot more frequently than Brigadoon. You might also visit the little German town of Mittenwald, an easy day trip from Seefeld.

For more information about these destinations, call the tourist information number in Seefeld (ℂ **05212/23-13**). Hours are Monday through Friday from 8:30am to 12:30pm and 2 to 5:30pm, and Saturday from 10am to 4pm.

WHERE TO STAY
EXPENSIVE
Hotel Astoria ★★   This luxurious, government-rated five-star choice stands on a beautiful elevated position in a large park with panoramic views of the

surrounding mountain ranges. It lies a 5-minute walk northwest of Seefeld's center. Because of its sunny and sheltered ambience, it's a favorite with well-heeled visitors in both summer and winter. Summer brings flowered terraces and gardens; winter brings the open fireplace in the lounge bar. The attractively furnished rooms have exceedingly comfortable beds and medium-size bathrooms with shower-tub combinations.

Saturday evenings are gala nights here, with candlelit dinners and music from the house band. Once a week, a Viennese *Heurige* or a Tyrolean evening with traditional buffet is presented.

Geigenbühel, A-6100 Seefeld. © **05212/22-720.** Fax 05212/22-72-100. www.astoria-seefeld.com. 56 units. Winter 304€–446€ double, 496€–538€ suite; summer 170€–290€ double, 246€–384€ suite. Rates include half-board. AE, DC, MC, V. Free outdoor parking; indoor parking 14€ during winter, 10€ during summer. Closed Apr–May 20 and Oct–Dec 20. **Amenities:** Restaurant; bar; pool; fitness center; sauna; solarium; room service; massage; babysitting; laundry; dry cleaning. *In room:* TV, minibar, hair dryer, safe.

Hotel Klosterbräu 🐾🐾🐾   The town's most unusual and elegant hostelry is constructed around a 16th-century cloister. The interior contains soaring vaults supported by massive columns. Rooms are encased in a towering chalet behind the front entrance, and windows look out over the midsummer buffet set up near the outdoor sun terrace. They come in a variety of sizes, but all are beautifully kept, with antiques and comfortable mattresses. Medium-size bathrooms have robes, shower-tub combinations, and bidets. Some rooms contain balconies opening onto mountain vistas, and nonsmoking rooms can also be reserved.

Restaurants on the premises include a country-style *Bräukeller* with regional furniture and live music, a rustic Tyrolean room with impeccable service, and a more formal dining room where guests sit below ancient ceiling vaults. Dishes include international and Austrian specialties. A la carte dinners go for 21€ to 45€, and reservations are necessary.

In the evening, chicly dressed patrons often drop in at Die Kanne nightclub, whose comedians and musical revues provide a high spot in the village's nightlife. A daily afternoon tea dance in winter allows hotel guests to meet one another.

Klosterstrasse 30, A-6100 Seefeld. © **05212/26-210.** Fax 05212/38-85. www.klosterbraeu.com. 120 units. Winter 276€–670€ double, from 420€ suite; summer 180€–290€ double, from 360€ suite. Rates include breakfast. AE, DC, MC, V. Free parking on street; garage parking 9€. Closed Apr–May and Oct–Nov. **Amenities:** 3 restaurants; bar; nightclub; 2 pools; fitness center; sauna; solarium; room service; babysitting; laundry; dry cleaning. *In room:* TV, minibar, hair dryer, safe.

MODERATE
Alpenhotel Lamm 🐾   The cozy interior of this 1940s hotel is decorated with ceiling beams, rural artifacts, and baroque sculpture. The best rooms are fairly elegant and spacious; all have balconies. Bathrooms are spotlessly maintained with shower-tub combinations. The hotel's restaurant, Zum Kirchenwirt, enjoys a good reputation among visitors, and dancing and music are offered daily in the Lammkeller beginning around 8:30pm.

Dorfplatz 28, A-6100 Seefeld. © **05212/24-64.** Fax 05212/28-34-34. www.alpenhotel.com. 88 units. Winter 198€–260€ double, 220€–320€ apt for 2; summer 112€–168€ double, 152€–176€ apt for 2. Rates include half-board. MC, V. Closed late Oct to Dec 10. **Amenities:** Restaurant; bar; fitness center; Jacuzzi; sauna; room service; babysitting; laundry; dry cleaning. *In room:* TV, minibar, hair dryer, safe.

Karwendelhof 🐾   The Wilberger family runs one of the most elegant hotels in Tyrol. The century-old Tyrolean parlors have parquet floors, beamed ceilings, and antique accents. The personalized, rustically furnished rooms are elegant yet simple. Some have balconies opening onto mountain vistas, but all are immaculately maintained and have colorfully tiled bathrooms with shower-tub combinations, some with bidets.

The hotel restaurant, Alte Stube, is completely covered in old paneling burnished to a rich mellow glow. Dishes include well-prepared beef, veal, and pork, accompanied by fresh vegetables and followed by regional cheeses and home-baked pastries. Meals cost 18€ to 36€, and reservations are necessary.

The hotel's K-Keller is one of the village's social centers. It's open only in winter 9pm to 2:30am. A casino in an adjoining building opens at 3pm every afternoon in winter.

Bahnhofstrasse 124, A-6100 Seefeld. ℂ 800/528-1234 in the U.S., or 05212/26-550. Fax 05212/26-55-44. www.karwendelhof.at. 42 units. Winter 114€–260€ double, 288€ suite for 2; summer 88€–168€ double, 194€ suite for 2. Rates include half-board. AE, DC, MC, V. Free parking on street; garage parking 8€ in summer, 12€ in winter. Closed Apr to mid-June and Oct–Dec 15. **Amenities:** Restaurant; bar; beer cellar; casino; fitness center; sauna; room service; babysitting; laundry; dry cleaning. *In room:* TV, minibar, hair dryer, safe.

Waldhotel   One of the oldest hotels in Seefeld, the Waldhotel has been fully renovated. Its location, at the edge of the resort adjoining the woods surrounding Seefeld, is about a 7-minute walk from the village center. All of the well-appointed rooms have balconies and terrific beds. The very best rooms have sitting areas; some of the smaller doubles are a bit cramped. Bathrooms, though small, are well maintained and equipped with shower-tub combinations. A panoramic garden restaurant and a terrace are favorite spots for lunch or tea. Dinners include a choice of four-course menus, and breakfast is a buffet. In winter, there's a curling rink, and the hotel is just a 3-minute walk from the cable cars leading to the slopes. Year-round, the place offers a variety of entertainment, such as a live Dixieland band or Tyrolean music.

Römerweg 106, A-6100 Seefeld. ℂ 05212/22-070. Fax 05212/20-01-30. www.waldhotel-seefeld.at. 50 units. Winter 120€–160€ double, 140€–220€ suite for 2; summer 68€–84€ double, 98€–112€ suite for 2. Rates include half-board. AE, MC, V. Parking garage 9€. Closed Apr and 2 weeks in Nov. **Amenities:** Restaurant; bar; sauna; babysitting. *In room:* TV, hair dryer.

INEXPENSIVE
Hotel Christina   A 5-minute walk from the town center is this comfortable, contemporary chalet with exposed wood and a rustic, homey character. It has an indoor pool accessible through big glass doors in the cellar. Many of the comfortably furnished rooms have balconies, and, after recent renovations, the rooms are better than ever, with new beds. Bathrooms here are excellent, if a bit small, with shower-tub combinations.

Reitherspitzstrasse 415, A-6100 Seefeld. ℂ 05212/25-53. Fax 05212/25-53-32. 14 units. Winter 98€–122€ double, 150€ suite for 2; summer 70€–82€ double, 125€ suite for 2. Rates include buffet breakfast. DC, MC, V. **Amenities:** Breakfast room; lounge; sauna; solarium. *In room:* TV, hair dryer.

WHERE TO DINE
Most guests book into a Seefeld hotel on the half-board plan, and most of the hotels listed above have excellent dining facilities, although you should call ahead to make reservations.

Gourmet Restaurant Ritter Oswald/Bräukeller ✿✿ CONTINEN-
TAL/TYROLEAN   There are two restaurants of charm and historic importance within the most legendary hotel of Seefeld. The more expensive of the two is the Ritter Oswald. Set on the hotel's lobby level and outfitted with Tyrolean artifacts, richly oiled paneling, hunting trophies, and alpine mementos, it's small

(60 seats), intimate, and cozy, with elaborate service rituals and food that mimics the grand cuisine you'd expect in, say, Salzburg or Vienna. Menu items change with the seasons but might delectably include filets of venison with a morel and port-wine sauce, strips of filet of veal served with herb-flavored cream sauce and spinach, and sophisticated variations on local freshwater trout. The less expensive and larger (150 seats) of the two is the cellar-level Bräukeller, which is capped with a 500-year-old vaulted stone ceiling that originally functioned as part of a monastery. Earthier and a bit more swashbuckling than the Ritter Oswald, it focuses on the hearty, folkloric cuisine of the Austrian Alps, with menu items that include *Tafelspitz* (boiled beef), liver and noodle soup, grilled lake char with seasonal vegetables, Wiener schnitzel, and braised beef with wild mushrooms. There's live Tyrolean-style music performed nightly in the Bräukeller. Whereas you might be subtly steered into buying wine with your meal in the Ritter Oswald, no one will object if you opt for beer as accompaniment for your meal in the Bräukeller.

In the Hotel Klosterbräu, Klosterstrasse 30. ⓒ 05212/26210. Reservations recommended in Ritter Oswald, not necessary in the Bräukeller. Main courses in Ritter Oswald 19€–28€; main courses in the Bräukeller 10€–23€. AE, DC, MC, V. Both restaurants daily 11am-2pm and 6-11pm. Closed: Mid-Mar to mid-June and Oct to mid-December.

Restaurant Wetterstein *(Value* TYROLEAN/AUSTRIAN   Locals praise the Tyrolean food served in the paneled dining room of this cozy 45-unit hotel, which was built in a chalet style in stages between 1920 and 1975. The restaurant produces particularly appealing versions of such dishes as Weiner schnitzels, medallions of venison with mushroom and herb sauce, braised beef with forest mushroom and red cabbage, liver-noodle or goulash soup, and roasted rabbit served with noodles. Pastries are elaborate and as highly caloric as you'd ever want, and the presentation of each dish is more elaborate than you'd expect within some of its nearby competitors.

In the Hotel Wetterstein. Mösererstrasse 120 at Klosterstrasse. ⓒ 05212/2283. Reservations recommended. Main courses 10€–21€. MC, V. Mid-Dec to mid-Mar daily 11am–9pm (last order). June to early Oct daily noon–2pm and 7–9pm. Closed mid-Mar to June and early Oct to mid-Dec.

SEEFELD AFTER DARK

Seefeld has plenty of nightlife options to keep you entertained after a day in the alpine outdoors. Consider a drink at a glass-sided, oversize replica of an Eskimo's igloo, **Bar Siglu,** Klosterstrasse (ⓒ 05212/26-21-186), where live music is presented in the early evening in ways that somehow make the drinks taste better. If you're tempted to go dancing after all those drinks, at least three discos thrive in Seefeld year-round. They include **Full Moon,** Klosterstrasse (ⓒ 05212/ 26-21), an enclave of high-energy dance music that's decorated to resemble the interior of a rather grim-looking tomb, and **Jeep Disco,** Klosterstrasse (ⓒ 05212/ 85-75-14), which is smaller, more intimate, and cozier than Full Moon. Jeep Disco's dance floor is centered on a brown Jeep that appears prominently as a decorative object. Most traditional and gemütlich of all is the alpine-style **Post Bar,** Bahnhofstrasse (ⓒ 05212/22-01-502). All three are open nightly around 10pm to around 6am, depending on business. Entrance is usually free.

In season, Seefeld bustles with typical wine and beer cellars, along with nightclubs and dance clubs that come and go. However, the major nighttime attraction is the **Spiel-Casino Seefeld,** at the Hotel Karwendelhof, Bahnhofstrasse (ⓒ 05212/23-40). It offers baccarat, blackjack, seven-card stud poker, a money wheel, American and French roulette, and 70 slot machines. Your admission is

20€—but that gives you the equivalent of 25€ in chips. It's open daily from 3pm to 3am.

Hotel Klosterbräu, Klosterstrasse 30, is the most sophisticated nightspot in town; its nightclub, **Die Kanne,** presents an international orchestra and a floor show daily in winter and 3 nights a week in summer from 9pm to 3am. In winter, the club opens at 5pm for a *Tanz-tee* (tea dance). The hotel also features international specialties in its restaurant, **Ritter Oswald Stube,** and a gemütlich atmosphere in its **Bräukeller,** open from 10am to midnight, presenting *Stimmung* (folk) music after 8pm.

7 The Ziller Valley 🟊🟊

Zillertal is the German name for the Ziller Valley east of Innsbruck, a resort mecca in summer and winter. Some say that this is the most beautiful valley in all of Tyrol. You might doubt this claim as you go through the first stretches of the Zillertal, but don't turn back. It gets more impressive as you travel deeper into the valley.

When you first enter the Zillertal during the warmer months, you'll pass rich meadowlands and sleek, healthy grazing cows. To the west are the **Tux Alps** and to the east are the **Kitzbühel Alps,** covered later in this chapter. As tempting as it might be to head for these alpine areas, continue farther into the Ziller Valley, which will suddenly grow narrower, with the scenery becoming more dramatic.

The people of the Zillertal are the finest singers in Austria, as generation after generation of valley families inherited magnificent voices and made use of their talents. Pass through the first of the little villages and resorts, since we think better ones lie ahead.

ZELL AM ZILLER

Zell am Ziller lies 479km (298 miles) west of Vienna and 60km (37 miles) east of Innsbruck. This is the first town that merits a stop, but don't confuse this resort with Zell am See in Land Salzburg. Zell am Ziller is the major town of the lower section of the Ziller Valley, and inns here are reasonably priced. Once it was a gold-mining town, but those days are long gone.

GETTING THERE   If you're coming directly to Zell am Ziller, you can **fly** to the nearest international airport, in Munich, and arrange further transportation from there.

Trains from Innsbruck travel frequently to **Jenbach,** which sits on the main rail line to Salzburg (trip time: 20 min.). At Jenbach, trains depart every hour for Zell am Ziller (trip time: 45 min.).

Most **bus lines** servicing Zell am Ziller originate in nearby towns and villages. However, three buses per day depart from Innsbruck's Hauptbahnhof for Zell am Ziller (trip time: 1¾ hr.). For **rail and bus information** in Zell am Ziller from other parts of Austria, call ⓒ **05244/60-60.**

If you're **driving** from Innsbruck, head east along Autobahn A12 to the junction with Route 169 and cut south.

VISITOR INFORMATION   The **tourist office** in the town center (ⓒ **05282/22-81;** www.zell.at) is open Monday through Friday from 8:30am to 6pm and Saturday from 9am to 5pm.

EXPLORING ZELL AM ZILLER

Like many other Austrian villages, Zell has a **Pfarrkirche (Parish Church)** 🟊, this one dating from 1782. A huge dome tops its octagonal design.

Once this village was known only as a summer holiday site, but more recently it has also become a winter sports resort. In 1978, the Kreuzjoch area was opened to skiers, and Zell am Ziller took its place on the tourist ski maps of Europe. In season, a free ski bus stops at the major hotels to transport guests to the slopes.

You can travel by gondola to a restaurant with a view of the **Gründalm** (1,022m/3,350 ft.) and then continue by chairlift to **Rosenalm** (1,761m/5,775 ft.), where another restaurant opens onto a panoramic view. From Rosenalm, a surface lift can take you to a lofty citadel 2,266m (7,430 ft.) above sea level.

Another ski area, the **Geriosstein**, more than 5km (3 miles) from Zell am Ziller, also has bus service, but not as frequently. From the bottom station, a cableway will lift you to 1,647m (5,400 ft.), where you can take a chairlift up to 1,836m (6,020 ft.).

WHERE TO STAY

Alpenhof Zellerhof ✿✿   The town's glossiest and most stylish big-city hotel is a modern adaptation of a traditional chalet, with several wood-trimmed bars and restaurants. These include Das Kleines Restaurant, one of the best places to dine in the city (see "Where to Dine," below); Pablo's, a pizzeria where pizzas emerge from a wood-burning oven; and a cafe, Zeller Fassl. A folkloric group, the Tiroler Abend, presents weekly performances in the Zeller Dorfstadl, and dancing follows the performance. The ample rooms are traditionally decorated and have comfortable beds. Each contains a small but efficiently organized private bathroom—usually with a shower stall. This is the only hotel in Zell am Ziller with its own covered garage.

Bahnhofstrasse 3, A-6280 Zell am Ziller. ✆ **05282/26-120.** Fax 05282/26-12-65. zellerhof@netway.at. 43 units. Winter 82€–146€ double; summer 90€ double. Rates include half-board. AE, DC, MC, V. Closed mid-Oct to mid-Dec. **Amenities:** 3 restaurants; 2 bars; cafe; pool; sauna; room service. *In room:* TV.

Hotel Bräu   At the edge of the town's most important crossroads, this ample chalet was originally built in the 15th century, and an extra wing was added in 1985. Rising five balconied stories, its ochre-colored facade is embellished with trompe l'oeil frescoes. Inside, it contains three different dining rooms (see "Where to Dine," below). Each comfortable guest room is outfitted with wood trim and plenty of Tyrolean charm. Modern extras have not been ignored. Rooms are a bit small, however, as are the bathrooms with shower-tub combinations.

Dorfplatz 1, A-6280 Zell am Ziller. ✆ **05282/23-13.** Fax 05282/23-13-17. www.tiscover.at/hotel-braeu. 36 units. 110€–130€ double. Rates include half-board. No credit cards. Closed Apr and Oct 15–Dec 20. **Amenities:** 3 restaurants; bar; sauna; room service; babysitting; laundry; dry cleaning. *In room:* TV, minibar, hair dryer, safe.

Hotel Tirolerhof   This five-story balconied chalet, built in the 1970s, has a desirable location right in the commercial center. The cozy rooms have comfortable beds and all the modern comforts, such as small but efficient bathrooms with shower-tub combinations. The owners are the Waidhofer family. On the premises is a Tyrolean disco as well as an intimate country restaurant. Local residents often gather in the evening for some serious beer drinking, and no one seems to mind if you join in.

Dorfplatz 8, A-6280 Zell am Ziller. ✆ **05282/22-27.** Fax 05282/22-27-95. 40 units. Winter 152€–194€ double; summer 130€ double. Rates include half-board. DC, MC, V. **Amenities:** Restaurant; bar; sauna; solarium; room service; massage; laundry; dry cleaning. *In room:* TV, hair dryer.

WHERE TO DINE

Hotel Bräu Restaurant AUSTRIAN   Lined up side by side on the street level of the Hotel Bräu, this trio of authentic Tyrolean dining rooms competes with one another for the most regional charm. You might want to check out each of them before deciding. They're called **Speisezimmer, Bräustübl,** and **Casino.** Full meals cost around 24€ and include solid Teutonic dishes, suitable for cold-weather days.

Dorfplatz 1. ℂ **05282/23-13.** Reservations required. Main courses 5€–21€. No credit cards. Daily 11:30am–2pm and 6–9pm. Closed Apr and Oct 15–Dec 10.

Das Kleines Restaurant ℱ AUSTRIAN/INTERNATIONAL   Located in the town's most stylish hotel, this restaurant serves some of the best food around. The main dining room contains a green ceramic stove and big windows. For even more charm, ask for a table in the darkly intimate *Stübl,* where row upon row of antique photographs adorn the wood paneling. Dishes are based on centuries-old Tyrolean recipes. You might begin with fried Camembert with cranberries and follow with a choice of three kinds of schnitzels, or else trout or perch from the hotel's own fish hatcheries. One of the chef's specials is hunter's pie, made with venison and two kinds of wild mushrooms in a creamy sauce. A different special is featured every day.

In the Hotel Alpenhotel Zellerhof, Bahnhofstrasse 3. ℂ **05282/26-12.** Reservations recommended. Main courses 7€–14€. AE, DC, MC, V. Daily 11am–2pm and 6–10pm. Closed mid-Oct to mid-Dec.

MAYRHOFEN ℱ

The road divides at Zell am Ziller, and to reach Mayrhofen, head southwest on Route 169 to the popular resort. After a visit here, we recommend that you return to Zell and then go southeast to **Gerlos.** But first, Mayrhofen.

This resort, standing at 633m (2,075 ft.), enclosed by towering alpine peaks and lying at the foot of the glaciers crowning the adjacent Alps, is a premier summer holiday spot and winter playground, the finest in the valley in terms of facilities and accommodations. Some of the area's best food is served here.

GETTING THERE   Following the routes used to reach Zell am Ziller, travelers from Innsbruck transfer at the railway junction at Jenbach. From Jenbach, **trains** depart every hour for the 1-hour ride south to Mayrhofen. From Mayrhofen many bus lines fan out into the nearby valleys. Unless you're coming from one of those obscure valleys, it's easier to take the train. Mayrhofen is 76km (47 miles) southeast of Innsbruck.

For **bus and rail information,** call ℂ 05244/60-60.

VISITOR INFORMATION   The **tourist office** in the town center (ℂ **05285/67-60;** www.mayrhofen.com) is open Monday through Friday from 8am to 6pm, Saturday from 9am to 6pm, and Sunday from noon to 2pm.

SUMMER SPORTS, SKIING & MORE

For decades, Mayrhofen has drawn summer holiday crowds with its endless opportunities for mountaineering, hang gliding, shooting, tennis, fishing, swimming in a heated outdoor pool, minigolf, cycling, and even summer skiing in the **Hintertux glacier area** at the top of the valley. Mayrhofen is also a mecca for mountain climbers during the nonskiing seasons.

In recent years, the resort village has become more a ski center. Starting from scratch, you can learn to ski at the resort school: The children's ski training is especially good here, and a kindergarten makes this an ideal family resort. Slopes for advanced skiers are available in the **Penkenjoch** section to the west of

Mayrhofen, with a cableway taking you to nearly 1,830m (6,000 ft.). From the top, you'll be rewarded with one of the most panoramic views of the Zillertal alpine range. There's also a restaurant with quite a view up here.

You can also take a cableway (departs south of Mayrhofen) up to ski in the **Ahorn** area (1,906m/6,250 ft.). There are seven surface lifts at the top, as well as another restaurant with a panoramic view.

Other winter activities include sledding on a natural toboggan run, curling, ice-skating, taking horse-drawn sleigh rides, going horseback riding, and playing sports in an indoor arena.

After your outdoor fun, you can spend your evening attending a tea dance or eating fondue. You can also hear some of that famous Ziller Valley singing at folk festivals in July and August. The dates change every year, so check with the tourist office. Another popular summer diversion is taking a ride on the narrow-gauge steam train between Zell am Ziller and Mayrhofen.

VENTURING INTO THE ALPS

From Mayrhofen you can also venture into the Alps around the Zillertal, where you'll be rewarded with some of the most spectacular scenery in Tyrol. By the time you reach Mayrhofen, the trail through the Zillertal that you've been following will have split into four different parts, each of which runs through a valley radiating off the Zillertal. Three of the valleys have the suffix *grund* (the German word for "ground") on their names: the **Stillupgrund,** the **Zemmgrund,** and the **Zillergrund.** The last takes its name from the alpine range.

You might not have time to explore all these valleys, but if you can make time for one, make it the fourth and loftiest valley, the **Tuxertal,** or Tux Valley, which cuts like a deep slash through the mountains. This valley reaches its end point at several glaciers, including the **Olperer,** 3,477m (11,400 ft.) high. You can take a bus from Mayrhofen to either the village of **Lanersbach** or on to **Hintertux,** both in the Tuxertal. The road runs west from Mayrhofen for some 21km (13 miles) to the end of the valley, where ski lifts branch off in several directions.

You come first to Lanersbach, the largest village in the Tuxertal, lying in a sunny, sheltered spot. From here you can take a chairlift to the **Eggalm plateau,** which has a restaurant at 2,001m (6,560 ft.) and offers one of the most scenic panoramas the Ziller Alps has to offer.

Hintertux, your ultimate destination, lies at the top of the valley, virtually on the doorstep of the towering glaciers. Because of thermal springs, Hintertux also enjoys a reputation as a spa. You might want to buy some wood carvings from the skillful craftspeople here.

You can ski on the glaciers in summer. A chairlift or a gondola from Hintertux will transport you to **Sommerbergalm** (2,074m/6,800 ft.), and once here, you can take a surface lift west to **Tuxer-Joch Hütte** (2,531m/8,300 ft.).

WHERE TO STAY

Alpenhotel Kramerwirt   This hotel's facade has green shutters, a painted illustration of a medieval figure, and a towerlike construction high above the roofline. The rustic interior contains a scattering of oriental rugs and antique chests. Some rooms have romantic four-poster beds and big bathrooms; others are designed in a more functional style with less spacious bathrooms, each with a shower-tub combination. Additional but less desirable rooms are located in a 1980s annex a short walk away. A folkloric nightclub, the **Andreas Keller,** is in the cellar. Live musicians entertain the drinkers and diners.

Am Marienbrunnen 346, A-6290 Mayrhofen. © 05285/67-00. Fax 05285/67-00-502. www.kramerwirt.at. 80 units. Winter 144€–200€ double; summer 96€–120€ double. Rates include half-board. MC, V. Parking 8€ in winter, free in summer. Closed mid-Oct to mid-Dec. **Amenities:** Restaurant; bar; nightclub; 2 Jacuzzis; sauna; room service; babysitting. *In room:* TV, hair dryer, safe.

Elisabethhotel ❅❅ *(Kids* Named after the youngish matriarch of the Thaler family, the owners, this stylish and luxurious hotel is a 3-minute walk from the village center. Its chalet-style facade is accented with carefully detailed balconies, heavy overhanging eaves, painted designs, and a tower. Rooms, the resort's finest, have charming Tyrolean motifs. Bathrooms are generally spacious and equipped with charming appointments, large tubs, showers, and cosmetic mirrors. On the premises is a cozy restaurant, Die gute Stube, and an airy, elegant bar named after one of Mozart's most memorably comic characters, Papageno. There's also a large terrace with a coffee shop and an Italian restaurant, Mamma Mia. In winter, a disco operates in the basement, and in summer there's a large garden to use, plus a children's playground.

Einfahrt Mitte 432, A-6290 Mayrhofen. © 05285/67-67. Fax 05285/67-67-67. www.elisabethhotel.com. 32 units. 187€–274€ double; from 420€ suite. Rates include half-board. AE, DC, MC, V. Closed Nov and May. **Amenities:** Restaurant; bar, nightclub; pool; fitness center; Jacuzzi; sauna; solarium; children's playground; room service; massage; babysitting; laundry; dry cleaning. *In room:* TV, minibar, hair dryer, safe.

WHERE TO DINE

Wirtshaus Zum Griena ❅ *(Finds* AUSTRIAN/TYROLEAN   This restaurant, strong on regional charm and cuisine, sits in a meadow above Mayrhofen's main colony of resort hotels. The two dining rooms are covered with pinewood planks that everyone claims were installed about 400 years ago. Even the tables are an unfinished series of smoothly sanded planks. If you can read German, you might still find the menu tough going, as it's written in a little-used Tyrolean dialect. Many dishes are based on butter-and-egg alpine recipes, sometimes laden with cream from high-altitude cows. Several involve baking in a ceramic pot, including noodles layered with cream and cheese. Ever had beer soup? You might opt for the cheese platter, a bowl of polenta, or one of the meat dishes. The Wiener schnitzel, in the words of the apron-clad waitress, comes "fresh from the veal" and is "very, very pretty."

Dorfhaus 768. © 05285/62778. Reservations recommended. Main courses 6€–12.90€. MC, V. June–Oct Tues–Sun 11am–10pm; Dec–May daily 11am–11pm. Closed Nov. Drive uphill (north) from the town center for 10 min. to the secluded suburb of Dorfhaus; turn left at a fountain and head several hundred feet down a 1-lane road flanked with a fence.

8 The Kitzbühel Alps ❅❅❅

Hard-core skiers and the rich and famous are attracted to this ski region. Such a dense network of lifts covers the Kitzbühel Alps that they're Austria's largest skiing area, with a series of superlative runs. The action centers on the town of Kitzbühel, but there are many satellite resorts that are much less expensive, including **St. Johann** in Tirol. Kitzbühel is, in a sense, a neighbor of Munich, 130km (81 miles) to the northeast: Most visitors to the Kitzbühel Alps use Munich's international airport.

KITZBÜHEL ❅❅❅

Edward, Prince of Wales (you might remember him better as the Duke of Windsor), might have put Kitzbühel on the international map with his 1928 "discovery" of what was then a town of modest guesthouses. Certainly his return a few years later with Mrs. Simpson caused the eyes of the world to focus on this town, and the "upper crust" of England and other countries began flocking here, placing a stamp of elegance on Kitzbühel.

At the time of this 20th-century renaissance, however, Kitzbühel was already some 8 centuries old by documented history, and a settlement existed here much, much longer than that. Archaeological finds have shown that during the Bronze Age—and until the 9th century B.C.—copper was mined and traded in nearby mountains. The settlement *Chizbühel* is first mentioned in documents of 1165, the name derived from the ruling family of Chizzo. Kitzbühel was a part of Bavaria until 1504, when it came into the hands of Holy Roman Emperor Maximilian I of Austria and was annexed to Tyrol.

A second mining era began in Kitzbühel in the 15th century—this time copper and silver—and the town became fat and prosperous for many decades. Numerous buildings from the mining days are still here, as are remnants of the town walls and three of the gates. In what used to be the suburbs of Kitzbühel, you'll see some of the miners' cottages still standing.

Kitzbühel is not a cheap place to stay, but to make things easier on your pocketbook, the local tourist office has come out with a **Guest Card** for summer visitors. This card is valid after being stamped at your hotel or guesthouse and entitles you to reductions, some quite substantial, on the price of many activities, plus some freebies.

GETTING THERE   Two and three **trains** per hour (many express) arrive in Kitzbühel from Innsbruck (trip time: 60 min.) and Salzburg (trip time: 2½ hr.).

Although it's serviced by at least nine local **bus lines** running into and up the surrounding valleys, most visitors arrive in Kitzbühel by train. The most useful of these bus lines runs every 30 to 60 minutes between Kitzbühel and St. Johann in Tirol (trip time: 25 min.). In addition, about half a dozen buses travel every day from Salzburg's main railway station to Kitzbühel (trip time: 2¼ hr.). For **regional bus information,** call ✆ 05356/627-15.

Kitzbühel is 449km (279 miles) southwest of Vienna and 100km (62 miles) east of Innsbruck. If you're **driving** from Innsbruck, take Autobahn A12 east to the junction with Route 312 heading to Ellmau. After bypassing Ellmau, continue east to the junction with Route 342, which you take south to Kitzbühel.

VISITOR INFORMATION   The **tourist office,** Hinterstadt 18 (✆ 05356/ 621-55; www.kitzbuehel.com), is open Monday through Friday from 8:30am to 6pm, Saturday from 8:30am to noon and 4 to 6pm, and Sunday from 10am to noon and 4 to 6pm.

EXPLORING THE TOWN

The town has two main streets, both pedestrian walkways: **Vorderstadt** and **Hinterstadt.** Along these streets, Kitzbühel has preserved its traditional architectural style. You'll see three-story stone houses with oriels and scrollwork around the doors and windows, heavy overhanging eaves, and Gothic gables.

The **Pfarrkirche (Parish Church)** was built from 1435 to 1506 and was renovated in the baroque style during the 18th century. The lower part of the **Church of Our Lady (Liebfrauenkirche)** dates from the 13th century; the upper part dates from 1570. Between these two churches stands the **Ölberg Chapel (Ölbergkapelle)** with a 1450 "lantern of the dead" and frescoes from the latter part of the 16th century.

Heimatmuseum, Hinterstadt 32 (✆ 05356/645-88), is the town's most visible showcase of its own culture and history. It lies within what was originally the town granary, constructed in the city's center on the site of an early medieval

Kitzbühel

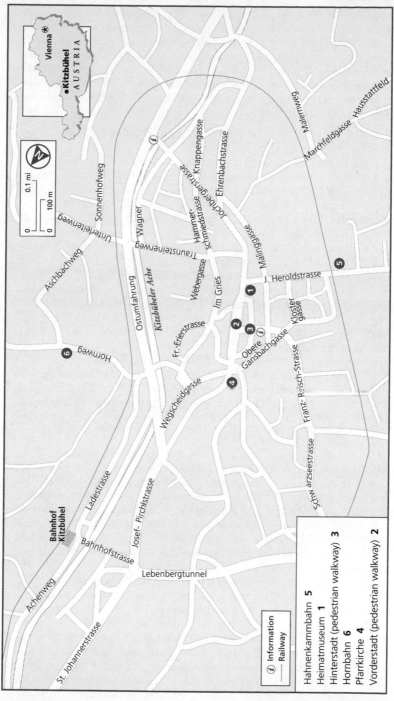

Hahnenkammbahn **5**
Heimatmuseum **1**
Hinterstadt (pedestrian walkway) **3**
Hornbahn **6**
Pfarrkirche **4**
Vorderstadt (pedestrian walkway) **2**

ⓘ Information
— Railway

castle. In 1998, it was enlarged with the incorporation of the town's oldest extant tower, a 14th-century stone structure once part of Kitzbühel's medieval fortifications. Inside you'll see artifacts based on the town's legendary mines, from prehistoric times and the Bronze Age through the Middle Ages, as well as trophies of the region's skiing stars, with lots of emphasis on its 19th- and early-20th-century development into a modern-day ski resort. The museum is open year-round Monday through Saturday from 10am to 1pm. Admission is 4€ for adults and 2€ for persons under 18.

SKIING GALORE AT THE KITZBÜHEL SKI CIRCUS

In winter, the emphasis in Kitzbühel, 702m (2,300 ft.) above sea level, is on skiing, and facilities are offered for everyone from novices to experts. The ski season starts just before Christmas and lasts until late March. With more than 62 lifts, gondolas, and mountain railroads on five different mountains, Kitzbühel has two main ski areas, the **Hahnenkamm** (renovated in 1995) and the **Kitzbüheler Horn** ★★. Cable cars (Hahnenkammbahn) are within easy walking distance, even in ski boots.

The linking of the lift systems on the Hahnenkamm has created the celebrated **Kitzbühel Ski Circus** ★★★, which makes it possible to ski downhill for more than 80km (50 miles), with runs that suit every stage of proficiency. Numerous championship ski events are held here, like the World Cup event each January, when top-flight skiers pit their skills against the toughest downhill course in the world, a stretch of the Hahnenkamm especially designed for maximum speed. Its name, Die Strief, is both feared and respected among skiers because of its reputation as one of the world's fastest downhill racecourses. A ski pass entitles the holder to use all the lifts that form the Ski Circus.

Skiing became a fact of life in Kitzbühel as long ago as 1892, when the first pair of skis was imported from Norway and intrepid daredevils began to slide down the snowy slopes at breakneck speeds. Many great names in skiing have since been associated with Kitzbühel, the most renowned being town native Toni Sailer, who was the triple Olympic champion in the 1956 Winter Games in Cortina.

MORE WINTER & SUMMER PURSUITS

Skiing, of course, is not the only winter activity here—there's also curling, skibobbing, ski jumping, ice-skating, tobogganing, hiking on cleared trails, and hang gliding, as well as indoor activities like tennis, bowling, and swimming. The children's ski school, **Schi-schule Rote Teufel,** Museumkeller, Hinterstadt (⑦ 05356/635-00), provides training for the very young skier. And don't forget the après-ski, with bars, nightclubs, and dance clubs rocking from teatime until the wee hours.

Kitzbühel has summer pastimes, too, with activities including walking tours, visits to the **Wild Life Park at Aurach** (about 3km/2 miles from Kitzbühel), tennis, horseback riding, golf, squash, brass-band concerts in the town center, cycling, and swimming. For the last, there's an indoor swimming pool, but we recommend going to the **Schwarzsee (Black Lake).** This *See,* about a 15-minute walk northwest of the center of town, is an alpine lake with a peat bottom that keeps the water relatively murky. Covering an area of 16 acres, with a depth that doesn't exceed about 8m (25 ft.), it's the site of beaches and **Seiwald Boosverleih,** Schwartzsee (⑦ 05356/623-81), an outfit that rents rowboats and putt-putt electric-driven engines in case you want to fish or sunbathe from within a boat. Obviously, everything is shuttered down tight from September to mid-May. (As of November 1998, water-skiing was banned on the lake, and the windsurfing school has moved to a larger lake in Carinthia.)

One of the region's most exotic collections of alpine flora is clustered into the jagged and rocky confines of the **Alpine Flower Garden Kitzbühel,** where various species of gentian, gorse, heather, and lichens are found on the sunny slopes of the Kitzbüheler Horn. Set at a height of around 1,830m (6,000 ft.) above sea level, the garden—which is owned and maintained by Kitzbühel as an incentive to midsummer tourism—is open from late May to early September daily from 8:30am to 5:30pm, and it is most impressive during June, July, and August. Admission is free, and many visitors see it by taking the Seilbahn Kitzbüheler cable car to its uppermost station and then descending on foot via the garden's labyrinth of footpaths to the gondola's middle station. (You can also climb upward within the garden, reversing the order of the gondola stations, although that would require a lot more effort.) The **Seilbahn Kitzbüheler cable car** (© **05356/69-51**), 14€ round-trip, departs from the Kitzbühel at half-hour intervals daily throughout the summer and winter. In spring and autumn, it operates Saturday and Sunday only.

SHOPPING

A promenade around the resort's center reveals shops containing all the luxury goods and sporting equipment a shopper could need to satisfy even serious binges of acquisitive lust. But if you're looking specifically for sporting goods, consider dropping into **Kitz Sport,** Jochbergerstrasse 7 (© **05356/622-04**). For Kitzbühel souvenirs and the most complete array of local handicrafts in town, head for **Samy's Souvenirs,** Untere Gänsbachgasse 7 (© **05356/629-66**), where you'll find locally handcrafted pewter, ironwork, ceramics, wood carvings, and a small selection of folkloric clothing for men and women. For an outlet with even greater amounts of women's *Trachten* (traditional clothing such as dirndls), head to **Sport Alm,** Josef Pirchl Strasse 9 (© **05356/710-38**). Traditional clothing for men, women, and children, as well as modern, conventional clothing for all occasions, is available at **Eden,** Vorderstadt 22 (© **05356/626-56**).

WHERE TO STAY

Although there's a wide range of hotels in Kitzbühel, reservations are absolutely mandatory in the high-season winter months, particularly the peak ski times such as February. As for Christmas in Kitzbühel, someone once wrote, "It's best to make reservations at birth."

Very Expensive
Romantik Hotel Tennerhof ⭐⭐⭐   High in the foothills of the mountains near the Hornbahn cable cars, and half a mile west of the town center, this comfortable, government-rated five-star chalet hotel evolved from a 17th-century farmhouse. The whole place is furnished in a Tyrolean style with great care and taste, offering good living and complete relaxation in a garden setting. The views from the outdoor cafe encompass the pool and the village. The owners, the Pasquali family, take a personal interest in their guests and see that a high standard of service is maintained. If you're a traditionalist, try one of the rooms in the original building, as they're the most intimate and cozy. All rooms are beautifully furnished, sometimes with antiques. Bathrooms come in a variety of sizes, all with shower-tub combinations.

The Romantik Hotel Tennerhof Restaurant (see "Where to Dine," below) offers wholesome food, with vegetables and herbs straight from the hotel's garden.

Griesenauweg 26, A-6370 Kitzbühel. (C) 05356/631-81. Fax 05356/63-18-170. www.tiscover.at/hotel. tennerhof. 48 units. Winter 248€–350€ double, 344€–800€ suite; summer 204€–300€ double, 300€–580€ suite. Rates include breakfast. Half-board (granted with a stay of 3 or more days) 28€ per person extra. AE, DC, MC, V. Closed Apr–May 14 and Oct–Dec 18. **Amenities:** Restaurant; bar; 2 pools; Jacuzzi; sauna; room service; massage; babysitting; laundry; dry cleaning. *In room:* TV, minibar, hair dryer, safe.

Expensive

Hotel Goldener Greif ✿

The ancestor of this hotel was built in 1271, and parts of it still remain within the massive walls of this well-known establishment. The hotel, next to the Spiel-Casino and 600 feet from the Hahnenkamm cable-car station, has many balconies and elaborate shutters. Owner Josef Harisch likes traditional charm with a good dose of luxury thrown in. The interior contains fireplaces, antique furniture, oriental carpets, Tyrolean paintings, and a Greif Keller in, of course, the cellar. The comfortable, attractive rooms have firm beds. Most rooms are quite spacious, and many have alpine oak furnishings, alcove seats, nonworking fireplaces, parquet floors, double-glazed windows, and (in some cases) a whirlpool. Bathrooms are midsize and contain bidets and shower-tub combinations. If you want to splurge a bit, you can request one of the deluxe suites, many with a hunting-lodge motif and their own Jacuzzis, private steam baths, and fireplaces.

The superb **Restaurant Goldener Greif** (see "Where to Dine," below) serves Austrian and regional cuisine.

Hinterstadt 24, A-6370 Kitzbühel. (C) 05356/643-11. Fax 05356/650-01. www.hotel-goldener-greif.at. 56 units. Winter 124€–244€ double, 198€–282€ suite; summer 78€–126€ double, 116€–142€ suite. Rates include breakfast. Half-board available for a supplement of 11€–17€ per person. AE, DC, MC, V. Free parking on street. Closed Apr–May and Oct–Nov. **Amenities:** Restaurant; bar; pool; fitness center; sauna; room service; massage; laundry; dry cleaning. *In room:* TV, hair dryer.

Hotel Schloss Lebenberg ✿✿

The core of this hotel is a medieval castle whose walls and turrets have been covered with stucco, and a modern extension has been added nearby. The entire complex sits on a hill looking over the village, less than a mile from Kitzbühel, with dozens of mountain paths originating at its door. Rooms, especially the suites, are elegantly furnished and come in a wide range of sizes, including some spacious enough for sitting areas with wrought-iron coffee tables. Many beds are canopied. French doors lead to private patios or balconies. The dozen or so large, Gothic-style castle rooms are the most sought after. Bathrooms are small but functional and equipped with shower-tub combinations. The hotel restaurant serves lunch and dinner, and provides a lavish breakfast buffet for guests.

Lebenbergstrasse 17, A-6370 Kitzbühel. (C) 05356/690-10. Fax 05356/644-05. www.tiscover.com/schloss-lebenberg. 120 units. Winter 290€–370€ double, 420€ suite; summer 190€ double, 220€ suite. Rates include half-board. AE, DC, MC, V. Free outside parking; garage parking 14€. Hotel bus picks up guests at train station. **Amenities:** Restaurant; bar; pool; fitness center; sauna; room service; babysitting; laundry; dry cleaning. *In room:* TV, hair dryer, safe.

Hotel Weisses Rössl

This hotel was originally built in the 19th century as an inn for the merchants passing through Kitzbühel by coach. Today it's impeccably maintained by the Klena family and its fine staff. Dozens of seating niches offer cozy intimacy, and a fireplace provides midwinter cheer a few paces from the heavily trafficked lobby. The fourth floor contains a panoramic terrace with one of the best mountain views in town. A 2-minute walk from the ski lifts, the hotel offers snugly equipped rooms with comfortable furniture and neatly kept bathrooms with shower-tub combinations. An a la carte restaurant serves well-prepared Austrian and international dishes.

Bichlstrasse 3–5, A-6370 Kitzbühel. © **05356/62-54-10.** Fax 05356/634-72. www.weisses-roessl.com. 65 units. Winter 215€–410€ double, 370€–700€ suite for 2; summer 145€–275€ double, 250€–420€ suite for 2. Rates include half-board. Closed Easter to late May and mid-Oct to mid-Dec. AE, DC, MC, V. **Amenities:** Restaurant; bar; pool; sauna; room service; babysitting; laundry; dry cleaning. *In room:* TV, mini-bar, hair dryer, safe.

Hotel Zur Tenne ★★
A sophisticated family from Munich operates this hotel, one of the resort's best. It combines Tyrolean gemütlichkeit with urban style and panache, and the staff shows genuine concern for its clientele. The hotel was created in the 1950s by joining a trio of 700-year-old houses. Rooms are as glamorous as anything in Kitzbühel: wood trim, comfortable beds, eider-downs, and copies of Tyrolean antiques. Many have working fireplaces and canopied beds for a romantic touch. Bathrooms are generally large, with vanity mirrors and shower-tub combinations.

In addition to intimate lounges, niches, and nooks, the hotel sports the most luxurious health complex in town, complete with a tropical fountain, two hot tubs, and a hot-and-cold foot bath.

The Zur Tenne Restaurant offers international cuisine with a Tyrolean flair (see "Where to Dine," below).

Vorderstadt 8–10, A-6370 Kitzbühel. © **05356/64-44-40.** Fax 05356/648-03-56. www.hotelzurtenne.com. 50 units. Winter 276€ double, 345€ suite for 3; summer 138€–212€ double, 278€ suite for 3. Rates include breakfast. Half-board 28€ per person extra in winter, 23€ in summer. AE, DC, MC, V. Free parking outdoors, 11€ in covered garage nearby. **Amenities:** 2 restaurants; bar; lounge; fitness center; 2 Jacuzzis; sauna; room service; massage; babysitting; laundry; dry cleaning. *In room:* TV, minibar, hair dryer, safe.

Sporthotel Bichlhof ★
Slightly more than 3km (2 miles) south of the resort's center, this 1970s hotel offers panoramic views over most of the valley. This tasteful chalet complex surrounds you with a decor of exposed paneling and patterned carpeting. The spacious rooms sometimes look Japanese in their simplicity. The most desirable ones open onto private balconies with views of the surrounding mountains. The average-size bathrooms have shower-tub com-binations.

The hotel's restaurant serves authentic Tyrolean cuisine, specializing in fish caught in its own lake. As part of its weekly programs, the hotel offers guided torchlit walks, Tyrolean buffets, and fondue evenings or barbecues.

Bichlweg, A-6370 Kitzbühel. © **05356/640-22-23.** Fax 05356/636-34. www.bichlhof.at. 47 units. Winter 240€–320€ double, from 284€ suite for 2; summer 140€–190€ double, from 240€ suite for 2. Rates include half-board. MC, V. Closed Apr–May and Nov. **Amenities:** Restaurant; bar; pool; 18-hole golf course; 2 tennis courts; fitness center; Jacuzzi; sauna; room service; massage; babysitting; laundry; dry cleaning. *In room:* TV, minibar, hair dryer, safe.

Moderate

Hotel Bruggerhof ★ *(Finds)*
About a mile west of the town center, near the Schwarzsee, is this countryside chalet with a sun terrace. Originally built as a farmhouse in the 1920s, it later gained local fame as a restaurant. The interior has massive ceiling beams and a corner fireplace. The owners, the Reiter family, run a well-maintained hotel. Rooms are comfortable and cozy and decorated in an alpine style. All have a well-lived-in look, although housekeeping is attentive. Firm beds are most inviting, although bathrooms, which contain shower-tub combinations, can be a bit cramped. Don't expect the smooth-running effi-ciency of a large-scale chain hotel, as everything here is family managed, idio-syncratic, and personalized—sometimes to the point of eccentricity.

Reitherstrasse 24, A-6370 Kitzbühel. © **05356/628-06.** Fax 05356/64-47-930. www.tiscover.at/bruggerhof. 25 units. Winter 150€–240€ double; summer 106€–140€ double. Rates include half-board. AE, DC, MC, V.

Closed Apr and Oct 15–Dec 15. **Amenities:** Restaurant; bar; pool; minigolf; 2 tennis courts; fitness center; Jacuzzi; sauna; solarium; room service; babysitting; laundry; dry cleaning. *In room:* TV, minibar, hair dryer, safe.

Hotel Schweizerhof ⚤ This recently enlarged hotel is a well-designed cross between a chalet and a mountain villa. The interior has some attractive antiques, oriental rugs, and beamed and paneled ceilings. The generally spacious rooms have terraces and lovely interiors; those in the newer wing are more up-to-date. Nonsmoking rooms are also rented, and some rooms are suitable for persons with disabilities. Management has tried to create the aura of a "living room" in the bedrooms, making you want to linger instead of using it just as a crash pad for the night. Of course, nothing in the room itself can compete with the private balcony overlooking the Steif or the imposing Kaiser Mountains. Bathrooms are medium in size, with shower-tub combinations. The hotel restaurant's food is Tyrolean and international, and the menu is varied and interesting. On some winter evenings, the public rooms seem more like a house party than a hotel. Summer brings tables and umbrellas out on the lawns. The hotel overlooks the children's ski school next to the Hahnenkamm cableway. It prides itself on its beauty and wellness center, which is very much a part of its allure.

Hahnenkammstrasse 4, A-6370 Kitzbühel. ✆ **05356/627-35.** Fax 05356/620-40-57. www.hotel-schweizer hof.at. 42 units. Winter 176€–226€ double, 204€–260€ suite for 2; summer 104€–192€ double, 124€–274€ suite for 2. Rates include half-board. AE, DC, MC, V. Closed Apr 5–May 18 and Oct–Dec 20. **Amenities:** Restaurant; bar; 18-hole golf course; health spa; Jacuzzi; sauna; room service; massage. *In room:* TV, hair dryer.

Hotel Zum Jägerwirt ⚤ The name of this place means "Hunter's Inn," and even if you don't like to hunt wild animals, you'll love the blazing fires and mellow paneling of this rustic, mellow hotel. The inn was indeed a hotel once catering to hunters, who are known in Austria for their appreciation of good food and atmosphere. The government-rated four-star hotel, 600 feet west of the town center, was recently enlarged and renovated. It has a bar area with hewn overhead beams. Double rooms are spacious and well furnished, while singles are rather small and might not be large enough to handle all your ski equipment. Heavy pine furniture, oriental rugs, and good beds make the place inviting, although time has taken its toll on the decor. Bathrooms are also small but have shower-tub combinations.

The hotel restaurant, Jägewirt, serves both Austrian and international specialties. In addition to an ample breakfast buffet, guests are treated in the evening to a large salad buffet, plus a bountiful dinner. The chef can cater to special diets.

Jochbergerstrasse 12, A-6370 Kitzbühel. ✆ **05356/698-10.** Fax 05356/640-67. www.hotel-jaegerwirt.at. 78 units. Winter 144€–246€ double, 242€–338€ suite for 2; summer 120€–176€ double, 206€–280€ suite for 2. Rates include half-board. AE, DC, MC, V. Parking garage 11€. Closed Apr–May and Oct–Dec 20. **Amenities:** Restaurant; bar; sauna; solarium; room service; massage; laundry; dry cleaning. *In room:* TV, minibar, hair dryer, safe.

Inexpensive
Gasthof Eggerwirt *(Value* Lying in Kitzbühel's lower altitudes, this lodging sits next to a gurgling alpine stream. Today country-baroque designs highlight the traditional stucco facade of a remodeled and much enlarged hotel, whose structure was actually built in 1658. Inside the Gasthof is clean, with well-maintained standards of simple, solid comfort in its rooms. Decor is rather functional, but all rooms have neatly kept bathrooms with shower-tub combinations; some rooms contain a private balcony. Considering the location, however, price is very good. There's a charming dining room (see "Where to Dine," below).

Goensbachgasse 12, A-6370 Kitzbühel. © **05356/624-55.** Fax 05356/62-43-722. www.eggerwirt-kitzbuehel.at. 20 units. Winter 96€–160€ double; summer 62€–100€ double. MC, V. Rates include breakfast. Closed Easter to May 20 and Nov. **Amenities:** Restaurant; bar. *In room:* TV, minibar, safe.

WHERE TO DINE

Many guests stay at Kitzbühel on the half-board plan. It's also fashionable to dine around, checking out the action at the various hotels. With one or two exceptions, most notably the Wirtshaws Uterberger-Stuben, all the best restaurants are in hotels.

Expensive

Hotel Restaurant Zur Tenne 🏔🏔 INTERNATIONAL   Large, elegantly paneled, and accented with a corner bar, this is one of the top restaurants of Kitzbühel. The light Tyrolean atmosphere invites you to relax and enjoy traditional dishes. A cooperative and polite young staff sees to your dining needs. Depending on the amount of sunlight streaming in, the most popular seating area is often the glass-sided extension. The restaurant's cachet and cuisine have improved dramatically in recent years. The delectable menu is likely to include carpaccio, a salad of juniper-smoked trout, filet of roast saddle of hare, medallions of venison, Hungarian goulash, and chateaubriand. A popular favorite is the Tenne special steak, served with Idaho baked potatoes and sour cream. A dessert specialty is an iced soufflé flavored with Grand Marnier.

Vorderstadt 8–10. © **05356/64-44-40.** Reservations recommended. Main courses 12€–28€. AE, DC, MC, V. Daily 11:30am–2pm and 6:30–10pm.

Restaurant Goldener Greif 🏔🏔 TYROLEAN   The setting is cozy and warm, and the cuisine is some of the best at the resort, with a menu that includes everything from a simple goulash to caviar. The dining room features vaulted ceilings, intricate paneling, ornamental ceramic stoves, 19th-century paintings, and, in some cases, views out over the base of some of Kitzbühel's busy cable cars. Menu items are savory and designed to satisfy appetites heightened by the bracing alpine climate. You might order veal steak with fresh vegetables, pepper steak Madagascar, or venison. Many kinds of grilled steaks are regularly featured. A "Vienna pot" is one of the chef's specials, and fresh Tyrolean trout is offered daily. Begin with a Serbian bean soup or decide on a fondue bourguignonne. All the meat, sausages, and smoked meat come from the hotel's own butcher.

Hinterstadt 24. © **05356/643-11.** Reservations recommended. Main courses 7€–30€. Fixed-price menu 18€–23€. AE, DC, MC, V. Daily 10am–2pm and 7–10pm. Closed mid-Apr to late May and mid-Oct to mid-Dec.

Romantik Hotel Tennerhof Restaurant 🏔🏔🏔 TYROLEAN   You'll walk a short distance from the town center before reaching this well-run hotel, which looks like a balconied hunting lodge. Rated by some critics as one of Austria's best restaurants, it has huge windows, whose view might give you pause between courses. House specialties include mushroom tarts, crayfish soufflé, tomato-cream soup, rabbit bouillon, saddle of lamb with polenta, veal medallions and asparagus, and, for dessert, curd-cheese dumplings and strawberries, freshly made sorbets, or a lemon soufflé that's renowned throughout the region. The kitchen staff is dedicated, talented, and hardworking, comfortable with both regional dishes and international specialties. You'll have a delightful time—and so will your palate.

Griesenauweg 26. © **05356/631-81.** Reservations required. Jacket required for men. Main courses 22€–26€. Fixed-price menus 45€–75€. AE, DC, MC, V. Daily noon–2pm and 7–9:30pm. Closed Oct–Dec 16 and Tues Mar–June and Apr–May 14.

Wirtshaus Unterberger-Stuben 🎯 INTERNATIONAL Throughout the 1980s and early 1990s, this was the preferred hangout for industry, media, and show-biz rich and famous. The stars of yesteryear long faded, the venue now attracts a scattering of lesser-known athletes, entwined couples, and hunters. Within a setting of old paintings and old paneling, you're likely to still be served a good meal—although the service has faded as well. If you see it on the menu, try a poppy-seed soufflé or any specialty from the many countries that once belonged to the Austrian Empire. The fresh fish and game are well prepared and savory. Dessert will feature (in summer) the succulent mountain berries of the region, or you might order the poached apples filled with white-chocolate mousse. The establishment is open for snacks, coffee, and drinks from 9am to midnight daily, except Tuesday in summer and the annual closings, but warm meals are served only during lunch and dinner hours.

Wehrgasse 2. ℂ 05356/661-27. Reservations recommended. Main courses 11€–25€; fixed-price menu 50€. V. Daily noon–1:30pm and 6–9:30pm. Closed June, Nov, and Tues in summer.

Moderate
The Dining Rooms in the Schloss Lebenberg 🎯 AUSTRIAN/INTERNA-
TIONAL Although this hotel offers comfortable rooms, we actually prefer the Schloss Lebenberg for its well-managed restaurant and its sense of history. Originally built in 1548, it was transformed in 1885 into Kitzbühel's first family-run hotel. Since then, the royal family of Monaco has graced the dining room, along with thousands of other lesser luminaries who have appreciated the savory cuisine. The most elegant of the hotel's three dining areas is the Gobelins Room, although the other dining rooms are equally appealing and a bit less intimidating. Always reliable specialties include cream of tomato soup with gin, Tyrolean-style calves' liver, Wiener schnitzels and roulades of beef, and many desserts, which often feature mountain berries.

Lebenbergstrasse 17. ℂ 05356/690-10. Reservations required. Main courses 11€–19€. AE, DC, MC, V. Daily noon–2pm and 6–9:30pm.

Florianistube *(Value* INTERNATIONAL/TYROLEAN Named after St. Florian, patron saint of the hearth, this restaurant is in one of the less ostentatious guest houses at the resort, and it welcomes outsiders. You dine in a cozy Tyrolean *Stube,* and the menu is comprehensive for such a *Gasthof*-type place—it might include typical Austrian or Tyrolean dishes, or tournedos with mushroom sauce, spaghetti with clam sauce, or fondue bourguignonne. Cooking is reliable and the ingredients are fresh, but don't expect a lot of imagination from the kitchen staff or finesse in the service rituals. In summer, a lunch or dinner buffet is served outside under the trees of the rear garden.

In the Gasthof Eggerwirt, Goensbachgasse 12. ℂ 05356/624-37. Reservations recommended. Main courses 8€–20€. AE, MC, V. Daily 11am–2pm and 6–10pm.

KITZBÜHEL AFTER DARK
If you're lucky enough to be in Kitzbühel during July or August, you can schedule your nightly promenade to coincide with the open-air concerts that begin every Tuesday, Thursday, and Friday at 8:30pm. Musicians position themselves against one edge of the Vorderstadt, whose edges are sealed off against motorized traffic. The result is an open-air all-pedestrian party with lots of folkloric and alpine overtones. Expect alpine folk music every Tuesday and Friday, and a venue of more international music (Dixieland or free-form jazz, or perhaps a New Orleans–style blues concert) every Thursday.

A Cafe: The Hottest Rendezvous Spot

Even before night falls, people make a mad dash for a seat at **Café Praxmair,** Vorderstadt (℡ **05356/62646**). One of the most famous pastry shops in Austria, it's known for its florentine cookies. Later in the evening, the Praxmair Keller offers the town's most permissive nightlife. It remains open all night, summer and winter. But if it's before 5 o'clock, the item to order is hot chocolate with a "top hat" of whipped cream. Coffee costs from 2€; pastries go for 1.60€ to 2.30€. The cafe is open daily from 10am to 1am; the cellar bar is open daily from 10pm to dawn.

Even if you arrive whenever a concert isn't scheduled, you can always enjoy Kitzbühel's collection of nightlife and drinking options, most of which line either edge of the resort's two most central avenues, Vorderstadt and Hinterstadt. A site whose decor you might immediately recognize as inspired by 1950s America (it contains an antique car and a replica of an old-fashioned gasoline station you might have found in a rural backwater of Tennessee) is **Highways Pub,** Im Gries 20 (℡ **05356/753-50**). A watering hole with a theme like that of a Victorian pub is **The Londoner,** Franz-Reisch-Strasse 4 (℡ **05356/714-28**), where old-fashioned paneling and hot music sometimes have late-night clients up and dancing on the tables. Two conventional discos, both of which are usually brimming with high-altitude energy, include **Royal Dancing,** Hinterstadt 9 (℡ **05356/75901**) and its almost equivalent nearby neighbor, **Olympic Disco,** Hinterstadt 6 (℡ **05356/721-43**). A more glamorous address, with a more aggressive policy about screening rowdies from the lines that sometimes form on weekends, is **Take Five Disco,** Hinterstadt 22 (℡ **05356/741-31**). Here, within a mostly black and artfully lit interior, you'll find one of the biggest settings for a disco in town.

In winter, every Thursday from 5:30pm to around 1am, the **Alpenhotel am Schwarzee** (℡ **05356/642-54**) sponsors live music that usually transforms the place into a fun and convivial dance. Admission is free at this party, held about 1¼ miles northwest of Kitzbühel's center, beside the lake.

Gatlo Bello, Hinterstadt 9 (℡ **05356/670-17**), is a popular rendezvous. Inside are two bars and good music from several different eras. If you're hungry, you can order homemade Hungarian goulash or Italian pasta. The drink list favors such tropical concoctions as planter's punch and piña coladas; five intriguing cocktails are made from champagne. Beer begins at 2.70€; drinks start at 5€. It's open daily from 4pm to 2:30am; however, on certain nights, especially in wintertime when there's a big crowd, it might close just before breakfast.

More than virtually any other watering hole in Kitzbühel, **Heurigenstadel Goldene Gams,** Vorderstadt (℡ **05356/666-80**), succeeds at emulating the nostalgic, old-fashioned aura of a Viennese *Heurige,* a wine house where schmaltz and laughter evoke the old days of the Austro-Hungarian Empire. The folkloric decor encourages a sense of community among the people who come here to drink, gossip, order wine, and listen, when it's provided, to zither music. It sells platters of hearty food for 6€ to 15€; carafes of wine begin at 3€. It's open daily from 9am to midnight (sometimes a bit later during midwinter).

Local residents who want to escape too constant a diet of evergreen music and ski-related raucousness head for the cool and quiet enclaves of Kitzbühel's most appealing piano bar, **The Piano Place,** in the Hotel Tennerhof, Griesenauweg

26 (© **05356/631-81**). It features live music in winter (Dec–Apr) every Wednesday through Sunday from 6pm to midnight; and in summer (late June to late Aug) every Thursday through Sunday during the same hours. Whisky with soda costs 6€, beer costs 3.50€, and the music is very, very drinkable.

A CASINO

Casino Kitzbühel   Although it offers a less ambitious roster of entertainment options than it did in years gone by, this remains the only (legal) gambling venue in Kitzbühel. You'll be required to show a passport before entering, after which you can wander among machines and croupiers devoted to roulette, blackjack, baccarat, poker, and the endless jangle of slot machines. There's also a bar on-site, where you might eventually search out a perch for the observation of the sometimes-sleepy gambling action at the tables.

It's open only about 6 months out of the year, from July 1 to mid-September, and from about a week before Christmas to the end of March. During those periods, it opens nightly at 7pm, and there's never any set closing time. Unlike some other Austrian casinos, men are not required to wear jackets or ties. In the Hotel Goldener Greif, Hinterstadt 24. © **05356/62300**. 20€ buys 25€ of welcome chips.

ST. JOHANN IN TYROL

St. Johann has neither the chic reputation nor the high prices of Kitzbühel. You'll save money if you stay here and go to Kitzbühel, 10km (6 miles) to the south, to enjoy the facilities there.

GETTING THERE   One **train** per hour (some express) arrives in St. Johann by way of Kitzbühel from Innsbruck (trip time: 1¼ hr.) and Salzburg (trip time: 2¾ hr.). Some trains from Salzburg require a transfer in the railway junction of Schwarzach–St. Veit. You can also take one of the half-dozen **buses** that run every day between St. Johann and Kitzbühel (30 min.). For **bus** or **train information** in Kitzbühel, call © **05356/640-55**. Buses also pull into St. Johann from Salzburg several times a day, stopping first at Kitzbühel (trip time: 1¾ hr.).

St. Johann lies 399km (248 miles) west of Vienna, 90km (56 miles) east of Innsbruck, and 90km (56 miles) southwest of Munich. If you're **driving** from Innsbruck, follow the A12 east to the junction with Route 312, which you take east to St. Johann.

VISITOR INFORMATION   The **tourist office**, Poststrasse 2 (© **05352/63335**; www.st.johann.tirol.at), in the town center, is open Monday through Friday from 8:30am to noon and 2 to 6:30pm, and Saturday from 9 am to noon.

EXPLORING ST. JOHANN

Lying between two mountains, the **Wilder Kaiser** and the **Kitzbüheler Horn,** this village is both a summer vacation center and a winter ski resort. In summer, it has a busy open-air swimming pool, and in winter, the good ski runs appeal to both beginners and experts. A ski school and ski kindergarten, plus cross-country ski trails, add to the attractions. Bars in the snow are also popular.

Many old Tyrolean houses fill the little town with charm, and some of the traditional inns have frescoed exteriors.

The Kaisergebirge, near St. Johann, also draws many mountain climbers.

WHERE TO STAY

Gasthof Post 🏱   Gasthof Post, in the town center adjacent to the village church, is about as solid a building as you'll find in Tyrol. It was first constructed in 1224, and parts of its original wooden ceiling beams are still in place. The interior is replete with stone and wood columns and bucolic charm. Rooms range from large to intimately small and are well furnished with good beds and small private bathrooms with shower-tub combinations; many open onto balconies. There's a large dining room for hotel guests and an a la carte restaurant with main courses ranging from 6€ to 17€.

Speckbacherstrasse 1, A-6380 St. Johann in Tirol. ℂ **05352/622-30.** Fax 05352/62-23-03. www.hotel-post.tv. 45 units. Winter 12€–150€ double; summer 66€–86€ double. Rates include half-board. AE, DC, MC, V. Closed Apr and Nov 16–Dec 18. **Amenities:** 3 restaurants; bar; pool; massage; room service; babysitting. *In room:* TV.

Hotel Fischer   In the village center, this solidly built four-story chalet was erected in 1972 with wooden balconies and a sun terrace framed by cascading vines. The sunny rooms are comfortable and cozy, although in some cases they're a bit on the small side. All have tiny bathrooms with shower-tub combinations. Housekeeping rates an A. The elaborately paneled dining room is open only to hotel residents, a fact that permeates it with the atmosphere of a private club. The Grander family, which renovated the hotel in 1997, is helpful and glad to point out nearby bars and clubs that might supplement the diversions available within the house cocktail lounge.

Kaiserstrasse 3, A-6380 St. Johann in Tirol. ℂ **05352/623-32.** Fax 05352/651-68. www.hotel-fischer.at. 36 units. Winter 104€–133€ double, 144€–164€ suite; summer 79€–120€ double, 124€–144€ suite. Rates include half-board. AE, DC, MC, V. **Amenities:** Dining room; bar; fitness center; sauna. *In room:* TV, hair dryer.

Hotel Park 𝕘 *Kids*   Well scrubbed and appealing, this modern, government-rated four-star hotel made few attempts to emulate the chalet-style architecture of many of its competitors when it was built in 1973. The result is an angular, well-accessorized hotel that's among the least expensive, with a hardworking family-derived staff. Skiers appreciate its easy access to the lifts, close to the larger of the town's two gondola stations. Most rooms look out over either the ski slopes or the mountains; the others overlook a pleasant garden. All have a cozy, warm feeling, although they are not overly large; each has a well-kept bathroom with a shower-tub combination. Our favorite feature in the sitting room is the copper-sheathed bonnet over the fireplace, built into a corner of two stucco walls. There's an attractive restaurant, The Park, serving Tyrolean and Austrian dishes. In summer, guests gravitate to the beer garden. The hotel is a good choice for families because it has a playground, and a supply of bicycles and mountain bikes is on hand.

Spechbacherstrasse 45, A-6380 St. Johann in Tirol. ℂ **05352/622-26.** Fax 05352/62-22-66. www.park.at. 54 units. Winter 126€–164€ double; summer 88€–104€ double. Rates include half-board. AE, DC, MC, V. Closed mid-Oct to mid-Dec and late Mar to late May. **Amenities:** Restaurant; bar; pool; sauna; bike rentals; playground; room service; babysitting. *In room:* TV, hair dryer, safe.

WHERE TO DINE
La Rustica ITALIAN   The decor and setting are solidly elegant yet rustic, a play on both the restaurant's name and its position within a building from the 1850s in the center of the resort. But unlike many restaurants, its menu incorporates a wider-than-expected gamut of food that includes 2 dozen kinds of pizzas, about 20 kinds of main-course pastas, and about 20 hearty meat dishes that go well with the bracing alpine air. Most are inspired by the culinary tenets of northern (usually alpine) Italy, with the exception of a pizza Margherita, whose simple tomato-with-basil-and-garlic ingredients derive from pure Neapolitan

models. Desserts are made on the premises. The clientele seems about evenly divided in its preference for either Chianti or beer.

Spechbacherstrasse 31. ℂ 05352/628-43. Reservations recommended. Main courses 9€–30€. AE, DC, MC, V. Thurs–Tues 11am–2pm and 5pm–midnight. Closed Apr and Oct.

9 East Tyrol ★★★

East Tyrol is not geographically connected to North Tyrol. When South Tyrol was ceded to Italy in 1919 in the aftermath of World War I, East Tyrol was cut off from the rest of the province by a narrow projection of Italian land that borders Land Salzburg.

Italy, including what used to be South Tyrol, lies to the south and west, with Land Salzburg to the north and Carinthia to the east. The little subprovince, of which Lienz is the capital, is cut off from its neighbors on the north by seemingly impenetrable Alps. East Tyrol is known as Östtirol in German.

Because of its isolated position, East Tyrol tends to be neglected by the average North American tourist, which is a shame. The grandeur of its scenery and the warm hospitality of its people make it worth visiting. It's crowned by the towering peaks of the **Lienz Dolomites** ★★, which invite exploration. The scenery along the **Drau** and the **Isel** valleys is spectacular. These two main valleys have many little side hollows worth exploring, especially the **Virgental.** You'll see alpine pastureland, meadows, relatively undiscovered valleys, and beautiful lakes.

The Romans occupied East Tyrol in ancient times. Later the Slavs moved into the area as settlers and made it a section of Carinthia. It has known many rulers, from the Bavarians to the French. Even Great Britain had a hand in running things here, when the Allies made East Tyrol a part of the British-occupied sector of Austria from 1945 to 1955.

Since 1967, it has been possible to reach East Tyrol by taking the 5km-long (3-mile) **Felbertauern Tunnel,** a western route through the Alps. If you're driving, you can come from the east or the west. From the **Grossglockner Road,** you take the Felbertauern Road and the tunnel. If you're driving from the north to Lienz, East Tyrol's capital, you can take the Felbertauern Road from Land Salzburg, passing through the tunnel. In summer, you might want to take the Grossglockner Road and the Iselberg Pass. This road runs along the boundary between East Tyrol and Carinthia.

It's also possible to take a train from Italy to East Tyrol. Corridor trains operate between Innsbruck and Lienz as well. As you pass through Italy on this trip, the trains are locked and you don't have to show your passport or clear Italian Customs.

Wood carving, long a pursuit in East Tyrol, is still practiced in tranquil chalets during the long winter months. You might want to shop for some pieces while you're here.

LIENZ ★

Don't confuse this city with Linz, the capital of Upper Austria. This **Lienz,** with an *e,* is the capital of East Tyrol. It sits at the junction of three valleys—the Isel to the northwest, the Puster to the west, and the Drau to the east. The old town of Lienz stretches along the banks of the Isel River, with Liebburg Palace, a 16th-century building, now the seat of local government, overshadowing Hauptplatz (Main Square).

GETTING THERE   From Innsbruck, Lienz-bound travelers can take the direct **Korridorzug train,** which involves no border formalities with Italy. The **Val Pusteria** is another connection, going via Italian territory to Lienz (trip time: 3½ hr.). From Salzburg, you'll have to change trains in the rail junction at **Spittal-Millstättersee** (3½ hr.). The **railway station** can be reached by calling © **05/1717.**

A confusing array of **buses** travels among the various villages of East Tyrol. One daily bus, after many stops, travels to Lienz from Innsbruck, and another travels from Zell am See. For **bus information** in Lienz, call © **04858/64944.**

From Kitzbühel (see section 8, above), you can **drive** to Lienz by traveling southeast along Route 161, which becomes Route 108. From Salzburg, take the A10 southeast to the junction with Route 100 near Seeboden and follow the signs west to Lienz. Lienz lies 434km (270 miles) southwest of Vienna, 180km (112 miles) south of Salzburg, and 222km (138 miles) southeast of Munich.

VISITOR INFORMATION   The **tourist office,** Europaplatz (© **04852/652-65;** www.tiscover.com/lienz), is open Monday through Friday from 8am to 7pm, and Saturday from 9am to noon and 5 to 7pm.

OUTDOOR ACTIVITIES

In winter, Lienz, at an elevation of 869m (2,850 ft.), attracts skiers to its two major ski areas: the **Hochstein** and the **Zertersfeld,** serviced by chairlifts and drag lifts. The height of the top station is 2,204m (7,225 ft.).

In summer, the town fills up with mountain climbers, mainly Austrians, who come to scale the Dolomites. This is a good base for many excursions in the area. For example, from Schlossberg you can take a chairlift up to **Venedigerwarte** (1,017m/3,335 ft.). You can explore the excavations of **Aguntum,** the Roman settlement, 5km (3 miles) east of Lienz, or swim in **Lake Tristacher,** 5km (3 miles) south of the city.

The Dolomites, actually the northwestern part of the Gailtal alpine range, lie between the Gail Valley and the Drau Valley: Their highest peak is the **Grosse Sandspitze** at more than 2,745m (9,000 ft.).

EXPLORING LIENZ

Schloss Bruck (Bruck Castle) and Osttiroler Heimatmuseum (Museum of East Tyrol)   The showcase of Lienz, and the focal point of its civic pride, is this former stronghold of the counts of Gorz, who controlled vast medieval estates from this strategically located castle that dominated most of the access routes to the Isel Valley. In the early 1500s, it fell to the Hapsburgs. It rises impressively about a half mile west of the town center and contains a museum devoted to the history, culture, sociology, and artifacts of the region. The **Rittersaal (Knight's Hall)** shows how the castle looked in the Middle Ages. The **Albin Egger-Lienz gallery** contains an art collection of the outstanding native painter Egger-Lienz (1868–1926). Another section displays artifacts unearthed at the archaeological site of the Roman town of Aguntum.

Iseltaler Strasse. © **04852/625-80.** Admission 7€ adults, 5€ students and seniors, 4€ children under 16. Easter to Nov 1 daily 10am–6pm; June 15–Sept until 6pm. Closed Nov–Apr.

St. Andrä (Church of St. Andrew)   If you have time, visit this church with its outstanding collection of 16th-century tombstones carved of marble quarried outside Salzburg. The last Gorz count is buried here. The church, consecrated in 1457, was restored in 1968. During the restoration, workmen uncovered murals, some dating from the 14th century. The church is the finest example of

Gothic architecture in East Tyrol. A **memorial chapel** honors the Lienz war dead. The renowned painter Egger-Lienz, mentioned above, is entombed here. Patriasdorfer Strasse. Free admission. Daily 9am–5pm.

SHOPPING

More energy seems to be devoted to folkloric clothing in Lienz than to virtually any other product in town. Consequently, you'll find lots of outlets scattered throughout the tourist zone, two of the best of which are **Oberhueber,** Johannesplatz 7–9 (© **04852/621-48**), and **Krismer,** André-Kranz-Gasse 4 (© **04852/624-97**). Either store has stacks of old-fashioned clothes (dirndls, lederhosen, loden coats, alpine hats with pheasants' feathers, embroidered suspenders, or whatever) that correspond to East Tyrolean traditions. And if you're hankering for a sampling of the local breads, cheeses, sausages, and *Bundnerfleisch* (air-dried alpine beef that's reminiscent of beef jerky), consider dropping into any of the well-stocked local delicatessens, a particularly worthwhile example of which is **Feinkost Zuegg,** Rechteiselkai (© **04852/66-99-30**).

WHERE TO STAY

Gasthof Goldener Fisch 🔆 *(Value*   Set within 600 feet of Lienz's center, this old-fashioned government-rated three-star hotel occupies what was originally built as the private home of a prosperous landowner in the 1880s. Today its ochre-beige facade remains basically the same as when it was originally erected, with jutting bay windows that the owners festoon with flowers throughout the summer. The ambience is pleasantly dowdy, matter-of-fact, and unpretentious. Rooms are old-fashioned and the beds are a bit soft, but housekeeping is good and the comfort level is fairly high. Bathrooms are small, with shower stalls. A cafe and restaurant serve traditional platters of food, coffee, and drinks daily from 7am to midnight. Meals have been served to virtually everyone in town at one time or another.

Kärtnerstrasse 9, A-9900 Lienz. © **04852/621-32.** Fax 04852/689-48. Goldfisch@magnet.at. 35 units. 66€–72€ double. Rates include buffet breakfast. MC, V. Closed Nov. **Amenities:** Restaurant; bar; sauna. *In room:* TV, hair dryer.

Gasthof-Hotel Haidenhof   This appealing hotel looks like a cross between an alpine chalet and a Mediterranean villa. The windows of the hotel's central section are bordered with painted Tyrolean designs, whereas on either side symmetrical wings stretch toward the surrounding forest. Views from the balconies of the well-furnished rooms encompass most of Lienz. Rooms are exceedingly comfortable, if a bit old-fashioned, with beautifully maintained small bathrooms with shower-tub combinations. On the premises are a sun terrace and a paneled restaurant serving regional specialties.

Grafendorferstrasse 12, A-9900 Lienz. © **04852/624-40.** Fax 04852/62-44-06. hotel.haidenhof@tirol.com. 25 units. 70€–95€ double. Rates include breakfast. Half-board 10€ per person extra. MC, V. Closed mid-Oct to mid-Dec. Drive 10 min. north of Lienz to the suburb of Gaimberg. **Amenities:** Restaurant; bar; lounge; sauna. *In room:* TV, hair dryer.

Hotel Post   This small-scale, family-run inn has a history of welcoming passersby that dates from the 1400s, when it functioned as an inn sheltering merchants and traders negotiating the mountain pathways. Today it's a calm, respectable, not terribly expensive hotel that decided several years ago to abandon the food and beverage business completely, except for the generous breakfast buffets. A small lobby leads into a garden with cafe tables in back. Your hosts, members of the Kranz and Lederer families, will welcome you whole-heartedly. This is a reasonably priced, reasonably comfortable, government-rated three-star hotel, less glamorous than the Romantik Hotel Traube (see below). Rooms are charming and cozy, equipped with small bathrooms containing shower-tub combinations. Each has been renovated in slow increments throughout the '90s.

Südtirolerplatz 7, A-9900 Lienz. ℰ **04852/625-05.** Fax 04852/625-05-50. 18 units. 67€–72€ double. Rates include breakfast. AE, DC, MC, V. **Amenities:** Breakfast room; bar; lounge. *In room:* TV.

Hotel Sonne   This hotel's modernized mansard roof rises from one end of Südtirolerplatz. In addition to a helpful staff, the hotel has terra-cotta floors, oriental rugs, a roof garden, and a sun-flooded restaurant with an outdoor terrace. The reservations system is tied in to the Best Western network. The cozy rooms have modern furniture and good beds. Bathrooms are small but come with shower-tub combinations. The hotel maintains a very good restaurant, the Restaurant Sonne, open daily from 11am to 2pm and 6 to 10pm. Main courses are 10€ to 25€.

Südtirolerplatz, A-9900 Lienz. ℰ **800/528-1234** in the U.S., or 04852/633-11. Fax 04852/633-14. www.hotelsonnelienz.at. 62 units. 106€–136€ double. Rates include breakfast. Half-board 15€ per person extra. AE, DC, MC, V. Free parking outside; garage parking 8€. **Amenities:** Restaurant; bar, sauna; solarium; room service; laundry; dry cleaning. *In room:* TV, minibar, hair dryer.

Romantik Hotel Traube 𝕬𝕬𝕬   This hotel's location, in the very center of town on a tree-lined street, couldn't be more ideal. The facade is painted a vivid red, with forest-green shutters and a canopy covering part of the ground-level cafe. Furnishings in the public areas are elegant and comfortable. The hotel was demolished in World War II but rebuilt in the 1950s. Rooms contain either antique furnishings or copies of traditional pieces. The comfort level is greater here than anywhere else in East Tyrol. Beds are luxurious and the bathrooms come in a range of sizes, all nicely maintained and equipped with shower-tub combinations. Many windows open onto views of the nearby mountains. On the premises are a well-furnished bar and two restaurants. One restaurant is quite formal (see below); the other, less expensive one offers Italian food.

Hauptplatz, A-9900 Lienz. ℰ **04852/644-44.** Fax 04852/641-84. www.tiscover.at/romantikhotel-traube. 51 units. 108€–168€ per person double. Rates include breakfast. AE, DC, MC, V. **Amenities:** 2 restaurants; bar; pool; sauna; room service; babysitting; laundry; dry cleaning. *In room:* TV, minibar, hair dryer, safe.

WHERE TO DINE

Romantik Hotel Traube 𝕬   AUSTRIAN/TYROLEAN/ITALIAN   Amid Tyrolean accents of flowered banquettes, gilded wall sconces, and big arched windows, this airy restaurant offers elegant meals in comfortable surroundings. The cuisine here is the best in town, based on fresh ingredients deftly handled in the kitchen. Menu items run an artful line between experimental new dishes and tried-and-true Tyrolean favorites. Examples include a terrine of smoked salmon with a honey-mustard sauce, an autumn salad that's dressed with olive oil and air-dried chunks of smoked lamb, filet of venison wrapped in bacon with potato terrine and brussels sprouts, and braised joint of lamb with a gratin of leeks and braised vegetables. A fish dish that's considered a delicacy of the house, despite the unappetizing translation of its name, is frogfish (*Seeteufel*) served on a bed of stewed tomatoes with risotto.

Hauptplatz 14. ℰ **04852/644-44.** Reservations required. Main courses 6€–20€; fixed-price menu 14€. AE, DC, MC, V. Daily 11am–2pm and 6–9:30pm. Closed Nov 1–Dec 22.

LIENZ AFTER DARK

No one ever seems to get thirsty in Lienz, where virtually every hotel and guest-house has a gemütlich-looking *Stube* lined with varnished pine that's ready, willing, and eager to dispense steins of beer and East Tyrolean folklore. But if you're interested in equivalent bars that play disco music where you might conceivably get up and dance, consider the **Stadtkeller,** Tiroler Strasse 30 (© **04852/628-52**), a site favored by patrons under 30, or the somewhat more dignified **Dolomitenkeller,** within the Dolomitenhotel, Dolomitenstrasse 2 (© **04852/629-62**). Both feature a woodsy, alpine-derived decor where dozens of steins of beer have been spilled over the years, and both have been known to extend the dancing even onto the tabletops. A disco with a different, Milanese-modern decor and a somewhat more international outlook is the **Joy Bar,** Hauptplatz 9 (© **04852/672-22**). Cover at all three is 5€ to 7€, which includes the first drink. Each is open nightly from around 8:30pm.

Incidentally, if your visit to Lienz happens to fall between early July and late September, at least part of your evening entertainment will be free. Every Saturday, Sunday, and Wednesday, beginning at 8pm, the city sponsors a 75-minute concert of traditional Tyrolean music, performed by musicians in *Trachten* (traditional Tyrolean garb), from a perch within the **Hauptplatz.** The only problem with these love fests of Tyrolean nostalgia is that they simply don't last long enough.

The second weekend in August in Lienz is the scheduled time for **Stadtfest,** a public celebration of the contributions of Lienz to East Tyrolean culture. Expect kiosks scattered throughout the town's historic center selling food, wine, beer, and enough sausages to ring the city. There's also an ongoing series of afternoon and evening concerts by singers and musicians in folkloric garb, warbling away, a la Maria von Trapp, their odes to Tyrolean nostalgia.

11

Vorarlberg

Austria's westernmost province is Vorarlberg, a land of mountain villages, lakes, deep valleys, and meadowlands. In autumn, one of the most beautiful spots on the continent is the plain of the Rhine Valley near Dornbirn. This region is Switzerland in miniature, and there are things to do here year-round. The three biggest attractions are the ski slopes that rival Switzerland's, the gorgeous Lake Constance, and the lush forests of the Bregenzerwald. The region's two best-known tourist centers, Lech and Zürs, are very expensive, but prices in the rest of the province are quite reasonable.

Vorarlberg's mountains make for great skiing, and slopes are linked together, offering miles and miles of trails. The Bregenz Forest, on the northern part of the Vorarlberg alpine range, has every bit as much charm and character as the Black Forest.

Two annual special events take place in Vorarlberg during the summer: the Music Festival at Hohenems, in the second half of June, which focuses on the works of Franz Schubert; and the Bregenz operas, presented on a large stage floating in Lake Constance.

From Tyrol, you head west to reach Vorarlberg: There's no better gateway to the province than either Zürs or Lech, which are both on Route 198, north of the Arlberg Tunnel. Parking in the Vorarlberg region is rarely a problem, and, unless otherwise noted, you park for free.

1 The Western Side of the Arlberg

We visited the east side of Arlberg in chapter 10 on Innsbruck and Tyrol, so it's time for us to tell you the "west side story" of this massif that separates Vorarlberg from Tyrol. This part of Austria is one of the major winter-sports meccas in Europe. The leading resorts on the Arlberg massif, the highest mountain range in the Lechtal Alps, include **Lech** and **Zürs**. With an **Arlberg ski pass,** you can use the 88 ski tows, chairlifts, and cable cars located in the entire Arlberg region.

Up through the **Flexen Pass,** you come to Zürs, a chic, elegant, refined resort with skiing at **Trittkoph** and **Mahdloch.** Lech is larger, with easier skiing on the **Kriegerhorn** and **Mohnenfluh.**

SKIING IN ZÜRS & LECH   Part of the Vorarlberg's popularity stems from its two most visible and stylish resorts, **Zürs** and **Lech.** Both resorts boast lofty altitudes that are high even by central European ski-resort standards; they enjoy access to more than 1,000m (3,280 ft.) of skiable hillside above Lech and almost

---

Did You Know?
Local legend has it that Vorarlberg—not Mount Ararat in the Middle East—is where Noah landed with his ark after the flood waters receded.

702m (2,300 ft.) of carefully maintained hillsides above Zürs, where midwinter snows accumulate in deep billowing drifts.

Zürs boasts straight downhill runs that have tested the skills of Olympic champions, as well as gracefully sculpted runs that pass rocky outcrops and copses of trees. Lech, positioned in the center of a roster of north- and east-facing bowls and slopes, offers a greater number of ski options that challenge intermediate skiers as well as the experts. Although they are competing resorts, Zürs and Lech cooperate with each other. Chances are that the ski pass you buy will allow you access to the slopes and chairlifts of both resorts.

The 20km (12½ miles) of ski trails running between the two resorts offer experiences on four different mountains, and there's enough variety to qualify the area as one of the most exciting ski transits in Austria. If there are complaints about the resorts (and they certainly don't involve a lack of snow), it's only because you have to ski back into one of the villages for lunch: Dining options on the slopes are limited.

Snowboarding in the Arlberg

Snowboarding techniques are taught at each of the ski schools in Arlberg's resorts. Shredders have free access to all of the region's slopes, and Lech even has several slopes that allow *only* snowboarders.

Favorite ski venues around Lech include the **Kriegerhorn** and the less-popular **Rüfikopf,** which has perilously steep slopes and is subject to avalanche danger after snowstorms. In Zürs, the best skiing lies to the east of the resort, in regions known as the **Hexenboden** and the **Trittkopf,** but because of the morning glare, these slopes are most appealing in the afternoon. Morning skiers usually head out to the **Seekopf** and **Zürsersee** areas, or the slopes running downhill from the **Muggengrat chairlift.**

Regardless of the resort you select, trails are usually impeccably groomed, the evening après-ski venues are the most stylish in Austria, and the Vorarlberg's scenery is among the most appealing in the world.

Zürs, Lech, and the nearby ski resort Oberlech are linked by 34 lifts (the whole region has 88 lifts), all of which can be traveled on only one ski pass. Lifts and runs are close together, and it's possible to ski between Lech and Zürs. A cable car, running daily from 7am to 1am, connects Oberlech to the heart of Lech: You can take a cable car from the heart of the resort to **Rüfikopf** (2,329m/7,635 ft.).

LECH ☆☆

Founded in the 14th century by émigrés from the Valais district of Switzerland, Lech still has its original *Pfarrkirche* (parish church) from that era. This archetype of a snug alpine ski village is practically joined to Oberlech, a satellite resort a little farther up the mountain. Lech stands at 1,443m (4,730 ft.); Oberlech is at 1,708m (5,600 ft.).

Zürs is more fashionable, but Lech has its own claim to fame: It played host to Prince Charles and his future wife, Princess Diana. Despite its reputation as a ski resort, Lech offers some great warm-weather activities, too. In summer, visitors come here to tour the **Upper Lech Valley,** which stretches for 56km (35 miles) to a scenic valley between the Lechtal and the Allgäu Alps.

Regardless of which resort you stay in, we suggest that you go to Oberlech on a sunny day and find yourself a spot in one of the big sun-terrace restaurants.

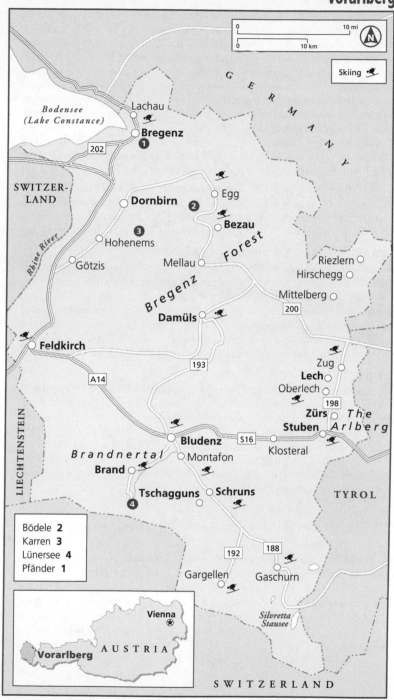

Vorarlberg

0   10 mi

0   10 km

Skiing

G E R M A N Y

Bodensee
(Lake Constance)

Lachau

Bregenz ❶

202

SWITZER-
LAND

Egg

Dornbirn ❷

Bezau

❸

Hohenems

Mellau

Bregenz Forest

Riezlern ○

Hirschegg ○

Götzis

Mittelberg ○

200

Damüls ○

Rhine River

Feldkirch ○

193

Zug ○

Lech ○

Oberlech ○

198

Zürs ○   *The*

Stuben   *Arlberg*

A14

Klosteral

Bludenz

S16

Brandnertal

○ Montafon

Brand

LIECHTENSTEIN

Tschagguns ○   **Schruns**

❹

TYROL

Bödele   **2**
Karren   **3**
Lünersee   **4**
Pfänder   **1**

192

188

Gargellen

Gaschurn

Silvretta
Stausee

Vienna
⊛

A U S T R I A

Vorarlberg

S W I T Z E R L A N D

407

GETTING THERE Set in the upper regions of the Arlberg Pass, Lech has no railway connections. Visitors are best advised to take the **train** to the rail stations at either end of the Arlberg Tunnel and then transfer to a bus that winds its way up the mountain passes to Lech. Passengers from either Vorarlberg or Tyrol should get off at Langen am Arlberg, the closest station to Lech. All Zurich–Vienna express trains stop here. Passengers then transfer to one of the half-dozen daily **buses** that depart for Lech (trip time: 25 min.). For bus information and schedules, call either the Lech tourist office (below) or the **Lech Post Office** (© 05583/22-40).

Lech is 90km (56 miles) southeast of Bregenz, 648km (403 miles) west of Vienna, and 200km (124 miles) east of Zurich. If you're **driving** from Tyrol, take Route 198 north after you pass through the Arlberg Tunnel.

VISITOR INFORMATION The **tourist office** (© 05583/216-10) is in the town center. It's open in winter Monday through Saturday from 9am to 6:30pm, Sunday from 10am to noon and 3 to 5pm; in summer Monday through Saturday from 8am to noon and 2 to 6:30pm, Sunday from 8am to noon and 3 to 5pm.

WARM-WEATHER EXPEDITIONS

From Mid-June to mid-September, Lech offers an **Activ-Inclusiv Program.** As part of this program, any hotel guest in Lech gains automatic free access to the five cable cars that run in the summer, the tennis courts, and the indoor pool. Daily guided hikes (of various difficulties) covering 5km to 11km (3–7 miles) are also included in the program. For more difficult rock-climbing excursions using rocks, pitons, and crampons, call **Herr Herbert** (© 05583/26-66), a guide who supervises the training at a local rock-climbing garden (*Klettergarten*).

SHOPPING

Most of the shops in Lech line the resort's main thoroughfare, the **Hauptstrasse,** and all steadfastly refuse to identify themselves with an individual street number. Lech offers sporting equipment from almost every important manufacturer in Europe. Three of the most impressive shops include **Sportalp** (© 05583/21-10), **Sporthaus Strolz** (© 05583/23-61), and **Pfefferkorn** (© 05583/22-24), all on Hauptstrasse. If you're interested in souvenirs or folkloric clothing, both Sporthaus Strolz and Pfefferkorn offer Austrian handcrafts, lederhosen, and traditional Austrian clothing.

WHERE TO STAY IN LECH

Hotel Berghof (see "Where to Dine in Lech," below) also rents rooms.

Very Expensive

Gasthof Post 𝄞𝄞𝄞 Queen Beatrix of the Netherlands has frequently visited this establishment, but even without its royal clientele, it's the noblest hotel in town. Behind the hotel's chalet facade ornamented with trompe-l'oeil murals, the Moosbrugger family displays many 18th-century items, including alpine painted chests and baroque sculpture. Rooms come in a variety of sizes, but all contain rustic decorations, double-glazed windows, beamed ceilings, excellent beds, and fine bathrooms with shower-tub combinations.

The hotel's convivial gathering places include a popular sun terrace and several bars. Zither and Austrian folk music are often presented in the peak winter months. Credit cards are accepted for dining, but not in the hotel.

Dorf 11, A-6764 Lech. © 05583/220-60. Fax 05583/22-06-23. info@postlech.com. 39 units. Winter 360€–650€ double, 520€–800€ suite; summer 190€–350€ double, 340€–400€ suite. Rates include half-board. AE, MC, V. Closed late Apr to mid-June and late Sept to Nov 30. Parking 10€. **Amenities:** 2 restaurants; bar;

pool; fitness center; health spa; Jacuzzi; sauna; room service; massage; babysitting; laundry; dry cleaning. *In room:* TV, minibar, hair dryer, safe.

Hotel Kristiania   The most advanced skiers are often attracted to this tranquil retreat because it was built by the family of Othmar Schneider, the Olympic ski champion. The many amenities here make this a worthy government-rated four-star hotel. Rooms facing south have balconies and mountain views, while north-facing rooms have views of the village and the valley, but no balconies. Bathrooms are well maintained and contain shower-tub combinations and robes.

The Kristiania is a 3- to 5-minute walk above the resort's center. Most guests leave their ski equipment at the Skiraum in the center of town, where someone will wax their skis for the following day, so that they don't have to lug them uphill to the hotel.

The hotel contains a restaurant for half-board guests, and another one for a la carte diners who call and reserve a table. Austrian and international cuisine is served.

A-6764 Lech. ℂ **05583/256-10.** Fax 05583/3550. www.kristiania.at. 34 units. 300€–480€ double; 410€–1,400€ suite. Rates include half-board. AE, DC, MC, V. Closed Apr 20–Dec 1. Parking 15€. **Amenities:** 2 restaurants; bar; pool; Jacuzzi; sauna; room service; massage; babysitting; laundry; dry cleaning. *In room:* TV, minibar, hair dryer, safe.

Hotel Krone 🏰🏰 *(Kids*   One of the two oldest and most historic hotels in Lech, this is the resort's only member of the Romantik chain, and as such it features large doses of genuine history and folkloric charm. Designed like a chalet in 1741, it was acquired by descendants of its present owners, the Pfefferkorn family, in 1865. The hotel's interior is attractively woodsy, with ceramic-tile stoves, oriental carpets, beamed ceilings, a spacious sun deck, and comfortable fireside chairs. Rooms are elegantly furnished, with exceedingly comfortable beds. Many have balconies, and the best of the doubles contain sitting rooms. Bathrooms have neatly kept shower-tub combinations.

Hotel guests enjoy the evening dance club, which is located in an adjoining wing to avoid disturbing the rest of the guests. Sometimes Tyrolean evenings are staged.

A-6764 Lech. ℂ **05583/25-51.** Fax 05583/25-51-81. www.kronelech.at. 51 units. Winter 216€–428€ double, 340€–680€ suite; summer 98€–185€ double, 152€–295€ suite. Rates include half-board. MC, V. Closed Apr 30 to late June and Sept 27 to late Nov. Parking 8€ in winter, free in summer. **Amenities:** Restaurant; bar; dance club; pool; fitness center; Jacuzzi; sauna; solarium; children's playrooms; room service; babysitting; laundry; dry cleaning. *In room:* TV, minibar, hair dryer, safe.

Expensive

Hotel Arlberg 🏰🏰🏰   Built in 1965, the Hotel Arlberg is a sprawling chalet well equipped for an alpine vacation in any season, and it's one of the only government-rated five-star hotels open during the summer in Lech. The interior offers regional antiques, crafted paneling, elegant accessories, and a baronial fireplace. Rooms are excellently furnished with antiques, rugs over thick carpeting, luxuriously comfortable beds, and double-glazed windows. Most are spacious and open onto big picture windows and individual balconies. Medium-size bathrooms are done in marble with corner tubs and dual basins.

The food served in the richly outfitted dining room is as generous as the decor itself. The Schneider family directs a team of chefs who prepare a daily European specialty, as well as Austrian-inspired foods—a wide variety of game and fish dishes, cream-flavored goulash, and cream schnitzels. Guests appreciate the intimate lighting in the bar after a day in the brilliant sunshine. Meals are also served, in season, on a flower-bedecked sun terrace.

A-6764 Lech. ℂ **05583/21-34.** Fax 05583/21-34-25. www.arlberghotel.at. 58 units. Winter 187€–273€ double, 232€–418€ suite; summer 100€–126€ double, 128€–169€ suite. Rates include half-board. AE, DC, MC, V. Closed Apr 20–June 22 and Sept 22–Nov 30. **Amenities:** 2 restaurants; 2 bars; 2 pools; tennis court; fitness center; health spa; sauna; room service; massage; babysitting; laundry; dry cleaning. *In room:* TV, minibar, hair dryer, safe.

Moderate

Hotel Lech and Pension Chesa Rosa   This very pleasant establishment, open year-round, is 5 minutes from the ski lifts. The interior of the two-chalet complex is handsomely paneled and accented with soft lighting. The recently renovated, medium-size rooms are comfortably furnished and have small but tidy bathrooms with shower-tub combinations. At the hotel restaurant, you can enjoy a fondue evening and a rustic dinner with zither music (Austrian and international cuisine is served). Special events include toboggan games at night, horse-drawn sleigh rides with torches, and even cocktail parties in cable cars.

A-6764 Lech. ℂ **05583/228-90.** Fax 05583/27-27. www.tiscover.at/hotel-lech.rosa. 40 units. 110€–240€ double. Rates include half-board. MC, V. **Amenities:** Restaurant; bar; tennis court; sauna; massage; babysitting; laundry; dry cleaning. *In room:* TV, hair dryer, safe.

PLACES TO STAY IN NEARBY OBERLECH

Whereas Lech boasts medieval roots and a status as a bona-fide alpine village, Oberlech is a relatively recent creation of modern tourism, and most of the hotels here are open only in winter. Some hardy souls struggle about half a mile uphill on foot from Lech to reach Oberlech, site of about 10 hotels and a grocery store. The situation is complicated by the fact that Oberlech's streets are reserved for pedestrians. The best way to reach Oberlech is to ride the **Bergbahn Oberlech cable car,** which operates daily from 7am to 1am (ℂ **05583/23-50** for information), from the center of Lech to Oberlech. Those with ski passes ride free, and everyone else pays 5.60€ round-trip.

If your hotel is in Oberlech, park your car at the base of the Bergbahn Oberlech (the cost of which is usually included in the price of your hotel), and carry your luggage to the cable car, whose operator will phone ahead to your hotel. An employee will usually meet you at the top to assist with your luggage.

Hotel Montana 🔆 *(Finds*   Above the village, this government-rated four-star hotel opens onto a large sun terrace looking out over Lech. The light-grained chalet has a stylish interior. Its cafe/bar area is an attractive place for a midafternoon drink. Furnished in an alpine style, the rather small rooms are exceedingly cozy on long, wintry alpine nights. Bathrooms are also small but have shower-tub combinations and adequate shelf space. Owner Guy Ortlieb, an expatriate Frenchman, organizes weekly farmer buffets and cocktail parties, and does what he can to make guests feel at ease. The hotel restaurant, **Zur Kanne,** serves a high-quality French cuisine and is reviewed below (see "Places to Dine in Nearby Oberlech & Zug").

A-6764 Oberlech. ℂ **05583/24-60.** Fax 05583/2460-38. www.lech.at/montana. 43 units. 240€–300€ double; 334€–390€ suite for 2. Rates include half-board. No credit cards. Closed Apr–Dec. Parking 15€. **Amenities:** Restaurant; cafe-bar; pool; sauna; room service; babysitting; laundry; dry cleaning. *In room:* TV, minibar, hair dryer, safe.

Sonnenburg   Built as one of the first hotels in Oberlech, and opening onto the village square, this large double chalet has wood-trimmed balconies, a sun terrace looking down the hillside, and a warm, intimate, and woodsy decor. The well-maintained rooms have modern comforts, though they lack alpine charm. Nonetheless, the hotel is a welcome retreat on a snowy night, and the bathrooms, though small, are equipped with shower-tub combinations and are handsomely cared for by the bevy of maids.

A short distance away—connected by an underground passage—stands the hotel's annex, Landhaus Sonnenburg, whose pleasantly furnished rooms rent for slightly less than those in the main building.

A-6764 Oberlech. © **05583/21-47.** Fax 05583/21-47-36. www.sonnenburg.at. 83 units. 117€–180€ double; 163€–208€ suite for 2. Rates include half-board. MC, V. Closed May–Nov. **Amenities:** 3 restaurants; 2 bars; pool; fitness center; sauna; room service; babysitting; laundry; dry cleaning. *In room:* TV, minibar, hair dryer, safe.

WHERE TO DINE IN LECH
Expensive
Bauernstube/Johannisstübe && AUSTRIAN/INTERNATIONAL These restaurants are the best recommended and most legendary in Lech, partly because of their age and partly because of their superb cuisine. The older of the two, Bauernstube, is reportedly the oldest building in Lech, a weathered and nostalgically evocative chalet from the 1400s that serves such traditional recipes as fondues (five different kinds), Swiss-style *raclettes,* and T-bone steaks.

The culinary star of the place, however, lies within the main body of the Goldener Berg Hotel, in a room (the Johannisstübe) that was dismantled from a 200-year-old chalet and reinstalled in this more modern building. Here, in a setting that's among the most glamorous in an admittedly glamorous town, you can enjoy carefully prepared international dishes that change according to the season—and the chef's inspiration. Examples include turbot with fennel and herb sauce, grilled sea bass with saffron sauce, filets of roebuck in port wine sauce, and homemade paté of foie gras studded with truffles.

In the Hotel Goldener Berg. A-6764 Lech. © **05583/22-05.** Reservations required. Main courses 25€–35€. Daily 11am–11pm (Bauernstube) and 7–11pm (Johannisstübe). MC, V. Closed May Nov.

Gasthof Post Restaurant && AUSTRIAN/NOUVELLE The Moosbrugger family, owners of the previously recommended Gasthof Post hotel, also presides over the restaurant, a member of Relais & Châteaux. Step into an old-fashioned imperial world of antiques, alpine paneling, and tile stoves. Many guests are on half-board, but nonresidents can select from two dining salons and choose from an a la carte menu or, perhaps more recommendable, a fixed-price menu. The latter is expensive, but you get top-quality ingredients prepared with care and flair. Game is featured in season, and Austrian classics, including a *Tafelspitz,* are always served. Other delicacies include lamb, fresh fish, venison, rabbit paté, international specialties, and an impressive dessert list.

Dorf 11, A-6764 Lech. © **05583/220-60.** Reservations recommended. Main courses 30€–60€; fixed-price menu 48€–55€. AE, DC, MC, V. Daily noon–2pm and 7–9pm. Closed mid-Apr to June 24 and Sept 20–Nov 30.

Hotel Berghof Restaurant & AUSTRIAN/INTERNATIONAL Peter Burger and his family run this popular government-rated four-star hotel dining room with white walls and wood trim. Big windows look out over the "baby lift" and the ski slopes. You might enjoy cream of cauliflower soup, saddle of lamb, *Tafelspitz,* a filet of chamois with salad greens and a red-wine dressing, or medallions of veal in calvados with curried potatoes. For dessert, perhaps you'll sample a soufflé of curd cheese. Year after year, this kitchen turns out respectable and well-prepared food that has pleased some of the most demanding palates in Europe.

The Berghof is also a good place to stay. Built in 1960 and enlarged and renovated in 1995, it offers 45 rooms, each comfortably and attractively furnished. Rates for half-board are 220€ to 316€ for a double room.

A-6764 Lech. ⓒ **05583/26-35.** Fax 05583/263-55. Reservations required. Main courses 16€–24€; 3-course fixed-price lunch 13€–20€; 5-course fixed-price dinner 27€–34€. MC, V. Daily noon–2pm and 7–9:30pm. Closed Apr 20–June 20 and Sept 20–Dec 1.

Restaurant Walserstuben ⚜ AUSTRIAN   You might want to escape your hotel dining room for at least one meal at this august establishment. The most elegant of the hotel's restaurants is in a fine dining citadel, the Wallisterstuben, and its smaller and more intimate salon is the Stube. Both rooms open onto a view of the mountains and contain antiques and well-oiled paneling. Prices in both are the same. Guests might begin with snails in wine sauce with garlic butter or a creamy garlic soup with bread croutons. The chef invariably prepares homemade al dente noodles, and you can count on such Austrian classics as Wiener schnitzel and *Tafelspitz;* game is featured in season. You might interrupt your repast with a palate-cleansing sorbet and later follow with a walnut parfait. The menu is well balanced and full of flavor, and you know that well-trained professionals are manning the stoves in the kitchen.

In the Hotel Schneider Almhof, Tannberg 59. ⓒ **05583/35-00.** Reservations required. Main courses 25€– 50€; fixed-price menu 68€. AE, DC, MC, V. Daily 12:30–2pm and 6:30–11pm. Closed Apr 24–Dec 9.

Moderate

Restaurant Panorama ⚜ AUSTRIAN   Located in the previously recommended Hotel Krone, this a la carte restaurant is patronized by many nonguests. The Pfefferkorns are your charming hosts. The restaurant affords views of the mountains or of the village center; many diners prefer a table in the main part of the restaurant, which has a row of large windows overlooking the river and, beyond it, the rendezvous point for the ski school. You could also sit in an additional pair of smaller and more intimate *Stubes.* Chef specialties include roast veal in a chicken-liver sauce and several regional recipes. One dish that invariably pleases is alpine trout from local streams prepared virtually anyway you desire. A mixture of innovative and traditional dishes keeps satisfied clients coming back for more. Dishes are rich in flavor and texture, and the chefs try to use very fresh ingredients.

In the Hotel Krone, A-6764 Lech. ⓒ **05583/25-51.** Reservations recommended. Main courses 8€–25€. MC, V. Daily 11:30am–2pm and 6:30–9:30pm. Closed Apr 30 to late June and Sept 27 to late Nov.

PLACES TO DINE IN NEARBY OBERLECH & ZUG

Auerhann ⚜ *Finds* AUSTRIAN/INTERNATIONAL   This restaurant prides itself on its role as the oldest dining spot in and around Lech. Set on the outskirts of town, in the hamlet of Zug, the 17th-century building was originally a farmhouse. The ambience is warm, woodsy, and undeniably authentic to alpine Austria's traditions. The restaurant serves large quantities of homemade noodle dishes (studded with ham, cheese, and herbs, among other things), three kinds of fondue (Chinese, bourguignonne, and cheese), the Swiss-inspired *raclette* that's served steaming and savory on bread with wine, fresh trout from nearby streams, game dishes (such as venison in red-wine sauce), plus wine and beer. Desserts tend toward traditional favorites like strudel smothered in vanilla sauce. The kitchen seems immune to passing fads and fancies in cuisine, and turns out consistently reliable dishes based on tried-and-true methods.

Zug. ⓒ **05583/27-54-14.** Reservations recommended. Main courses 9€–20€. MC, V. Winter Mon–Sat 11am–midnight; summer Tues–Sun 11am–midnight. Closed late Apr to June 30 and Oct 1–Dec 15.

Gasthof Rote Wand ⚜ AUSTRIAN/INTERNATIONAL   Lying in the hamlet of Zug (3km/2 miles north of Lech) near the onion-domed village church, this pleasantly old-fashioned place serves meals in an unpretentious

Beisl-style tradition. Prince Rainier and Caroline of Monaco, King Hussein of Jordan, and Princess Diana all dined at this rustic restaurant. A specialty of the house is *Spätzle* with cheese; roast veal and pork, warm cabbage salad, and *Tafelspitz* are also available. Some diners come for the fondue bourguignonne or *chinoise,* which you could precede with a soup made from puree of venison. If you're up for dessert, the hot curd strudel is heavenly.

In winter, if you call ahead, the owners will arrange for a horse-drawn sleigh to pick you up in Lech. A round-trip sleigh ride costs 60€ for up to four people; one-way costs 30€.

Zug. ℭ **05583/34-35.** Reservations required. Main courses 18€–30€. AE, DC, MC, V. Daily 10am–midnight. Closed late Apr to Nov 30.

Zur Kanne FRENCH/ALSATIAN   This restaurant is run by Alsace-born Guy Ortlieb, who operates the previously recommended Hotel Montana and sets very high standards. It's known for serving the best fish in the valley, including a filet of freshwater *fera* from Lake Constance. You might begin with homemade foie gras and then follow with filet of roebuck in red-wine sauce. The waiter presents a menu with no prices—the fixed-price menus are best. Many customers prefer to dine on the sun terrace, even during the chilly winter months.

In the Hotel Montana, Oberlech. ℭ **05583/24-60.** Reservations required for dinner. Main courses 19€– 24€; fixed-price dinner 40€–45€. MC. Daily noon–6pm and 7–9:30pm. Closed May–Nov.

LECH APRES-SKI & AFTER DARK

Lech has the finest après-ski life in Vorarlberg, and if you ever get bored here, you can check out the action at the satellite resorts or go over to Zürs.

The evening begins with a tea dance at the **Hotel Tannbergerhof** (ℭ **05583/ 22-02**), where Veronica Heller welcomes you and later in the evening you can dance to disco music. It's open from December to April 14 daily from 5 to 6:30pm and 9:30pm to 2am. Beer starts at 5€; hard drinks cost from 6€.

The previously recommended **Hotel Krone** (ℭ **05583/25-51**) is a major nightlife spot in Lech. Its magnet in winter is the **Side Step Bar,** where there's live music from the 1950s through the 1980s, and evergreen music is often featured. Beers cost 5€ to 8€. It's open daily from 9:30pm to 4am, and there's no cover. The hotel lounge also occasionally has a zither player. In summer, about twice a week, depending on demand, folkloric evenings are presented for 15€ per person, including the first drink.

Oberlech's **Red Umbrella,** operated by the December-to-April **Petersboden Sport Hotel** (ℭ **05583/32-32**), is the most famous afternoon rendezvous for skiers in the Lech area. The hydraulically operated red umbrella, approximately 36 feet wide, is set on a raised wooden deck. It's raised at 11am each morning and lowered each afternoon at 4 or 5pm, depending on business. Under the umbrella there's a circular bar where you can sit on a stool and order drinks such as *Jägertee* (laced with rum) or vodka *feigen* (with figs floating in it). Of course, in this cold, schnapps remains the favorite drink. The food here is simple and filling; a popular item is *Germknödel,* a jam-stuffed steamed dumpling covered with poppy seeds. Meals begin at 10€. If the weather is bad, you can retreat to the hotel to eat, drink, and warm yourself by a log fire.

STUBEN

This little village and winter resort is almost a suburb of Lech, lying on the southern fringes of the larger village on the west side of the Arlberg Pass. Stuben can be reached by bus, but the most romantic way to go from Lech is by horse-drawn sleigh.

The hamlet has been a way station for alpine travelers for many centuries, but in recent years, it has become a modern ski area with its own lift station on **Albona.** (It was the birthplace of Hannes Schneider, the great ski instructor.) Stuben is not as glamorous as Zürs, but its prices are much more reasonable and its location is just fine for skiers. Stuben has links with St. Anton in the Tyrol, as well as with Lech and Zürs.

Stuben is especially geared for family enjoyment, with children's ski courses, special meals, and hosts who help the small fry feel at home.

The helpful tourist office (© **05582/399**) is inside the Hotel Post in the Village center. It's open in winter daily from 9am to noon and 3 to 6pm; in summer Monday through Friday from 9am to noon.

GETTING THERE   Although a casual glance at some maps might lead newcomers to believe that Stuben lies on the main rail lines between Innsbruck and Bregenz, this is not the case. Stuben-bound passengers must get off the train at the tunnel's western mouth, **Langen am Arlberg,** and then take one of the dozen or so daily buses that wind their way upward during the 10-minute ride to Stuben.

Motorists should follow the directions to Lech and then follow signs to Stuben, which is 10k (6 miles) south of Lech and 24km (15 miles) east of Bludenz.

WHERE TO STAY IN STUBEN

Hotel Mondschein 𝕲𝕲   This building dates from 1739, when it was constructed as a rambling private home near the village church. Today it is the second-oldest hotel in Stuben, and its antique accents include forest-green shutters and weathered siding. The snug and cozy rooms have alpine accents and comfortable beds. Bathrooms are small but are equipped with a tub or shower. Crackling fires add to the ambience (and warmth), and secondary heating is provided by traditional ceramic-tile stoves. Radically renovated in 1971, the hotel is now a well-recommended government-rated three-star choice.

A-6762 Stuben. © **05582/511.** Fax 05582/736. www.mondschein.com. 46 units. 174€–258€ double. Parking 12€. MC, V. **Amenities:** Restaurant; bar; après-ski parties in mountain hut; indoor pool; fitness center; sauna; solarium; babysitting; laundry; dry cleaning. *In room:* TV.

Hotel Post 𝕲   When it was built in 1608, this comfortable, government-rated three-star hotel served as a shelter for tired mail-coach drivers. In 1995, Alexander Doaflinger began running the hotel, and today, with a hardworking staff, he welcomes winter-sports enthusiasts in a tradition maintained since the 17th century. Most of the rustically attractive public rooms have fireplaces and deep-seated chairs. On the premises are a dining room and two old *Stüblis*, or beer taverns, where people can drink and dine a la carte. In 1997, a third *Stüblis* was added to the existing two, using old timbers and antique panels removed from an older site for authenticity. The hotel is just at the edge of the village. Accommodations are spacious and decorated in a bright alpine style. All have comfy beds and small bathrooms with a shower or tub. Rooms at the nearby Hunting Lodge Post, or Jägdhaus (which is part of the hotel), cost the same but are slightly less desirable.

A-6762 Stuben. © **05582/761.** Fax 05582/762. 40 units. 95€–129€ double. Rates include half-board. Parking: 8€. DC, MC, V. Closed May to early Dec. **Amenities:** Restaurant; bar; sauna; steam bath; solarium; room service; massage. *In room:* TV, minibar.

ZÜRS 𝕲

An immaculate resort lying 4km (2½ miles) south of Lech in a sunny valley, Zürs (1,708m/5,600 ft.) consists of half a mile of typical white stucco Vorarlberger buildings with carved wood balconies. The resort, really a collection of extremely expensive hotels, is reached via the scenic **Flexen Road.**

Zürs is strictly a winter resort, and nearly all hotels close in summer. Because of its location, Zürs is avalanche prone, but these potential snowslides do not deter the loyal Zürs clientele.

Zürs (pronounced *Seurs*) is one of the world's most elegant resorts (more formal than Lech), and it's a favorite of royalty and film stars. Although Zürs is far more elite than either St. Moritz or Gstaad, it lacks their ostentatious attitudes. The resort has 130 ski instructors, and the snow here has been compared to talcum powder. Wealthy guests, many from South America, often have their own personal teachers.

A chairlift east of Zürs takes you to **Hexenboden** (2,349m/7,700 ft.), and a cable lift goes to **Trittkopf** (2,402m/7,875 ft.), which has a mountain restaurant and sun terrace.

In the west, a chairlift will take you to **Seekopf** (2,188m/7,175 ft.), and from the windows and terrace of the restaurant here, you can see the frozen **Zürser Lake.** A chairlift travels from Seekopf to the top station at 2,451m (8,035 ft.).

The year-round population of Lech is only 1,000 persons, but the year-round population of Zürs is just 100: Zürs is almost dead in the summer. Guests to Zürs are smug about returning season after season, some for as many as 30 years in a row, and it seems like everyone knows everyone else. Every hotel in Zürs has facilities that let guests ski directly up to a point near the hotel's entrance.

GETTING THERE   The two **buses** described in the Lech section stop in Zürs about 10 minutes before their scheduled arrival in Lech. Likewise, if you're **driving,** follow the same directions for Zürs as for Lech (see above). Zürs is 90km (56 miles) southeast of Bregenz, 34km (21 miles) east of Bludenz, and 43km (27 miles) west of Landeck in Tyrol. If you're arriving at the Zurich airport, as many do, Zürs is 240km (149 miles) east. Many of the hotels offer shuttle bus service from the airport to Zürs.

The nearest **railway station** is in the town of **Langen,** 14km (9 miles) away. It receives six or seven direct trains a day from Innsbruck (trip time: 1 hr., 20 min.). From Langen, yellow postal buses and taxis make frequent runs to and from Zürs.

VISITOR INFORMATION   The **tourist office** (© **05583/22-45**) is in the town center. It's open Monday through Saturday from 8am to 6:30pm.

WHERE TO STAY

Zürs is one of the most expensive ski resorts in the world—*prices are lethal.* If you're seeking bargains, you'll have to go to a more modest resort. The Hotel Hirlanda (see "Where to Dine," below) also rents rooms.

Very Expensive

Central Sporthotel Edelweiss ✦   This government-rated four-star property is one of the two oldest hotels in town, originally built in 1890 when Zürs was nothing more than a high-altitude farm with panoramic views. Overflow guests are housed in the hotel's annex, where prices are lower than in the main building, although the rooms here are not as good. Rooms are spacious and brightly painted, with handsome furniture and good, comfy beds. All the good-size bathrooms contain robes, bathtubs, and showers. Some also have a bidet.

The hotel has a restaurant reserved for residents on half-board, but also another dining spot, Restaurant Chesa, open to the general public.

A-6763 Zürs. ℂ **05583/26-62.** Fax 05583/35-33. www.edelweiss.net. 65 units. 253€–472€ double; 381€–711€ suite. Rates include half-board. No credit cards. Closed May to early Dec. Parking 11€. **Amenities:** 2 restaurants; bar; nightclub; fitness center; sauna; solarium; boutiques; room service; babysitting; laundry; dry cleaning. *In room:* TV, minibar, hair dryer, safe.

Hotel Zürserhof 🏵🏵🏵 An exclusive and private world unto itself, this hotel—the most luxurious of mountain refuges—consists of five separate chalets in the shelter of an alpine valley. Some of its more generous competitors cite it as the best hotel in central Europe, with virtually everything under one roof, and it really is a small, self-sufficient city in its own right. The hotel grew out of a house erected by the Count and Countess Valley Tattenbach in 1927. Film stars, royalty, and various VIPs from around the world have long been attracted to this destination, the hotel that put Zürs on the tourist map.

Accommodations consist of private apartments, many of which have stone fireplaces, bars, double-glazed windows looking out onto mountain views, and other opulent comforts. Rooms blend contemporary and rustic features perfectly. The spacious bathrooms have plenty of shelf space, robes, and shower-tub combinations. Suites have Roman-style baths. The public areas are decked out with old panels, antiques, and Persian carpets.

There's music almost every night in the cellar bar. The hotel's restaurant is reviewed below (see "Where to Dine," below).

A-6763 Zürs. ℂ **05583/25-13.** Fax 05583/31-65. www.zuerserhof.at. 98 units. 422€–678€ double; 620€–976€ suite for 2. Rates include full board. MC, V. Closed May to early Dec. **Amenities:** Restaurant; bar; pool; 4 tennis courts; fitness center; Jacuzzi; sauna; room service; massage; babysitting; laundry; dry cleaning. *In room:* TV, minibar, hair dryer, safe.

Sporthotel Lorunser 🏵🏵🏵 The late Princess Grace of Monaco used to send her children to this luxurious five-star hotel, and Queen Beatrix of the Netherlands sometimes stays here during her winter holidays. Designed with cedar shingles, stucco, and regional paintings around the windows, the five-story hotel has intricately carved ceiling beams, open fireplaces, and elegant accessories and furnishings. Most accommodations have one spacious bedroom with ample and rather luxurious beds topped with eiderdowns, plus a sofa and a painted armoire. Some of the junior suites also have a separate sitting area. Spacious bathrooms come with thick robes, showers and mostly oversize tubs.

The hotel serves some of the best food in Zürs, but the dining room is open only to hotel guests. In the right sunny weather, lunch can be served on a spacious terrace with an "ice bar." The constantly changing dinner menu features five courses served in a series of interconnected dining rooms. From the poultry liver parfait with apple nut salad to the main course of succulent stuffed breast of farmer's chicken flavored with tarragon, the cuisine is scrumptious. The chef has a motto: Serve only what's fresh, never repeat the menu, and always be inventive. Men most often wear jackets in the evening at the height of the season.

A-6763 Zürs. ℂ **05583/225-40.** Fax 05583/22-54-44. www.lorunser.at. 60 units. 278€–488€ double; 400€–606€ suite for 2. Rates include full board. No credit cards. Closed May–Nov. Parking 9€. **Amenities:** Restaurant, bar; health spa; sauna; room service; massage; babysitting; laundry; dry cleaning. *In room:* TV, hair dryer, safe.

Expensive

Hotel Enzian 🏵 Set above the bustle of Zürs, this symmetrical chalet offers a tasteful combination of wood walls, coffered ceilings, and fireplaces where you can snuggle up après-ski, plus a sauna where you can relax your tired muscles. Your sports-loving hosts do everything they can to create an informal ambience.

The well-appointed rooms and suites have many modern extras. The hotel's newer rooms (added in the early 1990s) are more luxurious and have more amenities than the rooms in the hotel's older core. Bathrooms are spacious, with towel warmers and tubs (except for eight rooms, which have showers). The hotel is at the edge of the village, on a hill behind a church and near the cable-car station—you can ski from the front door to all the lifts.

You'll enjoy a glass of *Glühwein* in the international alpine *Stube*. On the premises are two dining rooms, a cozy bar, and a sun terrace with waiter service.

A-6763 Zürs. ℂ **05583/224-20.** Fax 05583/34-04. www.hotelenzian.com. 36 units. 180€–300€ double; 240€–360€ suite for 2. Rates include half-board. MC, V. Closed May–Nov. Parking 8€. **Amenities:** 2 restaurants; bar; squash court; fitness center; health spa; sauna; game room; room service; massage; babysitting; laundry; dry cleaning. *In room:* TV, minibar, hair dryer, safe.

Hotel Erzberg ★★ (Finds)

Within its category, this is one of the most appealing hotels in Zürs. The hotel's location close to the ski lifts is ideal. Built in 1972, the comfortable interior features wrought iron, soft lighting, and softly burnished paneling crafted from local pines. Rooms are cozy and warm, and each contains a good bed and a well-equipped private bathroom with a shower-tub combination. Much of the bar's charm derives from the live music provided by the Wolff family.

Although there's a separate restaurant on the premises that's open to the public, hotel residents dine in their own dining room. But regardless of where it's consumed, the food is well prepared, flavorful, and served in generous quantities. The day begins with a buffet breakfast, and dinner is six courses, including a big salad buffet. Sometimes the hotel arranges special events, such as candlelight dinners and welcome cocktail parties.

A-6763 Zürs. ℂ **05583/26-44.** Fax 05583/26-44-44. www.hotel-erzberg.at. 26 units. 152€–280€ double; 270€–350€ junior suite. MC. Closed late Apr to early Dec. Free parking outdoors, 8.50€ in covered garage. **Amenities:** 2 restaurants; bar; sauna; room service; babysitting; laundry; dry cleaning. *In room:* TV, hair dryer, safe.

WHERE TO DINE

Hotel Hirlanda ★ AUSTRIAN   This hotel, originally built as a small inn in the 1920s, houses a popular restaurant frequented by ski instructors. The kitchen prepares hearty Vorarlberg fare as well as gastronomically delicate dishes. The grill uses different kinds of wood, which gives meat a pungent and savory flavor; the wine cellar is impressive as well. You might begin with onion soup served with cheese and croutons or perhaps lobster-stuffed ravioli. Spicy seasoned filet steaks are prepared on the wooden charcoal grill. Barbary goose with orange sauce is another delectable main course. The pastry chef concocts different surprises every night, perhaps Málage sabayon with mango slices. The owners keep the fireplace blazing to take the chill off the coldest winter's night.

About 20 cozy, alpine-style bedrooms are also rented. On the half-board plan, doubles cost 260€ to 314€, and suites are 320€ to 400€. You can pay with credit cards for meals, but not for rooms.

A-6763 Zürs. ℂ **05583/22/62.** Reservations required. Main courses 9€–25€. MC, V. Daily noon–2pm and 7–10:30pm. Closed May to early Dec.

Hotel Zürserhof Restaurant ★★★ INTERNATIONAL

A rich and famous clientele dines here, occasionally in black tie in season, especially for the twice-a-week galas. Though dress codes have been relaxed, few other hotels within central Europe match the Zürserhof's glamour and sophistication. The cuisine is of the finest international standard, and the service is the best at the resort. Even the unpretentious cuisine of rural Austria is expensive here (although well prepared). Main courses might include a delectable roast suckling pig, Viennese roast chicken, roast veal, bratwurst, and roast pork. Many guests prefer to dine in the *Stube*, which has a traditional alpine decor. The kitchen also prepares the most beautiful cheese buffet in town.

Zürs. ℰ **05583/25-13.** Reservations required. Main courses 20€–40€; fixed-price menus 40€–75€ at lunch. MC, V. Daily noon–2pm and 7–9pm. Closed May–Nov.

Restaurant Chesa INTERNATIONAL   This sporty, elegant place is run by the Strolz family. The restaurant is decorated in kaiser gold, yellow, and green, and its ambience is stimulating on a winter's night. Main courses include zander filet with a warm vinaigrette sauce or beef filet stuffed with goose liver and served with a sabayon of chives and quickly sautéed vegetables. The cheese board is impressive, as is the wine list. A fresh salad buffet is offered daily, along with whole-food selections for health-conscious guests. After dinner, many guests head to the basement disco for late-night entertainment.

In the Central Sporthotel Edelweiss, Zürs. ℰ **05583/26-62.** Reservations required. Main courses 12€–27€. MC. Daily noon–2pm and 7–9:30pm. Closed May–Nov.

ZÜRS AFTER DARK

After dinner, many hotel guests retreat to their hotel bars—or even up to their rooms—for privacy and R&R before braving the wilds of the Tyrolean Alps for another day of skiing. But if you're tempted to go dancing, the resort's two discos are **Vernissage,** in the Hotel Arcona Ski Club (ℰ **05583/22-71**), and the **Disco Zürserl,** in the Hotel Edelweiss (ℰ **05583/26-62**). Neither charges any cover; beers cost around 4€ each. Of the two, Vernissage is likely to be more crowded because of its location within the largest hotel in Zürs. Both open for business at 10pm and continue until the last client staggers home.

2 The Montafon Valley ⋆⋆

Montafon is a high alpine valley known for its sun and powdery snow. It stretches some 42km (26 miles) at the southern tip of Vorarlberg, with the Ill River flowing through on its way to join the Rhine. The valley, filled with mountain villages and major winter recreation areas, is encircled by the mountain ranges of Rätikon, Silvretta, and Verwall.

Montafon has been called a "ski stadium" because of its highly integrated ski region. One ski pass covers unlimited use of 70 cable cars, chairlifts, and T-bars in all four of the valley's main ski areas, as well as transportation among the resorts.

Hochjoch-Zamang offers skiing in the back bowls and down the front, and is the main mountain at Schruns (of Hemingway fame). Tschagguns has **Grabs-Golm** for some easier runs. **Silvretta-Nova** at Gaschurn and St. Gallenkirch is a superb ski circus on several mountains, and the **Schafberg** of Gargellen is secluded in a side valley.

EXPLORING SCHRUNS & TSCHAGGUNS ⋆

Schruns is the largest resort in the Montafon Valley, lying on the right bank of the Ill River. Tschagguns (a smaller resort) is on the left bank, and the two hamlets are so close (less than a mile apart) that they can be treated as one.

Although known for their winter sports, these towns are also popular in summer. The warm-weather allure here revolves around walking, hiking, and climbing in the alpine majesty of the Vorarlberg. Locals pride themselves on the nearness of **Pizbuin,** the highest peak in the Vorarlberg (more than 3,660m/12,000 ft. above sea level). Throughout the Montafon Valley, yellow-and-black signs point out natural attractions and destinations, and how long it will take to get there. For more information about climbing and hiking, call **Bergfuhrer Montafon** (© **066443/11445**), a local climbing club. Ski lift passes are also sold in the summer (for hiking and climbing, not skiing). These passes include unlimited lift rides as well as free access to all the valley's public pools. For more information, call the tourist office.

Above Tschagguns, at Latschau, you can take a cable railway or chairlift to **Grabs-Golm** at 1,388m (4,550 ft.), a small but fascinating ski region with several lifts, including a four-person lift going up to 2,135m (7,000 ft.). These slopes attract both beginners and experts, and they are known for World Cup races. While you're at Golm, you can stop at a rustic little restaurant or a modern self-service one, and then take the surface lift to Hochegga at 1,587m (5,202 ft.).

Ernest Hemingway spent winters at Schruns writing *The Sun Also Rises.*

GETTING THERE   Almost two dozen **trains** depart from Bludenz every day for Schruns (trip time: 22 min.). Schruns is the last stop on this line, and several buses head up into the nearby valleys from Schruns.

About two **buses** per day depart from Bludenz's railway station and arrive at Schruns in around 20 minutes. From the railway station in Schruns, about a dozen buses per day make the 3-minute trip to Tschagguns's main square, **Dorfplatz.** If you are laden with luggage, you might want to take a taxi.

Schruns is 698km (434 miles) west of Vienna and 63km (39 miles) southeast of Bregenz. From Bregenz, **drive** southeast along Autobahn A14 until you reach Bludenz. At Bludenz, follow the MONTAFON signs and head up the valley until you reach Schruns.

VISITOR INFORMATION   The **tourist office** (© **05556/72-16-60**) is located at Postfach 145, in the village center of Schruns. It's open in winter Monday through Friday from 8am to 6pm, Saturday from 9am to noon and 2 to 6pm, Sunday from 10:30am to noon and 2 to 6pm; in summer Monday through Friday from 8am to 6pm, Saturday from 9am to noon and 4 to 6pm, Sunday from 10:30am to noon.

WHERE TO STAY IN SCHRUNS

Hotel Krone *(Value* Owned by members of the Gmeiner family since 1847, this yellow baroque building has white trim, black shutters, and a hipped roof with at least one pointed tower. It's one of the few baroque structures in a resort loaded with chalets. The hotel has a shaded beer garden, a collection of rustic artifacts, and ornate paneling whose rich glow is reflected in the leaded windows. Rooms are pleasantly furnished, comfortable, and snug, with excellent beds and small shower-only bathrooms. The in-house restaurant, the Montafoner Stube, serves well-prepared and beautifully served cuisine. It's open daily for lunch and dinner, and it welcomes everyone.

Ausserlitz 2, A-6780 Schruns. © **05556/722-55.** Fax 05556/722-5522. www.austria-urlaub.com. 12 units. Winter 128€–140€ double; summer 110€–116€ double. Rates include half-board. MC, V. Closed 3 weeks in May and 3 weeks in Nov. **Amenities:** Restaurant; bar; room service; sauna. *In room:* TV, minibar, hair dryer, safe.

Löwen Hotel Schruns *★★* Built in 1974, this is the most lavish hotel in Schruns. The hotel's creative designers decided to give guests the best of both the alpine and modern worlds. The rambling chalet sits back on a large lawn in the

---

Finds **The Gathering Place of Town**

Feuerstein, Dorfstrasse, Schruns (☎ 05556/721-29), is the best-known place in town for ice cream and pastries. Housed in an antique building in the town center, the establishment serves attractively decorated pastries—some are miniature works of art. Coffee begins at 2.50€; pastries start at 2.20€. It's open daily in midwinter from 10am to 11pm; the rest of the year, it's open daily from 10am to 7pm (closed Easter–June and late Oct to mid-Dec).

---

center of town. The shrub-dotted lawn, however, actually rests on top of a modern steel, glass, and concrete construction. In many ways, this is a town social center and, except for outdoor recreation, it provides almost everything you need. Rooms are imaginatively designed and well furnished, with good, comfortable beds and small bathrooms equipped with shower-tub combinations.

The hotel contains the upscale Restaurant Français, which serves nouvelle cuisine, and the more casual and more gemütlich Restaurant Barga. The most desirable corner of the Restaurant Barga is the Montafoner Stube, where wood paneling and alpine accessories foster warmth and a sense of well-being. The hotel is the major after-dark venue in the area (see below).

Silvrettastrasse 8, A-6780 Schruns. ☎ 05556/71-41. Fax 05556/735-53. loewen-hotel@aon.com. 85 units. Winter 232€–292€ double, 290€–325€ suite; summer 174€–192€ double, 170€–205€ suite. Rates include half-board. AE, DC, MC, V. Closed Easter to mid-May and late Oct to mid-Dec. Free parking. **Amenities:** 2 restaurants; bar; disco; 2 pools; fitness center; Jacuzzi; sauna; salon; room service; babysitting; laundry; dry cleaning. *In room:* TV, minibar, hair dryer, safe.

WHERE TO STAY IN TSCHAGGUNS

Hotel Montafoner Hof 🏆🏆   This government-rated four-star hotel, run by the Tschohl family, is the premier resort at Tschagguns. A striking peach color on the outside, the Montafoner Hof (built in 1987) is decorated inside with Austrian woods to lend it an authentic alpine atmosphere; however, the hotel is completely modern in other respects. All of the well-furnished rooms come with good beds, lounge corners, and balconies with mountain views, plus small but well-organized bathrooms with ample shelf space and shower-tub combinations.

The Montafon Stube offers a rather glamorous fixed-price menu. The lobby bar and a hideaway near it, the Kaminstube, offer comfortable armchairs and sofas positioned in front of a blazing fireplace with lots of alpine artifacts. This is a popular après-ski venue.

Across the street, less expensive meals are served in the 4-century-old **Gasthof Löwen,** operated by the hotel's owner and closed only in July. The *Tagesmenu* (day's menu) costs 11€ to 15€, and because of its reasonable prices, the restaurant is also popular with local residents.

Dorfstrasse 852, A-6774 Tschagguns. ☎ 05556/710-00. Fax 05556/710-06. www.montafoner.com. 50 units. Winter 194€–268€ double, 222€–268€ suite for 2; summer 152€–216€ double, 174€–216€ suite for 2. Rates include half-board. No credit cards. Closed Easter to May 20 and Nov to Dec 20. **Amenities:** Restaurant; bar; 2 pools; fitness center; Jacuzzi; sauna; room service; babysitting; laundry; dry cleaning. *In room:* TV, minibar, hair dryer, safe.

SCHRUNS & TSCHAGGUNS AFTER DARK

Be aware that Schruns offers a wider range of nightlife than the smaller and sleepier Tschagguns, where a drink or two beside a flickering fire in any of the resort's hotels might be the most popular after-ski activity.

In Schruns, the previously recommended Löwen Hotel offers more energy and a greater number of options than anything else in town. Its disco, **Löwen Grube,** is open nightly from 9pm to at least 3:30am from December to late April. The evening invariably begins with a spate of live Montafon Valley evergreen music that's performed from 9 to 11pm. After that, disco rules till closing. Entrance is free, and beer costs around 4€ for a foaming mugful. A calmer, more contemplative bar that's undeniably cozy is the Löwen Hotel's **Kamin Bar.**

There are no equivalent discos in Tschagguns, although if you prefer something a bit quieter —or a bit earlier in the afternoon—there's a fire blazing in the Montafoner Hof's rustically appointed and very charming **Kaminstube** whenever temperatures justify it. It's open winter and summer every day from 3pm to 3am.

3 The Brand Valley 🖈🖈

Often visited from Bludenz (see above), the Brand Valley (Brandnertal in German) is one of Austria's most scenic valleys, a place of rare beauty surrounded by glaciers. The valley runs for almost 16km (10 miles) before reaching Brand, and along the way are romantic little villages and lush pastureland set against a panoramic alpine backdrop. This valley offers a wealth of inns and hotels, especially at Brand, and skiers are drawn to the mountain ranges, namely **Niggenkopf** and **Palüd.**

GETTING THERE   No rail lines run into Brand. The easiest way to reach the resort is by taking the **train** to Bludenz, from which about a dozen **buses** per day make the 30-minute trip to Brand. Each bus makes at least five different stops in Brand, whose city limits sprawl for several miles beside the valley's main highway.

Brand is 69km (43 miles) south of Bregenz, 10km (6 miles) southwest of Bludenz, and 171km (106 miles) east of Zurich. To reach it by **car,** follow the directions to Bludenz (see above) and then cut southwest along the road that's marked BRAND.

VISITOR INFORMATION   The **tourist office** (📞 05559/555) is in the town center. It's open in winter Monday through Saturday from 9am to noon and 2 to 5pm.

EXPLORING BRAND

A few centuries ago, exiles from the Valais, in Switzerland, settled this village at the mouth of the Zalimtal, near the Swiss border. At an elevation of 1,037m (3,400 ft.), Brand has long been a popular mountain health resort spread out along a mile stretch at the base of the Scesaplana mountain range. It's now a much-visited winter-sports center, the main resort of the **Rätikon district** of Vorarlberg.

You can take a cableway to the top of the **Tschengla,** at 1,249m (4,095 ft.), as well as a chairlift to **Eggen,** at 1,270m (4,165 ft.). From Eggen, it's easy to make connections to **Niggenkopf,** at 1,597m (5,235 ft.).

About 6km (4 miles) south of Brand, beside the only road leading south of town (it's an extension of the Hauptstrasses and is marked LUNERSEE), you'll find the **Lunersee Talstation.** Here, hardy souls can start a 1-hour climb leading steeply uphill to the **Lünersee (Lake Luner)** 🖈🖈, a glacial lake whose size has been increased with the construction of a dam and whose western edge abuts the frontier of Switzerland. If you find the climb daunting, you can take a cable car, which operates from 9am to 4:30pm daily from June to mid-October (snowfalls shut it down in winter). Round-trip fare for the 4-minute ride costs 7€; there's a cafe and snack bar at the top. Once you're there, you might opt for a relatively flat walk around the austere-looking lake, a trek that takes most hikers about 2 hours. Remember that the last cable car downhill departs at 5pm.

WHERE TO STAY & DINE

Hotel Scesaplana ✿   In the resort's center, this hotel has been tastefully modeled after a chalet, with wood accents, accommodating sun terraces, and balconied extensions. The hotel offers attractively furnished rooms in two categories. Type A includes cheerful twin rooms with modern furniture in the new part of the hotel (a third bed can be added) and semisuites in the building's old section. Type B includes standard rooms in the old building, most of which have balconies and sitting areas. All the guest rooms contain small, tidy bathrooms with shower-tub combinations.

There are three restaurants, a pub, and a cigar bar named Havana. A range of other sports are within easy reach, including riding, fishing, skiing, a nine-hole golf course, and carriage drives (many of them at an additional fee). The hotel restaurants are quite pleasant, and guests on the half-board plan receive a wide choice of specialties included with the evening meal.

A-6708 Brand. ✆ **05559/221.** Fax 05559/445. www.tiscover.at/scesaplana. 62 units. Winter 148€–286€ double; summer 118€–140€ double. Rates include half-board. MC, V. Closed Oct 20–Dec 20. Parking 4€. **Amenities:** 3 restaurants; 2 bars; pool; Jacuzzi; sauna; room service; massage; babysitting; laundry; dry cleaning. *In room:* TV, minibar, hair dryer, safe.

BRAND AFTER DARK

Nightlife is very casual in Brand, but when there are enough visitors in town, bars usually throw their doors open for a sometimes rollicking good time. The resort's nightlife centerpiece is the lobby level of the **Hotel Scesaplana** (✆ **05559/221**), where two bars divert and amuse the resort's many outdoor-loving visitors. The artfully raffish **Havana Bar** is a rambling, darkly paneled hideaway that manages, at least to some degree, to resuscitate the raunchy days of pre-Castro Cuba. Inside, you'll find potted palms, leather armchairs, and photographs depicting Fidel Castro, Winston Churchill, and Julia Roberts enjoying their favorite stogies. Havana Bar offers at least 30 different single-malt scotches, the requisite Cuba *libres,* at least 40 kinds of cigars—some of them intensely glamorous—and a staff that will absolutely never make you feel that smoking a cigar is inappropriate. Whisky costs 5€ to 10€. It's open Tuesday through Sunday from 9pm to 3am.

A few steps away lies the smaller and sudsier **Schwemme Bar,** a beery, folkloric pub that celebrates the rusticity of alpine Austria. You'll find several kinds of beer, many on tap, from Austria, Holland, Hungary, Italy, Germany, the United States, and France, with prices beginning at 4€. It's open nightly from 4 to 6pm and 8pm to 3am. Both of these bars are closed from late October to mid-December, when the hotel is closed.

4 En Route to Bregenz: Feldkirch & Dornbirn

If you're heading for Bregenz, Vorarlberg's capital, the Bregenz Forest, or Switzerland, you really should stop at Feldkirch and Dornbirn along the way. Arrive in Feldkirch in the morning, wander through the old town and castle, and stay the night before continuing on to Bregenz.

FELDKIRCH ✿: THE GATEWAY TO AUSTRIA

This venerable town, "the gateway to Austria," lies on the western edge of Vorarlberg. Unfortunately, many people rush on to other destinations, but we think this town dating back to medieval times is worth exploring. Feldkirch was once a fortified town that grew up at the "heel" of Schattenburg Castle, on a tributary of the Ill River.

GETTING THERE   Feldkirch sits atop an important junction in the Austrian railway network, with lines to Innsbruck and Bregenz, as well as a line running into Liechtenstein and Switzerland. Dozens of **trains** arrive every day from Innsbruck (trip time: 1¾–2½ hr.) and Bregenz (trip time: 35 min.). It's easier to arrive by train, but many local bus lines connect in Feldkirch.

Passengers who opt to fly to a point near Feldkirch usually land in Zurich. From the **Hauptbahnhof** in Zurich, trains depart every 2 hours, stopping at Feldkirch en route to either Innsbruck or Vienna.

By car, Feldkirch is 35km (22 miles) south of Bregenz (take the A14 south to reach it) and 121km (75 miles) east of Zurich (the nearest airport), from which it can be reached by taking Swiss motorway N13 to the Feldkirch exit.

VISITOR INFORMATION   The **tourist office** (© **05522/734-67**) is at Herrengasse 12. It's open year-round Monday through Friday from 8:30am to noon and 1:30 to 5:30pm; in summer it's also open Saturday from 9am to noon.

EXPLORING THE OLD TOWN & CASTLE

The **Old Town** ⋆, which can be explored in about an hour, is the attraction here—the New Town lies to the northeast. The heart of the Old Town is **Marktgasse (Market Street),** a rectangle with arcades. Many of the old houses facing Marktgasse are graced with oriels (large bay windows) and frescoed facades. A popular wine festival is held here on the second weekend of July, and the town fills up with revelers.

Among the curiosities of the Old Town is the **Katzenturm,** or Tower of the Cats, named for a defense cannon adorned with lion heads. The **Churertor (Chur Gate)** is another Feldkirch landmark. Sights include the **Domkirche,** a cathedral known for its 15th-century double nave, where you should stop in and see the *Descent from the Cross,* a 1521 painting by Wolf Huber of the Danube school.

Schattenburg Schloss (Castle), at Neustadt, can be reached by car (by heading up Burggasse), or you can climb the steps by the **Schloss-Steig.** The castle was once a fortress, and parts of it date from the turn of the 16th century. It's now a museum and restaurant. From the castle precincts, you have a panoramic view of the Valley of the Rhine.

Heimatmuseum (© **05522/719-82**), in Schattenburg Schloss, exhibits a wealth of furnishings of the region, ranging from those you'd have found in a farmer's shack to pieces that graced noblemen's halls. Also displayed are large collections of art and armor. The museum is open Tuesday through Sunday from 9am to noon and 1 to 5pm. Admission is 2.50€ for adults and 1€ for children.

WHERE TO STAY

Gasthof Lingg (see "Where to Dine," below) also rents rooms.

Hotel Alpenrose ⋆ *Finds*   In the heart of the Old Town and only a few minutes' walk from the pedestrian precinct, this hotel appeals to traditionalists. With a history going back 5 centuries, it has been run by the Gutwinski family since 1896. Accommodations come in various sizes and are quite stylish, with most containing small private bathrooms with shower units. Run with charm and flair, the hotel has an elevator, and there's a Biedermeier lounge for guests. The hotel's featured restaurant, Rosenbar, serves a regional cuisine.

Rosengasse 4–6, A-6800 Feldkirch. ⓒ **800/528-1234** in the U.S., or 05522/721-75. Fax 05522/72-17-55. 29 units. 101€–118€ double; 129€–141€ suite. Rates include buffet breakfast. AE, DC, MC, V. **Amenities:** 2 restaurants; bar; lounge; pool; exercise room; Jacuzzi; sauna; room service; massage; babysitting; laundry; dry cleaning. *In room:* TV, minibar, hair dryer, safe.

WHERE TO DINE

Gasthof Lingg ⚿ AUSTRIAN   Since 1878, this restaurant has enjoyed a good local reputation. The dining section is one floor above ground level in an old structure on the main square, whose medieval buildings are visible from the restaurant's windows. You could begin your meal with melon with shrimp, served in a homemade mayonnaise sauce, or else freshly made mushroom soup, and then follow with one of several well-prepared meat, fish, or game specialties from the traditional Austrian kitchen. The breast of fresh roasted goose is excellent.

The guesthouse also rents three double rooms, each with a shower and toilet. Including breakfast, a room for two costs 75€.

Am Marktplatz, A-6800 Feldkirch. ⓒ **05522/720-62.** Fax 05522/72-06-26. Reservations recommended. Main courses 7€–24€; fixed-price menu 10€–15€. AE, DC, MC, V. Tues–Sun noon–2:30pm; Tues–Sat 6–10pm.

DORNBIRN

In the heart of Vorarlberg, Dornbirn, the "city of textiles," is the province's largest town and commercial center. Only 11km (7 miles) south of the provincial capital, it sits on the outskirts of the Bregenz Forest, at the edge of a broad Rhineland Valley.

The city center, Marktplatz (Market Square), is graced by a 19th-century neoclassical parish church and by the Rotes Haus (Red House), a 1639 building that's now a restaurant.

GETTING THERE   Dornbirn is an express stop on the rail lines connecting Innsbruck with Bregenz. **Trains,** both local and express, arrive from either direction at 30-minute intervals throughout the day. It's easier to get here by train, but there's also a **bus** that travels from the railway station at Bregenz to Dornbirn about nine times throughout the day (trip time: 26 min.).

If you're **driving** from Bregenz, head south along the A14 until you reach the signposted junction with Route 190, where you'll head east for Dornbirn.

VISITOR INFORMATION   There's a **tourist office** (ⓒ 05572/221-88) in the center at Rathausplatz 1. It's open year-round Monday through Friday from 9am to noon and 1 to 6pm.

SEEING THE SIGHTS

If you're a car buff, you shouldn't pass up a visit to the **Rolls-Royce Museum** ⚿, 11A Gütle (ⓒ **05572/52652**), the world's largest museum dedicated to the world's most illustrious cars. Rolls-Royce collector Frank Vonier assembled the collection, and many of the swanky cars were once owned by celebrities, including such pop icons as John Lennon or such horrors as Generalissimo Francisco Franco, the longtime Spanish dictator. Many of the vehicles were also owned by members of the British royal family, including Queen Elizabeth and the late Queen Mother. The exhibition room is a converted old spinning mill built in 1862. The vehicles are spread over three floors where you can learn everything you'll need to know about the history of Rolls-Royce.

The most impressive vehicles are a seven-seater 1926 Phantom III, a continental 1933 Phantom II, and a 1936 Phantom III. Take the A14 motorway to

Dornbirn, exiting at Dornbirn Süd (South). Drive along Lustenauerstrasse, passing the Dornbirn Hospital, and follow the signs to Gütle. By public transport, take bus no. 4 from the center of Dornbirn. Admission is 8€ for adults, 7€ for senior citizens and 5€ for students. Children 6 to 16 pay only 4€, and a family ticket goes for 15€. It's open Tuesday through Saturday from 10am to 5pm.

The most exciting excursion in the area is to **Karren** (976m/3200 ft.), about 2km (1½ miles) from the heart of town. If you're pretty fit, you can make the climb in about 2 hours, but you can also take a cable car and get there in 5 minutes. From Karren, you can hike down to the **Rappen Gorge** 🐾, with the Ache River flowing through it.

WHERE TO STAY

Rickatschwende 🐾   This large, modern hotel lies on a steeply sloping hillside overlooking Dornbirn. It's composed of two interconnected buildings; one houses the restaurant, and the other contains the bedrooms. The atmosphere here is calm and quiet, and guests opt for walks in the nearby forest or in grassy meadows, or for any of the various spa cures offered by the on-site health therapists. Rebuilt in 2000, the building has rooms outfitted with warm colors, exposed wood, big windows, balconies, excellent beds, and small but efficiently arranged bathrooms with shower-tub combinations.

Bodelestrasse 1, A-6850 Dornbirn. 📞 05572/253-50. Fax 05572/253-50-70. www.rickatschwende.com. 47 units. 128€–256€ double. Rates include breakfast. Half-board 22€ per person extra. AE, DC, MC, V. From the center of town, drive toward Bödele for 5km (3 miles). **Amenities:** Restaurant; bar; pool; fitness center; health spa; sauna; room service; massage; laundry; dry cleaning. *In room:* TV, hair dryer, safe.

WHERE TO DINE

Das Rotes Haus 🐾🐾 AUSTRIAN/VORARLBERG   No other restaurant in the region offers such a historic setting for a meal. It was originally built in 1639 as a tavern and has functioned in the same role ever since. Its owners proudly define it as the oldest building that's open to the public in the Austrian Rheintal (this part of the Rhine Valley), and as such, strenuous efforts are made to preserve and protect the antique quality of its setting. You'll dine within one of five cozy dining rooms, each rustic and charming, but each with a slightly different decor. We prefer the Jagdstube, outfitted with hunting trophies, and the Ammanstube, which displays political memorabilia. Don't worry if either of these rooms are full: All five dining rooms are richly nostalgic. Local menu items include schnitzels, *Tafelspitz* (boiled beef), a main-course version of veal goulash, and a local noodle dish (*Kässpaetzle*) crafted from local cheeses and herbs. A note about the building's facade: In the 17th century, the dark red color of the exterior was created by mixing cow's blood or bull's blood with binders to create the dark red that—with some assistance from modern paint—still adorns the building's facade today.

Marktplatz 13. 📞 05572/31555. Reservations recommended. Main courses 12€–25€; set-price lunches 15€–18€. AE, DC, MC, V. Mon–Sat 11am–2pm; daily 6–10pm (last order). Closed Dec 24–Jan 6.

5 Bregenz 🐾🐾

(658km (409 miles) W of Vienna; 130km (81 miles) E of Zurich; 11km (7 miles) S of Lindau (Germany)

Bregenz, the capital of Vorarlberg, sits on terraces rising above the water at the eastern end of Lake Constance (Bodensee in German). Once the Roman town of Brigantium, Bregenz is now a major tourist spot that's both modern and historic. The modern part of town lies along the lake's shore, and the old town rises above it. In summer, the promenade along the Bodensee's shoreline is popular.

ESSENTIALS

GETTING THERE   Bregenz is the most important railway station in western Austria, where dozens of **trains** arrive from Zurich, Munich, Innsbruck, and Vienna throughout the day. The trip from Innsbruck takes about 3 hours and occasionally requires a change of train at Feldkirch. Although it's easier to arrive here by train, several bus lines make the trip to Bregenz. For **train and bus information**, call © **01/1717.**

If you're **driving** from Innsbruck, take Route 171 west (passing through the Arlberg Tunnel) into Vorarlberg, and then follow the S19 west until you hook up with the A14 autobahn going north.

VISITOR INFORMATION   At the **tourist office,** Bregenz-Tourismus, Bahnhoftrasse 14 (© **05574/495-90**), you can pick up a map for a walking tour of the Old Town. It's open year-round Monday through Friday from 9am to noon and 1 to 5pm, Saturday from 9am to noon.

SEEING THE SIGHTS

You can travel the Bodensee district by boat, venturing into Germany and Switzerland, which share Lake Constance with Austria. For a panoramic view of the lake and the town, with Switzerland looming in the background, take a cable car to **Pfänder** (see "Up the Mountain to Pfänder," below).

The **Unterstadt (Lower Town)** is Bregenz's shopping district, with traffic-free malls along the shore. In spring, the flower beds along the quays of the Unterstadt blaze with color.

The Upper Town is called both **Oberstadt** and **Altstadt.** Once the stronghold of the counts of Bregenz and Montford, this area is great for history buffs. If you're driving from the Lower Town, head up Kirchstrasse, Thalbachgasse, and Amstorstrasse, park, and then stroll back into the Middle Ages as you wander through the old quarter's quiet squares and narrow streets. Even before it was the Roman town of Brigantium, the Upper Town was the site of a Celtic settlement.

The **Pfarrkirche (Parish Church),** dedicated to St. Gall, stands on a hill south of the Upper Town. This 15th-century sandstone structure has a sunken nave from the 18th century.

 The Bregenz Music Festival

Bregenz is at its liveliest during the annual **Bregenz Music Festival.** This festival, held during a 4-week period in July and August, was established in 1946. Open-air and indoor concerts are given (some at the acoustically sophisticated Festspiele-und-Kongresshaus), but the most appealing productions are the lavish operas, operettas, and musical comedies. The more elaborate shows—with their ornately dressed actors and singers—are presented on a stage floating on the Bodensee. The audience looks on from a shoreside amphitheater that seats 6,500. Recent productions have included Verdi's *Un Ballo in Maschera* and such modern works as Bohuslav Martinu's *Greek Passion*. Tickets, from 33€ to 125€, are available at the Bregenzer Festspielehaus, Platz der Weiner Symphoniker 1 (© **05574/40-76**; www. bregenzerfestspiele.com).

Martinsturm (Tower Of St. Martin)   On the upper floor of this 13th-century tower is a local military museum. St. Martin's Chapel (founded in 1362), at the base of the tower, features 14th-century murals. Far more interesting than the art, however, is the view of the surrounding area from the top of the tower, which is capped with one of the largest all-wood cupolas in Austria.

Graf-Wilkhelm-Strasse ℭ **05574/466-32.** 2€ adults, 1€ children. May 1–Sept 30 daily 9am–6pm. Closed Oct 1–Apr 30.

Vorarlberger Landesmuseum (Vorarlberg Regional Museum) ✦ Here you'll find a rich collection of artifacts from throughout the province. Exhibits include relics from prehistoric and Roman days. You'll see Romanesque and Gothic ecclesiastical works of art from the churches in the district. Also make time to see the so-called portrait of the Duke of Wellington by Angelica Kauffmann.

Kornmarktplatz 1. ℭ **05574/460-50.** Admission 2€ adults, 1€ children. Tues–Sun 9am–noon and 2–5pm.

SHOPPING

Nose-to-the-grindstone Bregenz doesn't have a lot of shopping options, but you'll find a scattering of outlets within the Lower Town that might appeal to you. Foremost for sporting goods is **Sport Christian,** Leutbüel 2 (ℭ **05574/ 422-34**), where you'll find every type of equipment and clothing you'd need for every imaginable summer and winter sport. And noteworthy for traditional alpine clothing—lederhosen, dirndls, and woolen clothing suitable for men, women, and children in any season—is **Sagmeister,** Römerstrasse 10 (ℭ **05574/ 431-90**).

WHERE TO STAY

For the most luxurious accommodations in the area, stay at Deuring Schlössle (see "Where to Dine," below).

Gasthof Adler   Built around a century ago, this hospitable and unpretentious hotel is located half a mile south of the town center. Rooms contain painted furniture and exposed wood, and beds of good quality. The hallway bathrooms are well maintained and contain shower stalls. The restaurant, **Schnitzelhaus,** is a local hangout known for its plentiful food and reasonable prices; it's open for lunch and dinner Sunday through Friday. The Gasthof Adler specializes in Austrian and Teutonic food, serving a filling two-course *Tagesmenu,* or day's menu, priced at 8€.

Fluesl 11, A-6900 Bregenz. ℭ **05574/717-88.** Fax 05574/619-53. 8 units, none with bathroom. 49€ double. Rate includes breakfast. AE, DC, MC, V. **Amenities:** Restaurant; lounge. *In room:* No phone.

Hotel Mercure   Near the Festspielhaus, in the center opening onto the lake, this hotel, a member of a popular French hotel chain, is one of the town's most up-to-date. And it's in the same building as the local casino. The small rooms are of the bland hotel-chain variety but are comfortable. Some have balconies. Two are equipped for persons with disabilities. Bathrooms are small, with shower-tub combinations. The hotel's specialty restaurant, Le Gourmet, also operates an inexpensive cafeteria. Summer guests enjoy sitting out on the large umbrella-shaded terrace for drinks and food.

Platz d. Wiener Symphoniker 2, A-6900 Bregenz. ℭ **05574/46-10-00.** Fax 05574/474-12. www.accorhotel. com. 94 units. Sept–June 117€–141€ double, 214€ suite; July–Aug 170€–215€ double, 265€ suite. Rates include buffet breakfast. Half-board 16€ per person extra. AE, DC, MC, V. **Amenities:** Restaurant; bar; room service; babysitting; laundry; dry cleaning. *In room:* TV, minibar, hair dryer, safe.

Schwärzler Hotel ℛ   One of the best hotels in Bregenz, the elegant Schwärzler Hotel is a 5-minute drive east of the town center. Completely renovated, it has hosted famous visitors such as the late Arthur Ashe and José Carreras. Most of the handsomely furnished rooms are spacious and have balconies. Bathrooms are small but efficiently organized with shower. The **restaurant,** Schwärzler, is one of the most respected in the area, serving Swiss, Austrian, and international dishes. The hotel is known for its candlelight dinners and farmer buffets.

Landstrasse 9, A-6900 Bregenz. ⓒ 05574/49-90. Fax 05574/475-75. 82 units. 132€–196€ double; 168€–240€ per person suite. Rates include breakfast. Half-board 24€ per person extra. AE, DC, MC, V. Free parking. **Amenities:** Restaurant; bar; pool; sauna; room service; babysitting; laundry; dry cleaning. *In room:* TV, minibar, hair dryer, safe.

WHERE TO DINE

Berghaus Pfänder ℛ AUSTRIAN/INTERNATIONAL   Rebuilt in 1972 after a fire demolished its century-old predecessor, this is the most famous restaurant atop Pfänder (see "Up the Mountain to Pfänder," below). The restaurant's animal-loving owner is also the driving force behind the Pfänder Wildlife Park. From the dining room, you'll be able to peer over the landscapes of Germany and Switzerland. Operated by an Austrian and Australian-born team of family members, most of this restaurant is designed as an upscale self-service cafeteria. The food is well suited to the alpine air, and menu items include roasted pork with dumplings and sauerkraut, venison in its own gravy, Wiener schnitzels, fried calves' liver, and a complete roster of fresh pastries.

Auf dem Pfänder. ⓒ 05574/421-84. Reservations accepted. Main courses 6€–14€. No credit cards. Daily 9:30am–6:30pm. Closed Oct–Apr. Cable car from Bregenz; the restaurant is 100 ft. from the terminus.

Deuring Schlössle ℛℛ AUSTRIAN   In the center of Bregenz, at the highest point in the Old Town, this restaurant is one of Austria's finest. Through the efforts of its owners, the Huber family, the imposing, ivy-covered 600-year-old castle has provided exceptional food (and hotel rooms) since 1987. The establishment contains half-timbered detailing, a Renaissance-era fireplace, and an impressive wine list. Menu items are seasonal, varied, and thoughtful, such as cream soup with exotic fruits and pike perch with crab sauce, spinach, and buttered noodles; roasted breast of duck with wine sauce, ginger-flavored cabbage, and potato pancakes; and marinated whitefish from nearby lakes served with apple-cucumber salad and blinis. Dessert might be a hot paté of yellow cranberries served with poppy-flavored ice cream.

Some guests opt to spend the night in one of the 13 rooms. Accommodations are spacious and contain antiques, Persian carpets, parquet floors, and panoramic views of Lake Constance. Modern comforts have been added, and rooms come in a variety of sizes, with great beds and luxurious bathrooms with tub and shower. Our favorite guestroom is Gott im Espana in the tower, which is surrounded with windows. With its garden ambience, the place is both stylish and relaxing. Doubles are 264€ to 330€, and suites run 358€ to 430€. Rooms contain minibars, TVs, and phones. Half-board is an additional 35€ per person per day.

Ehre-Guts-Platz 4, A-6900 Bregenz. ⓒ 05574/478-00-80. Fax 05574/478-00-80. Reservations required. Main courses 17€–28€; tasting menu 78€. AE, DC, MC, V. Tues–Sun noon–2pm; daily 6:30–9:30pm.

Golden Hirsch ℛ AUSTRIAN   One of the most "folklorically conscious" dining rooms in town occupies an old-world house that was originally built as a tavern around 1800 and that has functioned in that venue ever since. Inside, you'll find one very large dining room whose seating expands during clement weather onto an outdoor terrace where the views extend out over the other historic buildings of Bregenz's historic core. Come here for the kind of cuisine that many Austrians associate with their grandmothers. Examples include giant Weiner schnitzels; *Tafelspitz* (boiled beef); local fish served with herbs and a white butter sauce; variations on noodle dishes, including versions with creamy ham and mushroom sauce; roasted beef with onions; and creamy goulash. Dishes that are a bit less obviously associated with the region include grilled turkey in a tomato-flavored Gorgonzola sauce and well-prepared pastas, some of them made with spinach-flavored tagliatelle. A particular specialty favored by residents of these parts is *Kisselfleisch,* composed of roasted pork served with sauerkraut, braised onions, and herbs.

Kirschstrasse 8. (℃) **05574/42815.** Reservations recommended. Main courses 10€–24€. AE, DC, MC, V. Wed–Mon 10am–midnight.

BREGENZ AFTER DARK

If you're in Bregenz on a summer night, you don't need nightlife: Few smoke-filled clubs could compete with a walk along the lakeshore and a visit to a cafe. However, if you'd like another diversion, you can visit the **Spiel-Casino Bregenz,** in the Hotel Mercure, Philharmonikerplatz 1 (℃ **05574/46-10-00**), where roulette, baccarat, and blackjack are played daily from 3pm to 3am. Parking in the garage is free, as is entrance to the casino. As a promotion, 21€ of chips costs 18€. Men must wear jackets and ties. The in-house restaurant, **Ialstaff,** offers a fixed-price four-course menu for around 47€.

UP THE MOUNTAIN TO PFÄNDER

Almost 300,000 visitors a year make the uphill trek to the mountain observation station of Pfänder, west of Bregenz. Pfänder is accessible by **road** (a meandering distance of 10km/6½ miles) or via the **Pfänderbahn cable car** (a straight-line transit of 4km/2½ miles) from the center of Bregenz. Celebrated as the second-oldest cable car in Austria, it was originally built in 1927 and was massively upgraded with almost double its original capacity in 1994. Operating year-round daily from 9am to 7pm, it departs from its lowest station, about 1,500 feet east of the **Kornmarkt I Bregenz,** and takes about 7 minutes to reach its summit. Round-trip fare is 9.50€ for adults and 4.50€ for children. Call (℃) **05574/421-60** for information about departure times.

At the summit, you'll find a scattering of shops and restaurants, the best of which is the **Berghaus Pfänder** (see "Where to Dine," above). Partly as a hobby for its builder, octogenarian and family patriarch Azi Kinz, and partly as an added attraction for its public image, the Berghaus maintains the **Pfänder Wildlife Park.** The owners emphasize that it is not a zoo. The park's large fenced-in areas are devoted to herds of red deer, wild boar, mountain goats, and wild sheep. Access to the Wildlife Park is free; it takes about 20 minutes to wander through its 10 hectares (26 acres) of rocky terrain. One of the highlights of the park is the twice-daily **Birds of Prey Show (*Greifvogel-Flugschau*),** during which ornithologists display the age-old hunting techniques of trained falcons, eagles, owls, and vultures. The 45-minute shows are presented from May to early October at 11am and 2:30pm. Tickets to the show are 5€ for adults and 2.50€ for children.

To get to this alpine complex by car from Bregenz, travel east of town (toward Lindau, Germany) along a narrow, twisting road through the mountains. Turn right, toward Lochau, where you'll pass a parish church, and turn right onto a secondary road leading to Pfänder. Cars usually park at a large lot near the summit. From here, you'll walk about 10 minutes to reach the panorama from the Berghaus Pfänder. From the Berghaus, an additional 15-minute walk leads to another, much smaller, alpine house with its own simple restaurant and a different panorama, the **Schwedenschanze belvedere.**

6 The Bregenz Forest ⭑

From Bregenz, you can make one of the most interesting scenic excursions in Vorarlberg—or in Austria, for that matter—deep into the **Bregenzerwald,** or Bregenz Forest. It's not as well known as Germany's Black Forest, but it has just as much charm and character.

The forest takes up the northern part of the Vorarlberg alpine range. A state highway splits the valley of the Bregenzer Ache River, making driving easy, but the true charm of the forest lies off the beaten path in the little undiscovered valleys cut by the river's tiny tributaries. Don't expect a proliferation of trees in the Bregenz Forest: The Austrians have cleared a lot of the woodlands to make meadows, where you'll see contented cows grazing and the Alps towering in the background.

One of the most frequented areas for sports and recreation is the Bödele, which lies between the Valley of the Ache and the Valley of the Rhine. Skiers are drawn to the highlands in winter.

BEZAU

The best-known village of the Bregenz Forest, Bezau is surrounded by a landscape that's scenic in any season. Be careful not to confuse Bezau with a village nearby, at the end of the neighboring valley, named Bizau.

In the spring, summer, and autumn, you can hike, go mountaineering, swim, fish for trout, or play tennis or minigolf. In winter there's alpine skiing, with the **Hinter-bregenzerwald ski ticket** covering a range of more than 50 lifts and cable railways. There are some 56km (35 miles) of cross-country ski trails, and you can also go tobogganing. A cableway from here will take you to the **Baumgartenhöhe,** at 1,632m (5,350 ft.).

GETTING THERE   Bezau has no railway connections. Most travelers take one of the many daily **trains** to Dornbirn, a 15-minute ride south of Bregenz. Around 20 **buses** depart every day from Dornbirn; the trip to Bezau takes about 50 minutes.

If you're **driving** from Bregenz, head south on the A14 to the junction with Route 200. Cut east along this winding road to Bezau, which lies 36km (22½ miles) from Bregenz.

VISITOR INFORMATION   The **tourist office** (© **05514/2129**) is in the center of town. It's open year-round Monday through Saturday from 8am to noon and 1:30 to 5pm.

WHERE TO STAY & DINE
Gasthof Gams   This dignified hotel has a facade of cedar shingles, white stucco, gables, and balconies. Although the core was built in 1648, guests will find an abundance of modern comforts, including a big garden and several antique-style sitting rooms. Rooms are well furnished and come in a variety of sizes; each year a few units are renovated. The most desirable open onto private balconies with scenic views. Beds are first-rate, and the small bathrooms have tub-shower combinations. The restaurant specializes in game, particularly venison. You'll also be offered seafood, such as a well-prepared filet of sole, along

Factoid

If you're passing through the valley on a Sunday, you'll see an occasional Vorarlberger going to church in his or her traditional garb. The headdress of the women is often striking, ranging from small crowns to wide-brimmed black straw hats. Unlike most of the rest of Europe, the people of this area wear white for mourning rather than black.

with filet steak, curry dishes, and desserts with fresh mountain berries. Full meals cost 22€ to 55€.

Platz 44, A-6870 Bezau. ℂ 05514/22-20. Fax 05514/22-20-24. www.hotel-gams.at. 41 units. 138€ double; 180€ suite for 2. Rates include half-board. V. **Amenities:** Restaurant; bar, lounge; pool; 3 tennis courts; Jacuzzi; sauna; solarium; room service; babysitting; laundry; dry cleaning. *In room:* TV, hair dryer, safe.

DAMÜLS

At an elevation of 1,427m (4,680 ft.), this town is one of the best places to ski in the Bregenz Forest. One skier who goes here every year describes it as "being for connoisseurs." Hotels organize weekly après-ski programs, so check to see what's going on during your stay. Damüls, the loftiest village in the forest, is an area of great scenic beauty, so a summer visit is also pleasant.

GETTING THERE From Bregenz, visitors should take a southbound 15-minute **train** to Dornbirn and then board one of the **buses** to Damüls. Buses depart around six times a day (trip time: 1½ hr.).

To get to Damüls from Innsbruck, you have to take a 2-hour train ride west to Bludenz and then board one of the nine daily buses that depart for the 90-minute ride to Damüls.

Damüls is 60km (37 miles) southeast of Bregenz, and a long 698km (434 miles) west of Vienna. To get to Damüls by **car** from Bezau (see above), drive southeast along Route 200 until you come to the junction with Route 193, and head southwest to Damüls.

VISITOR INFORMATION The **tourist office** (ℂ 05510/253) is in Kirchdorf, at the edge of the village center. It's open year-round Monday through Friday from 8:30am to noon and 1:30 to 6:30pm; in winter it's also open Saturday from 9:30am to noon and 3 to 5pm, Sunday from 10am to noon.

WHERE TO STAY & DINE

Hotel Damülser Hof This collection of modern chalets, each connected by covered passageways, sits in an alpine meadow a 5-minute walk uphill from the village church. Built in 1963 and renovated virtually every year since then, it boasts an elegant interior with enough variety in its decor to please most guests. The cozy public areas have intimate niches, soft lighting, and several fireplaces. Rooms are medium-size, comfortable, and well furnished, if rather impersonal. All units have well-kept bathrooms with shower-tub combinations.

A-6884 Oberdamüls. ℂ 05510/21-00. Fax 05510/543. www.damuelserhof.at. 50 units. Winter 144€–198€ double; summer 104€–120€ double. Rates include half-board. MC, V. Closed Nov and 1 week in Apr. Parking 8€ indoors, free outdoors. **Amenities:** Breakfast room; 2 bars; pool; tennis court; bowling alley; fitness center; sauna; room service; massage; babysitting; laundry; dry cleaning. *In room:* TV, hair dryer, safe.

12

Carinthia

If you like hiking or watersports or just lazing in the sun, Carinthia's beautiful countryside—gentle hills and steep mountains scattered with idyllic lakes—makes it a wonderful area to explore during the warmer months; it's also an ideal stopping point if you're heading south to Italy. The high mountains ringing Carinthia (or Kärnten, in German) create the province's natural borders, and the area has been likened to a gigantic amphitheater. Mountainous Upper Carinthia lies to the west and the Lower Carinthia Basin region slopes to the east. The province is bisected by the east-flowing Drau River, which becomes the Drava when it enters Slovenia; Villach is the biggest road and rail junction in the eastern Alps, and Klagenfurt is the capital of Carinthia.

If you're athletic, climb the gentle *Nocken* (hills) or head for the more demanding mountains. The region boasts more than 200 warm, clean lakes, and fishing is a popular pastime here, either in the lakes or in the colder mountain steams. The "Carinthian Riviera" is the name given to the main lake area, including the Wörther See, not far from Klagenfurt. Lake Ossiacher and Lake Millstatter are also in this area. Weissensee, another big lake, is less well known than the other three, but it's really the most scenic. The best way to see the lakes is to take one of the boats that operate from April to mid-October.

If you want to enjoy the lakes, visit Carinthia from mid-May to September, although the first 2 weeks in October are usually ideal, too. Hordes of visitors flock here in July and August, so make reservations in advance if you plan on visiting during those months.

Although the warm lakes are Carinthia's main attraction, the province also attracts some skiers to its mountains in winter. However, Carinthia's relatively mild winters don't always make for the best ski conditions. The ski season here lasts only from December to March. As a ski center, this province is much less expensive than Tyrol or Land Salzburg. Regardless of the season you visit, if you're driving, parking is rarely a problem: Unless otherwise noted, you park for free.

Archaeological discoveries prove that Carinthia was inhabited by humans far back in unrecorded time, and the Romans didn't overlook the area, either—their legions marched in to conquer alpine Celtic tribes in the kingdom of Noticum, establishing it as a Roman province.

For centuries, this area was home to ethnic groups from Slovenia, belonging to the kingdom of Germany and Avar-dominated Slavs from the east. Hoping to fend off invasions, the populace eventually invited Bavaria to become Carinthia's protector, and so it became part of the Holy Roman Empire.

When the Hapsburgs took Kärnten as a part of their rapidly expanding empire, it was a duchy of the Holy Roman Empire under the Bohemian aegis. To secure his control over the area, Ferdinand I of Hapsburg, soon to become emperor, married the heiress

Carinthia

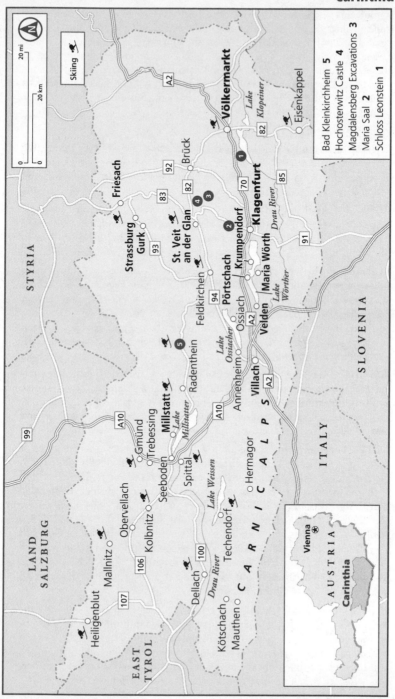

Bad Kleinkirchheim **5**
Hochosterwitz Castle **4**
Magdalensberg Excavations **3**
Maria Saal **2**
Schloss Leonstein **1**

Skiing

20 mi

20 km

Völkermarkt

Eisenkappel

Lake Klopeiner

A2

82

Brück

92

Friesach

83

82

70

85

Klagenfurt

Drau River

1

3

4

Strassburg

Gurk

93

St. Veit an der Glan

2

Krumpendorf

Pörtschach

Maria Wörth

91

STYRIA

Feldkirchen

94

Ossiach

Lake Ossiacher

Velden

A2

Lake Wörther

SLOVENIA

5

Radenthein

Annenheim

Villach

A2

A10

Millstatt

Lake Millstätter

Gmünd

Trebessing

A10

Seeboden

Spittal

A10

Hermagor

ITALY

99

Obervellach

Kolbnitz

Lake Weissen

Techendorf

C A R N I C   A L P S

LAND SALZBURG

Mallnitz

106

100

Dellach

Drau River

107

Heiligenblut

Kötschach

Mauthen

EAST TYROL

Vienna

AUSTRIA

Carinthia

to Bohemia and made Carinthia an imperial duchy. Later, Carinthia was designated a province of Austria.

The former country of Yugoslavia claimed southern Carinthia after World War I. During this time, some territory was ceded to Yugoslavia, and more was given to Italy, but all this land was later restored. In 1920, after the collapse of the Hapsburg Empire, the Slovenian minority in the south, along the Yugoslav border, voted to remain with Austria. Today a sizable minority of Carinthia's population is Slovenian, but the majority of it is German.

TIPS FOR ACTIVE TRAVELERS

If you spontaneously decide to spend a day boating, bicycling, or fishing, the staff at any local hotel will probably be able to tell you how to do it. Here's a list of outfitters who can help with advance planning and, in some cases, link you with a choice of specialized tours.

BIKING   Carinthia's gentle contours are ideal for cyclists, a fact you'll notice the moment you take to the district's highways. You can arrange both tours and rentals through the **Ossaich-Bodensdorf** railway station (© **04242/26954**). It's open Monday through Friday from 9am to 9pm, and Saturday from 9am to 2pm.

BOATING   The reception staff at virtually any lakeside hotel can arrange boating lessons and boat rentals, but two local experts are **Segel-und-Surfschule Wörthersee/Berger,** Seecorso 40, Velden (© **04274/269-10**), and **Herbert Schwieger,** 10 Oktober-Strasse 33, Pörtschach (© **04274/26-55**). These two outfits or any of the dozens of other *Bootverleih* (boat-rental agencies) can help you arrange windsurfing, canoeing, or sailing, and, where it's allowed, even rent you a motorized craft for fishing.

FISHING   Any local tourist office can provide you with the worthwhile pamphlet *"Kärnten Fischen,"* which explains the rules and procedures involved with a fishing expedition. Some hotels adjacent to important lakes offer fishing packages that include rooms, boat rentals, guides, and equipment in one price, and most hotel staffs are well versed.

GOLF   Some of the most appealing golf games in Austria are configured at sites that are relatively close to Carinthia's most beautiful lakes. From May to October (longer than at many other golf courses in the country), Carinthian golf is in full swing. The best of the district's golf courses include **Golfanlage Moosburg-Pörtschach,** A-9062 Moosburg (© **04272/83-48-60**). A nearby golf academy, **Golfakademie Moosburg-Pörtschach,** A-9062 (© **04272/82-30-20**), offers lessons on the same course. Two other fine courses are **Golfclub Bad Kleinkirchheim Golf Anlagen,** Zirkitzen 66, A-9546-Bad Kleinkirchheim (© **04275/595**), and **Golfclub-Austria Wörthersee,** Stallhofen 1, A-9062 Moosburg (© **04272/83-48-60**). Each of the courses mentioned above has 18 holes, a par of 72, and greens fees of 50€.

HIKING   Every lakeside resort has marked trails branching out over the mountains or through valleys. In summer, Carinthia is host to hordes of hikers, as Austrians flock here to take to the hills and mountains. The Ossiacher See area is especially suited for hiking, as are Hochosterwitz and Friesach. Some of the best hiking is possible from the towns of **Bad Kleinkirchheim, Feld am See,** and **Millstatt.** Ask at the local tourist office for information and maps.

SKIING   Carinthia doesn't have the mountains or facilities for skiing like Vorarlberg or Tyrol, but **Friesach** is emerging as a major ski area, attracting cross-country skiers in particular. The top ski resort is Bad Kleinkirchheim.

SWIMMING & WATERSPORTS   All the major lakes contain public beaches, and the waters are among the purest in Europe. You can drink from them safely, although we don't recommend this. In late summer, lake temperatures reach about 75°F (24°C), making them ideal for swimmers. If you'd like to combine your swimming with more serious watersports, check with such outfitters as **Segel-und-Surfschule Wörthersee/Berger,** Seecorso 40, Velden (℅ **04274/ 269-10**), or **Herbert Schwieger,** 10 Oktober-Strasse 33, Pörtschach (℅ **04272/ 26-55**).

TENNIS   Most major resorts such as Velden and Villach have their own courts; we particularly like Villach and its satellite areas for tennis. Try the courts at **Tennisplätz-ASKÖ, Landskron, Süduferstrasse** at Villach (℅ **04242/ 418-79**), or **Tenniscamp Warmbad** at Warmbad-Villach (℅ **04242/325-64**).

1 Klagenfurt ✴

38 miles (61km) NE of Italy; 19 miles (31km) N of Slovenia; 192 miles (309km) SW of Vienna; 87 miles (140km) SW of Graz; 130 miles (209km) SE of Salzburg

Klagenfurt is not an attraction in its own right; it's a sleepy city that's a great stopover point if you're driving around Carinthia's lakes. Arrive in Klagenfurt, get settled, and wander around the city's historic center. Stay the night, and then use Klagenfurt as the base of your explorations to **St. Veit, Hochosterwitz Castle, Magdelensberg,** the **Cathedral of Gurk,** and the region's lakes (see section 2, later in this chapter).

Klagenfurt, a university town dating from 1161, is the provincial capital and cultural center of Carinthia. Its charter was granted in 1252. The city was destroyed by fire in 1514 and was rebuilt and designated the duchy's capital in 1518. The medieval city was fortified with walls, which were torn down during the Napoleonic invasions in 1802.

The city center is quadrangular and rimmed with streets that were laid down where the city's walls once stood. The center of this quadrangle, and of the modern city, is **Neuer Platz,** presided over by a fountain in the shape of a ferocious dragon called Lindwurm, the city's symbol.

It can get very hot in the peak of summer, but if you're here, do as the Klagenfurters do and retreat to the nearby **Wörther See (Lake Wörther)** in the western sector of the city.

ESSENTIALS

GETTING THERE   By Train   Austrian Airlines serves Carinthia from Vienna, arriving at the **Klagenfurt Airport** (℅ **0463/41500** for flight information; www.klagenfurt-airport.at), northeast of the city, several times a day. Because Klagenfurt is a popular summer lakeside resort, **Austrian Airlines** adds summer flights from Zurich, Rome, and Frankfurt.

Klagenfurt, located on the lines connecting Vienna with Venice, Italy, and Zagreb, is the most important railway junction in southern Austria. It's also the focal point for several smaller rail lines whose passengers are eventually transferred to larger lines to Salzburg, Innsbruck, and Bregenz. Trains arrive from several different directions at intervals of 30 minutes or less throughout the day; call ℅ **0463/41500** for schedules.

By Bus   It's easier to take the train, but from Klagenfurt at least 20 different bus lines fan out into the surrounding region. For regional **bus information,** call ℅ **0463/58110** in Klagenfurt.

By Car If you're driving from Vienna, head south on Autobahn A2, cutting southeast at the junction with Route 17 and going through the Semmering mountain pass. Then follow Route 83 into Klagenfurt.

VISITOR INFORMATION The **tourist office** is in the **Rathaus,** or city hall (✆ **0463/53-72-23;** www.klagenfurt.at); to reach it from the rail station, head down Bahnhofstrasse. It's open Monday through Friday from 8am to 8pm, and Saturday and Sunday from 10am to 5pm.

If you are driving into Klagenfurt and want to leave the car, this city offers restricted parking zones where you can park for 90 minutes in specially marked "blue zones," so-called because of blue lines on the road. You have to use a parking voucher to stop in limited-parking zones. Vouchers can be purchased at banks, gas stations, or tobacconists. When you park, you must write in the time you arrived and display the voucher on the dashboard, inside the windshield.

EXPLORING KLAGENFURT
SEEING THE SIGHTS

Alter Platz, both a broad thoroughfare and a square, is lined with many baroque mansions. It's a pedestrian zone that's the center of the **Altstadt (Old Town),** and many crooked, narrow little streets and alleys open off the square.

The **Trinity Column** in Alter Platz dates from 1681; it was built to commemorate those who died from the plague. One of the most interesting buildings on the square is the 17th-century **Altes Rathaus (Old Town Hall).** It has a three-story arcaded courtyard. The **House of the Golden Goose (Haus zur Goldenen Gans),** on Alter Platz, dates from 1599.

The **Cathedral (Domkirche) of Klagenfurt** lies to the southeast of Neuer Platz. Construction on this building began in 1578, and the interior is richly adorned in stucco and has ceiling paintings from the 18th century. Next door to the cathedral, **Diozesanmuseum** ⚜, Lidmanskyg 10 (✆ **0463/536-30552**), is a small, often overlooked museum containing a remarkable collection of **religious art** ⚜⚜ from the 12th to the 18th centuries. Sculpture, tapestries, jewelry, artwork, and stained glass are on display here, including the oldest extant stained-glass window in the country, a portrait of Mary Magdalene from 1170. Some works of art in the museum are truly remarkable, including one-of-a-kind pieces such as a rare processional cross made of iron with traces of gilt. It dates from the 12th century. Diozesanmuseum is open Tuesday through Sunday from 9am to 4pm. Admission costs 2.50€ for adults and 1.50€ for children.

If you're traveling with children, consider an excursion to a nearby theme park, **Minimundus,** Villacherstrasse 241 (✆ **0463/211-94**). Here, scaled-down versions of the world's most famous buildings are artfully arranged in a layout that incorporates flower beds and whimsical interpretations of some of the world's most photographed buildings. Examples include small-scale versions of the Eiffel Tower, the Great Wall of China, Big Ben, and various European castles and Asian temples. Every model within the park measures approximately ½₅ the size of the original. Minimundus is open April through October. In April and October, it's open daily from 9am to 5pm. In May, June, and September, it's open daily from 9am to 6pm. In July and August, it's open daily from 9am to 9pm. Admission costs 11€ for adults and 6€ for children under 16.

Landesmuseum ⚜ At this provincial museum, you can see Roman artifacts, including votive stones, gleaned from excavations in Carinthia. Exhibits display art and artifacts from prehistoric times to the present. The most outstanding feature is a display of ecclesiastical art. See the skull of a rhinoceros, said to have been a model for the renowned Dragon Fountain in Neuer Platz.

Museumgasse 2. © **0463/536-30-552.** www.landesmuseum-ktn.at. Admission 3€ adults, 1.50€ seniors and children. Tues–Sat 9am–4pm; Sun and holidays 10am–1pm.

Landhaus   Originally an arsenal and later Carinthian state headquarters, this structure now houses the offices of the provincial government. Building was begun in 1574 and completed in 1590. The courtyard of the present building has two-story arcades, and the set of staircase towers has bulbous caps. Its **Grosser Wappensaal (Great Blazon Hall),** dating from 1739, was handsomely decorated by Joseph Ferdinand Fromiller. The painting on the hall's ceiling depicting 665 heraldic shields is executed in trompe l'oeil.

Landhaushof 1. © **0463/57-75-70.** Admission 1.50€ adults, .75€ children. Apr–Sept 9am–noon and 12:30–5pm. Closed Oct–Mar.

SHOPPING

The capital of Carinthia might surprise you with its quiet sense of prosperity and genteel good taste. Many of the interesting shops lie beside the **Bahnhofstrasse** and the pedestrian-only streets that radiate outward from the Alterplatz. Among the most appealing shops, you'll find **Kastner & Öhler,** Feldmarschal Konrad Platz 11 (© **0463/575-20**), where you'll see virtually every piece of equipment you'd need for the pursuit of sports in any season.

Kärntner Heimatwerk, Herrengasse 2 (© **0463/555-75**), is housed on the street level of a pink-and-white baroque building in the center of town. It offers the best collection of locally made handcrafts in Klagenfurt. Merchandise includes a selection of embroidery, ceramics, wrought iron, glassware, and textiles sold by the meter. It's open Monday through Friday from 8:30am to 6pm, and Saturday from 8:30am to noon.

WHERE TO STAY

Arcotel Hotel Moser Verdino ⭐   In the town center north of the Domkirche, the jutting tower of this hotel's elaborate pink-and-white facade was built in 1890 in a rich Art Nouveau design. For more than a century, it has been the town's leading hotel. Rooms were totally renovated in 1997, making them better than ever and restoring the hotel to its original prestige. Bathrooms have shower-tub combinations. The most popular cafe in town, Café Moser Verdino, is near the oak-trimmed lobby.

Domgasse 2, A-9020 Klagenfurt. © **0463/508-707.** Fax 0463/51-67-65. www.arcotel.at. 78 units. 114€– 171€ double. Rates include breakfast. AE, DC, MC, V. **Amenities:** Restaurant; bar; room service; babysitting; laundry; dry cleaning. *In room:* TV, minibar, hair dryer, safe.

Hotel Garni Blumenstöckl   Centrally located off Neuer Platz, this old-fashioned hotel (with a history that goes back 4 centuries) tends to be heavily booked in summer, so reservations are needed as far in advance as possible. One of this establishment's finest features is its elegant courtyard, where ornate wrought-iron balconies are supported by chiseled stone columns. The hotel offers peaceful and simply furnished rooms in a wide variety of sizes. The bathrooms are small, each with a tub and a shower. Only breakfast is served here. Parking is free on the street after 6pm.

10 Oktober Strasse 11, A-9020 Klagenfurt. © **0463/577-93.** Fax 0463/577-935. 14 units. 77€–80€ double. Rates include breakfast. No credit cards. Closed 2 weeks in Oct. **Amenities:** Breakfast room; lounge. *In room:* TV.

Hotel Sandwirt   All Austrian presidents elected since 1945 have stayed in this historic hotel, which was completely renovated in late 2001 and early 2002. In 1899, owner Paul Jamek's ancestors bought the centrally located neoclassical building constructed in the 1650s. Rooms vary widely in style and size but are usually high-ceilinged and comfortably old-fashioned; some, however, are very modernized. Most contain double beds, and each is equipped with a tiled bathroom with tub and shower.

Pernhartgasse 9, A-9020 Klagenfurt. © **800/528-1234** in the U.S., or 0463/562-09. Fax 0463/51-43-22. 40 units. 110€–145€ double. Rates include buffet breakfast. AE, DC, MC, V. Parking 4€. **Amenities:** Breakfast room. *In room:* TV, minibar.

Schloss Hotel Wörthersee ⚐   Despite its limited number of rooms, this is the most internationally famous hotel in Klagenfurt. Set across the road from the Wörthersee, it was originally built as a private villa in 1845 by a distant relative of Germany's counts of Thurn und Taxis. In 1892, a railway station (since demolished) was constructed nearby, and the building was bought and enlarged into a hotel. In 1982, the hotel was purchased by its present owners, the Strohschein family, who added what became the most popular restaurant in the region. In 1990, a German television series (*Schloss-Hotel Wörthersee*) filmed its most melodramatic scenes here.

Today the hotel is a combination of an Edwardian villa and a Teutonic castle, and a tunnel beneath the road leads to the hotel's private beach and a lakeside promenade that stretches for several miles. Most rooms have balconies and wood trim or paneling. All units have well-kept bathrooms equipped with shower-tub combinations.

The kitchens for the in-house restaurant **(Strohschein's Heuriger)** are supervised by the family matriarch, Hildstraud, and they produce some of the region's finest cuisine. Her elegant repertoire includes cream of broccoli soup with quail eggs, homemade paté de foie gras, and a white- and dark-chocolate mousse with a cocoa-cream sauce.

Villacher Strasse 338, A-9020 Klagenfurt. © **0463/211-58.** Fax 0463/21-15-88. www.schloss-hotel.at. 34 units. 60€–84€ double; from 84€ suite for 2. Rates include buffet breakfast. MC, V. Closed Jan. Head west from the center of Klagenfurt for 3km (2 miles) toward Villach. **Amenities:** Restaurant; bar; sauna. *In room:* TV.

WHERE TO DINE

Da Luigi ⚐ ITALIAN/SEAFOOD   One of the best restaurants in Klagenfurt focuses on dishes you'd expect to find in an upscale resort along the Adriatic, served with Italian panache in a mostly pink setting near Klagenfurt's Stadtstheater. Examples include grilled sea bass with balsamic vinegar and olive oil, and grilled daurade (a type of bream) served with a fresh tomato, white wine, and cognac sauce. The array of fresh shellfish, including crabs, oysters, clams, and about a half dozen other mollusks, is one of the best in town. The chefs at all times try to secure the freshest ingredients on the market. The wines come from throughout Europe, but there's a special emphasis on Austrian and Italian vintages.

Khevenhüllerstrasse 2. © **0463/51-66-51.** Reservations recommended. Main courses 9€–20€; set-price menu 45€–70€. MC, V. Mon–Sat 11:30am–2pm and 6–10pm.

Felsenkeller AUSTRIAN   Set about a mile north of town, this restaurant features a sophisticated, elegant, and relatively inexpensive set of menu items that are served within a big-windowed building originally constructed in the early 1600s as a storage shed for ice. Views sweep from the dining room out over the

Ossiacher See. Menu items rely on fresh seasonal ingredients and change with the inspiration of the chef. Good-tasting examples include a gourmet version of fish and chips wherein mussels are deep-fried and served with a Pinot wine sauce. Other choices include game, especially venison (in season), partridge, veal, pork, and usually at least one vegetarian dish a day.

Feldkirchner Strasse 141. © 0463/42-01-30. Reservations recommended. Main courses 5€–12€. DC, MC, V. Mon–Sat 10:30am–midnight.

Hamatle (Value CARINTHIAN   There's been a popular restaurant in this century-old building since the 1950s, and present management, in place since around 1995, does everything it can to preserve the nostalgia. The result is a cozy restaurant with grandmother-style (*Grossmutter Art*) cuisine and an obvious allegiance to the traditions of Carinthia. (Its name is the equivalent, in local dialect, of *Heimat,* which translates as "homeland.") There are two dining rooms, one on each of two floors, outfitted in a country-comfortable lake-district style. Menu items focus on noodles (usually in a creamy sauce and dotted with, among other things, ham, onions, and/or mushrooms); braised trout with butter sauce and herbs; succulent schnitzels of pork, chicken, or veal; and beefsteaks, any of which might be preceded by goulash soup.

Linsengasse 1. © 0463/555700. Reservations recommended. Main courses 7€–16€. Set-price lunch 7.10€; set-price dinner 19.30€. AE, DC, MC, V. Tues–Sun 11am-11pm.

Maria Loretto (🔆🔆 SEAFOOD   This is the kind of long-established restaurant where an extended local family might migrate, especially on a Sunday, for a breath of fresh air, a view over the lake, and a well-prepared roster of mostly fish dishes. The setting is directly beside the lake, within a pair of pale blue, vaguely baroque dining rooms whose style is best described as *romantische-gemütlich* ("romantic and cozy"). Menu items include a small selection of meats (especially Wiener schnitzels and grilled filet steak), and lots and lots of fish. Raw ingredients are hauled in from the North and Mediterranean seas, the Atlantic Ocean, and the freshwater lakes and streams of the surrounding region. Most of these are prepared in the simplest way possible (lightly grilled and seasoned with a garlic-flavored butter sauce), served with salad and boiled new potatoes, and accompanied with a young and fruity white wine, preferably Austrian or Italian. Consider prefacing any main course with such starters as onion or garlic soup, a carpaccio of tuna, whitefish, or beef; smoked trout; or perhaps succulent snails cooked in garlic-butter sauce with a gratin of cheese.

Lorettoweg 54. © 0463/24465. Reservations recommended. Main courses 13€–22€. Set-price menu 13.80€. V. Wed–Mon 11am–10pm. Closed Jan 10–Feb 28. From Klagenfurt's center, take bus marked STRAND-BAD KLAGENFURT/KLAGENFURT SEE.

Restaurant Lido AUSTRIAN   Although it originated in the 1980s as a rather grand and elegant restaurant, Lido has devolved into a much simpler, less pretentious bistro. Three kilometers (2 miles) west of the town center, beside the road leading to Villach, it offers simple but well-prepared fare: simple versions of Wiener schnitzel; cold platters of smoked fish, including local salmon and whitefish; crayfish salads; roasted lamb with rosemary and thyme; cold sliced beef in aspic; and an assorted roster of grilled fish.

Friedelstrand 1. © 0463/24-23-44. Reservations recommended. Main courses 12€–22€; set-price menus 14.50€–22.50€. AE, DC, MC, V. Tues–Sun 11:30am–2pm and 6–10pm.

Restaurant Oscar (🔆 AUSTRIAN/ITALIAN   Stalwart and reliable, with a reputation for solid, well-prepared Italian and Austrian food, this restaurant lies on the northern edge of Klagenfurt's commercial core and about 450m (1,500 ft.) from the local hospital. The dining room is large but cozy, trimmed with dark-stained wood and furnished with modern-looking tables and chairs and high-tech lighting. Menu items lean toward the Italian, with touches of Austrian specialties thrown in as well, and include homemade pastas, schnitzels, a savory roasted goose, hearty soups, a rich focus every autumn on game dishes, crepes (including flavorful versions with spinach and/or mushrooms), risottos, and roasted pork served with local cheeses and sage. The choice of fish is wide, with emphasis on meaty "noble" fish that include sea bass and sea trout. At least part of the design and allure of this restaurant was inspired by a trip that the then-owner took long ago to New York, where he was impressed with a restaurant named Oscar.

Sankt Veiter Ring 43. ℂ 0463/5001-77. Reservations recommended. Main courses 14€–18€; set-price lunch 6€; set-price dinner 29€; set-price dinner with wine 39€. AE, DC, MC, V. Mon–Sat 11am–2pm and 6–11pm.

KLAGENFURT AFTER DARK

The largest, grandest, and most formal theater in Klagenfurt is the **Stadttheater,** Theatergasse (ℂ **0463/552-66;** www.stadttheater-klagenfurt.at), which presents opera, classics of German theater, and chamber and orchestral music performed by visiting groups. Built in 1910, this building went through a 2-year renovation (ending in 1998) that has given it a new state-of-the-art interior.

If you're lucky enough to arrive in Klagenfurt between mid-July and late August, make a point of strolling through the Neuerplatz every evening after 9:30pm. Here, open-air movies of famous cultural events (from virtually everywhere) are presented without charge. Past presentations have included filmed concerts by Billy Joel, Liza Minnelli, Leonard Bernstein, Montserrat Caballé, Bruce Springsteen, and Tina Turner, and the Vienna Opera's presentation of various operas by Verdi. Kiosks around the square's perimeter offer snacks and drinks.

The rest of the year, take an evening stroll around the neighborhood of the **Pfarr-platz,** where you'll find most of Klagenfurt's nightlife options. The best of the lot includes **Bar Gallo Nero,** Pfarrhofgasse 8 (ℂ **0463/51-27-80**), where there's live music that never dips into anything too loud, too metallic, or too abrasive. A nearby nightclub that's a little more cramped and appealingly claustrophobic is the **Spectacle Bar,** Wienergasse 7 (ℂ **0463/564-19**). Nostalgic references to Ireland pour out of **Pub Molly Melone,** Theatergasse 7 (ℂ **0463/ 572-00**), where pints of Irish, German, and Austrian beer make the traditional ballads and fiddle music more appealing. And if you happen to be gay (male or female), Klagenfurt's only widely acknowledged gay bar is **Bar Absolut,** St-Veiter Strasse 3 (ℂ **0463-599-999**).

2 Cathedrals, Castles & More: Side Trips from Klagenfurt

ST. VEIT AN DER GLAN

The capital of Carinthia from 1170 until 1518, St. Veit an der Glan was where the dukes of Carinthia held power when the province was an imperial duchy. In the 15th century, high walls were built to fortify the city. To reach the town from Klagenfurt, drive 14km (9 miles) north on Route 83.

In the rectangular **Hauptplatz (Main Square)** at the center of town is a **Trinity Column** dating from 1715, erected to mark the town's deliverance from the plague. Also in this square is the fountain called **Schüsselbrunnen.** The bottom part of this fountain is believed to have been excavated at the old Roman city of Virunum. A bronze statue crowning the fountain depicts a 16th-century miner, which St. Veit has adopted as its symbol.

The **Rathaus (Town Hall)** has a baroque exterior, although the building dates from 1468, and an arcaded courtyard. Guided tours are conducted through the great hall Thursday through Tuesday from 8am to noon and 1 to 4pm, and on Wednesday from 8am to noon; it's closed Saturday and Sunday from November to April.

WHERE TO STAY & DINE

Rogner Dorint Hotel ★★★ (Finds   This is Carinthia's first art hotel, designed by Ernst Fuchs, doyen of Austria's Fantastic Realists. With a Tiffany-glass exterior, it is a luxurious, government-rated four-star establishment. This former ducal town has long been in need of accommodations to match its charm, and now it has a suitable hotel. The hotel is often a venue for seminars and conferences.

The public rooms are filled with art, and each of the bedrooms is decorated in a different color scheme. All bathrooms come with new equipment, each with a shower unit. The Zodiac restaurant offers impressive Styrian and continental cuisine, and there is grand comfort throughout the place.

Friesacherstrasse 1, A-9300 St. Veit an der Glan. ⓒ **04121/4660.** Fax 04212/4660-660. www.rogner. com. 60 units. 130€ double. Half-board 15€ per person extra. Rates include buffet breakfast. AE, MC, V. **Amenities:** Restaurant; bar; room service; babysitting; laundry; dry cleaning. *In room:* TV, minibar, safe.

HOCHOSTERWITZ CASTLE ★

St. Veit an der Glan stands at the center of the most castle-rich section of Austria, with more than a dozen of the fortress complexes lying within a 10km (6½-mile) radius of St. Veit. The best-known and most visited is **Hochosterwitz Castle** in Launsdorf-Hochosterwitz (ⓒ **04213/20-20**), about 10km to the east of St. Veit. The castle was first mentioned in documents of 860; in 1209, the ruling Spanheims made the Osterwitz family hereditary royal cupbearers and gave them Hochosterwitz as a fiefdom. When the last of that line was a victim of a Turkish invasion, the castle reverted to Emperor Frederick III, who bestowed it upon the area's governor, Christof Khevenhuller. In 1570, Baron George Khevenhuller, also the governor, purchased the citadel and fortified it against the Turks, providing it with an armory and adding the gates, a task completed in 1586. Since that time, the castle has been the property of the Khevenhuller family, as shown on a marble plate in the yard dated 1576.

The castle—the most striking in the country—stands in a scenic spot on a lonely, isolated hilltop 162m (530 ft.) above the valley. From the castle, you get an eagle's-eye view of the surrounding area, and to reach it you go up a 16th-century approach ramp and through a total of 14 fortified gates. You can look at the armor collection, visit a number of rooms, and wander through the portrait gallery.

Hochosterwitz Castle is open only from Easter to October daily from 9am to 5pm. Admission is 7€ for adults and 4€ for children. A regional cafe and restaurant are located in the inner courtyard.

THE EXCAVATIONS AT MAGDELENSBERG ★

You can also strike out from St. Veit and head south, back to Klagenfurt, on Route 83. If you turn left after 6km (4 miles) on a road marked MAGDE-LENSBERG and travel east, you'll reach the **Ausgrabungen (Excavations) at Magdalensberg** (ⓒ **04224/22-55**). About 14km (9 miles) from St. Veit,

Magdalensberg was a Celto-Roman settlement site and the oldest Roman habitation north of the Alps. The Romans built a town here when they came to trade in the final century before the birth of Christ. In 1502, a farmer made the first discovery of a settlement here when he found a bronze statue, now called the **Magdalensberg Youth** (on display in Vienna).

However, it was not until the late 19th century that excavation work began, and even then, collectors were mainly interested in discovering valuable Roman art objects. Serious archaeologists began to work the site during the Allied occupation of Austria after World War II.

As you explore the ruins, you can see the foundations of a temple, as well as public baths and some mosaics. Tours are conducted only May through October daily from 9am to 7pm. Admission is 4€ for adults and 2.50€ for children under 16.

A celebrated ritual (which has pagan origins), the "Four Hills Pilgrimage," starts from here every April. Complete with burning torches, the participants race over four hills, and the run must be completed within 24 hours.

At the summit of the mountain, the Austrians have erected a shrine honoring two saints: Mary Magdalene and Helen. From it, a panoramic view of the encircling mountain range, including the Klagenfurt basin, unfolds before you.

STRASSBURG

Returning once more to St. Veit, you can head northeast along Route 83, which becomes the E7. When you reach the junction with Route 93, turn west along the upper Gurk Valley road, passing through the hamlet of Strassburg, which was a walled town in the Middle Ages. There is a Gothic **Pfarrkirche (Parish Church)** here, and the **Heilig-Geist-Spital Church,** dating from the 13th century, has some well-preserved frescoes. Dominating the village is a castle built in 1147, but it's changed over the centuries. Once this was the headquarters of the powerful prince-bishops of Gurk. It has been turned into a local museum.

THE CATHEDRAL OF GURK 𝕒𝕒

A major pilgrimage site lies 3km (2 miles) to the west of Strassburg: the **Cathedral of Gurk Pfarramt Gurk (© 04266/823-60).** The cathedral is the principal feature of the little market town of Gurk, and from 1072 until 1787, this area was the bishop's see. The *Dom* (cathedral) is a three-aisled basilica erected between the mid–12th and early 13th centuries, and it's one of the best examples of Romanesque ecclesiastical architecture in the country. A set of towers with onion-shape domes rises nearly 43m (140 ft.).

The cathedral is rich in artwork, including the **Samson doorway** 𝕒, an excellent example of Romanesque sculpture dating from 1180. Some **16th-century carved panels** 𝕒 tell the story of St. Emma, an 11th-century countess who was canonized in 1938. The main 17th-century altar has dozens of statues, and there's a **1740 baroque pulpit** 𝕒. In the bishop's chapel you can see **Romanesque murals** 𝕒—other than the main altar, these are the most important art objects in the cathedral.

The cathedral is open daily from 9am to 6pm. You can take a guided tour in English of both the cathedral and the crypt for 2.60€. For 7€, you can include a visit to the bishop's chambers.

FRIESACH

After visiting the Cathedral of Gurk, you can take the same road east, back through Strassburg. Back on the E7, and depending on your time and interest, you can either turn north to visit the town of Friesach or else travel south again, passing through St. Veit en route to Klagenfurt.

If you opt for the Friesach detour, you'll find an interesting old town worth exploring. If you came from Vienna, Friesach might be your gateway to Carinthia. This is an ancient town whose first mention in historic annals occurred in the mid–9th century. The town once belonged to the prince-arch-bishops of Salzburg, who held on to it until the beginning of the 19th century. Lying in the broad Valley of Melnitz, this was once a major stopover for traders between Venice and Austria's capital.

In the historic center of town, you can see part of the 12th-century town walls and the remains of a water-filled moat. The Romanesque **Stadtpfarrkirche (Town Parish Church),** Wiener Strasse, was constructed in the 13th century and is noted for its stained glass in the choir. The town has a number of other interesting buildings, including a **Dominican monastery** from 1673, built on the site of a much older structure and containing a 14th-century church. The monastery lies north of the moat, and in summer, open-air plays are performed here. You can also visit the 13th-century **Heiligblutkirche (Church of the Holy Blood)** south of Hauptplatz, the main square of the town.

West of Friesach, a mile-long road or footpath takes you to the hill **Peters-berg,** where the 10th-century **Church of St. Peter** stands. Here you can visit a watchtower to see 12th-century frescoes, and you can also see the ruins of a cas-tle that belonged to the prince-archbishops of Salzburg. North of the town, on **Geiersberg,** is a second 12th-century castle, partially reconstructed but still mostly in ruins.

MARIA SAAL ⍟

Just outside of Klagenfurt, you can visit the pilgrimage church of **Maria Saal,** on a hill overlooking the Zollfeld Plain, some 10km (6½ miles) north of the provincial capital along Route 83.

Maria Saal was first built by Bishop Modestus around the mid–8th century. The present church, which dominates the valley with its twin towers made of volcanic stone, dates from the early part of the 15th century, when a defensive wall was constructed to ward off attacks from the east. In the latter part of that century, the Magyars tried to take the fortress-church, but, like the Turks in later years, they were unable to conquer it.

One of the church's most outstanding features is a "lantern of the dead" in the late Gothic style at the south doorway. There are some marble Gothic tombstones on the church grounds, and there's the *Karner* (charnel house), an octagonal Romanesque building with two tiers of galleries. The church has many objets d'art, but it is the 1425 image of the Virgin that has made it a pilgrimage site.

An interesting excursion to take from Maria Saal is to the **Herzogstuhl,** or Carinthian Ducal Throne, a mile to the north. A double throne on this ancient site was constructed from stones found at the Roman city of Virunum. The dukes of Carinthia used the throne to grant fiefs in medieval days.

THE VELLACH VALLEY

Southeast of Klagenfurt, the Vellach Valley leads to the Slovenian border, and your fellow visitors here are likely to be Slovenians. **Eisenkappel** is the major stopover in the valley. This town is surrounded by centuries-old forests and min-eral springs, and because of its position as a frontier town only 16km (10 miles) from the Austro-Slovenian border's Jezersko Pass, it also offers many cultural and historical attractions.

The southernmost of all Austria's market villages, Eisenkappel, also known as Selezna Kapla, its Slovenian name, is home to a large Slovenian ethnic population. It lies at the foot of Karawanken, 39km (24 miles) from Klagenfurt (or Celovec, as you're likely to hear it called in this valley). From Klagenfurt, drive south along Route 91 to the junction with Route 85. Cut east until you reach the junction with Route 82, and then head south to Eisenkappel.

There are many sky-blue lakes and white mountain peaks near Eisenkappel. **Lake Klopeiner** (see below), to the north of this town, is the warmest lake in Carinthia. Eight kilometers (5 miles) to the southwest you'll see **Trögerner Gorge.**

LAKE KLOPEINER

Surrounded by woodlands and shaped like an amphitheater, Lake Klopeiner lies south of the market town of Volkermarkt. To get there, drive east along Route 70.

The lake's waters sometimes reach 82°F (28°C) in summer, and the lake is fairly small—only 2km (1½ miles) long and less than a kilometer wide at its broadest point. In summer, it's flooded with fun-loving Austrians. To keep the sky-blue water free of pollution, the government does not permit motor-powered craft on the lake. The resorts that ring the lake are part of the community of **St. Kanzian.**

LAKE OSSIACHER

Follow Route 95 northwest of Klagenfurt, and pass through Moosberg and Feldkirchen to reach Lake Ossiacher (Ossiacher See). This body of water, some 11km (7 miles) long, is the province's third-largest lake. Its water temperature during the summer is only slightly cooler than that of Lake Wörther—a comfortable 79°F (26°C).

The lake is ringed with little villages that have become resorts by attracting summer visitors, mainly Austrians, who come to enjoy the sun and the water.

Our first stop, **Feldkirchen,** is an old town that once belonged to the Bamberg bishops. Located at a major crossroads, Feldkirchen grew and prospered from traders passing through the area, and pieces of the Middle Ages live on here, especially in the patrician houses and narrow streets. Visit the old quarter to see the Biedermeier facades that were added in the first part of the 19th century. The village has a Romanesque **Pfarrkirche (Parish Church)** with a Gothic choirand frescoes from the 13th century. Some small lakes near the town are worth visiting, if time permits.

Ossiach, a resort on the lake's south side, is small (pop. 650), but it's still the biggest settlement on the Ossiacher See. Ossiach has an 11th-century Benedictine abbey that was reconstructed in the 1500s. The monastery was dissolved a century or so ago, and **Carinthian Summer Festival** special events take place here.

On the lake's north shore are the **Sattendorf** and **Treffen** resorts, which are open year-round. Here you can breathe the pure mountain air and wander across alpine meadows deep into the forest. Vacationers can splash around in Lake Ossiacher or in indoor pools.

From the lake, you can make several easy excursions, including taking the **Kanzelbahn cable car** (10 min. from the resort) or driving to either Italy or Slovenia (20 min. to either destination). You can also make day trips to Klagenfurt (see section 1, earlier in this chapter) or Villach (see section 4, later in this chapter).

The little lakeside resort of **Annenheim** is on the north side of the Ossiacher See, near the end of the lake. From here, a cable car, the **Kanzelbahn,** takes you to **Kanzelhöhe** at 1,488m (4,880 ft.), where an observatory tower offers a panoramic view of the surrounding country.

3 Lake Wörther ⚡

The province's biggest alpine lake, 16km (10 miles) long, is the Wörther See, or Lake Wörther, lying west of Klagenfurt and linked to the city by a channel. In summer, it's a mecca for watersports enthusiasts.

This alpine lake's waters are quite warm—their temperature often exceeds 80°F (27°C) in midsummer. Beginning in May, Austrians swim here, something that rarely occurs in alpine lakes of most other provinces. The little villages around Wörther See are flourishing summer resorts, especially **Maria Wörth** and **Velden.**

KRUMPENDORF

This is just a small stop along the road, but you'll find some moderately priced hotels serving good food here. It's also well equipped for watersports. This resort does a thriving family business, and its hotels are spread out, vying for choice spots along the Wörther See.

GETTING THERE   Krumpendorf is both an express and a local stop on the train lines heading west from Klagenfurt to Villach. Two or three trains per hour arrive from both directions. The train ride from Klagenfurt takes about 8 minutes; call ✆ **0463/58110** for **train schedules.**

Although several daily buses depart from Klagenfurt's main railway station every day for the 15-minute ride to Krumpendorf, most travelers prefer the train. For **bus information,** call ✆ **0463/54340** in Klagenfurt.

If you're **driving** from Klagenfurt, head west on Route 83 to the first exit for Krumpendorf, 10km (6½ miles) west of Klagenfurt.

VISITOR INFORMATION   The **tourist office** (✆ **4229/23-13**) in the town center is open only in summer Monday through Friday from 8am to 5pm, Saturday from 9am to noon.

WHERE TO STAY & DINE

Strandhotel Habich ⚡ *Kids*   Set near the lake's edge in a parklike garden half a mile southwest of the town center, this hotel looks like a well-appointed private home. Built in the 1970s and administered by the Habich family, it's ideal for enjoying some summer fun by the lake. Inside, rustic paneling lends woodsy appeal and a homey atmosphere. The pleasant, medium-size rooms are comfortably furnished and well maintained. Bathrooms contain showers that are immaculately kept. On the premises are a lakeside swimming area, boating piers, a flowered breakfast terrace, and a children's play area.

Walterskirchenweg 10, A-9201 Krumpendorf. ✆ **04229/26-07.** Fax 04229/260776. strandhotel.habich@ epinet.at. 40 units. 110€–138€ double. Rates include half-board. No credit cards. Closed Oct 7–Mar. **Amenities:** Breakfast room; lounge; pool; 5 tennis courts. *In room:* TV.

PÖRTSCHACH

Known for its lakeside promenade, **Pörtschach** ⚡ is one of Carinthia's premier resorts. It's extremely sports-oriented, with water-skiing, sailing, riding, and golf. The resort, along Lake Wörther's north shore, is filled with many lavish villas, and a section of the town juts out on a tiny peninsula. In summer, the lakeside promenade's flower beds are a blaze of color. Southwest of the resort stands **Hotel Schloss Leonstain** (see below), and there are many lovely nature walks and scenic drives in the area.

GETTING THERE   Approximately two **trains** per hour, both local and some express trains passing between Klagenfurt and Villach, stop here throughout the day. The trip from Klagenfurt takes about 12 minutes; from Villach, it's about 15 minutes.

Buses depart several times a day from Klagenfurt for Pörtschach. The trip takes 25 to 40 minutes. For **bus information,** call ℭ **0463/543-40** in Klagenfurt.

If you're **driving** from Klagenfurt, head west along Route 83 for 14km (9 miles).

VISITOR INFORMATION   The **tourist office** in the center of the resort (ℭ **04272/28-10-15**) is open Monday through Friday from 8am to 7pm, and Saturday and Sunday from 9am to noon and 4 to 7pm.

WHERE TO STAY

Gasthof Joainig   A mile east of the town center, this gracefully detailed and generously proportioned establishment was built in 1911 as the country retreat of wealthy Austrian urbanites. There's a large bar/cafe/pastry shop here, as well as a big sun terrace and masses of beautiful summer flowers in boxes. Rooms are comfortable, if a bit small, with equally small bathrooms equipped with either tubs or showers.

Kochwirtplatz 4, A-9210 Pörtschach. ℭ **04272/23-19.** Fax 04272/237950. www.joainig.co.at. 21 units. 68€–82€ double. Rates include half-board. AE, DC, MC, V. Closed Nov. **Amenities:** Restaurant; bar; room service; laundry; dry cleaning. *In room:* TV.

Hotel Schloss Leonstain ᑫ   A century ago, inspired by the landscape surrounding this retreat, Johannes Brahms composed his *Violin Concerto* and his *Second Symphony* here. What you'll see today is a once-fortified 14th-century castle. Throughout the establishment are wrought-iron accents, old terra-cotta tiles, stone detailing, vaulted ceilings, and well-chosen furniture. Most rooms are furnished in an inviting, homey style, with rustic antiques and firm beds. A few, however, have a color scheme that's a bit jarring (painted in cobalt blue). Rooms come in a variety of sizes; some are duplexes. Bathrooms have shower-tub combinations.

The hotel restaurant offers the sort of candlelit ambience that many Austrians travel a long way to find. Served either inside or in the courtyard, the food is consistently good; specialties include filet of trout, Valencian fish soup, and veal cutlet with cream sauce. The homemade desserts are often accompanied by live music. Special buffets are presented on Sunday in the courtyard.

A-9210 Pörtschach. ℭ **04272/281-60.** Fax 04272/28-23. www.leonstain.at. 35 units. 138€–278€ double. Rates include breakfast. AE, DC, MC, V. Closed Oct–May 15. **Amenities:** Restaurant; bar; 5 tennis courts; fitness center; sauna; room service; massage; laundry; dry cleaning. *In room:* TV, safe.

Hotel Schloss Seefels ᑫᑫ   This is the most elaborate and most impressive hotel in the region, and it's only a 15-minute walk from Pörtschach's center. The hotel was originally built in 1860 as a private, neobaroque private villa. Between 1966 and 1970, the grandson of the original builders converted it into the town's only government-rated five-star hotel. Today, radiating outward from a copper-domed core, the hotel resembles a balconied chalet-style building that rambles along the lake's shore. Recent improvements include glassed-in patios, a small marina for motorboats and sailboats, and a spa. The cozy rooms are elegant and often outfitted with well-polished antiques, contemporary and traditional furniture, and thick carpets. Bathrooms are beautifully kept, with shower-tub combinations.

The hotel's dining room, Seestubel, features a *Tagesmenu* (day's menu); both Austrian and international dishes are served.

Töschling 1, A-9210 Pörtschach. © **04272/23-77.** Fax 04272/37-04. www.seefels.com. 73 units. 95€–205€ double; 300€–860€ suite for 2. Rates include half-board. AE, DC, MC, V. Closed Oct 4–May 1. Free parking outside. **Amenities:** 2 restaurants; bar; pool; fitness center; sauna; room service; babysitting; laundry; dry cleaning. *In room:* A/C, TV, minibar, hair dryer, safe.

Seehotel Werzer-Astoria 🚣 *(Kids* One of this hotel's most unusual buildings is the late-19th-century bathhouse, crowned with a latticed tower, that extends into the lake. It's protected as a historic monument and has welcomed bathers like Johannes Brahms. Today the bathhouse contains changing rooms, a lunchtime buffet, and a private rooftop platform hotel that guests can rent for nude sunbathing. This hotel is popular among Austrian families, and it's especially good for children. The sunny and spacious public rooms have big windows. The comforts, amenities, and furnishings of the rooms merit their government four-star rating. The best have lake views. The bathrooms are spotlessly maintained and equipped with shower-tub combinations.

There's a lake-view restaurant and a terrace with waiter service. The management plays host at Carinthian buffets and dinner dances.

Werzer-Promenade, A-9210 Pörtschach. © **04272/223-10.** Fax 04272/225-11-13. 132 units. 90€–210€ double; 180€–240€ suite for 2. Rates include breakfast. AE, DC, MC, V. Closed Oct 15–May 1. Free parking. **Amenities:** Restaurant; bar; pool; fitness center; sauna; room service; babysitting; laundry; dry cleaning. *In room:* A/C, TV, minibar, hair dryer, safe.

WHERE TO DINE

Rainer's Restaurant and Bar AUSTRIAN/ITALIAN The most consistently popular restaurant in Pörtschach occupies a simple but rambling building that can hold as many as 2,000 guests at a time. The clientele here is split between patrons of the cozy bar and the restaurant, where exposed wood contributes to the *gemütlichkeit* mood. The menu is composed of Austrian and Italian specialties, including spaghetti Bussara, made with scampi and fresh tomatoes in a style unique to the chef; roasted goose with red cabbage and semolina dumplings; and simply prepared fresh fish (including pike perch and whiting) from nearby lakes.

On Friday and Saturday nights, the bar here is dominated by live bands, which provide dance music from 10pm to 2am. Don't confuse this place (Rainer's Bar) with Rainer's Hotel, a completely separate entity.

Monte-Carlo Platz 1. © **04272/304-60.** Reservations recommended. Main courses 15€–32€. AE, DC, MC, V. Bar daily 5pm–5am; restaurant daily 7pm–1am.

VELDEN 🚣🚣: THE HEART OF THE AUSTRIAN RIVIERA

Velden, at the western end of the Wörther See, is the most sophisticated resort in Carinthia, and it's known as the heart of the Austrian Riviera. The resort has many landscaped parks that sweep down to the lakeside, and from most hotel rooms you'll have views of sparkling blue lake with the peaks of **Karawaken** in the background, marking the Slovenian and Italian borders.

GETTING THERE Velden sits astride the main routes that connect Klagenfurt with Villach, Salzburg, and Innsbruck. Dozens of trains stop throughout the day, and the trip from Klagenfurt takes 14 to 21 minutes. For information about **train schedules,** call © **043/1717** (in Austria only).

Velden has bus lines extending north and south, into small nearby villages, and east and west, paralleling the railway tracks to Klagenfurt and Villach. For **bus information,** call © **0463/543-40** in Klagenfurt.

If you're **driving** from Klagenfurt, head west along Route 83 for 23km (14 miles).

VISITOR INFORMATION   The **tourist office** in the village center (© **04274/21-03**) is open Monday through Thursday from 9am to 6pm, Friday from 9am to 8pm.

WHAT TO DO IN VELDEN

Naturally, the big attraction here is watersports, ranging from swimming in the warm alpine lake to water-skiing and surfing. The long swimming season begins May 1 and continues until the end of October. Instruction is available for all water activities. The most respected watersports outfitter in Velden is **Segelschule und Surfschule Berger,** Seecorso 40, Velden (© **04274/26-91**). They rent equipment—Windsurfers, small boats, and canoes or kayaks—and give instruction. Many resort hotels have tennis courts, and you can also play golf at an 18-hole course 6km (4 miles) from Velden in a hilly landscape.

Most guests spend their days playing in the lake and dance the night away. Five o'clock tea dances are popular, and you can also trip the light fantastic to the orchestral music on the lake terraces. Summer festivals are often staged in Velden, and balls and beauty contests keep the resort's patrons amused. Also, this is a fine area for taking scenic drives into the countryside. Contact the tourist office for more information about events and schedules.

SHOPPING

Despite its relatively small size, Velden has more cosmopolitan shopping options than you might think. Its boutiques reflect trends in Vienna, Paris, and, to some extent, Milan. The main shopping thoroughfare is **Am Corso** (the end of Am Corso closest to the lake is called **See Corso**); in addition to being the address of several of the town's bars and nightclubs, it's home to three terrific shops. For sporting goods of every conceivable type, stop in **Kretschman,** Am Corso 5 (© **04274/29-53**), and for folkloric clothing—including lederhosen, loden coats, and jaunty hats with pheasant feathers—try **Heerling,** See Corso 12 (© **04274/29-98**). If you're searching for glamorous evening gowns, head for **Tschebull,** Am Corso 21 (© **04274/49-47**).

WHERE TO STAY & DINE

Golf Park Hotel 🏵🏵   This grand hotel attracts Viennese celebrities, members of the Saudi Arabian royal family, tennis and ski stars, and film crews shooting movies at the region's historic monuments. Originally built in 1968, it has been enlarged and renovated since. The hotel sits in its own park beside the lake, offering peace, quiet, and impressive views of the valley below. Rooms are tastefully modern, each well furnished with comfy beds. Bathrooms have generous shelf space and either tubs or showers.

The heart and soul of the hotel is the well-recommended restaurant, where a verdant terrace opens up in warm weather. The chef concocts a tempting array of frequently changing specialties, which might include a mousse of smoked trout with caviar in a champagne-flavored gelatin, river crayfish in a dill-flavored yogurt, and a supreme of freshwater char with tarragon and fresh asparagus.

Seecorso 68, A-9220 Velden. © 04274/229-80. Fax 04274/229-86. www.golfparkhotel.at. 90 units. 146€–274€ double; from 274€ suite for 2. Rates include half-board. AE, DC, MC, V. Closed Oct–May 15.

Amenities: Restaurant; bar; pool; fitness center; sauna; room service; babysitting; laundry; dry cleaning. *In room:* TV, minibar, hair dryer, safe.

Hotel Alte Post-Wrann ✎   For many years, this hotel was the provincial headquarters for the postal routes from Vienna to Venice. Renovated, enlarged, and improved many times since, the hotel retains its stone-trimmed arched windows. Unlike many of the region's hotels, this one is open year-round. The sunny rooms are comfortable and conservatively furnished, and come in a variety of sizes—some quite large. All beds are excellent. Bathrooms generally have tubs or showers.

The entrance to the hotel's **Wrann** restaurant is marked by massive beams; during summer, seating is in the garden. Here, under a canopy of trees, you can order a range of traditional Austrian and regional recipes. The summer-only restaurant, **Vinoték,** is fashioned after a Viennese *Heurige* (wine tavern) and specializes in local wines.

Europaplatz 4–6, A-9220 Velden. ✆ 04274/2141. Fax 04274/511-20. www.wrann.at. 36 units. 88€–120€ double; 104€–152€ suite. Rates include half-board. DC, MC, V. **Amenities:** Restaurant; bar; pool; fitness center; sauna; room service; babysitting; laundry; dry cleaning. *In room:* TV, minibar, hair dryer, safe.

VELDEN AFTER DARK

The most visible and (on weekends) busiest nightlife spot is the **Casino Velden,** Am Corso 17 (✆ 04274/20-64). Built in the 1980s with lots of glass overlooking the busy lakefront boulevard and the lake, the casino contains a series of roulette, blackjack, and baccarat tables, jangling slot machines, and a convention center. There are also two bars (one of which features live music), and a restaurant where you can lick your wounds after losing at the gambling tables.

You must present your passport to enter, and men must wear a jacket and tie. Visitors must be at least 18 to enter. The complex is open daily from noon to 3am. Games of chance include blackjack, baccarat, stud poker, and American and French roulette, as well as slot machines. Entrance is free, but for paying 25€ at the door, you're granted 30€ worth of chips.

Don't think, however, that you have to enter the precincts of the casino to be amused and entertained. The **American Bar** (also known as the **Schinackl Bar,** Am Corso; ✆ 04274/512-33) is the de facto social centerpiece for the town, where you'll see virtually everyone, either drinking at the bar with you or during their promenades up and down the lakefront. Set almost adjacent to the casino, it's open nightly from 8pm to 4am, features both indoor and outdoor areas, and presents live music every night beginning around 9:30pm. A *Schinackl,* incidentally, is a vernacular name for a style of rowboat used to catch fish in Carinthia.

Disco, anyone? If you're young at heart, you might enjoy the **Red Bull Disco,** Klagenfurter Strasse 17 (✆ 4274/20-34), where high-volume music, sometimes heavy metal, brings influences from faraway London and Los Angeles to otherwise sleepy Velden. The Red Bull is open nightly from 10pm to around 4am, usually without any charge.

MARIA WÖRTH ✎

Maria Wörth is one of the best bases for visiting Carinthia's largest alpine lake, the Wörther See. Part of this village, on the southern side of the lake across from Pörtschach, juts out into the lake on a rocky peninsula, providing a good view of the area. In addition to enjoying the lake, you can visit the golf courses in the nearby hamlet of Dellach.

The village's Gothic **Pfarrkirche (Parish Church)** has a baroque interior and a Romanesque crypt. It's noted for its 15th-century main altar. The circular *Karner* (charnel house) in the yard, with a round tower, was built in 1278.

Nearby is another noted church, the **Rosenkranzkirche,** from the 12th century, often referred to as "the winter church." It has some Romanesque frescoes of the Apostles from that century.

GETTING THERE   To reach Maria Wörth, take the **train** to either Velden or Klagenfurt, and then board one of the dozens of buses that depart throughout the day for Maria Wörth (trip time: 25–45 min.). For **bus information,** call ✆ **0463/543-40** in Klagenfurt.

If you're **driving** from Klagenfurt, head south on Route 91 and take the first exit marked MARIA WÖRTH. Follow an unclassified road running along the southern tier of the lake. The drive takes about 15 to 20 minutes.

VISITOR INFORMATION   The **tourist office** in the town center (✆ **04273/22-40**) is open Monday through Friday from 8:30am to 1:30pm and 3 to 6pm, and Saturday and Sunday from 10am to noon and 3 to 6pm.

WHERE TO STAY & DINE

Hotel Astoria   A small Austrian chain owns this attractively designed hotel, which is open only during the summer. Set beside a peninsula, the hotel has a pointed tower and its own piers, one of which is covered with deck chairs and, during good weather, oriental rugs. The comfortable, medium-size rooms are pleasantly furnished and have excellent beds. Although small, bathrooms are efficiently organized with shower-tub combinations and adequate shelf space.

A-9082 Maria Wörth. ✆ **04273/22-79.** Fax 04273/22-79-80. 50 units. 82€–172€ double. Rates include half-board. V. Closed Sept 28–May. Parking 8€. **Amenities:** Restaurant; bar; pool; sauna; massage; laundry; dry cleaning. *In room:* TV, hair dryer, safe.

Strandhotel Harrich *(Kids)*   Located on the lake, this 1950s hotel has balconies along its facade. The private lakefront beach is a favorite among vacationing Austrian families and is known for its exceptionally good value. The hotel sits amid a well-planned garden, with a sun terrace cantilevered above the slope of the hillside. There's also a grassy lakeside area with a scattering of deck chairs. The comfortable small and medium-size rooms are equipped with firm beds and small shower-only bathrooms. Suites are rented to a maximum of four guests.

A-9082 Maria Wörth. ✆ **04273/22-28.** Fax 04273/222-81-38. 34 units. 88€–99€ double. Rates include half-board. AE, MC, V. Closed Oct 15–Apr 15. **Amenities:** Restaurant; bar; pool; fitness center; sauna; room service; babysitting. *In room:* TV, hair dryer, safe.

4 Villach ⓐ

48km (30 miles) W of Klagenfurt; 140km (87 miles) SE of Salzburg

Villach, in the center of the Carinthian lake district, is a great place from which to explore the rest of the district. It's also the gateway to the south, and it's easy to make day trips to Slovenia or Italy from here. If you were planning on continuing south anyway, this is also a good stopover point. This town, the second-largest in Carinthia, lies in a broad basin along the Drau River. There was a settlement here in Roman times, and Villach belonged to the bishops of Bamberg (a distant see near Nürnberg, Germany) from the 11th century until Maria Theresa acquired it for the Hapsburgs. Today it's an industrial town.

GETTING THERE   Villach is an important railway junction for four different lines connecting central and southern Austria with Italy, and **trains** arrive throughout the day from Vienna (trip time: 4½ hr.) and Klagenfurt (trip time: 25 min.). Although it's easier to take the train to Villach, several different bus lines fan out into the surrounding countryside. For **train information,** call ✆ **05/1717;** and for **bus information,** call ✆ **04242/267710.**

If you're **driving** from Klagenfurt, Villach is about 56km (35 miles) west on the Autobahn A2.

VISITOR INFORMATION The **tourist office,** Europaplatz 2 (✆ **04242/ 42000),** is open Monday through Friday from 8am to 6pm, and Saturday from 10am to 2pm.

EXPLORING VILLACH & THE VILLACHER ALPS ✪

At the center of the Altstadt (Old City) is **Hauptplatz (Main Square).** There's a bridge over the Drau at Hauptplatz's north end, and the **Pfarrkirche (parish church),** dedicated to St. Jacob, is at the south end. The church is a mixture of styles, with a baroque altar and Gothic choir stalls. Like most towns of its size, Villach has a **Trinity Column,** dating from 1739, commemorating deliverance from the plague.

Theophrastus Bombast von Hohenheim (1493–1541), a Swiss-born chemist and physician better known as Paracelsus, lived in Villach as a youth while his father practiced medicine.

In the **Schillerpark,** on Peraustrasse, there's a large panoramic relief of the province, the **Relief von Kärnten,** that's on view from May 2 to the end of October (except Fri, Sun, and holidays) from 10am to 4:30pm.

Villach is a good center from which to explore the Carinthian lake district, including the **Villacher Alps,** an 18km (11-mile) journey via the Villacher Alpenstrasse toll road (12€ each way). There are panoramic views in many directions, and the best viewing spots are marked. At the end of the road you'll find a chairlift that will take you to the summit of **Dobratsch** (2,166m/7,100 ft.), which offers one of the most famous views in Austria. At the top, a network of hiking paths fans out.

If you're in Villach in summer, you might want to drive southeast to **Lake Faaker (Faaker See),** a small body of water that's popular with swimmers and water-skiers. This lake's waters frequently reach 79°F (26°C) in July and August. From Villach, follow the signs to Faak.

WHERE TO STAY

Romantik Hotel Post ✪✪   Rich in Carinthian history, this hotel was built in 1500, and some original elements, like the rich vaulted ceilings, have been incorporated into the hotel. The facade is a Teutonic fantasy of carved stone detailing, Ionic columns, and intricately patterned wrought iron. Between 1548 and 1629, this was the town palace of one of Carinthia's richest families. During that period, the house hosted an emperor, a king, an archduke, and later an empress (Maria Theresa). Later still, the nephew of Napoléon I dropped in and signed a registration slip that still belongs to the hotel. On the premises is a baronial fireplace, an arcaded courtyard shielded from the sun by an ancient collection of chestnut trees, and a host of elegantly furnished rooms. As befits a building this large, rooms come in various sizes, and each has a marvelously comfortable bed. Bathrooms are rather luxurious and contain shower-tub combinations.

The establishment pays special attention to its traditional cuisine, much of which is heavily laced with cheese, butter, and cream. These include *Tafelspitz*

Thermal Waters to Keep You Young

From the heart of the Old Town in Villach, it's a 4km (2½-mile) drive to **Warmbad-Villach,** a town known for its thermal swimming pools and mineral springs. This spa, on the southern fringe of Villach, is the only place where visitors can swim at the source of the thermal waters, which are supposed to counteract the aging process.

The warm springs at Warmbad were used by the ancient Romans, and there was a road that passed through Warmbad en route to Italy. During the Middle Ages, Villach became a thriving market town, and Warmbad's springs were not commercialized.

Beginning with Europe's spa craze in the late 19th century, a handful of spa hotels sprung up around Warmbad-Villach, the first of which was the Kurhotel Warmbaderhof. We've recommended a few spa hotels below.

The **Kurhotel Warmbaderhof,** Kadischenallée, Warmbad Villach (© 04242/300-10; fax 04242/300-180; www.warmbad.at), is the largest and most dignified of the hotels that have sprung up near Warmbad's famous springs. Built 200 years ago, and enlarged and modernized since, it boasts a covered passageway leading directly to the town's spa facilities. Set amid gardens in the town center, the hotel offers its own heated swimming pool with a ceiling shaped like a continuous barrel vault, and an angular outdoor pool connected with the indoor pool. Hotel staff organizes different sporting activities, local and regional walking tours, and evening dances on the flowering outdoor terrace. The two hotel restaurants serve well-prepared food. Most of the 116 rooms and 12 suites are in a modern wing attached to the establishment's historic core and are conservatively furnished. The double rate is 164€ to 228€; a suite runs 320€ to 390€. Rates include half-board, and there's free parking. The hotel is closed 3 to 4 weeks in November and December.

Standing in a large park, **Der Karawankenhof,** Kadischenallée (© 04242/300-20; fax 04242/30-02-61; www.warmbad.at), offers a

(boiled beef), schnitzels (sometimes stuffed with cheese and ham), and recipes with local venison, including soups, patés, and stews. The hotel also offers a health-conscious cuisine. Dining choices include the restaurant Postillion, the Postcafé, the Jägerstüberl, and the garden restaurant Orangerie. In July and August, piano music and candlelit dinners are offered in the garden courtyard.

Hauptplatz 26, A-9500 Villach. © 04242/26-10-10. Fax 04242/26101-420. romantik-hotel@magnet.at. 77 units. 120€ double; 205€ suite. Rates include breakfast. AE, DC, MC, V. **Amenities:** 4 restaurants; bar; fitness center; sauna; room service; laundry; dry cleaning. *In room:* TV, minibar, hair dryer, safe.

WHERE TO DINE

Some of the best food in Villach is at the **Romantik Hotel Post** (see above).

Steakhouse Rob Roy STEAKHOUSE   The decor might be British and the list of carafe wines might be French, Austrian, and Italian, but the menu is pure steakhouse. The portions of the various meats served here are so generous that you might want to pass over the relatively standard appetizers. The beef is very battery of health and spa facilities (it's connected to these facilities by an underground passage). The "bath world," as they call it here, consists of whirlpools, indoor and outdoor swimming pools, a fitness center, a gym, a sauna, massage, and other facilities. The restaurant serves excellent cuisine. This sizable four-star modern hotel, open all year, rents 70 well-furnished rooms and 10 suites; the double rate is 138€ to 170€. Rates include half-board, and parking is free outdoors and 5€ indoors.

Josefinenhof Hotel ⚑, Kadischenallée 8 (© **04242/300-30**; fax 04242/ 3003-89; www.josefinenhof.at), functions as a government-rated four-star hotel with its own spa, fitness, and conference facilities. Although much of this hotel was built in the 1960s, its original core was established in the 1700s as a hospital. Its sun terrace stretches toward the hotel's private park. You can enjoy treatment at the hydrotherapy and beauty center or partake of a host of health and medical services. The 52 comfortable rooms and nine suites have rows of sun-flooded windows and balconies. Bathrooms are well equipped with robes and hair dryers. The double rate is 204€ to 212€, and a suite runs 224€ to 232€. Rates include full board, and there's free parking.

GETTING THERE Warmbad, no more than a cluster of buildings on routes heading into Italy, is 4km (2½ miles) south of Villach, and virtually everything in town stems from tourism. A **red bus** (marked WARMBAD when it goes to Warmbad and BAHNHOF as it heads back to Villach) runs between the towns at 30-minute intervals all day long; the trip takes 10 to 12 minutes. In Villach, the railway station acts as the stop for the red bus, although it stops almost everywhere else in between the towns.

There are also trains that come from Villach's main railway station at 30-minute intervals. For information about train schedules and fares, call © **04242/20-20-31-99.**

tender and grilled to perfection. There's also a succulent version of pork Provençal. The traditional desserts are apple pie and crepes. The restaurant also offers 10 simple rooms and suites, at rates of 50€ to 95€ for double occupancy. Ossiacher Zeile 46. © **04242/371-34.** Reservations required. Main courses 11€–22€. AE, MC, V. Thurs–Mon 6pm–11pm.

5 Lake Millstatter ⭑

The second-largest lake in the province, Millstatter See is 13km (8 miles) long, 2km (1 mile) wide, and 140m (460 ft.) deep. This beautiful blue lake, east of Spittal, is set against a backdrop of the forested **Seerücken** (866m/2,840 ft.) to the south and **Nockberge** to the north. Reflected in the lake are the distant peaks of the Reisseck and Kreuzeck.

MILLSTATT AM SEE

About midway along the lake's northern rim, **Millstatt am See** and **Seeboden** are the principal lake resorts. Most hotels here are open only during the warmer months, and prices are highest in July and August, when reservations are absolutely mandatory. Prices are often reduced in late spring and early autumn, when it's easier to find a room. An **organ-music festival** is held here May to September.

GETTING THERE   Because Millstatt has no train connections, most travelers take a **train** to Spittal an der Drau from Klagenfurt (trip time: 1 hr.) or Salzburg (trip time: 2 hr.). (On many maps and timetables, this railway junction is referred to as Spittal-Millstattersee.) From Spittal's railway station, passengers catch one of the **buses** that depart around 16 times a day for the 20-minute trip to Millstatt am See.

Millstatt is 299km (186 miles) southwest of Vienna and 90km (56 miles) west of Klagenfurt. To **drive** here from Villach, head northwest along the A10, bypassing Spittal. At the turnoff for Seeboden, head east along the northern perimeter of the lake, following Route 98.

VISITOR INFORMATION   The **tourist office** in the village center (© 04766/20-22) is open Monday through Friday from 8am to 5pm, and Saturday and Sunday from 10am to noon and 3 to 5pm.

VISITING THE ABBEY

Other than the lake, Millstatt's main attraction is the *Stift* (abbey) ★, which was founded in 1080 as a Benedictine monastery. Near the end of the 15th century, it was taken over by Jesuits. One part of the monastery has been used as a hotel (the **Hotel Lindenhof**) since 1773, and it was once the mansion of the Grand Master of the Knights of St. George.

In the abbey courtyard stands a 1,000-year-old "Judgment" lime tree. The cloister, which has Gothic vaulting and Romanesque arches, is reached from the east side of the court. The abbey contains a fresco of the Last Judgment, a masterpiece of Austrian Renaissance art. The abbey church (Stiftskirche) has a Romanesque doorway that is the complex's major architectural attraction.

WHERE TO STAY & DINE

Hotel Alpenrose ★ *Finds*   Enjoying a splendid scenic setting with a view of the valley and the mountains, the Hotel Alpenrose is in the tiny alpine village of Obermillstatt, 2km (1½ miles) from the center of Millstatt. This is the first "biohotel" to open in Austria, and the Theuermann family (your hosts) is involved in holistic medicine, macrobiotic diets, and yoga. They run a good hotel and restaurant in a chalet-inspired building that contains well-furnished rooms, each with a balcony. The owners prefer not to provide radios or TVs "to ensure tranquillity," but they do offer good beds, along with small bathrooms with well-kept shower units. On the premises are an array of carefully monitored new-age programs, including yoga lessons and biotraining in the care of both body and soul. Needless to say, smoking is not permitted at the hotel.

Obermillstatt, A-9872 Millstatt am See. © 04766/25-00. Fax 04766/34-25. www.biohotel-alpenrose.at. 30 units. 87€ per person. Rates include vegetarian half-board and 1 massage. No credit cards. **Amenities:** Restaurant; lounge; pool; spa; sauna; laundry; dry cleaning. *In room:* hair dryer, safe.

Hotel am See Die Forelle ★   This attractive, four-story hotel has a history dating from around 1900, when a private villa and an unpretentious guesthouse were combined to form one building. Today, much enlarged and improved over the years, the hotel has a lakeside terrace sheltered by chestnut trees and a reputation as one of the finest hotels on the Millstatter See. The hotel's interior contains bright, medium-size rooms (all but 10 have lake views) equipped with good beds. The small bathrooms have tubs or shower stalls. There's a big, well-maintained lawn that leads down to the lakefront beach. The Aniwanter family serves excellent cuisine, with fixed-price four-course meals and a la carte dishes.

A-9872 Millstatt am See. ℂ **04766/20-50.** Fax 04766/20-50-11. www.hotel-forelle.at. 81 units. 112€–216€ double. Rates include half-board. DC, MC, V. Closed mid-Oct to early May. **Amenities:** Restaurant; bar; pool; whirlpool; Jacuzzi; sauna; room service. *In room:* TV, hair dryer, safe.

Hotel Post   This hotel, in Millstatt's center, is designed like a baroque country villa. The interior contains an open fireplace and a mixture of Victorian and contemporary furniture. The renovated rooms are comfortable and well maintained. Another set of rooms, added in 1985, offers much comfort; each has a south- or west-facing balcony. Regardless of your room assignment, you will find small but tidy bathrooms equipped with shower-tub combinations. In each of the south-facing rooms, there's a separate recess to sleep one or two children, as well as a stove and a fridge. The hotel has a restaurant with well-polished knotty-pine paneling and massive chandeliers.

Marnockstrasse 38, A-9872 Millstatt am See. ℂ **04766/21-08.** Fax 04766/27-77. post-millstatt@carinthia. com. 30 units. 86€–118€ double; 124€–180€ suite. Rates include breakfast. MC, V. Closed Nov–Apr. **Amenities:** Restaurant; bar; pool; sauna; babysitting; laundry; dry cleaning. *In room:* TV.

13

Styria

In Styria, the "green heart of Austria," forests cover about half the country, and grasslands and vineyards blanket another quarter. This is one of Austria's bargain provinces—even its top hotels charge only moderate prices. Trout fishing, mountain climbing, and hiking are popular summer activities, and in the past decade Styria has been emerging as a ski area. (It has a long way to go before it will rival Land Salzburg or Tyrol, however.) Schladming/Rohrmoos is a skiing center of Dachstein-Tauern, in the upper valley of the Enns River.

Interesting areas to visit in Styria include Bad Gleichenberg, the most important summer spa in South Styria, set among parks and mineral waters; and Bad Aussee, an old market town and spa in the heart of the lush Salzkammergut. Also worth a visit are Murau, a winter ski region and a good center for driving tours of the surrounding countryside, and Mariazell, Austria's pilgrimage center. If you're driving around this area, you should know that parking is rarely a problem, and you park free unless otherwise noted.

Styria (Steiermark in German) is the second-largest province in the country. It borders Slovenia and Hungary, as well as the Austrian provinces of Burgenland, Lower Austria, Upper Austria, Land Salzburg, and Carinthia.

Northwestern Styria includes the alpine ranges of the Salzkammergut, while its eastern section resembles the steppes of Hungary. The Dachstein features mammoth glaciers.

Throughout history, this rich land of valleys and rivers, mountain peaks and glaciers has been sought after. It was greedily attacked by Huns, Hungarians, and Turks, among others, and even in Celtic times people knew that the mountains of Upper Styria were a valuable source of iron ore, which the tribes used for their weapons and other important goods. The Romans also exploited the rich deposits, and the Crusaders used armor made from Styrian iron to fight the "infidel" in the East. Iron resources shaped Styria's economy, and today it's Austria's leading mining province.

Styria is a province deeply steeped in tradition, and the costume that some of the men still occasionally wear demonstrates this point. Derived from an original peasant costume, it's made of stout greenish-gray cloth with Styrian green material used for the lapels and the stripe down the outside of the pant legs.

Graz, the capital of Styria, is the second-largest Austrian city, and in imperial times it was known as the place to which state officials retired—the city even acquired the nickname Pensionopolis (City of the Retired).

TIPS FOR ACTIVE TRAVELERS

Within Styria's borders are the alpine ranges of the Salzkammergut and steppe country resembling that of the Great Hungarian Plain. This conglomerate of river valleys, mountain peaks and glaciers, and verdant sun-drunk vineyards is a great place to pursue outdoor activities. Graz serves as a good base for stockpiling

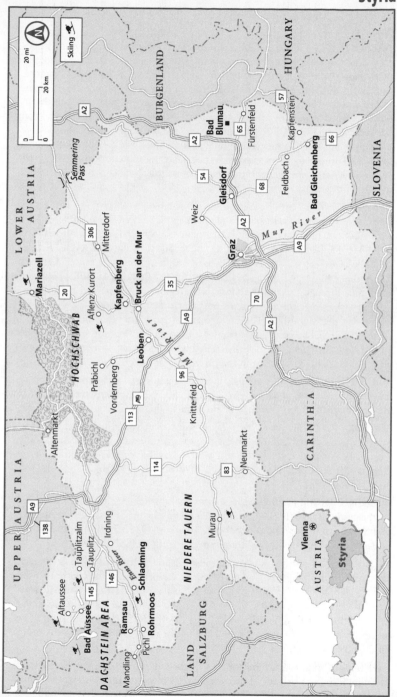

Styria

20 mi

20 km

Skiing

HUNGARY

BURGENLAND

LOWER AUSTRIA

SLOVENIA

A2

Semmering Pass

57

Bad Blumau

Fürstenfeld

Kapfenstein

66

65

A2

54

Gleisdorf

Feldbach

Bad Gleichenberg

68

Weiz

A2

306

Mitterdorf

Mur River

Graz

A9

Mariazell

Kapfenberg

35

20

Aflenz Kurort

Bruck an der Mur

70

HOCHSCHWAB

A9

A2

Leoben

Mur River

Präbichl

96

Vordernberg

Knittefeld

113

CARINTHIA

Altenmarkt

114

UPPER AUSTRIA

83

Neumarkt

A9

138

Irdning

NIEDERE TAUERN

Tauplitzalm

Murau

Tauplitz

Altaussee

146

Schladming

145

Bad Aussee

Ramsau

Vienna ✷

Rohrmoos

AUSTRIA

Styria

DACHSTEIN AREA

Pichl

Mandling

LAND SALZBURG

supplies and planning your excursions. Here are the essentials for planning an outdoorsy vacation in Styria.

BALLOONING   Styria is home to several hot-air ballooning outfits. For an entirely different perspective on life in general—and Austrian landscapes in particular—ask a local entrepreneur to take you up for a 90- to 120-minute escapade over the region's rooftops and lakes, preferably with a bottle of champagne and a good companion. The oldest outfitter in Styria (established in 1976) is **Gerd Skreiner's Union Aeronautic Styria,** Postfach 3, A-8182 Puch bei Weiz (✆ **03177/21-76**). Located in a village adjacent to the Stubenbergsee (a local lake), 40km (25 miles) east of Graz, it maintains six balloons. Excursions cost 220€ per person for the first flight and 130€ for subsequent flights. Flights can be conducted, weather permitting, in any season. Each balloon holds a pilot and up to three passengers.

BIKING   Cycling enthusiasts will be pleased by Styria's terrain. The gentle undulations of the eastern plain and the historic scenery make for a pleasant ride. You can rent a bicycle at Graz's main railway station, **Hauptbahnhof** (✆ **0316/78-48-508**), or through an independent operator, **Bicycle,** Kaiser-Franz-Josef-Kai 66 (✆ **0316/82-13-570**), near Graz's town center. Contact **Eurobike,** Mühlstrasse 20, A-5162 Oberturn (✆ **06219/744-40**), to arrange bike tours through some of the most scenic regions of Austria and Italy. A particularly appealing trip is an excursion known as the Muradweg, a week-long trek along the Mur River. The average age of participants in this tour ranges from 50 to 60. The cost ranges from 420€ to 512€, depending on the hotel you choose. Overnight accommodations, some meals, equipment rental, and luggage transfers are included in the price.

BOATING   The region's many lakes are great places for experienced and novice boaters. **Hotel Backenstein,** Bräuhof 156, A-8993 Grundlsee (✆ **03622/85-45**), offers packages that include boat rentals, lessons, and accommodations.

CANOEING   White-water enthusiasts will be enchanted by the clean, crisp waters of the glacial runoff. Although water temperatures can be brisk, any hearty paddler will tell you the best way to stay warm is to paddle furiously. **Sportagentur Strobl,** Hauptplatz 3, A-8940 Liezen (✆ **03612/253-43**), will help set you adrift.

FISHING   If you want to spend an afternoon fishing, cast your luck with one of the guide services that can be arranged for you by the **Tourismusver Ausseer Land,** Bahnhustrasse 132, A-8990 Bad Aussee (✆ **03622/540-40**), or **Tourismusregionalverband Murau,** Bundesstrasse 13 (✆ **03537/23-64**).

GOLF   Styria's gently undulating landscapes are well suited for golf courses, many of which allow nonmembers to reserve tee-off times if the course isn't too busy. Two of the region's most appealing golf courses are **Golfclub Gut Murstätten,** A-8403 Lebring (✆ **03182/35-55**), a half-hour drive south of Graz; and the **Golfclub Murhof,** A-8130 Frohnlieten (✆ **03126/30-10**), a half-hour drive north of Graz. Additionally, any hotel or tourist office can point you to dozens of other golf courses.

HIKING   Alpinists who toil for their highs will want to experience some of the climbs in the Dachstein-Tauern region. It's best to scale the steep rock faces of the Alps with an experienced guide. A guide (or just some climbing buddies) can be located for you by **Alpin- und Abenteuerclub Dachstein,** Schilldletten 88, A-8972 Ramsau (✆ **03687/81-59-80**).

SKIING   The Dachstein glacier enables year-round skiing in Styria. Cross-country skiers will find this a great diversion in summertime. For general and booking information, contact **Tourismusverband Ramsau** (© **03687/818-33**). The Dachstein-Tauern (see later in this chapter) and Salzkammergut regions have winter ski facilities.

TENNIS   If you want to play tennis, **Sporthotel Matschner** in Ramsau (© **03687/81-72-10**) offers guests hotel and tennis packages, as do many other hotels with courts (see hotel reviews throughout this chapter).

1 Graz

200km (124 miles) SW of Vienna; 138km (86 miles) NE of Klagenfurt; 285km (177 miles) SE of Salzburg

Graz, Styria's capital, blends modern life and historical architecture in a wonderful mix of past and present. The city's history dates from prehistoric times, when its location at a ford across the Mur River was a major factor in its development. Romans, Slavs, and Bavarians all had a hand in shaping the town.

Graz is a great place to stay for a number of reasons. It's easy to make day trips into the countryside from here, and there's plenty to see and do. Visit the Schloss, go hiking or hot-air ballooning, or stop in at one of the museums. If you're visiting in the fall, you might want to attend the **Steierischer Herbst (Styrian Autumn)** festival, which features contemporary art, music, and literature. The arts festival has a reputation for being avant-garde, presenting everything from jazz to mime.

Fearing floods, early settlers established fortifications on the steep dolomite hill overlooking the river's ford. The city's name is derived from the Slavic word *gradec,* meaning "little fortress." A small castle was built on the hill, which is now the Schlossberg. The town is first mentioned in documents from the early 12th century. Graz has been ruled by many governments, including those of Germany, Bohemia, Hungary, the Babenbergs, and the Hapsburgs.

The medieval town developed at the foot of the Schlossberg and some of the late Gothic period structures remain. These buildings were constructed when Emperor Frederick III used Graz as a capital after the Hungarians forced him out of Vienna. The *Burg* (castle) and the cathedral, along with the city's narrow-gable roofs and arcaded courtyards, all contribute to its charm.

Life wasn't always kind to the people of Graz. In 1480, the little town was afflicted by the "Plagues of God"—locusts, the Black Death, the Turks, and a threat from the Hungarians.

When the Hapsburg inheritance was divided into Austrian and Spanish branches in 1564, Graz became the prosperous capital of "Inner Austria" and the residence of Archduke Carl, who ruled Styria, Carinthia, and Italian Hapsburg lands. Carl had the town's fortifications strengthened in the Italian style, with bastions and moats.

A Jesuit college and Lutheran school were both active by the end of the 16th century. The astronomer Johann Kepler (1571–1630) began his teaching career at the Lutheran school. Fine arts and commerce flourished in Graz, bringing honor and riches to the city, and that prosperity is reflected in palaces and mansions built during that period. Italian Renaissance architects were making their impact here around the time Emperor Ferdinand II moved his court to Vienna in 1619.

The city walls were demolished in 1784, and the slopes they'd stood on were planted with trees. Napoléon's armies made three appearances here, and Austria's defeat by his forces at the Battle of Wagram (1809) resulted in a treaty that forced Graz to level the Schlossberg's battlements. Only the **Uhrturm (Clock Tower)** and the **bell tower** were saved, rescued by payment of a high ransom by the citizens of Graz. The Schlossberg became the beautiful park you see today.

During World War II, the city saw much bombing and devastation. However, in 1945, Graz was allotted to the British, and reconstruction began.

Today Graz has some 250,000 inhabitants, and it supports thriving breweries, machine factories, trading companies, and service industries. The **Graz Fair** is an important commercial and industrial event in southeastern Europe. Graz's three universities, opera house, theater, museums, concert halls, and art galleries comprise Styria's cultural center.

ESSENTIALS

GETTING THERE   **By Plane**   Austrian Airlines (✆ 0316/29-16-69) offers daily flights from Vienna to **Thalerhof International Airport** (✆ 0316/29-02), 18km (11 miles) south of Graz. **Tyrolean Air** and **Lufthansa** also serve the airport. There's a white-sided, 15-passenger minivan that makes six trips a day between Graz's airport and the city center. A one-way trip costs 2€ per person. Departures coincide with the arrival of incoming flights, but the trips aren't frequent enough. The much more convenient cab ride from the airport to the city center (for up to four passengers) costs around 20€.

By Train   Graz is Austria's southern center for rail lines between Vienna and Slovenia. It's also the junction for secondary rail lines that extend to Budapest and a series of valleys in western Styria. At least 10 trains depart every day from Vienna's Südbahnhof for Graz (trip time: 2½ hr.). Through connections, it's easy to get here from other Austrian cities such as Innsbruck, Salzburg, and Klagenfurt.

In addition, about one local train per hour arrives in Graz from minor rail lines in western Styria's isolated valleys and from the more populated areas of eastern Styria and the Hungarian border. For rail information, call ✆ 05/1717.

By Bus   Graz is also the departure point for about 100 different bus lines, most of which head toward hamlets and small villages. For bus information, call ✆ 0316/59-87. Because of its excellent train connections, however, most travelers arrive by rail.

By Car   If you're driving from Vienna, take Autobahn A2 south. The autobahn doesn't stretch all the way to Graz; part of it is Route 54, which becomes Autobahn A2 again northeast of Graz.

VISITOR INFORMATION

The **Graz City Tourist Office,** Herrengasse 16 (✆ 0316/807-50; www.graz tourismus.at), will book hotel rooms and provide information about the area. Hotels throughout Styria can be booked here. It's open Monday through Friday from 9am to 7pm, Saturday from 9am to 6pm, and Sunday from 10am to 3pm.

CITY LAYOUT

The **Old Town (Altstadt)** lies on the left bank of the Mur, centered on **Hauptplatz (Main Square).** To the south of this landmark plaza looms the **Rathaus (Town Hall).** Southeast of Hauptplatz is **Herrengasse,** a pedestrian area used by local shoppers, and this street comes to an end at **Platz am Eisernen Tor,** with its column mounted by a figure of the Virgin dating from the 17th century.

At the eastern end of the **Opernring** is the municipal park, **Stadtpark,** dating from the 19th century. Northeast of Hauptplatz looms the **Burg,** a 15th-century imperial stronghold. South of the Burg rises the late Gothic **Graz cathedral,** and

Graz

0.25 mi

0.25 km

Vienna
AUSTRIA
Graz

ATTRACTIONS ●
Burg **28**
Domkirche (Cathedral) **29**
Griesplatz **3**
Hauptplatz **14**
Jakominiplatz **23**
Landhaus **18**
Landesmuseum Joanneum **19**
Landeszeughaus **17**
Mariahilferkirche **6**
Mausoleum of Emperor Ferdinand II **30**
Paulustor **10**
Platz am Eisernen Tor **22**
Rathaus **15**
Schlossberg **8**
Uhrturm **11**

ACCOMMODATIONS ■
Austria Trend Hotel Europa **1**
City Hotel Erzherzog Johann **13**
Grand Hotel Wiesler Graz **4**
Hotel Drei Raben **2**
Hotel Gollner **33**
Hotel Grazerhof **20**
Hotel Weitzer **5**
Romantik Parkhotel **31**
Schlossberg Hotel **7**

DINING ◆
Café Glockenspiel **24**
Café Leinich **32**
Das Wirtshaus Greiner **9**
Gambrinuskeller **26**
Goldene Pastete **27**
Johan **16**
Krebsenkeller **12**
Landhaus-Keller **21**
Maroni **25**
Restaurant Casserolle **5**

south of the cathedral is the baroque **mausoleum** of Emperor Ferdinand II, who died in 1637.

Rising above the Altstadt is the Schlossberg, which can be reached by the cable railway.

GETTING AROUND

Graz City Transport (© 0316/82-06-06) operates streetcar and bus service throughout the city. **Jakominiplatz,** on the river's eastern bank, and **Griesplatz,** on the western bank, are the points where most streetcar lines intersect.

For information on Postal Buses, contact the **Graz City Tourist office,** Herrengasse 16 (© 0316/807-50).

The city's largest underground parking lot is the **Tiefgarage Andreas-Hofer-Platz,** on the Andreas-Hofer-Platz (© 0316/82-91-91). Parking costs 27€ for a full day or 8€ per hour. Within the city's historic center, you can park in the blue zones—indicated by a blue line painted beside the curb—for up to 3 hours. Parking costs .75€ per half-hour. You can either put coins in a parking meter or buy parking vouchers from tobacco shops or post offices. To use the voucher, fill in the blanks with the date and the time you parked in a spot, and leave it on the dashboard so it's visible through the windshield.

Major car-rental agencies in Graz (all represented at the airport) include **Avis,** Schögelgasse 10 (© 0316/81-29-20); **Budget,** Bahnhofgürtel 73 (© 0316/290-2342); and **Hertz,** Andreas-Hofer-Platz (© 0316/82-50-07).

Taxi service is available by hailing a cab on the street, lining up at any of the city's clearly designated taxi stands (the largest is in front of the main railway station), or calling © 878 (which gains access to the biggest company in Graz), 983, or 889.

 FAST FACTS: **Graz**

Babysitters Most hotels will set up visitors with a qualified babysitter, but if not, call **UNIKID,** Maxmellallee 11 (© 0316/380-1064).

Currency Exchange The best rates are offered at the main post office (see below).

Dentists & Doctors Your hotel will provide the name of one, but if you call the local hospital, **Landeskrankenhaus,** Riesstrasse 1 (© 0316/3850), you can also get the names of English-speaking doctors and dentists on call for local emergencies.

Drugstores The biggest and most central store is **Kastner & Öhler,** Sackstrasse 7–13 (© 0316/87-00). Hours are Monday through Friday from 9am to 6:30pm and Saturday from 9am to 7pm.

Emergencies Call © **133** for the police, **122** for the fire department, or **144** for an ambulance.

Hospitals The two best medical facilities in Graz include the **Krankenhaus der Elisabethinen,** Elisabethinergasse 14 (© 0316/706-30), and the larger **Landeskrankenhaus,** Riesstrasse 1 (© 0316/3850). Both have emergency rooms, and many staff members speak English.

Internet Access The most convenient location is **Café Zentral,** Andreas-Hofer-Platz 9 (© 0316/83-24-68), open Monday through Saturday from 6:30 to 10pm. It charges 4€ per hour.

Luggage Storage There are luggage-checking facilities on the main floors of both the railway station and the bus station. Depending on the size of your luggage, you can either store your luggage at the storage office for 2€ per day, or you can rent lockers for 2€ to 5€. The service is available daily from 6am to midnight.

Police Call ℂ 133 for the police.

Post Office The main post office, **Neutorgasse 46 (ℂ 0316/88-00)**, is open Monday through Friday from 7am to 9pm and Saturday from 8am to 2pm. There's also a post office next to the main railway station (Hauptbahnhof).

Restrooms Restrooms in the city center are labeled wc (water closet). Toilets are also found at bus, rail, and air terminals; at major museums; and in cafes, where it's polite to buy some small item such as coffee.

Safety Graz traditionally has been one of Europe's safest cities. However, crime is rising, so take the usual precautions: Wear a money belt and safeguard your valuables.

Taxes Graz imposes no special city taxes other than the value-added tax imposed on all goods and services in Austria.

Transit Information Call ℂ **0316/82-06-06**.

Useful Telephone Numbers For the airport, call ℂ **0316/2902**; for train information, ℂ **05/1717**.

EXPLORING THE TOWN

Much of Graz's Old Town has been well preserved (more so than the old districts of Austria's other similar-size cities), and many visitors take tours through this section of town. Major sights include **Hauptplatz (Main Square),** in the heart of the city, surrounded by ancient houses with characteristic brown-tile roofs and narrow gables. The most notable house is the **House of Luegg** at the corner of Sporgasse, known for its arcades and facade dating from the 17th century.

A few steps down Herrengasse, the wide shopping and business street, is the **Landhaus,** seat of the provincial government, a 1565 Renaissance masterpiece. An especially prominent window above the main gate intensifies the gate's effect. The south side of the courtyard ends in an arcade that runs the length of the court. The arched Renaissance fountainhead was poured in bronze near the end of the 16th century.

Paulustor (Paul's Gate), set between the remnants of the Graz's rampart, dates from the time Italian architects fortified the city. The side of the gate facing the city is plain, but the other side is decorated with the large coats-of-arms of Archduke Ferdinand and his first wife, Anne of Bavaria.

Burg (Castle)   One of the most visible buildings in town, the castle was built in 1499 for Emperor Maximilian I. The Burg is devoted exclusively to offices of the Austrian and Styrian provincial governments and is not open to visitors. It does, however, contain an unusual winding staircase, the **Wendeltreppe,** whose corkscrew (helix) shape is a marvel of medieval stonework. The concierge will usually allow visitors to enter for a peek.

Northeast of Hauptplatz in the Old Town. Free admission. Mon–Fri 9am–5pm. Tram: 3 or 6.

Domkirche (Cathedral)   This church was originally the Romanesque Church of St. Aegydius. It was a fortified structure outside the town walls that was first referred to in a late-12th-century document. In the 15th century, Frederick III had the church converted into a spacious three-bayed city parish church in the late Gothic style, although it ended up with a wooden turret instead of a Gothic spire. Archduke Carl of Inner Austria attached the church to his residence, the Burg, and later entrusted it to the Jesuits. After the dissolution of that order in Austria, it became the cathedral church of the bishops of Seckau. Inside you'll see two shrines (ca. 1475) made in Mantua, and a baroque high altar, the 18th-century creation of Fr. Georg Kraxner.

Burggasse 3. (C) **0316/82-16-83.** Free admission. Mon–Sat 6:30am–7:45pm; Sun 7am–7pm. Tram: 3 or 6.

Landesmuseum Joanneum This major attraction has galleries at different locations. The **natural history displays**—geology, botany, zoology—are at the old Joanneum building, Raubergasse 10 ((C) **0316/80-17**). The **Old Gallery,** with collections featuring paintings from medieval times to the 18th century, and the **arts-and-crafts department** are in the new Joanneum building at Neu-torgasse 45 ((C) **0316/80-17-47-80**). The **New Gallery,** on the third floor of the former Heberstein town house, Sackstrasse 16 ((C) **0316/82-91-55**), shows art from the 19th century to the present.

At the **Eggenberg Palace** (see Schloss Eggenberg, below) you'll find the pre-history and early history departments, including an extensive collection of Roman stones in an open-air pavilion in the park, the **Münzenkabinett,** a coin collection, and the **Styrian Hunting Museum.**

Departments at various addresses. Admission 8€ adults, free for children under 14. Mon–Fri 9am–4pm; Sat–Sun 9am–noon. Tram: 1, 3, 4, 5, or 6. Bus: 31.

Landeszeughaus (Armory) As the capital, Graz has always been militarily important, and for more than 2 centuries it was a bulwark against the Turks. The armory, built between 1642 and 1645 by Anton Solar, dates from the Turkish wars. The early baroque gate, created by Giovanni Mamolo, is flanked by stat-ues of Mars and Minerva (war deities), and the building's four upper floors are separated by their original wood-beam ceilings. There's also a vaulted cannon hall on the ground floor.

Now a museum displaying 3 centuries of weaponry, the Landeszeughaus contains some 30,000 harnesses, coats of mail, helmets, swords, pikes, muskets, pistols, harquebuses, and other implements of war. In 1749, Empress Maria Theresa, in recognition of Styrian military service and strategic significance, allowed this arsenal to remain when the others in her empire were destroyed.

Herrengasse 16. (C) **0316/80-17-98-10.** Admission 4.30€ adults, 2.90€ seniors and students, free for chil-dren under 6. Apr–Oct Tues–Sun 9am–5pm; Nov–Mar Tues–Sun 10am–3pm. Tram: 3 or 6.

Mariahilferkirche (Church of Our Lady of Succor) Built for the Minorite brothers, this church sits on the right bank of the Mur River. Pietro de Pomis carried out its reconstruction in the early 17th century and painted the cele-brated altarpiece depicting St. Elizabeth interceding with the Virgin Mary. This painting made the church a pilgrimage site.

Mariahilferplatz 3. (C) **0316/71-31-69.** Free admission. Daily 7am–8pm. Tram: 3 or 6.

Mausoleum of Emperor Ferdinand II Next to the Domkirche is one of Graz's most remarkable buildings. Begun in 1614 and completed in 1638, this structure was intended as the tomb of the emperor and his first wife. The church, with a crossing cupola and a vaulted tomb chapel, is regarded as the best example of mannerism in Austria. The high altar is an early work of

J. B. Fischer von Erlach, done from 1695 to 1697. The tomb's central sarcophagus, intended for Ferdinand's parents, contains only his mother's remains.

On Bürgergasse. (C) 0316/82-16-83. Free admission. July–Sept daily 11am–3pm; off-season daily 11am–noon and 2–3pm. Tram: 3 or 4.

Schlossberg   Overlooking Graz, this formerly fortified hill rises to a height of 473m (1,550 ft.) above sea level. As mentioned above, in 1809 the fortifications were leveled as the terms of Austria's treaty with Napoléon. You can take a **cable railway** ((C) 0316/88-74-13) to the restaurant on top of the hill, or you can climb the winding stairs. From the top, you'll be able to look down on the city and its environs. Guided tours of the citadel start from the bell tower opposite the upper station of the cable railway. Although you can visit the Schlossberg year-round, no guided tours are offered from November to April.

During the summer, concerts are held on a wooden stage constructed within the castle's ramparts. Tickets are not cheap—from 12€ to 75€. Upcoming concerts are announced every season. For more information about schedules, call the tourist office.

The **Uhrturm (Clock Tower)** on the citadel is a curiosity rising above the walls of the former **Citizens' Bastion.** It acquired its appearance between 1555 and 1556, when the original Gothic tower was remade in the Renaissance style: The builders added a circular wooden gallery with oriels and four huge clock faces.

(C) 0316/872-49-02. Admission to tours 2€ adults, 1€ ages 6–15 (free 5 and under). Tours given daily on the hour 9am–5pm. No tours Nov–Apr. Take the Zahnradbahn from Kaiser-Franz-Josef-Kai 38; departs every 15 min. The ascent takes 5–10 min. Round-trip fare 2€ adults, 1€ children under 16. Cable car operates Apr daily 9am–11pm; May–June daily 8am–11pm; July–Aug daily 8am–midnight; Sept daily 9am–10pm; Oct–Mar daily 10am–10pm.

NEARBY ATTRACTIONS

Piber Stud Farm   The most important stud farm in Austria lies some 24km (15 miles) west of Graz. Lipizzaner horses are bred and trained here, and the result is quite magnificent. General Patton rescued these horses and their very special lineage from doom during a daring raid to retrieve them from behind Soviet lines at the end of World War II. When their early training is complete, the horses raised on this farm are sent to the Spanish Riding School in Vienna.

Piber Bundesgestvet, Piber, near Koeflach. (C) 03144/33-23. Admission 10€. 75-min. tours given daily 9am and 1:30pm. Closed to the public Nov–Easter. If you're driving, head west from Graz along Route 70 until the marked turnoff to Piber along an unclassified road.

Schloss Eggenberg (Eggenberg Palace)   About 3km (2 miles) west of the center of Graz, this square 17th-century palace has towers at its four corners and an accentuated facade over the main gate. The building sits in a large park that's now used as a game preserve. The four wings of the baroque structure surround a large court with arched arcades and two smaller courts separated by the palace church. You can take guided tours of the baroque state apartments on the second floor.

The ground floor of the south wing houses the Landesmuseum Joanneum's department of prehistory and early history, with a good collection of Styrian antiquities and coin collections.

Eggenberg Allée 90. (C) 0316/58-32-640. Admission 5.70€ adults, 2.80€ children under 14. Palace tours given Apr–Oct daily 10 and 11am, noon, and 2, 3, and 4pm (no tours Nov–Mar). Landesmuseum collections open daily 9am–1pm and 2–5pm. Tram: 1.

AN OPEN-AIR MUSEUM

Österreichisches Freilichtmuseum (Austrian Open-Air Museum) ⍟
(© 03124/53-700), about 16km (10 miles) north of Graz in Stübing, is set in
a wooded valley branching off the Mur Valley. Here you'll find buildings, some
of which are 400 years old, from all the Austrian provinces. The 85 authentic
structures include a smokeroom house (Rauchstubenhaus) from East Styria, a
smokehouse (Rauchhaus) from Land Salzburg, and circular, triangular, and rectangular houses. All the houses are maintained by the Styrian provincial and
Austrian national governments.

Architectural enthusiasts will find that this museum has an intriguing display
of the regional variations of building traditions. Because of the park's sprawling
size, just over 100 acres, the buildings—mostly farmhouses, barns, and farm-
related storage or food-processing sheds—are set within the rural habitats that
originally produced them. Despite its location in the verdant heart of Styria, the
curators have tried to showcase buildings that derived throughout the country—
from Vorarlberg, Austria's most westerly province, to Burgenland, a marshy low-
lying province similar to the plains of neighboring Hungary.

The museum is open from early April to late October Tuesday through Sunday from 9am to 5pm. Admission is 5.70€ for adults and 2.50€ for children.
You can take a train from Graz toward Bruck an der Mur and get off at the
station marked STÜBING, a local (*not* express) stop. After that, it's a 40-minute
walk, or you can take a taxi. About 10 buses head to Stübing each day from
Graz's Lendplatz (on the western bank of the Mur River, a 5-min. walk west of
Old Town); the trip takes 35 minutes.

SHOPPING

You might begin your shopping expedition at Hauptplatz, the main square in
the center of town. The major shopping streets, including Herrengasse, branch
off from here. The major item to buy here is Styrian clothing in its famous gray-
and-green hues. Stores offer a good selection of dirndls and hats in particular, as
well as local handcrafts and leather clothing. Stores are generally open weekdays
from 9am to 6pm and on Saturday from 9am to noon.

Brühl and Söhne   You'll find high-quality, but also high-priced, Styrian
clothing for men, women, and children here. The inventory includes fashionable dirndls, coats, skirts, hats, vests, suits, and accessories. Am Eisernentor 1.
© 0316/82-16-16-0. Tram: 1, 3, 4, 5, 6, or 7.

Steirisches Heimatwerk   This large store sells only Austrian-made items, a
big selection of regional clothing, fabrics, shoes, and cookbooks, as well as
objects made from glass, ceramics, and wood. Some more unusual items include
depictions of the local saints hand-painted in small wooden frames. Paulustorgasse
4. © 0316/827-1060. Bus: 30.

WHERE TO STAY

Accommodations range from first-class hotels to camping sites. There are many
reasonably priced family hotels and inexpensive lodgings in Graz, and even the
top hotels will seem surprisingly inexpensive.

EXPENSIVE

Grand Hotel Wiesler Graz ⍟⍟   On the River Mur, this historic hotel is the
most desirable (and only deluxe) hotel in town. It's the choice of Arnold
Schwarzenegger whenever he comes back home to visit Graz. After you register,
an employee brings fruit and tea to your room. The view from the neoclassical

windows encompasses many of the medieval city's baroque spires that soar toward the mountains on the opposite side of the river. The comfortable medium-size rooms come with wide, firm beds, thick carpeting, and wooden furnishings. Bathrooms are fairly spacious, with combination tub and shower. The Wiesler's restaurant offers good food and an attractive decor. There's an informal snack bar for sit-down food, plus the Café Jugendstil, where you can read international newspapers while enjoying fresh pastries and rich coffee. The bar serves up piano music and special drinks.

Grieskai 4–8, A-8010 Graz. ℂ 0316/7066. Fax 0316/70-66-76. www.hotelwiesler.com. 98 units. 185€–229€ double; 259€–629€ suite. Rates include buffet breakfast. AE, DC, MC, V. Parking 10.50€. Tram: 3 or 6. **Amenities:** Restaurant; cafe, bar; sauna; solarium; room service; babysitting; laundry; dry cleaning. *In room:* TV, minibar, hair dryer, safe.

Schlossberg Hotel 🌟🌟 *(Finds)* Housed behind a beautifully embellished cerulean facade, this 15th-century baroque inn is both unusual and charming, and it's our favorite hotel in town. (It has more atmosphere than the Grand Hotel Wiesler Graz.) The owner's wife decorated this formerly decrepit rooming house herself in 1982 with 19th-century furniture. There's an early Biedermeier ceramic stove in the bar area, several pieces of baroque sculpture set in well-placed niches, and a courtyard with a lion's-head fountain. The medium-size rooms are among the town's most inviting, and many open onto private balconies. The bathrooms contain shower-tub combinations and adequate shelf space.

Guests can enjoy drinks 24 hours a day on a terrace with a panoramic view of Graz. Breakfast is the only meal served, and it's offered in a beautiful winter garden.

Kaiser-Franz-Josef-Kai 30, A-8010 Graz. ℂ 0316/807-00. Fax 0316/807-070. www.schlossberg-hotel.at. 54 units. 182€–225€ double; 300€–370€ suite. Rates include buffet breakfast. AE, DC, MC. Parking 12€. Tram: 4 or 5. **Amenities:** Breakfast room; bar; pool; fitness center; sauna; room service; massage; babysitting; laundry; dry cleaning. *In room:* TV, minibar, hair dryer, safe.

MODERATE

Austria Trend Hotel Europa Opened in 1986, this five-story hotel is the largest and, in many ways, the most convenient in Graz. It lies adjacent to the railway station, a 20-minute walk south of the town's medieval center. The medium-size rooms are comfortably modern. The small bathrooms have shower-tub combinations and adequate shelf space. After you arrive, you can relax at the intimate bar, Bella Grazia, where snacks and drinks are served. A covered shopping center is attached to the hotel.

Bahnhofgürtel 89, A-8020 Graz. ℂ 0316/707-60. Fax 0316/707-6606. www.austria-trend.at/eug/eugset. htm. 118 units. 102€–138€ double; 163€–203€ suite. Rates include breakfast. AE, DC, MC, V. Parking 9.60€. Tram: 1, 3, 6, or 7. **Amenities:** Breakfast room; bar; sauna; laundry; dry cleaning. *In room:* TV, minibar, hair dryer.

City Hotel Erzherzog Johann Standing near the Old Town's pedestrian zone, this hotel dates from the 16th century. It was built as a *Gasthof* and named after the most powerful figure (Erzherzog Johann) in Styria at the time. The elegant establishment arranges its rooms around a skylighted atrium surrounded by curving wrought-iron balconies and plants. The newer rooms tend to be more spacious and tranquil, while the others (especially the singles) are rather standardized and a bit small. The housekeeping is quite good; bathrooms are small and offer shower-tub combinations but minimum shelf space.

Sackstrasse 3–5, A-8010 Graz. ℂ 0316/81-16-16. Fax 0316/81-15-15. www.erzherzog-johann.com. 64 units. 145€–210€ double; 255€–330€ suite. Rates include breakfast. Half-board 20€ per person extra.

AE, DC, MC, V. Parking 15€. Tram: 3 or 6. **Amenities:** Restaurant; bar; sauna; room service; babysitting; laundry; dry cleaning. *In room:* TV, minibar, hair dryer.

Hotel Gollner   Although the Gollner was originally built in the late 1800s, renovations have created an ambience of bland modernity and dependable comfort. This hotel is popular with the artists performing at the opera house next door. The comfortable, high-ceilinged rooms are filled with contemporary furniture and come in a variety of sizes. Bathrooms are small, with shower-tub combinations and adequate shelf space. The hotel has a garden terrace on its rooftop and another garden in back. In the historic heart of the town, the hotel stands adjacent to the opera, near Herrengasse. Breakfast is the only meal served.

Schlögelgasse 14, A-8010 Graz. ✆ **0316/82-25-21-0.** Fax 0316/822-52-17. www.hotelgollner.at. 45 units. 115€–145€ double. Rates include breakfast. AE, DC, MC, V. Parking 10€. Tram: 3 or 6. **Amenities:** Breakfast room; bar; sauna; room service; laundry; dry cleaning. *In room:* TV, hair dryer.

Hotel Weitzer   Standing on the River Mur, this hotel (not to be confused with the Grand Hotel Wiesler) consists of two buildings connected by an overhead glass tunnel. The same family has run the whole complex for four generations. Rooms are well lighted and comfortably furnished. Some of the more spacious accommodations offer queen-size beds, whereas a dozen corner rooms are filled with paired double beds. All bathrooms have neatly kept shower-tub combinations. The third floor is the nonsmoking floor. For the best views, ask for one of the fifth-floor rooms.

Restaurant Casserolle, on the ground floor, is one of the best restaurants in town (see "Where to Dine," below). The hotel also offers the Floriani, a rustic wine tavern, and the Kaffeehaus, in typical Viennese style, along with a lobby bar for cocktails and after-dinner drinks. The hotel is a member of the Steigenberger Reservations System.

Grieskai 12–14, A-8011 Graz. ✆ **800/223-5652** in the U.S., or 0316/70-30. Fax 0316/703-88. www.weitzer. com. 200 units. 136€–181€ double; 207€–375€ suite. Rates include buffet breakfast. AE, DC, MC, V. Parking 10.60€. Tram: 1, 3, 6, or 7. **Amenities:** Restaurant; wine tavern; bar; sauna; solarium; room service; massage; babysitting; laundry; dry cleaning. *In room:* TV, minibar, hair dryer.

Romantik Parkhotel ⌖   Although it was built in 1574, this hotel looks much newer because of frequent renovations. It lies within a 10-minute walk east of the city center, near the opera house. The interior is filled with baronial accessories, including suits of armor, hanging tapestries in the beamed dining room, and a scattering of antiques. Rooms are comfortable and traditionally furnished with double-glazed windows, plush carpeting, antiques, good beds, and small bathrooms with shelf space and shower-tub combinations. A garden in back provides a midsummer escape.

Leonhardstrasse 8, A-8010 Graz. ✆ **0316/363-00.** Fax 0316/36-30-50. romantic@parkhotelgraz.at. 71 units. 116€–172€ double; 175€–232€ suite. Rates include breakfast. AE, DC, MC, V. Tram: 1, 3, 6, or 7. **Amenities:** Restaurant; bar; pool; sauna; room service; laundry; dry cleaning. *In room:* TV, minibar, hair dryer, safe.

INEXPENSIVE

Hotel Drei Raben *(Value*   This five-story hotel was originally built as an apartment house around 1900, and later it was modernized and transformed into a hotel. Within a 5-minute walk from the railway station and a 10-minute walk from the Old Town, the hotel offers modern comfort and well-furnished, medium-size rooms. Only 19 rooms have a tub-shower combination; the rest have shower-only bathrooms. Housekeeping rates a plus here. On the premises is a local branch of Wienerwald, a chain restaurant specializing in all-day dining, roast chicken, and reasonable prices aimed at the family trade.

Annenstrasse 43, A-8020 Graz. ⓒ **0316/71-26-86.** Fax 0316/71-59-596. www.vivat.at/3raben. 51 units. 93€–99€ double; 115€–127€ triple. Rates include buffet breakfast. AE, DC, MC, V. Parking 7.20€. Tram: 3 or 6. **Amenities:** Restaurant; bar. *In room:* TV, hair dryer.

Hotel Grazerhof   This four-story hotel in a central location boasts a 17th-century foundation, 19th-century walls, and a congenial atmosphere. Many Austrian visitors stay here. Rooms are simple and comfortable, but since there's no elevator, you might huff and puff a bit to reach those on the uppermost floor. Each year a selection of rooms is renovated. Accommodations are a bit small, but each room has a neatly kept bathroom with a shower unit. Corridor bathrooms are adequate and well maintained. On the premises is a very popular restaurant favored by locals, with set menus that range from 10€ to 15€.

Stubenberggasse 10, A-8010 Graz. ⓒ **0316/82-43-58.** Fax 0316/819-633-40. 25 units. 87€ double. Rates include breakfast. AE, DC, MC, V. Parking 22€. Tram: 3 or 6. **Amenities:** Restaurant; bar. *In room:* TV.

WHERE TO DINE

The variety of restaurants in Graz is enormous, ranging from first-class establishments to beer halls to student hangouts. Prices in even the top restaurants are moderate. You can dine in the hotels (which have some of the best food in town) or in cozy pubs and intimate bistros.

We suggest skipping typical international cuisine and concentrating on genuine Styrian specialties such as *Wurzelfleisch,* a kind of stew, or the different kinds of *Sterz,* a German version of kasha (made with cracked buckwheat or corn). The homemade sausages are generally excellent. Vienna is noted for its *Hendl* (chicken) dishes, but Graz chefs also do chicken extremely well.

The art of beer brewing is cultivated in Graz. Residents especially like the local Puntigam or Reininghaus beer, as well as the Gösser beer, brewed in Upper Styria.

You might want to try Styrian wine, whose grapes grow on steep, sunny slopes. Important varieties such as Welschriesling, Muskat-Sylvaner, Traminer, and the Schilcher (which grows only in a limited area in West Syria) have received international recognition. Many wine restaurants provide background music in the evening.

EXPENSIVE

Johan 👯 CONTINENTAL/NEW AUSTRIAN   Although it's set on the ground floor of a medieval building behind the Rathaus (Town Hall), you might get the feeling that you're in an underground cellar here, thanks partly to a majestic-looking vaulted stone ceiling and some very impressive masonry. Long, narrow, vaguely monastic, and permeated with a sense of the Middle Ages, it's the premier and most stylish restaurant of Graz, with a clientele whose names appear in the society section of the local newspaper. Its sophisticated touches of postmodern design put the place firmly in the 21st century. There's an elongated bar—almost 100 feet of it—crafted from beechwood, theatrical lighting, and food that's on the nouvelle side of the culinary equation. Menu items are much worked over, frequently adapted to the seasons and stylish. The best examples, depending on the time of year you arrive, include a divine breast of wild goose glazed with Pinot Grigio and a confit of goose liver; a mélange of sweet potatoes, Jerusalem artichokes, and poached carp dumplings; a platter containing three different preparations of veal served with a parsley and salsify *Rösti* (a patty sautéed to crispy golden brown) and a creamy version of red lentils; and filet of beef with crabmeat, roast onions, and white-bread dumplings. You'll recognize the outside of this place thanks to a baroque overlay that was added to the building's original medieval core, and a flickering torch that blazes near its entrance.

Landhausgasse 1. ℭ 0316/821312-0. Reservations required. Main courses 19€–22€. AE, DC, MC, V. Tues–Sat 6–11:30pm.

Restaurant Casserolle ℜ AUSTRIAN   One of the finest hotel dining rooms in Graz, this prestigious restaurant on the banks of the Mur offers a "taste of Styria." To go completely local, ask the waiter to bring you a Styrian Old Slivovitz, a schnapps made from plums. You can follow with a selection of either hot or cold appetizers, perhaps Styrian *Speck,* which is delicately cured and finely sliced ham garnished with grated horseradish. A homemade chicken-liver paté with Cumberland sauce is also recommended, or you could begin with one of the day's soups, perhaps a clear oxtail broth laced with sherry. Both freshwater and sea fish are offered, ranging from John Dory to grilled filet of pike perch. One of the chef's specialties is veal Casserolle, served in a casserole with Swiss-style sautéed potatoes. One entire section of the menu is taken up with Austrian beef specialties, not just the typically Viennese *Tafelspitz* (boiled beef), but tournedos with a truffle-cream sauce and even chateaubriand (which requires two diners). Boiled beef *Goldener Ochs* (a slice of boiled prime beef) is even better than the *Tafelspitz.* You can have a sweet dessert, such as a traditional apple strudel, or finish your meal, as many locals do, with a small cheese plate, perhaps Austrian Emmentaler, a mild nut-flavored cheese.

In the Hotel Weitzer, Grieskai 12–14. ℭ 0316/70-30. Reservations recommended. Main courses 10€–35€. AE, DC, MC, V. Daily noon–2pm and 6–10pm. Tram: 1, 3, 6, or 7.

MODERATE

Das Wirtshaus Greiner AUSTRIAN   About a mile north of the town's center, this cozy and historic setting occupies an old-fashioned building whose foundations date back to the early 1600s. Inside, you'll find a light and well-maintained set of dining rooms where the staff prepares meticulous versions of, among others, parfaits of venison with orange and pistachio marmalade; roasted quail with alpine berries; filet of zander with a wine, butter, and herb sauce; and roasted goose with caramelized onions.

Grabenstrasse 64. ℭ 0316/68-50-90. Reservations recommended. Main courses 5.50€–18.90€. MC, V. Mon–Fri 11:30am–2pm and 6–10pm. Tram: 4, 6, or 7.

Goldene Pastete ℜ AUSTRIAN   Our favorite restaurant in Graz is in a five-story 1751 building of pink stucco and green shutters. Window boxes bursting with flowers adorn its exterior, while the interior is a fantasy of rustic artifacts and Styrian folklore. Managed by the hardworking Patterer family, it's the oldest inn in Graz, with three dining rooms on three different floors. There's also an outdoor terrace near the garden for warm-weather dining.

The menu lists a flavorful choice of Austrian dishes, all well prepared. Specialties include prosciutto with melon, very fresh salads, pasta, calamari, *Tafelspitz,* several kinds of schnitzels (including a version with ham and cheese), several kinds of fish (including zander in Riesling sauce), and grilled beefsteaks. In the autumn, wild game dishes like venison appear on the menu. The onion-flavored roast beef is a perennial favorite, and gourmets flock here for the fresh trout, which is grilled perfectly in its natural juices and served without sauce.

Sporgasse 28. ℭ 0316/82-34-16. Reservations recommended. Main courses 11€–14€. AE, DC, MC, V. Mon–Fri 11am–midnight. Tram: 1, 3, or 6.

Landhaus-Keller ℜ AUSTRIAN   This restaurant is in one of the most historic buildings in Graz, in the city center near the casino. (Its entrance is at the rear side of the Landhaus; its neighbor is the Zeughaus, the Armory.) In summer, outdoor tables are set up in a flowered courtyard with a view of a baroque church's arcade. The building was constructed in the early 16th century, and since then the cellars have hosted such famous guests as Metternich, Franz and Eduard Sacher, and the Duke of Wellington. A dimly lit corridor passes three rustic and authentically Teutonic dining areas (there are six if you count the nooks and crannies), ranging from the Hunters' Room to the Knights' Room.

A wide and well-prepared selection of seafood, veal, beef, pork, and chicken dishes is served. Specialties are usually based on old Styrian recipes. You might begin with sour-cream soup with scorched polenta, meatballs with sauerkraut, Styrian cheese dumplings in beef broth, and browned omelets with blueberries. Specialties of which the chef is particularly proud include Styrian beef with chanterelles and smoked *Saebling* (salmon trout) with horseradish sauce.

Schmiedgasse 9. © 0316/830276. Reservations recommended. Main courses 14€–22€; fixed-price menu 32€–38€. DC, MC, V. Mon–Sat 11:30am–midnight. Closed holidays. Tram: 9.

INEXPENSIVE

Gambrinuskeller INTERNATIONAL   The decor, like the menu here, combines elements from rustically conservative Austria with overtones of the Middle East and the Balkans. A stainless-steel deli-style case separates the busy kitchens from the dining areas. The unusual menu offers Brazilian, Persian, and Italian foods, too. You might enjoy churrasco (Brazilian barbecue) of pork, Iranian-style kebabs, Italian pasta dishes, and grilled steaks. Dessert could be anything from baklava to apple strudel. The cuisine is marvelous change-of-pace fare, although the chefs perhaps extend themselves too much by offering such widely varied menus. In summer, the garden attracts diners and drinkers.

Färbergasse 6–8. © 0316/81-01-81. Reservations not required. Main courses 3.50€–16€. AE, DC, MC, V. Tues–Sat 10pm–midnight. Tram: 1, 3, 4, 5, 6, or 7.

Krebsenkeller (Value) AUSTRIAN/INTERNATIONAL   Many diners select this restaurant as much for its architecture as for its simple, wholesome food. Built in 1538, Krebsenkeller's entrance lies beneath a covered passageway that ends in an enclosed courtyard. Cafe tables spill from beneath a grape arbor into the courtyard-style garden. There's ample seating indoors in a series of dining rooms, including an underground *Keller* (cellar), a street-level *Stüberl* (tavern), and a gemütlich room known locally as the Osteria. Menu items include grilled dishes prepared in varying degrees of spiciness, a variety of homemade soups, fresh salads, fresh fish, and wild game. Dine as the residents do and order the savory kettle of goulash or the boiled pork with a cabbage salad. For dessert, the best choice is a crepe stuffed with marmalade, chocolate, or ice cream and covered with either a hot strawberry sauce or a cranberry sauce.

Sackstrasse 12. © 0316/82-93-77. Reservations recommended. Main courses 7.90€–13.70€; fixed-price menus 7€–15€. DC, MC, V. Daily 10am–midnight. Tram: 1, 3, or 6.

Maroni AUSTRIAN/ITALIAN   Its decor combines very old stonework and masonry that's offset with modern paintings and accessories that define it as urbanized and hip. As such, it fulfills a double function as a restaurant where Italian and Austrian specialties are enjoyed by folks of all ages, and a bar where the young and the restless can hobnob with one another over American martinis. The menu changes every 2 weeks but usually focuses on Austrian specialties that include Wiener schnitzels, *Tafelspitz,* trout with potatoes, and fried beefsteak with onions. Also look for pastas and risottos, very fresh salads, and marinated seasonal vegetables served in a way that will remind you of the agrarian bounty of the

Mediterranean. Cocktails at the bar range in price from 6€ to 9€. On Friday and Saturday, a DJ provides dance music in the bar from 9pm to 3am.

Mehlplatz 1. ℂ 0316/82-87-02. Reservations recommended. Main courses 12€–15€. AE, DC, MC, V. Daily 11:30am–3pm and 6–11:30pm. Tram: 1, 3, or 6.

CAFES

Café Glockenspiel, Glockenspielplatz 4 (ℂ 0316/83-02-91; tram: 1 or 3), is situated on a square filled with neoclassical and Art Nouveau buildings. A clock tower on the square plays three times day, at 11am, 3pm, and 6pm, and the cafe is on the ornate tower's ground floor, with tables out front in fair weather. A formally attired waiter will take your order for coffee, light snacks, or sandwiches. The comfortable interior contains serpentine banquettes, mahogany paneling and tables, original lithographs, and paintings. Coffee and pastries range from 1.90€ to 8€. It's open Monday through Saturday from 8am to midnight, and Sunday from 1 to 9pm.

Perfect on a summer day (and with a view looking over the open-air market), the popular **Café Leinich,** Kaiser-Josef-Platz 4 (ℂ 0316/83-05-86; tram: 3 or 6), has served good coffee and homemade pastries (rich concoctions using an abundance of fresh fruit and berries) since 1891. Coffee and pastries start at 1.90€. It's open Monday through Friday from 7am to 7pm and Saturday from 7am to 2pm.

GRAZ AFTER DARK

One of the most visible and frequently showcased buildings in Graz is the **Opernhaus (Opera House),** Opernring (ℂ 0316/80-00; tram: 1 or 7). It's the year-round home of Graz's opera company, of which local residents are justifiably proud. The faux-baroque theater was designed "in the style of Fischer von Erlach" at the end of the 19th century. Recent performances have included *Lucia de Lammermoor, Cavelleria Rusticana, Rigoletto,* and even Broadway musicals. Depending on the event and your seat, tickets are 21€ to 36.50€.

THE BAR & CLUB SCENE

Sometimes restaurants combine dancing and nightclub shows, so you might be able to spend an entire evening at one address. The cafes often have music as well.

The area around **Farbergasse-Mehlplatz** is the most popular place for people from all walks of life, and the city's greatest cluster of bars and restaurants is here. Locals refer to it as their "Bermuda Triangle."

The city often offers some excellent jazz, but performances are not always rigidly scheduled, and certainly not every night of the week. It's best to call to find out if a jazz program is being presented at the time of your visit. Your best bet is **Das Neue Wist,** Mosterhofgasse 34 (ℂ 0316/83-66-66-0; tram: 1 or 7).

Gamlitzer Weinstube   This is the most visible *Weinstube* (wine tavern) in town, established 300 years ago. The food is plentiful, inexpensive, and designed to accompany the wines (many from Styria) served here. Meals begin at around 12€ each, and wine sells for 1.80€ and up per glass. In summer, most of the establishment's business is conducted at tables and chairs outdoors. It's open Monday through Friday from 9am to 11pm.

Mehlplatz 4. ℂ 0316/83-25-44. Tram: 1, 3, 6, or 7.

Glockenspielkeller   Among the town's most frequented places (day or night) is this *Keller* (cellar) established in 1979 in a 300-year-old building. It occupies both a cellar and a paved garden-style terrace out in front. In the restaurant, a

Tagesmenu (daily menu) costs 7€ and is one of the city's best dining values. Although many patrons come here just to drink, this spot is also a full-fledged restaurant, serving old-fashioned Austrian and Styrian dishes, with main courses costing from 7€ to 13€. Coffee costs 1.50€, and a glass of wine costs 1.80€. The cellar is open from 11am to 1am.

Mehlplatz 3. ℭ **0316/82-87-01.** Tram: 3 or 6.

M-1   One of the most desirable bars in Graz, M-1 is located behind large glass windows on the rooftop of a historic building in the town's nightlife district. Views from the comfortable chairs encompass a postmodern design and breathtaking scenery. The crowd is congenial, and recorded music contributes to the place's big-city style. Beer costs 3.40€. It's open daily from 10am to 2am.

Färberplatz. ℭ **0316/81-12-33.** Tram: 3 or 6.

A CASINO

One of the premier nightlife venues in Graz is contained within its casino, **Casino Graz,** Landhausgasse 10 (ℭ **0316/83-25-78**). Set at the corner of the Schmiedegasse, in the historic core of town, it's a modern (ca. 1984) building whose chief venue is the availability of its slot machines (open daily 11am–3am) and its roulette wheels and blackjack tables (open daily 3pm–3am). To enter, you'll have to be over 18 and present appropriate ID. Jackets and ties are usually required for men, although ties are optional June through September. Entrance is free, although you'll be offered the opportunity to buy 20€ worth of chips for the price of 17€. On the premises are a restaurant and a piano bar; within one of the building's many meeting rooms, cabaret shows are occasionally presented. Take your passport.

2 Bad Gleichenberg ⟨⭐⟩

195km (121 miles) S of Vienna; 64km (40 miles) SE of Graz

The oldest and most important summer spa in South Styria (with a history of water treatments dating from Roman times), **Bad Gleichenberg** lies southeast of Graz. The countryside here, near Slovenia's border, is relatively flat, a low-altitude setting of rolling hills and vineyards. This is one of the most interesting and least-known parts of Austria to explore.

Untersteienmark, or Lower Styria, where this spa is located, was much larger in the days of the Hapsburgs. Much of its territory was lost to Yugoslavia following the breakup of the empire after World War I.

Bad Gleichenberg sits in a scenic valley opening to the south. In the area's landscaped parks you'll see exotic plants, including the giant sequoia. You can partake of the mineral waters of the Emma, Konstantin, and Johannisbrunnen springs and even take a bottle home with you. The spa has flourished for 160 years, longer than any other spa in Styria. The clientele here tends to be middle-aged or elderly, and there's an emphasis on low-key activities. The calm is punctuated with an entertainment program and special tours in the environs. Hotels ring the spa facilities, which mark the resort's center. Mud baths and long soaks in the thermally heated waters are big here, along with rest and relaxation.

ESSENTIALS

GETTING THERE   By Train   Bad Gleichenberg lies at the end of a minor rail line stretching eastward from Graz. Passengers board an eastbound train in Graz and head toward the Hungarian border town of Szentgotthárd, changing trains at Feldbach (trip time: 50–60 min.). From Feldbach, about five trains a day continue to the Bad Gleichenberg. (Fortunately, because rail connections from Feldbach to Bad Gleichenberg aren't always convenient, passengers can also board one of the eight Bad Gleichenberg–bound buses that depart from Feldbach's railway station every day.) The trip from Feldbach to Bad Gleichenberg by bus or train takes an additional 30 to 35 minutes.

By Bus There's one early morning bus, departing daily at 7:30am for Bad Gleichenberg from Vienna's Wien Mitte bus station (trip time: 3 hr.). From Graz, four buses depart Monday through Saturday at 8:25am, 10:30am, 12:15pm, and 4:35pm from in front of the main railway station for Bad Gleichenberg (trip time: 2 hr.).

By Car If you're driving from Graz, take the A2 east to the junction with Route 68, which you take south to the junction with Route 66. Continue south on Route 66 to Bad Gleichenberg.

VISITOR INFORMATION The **tourist office** in the town center (© **03159/ 22-03**) is open Monday through Friday from 8am to 6pm and Saturday from 8am to 2pm.

WHERE TO STAY & DINE

Hotel Gleichenberger Hof *(Value)* This cozy 1970s chalet is set in a forested area with a masonry sun terrace stretching below the facade. It's located in the town's center near the spa facilities. The interior has rustic yet modern accessories, including a piano bar and an open fireplace, and all rooms have balconies. The medium-size rooms are tastefully and comfortably furnished. Bathrooms are small but tidily maintained, with shower-tub combinations and adequate shelf space. The restaurant is open to nonguests for lunch only.

Bergstrasse 27, A-8344 Bad Gleichenberg. © **03159/24-24.** Fax 03159/295-56. 27 units. 111€–117€ double; 133€–140€ suite for 2. Rates include half-board. V. Closed Jan 7–Feb 17 and Nov 23–Dec 23. **Amenities:** Restaurant; bar; room service; babysitting; laundry; dry cleaning. *In room:* TV, minibar, hair dryer, safe.

Schloss Kapfenstein *(Finds)* As an alternative to staying in Bad Gleichenberg, you can go east to Kapfenstein and its *Schloss* hotel near the Slovenian border. The 10km (6-mile) trip takes 20 minutes. Drive south from Bad Gleichenberg along Highway 66, and then cut east along the unnumbered provincial highway (*Bundesstrasse*) that's marked KAPFENSTEIN. This solidly built castle has a hipped roof and a curving extension that's almost as old as the main building itself. Set in the middle of forests and rich fields, the castle offers rooms filled with antique furniture and all the modern comforts, such as good, firm beds and neatly kept bathrooms with shower units.

If you want, you can dine on the castle's terrace, which offers a view of the village below. Specialties are based on regional dishes such as roast hen, homemade blutwurst and other sausages, and apple strudel. The Winkler family makes its own wine, a very delicate and famous vintage.

A-8353 Kapfenstein. © **03157/2332.** Fax 03157/31-31-4. 8 units. 100€–136€ double. Rates include half-board. MC, V. **Amenities:** Restaurant; bar; pool; fitness center; sauna; solarium; room service; massage; babysitting; laundry; dry cleaning. *In room:* TV, minibar, hair dryer, safe.

3 Mariazell ★

150km (93 miles) SE of Vienna; 140km (87 miles) N of Graz

Mariazell is the most celebrated pilgrimage center in Austria, in addition to being a winter playground and a summer resort. It's the national shrine of Austria, Hungary, and Bohemia.

ESSENTIALS

GETTING THERE   By Train   Mariazell is at the terminus of a secondary train line that originates in the capital of Lower Austria, St. Pölten, 52 miles (84km) to the north. St. Pölten, which sits astride the main rail lines connecting Vienna and Salzburg, receives dozens of trains from Vienna (trip time: 45 min.) and Salzburg (trip time: 2½ hr.) throughout the day. From St. Pölten, about half a dozen trains head south to Mariazell (trip time: 2½ hr.).

By Bus   About half a dozen buses depart every day from Vienna's Wien Mitte bus station for their final destination at Mariazell (trip time: 2¼–4 hr.).

If the train schedule between St. Pölten and Mariazell is inconvenient, you can take one of the several daily buses that parallel the same route (trip time: 1½ hr.). In addition, two buses depart daily from the Graz railway station to Mariazell (trip time: 3 hr.). For bus information, call © **0316/82-0606.**

Finally, buses depart several times a day for Mariazell from the important railway junction of Mürzzuschlag (trip time: 1½ hr.), which is set on the main rail lines between Vienna and Graz.

By Car   If you're driving from Graz, head north along Autobahn A9 until you reach the junction with the S35 north. Continue north to the junction with Route 20, which leads into Mariazell.

VISITOR INFORMATION   The **tourist office,** Hauptplatz 13 (© **03882/ 23-66**), is open Monday through Friday from 9am to 5pm, Saturday from 9am to 3pm, and Sunday from noon to 3pm.

SEEING THE SHRINE

The pilgrimage destination is the **Mariazell Basilica** on Hauptplatz (© **03882/ 2595**), dating from the dawn of the 13th century, with three prominent towers. The goal of the pilgrimage, however, was to come and pray and make votive offerings to the statue of the Virgin, which is mounted on the altar.

The church was originally constructed in the Romanesque style, and then a Gothic choir was added in the late 14th century. The bulbous domes are baroque, a style added to most of Austria's churches in the 17th century. Both Fischer von Erlachs, senior and junior, aided the Mariazell transformation. The grave of the world-famous Hungarian Cardinal Mindszenty is in the church; there's also the Mindszenty Museum. In 1983, Pope John Paul II visited Mariazell and the cardinal's burial place.

In the treasury are votive offerings accrued over some 600 years. The Chapel of Grace is the national shrine of Austria. Miracles are attributed to its statue of the Virgin, giving rise to fame that has spread all over Europe. The altar on which the statue is mounted was designed by the younger von Erlach. In summer, large groups gather on Saturday night for torchlight processions to the church.

The treasury is open only from May to October Tuesday through Friday from 10:30am to noon and 2 to 3pm, and Saturday and Sunday from 10am to 4pm. Admission is 2.50€.

Over the years, Mariazell has attracted much royalty—some of the Hapsburgs, in particular, were fond of this village.

OUTDOOR ACTIVITIES

Many parents take their children to Mariazell to teach them how to ski. For generations, Mariazell has been a winter vacation center for the whole family. Here you'll find all the components of a modern winter-sports and recreation center:

Bad Blumau: Austria's Most Whimsical Spa

Trust us, you've never been to a place like this before. If you make the 90-minute trip south from Vienna to Blumau, or the slightly shorter trip from Graz, through the green rolling hills and blond fields of Styria, you will come to a dip in the road, a little town, and one of the most marvelous sights you have ever seen: **Bad Blumau** 🏵🏵🏵.

Imagine this: trees bubbling out of rooftops, mad yellow and white towers topped with onion domes, a lake-size pool with hidden fountains spraying thermal waters at random, hallway floors canted like coffee mugs turned on their sides. It's the world's largest inhabitable artwork, a 271-room spa with the sort of architecture you might expect if you hired a creative child and gave him a shovel, a set of Lego blocks, a blowtorch, and a roadside ditch. But in this case, the child just turned 70, his name is Friedensreich Hundertwasser, and he has littered Austria with his creations, among them the gaily colored Hundertwasserhaus at the edge of the Ring in Vienna. (See "Other Top Attractions" in chapter 4.)

Although it's a work of art, Bad Blumau is also a functioning spa. The rooms are comfortable, with minibars and safes; bathrooms are well maintained with tub and shower combos. The suites have just about the only level floors in the place.

The therapies here tend to drift toward the new age. Although you can happily glut yourself on shiatsu and Swedish massage, try having an attendant dip you in mare's milk, whey (yuck!), or the essence of evening primrose, and then suspend you in a heat box for a good half-hour. The 3-hour "resurrection therapy" session involves gongs, a box of pebbles, hypnotism, and more than a few euros.

avalanche-controlled grounds for skiers of all skill levels, a cableway, a chairlift, numerous surface lifts, a natural toboggan run, a skating rink, a ski school, and a ski kindergarten.

Its high altitude and good, brisk climate also make this a favored summer vacation site. You can go walking on some 201km (125 miles) of footpaths or go mountaineering, swimming, rowing, sailing, windsurfing, canoeing, fishing, horseback riding, glider flying, and camping. You can also play tennis or golf.

For the area's most dramatic views, you can take the **Seilbahn Mariazell-Bürgeralpe,** Wienerstrasse 28 (© **03882/25-55**), to the Bürgeralpe at 1,272m (4,170 ft.). Leaving from the center of town, cable cars depart about every 20 minutes. They run in July and August daily from 8:30am to 5:30pm; in September daily from 8:30am to 5pm; in May, June, October, and November daily 9am to 5pm; in December daily from 8am to 4pm; and from January to April daily from 8am to 4pm. A round-trip costs 6€.

WHERE TO STAY & DINE

Hotel Goldene Krone   Next to the basilica is a well-managed, government-rated three-star hotel that was established as an inn in the 1300s. Rebuilt several times and renovated again in 1991, the inn's in a substantial old Styrian house with stone trim. The interior has a contemporary bar area with decorative masonry. Rooms are a bit small, but they're well maintained and equipped with

The saunas are coed and naked. Don't be ashamed; no one else is. Also, they're the best part of the complex—you get to choose from Roman and Finnish saunas, Turkish baths, the Aromasauna, and the Biosanarium, which involves gassy peppermint and blinking lights. Likewise, in the health areas, you're apt to receive treatments from an attendant who is young, of the opposite sex, and (don't worry) utterly professional. The pool has lockers for both day-trippers and overnight guests.

You'll eat well, if not entirely healthfully: The buffet is full of meat and cheese, all delicious, but doubtless engineered to fatten all the happy Germans who fill the place. The a la carte menu advertises itself as "international," but let's just say it never made it to California.

The spa also offers child care, shopping, a hairdresser, laundry service, and parking. Conference and fitness rooms are also available. Blumau and the baths, A-8283 Blumau 100, are about 130km (81 miles) south of Vienna and 50km (37 miles) east of Graz (𝒞 **43-3383-5100-9445**; fax 43-3383-5100-808; www.blumau.com). Rates are 140€ to 170€ for a double and 195€ to 250€ for an apartment; half-board is 20€ extra. Rates include buffet breakfast and free use of all thermal bath and sauna facilities, service charge, and tax. Spa treatments and visitor tax are not included.

To get from Graz to Bad Blumau, take the Autobahn (A2) east and follow the signs to the spa (it's well marked).

good, firm beds and small bathrooms with shower-tub combinations but minimum shelf space. The restaurant, which serves Austrian national dishes along with Styrian specialties, is open to nonguests daily from 7am to 11pm, with main courses 6.50€ to 14€.

Grazerstrasse 1, A-8630 Mariazell. 𝒞 **03882/25-83.** Fax 03882/25-83-33. www.krone.at. 20 units. 59.60€ double. Rates include breakfast. Half-board 10.20€ per person extra. AE, DC, MC, V. Closed Mar. **Amenities:** Restaurant; lounge; room service; laundry; dry cleaning. *In room:* TV.

4 Bad Aussee ⟨★⟩

196km (122 miles) NW of Graz; 299km (186 miles) SW of Vienna; 80km (50 miles) SE of Salzburg

Surrounded by a lake, mountains, and woods, **Bad Aussee** is an old market town and spa in the "green heart" of the Salzkammergut. Unlike spa towns such as Bad Gleichenberg, Bad Aussee has developed into a resort relatively recently. It also doesn't place much emphasis on the medical/recuperative therapies that are all the rage at other resorts. Instead, most of the clientele comes here for its high altitude—650m (2,131 ft.) above sea level, nearly twice that of Bad Gleichenberg—and its profusion of hiking trails that are clearly marked with green-and-white signs. Guests here tend to be younger and more vigorous than those at the more sedentary Bad Gleichenberg.

From this spa, you can explore the **Altaussee,** one of the most beautiful bodies of water in Styria, which faces the Totes Gebirge.

Bad Aussee lies amid a network of lakes in the Valley of Traun, with the peaks of the Totes Gebirge and the Dachstein massif visible in the distance. The best time to visit is in June, when fields of narcissus burst into bloom, one of the most spectacular signs of spring coming to Europe.

Despite the relative lack of interest in spa rituals here, Bad Aussee does emphasize the saltwater and freshwater springs that are tapped by many of the town's hotels. Waters from the Bad Aussee Glaubersalt spring are said to be effective for losing weight, partly because a pint or so will usually manage to curtail the most stalwart of appetites. Salt mined in the nearby hills and added to bathwater is also supposed to relieve aches and pains.

Bad Aussee, at the confluence of a pair of upper branches of the Traun River, is the capital of the Styrian section of the Salzkammergut. Only 5km (3 miles) north is the Altaussee, with the spa town of Altaussee on its shore.

One of Austria's most beautiful areas, the town is a good center for walking and climbing in summer. Although Bad Aussee has long been known as a summer spa resort, it has also developed into a winter ski center. Several ski lifts are located nearby, making it attractive to ski enthusiasts.

Bad Aussee's best-known association is with Archduke Johann of the House of Hapsburg. In 1827, he married the daughter of a local postmaster, a cause célèbre rivaling the later romance of the Duke and Duchess of Windsor. There's a statue of the "Prince of Styria," Johann, in the Kurpark.

ESSENTIALS

GETTING THERE   By Train   Bad Aussee sits astride a secondary rail line running between the Austrian junctions of Stainach-Irdning (which services passengers arriving from Graz and Vienna) and Attnang-Puchheim (which services passengers arriving from Salzburg and Linz). The trip from Graz to Stainach-Irdning takes about 2½ hours. At Stainach-Irdning, passengers transfer onto any of a dozen northbound trains for Bad Aussee (trip time: 40 min.).

Passengers starting in Salzburg or Linz can take any of the dozens of daily trains to Attnang-Puchheim and then transfer to a southbound train. This train passes through several resorts in Upper Austria—most notably, Bad Ischl and Bad Goisern—before reaching Bad Aussee (2½ hr.).

By Bus   Because of its good (albeit complicated) rail connections, most visitors arrive in Bad Aussee by train. The most useful of the handful of bus lines running into Bad Aussee, however, is the one that runs from Styria across the border of Upper Austria into the resort of Bad Ischl (see chapter 9) several times a day (trip time: 45 min.).

By Car   Driving from Graz, take Autobahn A9 northwest and continue in the same direction as it becomes Route 113. Follow that highway's extension, which becomes Route 146, but cut west at the junction of Route 145 toward Tauplitz.

VISITOR INFORMATION   The **tourist office** in the village center at Bahnustrasse 132 (© **03622/523-23;** www.ausseerland.at) is open Monday through Friday from 8am to 8pm and Saturday from 9am to noon and 4 to 7pm.

WHERE TO STAY & DINE

Erzherzog Johann ✯✯   In the center of town, this government-rated four-star hotel is the resort's finest. The conservatively designed building has stone detailing and an arched entranceway, and its rustic interior offers fireplaces, beamed ceilings, and comfortably up-to-date furniture. Rooms are a bit small, with a balcony, good beds, and small bathrooms (usually with shower-tub combinations). Housekeeping gets high marks. The hotel restaurant serves a sampling of excellent Austrian and international dishes, with fresh ingredients used whenever possible. Main courses are 7€ to 16€ and are served daily from noon to 2pm and 6:30 to 9:30pm. The area's sporting facilities are easily accessible from here.

Kurhausplatz 62, A-8990 Bad Aussee. © **03622/52507.** Fax 03622/52507-680. www.erzherzogjohann.at. 62 units. 158€–198€ double. Rates include half-board. AE, DC, MC, V. Free parking. **Amenities:** Restaurant; bar; room service; pool; fitness center; health spa; sauna; massage; beauty treatments; babysitting; laundry; dry cleaning. *In room:* TV, minibar, hair dryer.

Hotel-Pension Villa Kristina ⚜ *Value*   This charming and personal establishment was built in 1892 as a simple inn for the many hunters who frequented the region. Friedl Raudaschl bought the place in the 1970s, updated its plumbing and electricity, and named it after his wife, Krista, who continues to manage it with him today. The hotel lies on ample private grounds studded with very old trees beside the River Traun and the road leading to Altaussee, about a 10-minute walk from Bad Aussee. Inside and out, the steep-roofed, wood-trimmed house is loaded with handcrafted details. Tastefully appointed medium-size rooms are filled with a certain Eastern Austrian charm, although modern luxuries have been looked after as well, including efficiently organized bathrooms, with shower-tub combinations. The most desirable guest rooms have private balconies with great views. The hotel has a home library and a piano. Meals are served only to guests who request meals in advance.

Altauseerstrasse 54, A-8990 Bad Aussee. © and fax **03622/520-17.** www.villakristina.at. 12 units. 80€–98€ double. Rates include breakfast. AE, DC, MC, V. Closed Apr and Nov–Dec 18. **Amenities:** Restaurant; bar; pool; room service; laundry; dry cleaning. *In room:* TV.

5 Dachstein-Tauern

The province's major ski area, Dachstein-Tauern, lies in northwest Styria. The Dachstein, in the Salzkammergut, is a gigantic alpine mountain range cutting across Land Salzburg, Upper Austria, and Styria, with mammoth glaciers lying between its peaks. The Enns River separates the Dachstein and the Tauern massifs. Championship ski races are held here, and it's a great place for powder skiing.

SCHLADMING & ROHRMOOS

To see more of West Styria, stay in either Rohrmoos or Schladming, south of Bad Aussee, and use these resorts as a center for exploring the alpine mountain range of Dachstein-Tauern.

GETTING THERE   This skiing center is in the Dachstein-Tauern recreation and winter-sports area on Route 308 and the Vienna-Bruck/Mur-Graz rail line. It's easy to reach. The center of Rohrmoos is 2km (1 mile) south of the center of Schladming, but the edges of the two resorts touch one another; for most practical purposes, they are considered one.

At least one **train** per hour reaches Schladming from Graz (trip time: 2½ hr.) or Salzburg (trip time: 1¼ hr.). Some trains from Graz might require a transfer at Selzthal, and some trains from Salzburg require a transfer in Bischofsofen.

Many **bus routes** begin in Schladming and wind into the surrounding hills and valleys; many of the town's residents use these buses. The only exception is the bus that travels from Schladming to Ramsau (see below). Rohrmoos has no rail connections, but many different buses travel throughout the day along the northeast to southwest stretch of the valley between Schladming and Rohrmoos, making frequent stops at the hotels that line the valley's main road.

Although it's in the northwestern corner of Styria, Schladming/Rohrmoos is most often visited by people **driving** from Land Salzburg. To get here, take the A10 south from Salzburg to the junction with Route 308, heading east. Schladming is 299km (186 miles) southwest of Vienna and 203km (126 miles) northwest of Graz.

VISITOR INFORMATION The **tourist office** in Schladming (© 03687/ 222-68) is open Monday through Friday from 9am to 6pm and Saturday from 9am to 3pm.

SKIING, HIKING & MORE

The **Planai** (1,902m/6,235 ft.) and the **Hochwurzen** (1,851m/6,070 ft.) have fast downhill runs and ski slopes, equipped with a cableway, five double chairlifts, a connecting three-seat chairlift, ski buses, and 15 surface lifts, at all altitudes. Some 22,000 people per hour can be transported.

The **Dachstein-Südward cableway** makes skiing at 2,704m (8,865 ft.) possible in summer. There are ski schools, and you can leave small children at the ski kindergarten, which has a children's surface lift.

Miles of winter footpaths make for good, invigorating walking. You can also enjoy horse-drawn sleigh rides, tobogganing, ski-bobbing, curling, game-feeding trips, and many other winter activities. Cafes and bars offer lively après-ski activities, as do the hotels. In summer, you'll enjoy mountaineering, swimming, tennis, bowling, and top-quality entertainment, along with warm Styrian hospitality. Golf (an 18-hole course), rafting, and parasailing are other sports practiced in fair weather.

Schladming is an ancient town in the upper valley of the Enns River, lying between Dachstein to the north and Schladminger Tauern to the south. It was a silver- and copper-mining town in medieval times. Old miners' houses are still standing. The Pfarrkirche (Parish Church) is late Gothic, and the town's 1862 church is the largest Protestant church in Styria.

WHERE TO STAY & DINE IN THE AREA

Gasthof Sonneck This chalet has white walls, big windows, and wooden balconies. You can relax with a cup of coffee on a flagstone-covered terrace. The interior is rustically outfitted with glowing pine and tasteful furniture. The comfortable small rooms—furnished with modern, built-in pieces—look out over the mountains and have balconies. Bathrooms are also small but efficiently organized with shower-tub combinations and more than enough shelf space.

Rohrmoos 112, A-8970 Schladming. © 03687/612-32. Fax 03687/61-23-26. www.sonneck.at. 20 units. Winter 88€–129€ double; summer 67€–76€ double. Rates include half-board. No credit cards. Closed Oct–Nov. **Amenities:** Restaurant; bar; lounge; sauna; solarium. *In room:* TV, hair dryer, safe.

Hotel Alte Post ★★ This chalet-style, government-rated four-star establishment has a center-of-town location, a history that dates from 1618, and a popular restaurant with a nouvelle/traditional Austrian cuisine menu. Rooms are among the finest in town, although only moderate in size. Each is traditionally furnished with many modern touches. Bathrooms, though small, are neatly arranged with generous shelf space and shower-tub combinations. In the restaurant, you might enjoy a mousse of chicken liver with leaf lettuce or a combination of wild salmon and fresh asparagus baked in an orange sauce, or perhaps a ragout of snails or aiguillettes of venison in a creamy sauce. Even if you're staying at the hotel, reservations in the formal dining room are advised for a la carte dishes, which are 10€ to 17€, or for fixed-price menus, which cost 22€. Hot food is served daily from 11:30am to 2pm and 6 to 10pm. Less formal meals and afternoon snacks are available in the rustic Knappenstube.

Hauptplatz 10, A-8970 Schladming. ② 03687/225-71. Fax 03687/22-57-18. www.alte-post.at. 40 units. Winter 121€–197€ double (includes half-board); summer 108€–124€ double (includes breakfast). AE, DC, MC, V. Closed Nov and 2 weeks in Apr. **Amenities:** Restaurant; bar; sauna; room service; laundry; dry cleaning. *In room:* TV, minibar, hair dryer.

Hotel Schwaigerhof   Located on a hillside with a mountain view, this five-story chalet, built in stages from 1975 to 1981, is attractively embellished. It sports a prominent aerie for a stork's nest on its gently sloping roof. The comfortably furnished rooms, decorated with modern pieces, are either small or medium in size. Bathrooms are a bit cramped but have shelf space and shower-tub combinations. A host of sporting facilities is available nearby. The Stocker family is your host.

A8970 Rohrmoos. ② 03687/61-42-20. Fax 03687/614-22-52. 42 units. Winter 144€–184€ double, 224€ suite; summer 100€–120€ double, 164€ suite. Rates include half-board. AE, MC, V. Parking 7€. **Amenities:** 2 restaurants; bar; pool; fitness center; Jacuzzi; sauna; laundry; dry cleaning. *In room:* TV, minibar, hair dryer, safe.

RAMSAU

At the foot of the mighty Dachstein massif, which reaches a height of nearly 3,050m (10,000 ft.), Ramsau is an emerging ski resort, rivaling but not yet surpassing Schladming (see above). On a high plateau to the north of Schladming, Ramsau is completely devoted to skiing in winter and, to a lesser extent, trekking and hill-climbing in summer. Trails around the resort are clearly marked with white-and-green signs. The prices here are, in general, lower than those at Schladming.

GETTING THERE   Ramsau has no train connections, but about two **buses** per hour from Schladming arrive here throughout the day. The trip up the valley roads takes about 20 minutes. If you're **driving,** you can take a winding, unclassified, but signposted road north from the center of Schladming.

WHERE TO STAY & DINE

Almfrieden Wander- und Langlauhof Hotel *(Value)*   Set at the base of a rock-strewn mountain, this chalet looks out over a grassy meadow and a nearby sun terrace covered with umbrellas. The government-rated three-star hotel, built as a comfortable and cozy inn in 1926, is rustically paneled with pine boards and dotted with open fireplaces and mountain chairs. The snug and cozy rooms are decorated with traditional modern furniture. Rooms are small but well equipped with comfortable wooden beds and a table and chairs where breakfast can be served. Many open onto private balconies that catch the sun. Bathrooms are also a bit small, but they have adequate shelf space and shower-tub combinations. The cuisine served here is among the finest in the area, with good Austrian and Italian wines and both Stryian and continental dishes. Guests here can also try marksmanship on the indoor rifle range.

A-8972 Ramsau. ② 03687/817-53. Fax 03687/81-75-36. www.almfrieden.at. 36 units. Winter 110€– 124€ double; summer 88€–96€ double. Rates include half-board. MC. Closed Easter–May 15 and Nov–Dec 20. **Amenities:** Restaurant; bar; lounge; pool; sauna; solarium; room service; laundry; dry cleaning. *In room:* TV.

Sporthotel Matschner   Built in 1967 and renovated and much improved since then, the Matschner is one of the resort's largest hotels. Located in the town center, it's a double chalet with many flowered balconies. The hotel offers cozy, beautifully maintained, well-furnished rooms with good beds. The rooms open onto private balconies with a view. Bathrooms are small but contain well-kept shower-tub combinations and have enough shelf space for your stuff. The hotel provides easy access to many nearby sporting facilities.

A-8972 Ramsau. *©* **03687/817-21.** Fax 03687/82-666. www.matschner.at. 60 units. Winter 134€–238€ double; summer 116€–150€ double. Rates include half-board. V. Closed Easter–May 15 and Nov 8–Dec 15. **Amenities:** Restaurant; bar; pool; sauna; babysitting; laundry; dry cleaning. *In room:* TV, minibar, hair dryer, safe.

Appendix:
Language Lessons

English is widely spoken throughout Austria, especially in cities such as Vienna and Salzburg and at all the major resorts. Children are taught English in school. However, when you encounter someone who doesn't speak it, the following might be useful. Even attempting to use a little German is a nice sign of respect toward your hosts.

1 Basic Phrases & Vocabulary

English	German	Pronunciation
Hello	**Guten Tag**	goo-ten-tahk
How are you?	**Wie Geht es Ihnen?**	vee gayt ess ee-neen
Very well	**Sehr gut**	zayr goot
Thank you	**Danke schön**	dahn-keh-shern
Good-bye	**Auf Wiedersehen**	owf vee-dayr-zayn
Please	**Bitte**	bit-tuh
Yes	**Ja**	yah
No	**Nein**	nine
Excuse me	**Entschuldigen Sie**	en-shool-di gen zee
Give me	**Geben Sie mir**	gay-ben zee meer
Where is . . .	**Wo ist . . .**	voh eest
the station?	**der Bahnhof?**	dayr bahn hoft
a hotel?	**ein Hotel?**	ain hotel?
a restaurant?	**ein Restaurant?**	ain res-tow-rahng
the toilet?	**die Toilette?**	dee twah-let-tuh
To the right	**Nach rechts**	nakh reshts
To the left	**Nach links**	nakh leenks
Straight ahead	**Gerade aus**	geh-rah-deh-ows
I would like . . .	**Ich möchte . . .**	ikh mersh-ta
to eat.	**essen.**	ess-en
a room	**ein Zimmer.**	ain tzim-mer
for one night.	**für eine Nacht.**	feer ai-neh nakht
How much is it?	**Wieviel kostet?**	vee-feel kaw-stet
The check, please.	**Zahlen, bitte.**	tzah-len bit-tuh
When?	**Wann?**	vahn
Yesterday	**Gestern**	geh-stern
Today	**Heute**	hoy-tuh
Tomorrow	**Morgen**	more-gen
Breakfast	**Frühstück**	free-shtick
Lunch	**Mittagessen**	mi-tahg-gess-en
Dinner	**Abendessen**	ah-bend-ess-en

2 Numbers

1	**eins** (aintz)	15	**fünfzehn** (fewnf-tzayn)
2	**zwei** (tzvai)	16	**sechzehn** (zex-tzayn)
3	**drei** (dry)	17	**siebzehn** (zeeb-tzayn)
4	**vier** (feer)	18	**achtzehn** (akh-tzayn)
5	**fünf** (fewnf)	19	**neunzehn** (niyn-tzayn)
6	**sechs** (zex)	20	**zwanzig** (tzvahn-tzik)
7	**sieben** (zee-ben)	30	**dreissig** (dry-tzik)
8	**acht** (ankht)	40	**vierzig** (feer-tzik)
9	**neun** (noyn)	50	**fünfzig** (fewnf-tzik)
10	**zehn** (tzayn)	60	**sechzig** (zex-tzik)
11	**elf** (ellf)	70	**siebzig** (zeeb-tzik)
12	**zwölf** (tzvuhlf)	80	**achtzig** (akht-tzik)
13	**dreizehn** (dry-tzayn)	90	**neunzig** (noyon-tzik)
14	**vierzehn** (feer-tzayn)	100	**hundert** (hoon-dert)

3 Menu Terms

SOUPS (*SUPPEN*)

Erbsensuppe   pea soup

Gemüsesuppe   vegetable soup

Gulaschsuppe   goulash soup

Kartoffelsuppe   potato soup

Linsensuppe   lentil soup

Nudelsuppe   noodle soup

MEAT (*WURST, FLEISCH & GEFLÜGEL*)

Aufschnitt   cold cuts

Brathuhn   roast chicken

Bratwurst   grilled sausage

Deutsches   beefsteak, hamburger

Ente   duck

Gans   goose

Geflügel   poultry

Kalb   veal

Kassler Rippchen   pork chops

Lamm   lamb

Leber   liver

Ragout   stew

Rinderbraten   roast beef

Rinderfleisch   beef

Schinken   ham

Schweinebraten   roast pork

Truthahn   turkey

Wurst   sausage

FISH (*FISCH*)

Aal   eel

Forelle   trout

Hecht   pike

Karpfen   carp

Kerbs   crawfish

Lachs   salmon

Makrele   mackerel

Rheinsalm   Rhine salmon

Schellfisch   haddock

Seezunge   sole

EGGS (*EIER*)

Eier in der Schale   boiled eggs

Rühreier   scrambled eggs

Spiegeleier   fried eggs
   mit Speck   with bacon

Verlorene Eier   poached eggs

VEGETABLES (*GEMÜSE*)

Blumenkohl cauliflower
Bohnon beans
Bratkartoffeln fried potatoes
Erbsen peas
Grüne Bohnon string beans
Gurken cucumbers
Karotten carrots
Kartoffelbrei mashed potatoes
Kartoffelsalat potato salad

Kohl cabbage
Rote rüben beets
Rotkraut red cabbage
Salat lettuce
Salzkartoffeln boiled potatoes
Spargel asparagus
Spinat spinach
Tomaten tomatoes

FRUITS (*OBST*)

Ananas pineapple
Apfel apple
Apfelsine orange
Banane banana
Birne pear

Erdbeeren strawberries
Kirschen cherries
Pfirsich peach
Weintrauben grapes
Zitrone lemon

BEVERAGES (*GERÄNKE*)

Bier beer
  ein dunkles a dark beer
  ein helles a light beer
Schokolade chocolate

eine Tasse Kaffee a cup of coffee
eine Tasse Tee a cup of tea
Milch milk
Wasser water

CONDIMENTS & TABLE ITEMS

Brot bread
Brötchen rolls
Butter butter
Eis ice
Eissig vinegar
Gabel fork
Glas glass
Knödel dumplings
Löffel spoon
Messer knife

Pfeffer pepper
Platte plate
Reis rice
Sahne cream
Salz salt
Senf mustard
Tasse cup
Vorspeisen hors d'oeuvres
Zucker sugar

COOKING TERMS

blutig rare
gebacken baked
gebraten fried
gefüllt stuffed
gekocht boiled

geröstet roasted
gut durchgebraten well-done
heiss hot
kaltes cold

Index

FROMMER'S® COMPLETE TRAVEL GUIDES

Alaska
Alaska Cruises & Ports of Call
Amsterdam
Argentina & Chile
Arizona
Atlanta
Australia
Austria
Bahamas
Barcelona, Madrid & Seville
Beijing
Belgium, Holland & Luxembourg
Bermuda
Boston
Brazil
British Columbia & the Canadian
  Rockies
Budapest & the Best of Hungary
California
Canada
Cancún, Cozumel & the Yucatán
Cape Cod, Nantucket & Martha's
  Vineyard
Caribbean
Caribbean Cruises & Ports of Call
Caribbean Ports of Call
Carolinas & Georgia
Chicago
China
Colorado
Costa Rica
Denmark
Denver, Boulder & Colorado
  Springs
England
Europe
European Cruises & Ports of Call
Florida

France
Germany
Great Britain
Greece
Greek Islands
Hawaii
Hong Kong
Honolulu, Waikiki & Oahu
Ireland
Israel
Italy
Jamaica
Japan
Las Vegas
London
Los Angeles
Maryland & Delaware
Maui
Mexico
Montana & Wyoming
Montréal & Québec City
Munich & the Bavarian Alps
Nashville & Memphis
Nepal
New England
New Mexico
New Orleans
New York City
New Zealand
Northern Italy
Nova Scotia, New Brunswick &
  Prince Edward Island
Oregon
Paris
Philadelphia & the Amish Country
Portugal
Prague & the Best of the Czech
  Republic

Provence & the Riviera
Puerto Rico
Rome
San Antonio & Austin
San Diego
San Francisco
Santa Fe, Taos & Albuquerque
Scandinavia
Scotland
Seattle & Portland
Shanghai
Singapore & Malaysia
South Africa
South America
South Florida
South Pacific
Southeast Asia
Spain
Sweden
Switzerland
Texas
Thailand
Tokyo
Toronto
Tuscany & Umbria
USA
Utah
Vancouver & Victoria
Vermont, New Hampshire &
  Maine
Vienna & the Danube Valley
Virgin Islands
Virginia
Walt Disney World® & Orlando
Washington, D.C.
Washington State

FROMMER'S® DOLLAR-A-DAY GUIDES

Australia from $50 a Day
California from $70 a Day
Caribbean from $70 a Day
England from $75 a Day
Europe from $70 a Day

Florida from $70 a Day
Hawaii from $80 a Day
Ireland from $60 a Day
Italy from $70 a Day
London from $85 a Day

New York from $90 a Day
Paris from $80 a Day
San Francisco from $70 a Day
Washington, D.C. from $80 a Day

FROMMER'S® PORTABLE GUIDES

Acapulco, Ixtapa & Zihuatanejo
Amsterdam
Aruba
Australia's Great Barrier Reef
Bahamas
Berlin
Big Island of Hawaii
Boston
California Wine Country
Cancún
Charleston & Savannah
Chicago
Disneyland®
Dublin
Florence

Frankfurt
Hong Kong
Houston
Las Vegas
London
Los Angeles
Los Cabos & Baja
Maine Coast
Maui
Miami
New Orleans
New York City
Paris
Phoenix & Scottsdale

Portland
Puerto Rico
Puerto Vallarta, Manzanillo &
  Guadalajara
Rio de Janeiro
San Diego
San Francisco
Seattle
Sydney
Tampa & St. Petersburg
Vancouver
Venice
Virgin Islands
Washington, D.C.

FROMMER'S® NATIONAL PARK GUIDES

Banff & Jasper
Family Vacations in the National
  Parks
Grand Canyon

National Parks of the American
  West
Rocky Mountain

Yellowstone & Grand Teton
Yosemite & Sequoia/ Kings Canyon
Zion & Bryce Canyon

FROMMER'S® MEMORABLE WALKS

Chicago	New York	San Francisco
London	Paris	Washington, D.C.

FROMMER'S® GREAT OUTDOOR GUIDES

Arizona & New Mexico	Northern California	Vermont & New Hampshire
New England	Southern New England	

SUZY GERSHMAN'S BORN TO SHOP GUIDES

Born to Shop: France	Born to Shop: Italy	Born to Shop: New York
Born to Shop: Hong Kong,	Born to Shop: London	Born to Shop: Paris
Shanghai & Beijing		

FROMMER'S® IRREVERENT GUIDES

Amsterdam	Los Angeles	San Francisco
Boston	Manhattan	Seattle & Portland
Chicago	New Orleans	Vancouver
Las Vegas	Paris	Walt Disney World®
London	Rome	Washington, D.C.

FROMMER'S® BEST-LOVED DRIVING TOURS

Britain	Germany	Northern Italy
California	Ireland	Scotland
Florida	Italy	Spain
France	New England	Tuscany & Umbria

HANGING OUT™ GUIDES

Hanging Out in England	Hanging Out in France	Hanging Out in Italy
Hanging Out in Europe	Hanging Out in Ireland	Hanging Out in Spain

THE UNOFFICIAL GUIDES®

Bed & Breakfasts and Country
  Inns in:
  California
  Great Lakes States
  Mid-Atlantic
  New England
  Northwest
  Rockies
  Southeast
  Southwest
Best RV & Tent Campgrounds in:
  California & the West
  Florida & the Southeast
  Great Lakes States
  Mid-Atlantic
  Northeast
  Northwest & Central Plains

Southwest & South Central
  Plains
  U.S.A.
Beyond Disney
Branson, Missouri
California with Kids
Chicago
Cruises
Disneyland®
Florida with Kids
Golf Vacations in the Eastern U.S.
Great Smoky & Blue Ridge Region
Inside Disney
Hawaii
Las Vegas
London

Mid-Atlantic with Kids
Mini Las Vegas
Mini-Mickey
New England and New York with
  Kids
New Orleans
New York City
Paris
San Francisco
Skiing in the West
Southeast with Kids
Walt Disney World®
Walt Disney World® for Grown-ups
Walt Disney World® with Kids
Washington, D.C.
World's Best Diving Vacations

SPECIAL-INTEREST TITLES

Frommer's Adventure Guide to Australia &
  New Zealand
Frommer's Adventure Guide to Central America
Frommer's Adventure Guide to India & Pakistan
Frommer's Adventure Guide to South America
Frommer's Adventure Guide to Southeast Asia
Frommer's Adventure Guide to Southern Africa
Frommer's Britain's Best Bed & Breakfasts and
  Country Inns
Frommer's Caribbean Hideaways
Frommer's Exploring America by RV
Frommer's Fly Safe, Fly Smart
Frommer's France's Best Bed & Breakfasts and
  Country Inns
Frommer's Gay & Lesbian Europe

Frommer's Italy's Best Bed & Breakfasts and
  Country Inns
Frommer's New York City with Kids
Frommer's Ottawa with Kids
Frommer's Road Atlas Britain
Frommer's Road Atlas Europe
Frommer's Road Atlas France
Frommer's Toronto with Kids
Frommer's Vancouver with Kids
Frommer's Washington, D.C., with Kids
Israel Past & Present
The New York Times' Guide to Unforgettable
  Weekends
Places Rated Almanac
Retirement Places Rated